Training: Research
and Practice

To Chris, Sean and Tanya

Training: Research and Practice

J. Patrick

School of Psychology
University of Wales
College of Cardiff
Cardiff, UK

ACADEMIC PRESS
Harcourt Brace Jovanovich, Publishers

London   San Diego   New York   Boston
Sydney   Toronto   Tokyo

ACADEMIC PRESS LIMITED
24/28 Oval Road
London NW1 7DX

United States Edition published by
ACADEMIC PRESS INC.
San Diego, CA 92101

A catalogue record of this book is available from the British Library.

ISBN 0–12–546660–9

Typeset by J&L Composition Ltd, Filey, North Yorkshire
and printed by TJ Press Ltd, Padstow, Cornwall

Contents

Preface

Training is an increasingly important, yet diffuse subject, which is relevant to industrial, occupational, educational, business and recreational contexts. This book attempts to bring together, in a context-free manner, as far as possible, the rationale underpinning the development and practice of training. It is aimed at "students", in the widest sense, including not only undergraduates and postgraduates but also researchers and inquiring practitioners. The perspective adopted is a psychological one, although the book is intended as a text for students not only in psychology but also in ergonomics, human factors, education, business and management-related disciplines.

Any book is a result of many compromises by the author and it is sensible to make these explicit, even though some may be regarded as ill-conceived or poorly implemented. The first, and perhaps most important one, concerns the balance between theory and research evidence on the one hand and practice on the other. The view taken is that there are many texts concerned with the practical aspects of training but few which discuss its foundations and the evidence for and against what might loosely be termed "training principles and techniques". Also, providing the reader with prescriptions without their rationale can be problematic when some have to be selected and adapted for new training situations. Therefore this book reviews theoretical principles, techniques and accompanying evidence concerning the development of training. In so doing, it identifies and synthesises the content of psychology which is applicable to training and therefore of relevance to the practitioner. The distinction between psychology and applied psychology is not an easy one and this is discussed further in Chapter 1. The overall message of the book is that there is room for improvement not only in the practice of training but also in our understanding of its theoretical and empirical basis.

A second issue concerns the disciplines and areas of psychology relevant to training. It is unfortunate that we are all prisoners of a society and educational system which reinforce boundaries between subjects. Indeed this is the very way in which we attempt to survive amidst an ever increasing bombardment of information and proliferation of "labels". Whilst this book does not overcome these problems, it does, in a limited way, bring together areas of both psychology and application which are not usual bed-fellows. One aim is to integrate ideas from cognitive psychology with those from the more traditional areas on which training draws; that of occupational/industrial psychology, human factors and ergonomics. The former contributes important notions concerning the acquisition, transfer and retention of skill and expertise whereas the latter provides many well established techniques for job/task analysis, evaluation etc. In the study of training there is a need for further rapprochement between these areas of psychology.

A third issue concerns the balance in this book between recent and older literature concerning training. The overriding criterion guiding selection was the contribution which a theory or technique makes to our understanding of how training should be developed. One consequence of the proliferation of fashionable labels and supposedly new areas, is that the wheat has to be separated from the chaff and more recent ideas have to be examined in terms of older ones. Our understanding of training has been slow and cumulative over many decades and has not been linked to developments in technology, although technology has extended the means by which training can be delivered. Some of the literature is not easily accessible because it is either old or resides in obscure technical reports. An effort has been made to provide quotations and examples concerning its most important aspects. In this respect, at least, I hope the complaints of my own students will diminish in the future.

Finally, this book has benefitted from an earlier one written by Rob Stammers and myself. I am also grateful to Tom Singleton for some comments on an earlier draft. In addition I am indebted to many colleagues for their encouragement and discussion, in particular, John Annett, Keith Duncan, Jacques Leplat and Tom Singleton.

J. Patrick

Acknowledgements

The following figures and tables are reproduced with permission from material published elsewhere. The sources are as follows:

Figure 2.1 and Table 2.1: Ericsson, K.A. and Polson, P.G. (1988). A cognitive analysis of exceptional memory for restaurant orders. In Chi, M.T.H., Glaser, R. and Farr, M. (Eds) *The nature of expertise.* Hillsdale, NJ: Lawrence Erlbaum Associates.

Figure 2.2: Welford, A.T. (1968). *Fundamentals of skill.* London: Methuen & Co.

Figure 2.4: Crossman, E.R.F.W. (1959). A theory of the acquisition of speed-skill. *Ergonomics,* **2**, 153–166.

Figure 2.5: Schmidt, R.A. (1975). A schema theory of discrete motor skill learning. *Psychological Review,* **82** (4), 225–260. (© 1975 by the American Psychological Association. Reprinted (or adapted) by permission.)

Figure 2.6: MacKay, D.C. (1982). The problems of flexibility, fluency, and speed accuracy trade-off in skilled behaviour. *Psychological Review,* **89**(5), 483–506. (© 1982 by the American Psychological Association. Reprinted (or adapted) by permission.)

Figure 2.7: Reprinted with permission of the publisher from Miller, George A., Eugene Galanter and Karl H. Pribram, *Plans and the structure of behavior.* 1960. Reprint. New York: Adams, Bannister, Cox, 1986. All rights reserved pp. 34 & 36.

Figure 2.8: Pew, R.W. (1966). Acquisition of hierarchical control over the temporal organisation of a skill. *Journal of Experimental Psychology,* **71**, 764–771. (© 1966 by the American Psychological Association. Reprinted (or adapted) by permission.)

Figures 2.9 and 2.10: Schneider, W. and Shiffrin, R.M. (1977). Controlled and automatic human information processing: 1. Detection, search and attention. *Psychological Review,* **84**, 1–66. (© 1977 by the American Psychological Association. Reprinted (or adapted) by permission.)

Table 2.3: Norros, L. and Sammatti, P. (1986). *Nuclear power plant operator errors during simulator training.* Research Report 446. Espoo: Technical Research Centre of Finland.

Figure 3.1: Roscoe, S.N. (1971). Incremental transfer effectiveness. *Human Factors,* **13**(6), 561–567. Reprinted with permission by the Human Factors Society, Inc. All rights reserved.

Figure 3.3: Gick, M.L. and Holyoak, K.J. (1987). The cognitive basis of knowledge transfer. In Cormier, S.M. and Hagman, J.D. (Eds). *Transfer of learning: contemporary research and applications*. New York: Academic Press.

Figure 3.4: Anderson, J.R. (1987). Skill acquisition. Compilation of weak-method problem solutions. *Psychological Review*, **94**, 192–210. (© 1987 by the American Psychological Association. Reprinted (or adapted) by permission.)

Figure 3.5: McKenna, S.P. and Glendon, A.I. (1985). Occupational first aid training: decay in cardiopulmonary resuscitation (CPR) skill. *Journal of Occupational Psychology*, **58**, 109–117.

Figure 4.1: Annett, J. (1968). A systems approach. In *Planning industrial training*. London: National Institute of Adult Education.

Figure 4.2: Patrick, J. (1980). Job analysis, training and transferability: some theoretical and practical issues. In Duncan, K.D., Gruneberg, M.M. and Wallis, D. (Eds) *Changes in working life*. Chichester: John Wiley & Sons. Adapted from Eckstrand, G.A. (1964). Current status of the technology of training. Report AMRL-TDR-64-86. Wright-Patterson Air Force Base Aerospace Medical Laboratories. (Reproduced by permission of John Wiley & Sons Limited.)

Figures 4.4 and 9.15: Patrick, J., Michael, I. and Moore, A. (1986). *Designing for learning – some guidelines*. Birmingham: Occupation Services Ltd. (Reproduced by permission of the Controller of Her Majesty's Stationery Office.)

Figure 4.5: Merrill, M.D., Reigeluth, C.M. and Faust, G.W. (1979). The instructional quality profile: a curriculum evaluation and design tool. In O'Neil, H.F. Jr (Ed.) *Procedures for instructional systems development*. New York: Academic Press.

Figure 5.2: Seymour, W.D. (1966). *Industrial skills*. London: Pitman.

Figure 5.3: Brehmer, B. (1987). Development of mental models for decision in technical systems. In Rasmussen, J., Duncan, K. and Leplat, J. (Eds) *New technology and human error*. Chichester: John Wiley & Sons. (Reproduced by permission of John Wiley & Sons Limited.)

Table 5.2: Bouchard, T.S. Jr (1976). Field research methods: interviewing, questionnaires, participant observation, systematic observation, unobtrusive measures. In Dunnette, M.D. (Ed.) *Handbook of industrial and organisational psychology*. Chicago: Rand McNally. (Reprinted New York: John Wiley & Sons.) (Adapted by permission of M.D. Dunnette.)

Figure 6.2: Annett, J., Duncan, K.D., Stammers, R.B. and Gray, M.J. (1971). *Task analysis*. Training information No. 6. London: HMSO. (Reproduced with permission of the Controller of Her Majesty's Stationery Office.)

Figure 6.6: Asher, J.J. and Sciarrino, J.A. (1974). Realistic work sample tests: a review. *Personnel Psychology*, **27**, 519–533.

Table 6.7: Robertson, I.T. and Kandola, R.S. (1982). Work sample tests: validity, adverse impact and applicant reaction. *Journal of Occupational Psychology*, **55**, 171–183. (© 1982 by the American Psychological Association. Reprinted (or adapted) by permission.)

Table 6.8: Robertson, I.T. and Downs, S. (1979). Learning and the prediction of performance: development of trainability testing in the United Kingdom. *Journal of Applied Psychology*, **64** (1), 42–50. (© 1979 by the American Psychological Society. Reprinted (or adapted) by permission.)

Figure 7.3: Mallamad, S.M., Levine, J.M. and Fleishman, E.A. (1980). Identifying ability requirements by decision flow diagrams. *Human Factors*, **22**, 57–68. (Reprinted with permission by the Human Factors Society, Inc. All rights reserved.)

Figure 7.5: Fleishman, E.A. and Rich, S. (1963). Role of kinesthetic and spatial-visual abilities in perceptual-motor learning. *Journal of Experimental Psychology*, **66**, 6–11. (© 1963 by the American Psychological Association. Reprinted (or adapted) by permission.)

Figure 7.6: Bainbridge, L. (1989). Multi-plexed VDT display system: a framework for good practice. In Weir, G.R.S. (Ed.) *HCI and complex systems*. London: Academic Press.

Figures 7.7 and 7.9 and Table 7.8: Rasmussen, J. (1986). *Information processing and human–machine interaction: an approach to cognitive engineering*. Amsterdam: Elsevier Science Publishers.

Figure 7.8: Norman, D.A. (1986). Cognitive engineering. In Norman, D.A. and Draper, S.W. (Eds) *User centered system design*. Hillside, NJ: Lawrence Erlbaum Associates.

Figures 7.11 and 7.12, Tables 7.10 and 7.11: Pew, R.W., Miller, D.C. and Feehrer, C.E. (1981). *Evaluation of proposed control room improvements through analysis of critical operator decisions*. EPRI NP–1982. Palo Alto, CA: © 1981 Electric Power Research Institute.

Table 7.4: McCormick, E.J., Jeanneret, P.R. and Mecham, R.C. (1969). *A study of job characteristics and job dimensions as based on the Position Analysis Questionnaire*. Report No. 6. Lafayette, Indiana: Occupational Research Center, Purdue University.

Table 7.5: Marquardt, L.D. and McCormick, E.J. (1974). *The job dimensions underlying the job elements of the Position Analysis Questionnaire (PAQ)*. Report No. 4, Lafayette, Indiana: Occupational Research Center, Purdue University.

Tables 7.6 and 7.7: Fleishman, E.A. and Quaintance, M.F. (1984). *Taxonomies of human performance*. Orlando, FL: Academic Press.
Adapted from Guilford, J. and Hoepfner, R. (1971). *The analysis of intelligence*. New York: McGraw-Hill, Inc.

Figure 8.2: Gagné, R.M. (1970). *The conditions of learning*, 2/e. New York: Holt, Rinehart and Winston. (© 1970 by Holt, Rinehart and Winston, Inc. Reprinted by permission of the publisher.)

Figure 8.3: Rowntree, D. (1988). *Educational technology in curriculum development*, 2/e. London: Paul Chapman Publishing Ltd.

Figure 8.4: Gagné, R.M. (1985). *The conditions of learning and theory of instruction*, 4/e. New York: Holt, Rinehart and Winston. (© 1985 by Holt, Rinehart and Winston, Inc. Reprinted by permission of the publisher.)

Figure 8.5 and Table 8.5: Merrill, M.D. (1983). Component display theory. In Reigeluth, C.M. (Ed.) *Instructional design theories and models. An overview of their current status*. Hillsdale, NJ: Lawrence Erlbaum Associates.

Figure 8.6: Landa, L. (1987). A fragment of a lesson based on the Algo-heuristic theory of instruction. In Reigeluth, C.M. (Ed.) *Instructional design theories in action: lessons illustrating selected theories*. Hillsdale, NJ: Lawrence Erlbaum Associates.

Table 8.3: Gagné, R.M. and Briggs, L.J. (1974). *Principles of instructional design*. New York: Holt, Rinehart and Winston. (© 1974 by Holt, Rinehart and Winston, Inc. Reprinted by permission of the publisher.)

Table 8.4: Gagné, R.M. and Briggs, L.J. (1979). *Principles of instructional design, 2/e*. New York: Holt, Rinehart and Winston.

Table 8.6: Collins, A. (1985). Teaching reasoning skills. In Chipman, S.F., Segal, A.W. and Glaser, R. (Eds) *Thinking and learning skills. Volume 2, Research and open questions*. Hillsdale, NJ: Lawrence Erlbaum Associates.

Figure 9.1: Patrick, J. and Fitzgibbon, L. (1988). Structural displays as learning aids. *International Journal of Man–Machine Studies*, **28**, 625–635.

Figure 9.2: Reigeluth, C.M., Merrill, M.D., Wilson, B.C. and Spiller, R.T. (1980). The elaboration theory of instruction: a model for sequencing and synthesising instruction. *Instructional Science*, **9**, 195–219. Reprinted by permission of Kluwer Academic Publishers.

Figure 9.3: This figure is reprinted with permission from the *Research Quarterly for Exercise and Sport*, vol. 9. The Research Quarterly for Exercise and Sport is a publication of the American Alliance for Health, Physical Education, Recreation and Dance, 1900 Association Drive, Reston, VA 22091.

Figure 9.5: Mané, A.M., Adams, J.A. and Donchin, E. (1989). Adaptive and part–whole training in the acquisition of a complex perceptual-motor skill. *Acta Psychologica*, **71**, 179–196.

Figure 9.6: Frederiksen, J.R. and White, B.Y. (1989). An approach to training based upon principled task decomposition. *Acta Psychologica*, **71**, 89–146.

Figure 9.7: Nettelbeck, T. and Kirby, N. (1976). A comparison of part and whole training methods with mildly mentally retarded workers. *Journal of Occupational Psychology*, **49**, 115–120.

Figures 9.9 and 9.10: Atkinson, R.C. (1972). Ingredients for a theory of instruction. *American Psychologist*, **27**, 921–931. (© 1972 by the American Psychological Association. Reprinted (or adapted) by permission.)

Figure 9.11: Atkinson, R.C. and Paulson, J.A. (1972). An approach to the psychology of instruction. *Psychological Bulletin*, **78**, 49–61. (© 1972 by the American Psychological Association. Reprinted (or adapted) by permission.)

Figure 9.14: Lewis, B.N., Horabin, I.S. and Gane, C.D. (1967). *Flow charts, logical trees and algorithms for rules and regulations. CAS Occasional Paper No. 2*. London: HMSO. Reproduced with the permission of the Controller of Her Majesty's Stationery Office.

Figure 9.16: Marcel, A. and Barnard, P. (1979). Paragraphs of pictographs: the use of non-verbal instruction for equipment. In Kolers, P.A., Wrolstrad, M.E. and Bouma, H. (Eds) *Processing of visible language*. Volume 1. New York: Plenum Press.

Table 9.1: Reigeluth, C.M. and Stein, F.S. (1983). The elaboration theory of instruction. In Reigeluth, C.M. (Ed.) *Instructional-design theories and models. An overview of their current status*. Hillsdale, NJ: Lawrence Erlbaum Associates.

Table 9.2: Frederiksen, J.R. and White, B.Y. (1989). An approach to training based upon principled task composition. *Acta Psychologica, 71*, 89–146.

Table 9.3: Baddeley, A.D. and Longman, D.J.A. (1978). The influence of length and frequency of training session on the rate of learning to type. *Ergonomics, 21*, 627–635.

Figures 10.1 and 10.2: Jordan, T.C. and Rabbitt, P.M.A. (1977). Response times to stimuli of increasing complexity as a function of aging. *British Journal of Psychology, 68*, 189–201.

Figure 10.4: Pask, G. and Scott, B.C.E. (1972). Learning strategies and individual competence. *International Journal of Man–Machine Studies, 4*, 217–253.

Figure 10.6: Holley, C.D., Dansereau, D.F., McDonald, B.A., Garland, J.C. and Collins, K.W. (1979). Evaluation of a hierarchical mapping technique as an aid to prose processing. *Contemporary Educational Psychology, 4*, 227–237.

Figure 10.7: Braby, R. and Kincaid, J.P. (1978). *Use of mnemonics in training materials: a guide for technical writers*. TAEG Report No. 60: Orlando, FL: Training Analysis and Evaluation Group, Naval Training Systems Center.

Figure 10.8: Dansereau, D.F. (1985). Learning strategy research. In Segal, J.W., Chipman, S.F. and Glaser, R. (Eds) *Thinking and learning skills, Volume 1: relating instruction to research*. Hillsdale, NJ: Lawrence Erlbaum Associates.

Figure 10.9: Brown, A.L. and Palincsar, A.S. (1989). Guided, cooperative learning and individual knowledge acquisition. In Resnick, L.B. (Ed.) *Knowing, learning and instruction. Essays in honor of Robert Glaser*. Hillsdale, NJ: Lawrence Erlbaum Associates.

Table 10.1: Newsham, D.B. (1969). *The challenge of change to the adult trainee*. Training Information Paper 3. London: HMSO. Reproduced with the permission of the Controller of Her Majesty's Stationery Office.

Table 10.3: Rigney, J.W. (1978). Learning strategies: a theoretical perspective. In O'Neil, H.F. Jr (Ed.) *Learning strategies*. New York: Academic Press.

Table 10.4: Weinstein, C.E. and Mayer, R.E. (1986). The teaching of learning strategies. In Wittrock, M.C. (Ed.) *Handbook of research on teaching. Third Edition*. New York: Macmillan. (Reproduced with permission of Macmillan Publishing Company, a Division of Macmillan, Inc. (© 1986 by the American Educational Research Association.)

Figure 11.1: Braby, R., Parrish, W.F., Guitard, C.R. and Aagard, J.A. (1978). *Computer-aided authoring of programmed instruction for teaching symbol recognition*.

TAEG Report no. 58. Orlando, FL: Training Analysis and Evaluation Group, Naval Training Systems Center.

Figures 11.3 and 11.4: Kay, H., Dodd, B. and Sime, M. (1968). *Teaching machines and programmed instruction.* Harmondsworth: Penguin. (Harry Kay, Bernard Dodd and Max Sime, 1968. Reproduced by permission of Penguin Books Ltd.)

Figures 11.5 and 11.6: Merrill, M.D. (1988). Applying component display theory to the design of coursework. In Jonassen, D.H. (Ed.) *Instructional designs for microcomputers coursework.* Hillsdale, NJ: Lawrence Erlbaum Associates.

Figure 11.7: Crawford, A.M. and Crawford, K.S. (1978). Simulation of operational equipment with a computer-based instructional system: a low cost training technology. *Human Factors,* **20**, 215–224. (Reprinted by permission of the Human Factors Society, Inc. All rights reserved.)

Figure 11.8: Finnegan, J.P. (1977). Evaluation of the transfer and cost effectiveness of a complex computer-assisted flight procedures trainer. Technical Report ARL–77–7/AFOSR–77–6. Illinois: Institute of Aviation.

Figure 11.9: Carbonell, J.R. (1970). AI in CAI: an artificial-intelligence approach to computer-assisted instruction. *IEEE Transactions on man–machine systems,* **11**, 190–202. (© 1970 The Institute of Electrical and Electronics Engineers, Inc.)

Figure 11.10: Brown, J.S. and Burton, R.R. (1978). Diagnosing models for procedural bugs in basic mathematical skills. *Cognitive Science,* **2**, 155–192.

Figure 11.11: Brown, J.S., Rubenstein, R. and Burton, R. (1976). *Reactive learning environment for computer assisted electronics instruction.* Report No. 3314. Cambridge, MA: Bolt, Beranek and Newman Inc.

Table 11.1: Skinner, B.F. (1958). Teaching machines. *Science,* **128**, 969–977.

Tables 11.2 and 11.3: Hartley, J. (1966). Research report. *New Education,* **2**(1), 29–35.

Figures 13.1 and 13.3: Hamblin, A.C. (1974). *Evaluation and control of training.* London: McGraw Hill.

Figure 13.2: Borich, G.D. and Jemelka, R.P. (1981). Evaluation. In O'Neil, H.F. Jr (Ed.) *Computer-based instruction. A state-of-the-art assessment.* New York: Academic Press.

CHAPTER 1

Introduction

Society poses many different training problems. In order to solve these training problems efficiently, we need to encourage the study of training and delineate its subject matter. Principles need to be identified for the development of training programmes which are not problem specific but generalise to a range of training problems. Despite some notable contributions (e.g. Goldstein, 1986; Holding, 1965), further progress is necessary in defining the study of training and articulating the evidence on which training principles are based. This is increasingly necessary as both politicians and industrialists are becoming more aware of the importance of good training practice in a rapidly changing technological society.

The perspective adopted in this book is that training is an important area of applied psychology. Essentially, training is concerned with the learning or acquisition of new skills and therefore psychological theories and studies which cover this topic have to be reviewed and synthesised. In this introductory chapter the following six questions will be addressed:

1. What is training? How is training different from learning?
2. Is there any difference between training and education?
3. What is the relationship between training, personnel selection and ergonomics/human factors?
4. What are the contexts of training?
5. In what sense is training an area of applied psychology?
6. What is the content of this book and how is it organised?

Each question is dealt with in subsequent sections of this chapter. Some readers may find it helpful to consult first Section 1.6 which provides an overview of the content and organisation of this book.

1.1 WHAT IS TRAINING?

The aim of training is to develop new skills, knowledge or expertise. This view is reflected in definitions of training. For example, the

1

Department of Employment's *Glossary of Training Terms* (1971) defined training as:

> The systematic development of the attitudes/knowledge/skill behaviour pattern required by an individual in order to perform adequately a given task or job ... (p. 29; italics omitted).

In a review of training, Goldstein (1980) defined training as:

> The acquisition of skills, concepts or attitudes that result in improved performance in an on-the-job situation (p. 230).

Training is therefore intimately concerned with the theories or principles of learning and skill acquisition. However, both definitions suggest that training is more than just this, and that such learning has to be manifested in improved performance at some task. Goldstein's definition is possibly too restrictive since it specifies that such improved performance is in an on-the-job situation. Whilst undoubtedly most training is concerned with improving performance in an occupational or normal work situation, this is not always the case. Thus training might be designed to improve either a sportsperson's or disabled person's performance, neither of which involve an occupational context. The important point is that training is more than just learning since training has, or should have, the goal of improved performance at some specified task. Learning is therefore a necessary but not sufficient condition for training to take place.

Let us conclude these introductory remarks with some discussion of what is meant by learning and performance. If we ignore the many definitions of learning which cover theoretical explanations of the phenomenon, we can usefully adopt an operational definition from Bower and Hilgard (1981):

> Learning refers to the change in a subject's [person's] behaviour or behaviour potential to a given situation brought about by the subject's [person's] repeated experiences in that situation, provided that the behaviour change cannot be explained on the basis of the subject's [person's] native response tendencies, maturation, or temporary states (such as fatigue, drunkenness, drives, and so on) (p. 11). (Square parentheses added.)

Note that this definition emphasises the relative permanency of learning.

An important point for those interested in training is the nature of the concept of learning and its distinction from performance. We cannot directly observe learning which has the status of a hypothetical construct. We can, however, observe and measure a person's changing performance and when appropriate, we can infer that such changes are a consequence of learning. However, levels of learning and performance are not necessarily equivalent. Performance may not accurately reflect learning because of factors impinging upon the performance situation. For example, a student who writes a poor examination paper may claim with justification (or not!) that performance was influenced by motivation, anxiety or medical circumstances such that performance was not an accurate reflection of learning. Also learning will only be manifested in changed performance if an appropriate opportunity is available to the student or trainee. Alternative routes of navigating between two towns may have been learned but this will only be evident when the trainee is given appropriate verbal questions or some practical test. Similarly a fault-finder may have been trained to cope with a complex fault which he has not yet had the opportunity of demonstrating in the operation of the actual plant or equipment. Hence for various reasons, performance may not reflect learning which needs to be borne in mind in any training situation.

1.2 TRAINING, EDUCATION AND INSTRUCTION

Given our discussion of the nature of training, how is training different from education? This is a teasingly difficult question which might reasonably be asked by any student of training. It can be argued that both education and training are concerned with encouraging the development of new skills and knowledge. However, the aim of education has been viewed traditionally as broader than that of training. This is evident if we compare the previous definitions of training (p. 2) with the following definition, from the Department of Employment's *Glossary of Training Terms* (1971), that education is:

> Activities which aim at developing the knowledge, moral values and understanding required in all walks of life rather than knowledge and skill relating to only a limited field of activity. The purpose of education is to provide the conditions essential for young persons and adults to develop an understanding of the traditions and ideas influencing the society in which they live, of their own and other cultures and of the laws of nature, and to acquire linguistic and other skills which are basic to learning, personal development, creativity and communication (p. 8; italics omitted).

According to Glaser (1962), a distinction can be drawn between training and education on the basis of two criteria: (1) the degree of specificity of objectives, and (2) whether one's aim is to minimise or maximise individual differences. Training, as implied by its definitions, has a specific objective which is to improve performance at a particular task which contrasts with the more wide-ranging aim of education. It would be extremely difficult to get educationalists to agree on common educational objectives and what educational curricula best serve these objectives. One such discussion led to the development of Bloom's well-known *Taxonomy of Educational Objectives* (Bloom, 1956) and more recently Resnick (1987) has questioned how education curricula should best develop higher-order thinking and reasoning skills. Also training intends to raise a group of trainee's performances to the *same* level whilst education does not share this goal and capitalises upon individual differences, enabling different talents to prosper, at least in theory.

This view of the difference between education and training is a traditional one. There is some evidence that this gap may be narrowing. On the one hand, training, particularly for some complex industrial tasks which cannot be automated, needs to be more wide-ranging than ever before. The tasks confronting the process control operator or the trouble-shooter in a complex plant often require many types of knowledge. On the other hand, in the UK, there is a surge of interest in ensuring that educational curricula are more relevant vocationally, e.g. in the teaching of mathematics. Hence one has to be cautious of rigid characterisations of either training or education.

There is no sharp academic distinction between education and training. Some writers (e.g. Glaser, 1962; Mager, 1962) have suggested that both training and education are concerned with the development of systematic instruction and that the term "instruction" is acceptable to both areas. Both training and educational programmes need the objectives of instruction to be specified clearly, together with the nature of the instructional exercises. The nature of these instructional activities is not fundamentally different even though their contexts may differ.

1.3 TRAINING, PERSONNEL SELECTION AND ERGONOMICS

In this book, it is assumed that training is the most appropriate solution to some applied problem. However, in the occupational context it is important to remember that training is only one of three potential solutions, each of which needs careful consideration. If performance at a task or job is problematic, then the following options are available:

1. Select persons who have the appropriate abilities, attitudes or previous training to cope with the task(s).
2. Train persons to become skilled at performing the task(s).

3. Design, or redesign, the task(s) in order to reduce or change the performance requirements.

The first option is concerned with the topic of personnel selection whilst the third option deals with ergonomics, human factors, or human–machine interaction. Any one of these three solutions may be used to solve the problem, or, of course, a mixture of all three. Often choice of solution is dictated by factors in the real world which are beyond the control of the applied psychologist. Such factors include:

(a) availability of labour and financial resources;
(b) current practice or tradition in an organisation;
(c) time constraints;
(d) availability of expert advice;
(e) expected life of equipment, manufacturing process etc;
(f) attitudes of those involved; and
(g) current fashions in the human resources area.

The area of training interacts with both the areas of personnel selection and ergonomics. Trainees may have been selected to participate in a training programme. Such selection will have taken place on the basis of the relevance of either their abilities/aptitudes or their previous experience of the task(s) to be trained. In either case such selection information will influence training decisions. The scope or content of training will be different for a new recruit, in contrast to a person who has mastered some but not all of the task(s). Similarly some individual difference variables, such as intelligence, may affect how a training programme is designed. Hence there is a close relationship and trade-off between selection and training. The more stringent or successful the selection process, then the less training that is required and vice versa. It should be noted that whilst training and personnel selection are distinct areas of applied psychology, they do share some techniques. A common requirement in both areas is that some analysis is carried out which identifies the nature of the task(s) or job in question. Different analysis techniques are discussed in Chapters 5–8, and some of these such as trainability testing, the Critical Incident Technique and tests of ability have been more frequently used for personnel selection than training.

One might assume that humans do not have to be trained to operate poorly designed systems or equipment. This assumption would be incorrect. It is an unfortunate fact that human factors advice is frequently absent at the design stage of even complex systems (Rasmussen and Rouse, 1981). Despite the increasing application of psychology to user-interface design (e.g. Gardiner and Christie, 1987; Norman and Draper, 1986), training still has to equip humans to perform tasks which are sometimes unnecessarily difficult or complex due to a poorly designed display or control system. One solution which falls short of redesigning or replacing the system is to provide the person with some form of job aid. This might take the form of written or pictorial material, some algorithm or decision tree, or some on-line decision support such as that provided to operators of complex industrial processes (Hollnagel, Mancini and Woods, 1986). Such aids change the nature of the task and hence the type and amount of training required. Training is therefore influenced by and overlaps with other areas of applied psychology. This theme is further elaborated in Chapter 4 which adopts a systems approach and discusses how training as a system interacts with other systems.

Finally let us consider the intriguing problem of what might be labelled the *training paradox*. The paradox is as follows. One fundamental tenet of training is that some form of *analysis* of the task or job is necessary *before* a training programme can be developed. No training is possible without analysis. Analysis reveals the components of a task and determines both the objectives and content of any training programme. Ideally such an analysis should identify exactly how the task should be performed. However, if such a prescriptive and detailed analysis is available, why is it necessary to train? Surely a better solution is to capture this expertise in some automatic device, possibly a so-called expert system, which then circumvents any frailties of the human performer (e.g. bias, limited working memory). The paradox is that what is a prerequisite for training (i.e. analysis) is also a reason why training is not necessary. This is indeed a powerful argument which is logically correct. However, there are various practical points which make things less straightforward. First, no analysis of any task, other than a trivial one, is ever as complete as one would wish from a psychological perspective. In order to achieve this goal, psychology would have to be a more complete and predictive science than it currently is and this is unlikely to be the case for many decades. The inescapable implication therefore is that training has to be devised for tasks which are not completely analysed. Few people in the training community would be comfortable with this conclusion. Of course, developing an automatic solution for an incompletely analysed task is arguably more difficult and risky than allowing an intelligent trained person to do what a human is reasonably good at: improvising on the basis of knowledge and experience. The second point, which has the same implication as the first, is that some complex tasks have so many possibilities, some of which are not easily predicted, that the person has to be trained to cope with unfamiliar or novel situations. Again the argument is that the human is better able to do this because of reasoning and problem solving skills rather than an "intelligent" but constrained automatic device. The consequence of this argument is again the same. Training is only necessary for ill-defined or fuzzy tasks for which a fully prescriptive analysis is not available.

1.4 CONTEXTS OF TRAINING

The need for training is pervasive and is not restricted to particular contexts of society. This is certainly true if we accept the argument put forward in Section 1.2 that there is no fundamental difference between training and education and that both involve the development of systematic instruction, albeit in different contexts. The most important context for training is the occupational one in which tasks or jobs have to be mastered by young and old alike. Training is necessary for new recruits to an organisation. Retraining of experienced personnel is required to cope with new tasks, perhaps created by new technology or new procedures, staff redeployment or the gradual forgetting of skills which need to be refreshed. Training needs to be a continuous process given the rate of technological change in our present society, unlike the days in which an "apprenticeship" in industry was a preparation for a job which did not change dramatically. Training takes place at all levels within an organisation and includes operators, foremen and supervisors, clerical and administrative staff, sales personnel, research workers and management.

Job titles can be very misleading indicators of job content. People with different job titles do not necessarily require different training any more than people with the same job title need the same training. Job titles are often adopted for historical and idiosyncratic reasons and are influenced by the size of the organisation and the industrial context in which it operates. One example which springs to mind was that of a secretary in a university psychology department. A task analysis of her job revealed that the conventional secretarial tasks in the job were less important than the managerial tasks. The description of her job as "secretary" grossly underestimated what amounted to a pivotal role in maintaining the smooth running of the department!

Occupational contexts of training embrace all types of industry. Thus training is just as relevant to manufacturing industry as it is to the service industries and commerce (e.g. insurance, banking and hotel and catering). Some occupations fall outside of industry, such as local government, health care and the armed services. Thus occupational training involves most people in society at least sometime in their lives. Training is a major and continuous activity in the armed services in which changes in manpower and technology take place regularly. This is supported by a large research and development activity in military establishments which has contributed not only to innovations in equipment, but also to research in training and the development of training principles.

Another context is that of sports activities, which involves either occupational or leisure contexts. The study of how to coach or instruct performers of different sports has had a long and close relationship with psychology (e.g. Knapp, 1963). Most sports involve tasks of a perceptual-motor or motor character, i.e. physical movement and coordination of one form or another. These tasks have remained largely unchanged over the decades. This has not been the case in industry where in the first sixty years of this century, many industrial tasks were manual in nature. More recently many of these tasks have been automated and the need for motor skills has been replaced by the requirement for supervisory, monitoring and problem solving skills. This change in the nature of tasks performed, not only in industry but also society generally, has been reflected in psychology's changing interest from perceptual-motor skills in the 1940s to 1960s, to more cognitive skills in the 1970s onwards. Bainbridge (1987) pointed out many ironies which have accompanied this shift towards automation in many industries. The motivation to automate an industrial process is often based on the belief that it is better to eliminate the human, who is inefficient and prone to error. However, as Bainbridge argued, this means that the tasks which remain after automation are not only by definition the most difficult ones but their performance is made more difficult because the operator is called upon to intervene only occasionally and then often in emergency circumstances with the problem of time-stress.

Training takes place in all contexts of society. It embraces tasks which require perceptual-motor, cognitive, management/supervisory and social skills plus contexts in which attitudes have to be trained. Training is not only relevant to those in "normal" employment but also young and old persons; women at home; and special groups of the population such as the disabled or long-term unemployed. The trainers will vary according to context. In sports these may be professional instructors or coaches who have themselves been trained how to train. Training in industry may be delivered by outside organisations or provided in-house by trainers, supervisors or indeed by colleagues on an informal basis. It is unfortunate that much industrial training takes place on-the-job, i.e. in the normal work situation, which therefore limits the extent to which training can be organised systematically and incorporate helpful training principles.

The approach adopted in this book is to consider how to develop training irrespective of the nature of the task and context. This ideal cannot, of course, be attained, since some contexts tend to be associated with certain types of task which in turn use only a subset of all possible training principles or techniques. Nevertheless, there is a strong argument that the development of any systematic training programme involves the same instructional process or set of questions to be answered by the training designer. These questions do not change, even though the solutions to them may be strongly influenced by the training context. This philosophy is elaborated further in Chapter 4, where a systems approach is used to identify the questions or stages in the development of training materials.

1.5 TRAINING AND APPLIED PSYCHOLOGY

It has already been stated that training is one important area of applied psychology. Training exemplifies the aims and difficulties facing the applied psychologist. What then is meant by applied psychology? How is applied psychology different from psychology? Such questions plunge us into problems of definition and much controversy which I would argue has never been resolved satisfactorily. Perhaps some comfort can be drawn from Miles (1957) who pointed out that there are at least 12 alternative definitions of the term "definition"!

Two approaches to defining applied psychology have been to distinguish either different types of psychologist or different types of research. Hence psychologists might be divided into the supposed "pure" or academic psychologist, the applied psychologist and the practitioner. They vary in their concern with theoretical as opposed to practical issues. Whilst this may have some appeal, it is increasingly the case these days that academic psychologists are not divorced from practical problems. Also it will be argued below that the applied psychologist is necessarily involved in the activities of both the practitioner and academic psychologist. Similar arguments can be made against attempts to identify and label different types of research. For example, Clark (1972) distinguished between pure basic, basic objective, action, evaluation and applied types of research. The psychologist who is involved in training research might be involved in all or any mixture of these dependent upon his/her role and the nature of the practical/research problem. For example, if a problem of how to design a training programme cannot be resolved by an examination of the scientific literature, then some experimental study may have to be undertaken to find the answer. Such a study has to be designed properly so that it is internally valid, otherwise any conclusions derived from it will be unsound. Another, classical, argument against simplistic research distinctions is that there is no better way to tackle practical problems than by developing a good theoretical understanding of how people function, i.e. advancing the explanatory power of psychology's theories. This argument has been recently expressed by Broadbent (1990) in the context of avoiding catastrophes in hazardous situations:

> More generally, we can only guard against real-life errors by a theoretical understanding of the manner in which the human controller functions. It would not be safe to accept a chemical plant process merely because it seems to produce the correct product in one set of background conditions; to be sure that it will avoid instability in some other circumstances, we need to understand the underlying equations. In the same way the human component of the control loop needs to be analysed, if we are to be sure that a person who can carry out some emergency procedure on leaving the training school can also do so a year later, in the middle of the night, and in danger of death (p. 494).

Applied psychology is certainly interested in the *applicability* of findings either from research studies generally or from specifically designed investigations. It is driven by the goal of solving "real world" problems. However, principles which have been established in laboratory settings often do not stand up when applied to real training problems (Gagné, 1962). The applied psychologist is interested in improving this interchange between psychology and practical problems such that psychology is more applicable and also that practical problems capitalise on what solutions are available. This is certainly true of training. It is misleading to imagine that there is some area of applied psychology which is separate from psychology and which has its own theories and methods. Rather the applied psychologist is more sensitive to practical problems both in the development and application of psychological theories and methods. Applied psychology has two important concerns which are in addition to those of psychological science:

1. The *content* of psychology which is applicable.
2. The *process* of solving practical problems which involves the application of some of the *content* of psychology.

First, the applied psychologist aims to develop, identify and synthesise the content of psychology which is *applicable* and therefore of potential practical significance. Thus applied psychology uses extra criteria to identify a part of psychology as its subject matter. The main criterion employed in psychology is whether findings are of statistical significance. Additionally, applied psychology requires that the content of psychology (i.e. its theories, variables and techniques) satisfy the criteria of:

(a) robustness;
(b) generality;
(c) practical significance.

Psychological findings have to be robust when transported from the laboratory because practical situations will never correspond exactly and will have extra "noise" or more nuisance variables. One result is an impetus for more research to be carried out which has "ecological validity". As the term suggests, this involves studying psychological effects in their more natural settings rather than the laboratory. Chapanis (1988) has considered this problem of robustness in terms of how well research findings generalise and has listed features of the studies which limit the generalisation of their findings. He reached two conclusions. Firstly, studies should include greater variability of subjects, tasks, response variables and conditions. Secondly, more studies should be aimed at replicating other studies using changed tasks, procedures etc. These are important suggestions for those engaged in applied psychology.

The second criterion of *generality* is different from Chapanis' point concerning the generalisation of findings from the laboratory to the real world. Generality, as defined here, concerns the extent to which a psychological finding or principle is relevant to many practical problems as opposed to few. In this sense, the fact that people forget is a finding which is pervasive to many practical problems. The memory variable therefore has considerable relevance and generality. The third criterion of *practical significance* is concerned with utility. Psychological principles may be robust and also have generality, whilst lacking in their practical significance. This is because the psychological variables involved in these principles make too small a contribution to performance to be of practical significance. On the one hand, memory is a powerful variable which may affect performance by as much as 50%, whereas one can imagine a training variable which affects the rate of learning by only 1%. (This is known as the "strength of effect" of a variable, as opposed to its conventional statistical significance, and can be measured by formulae provided by, for example, Hays, 1973 and Keppel, 1973.) A variable which accounts for little variation in performance is unlikely to be of interest to the applied psychologist. This book can be seen as an attempt to identify psychological theories and variables which meet these three criteria in the contexts of training. Unfortunately, there are no scientific methods to help us in this task. Value judgements are therefore inevitable.

Second, the applied psychologist is concerned with the *process* of solving practical issues (i.e."how"). This involves skills additional to those of the psychologist and includes:

1. *Predicting future needs and problems.* Thus the psychologist involved in training has to plan for future training requirements rather than just react to current needs. Unfortunately techniques for predicting future technical developments and training requirements, such as the Delphi technique, have, not surprisingly, somewhat poor scientific reputations.
2. *Problem-solving.* Practical problems in training are not easily divided and linked to pre-arranged psychological solutions. A practical training problem may require knowledge to be distilled from both *within* and *outside* psychology and a specific solution developed.
3. *Understanding organisational change.* Most training takes place within some type of organisation. There are many organisational variables which influence what is an acceptable training solution, and whether a training solution is implemented and assimilated into the long-term operation of that organisation. Good training programmes may flounder because of a failure to: (a) appreciate conflicts of interests in an organisation; (b) communicate to those responsible for or involved in changes in training practice; (c) manage adequately the introduction of new training practices.

In conclusion, the question of what is applied psychology has only been answered indirectly. Applied psychology is not a separate area from psychology but is where psychology passes a threshold of being applicable to practical problems as in the development of training. This threshold is dictated by the desire to solve training problems. The applied psychologist involved in training therefore uses extra skills in comparison to the academic psychologist. These are concerned with identifying and developing the principles and techniques of psychology which are likely to be applicable to training. (Wallis, 1966, termed this body of knowledge, a "technology of training".) The applied psychologist might also be involved in developing a training solution to a company's problem which in turn requires further skills of the practitioner and consultant. Hence the applied psychologist might be involved in not only training research but also its application and possibly even the development of a training programme. It is less likely that the same psychologist will also be the trainer and it is more likely that the psychologist will be training the trainer in, for example, new training techniques. However, there is no reason why an instructor or trainer should not also be a psychologist and this might result in some improvement in the practice of training.

1.6 OVERVIEW OF THE CONTENT AND ORGANISATION OF THIS BOOK

This book is divided into four parts:

1. An introduction to training covering basic psychological issues and a systems approach to the development of training (Chapters 2 to 4).
2. The *analysis* of tasks, jobs or expertise in order to develop the *content* of training (Chapters 5 to 8).
3. How training should be structured and sequenced and the variety of training "methods" which might be used in the *design* of a training programme (Chapters 8 to 12).
4. The evaluation of training (Chapter 13).

Chapter 8 has information about both the analysis and design of training and therefore bridges Parts 2 and 3. The sequence of Parts 2 to 4 reflects the order in which activities take place in the development of any one training programme. This reflects the sequence of stages in the development of training materials as advocated by ISD (Instructional Systems Development) models which are discussed in Chapter 4. Initially, some type of analysis is necessary to determine the nature of a task and what has to be learned. This activity precedes the design of training which is, in turn, followed by some evaluation of how well the training programme has achieved its objectives. Whilst each chapter provides a review of a separate topic, the student who is new to training is advised to read Part 1 first and also to read the introductory chapters to Parts 2 and 3 (i.e. Chapters 5 and 8 respectively) before reading the remaining chapters. Below is a brief summary of the content of the four parts of this book.

Part 1: Introduction

Two different introductions to training are provided. Chapters 2 and 3 adopt a *psychological* perspective that the main goal of training is concerned with the acquisition, transfer and retention of skills and knowledge. Chapter 2 examines what is meant by the terms "skill" and "expertise". It provides an overview of different theoretical approaches to learning and skill acquisition ranging from those in the old behaviourist tradition to more recent cognitive explanations. The quantitative relationship between the amount learned and the number of training sessions is explored together with the various qualitative changes which occur in the transition from novice to expert. The skilled or expert performer can smoothly execute and adapt performance in a manner which is "automatic" such that less attentional and working memory resources are required in comparison to the novice. In addition the number and type of errors made by novices and experts differ.

Chapter 4 provides a nonpsychological introduction to training using the systems approach. A system is defined in terms of its objectives. A system can be divided into its subsystems which fulfil certain functions and inter-relate with each other in order to meet the overall system objectives. This systems approach is used in two ways. First, *training* itself can be viewed as a system which interacts with other systems such as personnel selection, ergonomics, etc. Second, *the development of training* can also be seen as a system and the various functions or activities within it can be specified and inter-related. This approach is captured in what are known as Instructional Systems Development models, some of which are discussed in Chapter 4. These models emphasise the need, for example, to identify needs and specify training objectives, to analyse the task or job to be trained and to design and evaluate the training programme. These models not only specify the nature of training development activities but also their logical sequence. It has already been mentioned that the order of Parts 2 to 4 of this book generally follows this sequence.

Part 2:　Analysis

Chapters 4 to 8 concentrate on the problem of how to analyse a task, job or skill in order to determine the content of a training programme. This area is not well treated by most books and can be a minefield for the new student of training. Hence Chapter 5 provides a methodological overview of how types of analysis vary and which aspects of an analysis are most important. Some readers may find part of this chapter difficult and abstract, particularly if they have no experience of specific analysis techniques. A major distinction is made between analyses which are task-oriented (or nonpsychological) and those which are psychological. Data collection methods and sources of information for any analysis are also discussed together with questions of reliability, validity and utility. Chapter 6 reviews task-oriented types of analysis including the well-known Critical Incident Technique, Hierarchical Task Analysis, task taxonomies and work sampling or trainability testing. Chapter 7 covers three different types of psychological analysis: an information-processing approach, an abilities requirements approach and more recent, ad hoc analyses which are now termed "knowledge representation". R.B. Miller's 25 task functions is an example of the use of an information processing approach for analysis and so is McCormick's Position Analysis Questionnaire. Each of the techniques discussed is reviewed in terms of its main features, examples are provided, and its advantages and disadvantages are discussed. Whilst there are many analytical techniques, some improvisation and ingenuity is needed in order to analyse complex tasks. In Section 7.3, some examples of this are discussed which include analysis of the decision-making of nuclear power plant operators in various incidents.

Chapter 8 is a bridge between Parts 2 and 3 of the book concerned with analysis and design. Another important psychological approach to analysing a task is to break it down into the types of learning required. The most famous proponent of this approach is Gagné who, over the years, has discussed different types of learning and the nature of the internal and external conditions required for them to flourish. Gagné was therefore not only concerned with the analysis of tasks, but also the design of training, which included the sequence of training content. In a similar vein is Merrill's Component Display Theory which also makes distinctions between different types of learning.

Part 3:   Design of training

The remainder of Chapter 8 discusses further theories of training or instructional design, including Landa's Algo-heuristic theory of instruction and Collins' theory of Inquiry Teaching. All of these theories dwell upon the cognitive factors which influence the design of training. One theory which focuses on the motivational factors in the design of training is Keller's ARCS model, which is also discussed in Chapter 8.

Chapter 9 reviews some of the more traditional "methods" of training such as the potency of providing the trainee with knowledge of results within some practice regime. Other training methods are pretraining techniques, demonstrations, guidance and cueing. One long-standing question has been concerned with how to design practice. Is it better to train the task as a whole or break it down into parts which are trained

separately? Another issue is how training might be adaptive to accommodate the increasing competence of a trainee during training. These
and related topics are discussed in Chapter 9.

Chapter 10 discusses training design from the trainee's standpoint.
This covers the more traditional role of individual difference variables
in training (e.g. age, IQ), plus an approach which grew up in the 1970s
labelled the "learning strategy" movement. The message of this movement was not a new one. It emphasised that training should be more
concerned with the *process* of training rather than the learning *products*
achieved by trainees after training. Training should identify the
different cognitive strategies required by trainees to master new tasks
(i.e. learning strategies). Rigney (1978) provided a penetrating account
of how appropriate strategies might be encouraged through the use of
what he termed "orienting tasks" included either in the training material
or separately from it. Some examples of work in this tradition are
reviewed.

There is a long history of attempts to automate training. These
include the programmed learning movement in the 1950s, the development of computer-based training in the 1960s and 1970s and the design
of so-called intelligent tutoring systems in the 1980s onwards. Chapter
10 attempts to unravel these different labels and discusses which
training activities a computer or automatic device can usefully support.
The computer can not only fulfil totally or partially the role of tutor, but
can also act as manager to a training programme, or provide support for
the trainers or training designers.

Simulation is an important topic in training since it is often not
possible or desirable to train a person in their normal "on-the-job"
situation. Then some simulation of the job or task has to be constructed in order to provide training "off-the-job". Chapter 12 discusses various aspects of simulation including why it may be necessary,
what types of simulation exist and what degree of similarity (or fidelity)
a simulation should have with the real task in order to facilitate
training.

Part 4:   Evaluation

This topic is dealt with in Chapter 13. Evaluation models and procedures are well covered by many other texts. Therefore types of
evaluation which are relevant to training are discussed briefly together
with the design of training evaluation studies. It is unfortunate that good
evaluation studies of training are somewhat rare.

REFERENCES

Bainbridge, L. (1987). Ironies of automation. In Rasmussen, J., Duncan, K.D. and Leplat, J. (Eds), *New technology and human error*. Chichester: John Wiley & Sons.

Bloom, B.S. (Ed.) (1956). *A taxonomy of educational objectives. Book 1: Cognitive domain*. New York: McKay. (Reprinted in 1972 by Longman.)

Bower, G.H. and Hilgard, E.R. (1981). *Theories of learning*. 5th edition. Englewood Cliffs, NJ: Prentice-Hall.

Broadbent, D.E. (1990). Effective decisions and their verbal justification. In Broadbent, D.E., Reason, J. and Baddeley, A. (Eds) *Human factors in hazardous situations*. Oxford: Clarendon Press.

Chapanis, A. (1988). Some generalizations about generalization. *Human Factors*, **30**, 253–267.

Clark, P.A. (1972). *Action research and organizational change*. London: Harper and Row.

Department of Employment. (1971). *Glossary of training terms*. 2nd edition. London: HMSO.

Gagné, R.M. (1962). Military training and principles of learning. *American Psychologist*, **17**, 83–91.

Gardiner, M.N. and Christie, B. (Eds) (1987). *Applying cognitive psychology to user-interface design*. Chichester: John Wiley and Sons.

Glaser, R. (1962). Psychology and instructional technology. In Glaser, R. (Ed.), *Training research and education*. New York: Wiley. (Reprinted in 1965.)

Goldstein, I.L. (1980). Training in work organizations. *Annual Review of Psychology*, **31**, 229–272.

Goldstein, I.L. (1986). *Training in organizations: Needs assessment, development and evaluation*. Monterey, CA: Brooks Cole.

Hays, W.L. (1973). *Statistics for the social sciences*. 2nd edition. New York: Holt, Rinehart and Winston.

Holding, D.H. (1965). *Principles of training*. Oxford: Pergamon.

Hollnagel, E., Mancini, G. and Woods, D.D. (Eds) (1986). *Intelligent decision support in process environments*. Berlin: Springer-Verlag.

Keppel, G. (1973). *Design and analysis: A researcher's handbook*. Englewood Cliffs, NJ: Prentice-Hall.

Knapp, B. (1963). *Skill in sport: The attainment of proficiency*. London: Routledge and Kegan Paul.

Mager, R.F. (1962). *Preparing instructional objectives*. Palo Alto: Fearon Publishers.

Miles, T.R. (1957). On defining intelligence. *British Journal of Educational Psychology*, **27**, 153–165.

Norman, D.A. and Draper, S.W. (Eds) (1986). *User-centred system design*. Hillsdale, NJ: Lawrence Erlbaum.

Rasmussen, J. and Rouse, W.B. (Eds) (1981). *Human detection and diagnosis of system failures*. New York: Plenum Press.

Resnick, L.B. (1987). *Education and learning to think*. Washington, DC: National Academy Press.

Rigney, J.W. (1978). Learning strategies: A theoretical perspective. In O'Neil, H.F. Jr (Ed.), *Learning strategies*. New York: Academic Press.

Wallis, D. (1966). The technology of military training. In Jessop, W.M. (Ed.), *Manpower planning*. New York: American Elsevier.

CHAPTER 2
Learning and skill acquisition

Training attempts to "engineer" an optimal learning environment for the tasks which have to be mastered. Therefore understanding how people acquire new skills or adapt old ones is central to training. In this chapter we examine the nature of skill and how it is acquired. This covers not only quantitative relationships between practice and skill but also important qualitative changes which occur as skill is developed. These qualitative changes mark the shift from novice to expert performance. They also have important implications for those designing and monitoring training programmes. Different psychological theories which describe or explain skill acquisition are also reviewed briefly.

2.1 SKILL AND EXPERTISE

Skill in a psychological sense is not to be equated with the layperson's view, which has traditionally referred to motor skill, acquired possibly through apprenticeship in industry. In psychology, the notion of skill is more wide-ranging and defies simple definition. Few people would have difficulty in acknowledging the high pinnacles of skill or expertise of a virtuoso musician, a chess grandmaster or an international gymnast. Such pinnacles of skilled performance are achieved after extensive training. On the other hand, the skills involved in speaking, walking or making an omelette (which is a favourite task for analysis) are more commonplace, but of no less interest to psychologists. Even these everyday skills pose a variety of problems to the unskilled performer. For example, walking includes learning to coordinate leg movements with changes in the balance of the body, perceiving any impending obstacles and making appropriate adjustments in the direction, rate or size of steps taken. Such a task might appear so complex that it is surprising that we ever learn to walk with such subtle flexibility without (usually!) falling over and without seemingly paying attention to the activity of walking.

How do we define skill? Definitions are difficult and dangerous things. The Department of Employment's *Glossary of Training Terms* (1971) defined skill as follows:

An organised and co-ordinated pattern of mental and/or physical activity in relation to an object or other display of information, usually involving both receptor and *effector* processes. It is built up gradually in the course of repeated *training* or other experience. It is serial, each part from second to second is dependent on the last and influences the next. Skills may be described as perceptual, motor, manual, intellectual, social etc according to the context or the most important aspect of the skill pattern (p. 26).

Skill is not an all-or-none but rather a relative term. People vary in their level of skilled performance with respect to a task. Skill cannot be observed directly but can only be inferred from performance. It is a hypothetical construct (as is learning, discussed in the previous chapter), and its manifestation can therefore be helped or hindered by situational and affective factors. As the definition above suggests the term skill can be applied to a range of performance situations. It includes the relatively gross bodily movements of walking and finger dexterity (motor skill); the coordinated activities of driving (perceptual-motor skill); arithmetic manipulation to problem solving (cognitive skill) through to social skills. Categorisation into "cognitive", "perceptual", or "motor" skill is only a shorthand means of labelling the dominant features of a task. Thus as Holding (1965) suggested, perceptual-motor tasks vary along a continuum in terms of their "perceptual" and "motor" components. When the stimulus elements are more dominant they are labelled "perceptual" as, for example, in the visual discrimination of one type of aircraft from another. On the other hand, skills which involve bodily movement, such as gymnastics, are classified as "motor". "Cognitive" skill depends on mental processes such as decision-making or reasoning and is required for tasks such as chess, geometry proofs and fault-finding. Even in cognitive skill some perceptual and motor elements are necessary, although they are minimal. Types of skill are therefore used only as descriptors of the dominant psychological features of tasks.

Skilled performance has various attributes about which most writers are agreed:

1. *Skills are learned or trained.* This is reflected in the previous definition of skill. Skills develop through either formal learning/training or haphazard practice and experience. The time and effort required to master a task and become highly skilled is not trivial. Anderson (1982) asserted that at least 100 hours of learning are needed to acquire any significant cognitive skill. Years of instruction and experience are required to produce chess grandmasters or internationally recognised musicians. As skill is developed, both quantitative and qualitative changes occur in the nature of skilled performance, which are the subject of later parts of this chapter.

2. *Skill implies some coordinated physical or cognitive activity to achieve a goal.* There are two important points in this statement. First, skilled performance is highly organised and characterised by such features as efficiency, smoothness, accuracy etc. For example, a skilled driver is able to perceive and anticipate changes in the traffic situation ahead, and translate decisions into an unhurried coordination between the gear, brake and steering controls. Such behaviour contrasts with that of a learner who is initially unable to coordinate arm and leg movements, let alone in response to a changing traffic situation.

The second point is that skill is always goal-oriented in the sense that it enables one to execute a task or a class of tasks. Skilled performance therefore importantly involves knowledge about *how* to carry out tasks. Hence we speak of an operator skilled at process control, a technician skilled at fault diagnosis, a manager skilled at running a factory and so on.

3. *Skill implies flexible or adaptive performance.* A musician who performs *one* and only one piece of music, albeit excellently, is not skilled. Skill suggests that a person is able to perform in a range of situations in which behaviour can be adjusted appropriately to meet changing task requirements. Hence a skilled chess player will be capable of responding with different strategies to his opponent's moves. A skilled tennis player will not only be able to adjust his game at a tactical cognitive level with respect to his opponent but will also be able to make the associated physical changes in serve or stroke play. The skilled performer is able to review and reformulate his actions and even develop new procedures to cope with unexpected or novel task situations. The skilled performer has a large repertoire of potential behaviour. Strategies are used to identify, select and monitor these to fulfil the changing requirements of a task. In playing tennis or squash, speaking or playing a musical instrument, the skilled performer selects and controls the temporal and spatial patterning of movements in such a way that future action is anticipated and current performance is unhurried. A good example of this is given in an analysis of the movement patterns of novice and expert typists by Gentner (1988). Expert typists were able to overlap their execution of movements not only using fingers of different hands, but also of the same hand.

In the last 10 years or so, the term "expertise" has been used as a synonym for "skill". Expertise was originally associated with human performance, usually in a cognitive domain and became the focus of much attention in the development of so-called expert systems, which attempted to mimic human expertise. Thus expertise had to be analysed and described before it could be put into an automatic device or decision support system. This was problematic. Unfortunately experts, as opposed to experienced persons, are not as readily available as some envisage, particularly in industrial domains in which technological change makes it difficult for such expertise to develop. Even if an expert is available, it is not easy to capture such expertise in a form which is useful either to a novice or to a person developing a training programme. An expert is often unable to describe the nature of such expertise and how it was developed. (For a further discussion of this topic, refer to "verbal report" pp. 154–157.)

Analyses of skill or expertise can too easily capture only the superficial characteristics rather than the deeper cognitive mechanisms which account for the qualitative differences between expert and novice performance. Some fascinating accounts of expertise are available, including a discussion of the nature and acquisition of radiological diagnostic expertise (Lesgold, 1984; Lesgold et al., 1988). Lesgold was interested in how X-ray films were examined and how diagnostic expertise might be trained. Significantly, Lesgold (1984) commented that even if thousands of rules were found to describe such a skill, then it would "leave an expert with very brittle knowledge, knowledge that does not readily adapt to new situations" (p. 81). Lesgold described several qualitative differences between his experts, partially trained staff and novices which he interpreted in terms of the development of a relevant schema. Novices had difficulty in visual recognition of diseases due to the variation inherent in the same diseases, noise in the film, and relating this to normal anatomy; their schema was less well developed for interpreting symptoms and knowing where and what to look for; they also initially used a probabilistic strategy rather than reasoning by a deeper analysis of the problem. Such notions illustrate the complexity of radiological expertise and begin to identify the types of knowledge which are required to develop it.

Accounts of expertise in different domains can be found in the classic studies of chess expertise by De Groot (1965, 1966) and in the various chapters of *The Nature of Expertise* by Chi, Glaser and Farr (1988). De Groot found, to his initial surprise, that grandmasters were not superior to less expert players in either the number of possible moves they considered or how far forward they analysed the consequences of each move. Why then were grandmasters better in the moves they made? The answer began to reveal itself when De Groot discovered that masters were better than less expert players at reconstructing the position of pieces on a board after viewing it for five seconds. This superiority disappeared when the pieces were randomly arranged on the board and did not compose a meaningful chess pattern. These studies, and others in this domain, suggested that chess masters were able to encode more positions more quickly as a consequence of the manner in which their knowledge was organised.

Similarly, Ericsson and Polson (1988) described the astounding memory skills of a headwaiter, named JC, who was able to remember full dinner orders from as many as 20 people seated at several tables without using paper and pencil. Ericsson and Polson demonstrated JC's expertise using a simulated restaurant situation in which cut-out faces on a table represented the customers. The "waiter" requested the order from each "customer" which was read by the experimenter. An order was made up of an entrée (seven types, e.g. Steak Oscar, Teriyaki), the degree to which it is to be cooked ("temperature", five ratings from well-done to rare), a salad dressing (five types, e.g. blue cheese, thousand island) and one starch (three types, e.g. french fries, rice). JC's performance was dramatically better in the simulated restaurant than that of

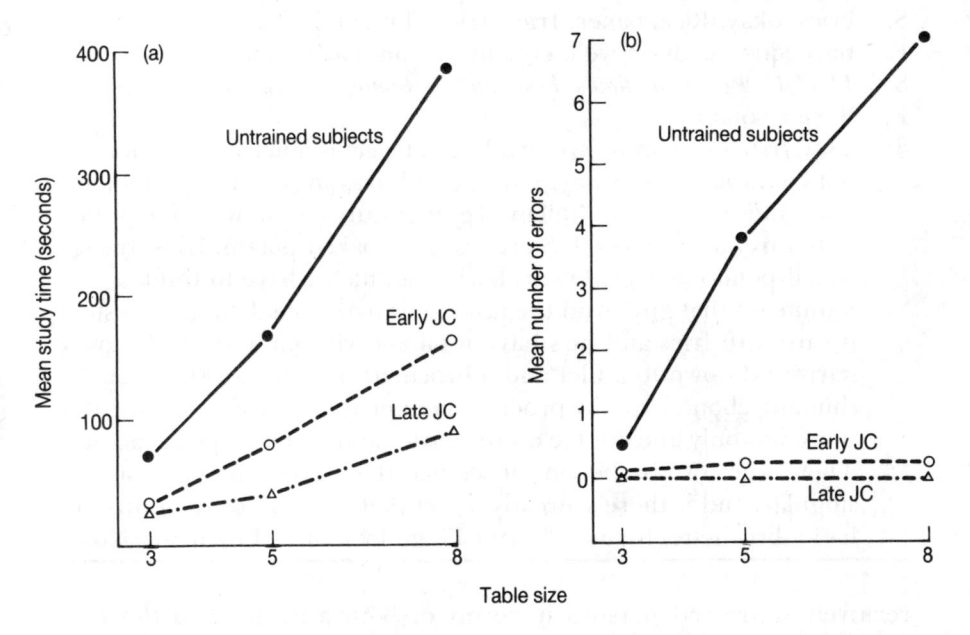

Figure 2.1 (a) Speed and (b) accuracy of taking restaurant orders as a function of table size for untrained subjects and JC early and late in the study (Ericsson and Polson, 1988).

Table 2.1   An example of JC's comments during and after taking
dinner orders from a table with five persons (Ericsson and Polson, 1988)

E: Why don't you start thinking out loud.

S: Oh, it is five. I thought it was going to be eight. These five people
     look like they don't fit together. That's unusual. Out of your real
     estate magazine. This guy, the first guy looks like he's way out of
     place with this group of people so we'll see how easy his order is.
     Okay. Go.

E: Steak Oscar, well done, thousand island, rice.

S: Okay. *Well done and rice seem to fit that guy. Steak Oscar doesn't.* Next.

E: Barbeque, well done, bleu cheese, baked potato.

S: *That sounds fairly standard. TB is my salad dressing notation* and next.

E: Filet mignon, medium well, thousand island, fries.

S: *TBT, rice, baker, fries. Temperatures are making an easy pattern.* Next.

E: Filet mignon, rare, oil and vinegar, fries.

S: *TB.* What's the salad dressing?

E: Thousand Island.

S: TBTO. Starch for no. 4?

E: Fries.

S: Fries, okay. Rice, baker, fries, fries, TBTO. Next.

E: Barbeque, medium well, creamy Italian, baked potato.

S: *TBTOH. Barbeque, that's the second barbeque, medium well,* starch?

E: Baked potato.

S: *Okay, fries, rice, starches are easy.* Done. It seems much easier when I'm
     not counting, by the way. Okay, salad dressings. Thousand, bleu,
     thousand, oil, creamy Italian. Temperatures: well, well, medium-
     well, rare, medium-well. Starches: rice, baked potato, fries, fries,
     baked potato. Steaks: Oscar, barbeque, filet, I have to think a
     minute on that guy. And the last one is barbeque. Um, no. 4's steak
     is rare with fries and he's having oil and vinegar and uh, I have it
     narrowed down to a filet and a brochette are the two that I'm
     thinking about. Now, by process of elimination, it seemed to me that
     there was only one double on this order and that was the barbeques.
     There were two barbeques, it seemed that everything else was
     singular, and if there's already a filet that I'm sure of then this guy
     had a brochette, for no. 4. And I'll go by that. A brochette. No.

relatively untrained persons in terms of both accuracy and the time
required to take the orders (Figure 2.1a, b). The nature of this expertise
lay in the memory processes used. JC organised the orders into two
dimensions: one concerning characteristics associated with the person

who ordered and the other describing the types of item required (Table 2.1). In addition, as the orders were given, JC organised them into groups of four and used various tricks to remember items within each category. For example, if four salad dressings for consecutive orders were *b*lue cheese, *o*il and vinegar, *o*il and vinegar and *t*housand island, these could be remembered by the word BOOT. The temperatures of a series of four steaks were remembered as a visuo-spatial pattern (rather like a piece of music) with the highest temperature (well done) represented as the highest point on a five line scale.

Evidence for these memory tricks and JC's approach to coding the orders can be found in JC's report in Table 2.1. This "think aloud" report was made up of one part which occurred as the orders were being taken and another part which covered JC's report on the orders and how he thought he remembered them. Two interesting findings from the Ericsson and Polson study were that JC was surprisingly knowledgeable about his own memory skills and also that these skills did generalise to other memory tasks with the same structure but with different content.

Let us conclude this discussion of skill and expertise with some generalisations about expertise from Chi, Glaser and Farr (1988):

1. Experts excel mainly in their own domains.
2. Experts perceive large meaningful patterns in their domain.
3. Experts are fast; they are faster than novices at performing the skills of their domain, and they quickly solve problems with little error.
4. Experts have superior short-term and long-term memory.
5. Experts see and represent a problem in their domain at a deeper (more principled) level than novices; novices tend to represent a problem at a superficial level.
6. Experts spend a great deal of time analysing a problem qualitatively.
7. Experts have strong self-monitoring skills.

2.2 AN OVERVIEW OF PSYCHOLOGICAL APPROACHES TO LEARNING

During this century many perspectives on the mechanisms underlying learning and skill acquisition have been proposed. In Section 2.4, theories of skill acquisition are discussed. However, it may be helpful, particularly for nonpsychologists, to sketch some of the main developments in the psychology of learning and their implications for training. Inevitably such an overview is selective and does not discuss theoretical issues in detail.

One finds an iterative relationship between developments in psychology and changes in society which psychology attempts to understand and explain. Changes in the needs of society (e.g. during a war) in terms of the nature of the tasks and skills to be mastered have an influence on the studies performed by psychologists. Sometimes this effect is sharp, whilst at other times it may be gradual.

For convenience, the study of the psychology of learning might be divided into three periods. The early period, from the beginning of this century to the 1950s, was dominated by the behaviourist tradition and principles of reinforcement. A middle period can be identified in which the "black box" between stimulus and response was elaborated in terms of information-processing models stimulated by cybernetic theory. Out of this movement grew a stronger interest in the description and modelling of mental events, which is now the domain of cognitive psychology and which extends up to the present day. There is no sharp division between these periods, particularly the last two. Indeed, the roots of cognitive psychology can be traced back to the work of those such as Bartlett (1932), Bruner, Goodnow and Austin (1956), and beyond.

Let us briefly consider each of these periods and their main ideas with respect to training.

The early period

This period was characterised by the desire that psychology should be distinguished from philosophy and be the science of human behaviour. There were many different theories and concepts used to explain learning. Two distinctions can be drawn. Firstly, the more cognitively oriented concepts of Kohler, Tolman and others contrasted with the stimulus–response approach of Thorndike, Hull, Guthrie and Skinner. Secondly, it was postulated that learning occurred through either the principle of contiguity (i.e. association) as proposed by Guthrie and Tolman, or the principle of reinforcement expounded by Thorndike, Hull and Skinner. Undoubtedly the most dominant and long-lasting approach was to conceptualise learning as the process of reinforcement of stimulus–response connections. The publication of *Animal Intelligence* by E.L. Thorndike in 1898 laid the foundation of the reinforcement position. Having observed the consistent behaviour of cats escaping from puzzle boxes, he proposed that learning was a result of the gradual strengthening of connections between a stimulus (S) and a response (R). Thorndike proposed three laws to explain learning: the law of readiness, the law of exercise and the law of effect. The law of exercise or practice holds that the repetition of S–R situations tends to strengthen a habit or skill. Interestingly, this law was renounced after 1930. By far the most important law was the law of effect which said that "if the connection is made and is accompanied by a satisfying state of affairs, the strength of the connection is increased; if the connection is made and followed by an annoying state of affairs, its strength is decreased". Later this theory became asymmetric such that the effect of an annoying state of affairs was not as strong as a satisfying one. Reinforcement theory was further elaborated by Hull (1943) who linked reinforcement with a reduction in biological drive and Skinner (1953) who emphasised the role of reinforcement in operant conditioning situations as the basis of controlling behaviour. Skinner's works have been very influential both in the study of learning and in its application, for example, in the emergence of programmed learning, which is discussed in Chapter 11.

From a training perspective, a key feature of the reinforcement position is that learning involves the strengthening of S–R connections which occurs automatically when followed by a satisfying state of affairs after the occurrence of a correct response (positive reinforcement). Training was seen as arranging the circumstances for appropriate stimuli, responses and reinforcers to become linked and inevitably learning ensued. The responsibility of learning therefore fell upon the trainer for contriving the appropriate training situation, which was imposed on a relatively "passive" trainee.

In this thumbnail sketch of reinforcement theory it is not possible to represent adequately the subtleties of the theories or their criticisms. Some of the philosophical, logical and empirical objections are covered by Postman (1947). In some simple human learning situations it was possible to identify stimuli and responses and to provide positive reinforcement in terms of "good", "right", sweets, money etc. There was disagreement over the extent to which the reinforcement paradigm, developed in animal studies, was maintained when applied to human learning. A substantial number of empirical studies of verbal and motor learning suggested that what the learner required to master a task was *information*. Reinforcement was important not so much because of its motivational value, as argued by reinforcement theorists, but because of its informational content. Reinforcers such as "good" and "right" provide information concerning the correctness of a response. Unfortunately it is not possible to design a study which separates these competing interpretations, since reinforcement which is assumed to provide information may also be motivational and vice versa. It also became evident that information given to a trainee does not have to be provided *after* the execution of a response in order to facilitate learning. Demonstrations of what should be done in a task or in guiding the trainee were found to be equally successful methods of training. Consequently the law of effect had to be rejected in its strong form as an underlying mechanism of learning or a universal law of learning. On the other hand, it can be accepted in a weaker form as a law of performance. Nowadays there are still many training situations (e.g. those involving people with mental handicap or behavioural problems) in which reinforcement principles are claimed to be useful in developing appropriate behaviours. However, there is a general acceptance that such theories no longer help in understanding or explaining the complex nature of human skilled behaviour in either laboratory or applied contexts.

The middle period

The most important feature of the 1960s and 1970s from a training perspective was the information-processing model of skill (e.g. Welford, 1968). It brought together the two concepts of information and feedback control. The origins of the notion of feedback are to be found in Wiener's *Cybernetics* which conceptualised the human as a self-governing system in both physiological and psychological terms. Feedback control was the means by which a system was regulated. Consequently, the output of the system is used to control the input to the system, as in a thermostat. The concepts of information were set out by Shannon (1948) in so-called communication theory and summarised in Fitts and Posner (1967). A signal contains information which is defined in terms of the amount of uncertainty which it eliminates. The signal is encoded and transmitted along a communication channel at a particular rate. The signal is subject to "noise" or distortion and the rate at which information can be transmitted is limited. Subsequently, the signal is decoded and received. This communication theory metaphor was applied to human skilled performance. Its great attraction was that quantitative measures of information processing could be derived which could be compared between different tasks.

In the information-processing model of skill represented in Figure 2.2, there are various implications for those interested in promoting learning or training. Information is input via a person's sense organs and is then processed through stages of perception, memory, decision-making before some behaviour is initiated via the effector organs (arms, vocal cords etc.). As discussed earlier different tasks or skills will vary in

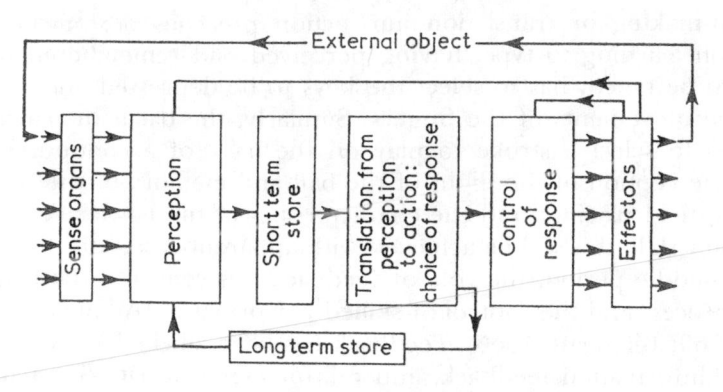

Figure 2.2 Information-processing diagram of the human sensori-motor system with only a few of the many feedback loops which exist (adapted from Welford, 1968).

their requirements at different stages. Therefore, the trainer has to be aware of which stage or stages will be problematic in learning the new task. Out of the multitude of task-related information impinging upon the trainee via his receptor organs, relevant information has to be filtered, interpreted, organised and eventually translated into an appropriate course of action. The ease and precision with which this is accomplished will differentiate the skilled from the unskilled performer. Training of tasks with a high perceptual component will focus on helping the trainee to attend to, discriminate and interpret relevant information. For example, in perceptual (auditory or visual) detection tasks in which a "signal" has to be detected against a "noisy" background, cueing has had some success as a training method (Aiken and Lau, 1967). In this method the trainee is informed *when* a "signal" is about to occur.

Memory processes are also fundamental to skilled performance, as was evident in our previous discussion in this chapter. A distinction is made between short-term or working memory and a longer-term store, both of which are involved in learning a new task. In the former, information decays rapidly without adequate rehearsal. Overload in working memory is often a problem in the early stages of training. For example, in learning to type, the "rules" of typing and the position of the keys have to be recalled whilst information is perceived, held in working memory and then typed. The increasing fluency of a typist is marked by the ability to hold larger and larger chunks of information in working memory as the rules of typing, key positions and movement patterns are transferred to a longer-term store as learning progresses.

Decision-making or translation into action precedes performance. The person learning to type, having perceived and remembered the message to be typed, has to select the keys to be depressed and then control the movements of the fingers. Similarly, the batsman playing cricket has to select a stroke to play on the basis of a continuously changing perception of the flight of the ball and memory of the pitch conditions, field placings and the characteristics of the bowler. With a high level of skill, this will be achieved with apparent ease.

In this middle period, the role of feedback was central to both the learning process and the control of skilled performance (Adams, 1968; Annett, 1969; Bilodeau, 1966). Feedback has been labelled knowledge of results, information feedback, and reinforcement to cite but a few terms. An important distinction for training purposes is that between intrinsic and extrinsic feedback made by Annett (1961) (see Figure 2.3). This dichotomy is often confused with that between internal (e.g. proprioceptive) and external (e.g. auditory, visual) feedback. Intrinsic feedback may involve internal or external feedback and refers to information which is available to the person as a consequence of *normal execution of the task*. As the name implies, feedback which is not normally available but is introduced to facilitate training is labelled extrinsic feedback. In order to clarify this dichotomy, let us consider coaching a person to long-jump. The long-jumper will always have information from the approach (e.g. sight of the take-off board), flight in the air (e.g. balance) and the final landing position (e.g. distance) which is all intrinsic feedback from the act of long-jumping. This feedback is important in enabling adjustments

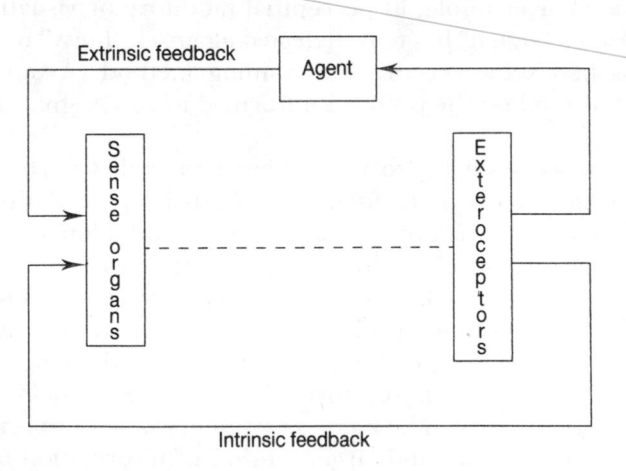

Figure 2.3 Extrinsic versus intrinsic feedback associated with performance.

to be made both during and between jumps. Extrinsic feedback may be supplied by another person, a machine or both. A coach may suggest alterations in run-up or style, whilst a video recording will enable the long-jumper to evaluate his or her own performance. In both cases such extrinsic feedback is not normally available and will be withdrawn after training. Therefore critical research questions of this period were: when and what sort of extrinsic feedback optimised learning? How can the trainee avoid becoming dependent upon it and how should it relate to the intrinsic feedback which is normally available to the trainee? For a discussion of these issues in the context of training, the reader is referred to Stammers and Patrick (1975). Some of the main implications for training arising from this literature are summarised in Chapter 9.

The emergence of cognitive psychology

The contrast between cognitive psychology and the behaviourist principles of reinforcement in the early period is stark. The reinforcement learning paradigm conceptualised the trainee as being passive. Learning was achieved through the presentation of reinforcement which *effected* learning. Given the appropriate training conditions, learning was largely an automatic process. These notions were challenged by studies carried out in experimental psychology, subsequently labelled cognitive psychology. The role of the learner changed. He/she was conceptualised as being active, not in the sense of performing, but by bringing to bear different strategies, perspectives and interpretations on the subject matter in the search for a coherent understanding. For example, people develop "schemata" which organise new and old perceptions of types of objects, people etc. People develop "scripts" for certain situations (Schank and Abelson, 1977) which are potent in determining what is remembered (e.g. Bower, Black and Turner, 1979). Even in a reaction time task, the person's expectations and assumptions result in subtle changes in speed–accuracy trade-offs which affect reaction time (Rabbitt, 1981).

The cognitive strategies which a person uses in manipulating information associated with a task are important. The information-processing model of skill suggested that information inevitably passed through intervening stages such as perception, memory and decision-making which impose various capacity limitations. This preoccupation with structure ignored the influence of "strategies" which an individual might utilise. Broadbent (1987) made a similar point, stating that structures or invariant mechanisms proposed by some psychological theorists tend to hide the flexibility of performance and the variety of resources which are used for task performance. Therefore during training, the learner will bring old and develop new cognitive strategies which will determine the effectiveness of both learning and subsequent performance of the new task. Hence training has to ensure that appropriate cognitive strategies are developed during training which support performance for, sometimes novel, task situations after training.

Cognitive psychology in its early development was primarily concerned with how information is represented, for example, in long-term memory. It was only in the late 1970s onwards that the question of how people acquire new knowledge was addressed. This later focus on the dynamics of learning is reflected in the chapters of *Cognitive Skills and their Acquisition* edited by J.R. Anderson (1981). Cognitive skills include such tasks as algebra manipulation, geometry proofs and problem-solving. There was also a shift towards defining and explaining the types of knowledge which support such cognitive skills. This is most explicit in Anderson's ACT theory of skill acquisition (1982) in which declarative (i.e. factual) knowledge is transformed and compiled into procedural knowledge which underpins skilled performance or expertise. Anderson's theory is discussed in Section 2.4.

In order to give a flavour of the cognitive approach to skill acquisition, let us conclude this overview with an account by Rumelhart and Norman (1978). They suggested that complex human learning occurs through the development or modification of schemata which are the means by which information is represented in a person's knowledge base. They identified three types of learning: accretion, tuning and restructuring. Accretion occurs when new information is encoded in terms of existing schemata. Tuning involves the modification of existing schemata, whilst restructuring (or structuring) refers to the later stages of knowledge development in which a schema is refined in its application to specific situations. This tuning also allows performance to become more automatised. (Automatisation is a characteristic of the later stages of skill acquisition and is discussed in Section 2.5.) Rumelhart and Norman (1981) argued that learning by analogy often underlies the development of a new schema. The instructional implication is that an appropriate conceptual model has to be found and provided to the trainee. More recently, it has become popular to talk about a person's "mental model" of a domain although the term has various connotations. Thus an operator of, say, a nuclear power plant is said to have a "mental model" of the plant which provides an understanding of how it works. Such mental models may be grossly wrong or just contain a few misconceptions. Recently White and Frederiksen (1987) suggested that training should be sequenced to take the trainee through a series of mental models of how a system works which become progressively more complex. The aim of training is therefore to ensure that relevant and correct mental models are available to and selected by the trained person. These notions are relevant to the transfer of training which is explored in Chapter 3.

Summary

In this sketch of psychological approaches to learning, three periods have been distinguished, even though chronologically there are no sharp boundaries. The important point is that there have been shifts in the concepts used and mechanisms proposed to explain learning. Two trends are particularly apparent. Firstly, the learner is no longer conceptualised as passive in a training regime which "effects" learning through the principle of reinforcement. Rather the learner actively brings to bear old and new schemata and strategies to understand a new task. Consequently, training has to be more subtly engineered from a cognitive perspective. Secondly, it is difficult to focus only on behaviour or S–R elements in order to explain complex performance. Hence the information-processing approach distinguishes between different psychological processes occurring between stimulus and response.

These shifts in perspective partly reflect changes in the tasks which psychological studies and theories have addressed. In a society with manually operated devices, there was an emphasis on understanding motor skills. During and after the Second World War, studies of the acquisition and transfer of tracking skills proliferated. More recently, with the automation of many repetitive tasks, there is a greater interest in the more intellectual or cognitive requirements of those tasks or jobs remaining. Nowadays the operator in manufacturing industry assumes a supervisory role which involves monitoring the manufacturing process and intervening only when problems arise. Ironically, this intermittent intervention means that the operator is ill-prepared to solve the problems which are most difficult and automation cannot solve (see Bainbridge, 1982, for a discussion of many such ironies of automation). Of course these changes have not penetrated all contexts of society such as in the training of sports and athletic skills.

It should not be assumed that changes in our approach to understanding learning implies that the older psychological principles are defunct. Psychological perspectives have changed and the skills and tasks requiring explanation are better understood by their contemporary theories. Reinforcement principles when applied to situations which can be encapsulated by some simple behavioural analysis will still work to produce changes in performance. Extrinsic feedback or knowledge of results remains one of the most potent variables to be manipulated in training and there is no reason to suspect that its potency will be diminished when applied to cognitive rather than perceptual or motor components of skill. It will, however, be more difficult to analyse cognitive skills and provide the trainee with extrinsic feedback for components of these skills.

2.3   THE LEARNING CURVE AND PRACTICE

The power law relationship between practice and improvement in skill is of fundamental concern not only to research into learning processes but also to the design of training programmes. This relationship can be described by a learning curve in which the level of performance of a skill or task is plotted against the amount of practice provided. Comparisons of the learning curves for a variety of tasks reveal the same phenomenon. Learning is initially rapid, but more and more practice is required to achieve the same improvement later in training. In other words, whilst initial improvements in performance are typically dramatic, there is a diminishing return from investment in practice. Improvement does not stop with extended practice, but it becomes progressively smaller. Some psychologists have been interested in formally describing these learning curves in mathematical terms and determining their similarity across a range of tasks. A review by Newell and Rosenbloom (1981) suggested that the relationship between skill acquisition and practice can be generally described by what is termed a "power law". We will explore what this means and also discuss different explanations of this phenomenon.

First, it is worthwhile dispelling some misconceptions which may arise from the old adage that "practice makes perfect" which relates directly to this topic. Practice per se is of little value. As Sir Frederick Bartlett put it (cited by Welford, 1968), "It is not practice but practise the results of which are known that makes perfect". Knowledge of results or extrinsic feedback has already been mentioned in Section 2.2 as an important factor in learning. Many theorists give it a prominent role in skill acquisition (see Section 2.4). Hence when we speak of practice, it is assumed that this is accompanied by some appropriate knowledge of results or extrinsic feedback, otherwise learning may not occur.

Some of the earliest studies concerning learning curves were carried out by Bryan and Harter (1897, 1899) who monitored the progress made by students who were being trained as telegraphers to send Morse code. As Fitts and Posner (1967) pointed out, such a task involved learning a new set of perceptual-motor skills (perceiving the dots and dashes and subsequently manipulating the sending key) and developing a new set of language skills which had to be superimposed on existing ones. Bryan and Harter noticed that after improvement in the rate of receiving messages, there was no apparent increase for a couple of weeks which they labelled "a plateau". Subsequently the learning curve started upward again. Their conclusions were appealing. They argued that such a skill involved a hierarchy of habits (or skill components) and that a plateau signified a shift from one level to the next. So that receiving code initially starts at the letter level whereas with practice, it subsequently becomes possible to group the letters into words or phrases. A plateau therefore would occur when the trainee had become as proficient as possible at the letter level but had not yet mastered the word/phrase level to improve performance further. Subsequent studies by Taylor (1943) and Keller (1958) demonstrated that such plateaus were not inevitable. Nevertheless the idea that learning some skills involves progression through a series of hierarchically organised subskills has been of enduring significance (see pp. 55–58).

The power law relationship between performance and practice is carefully described by Newell and Rosenbloom (1981). Such a relationship had been observed previously although its ubiquitous nature had largely gone unnoticed. For example, De Jong (1957) suggested that the time to perform a repetitive task reduced exponentially until it reached some value beyond which improvement was impossible. The power law predicts that the logarithm of the time to perform a task is a linear function of the logarithm of the number of times the task is practised. Newell and Rosenbloom provided two main equations for this power law:

$$T = BN^{-\alpha} \tag{1}$$
$$\log (T) = \log (B) - \alpha\log (N) \tag{2}$$

T is the speed of performance, N is the number of practice trials, B is the speed on the first trial and α is the slope of the line (i.e. the learning rate).

This relationship holds true across an impressive range of tasks including perceptual-motor skills such as mirror-tracing (Snoddy, 1926), perceptual identification (Neisser, Novick and Lazar, 1963) and choice reaction time (Klemmer, 1962; Seibel, 1963). The power law relationship also holds for editing text (Moran, 1980) and more complex cognitive tasks such as learning to perform geometry proofs (Neeves and Anderson, 1981). The appeal of such a law from a training perspective is obvious. It provides a means of calculating the amount of practice required to achieve specified levels of performance. The law predicts that improvement will be initially rapid but will continue to improve at a decreasing rate with more and more practice. Schneider (1985) provided an example of using the power law to predict reaction time with increased practice,

> ... if reaction time to perform a response decreased from 10s to 5s over the first 100 trials of training, at 440 trials response time will be 4s, at 3978 trials response time will be 3s and a total of 10,000 trials of training would be necessary to reduce reaction time to 2.5s (p. 291).

The most famous data which conform to the power law of practice were provided by Crossman (1959) in a study of cigar-making by female operators. In Figure 2.4, the machine cycle time (indicating speed of performance) is plotted against the amount of practice as indicated by the number of cigars produced. Note that the maximum amount of practice was equivalent to producing 20 million cigars! Besides this, another interesting feature of the study was that improvements, albeit small ones, were still taking place with up to two years of practice. As Newell and Rosenbloom observed, the data deviate from the log–log line

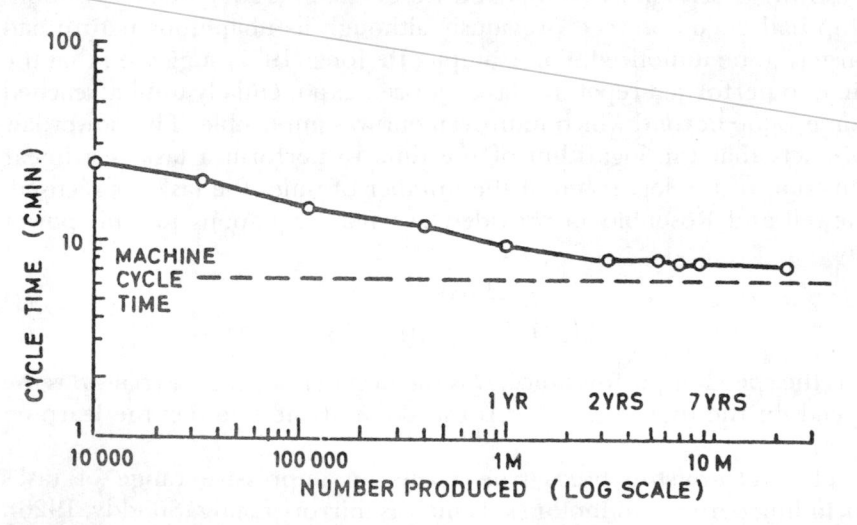

Figure 2.4 Improvements with practice in speed of cigar-making (Crossman, 1959).

at higher levels of practice due to the physical reality that performance is limited by the cigar-making machine cycle time. Indeed the power laws as stated in Equations (1) and (2) above make two assumptions. Firstly, that the task can be performed in an arbitrarily small time after enough learning and secondly, that the first practice trial reflects the beginning of learning. The first assumption does not hold up in Crossman's study and there may be many tasks for which some prior learning has occurred. Hence data may deviate from the power law, particularly at the beginning of practice and also when speed of performance approaches its asymptote. For these reasons, Newell and Rosenbloom proposed a more general form of the power law which is

$$T = A + B (N + E)^{-a} \qquad (3)$$

where A is the speed as performance approaches an asymptote at high levels of practice and E is the number of practice trials that occurred prior to the first trial on which performance was measured (i.e. reflecting prior experience).

From a training perspective the power law offers the possibility of calculating the cost–benefit relationship from investment in extended practice or training. Also in complex tasks it may be possible to analyse and provide extended practice for the more difficult subtasks involved. Card, Moran and Newell (1983) used this approach to predict performance improvements in an editing task.

It is not unusual in psychology to be certain of the empirical characteristics of a phenomenon, such as the power law, but to be equally uncertain as to why it occurs. Pragmatists involved in training will argue that it matters little what the explanation is. On the other hand, for the sake of completeness and maybe to satisfy the inquiring mind, some of the theoretical explanations proposed will be discussed briefly.

Explanations of the power law

Three types of explanation have been put forward which we will call "mixed components", "selection" and "exhaustion" models. The mixed component model is described by Newell and Rosenbloom (1981):

> Performance depends on a collection of mechanisms in some monotone way [i.e., an increase in the time taken for any mechanism increases (possibly leaves unchanged) the total performance time.] The learning mechanisms that improve these performance mechanisms will have a distribution of rates of improvement – some faster, some slower. At any moment total system learning will be dominated by the fast learners, since

a fortiori they are the fast ones. However, the fast learners will soon make little contribution to changes in total performance, precisely because their learning will have been effective (and rapidly so, to boot), so the components they affect cannot continue to contribute substantially to total performance. This will leave only slow learners to yield improvement. Hence the rate of improvement later will be slower than the rate of improvement initially. This is the essential feature of the log-log law – the slowing down of the learning rate. Hence learning in complex systems will tend to be approximately linear in log-log space (p. 35).

Hence as the name suggests, the mixed component model proposes that some parts of the task will be learned quickly but with increased practice there will be fewer and fewer "slower" components to be learned, which explains the diminishing returns predicted by the power law. From a training perspective the mixed component model implies that it is important to analyse the different components of a task such that training might focus more resources on those which are more difficult and will normally be acquired at a slower rate.

The selection model proposes that skill increases with practice because the likelihood of selecting the optimal method increases. (Method not only includes any physical aspects of performance but also the cognitive basis of performance.) Crossman (1959) proposed such a notion from an analysis of data collected from studies of repetitive manual skills (e.g. cigar-making) where speed was at a premium. He was impressed with the decreased cycle time with practice and suggested that "practice exerts a selective effect on the operator's behaviour favouring those patterns of action which are quickest at the expense of others". Performance improves at a decreasing rate as the probability of selecting the optimal method increases with practice. As Welford (1968) pointed out, Crossman's theory is too rigid in the sense that it assumes that the trainee selects from a fixed set of methods which are available at the outset of learning. It is more likely that as training takes place "methods" are developed and revised in a more exploratory fashion.

Two main types of selection models have been identified by Restle and Greeno (1970) called replacement and accumulation models. In the replacement model, as the name suggests, learning occurs through a process of correct responses replacing incorrect ones. In contrast, in the accumulation model, as originally proposed by Thurstone (1919), learning occurs because more and more correct responses are added to the person's repertoire, which come to dominate the incorrect responses, which remain constant. The implications of selection models for training are that the trainer needs to ensure that optimal methods are available to the trainee for selection. This in turn suggests that training might initially either demonstrate or guide the trainee through the correct method(s) or concentrate on enabling the trainee to differentiate the optimal one(s).

The "exhaustion" model, as the name suggests, proposes that the rate of learning decreases with practice because there is less room for further improvement. It might be that improvements are more difficult to find, there is less time for improvement, improvements are less effective or improvements are less applicable or indeed some combination of these. Newell and Rosenbloom (1981) proposed what they term a "chunking" theory of learning which is a form of exhaustion model in which improvements become less applicable. The idea of a chunk stems largely from the memory literature in which a chunk is a means by which a person acquires and organises knowledge about similar aspects of a task. Newell and Rosenbloom proposed that with practice, small chunks are learned and subsequently combined into larger ones which are more specialised. Research concerned with the perception and retention of chess positions relates to Newell and Rosenbloom's theory. Thus an expert can be said to have more chunks with which to encode the position of a chess piece than a novice. Some estimate that there are as many as 50,000 chunks available to the expert for this purpose.

Therefore there is agreement that a power law of practice exists but no consensus as to the mechanisms underlying this phenomenon. Three different theoretical models have been discussed. It may be that all of them have some truth as they are not necessarily mutually exclusive. The nature of the task and the trainee's previous experience may contribute to the applicability of different explanations. It should be remembered that the power law of practice has primarily been demonstrated using speed, rather than accuracy, as the measure of performance. It does not, of course, follow that all learning can be described by a power law, nor that practice will necessarily produce learning. Generally the law focuses on the quantitative relationships between practice and performance. The competing explanations do offer some understanding of this phenomenon, although they tend to be judged mathematically rather then whether such explanations have psychological validity. There are important qualitative changes which occur during skill acquisition which the power law does not address. These, together with some general theories of skill acquisition, will be discussed in Sections 2.4 and 2.5.

2.4 THEORIES OF SKILL ACQUISITION

Theories of skill acquisition or learning are different from theories of instruction or training design. The former focus on the processes of learning which involve qualitative changes with practice. They do not necessarily address the question of *how* to design training. In contrast, theories of instruction are concerned explicitly with issues facing the training designer. They are interested in specifying which training methods should be used under which circumstances to achieve particular learning goals. From a training perspective, these theories are more relevant to the problems of how to design training for different learning situations. However, despite the enthusiastic claims of some instructional theorists, no comprehensive and validated set of design principles yet exists. Since these theories are relevant to training design, they are discussed in Chapter 8.

The student confronted with a range of quite different theories of learning or skill acquisition might reasonably ask how to decide which one is relevant to a specific training situation. Are they alternatives or mutually exclusive? To answer this question one has to understand that different traditions and paradigms have developed in different areas of psychology. The constructs and mechanisms used to explain learning vary considerably from one area to another. In addition, theories developed during one era reflect the dominant psychological ideas of that time. Early learning theories focus on S–R connections, whilst Anderson's ACT theory emphasises the role of propositions and rules in the knowledge acquisition process. Hence the answer to the question of which theory to select is that theories are generally not competitive, but address different tasks and situations. Logan (1988) conveyed this notion using the analogy of choosing which statistical test to use:

> Choice among theories is something like choice among statistical tests. One considers the assumptions of the statistical model and determines whether they can be satisfied in a given situation. If so, one uses the test; if not, one chooses another test. Analysis of variance, for example, is not wrong or inaccurate because it cannot deal with data from Bernouli trials; it is simply inappropriate. When two different tests can be used on the same data, one can ask which is more powerful and more accurate... (p. 517).

Theories differ in their scope. Some, for example those proposed by Adams (1971) and Schmidt (1975), have been developed primarily to explain the acquisition of movements and the development of motor control. The theory proposed by MacKay (1982) was developed from studies in the area of speech production whilst Anderson's theory is more cognitively oriented, focusing on, for example, how we learn to do geometry proofs and arithmetic problems. Most theories aspire to generality outside of the area in which they were developed, but inevitably they have difficulties in making such a transition.

Finally, a pervasive characteristic of theories of skill acquisition is that they are more *descriptive* rather than *predictive* in nature. They describe the changes which occur during learning, but do not enable one to predict *when* such changes will occur. This is a major shortcoming, especially from a training perspective.

A selection of theories of skill acquisition is discussed below in chronological order.

Fitts' three-phase theory

The three-phase theory proposed by Fitts (1962) has undoubtedly been the most influential theory of skill acquisition for those interested in training. The theory was developed from his own experiments and the opinions of pilot trainers and sports coaches concerning the problems and nature of skill acquisition observed in their trainees. As a result, Fitts postulated that the development of skill progressed through three phases or stages:

1. the cognitive phase;
2. the fixation or associative phase;
3. the autonomous phase.

Fitts admitted that these phases overlapped and that transition from one phase to the next is a continuous process. We can only be certain that the first and third phases do not overlap.

The first, cognitive, phase is concerned with the initial "intellectualisation" process involved in learning a new task. In this phase both the trainer and trainee attempt to verbalise what has to be learned. Whilst the trainee is given some expectations about the nature of the task, and any procedures involved, initial performance is error prone and further advice or demonstration has to be provided by the trainer. This phase applies to the acquisition of many nontrivial tasks in which the trainee has to understand what is involved in the task before performance can be attempted. This includes any formal procedures which govern how a task is executed, such as the rules of chess or squash. The trainee learns gradually what is permitted in addition to *how* a chess move or squash stroke is executed. Such an intellectualisation component might be large in complex tasks, such as process control operations, whilst being minimal in others. Unfortunately, Fitts' formulation does not enable one to predict how important this phase and subsequent phases are in learning a new task.

In the fixation or associative phase, correct patterns of behaviour are slowly established by practice with errors being gradually eliminated.

Generally this phase lasts longer than the preceding cognitive one. Fitts gives us some idea of the envisaged duration of this phase for typing.

> In the case of a typist it would extend from the point at which the student has learned the position of the different keys and how the fingers are used in striking them to the point where he/she has perhaps graduated from his/her first typing course and reduced his/her errors to less than 1 per cent and has acquired a fair degree of typing speed (Fitts, 1962, p. 188).

The final autonomous phase of skill acquisition has two main features according to Fitts:

(a) gradually increasing speed of performance in tasks where it is important to improve time or accuracy scores far beyond the point where errors, as ordinarily defined, can be detected, and
(b) gradually increasing resistance to stress and to interference from other activities that may be performed concurrently (Fitts, 1962, p. 188).

During this autonomous phase, skill becomes more automatic and requires fewer psychological resources such as memory and attention. The trainee relies less and less on verbal mediation of the skill and indeed may be quite unable to verbalise how or what has been performed. In some tasks, visual feedback becomes less important and the person has extra capacity to perform other tasks simultaneously. Larger and larger chunks of behaviour can be "programmed" and executed without conscious awareness. The everyday intuitions of, for example, driving a car illustrate these points. Assuming that you are a skilled driver, how often have you arrived at a destination without seemingly being aware of driving there? Also, how aware are you of movements of the clutch, gear and brake in comparison to the early stages of learning when you struggled to master their coordination? The skilled driver is able to perform other tasks simultaneously with apparent ease, for example, using a car phone (even though this might not be a good idea if an emergency situation arose). These ideas of automatic behaviour, sometimes referred to as automaticity or automatisation, relate to and have been extended by contemporary ideas in cognitive psychology (e.g. Logan, 1985; Schneider and Shiffrin, 1977). A distinction has been made between automatic processing, which occurs in the final phase of skill acquisition, and controlled processing, which occurs earlier on. This distinction and evidence for it, are discussed in Section 2.6.

Closed-loop theory of motor learning (Adams, 1971, 1987)

As this title suggests, Adams considered that the basis of skill acquisition was in the learning of simple graded movements. The closed-loop

theory postulates two constructs to explain learning: a perceptual trace
and a memory trace (Adams, 1971). Execution of a movement generates
its own representation or perceptual trace which is made up of the
feedback characteristics of movement (e.g. visual and proprioceptive
information). This perceptual trace is adjusted on successive repetitions
on the basis of the response-produced feedback and any extrinsic
feedback supplied by the trainer. Execution of a movement is controlled
by a matching process between the on-going feedback of the current
movement and the perceptual trace. Since no response-produced feedback is available at the beginning of a movement, a second construct, the
memory trace, is needed to explain the selection and initiation of the
movement and its accompanying perceptual trace. The memory trace is
a modest motor programme. An incorrect memory trace also explains
how errors may occur when the perceptual trace is well established later
in learning.

Another aspect of Adams' theory, at least as originally formulated in
1971, is that learning proceeds through two stages: the verbal-motor and
then the motor. The verbal-motor stage encompasses both the cognitive
and associative phases proposed by Fitts. In this stage, extrinsic feedback
is important in developing a more accurate perceptual trace of the
required movement. Verbal information is important both in terms of
general instructions concerning the trainee's task and also extrinsic
feedback about previous movements. In the second motor stage of
learning the perceptual trace is well established and such verbal information becomes redundant. The theory accords a prominent position to
the effect of feedback on learning. There is indeed a considerable
weight of evidence in the literature demonstrating the potency of
feedback as a learning variable summarised by Annett (1969), and
subsequently by Adams (e.g. 1971, 1984, 1987) and many others. To
accept the importance of feedback does not, of course, necessarily lead
one to agree with Adams' theory. It is not possible to point to any one
empirical study which unequivocally demonstrates the existence of a
perceptual and memory trace.

The fact that the theory proposed by Adams is restricted to the
learning of movements is not in itself an important criticism. More
significant are some of the points made by Schmidt (1975) which led him
to formulate his own schema theory of learning which is discussed
below. Two major criticisms are worth mentioning. First, it is difficult for
Adams' theory to account for how learning can occur without the
"correct" perceptual trace being developed by experiencing the correct
movement. Evidence exists that trainees are able to "abstract" what
constitutes the correct movement from the feedback associated with

incorrect ones without necessarily ever experiencing the correct movement. A similar problem concerns explaining how a person can generate a novel movement which, by definition, will not have a corresponding perceptual trace to guide its execution. Clearly in many racquet and ball games, the skilled performer is able to generate novel movements which have not been executed previously. Secondly, the theory suffers from lack of parsimony since it has to postulate that for every movement there exists its own perceptual or memory trace. As Schmidt pointed out, this presents a massive storage problem if there is a one-to-one mapping between stored states and movements to be executed.

A schema theory of motor learning (Schmidt, 1975)

Schmidt's theory attempted to overcome the problems associated with Adams' theory discussed above by utilising the concept of a schema originally introduced by Bartlett (1932). Essentially, a schema organises experiences derived from our environment and guides future action. It enables us to abstract and generalise. For example, we build up a schema of what a dog is which enables us to recognise familiar breeds and classify unfamiliar ones. Similarly, Schmidt suggested that we develop a motor response schema. This not only explains how a vast repertoire of different movements can be recalled, but also how it is possible to generate new ones. There are four aspects of a movement which make up this motor schema. They are:

(i) *The initial conditions*: information about the limb position, position of the body etc., coupled with the state of the environment in which the movement is to be produced.

(ii) *Response specifications*: information about the dimensions of a response such as its force, speed and direction. It is assumed that there is a general motor programme for generating movements and that these dimensions represent how this can be varied from one performance situation to another.

(iii) *Sensory consequences*: this is any feedback generated by the movement itself, e.g. visual, auditory and proprioceptive consequences.

(iv) *Response outcome*: this is information concerning the success or otherwise of a movement and is made up of any extrinsic feedback which may be available and any subjective impressions gained by the performer.

For every movement produced, these four aspects are stored and gradually as more movements are executed, the person begins to

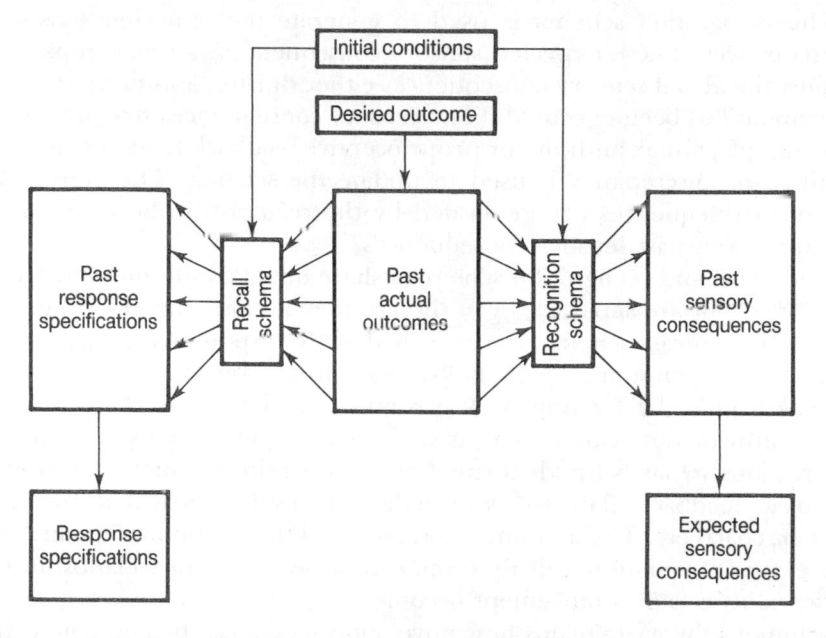

Figure 2.5 Recall and recognition schemata and their relationships with sources of information (Schmidt, 1975).

abstract information about the relationship between these four dimensions. The strength of the relationship between these dimensions increases with successive repetitions of the same movement type. Schmidt distinguished between the schema required for recall and the schema needed for recognition as indicated in Figure 2.5. Consider a person who is about to throw a ball and who has had considerable experience of throwing such a ball. In Schmidt's terms the person has a well-developed schema. In order to plan the movement which is required, two inputs are necessary to the schema: the initial conditions (i.e. the state of the person and the environment) and the desired outcome (i.e. where the ball should land). The specifications of how to perform such a movement are determined from the relationship between past movement specifications and their associated outcomes. This may involve some interpolation among past specifications as the exact movement required may not have been previously encountered. Novel movements are thus possible given this theoretical formulation. When the response specifications have been determined, the movement is then carried out by means of a "motor programme" which executes the necessary response specifications.

The recognition schema is used to generate the expected sensory consequences. These expected sensory consequences can be compared against the actual sensory consequences either during, and/or after, the movement has been executed. (The sensory consequences may involve, for example, visual, auditory or proprioceptive feedback from the movement.) Any discrepancy is used to update the schema. The expected sensory consequences are generated by the relationship between past outcomes and past sensory consequences.

The recall and recognition schemata share initial conditions and past outcomes, but are separate, even though they are associated with each other. The recall schema is concerned with response specifications, whilst the recognition schema looks after sensory consequences. Learning takes place by feeding back error information to both schemata. Error information can either arise from the performer's subjective impressions (what Schmidt termed subjective reinforcement) or from extrinsic feedback (labelled knowledge of results) provided by the trainer, coach etc. The amount of practice and the extent and quality of the error information will determine how accurate the relationships between aspects of a movement become.

Schmidt's theory explains how novel movements can be generated. It stresses the flexible nature of motor skill and its generative and constructive nature. It does not address the issue of how motor schemata originate which would involve a developmental perspective. Those interested in some further discussion of both the theory and the empirical evidence should consult Schmidt (1982a, b) and Shapiro and Schmidt (1982).

MacKay's theory (1982)

MacKay's interests originated in the area of speech production. He was intrigued with the question of how fluency and flexibility develop in speech production. For a detailed discussion of Mackay's theory, the reader should consult MacKay (1982). A brief description follows.

The theory postulates that a hierarchy of different types of interconnected nodes underlies the learning and production of complex skill (Figure 2.6). Nodes are divided into at least two independently controlled systems. One, at the top of what he terms the action hierarchy, is made up of mental nodes which correspond to cognitive units for controlling parts of a movement or behaviour pattern. In speech production the mental nodes represent units such as phrases, words, syllables and phonemes, and together form the mental

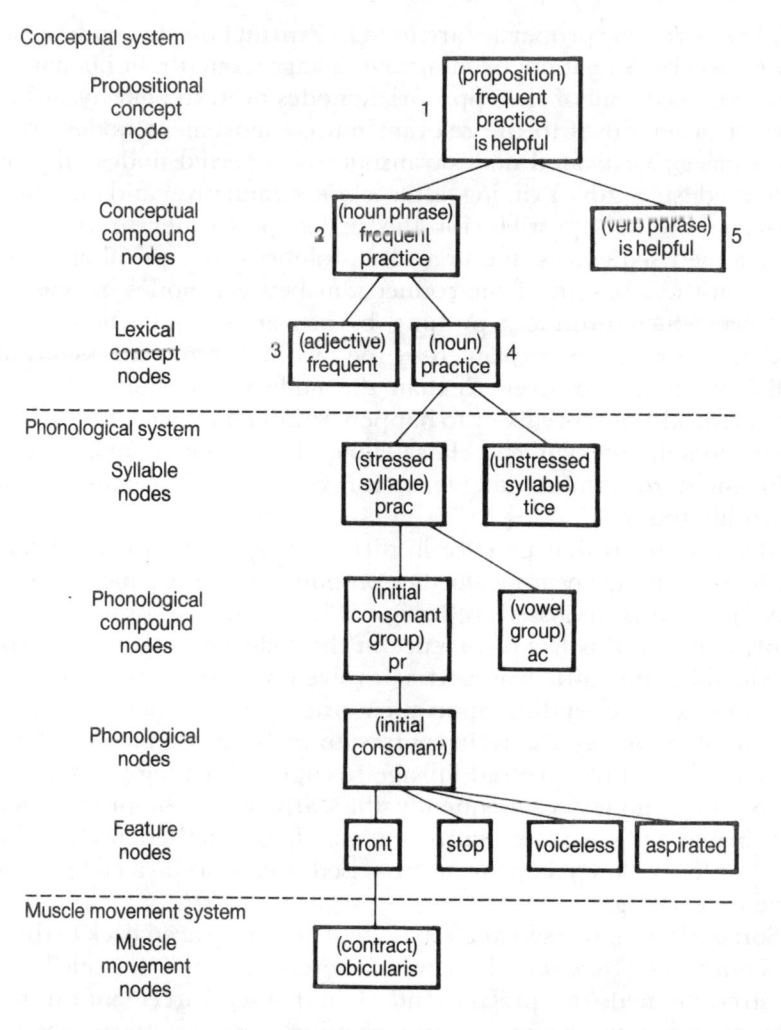

Figure 2.6 An action hierarchy consisting of nodes in the conceptual, phonological and muscle movement systems for producing aspects of the sentence "Frequent practice is helpful". The numbers indicate the order of activation of the nodes shown. Syntactic domain appears in parentheses. (From MacKay, 1982.)

representation of a sentence. A second is made up of nodes which are directly related to the specific muscle patterns which produce the behaviour. In the case of speech production this includes the tongue, larynx, velum and lips.

Three dynamic properties are used to explain how this node structure system works: activation, priming and linkage strength. For behaviour to occur correctly, all of the appropriate nodes need to be activated in the correct order down to the relevant muscle movement nodes. Priming takes place as activated nodes transmit to connected nodes, to produce increased strength. Priming effects are cumulative and are used to explain how it is possible for the skilled performer to run off fast preplanned sequences due to a sort of anticipatory priming effect. In addition the strength of the connections between nodes increases with practice which produces priming by activating connections between nodes. Errors can be explained by the fact that some extraneous nodes will have a greater strength than the node which should have been activated. This is more likely to happen within nodes which belong to the same domain or syntactic class. Hence in speech errors, nouns are substituted for nouns and verbs for verbs which is indeed what is generally found.

MacKay stated that practice in different types of speech production conformed to the linear log–log law proposed by Newell and Rosenbloom (1981) which is discussed in Section 2.3. The theory provides another explanation of this law of practice in the following manner. In speech production, the different nodes involved will vary in their rates of improvement depending upon their prior practice. Some unpractised nodes will improve rapidly, in contrast to well-practised nodes which will have no room for increased linkage strength. Learning is a function of all of these nodes. Consequently the early stages of practice will be dominated by the rapid improvement of unpractised nodes whereas later on only slowly improving practised nodes are available to contribute to learning.

Some of the notions in MacKay's theory can be traced back to the work of Thorndike (1898) and his laws of exercise and effect. Node links can be strengthened with practice and of course reinforcement can lead to strengthening via activation and priming. One interesting aspect of Mackay's theory is that it can explain how mental practice can result in subsequent behavioural improvements, since the interconnections between some mental nodes may be strengthened by mental practice. The theory provides a novel conceptualisation of what occurs between the stimulus and response during learning. It is well tailored to explaining the results in the area of speech production, although MacKay argued for its general applicability to skill acquisition. The major difficulty for the theory is determining how to use it in a new domain. In other words, how does one determine which mental, muscle and other nodes and interconnections are used in certain skills? In speech production, it is argued that mental nodes correspond to grammatical distinctions such as proposition, noun or verb phrase, adjective or noun. This is convenient and useful, even though it might be argued that other, especially higher order, mental/cognitive distinctions may be important. Also in other domains, nodes may not be so easily subdivided in correspondence to behaviour in that domain. What node structures represent problem-solving, car-driving etc.? Much work remains to be done to demonstrate that the node structure approach has generality.

Anderson's theory of cognitive skill acquisition

A most influential theory of skill acquisition has been proposed by Anderson during the last decade (Anderson, 1982, 1983, 1987). The stages of skill acquisition suggested by Anderson are similar to, as Anderson acknowledged, those in Fitts' three-phase theory published twenty years earlier. (A discussion of Fitts' theory is given earlier in this section.) Nevertheless, the hypothesised processes which are responsible for the transition from novice to expert are quite different from those suggested by Fitts. In one sense, Anderson has elaborated Fitts' ideas in greater detail using the vocabulary of cognitive psychology. The theory addresses the *cognitive* basis of skills and to its credit, has provided a framework for understanding a range of skills including computer programming, text editing, making geometry proofs, performing arithmetic and playing chess.

Before embarking on a description of this theory, it is necessary to introduce two notions:

1. The distinction between declarative and procedural knowledge.
2. The nature of a production system.

The characteristics of declarative knowledge are quite different from those of procedural knowledge. Declarative knowledge is essentially factual knowledge which can be stated and made explicit. Examples include: the fact that there are five main controls in my car – the clutch, the brake, the accelerator, the steering wheel and the gearstick; the explanation of how the ignition and carburettor systems combine to produce movement of the piston in an engine. In contrast, procedural knowledge is concerned with *how* to do something which is often implicit and not easily verbalised by the performer, e.g. driving a car; diagnosing malfunctions in a car. This procedural knowledge is the cognitive basis for skilled performance. In Ryle's terms (Ryle, 1949), declarative knowledge is equivalent to "knowing *that*" something is true, whereas procedural knowledge is equivalent to "knowing *how*" to do something. Anderson's theory is concerned with how procedural knowledge is developed from declarative knowledge and how it is turned into the fast, accurate and flexible routines of skilled performance.

A production system is made up of a set of productions or rules of the form:

IF condition X is met,
THEN execute Y.

Hence when condition X is satisfied by the current state, the THEN part is executed, i.e. whatever is specified as Y. IF...THEN rules have been used by psychologists to explain the nature of expertise and, in Anderson's case, also its acquisition. Experts have more, more detailed and accurate rules than novices in the area of their expertise which guide their skilled performance. Rules have been particularly useful in explaining the nature of problem-solving expertise. Hence an experienced car mechanic will have a large repertoire of rules which enables faster diagnosis of car malfunctions than the average motorist. We might all recognise the following rule:

IF the goal is to start the car
and the engine will not fire
and the fuel indicator is near empty
THEN fill the car with petrol.

Anderson's theory explains how skill acquisition is a process of developing and refining such rules in the transition from declarative knowledge to a highly tuned procedural knowledge. Anderson proposed that there are three main stages in the development of skill, each of which is discussed below:

1. The declarative stage.
2. The knowledge compilation stage.
3. The tuning stage.

1. The declarative stage. Initially, the trainee only has some facts concerning the new task (i.e. declarative knowledge). Task performance is attempted by using these facts in conjunction with general problem-solving procedures (as opposed to procedures tailored to carrying out the task). Sometimes analogies are useful in working out how to tackle the task. Task performance at this stage will make heavy demands on working memory and attentional resources and will be slow, inaccurate and effortful. Anderson (1985) provided an example of a person learning to drive who rehearses declarative knowledge concerning the location of the gears and the sequence of movements involved in changing gear. The following general rule may be used to figure out how to drive the car forward:

> IF the goal is to achieve a state X
> and M is a method for achieving state X
> THEN set as a subgoal to apply M (Anderson, 1985, p. 234).

The learner knows that the gearstick has to be moved to the upper left of a figure H to get forward motion. Application of the above general rule would result in a subgoal being set of moving the gearstick to the upper left of the H.

The examples provided by Anderson of difficulties experienced during this declarative stage (e.g. in making a geometry proof, Anderson, 1982, pp. 374–380) are illustrations of poor training practice. This is not unusual. Instructions given to a trainee often do not specify adequately *how* the task should be performed. This is only possible after a systematic analysis of the task has been completed which is the subject of Chapters 5–8 of this book. However, even if good analysis eliminates any discrepancy between what the trainee is told and what is needed to perform the task, it is still necessary for the trainee to develop the appropriate procedure by "doing" the task. Only then will procedural knowledge develop.

2. The knowledge compilation stage. By the end of this stage, the trainee has developed specific procedures (procedural knowledge) for performing the task. Thus a person learning to drive will have a rule for driving forward such as:

> IF the goal is to drive forward from stationary
> THEN set as subgoals
>   1. Disengage the clutch.
>   2. Move the gearstick to the upper left of the H.
>   3. Engage the clutch.
>   4. Press the accelerator. (Adapted from Anderson, 1985, p. 235.)

Any task-specific procedure, made up of many rules, is developed by what Anderson termed *knowledge compilation* which translates declarative knowledge into procedural knowledge. There are two important processes in knowledge compilation which contribute to the acceleration of skilled performance with practice.

(a) *Composition* is a process by which adjacent rules are collapsed or merged into a single more direct rule. Thus rules 1 and 2 below can be merged to create rule 3.

Rule 1   IF the goal is to avoid a collision
                  and it is not possible to swerve
              THEN set as a subgoal stopping the car.

Rule 2   IF the subgoal is to stop the car
              THEN hit the brake.

Rule 3 = rule 1 + rule 2
              IF the goal is to avoid a collision
                  and it is not possible to swerve
              THEN hit the brake.

There are various types of composition which need not concern us here.

(b) *Proceduralisation* is the other process of knowledge compilation which enables a rule to incorporate more task relevant information. If a rule is used repeatedly in a particular context then a new rule is created with the details of that context. Therefore if rule 3 above was used repeatedly to avoid hitting pedestrians in crowded streets, the following more specific rule would be developed:

              IF the goal is to avoid hitting a pedestrian
                  and it is a crowded street
              THEN hit the brake.

The advantage of such proceduralisation is that the person does not have to recall information into working memory in order to execute the rule. The more general rule 3 covers various types of collision and the different situations in which it is not possible to take avoiding action. The proceduralised version of rule 3 is more specific and therefore can be executed faster.

3. The tuning stage. Even when knowledge has been compiled into a procedural form, improvement still occurs as the skill is tuned or adjusted. There are three mechanisms which accomplish this tuning or procedural learning:

> A *generalisation* process by which production rules become broader in their range of applicability, a *discrimination* process by which the rules become narrower, and a *strengthening* process by which better rules are strengthened and poorer rules weakened (Anderson, 1982, p. 390; italics added).

Generalisation enables a new general rule to be created which captures what two or more specific rules have in common. Discrimination is the reverse of generalisation, since it seeks out the attributes which discriminate between rules which have been successfully and unsuccessfully applied. Finally, each rule is assumed to have a strength which affects whether it is likely to be used in the future when it is competing with other rules. The strength of a rule is increased when it is used and decreased when it is unsuccessfully used. All of these tuning mechanisms take account of feedback concerning whether or not performance was successful. (The importance of feedback as a learning variable is discussed in Section 9.3).

Anderson's three stages can be mapped onto those proposed in Fitts' three-phase theory. The declarative stage is equivalent to Fitts' cognitive stage, whilst knowledge compilation is equivalent to Fitts' associative phase. Further learning occurs even after knowledge is in a procedural form. This is labelled tuning by Anderson and the autonomous stage by Fitts. Another similarity and criticism of both theories is that they are descriptive rather than predictive. Plausible accounts are provided of qualitative changes in the development of a range of skills, but these do not enable one to predict how long each stage will take for one particular skill. Hunt (1989) reached a similar conclusion about Anderson's theory:

> The ACT* model has been applied to a wide variety of phenomena varying from recognition memory experiments to problem solving in geometry and computer programming. The applications are more demonstrations of consistency of the theory with gross observations than demonstrations of detailed, accurate predictions. The breadth of the theory's applications is impressive (Hunt, 1989, p. 612).

Skill acquisition according to Anderson is concerned with the development and refinement of rules. Construction of these rules is accomplished by "doing" the skill, an aspect which other theorists have also emphasised (cf. Anzai and Simon, 1979). The implication for training is obvious. Training, through careful analysis, should attempt to identify and pass on to the trainee the rule structure underlying skilled performance, thus minimising the difficulty of constructing task-specific procedures. The declarative and knowledge compilation stages are difficult, slow and require considerable effort on the part of the trainee. There exists a trade-off between the quality of material provided during training and the cognitive gymnastics required of the trainee. The better the training material, the less is required of the trainee during the declarative and compilation stages and vice versa. Even if the rules and how they operate can be defined in advance of training, it is still necessary for the trainee to internalise them by practice and modify them appropriately with changes in the task/environment. An important implication of Anderson's theory is that training must provide an opportunity for performing the task. Skill is developed by "doing" for which there is no substitute.

Another point which should be made is that Anderson uses a computer metaphor to understand the development of skill. Thus the building blocks of cognition are rules. Initially, rules are interpreted with factual knowledge until they are compiled into specific procedures which can be executed automatically. This view of the cognitive basis of skill should be applauded because of its utility in explaining the nature and acquisition of skill in various domains. However, it should not become too restrictive in allowing us to represent skill acquisition in different and even more useful ways in the future.

Finally, Anderson's theory assumes that learning has to pass through a declarative stage before procedural knowledge can be achieved. This assumption is contentious as various writers have argued that some knowledge is implicit and cannot be verbalised, as opposed to knowledge which is explicit which can be verbalised (for a discussion of this topic, see Broadbent, 1990). Implicit knowledge may be acquired in a different manner to explicit knowledge which does not involve a transition from working memory to long-term memory as suggested by Anderson (Hayes and Broadbent, 1988).

2.5 FURTHER QUALITATIVE CHANGES IN SKILL ACQUISITION

The preceding sections of this chapter have already mentioned some important qualitative changes which occur during skill acquisition. Old knowledge is reorganised and integrated with new knowledge which is accompanied by the development of new knowledge structures involving goals, plans, schemata, etc. Earlier in this chapter we learned how JC's exceptional memory for restaurant orders was the consequence of strategies which had been developed for coding orders. Similarly, Lesgold emphasised how radiological expertise was developed through the development and refinement of a schema which guided an expert's perception and interpretation of an X-ray picture. Those responsible for training have to attempt to discover the nature and organisation of knowledge which underpins skilled performance of the tasks to be trained.

Each theory of skill acquisition (Section 2.4), discusses the qualitative changes which occur during the learning of some tasks. Even though the emphasis of each theory is different, some generalisations do emerge. All agree on the shift from the stuttering and clumsy attempts of the novice to the refined and organised performance of the expert. During the initial stage of skill acquisition, the trainee is dependent upon (verbal) instructions, information from the task and also feedback concerning the success or otherwise of performance. The quality of the training material and the abilities and experience of the trainee will determine just how much of a struggle these initial attempts at under-standing and performing the task are. At this stage high demands are made of working memory, a point emphasised by Anderson's theory, in which the trainee has to construct task-relevant procedures. There is not only a quantitative reduction in the trainee's workload (i.e. processing requirements) as skill develops (e.g. Bainbridge, 1989) but also a qualitative change (e.g. Logie *et al.*, 1989). During training, a trainee learns what information is relevant and what is irrelevant in the task environment. Relevant information is coded with increasing efficiency into larger and more discriminating patterns. This not only means that more can be stored in working memory but also that these patterns are more likely to be matched with those in long-term memory. The trainee "knows" what to look for and how to respond and becomes less dependent upon verbal advice and feedback from the trainer. Methods or procedures are built up for tackling the task which are as versatile as is necessary to cope with variations in the task presented or experienced by the trainee. Gradually these mental procedures dictate what the trainee attends to, how it is interpreted and the course of action taken. Whilst they lead to fast task performance, they can have negative effects and may result in rigid or stereotyped behaviour which is inappropriate when the task is varied slightly. Errors committed by a trained person are likely to be of a quite different kind to those made by an untrained person. This is discussed in the last section of this chapter.

Hierarchical nature of skill

We have mentioned that one feature of skilled performance is that it is highly organised. Psychologists generally agree that this organisation is hierarchical in nature (e.g. Anderson, 1982; Miller, Galanter and Pribram, 1960). It is helpful to use a computer analogy to explain what is meant by this:

> The opportunity to develop complex programs to govern the operations of large electronic data-processing systems has led to new conceptions of how skilled performance may be organized in man. The operation of such systems is governed by a program or sequence of instructions. Parts of the program may be repeated over and over again. These short, fixed sequences of operations are written as *subroutines* which may be called into

play as units by the overall program. Such subroutines may be repeated over and over again until some predetermined point is reached or until interrupted by the overall program. These fixed sequences are under the control of a higher level or *executive program* which provides the overall logical or decision framework that gives the system its flexible and adaptive characteristic. In much the same way, some sequences of movement become fixed units within complex human activity. These fixed units are quite automatic, and may be incorporated as components in many different activities. The timing and order of these units will vary with different skills and provide the unique character of each activity. Learning skills involves a new integration and ordering of units, many of which may be transferred as a whole from other activities (Fitts and Posner, 1967, pp. 10–11).

There are two important implications of skills being hierarchically organised. The first is that during skill acquisition, what we might term "action units" (cognitive and/or physical), are gradually learned and assembled into larger action units in a hierarchical structure. The notion of larger units, groupings or chunks can be traced back to the ideas of Bryan and Harter (1897, 1899). The second implication is that "action units" at one level are controlled by "action units" at the next higher level. Hence with skill acquisition, control passes to higher and higher levels. Some have labelled the highest level processes *metacognitive*, indicating that they select and execute the appropriate lower-level cognitive processes or "action units". When skill becomes highly developed, it also tends to become "automatic" and the skilled performer is often not consciously aware of how it is organised. Thus the expert may be unable to verbalise the basis of his expertise and his verbal descriptions are qualitatively quite different from those of the novice who is struggling to learn lower level "action units".

Take piano-playing as an example. Initially striking a single key on the piano might be an "action unit" which is controlled on the basis of a simple feedback loop. However, this "action unit" becomes a subordinate element of playing a chord which in turn might be part of playing a piece of Chopin. Even striking the single key can be analysed into its subordinate "action units", such as moving the hand into position and using the correct finger at the correct speed etc.

Psychologists have used different vocabularies for describing this hierarchical nature of skill. Anderson's (1982) theory of skill acquisition uses IF...THEN type rules, as its "action units", which are organised in a hierarchical goal structure. High-level rules may set the subgoals to be executed. Miller, Galanter and Pribram (1960) suggested, in a classic account, that the building blocks for the hierarchy were plans or TOTE units. TOTE stands for *Test, Operate, Test, Exit* (Figure 2.7a). The "test" phase assesses whether there is a discrepancy between the actual and desired state, and if there is, the "operate" phase executes the necessary activity. This is an iterative process until a subsequent "test" confirms that a discrepancy between the actual and desired states no longer exists. TOTE units exist at different levels as illustrated by the example of hammering a nail (Figure 2.7b). The TOTE of hammering has embedded within it two lower order TOTEs concerned with lifting the hammer and striking the nail. The higher-order TOTE plans how these two lower-order TOTEs are executed if the nail is not flush. When the nail is flush then control passes to another TOTE. One must remember that the TOTEs in Figure 2.7b might themselves be controlled at a higher level by a plan to "fix a piece of wood" which in turn might be part of a plan to "repair the garden fence".

The idea that skilled performance is hierarchically organised has important implications for training. When skill is being acquired or for some reason skilled performance breaks down, some form of analysis is necessary to pinpoint where the person is having difficulty. A person may lack an effective plan, in terms of either sequencing lower level units or monitoring their successful completion. Alternatively, the

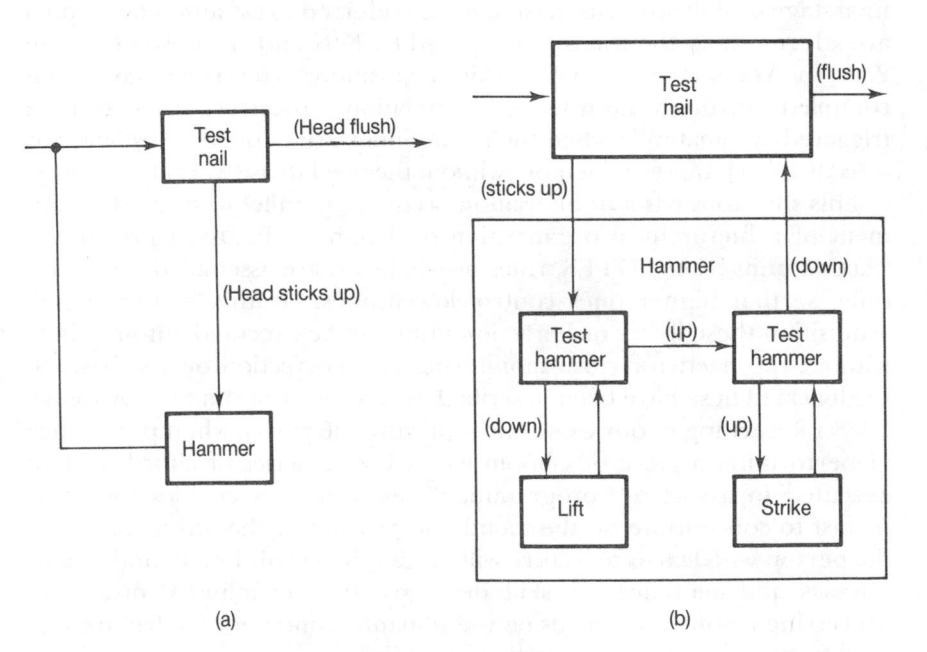

(a)   (b)

Figure 2.7   (a) The TOTE unit; (b) a plan or TOTE hierarchy for hammering a nail (Miller *et al.*, 1960).

nature of the action units might be unknown or mistaken. The challenge for any training analysis is identifying this essentially covert hierarchical structure. Some analysis techniques (e.g. Hierarchical Task Analysis, see Section 6.1) do produce a hierarchical structure, although it does not necessarily reflect the *psychological* organisation of skilled performance. From a training perspective, it is useful to identify what goals, subgoals and so on, the trainee should master since this will begin to delimit how such goals are achieved, which is fundamental to the development of training content.

Automatic and controlled processes

An important characteristic of skilled or expert performance is that little attention is required and the person is able to switch control to some sort of "automatic pilot". Language skills such as speaking and perceptual-motor skills such as riding a bicycle or driving a car provide intuitive evidence of this. Thus the skilled person has spare "capacity" to "time-share" and perform another task at the same time. These features of the final stage of skill acquisition (sometimes referred to as "automatisation") are addressed by the theories proposed by Fitts and Anderson (Section 2.4). In Anderson's theory of skill acquisition, after rules have been compiled (through knowledge compilation processes), they can be triggered automatically when the if-conditions are satisfied. This happens directly from long-term memory without the need to use working memory.

This shift towards automatisation occurs in parallel with the development of a hierarchical organisation of action as discussed previously. "Action units", i.e. TOTES, rules or whatever, are assembled hierarchically, so that higher ones control lower ones. Gradually during skill acquisition these lower order action units can be executed automatically without the need for close monitoring and correction on the basis of feedback. (These have been described as "motor programmes" by Keele, 1968.) Returning to our example of playing the piano, when proficiency of performing a piece of Chopin is reached, a series of chords can be executed in a sort of "programmed" fashion. This enables the good pianist to concentrate on the mood and rhythm of the music. Similarly the person who learns to lecture will gradually reel off longer and longer phrases and sentences as skill develops, thus enabling control and processing resources to focus on the semantic content of the lecture and modification to it to suit a particular audience.

A classic study by Pew (1966) demonstrated this shift in the nature and level of control when a tracking task was learned. A target moving across an oscilloscope had to be kept as close as possible to a central position by pressing two keys which resulted in an acceleration of the target either to the left or right. Early in training, control was poor because the person pressed a key and waited to see the results of this action before initiating their next response, i.e. control is dependent on feedback or is "closed loop". Inter-response times were therefore too long and control was poor as indicated by the records of two persons, HN and RU (Figure 2.8a). At this stage, as Pew observed, each new response was initiated to compensate for the inadequacies of the previous one. Later in training, two strategies for controlling the target developed which reflected the transition to an "open-loop" or more predictive type of control. These strategies reflected a "pattern" of actions which were monitored and corrected as such rather than a sequence of individual movements. The two strategies which emerged are illustrated by the records of HN and RU (Figure 2.8b). HN responded more frequently than earlier in training but occasionally paused a little longer to make a single response which corrected the drift of the target away from the centre. A second strategy, adopted by RU, was to correct any drift of the target by pressing one key slightly longer than the other one. This was a better strategy since it did not result in an increase in inter-response time. Pew's study illustrated that as skill became hierarchically organised, control moved to the level of patterns such that individual responses were made automatically with minimal attention devoted to monitoring their execution. It is significant that even in the performance of a simple task, which

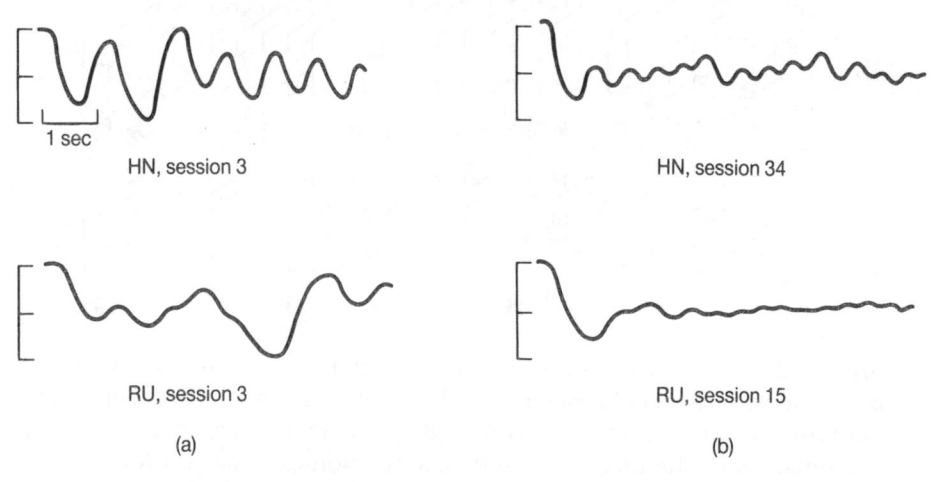

Figure 2.8   Performance of HN and RU, (a) early and (b) late in training (Pew, 1966). The vertical axis represents displacement of the target from the centre of the oscilloscope and the horizontal axis indicates time.

had no obvious way of being organised, new strategies were developed by trainees which resulted in increased efficiency. Pew's finding of a shift from a "closed-loop" type of control to a more predictive "open-loop" form later in training has been corroborated by many studies concerned with the acquisition of process control skills (e.g. Moray, Lootsteen and Pajak, 1986).

More recently a series of studies by Schneider and Shiffrin (Schneider and Shiffrin, 1977; Shiffrin and Dumais, 1981; Shiffrin and Schneider, 1977) have described processes which require minimal attention as *automatic* in contrast to *controlled* processes which require considerable attention. *Automatic* processes develop after extensive training and are said to be fast, effortless, not under conscious control and can be executed in parallel with other activities. On the other hand, *controlled* processes are slow, consciously regulated and require considerable effort and attention. These ideas have generated much discussion and controversy. Some have rejected this distinction (e.g. Ryan, 1983) whilst others have interpreted the evidence in different ways (e.g. Cheng, 1985; Logan, 1988). It is therefore worthwhile briefly considering the nature of the studies which demonstrated these differences in type of processing.

In their experiments, Schneider and Shiffrin presented visual displays, containing 1, 2 or 4 characters (letters or numbers). Twenty displays were presented quickly, one at a time (Figure 2.9). Before each

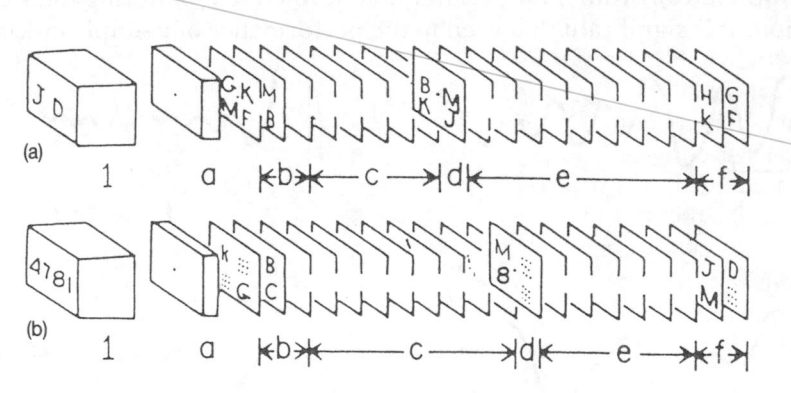

Figure 2.9 Two examples of visual search paradigm. (a) is varied mapping with target characters J and D (frame size = 4). (b) is consistent mapping with target characters 4, 7, 8 and 1 (frame size = 2). (1) is the presentation of the target characters; a: fixation dot goes on for 0.5 sec; b: three frames which never contain the target(s); c: distractor frames; d: target frame; e: distractor frames; f: frames which never contain the target (Schneider and Shiffrin, 1977).

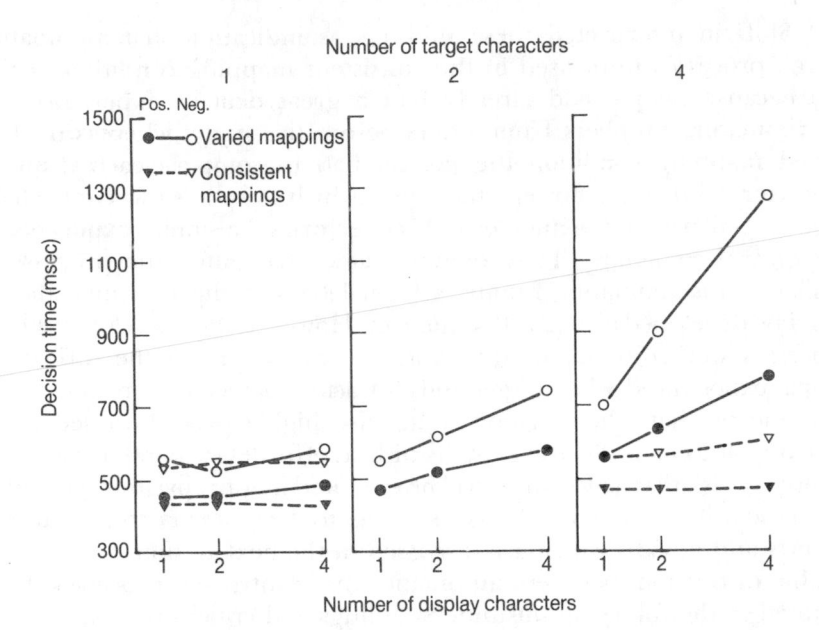

Figure 2.10 Decision times for correct answers as a function of number of target characters (1, 2 or 4) and number of characters on each display (1, 2 or 4). Pos., target present; Neg., target absent. (Schneider and Shiffrin, 1977).

sequence, the person was given a target set of 1, 2 or 4 character(s) to search for and his/her task was to indicate whether any target character was present in any of the displays. The important feature of the experiment was the relationship between the target and distractor characters in the displays. In a "consistent mapping" condition the target character was always from a different set of characters to that used for the distractor items. Hence, in this condition, if a number had to be detected as the target, then the number was displayed amongst letters (Figure 2.9b). The person therefore knew that every number detected must be a target. In the varied mapping condition, the target and distractor characters were selected from the same set. Hence a person may be asked to detect the target letters JD from other letters (Figure 2.9a). Two other factors were varied: the number of target characters (1, 2 or 4) and the number of items in the display (1, 2 or 4). It was found that decision time was faster in the consistent mapping condition and was little affected by an increase in the number of target or display characters (Figure 2.10). In contrast, under varied mapping, decision speed was slower and was affected by both of these factors. Schneider and Shiffrin interpreted these findings as indicating that automatic search processes were used in the consistent mapping condition. This was because people had already had a great deal of experience in discriminating numbers from letters before the study, whereas in the varied mapping condition the person had to compare each display character with each target character, which was a slow controlled process. Shiffrin and Schneider (1977) performed a similar experiment but only used letters. They demonstrated that automatic processes, similar to discriminating numbers from letters in the previous study, could be developed after 2100 sequences. However once developed such processes were difficult to suppress, as was evident in the difficulty people experienced when target and distractor characters were reversed. This means that when "action units" are highly proceduralised and executed automatically, the benefits of fast, effortless action have a cost. There is a risk that action units will be executed inappropriately, possibly when the task is changed. This issue relates to the types of error made by experts and novices which are discussed in the next section.

The distinction between automatic and controlled processes has resulted in the following misunderstandings and criticisms:

1. Skill should not be equated with automatic processes. Rather automatic processes are one aspect of skilled performance, albeit an important one. Schneider's and Shiffrin's experiments used *simple visual* displays and it is not clear how far these results can be extended to other modalities. It is likely that in any complex task there will be a mixture of components requiring both automatic and controlled processes.
2. An automatic process is often assumed to imply that a person lacks control. This is misleading. As skill becomes progressively more hierarchically organised, more automatic processes occur and control passes to a different higher level. Thus lack of control at a lower level of an "action unit" is not incompatible with control at a higher level.
3. Some have argued that there is a continuum between automatic and controlled processes such that some processes are *partially* automated (Norman and Shallice, 1980).
4. Arguably, Schneider and Shiffrin have overemphasised the change in *processing* with skill acquisition at the expense of changes in the structure of skill. Trainees develop new methods for carrying out a task and relinquish older, less successful ones. Hence new knowledge is developed and organised with respect to goals involved in the task. This argument has been put forcibly by Cheng (1985) who argued that Schneider and Shiffrin's distinction between automatic and controlled processes could be attributed to changes in the nature of

the method used rather than the processing. More recently Logan (1988) has put forward what amounts to a theory of skill acquisition which is specifically addressed to the issue of automatisation. Logan, like Cheng, focuses on the changes in *knowledge* which occur with training rather than changes in processing. According to Logan, skilled performance is based on memory for stored instances of the task (in a similar but more complex fashion than Adams' theory). Each time a task is executed a trace is stored and with training more detailed traces are stored and retrieved from memory more quickly.

Types of error

The errors made by an expert or highly trained person are quantitatively and qualitatively different from those of a novice or an untrained person. By definition, experts commit fewer errors than novices as has been evident in the examples discussed in Section 2.1 (e.g. JC's exceptional memory for restaurant orders and the diagnosis of X-ray pictures by experts). What is more interesting to the psychologist, and of potential benefit to the trainer, are the qualitative differences in the nature of errors, some of which reflect different levels of skill.

Identifying the nature of errors is important in both the analysis of a task prior to training and also in the performance of a task during training. It is important to try and identify which aspects of a task are responsible for the errors of the job incumbent or the trainee. Training is a diagnostic process in which trainee's errors provide the trainer (or device, if it is computer-based training) with evidence of the trainee's difficulties. The trainer uses this information to diagnose the trainee's weaknesses and provide remedial material which attempts to eliminate them. This is the philosophy underlying much good training practice whether training is provided by human, machine or a mixture of both. The diagnostic role of a good tutor is emphasised by Collins' theory of inquiry teaching (pp. 304–309) and, of course, is fundamental to the important principle of providing the trainee with intelligent advice or feedback concerning performance (Section 9.3).

One approach to identifying types of error is to use an information-processing model (of the sort represented in Figure 2.2). Errors can occur in any of the psychological processes involved in performing a task beginning with the perception of some information and ending with the execution of some action. Errors may take place in the information-processing activities of monitoring, memory, decision-making, reasoning etc. How a task can be analysed using information-processing categories is discussed in Section 7.1. A similar approach is to conceptualise a task as comprising a series of common stages. These stages can then be used to map out where errors are occurring. Two examples are given by Norman (1986) and Rasmussen (1986) in Table 2.2.

Table 2.2   Cognitive stages required by a task

Norman's seven stages of user activities	Rasmussen's mental activities between initiation of response and action
Establishing the goal	Activation; detection of need
Forming the intention	for action
Specifying the action	Observe information and data
sequence	Identify present state of the system
Executing the action	Interpret consequences for current
Perceiving the system	task, safety, efficiency, etc.
state	Define task; select change of system
Interpreting the state	condition
Evaluating the system	Formulate procedure; plan sequence
state with respect to	of actions
goals and intentions	Execute; coordinate manipulations

Norman's stages are oriented towards human–computer interaction tasks, whereas Rasmussen's have been used in problem-solving contexts, particularly in the control and diagnosis of industrial processes. These two approaches are discussed further in Section 7.3 in terms of how task-related knowledge might be represented and analysed.

Goodstein (1986) reported a study by Norros and Sammatti in which nuclear power plant operators were trained using a simulator. Crews of operators had to deal with various "disturbances" or faults which could be introduced into the simulated plant. Their performance was analysed in terms of deviations from an optimal sequence, and errors were classified into different types and their likely causes. In one study the fault was a break of the manifold of the steam generator and in total "155 errors were identified varying from 9 to 19 per crew". These errors were classified in terms of two dimensions: one dimension concerned the information-processing stage at which errors occurred – observation of the symptoms, diagnosis of the fault, decision-making concerning what should be done, execution of some corrective action, and feedback concerning the results of this action; and the second dimension attempted to pinpoint the different causes of these errors – control room layout,

Table 2.3 Distribution of errors in operating a simulated nuclear power plant having one fault (Norros and Sammatti, 1986)

Error categories	Decision function					n	%
	obs	dia	dec	exe	fb		
1. Control room layout							
11 Separated displays and controls	1				1	2	
12 Unclear layout of panels	1			1		2	
13 Displays difficult to understand							
14 Information missing					1	1	
	2			1	2	5	3.2
2. Procedures							
21 Error in procedures							
22 Deficiencies in procedures	2	1	5	9		17	11.0
23 Contradictions in procedures			1	1		2	
24 Procedures not used			6	2		8	5.2
	2	1	12	12		27	17.4
3. Cooperation							
31 Insufficient concentration			1		2	3	
32 Insufficient communication			7	4		11	7.1
33 Unclear division of tasks							
34 Lack of operational strategy			11			11	7.1
			19	4	2	25	16.2
4. Knowledge and action control							
41 Insufficient process knowledge	3	1	11	6	2	23	14.9
42 Deficiencies in processing information	3		1		1	5	
43 Inaccurate diagnosis		6	1			7	
44 Incorrect action							
45 Omission			4	12	4	20	12.9
46 Delay in decision or action			14	6		20	12.9
47 Significance not understood	1	1	1			3	
48 Lack of supervision				6	2	8	5.2
	7	8	32	30	9	86	55.5
5. Action disturbances							
51 External disturbances							
52 Stress							
53 Operator incapacitated							
						0	0
6. Simulator effect							
61 Differences between controller and simulator	2			6		8	
62 Attitudes towards simulator				4		4	
	2			10		12	7.7
	13	9	63	57	13	155	100
	8.4	5.8	40.6	36.8	8.4	100	

obs: observation; dia: diagnosis; dec: decision; exe: execution; fb: feedback.

procedures, cooperation amongst the crew, knowledge of the plant and actions required, factors affecting operators' actions, and the effect of using the simulator. The results are given in Table 2.3. This sort of detailed information concerning performance errors, in this case for only one fault, has considerable diagnostic value. It can be used to not only debrief each crew with respect to their particular weaknesses, but also to gauge more generally where training can be most profitably targetted.

Over the past decade, errors have been highlighted by the work of Reason (e.g. 1984b, 1987a, b) and Norman (e.g. 1981, 1986) which has provided some fascinating theoretical insights from everyday examples. A dichotomy is drawn by these psychologists between two types of error:

1. *Mistakes.* These are planning failures. A person carries out some action which *was* intended but the action fails to achieve the desired goal. For example, one might hit the wrong computer key whilst editing because one incorrectly thought that it performed a particular function.
2. *Slips.* These occur when an action is performed which was *not* intended. For example one might hit the wrong key unintentionally whilst editing because it was adjacent to the correct key when one's attention was distracted.

This distinction between mistakes and slips is not as straightforward as it might appear, although that need not concern us here. It is important to note that, in the example of hitting the wrong key, it is not possible to differentiate whether this was a mistake or a slip from observation of the action alone. The action is identical in both situations although the training implications are quite different. If it was a mistake, some extra knowledge is required, whereas if it was a slip there is no knowledge deficit but rather a need for the person to monitor his/her action more closely. In more complex tasks which involve a variety of cognitive processes, it is naturally much more difficult to be sure about the reason(s) for errors.

Mistakes. These are the result of incorrect plans of action. In other words, the person did what he/she intended to do but this was incorrect. Mistakes characterise the early stages of skill acquisition (Fitts' cognitive and Anderson's declarative stages) in which the trainee might either misunderstand what the goal and intermediate goals of performance should be, or have no adequate methods for achieving them. Management training is an example in which it is notoriously difficult to specify what the intermediate goals of a manager should be. Those learning to play chess, bridge, tennis or squash have to learn the rules of the game which determine not only what actions are legitimate, i.e. within the rules and those which are not, but also what constitutes "winning". During this early, "intellectualisation" stage of training, the trainee is often unreasonably bombarded with new instructions, procedures and the like. It is not surprising, given the limitations of working memory, that some information is lost, as the trainee struggles in his initial attempts at the task. Those involved in training need to be aware of these potential difficulties and training should be designed to minimise mistakes caused by information overload by providing:

small chunks of information which can be rehearsed;
redundancy or repetition of information;
information which is as directly relevant as possible to both the goal and methods of performance;
materials that are coherent and logical.

Mistakes are not always associated with unskilled performance. Mistakes have been committed by skilled nuclear power plant operators in various incidents which were analysed by Pew, Miller and Feehrer (1981). In the famous Three Mile Island accident, operators failed to diagnose that a relief valve was open and mistakenly interpreted it as being shut. The skill of a process control operator is often reflected in the extent to which both the side-effects and long-term consequences of actions are taken into account (e.g. Herry, 1987).

Mistakes can occur in any of the activities of a task. We have mentioned that information overload creates problems for the novice, whilst even highly skilled persons may reason incorrectly, resulting in mistakes. In a sense, it is very human to make such mistakes. Some problems are so complex, that they are difficult for a person to handle in a rational manner (Reason, 1987a). A person does not have unlimited mental resources in dealing with a problem. People tend to reduce the cognitive strain by simplifying the task confronting them and this can introduce a variety of biases resulting in mistakes. Below are some of these biases (adapted from Reason, 1987b):

1. A tendency to interpret information in terms of recent events, previous successes, and theories which have not been proven.
2. A selective examination of all the available information.
3. Inadequate time devoted to planning what should be done.
4. A low ability to assess statistical information which is linked to poor anticipation and prediction of future events.
5. A poor ability to work out the causal relationships between events.
6. Resistance to change a course of action despite the availability of contradictory information.

When training is being devised for a task, it is important to try and anticipate where mistakes are likely to occur or identify the nature of the mistakes being committed by persons currently performing the task. In a sense the biases elaborated by Reason characterise "natural" human tendencies and therefore training people to overcome them in the context of a particular task is a daunting, but not impossible, goal. In some cases task redesign will be necessary to reduce the possibility of such biases operating.

Slips.   Slips are relatively rare in comparison with the frequency with which mistakes occur. This means that slips are less important from a training perspective although they are no less interesting. Slips are a type of error where the person does something which was not intended. Slips are associated with high levels of skill or "automatic" behaviour and are quickly detected as errors by the person performing them. It is difficult to resist quoting, as an example, the frequently cited observation of James (1890) which illustrates the price we sometimes have to pay for the benefits of being skilled:

> Not only is it the right thing at the right time that we involuntarily do, but the wrong thing also, if it be an habitual thing. Who is there that has never wound up his watch on taking off his waistcoat in the daytime, or taken his latch-key out on arriving at the doorstep of a friend? Very absent-minded persons on going to their bedroom to dress for dinner have been known to take off one garment after another and finally get into bed ... (p. 115).

Slips have been discussed and categorised by Reason (1984a,b) and Norman (1981), both of whom have provided some fascinating examples together with some theoretical insights into why they occur. The above examples from James demonstrate how actions from different tasks can become intermingled. In the preceding section of this chapter we discussed how increasing skill leads to higher levels of control such that lower level action sequences can be run off with little attention required. Sometimes the beginning of one action sequence is taken over or "captured" by another stronger one. This results in an intrusion error as illustrated in James' examples. As Reason (1984b) observed, this sort of slip is associated with well practised actions which are often carried out in familiar surroundings and the person therefore is not required to monitor his or her own actions closely. Besides intrusion errors, slips may manifest themselves in different ways; the correct action is carried out but with respect to the wrong object; an action is repeated unnecessarily; and an action is omitted from a sequence. Some examples of different slips, together with possible reasons for them, are taken from Reason (1984a,b):

1. *Double-capture slips* which involve one stronger habit/skill which intrudes into another one as in the examples from James, previously discussed. Four situations in which these strong habit intrusions may arise are:
   (a) When a change of goal demands a departure from some well-established routine, e.g.: "I had decided to cut down my sugar consumption and wanted to have my cornflakes without it. But I sprinkled sugar on my cereal just as I had always done."
   (b) When changed circumstances require a modification of an established action pattern, e.g.: "We now have two fridges in our kitchen, and yesterday we moved our food from one to the other. This morning I repeatedly opened the fridge that used to hold our food."
   (c) When we enter a familiar environment, e.g.: "I went into my bedroom intending to fetch a book. Instead, I took off my rings, looked into the mirror and came out again without the book."
   (d) When features of our present circumstances contain elements common to those in highly familiar circumstances, e.g.: "I found myself on a friend's doorstep trying to fit my latch-key into the lock."
   (a–d adapted from Reason, 1984a).
2. *Place-losing errors* in which one fails to pay sufficient attention to a well-practised routine and "forgets" the stage one is at in carrying out the task, e.g.: "I was spooning tea into the teapot, and realised I had no idea of how many spoonfuls I'd put in."
3. *Lost goal errors* which occur when one temporarily forgets one's intention, e.g.: "I stopped halfway down the stairs. I couldn't remember what I was going for."
4. *Blends* in which the actions associated with two tasks being performed at about the same time become mixed, e.g.: "During a morning in which there had been several knocks on my office door, the phone rang. I picked up the receiver and bellowed 'come in' at it."
5. *Reversals or behavioural spoonerisms* in which the correct action of a task is performed but to an inappropriate object, e.g.: "I unwrapped a sweet, put the paper in my mouth and threw the sweet into the wastepaper basket."

Undoubtedly these sort of errors are all too embarrassingly familiar. The important point from a training perspective is that these slips will occur *after* a person has been trained to a high level of skill. By definition they are infrequent. They are a reflection of the absent-minded professor syndrome. Since such errors are usually quickly detected by the person making them, generally little damage will be done. An exception will be when a wrong action is carried out in an intolerant environment and the error is not detected by the performer.

One interesting question is the extent to which training can be provided which enables people to avoid making slips or whether slips are an inevitable consequence of being skilled. Even if training or an instruction to be more careful is not effective, changes in the design of tasks involving a high error cost can often be made to accommodate the dangers posed by slips. Thus a computer may require the person to restate the intended action as when a computer disk is being formatted. Alternatively, it is possible that certain actions are required to be carried out by a group or referred to a supervisor before they can be initiated.

REFERENCES

Adams, J.A. (1968). Response feedback and learning. *Psychological Bulletin*, **70**, 486–504.

Adams, J.A. (1971). A closed-loop theory of motor learning. *Journal of Motor Behaviour*, **3**, 111–149.

Adams, J.A. (1984). Learning of movement sequences. *Psychological Bulletin*, **96**, 3–28.

Adams, J.A. (1987). Historical review and appraisal of research on the learning, retention and transfer of human motor skills. *Psychological Bulletin*, **101**(1), 41–74.

Aiken, E.G. and Lau, A.W. (1967). Response prompting and response confirmation. A review of recent literature. *Psychological Bulletin*, **68**, 330–341.

Anderson, J.R. (Ed.) (1981). *Cognitive skills and their acquisition*. Hillsdale, NJ: Lawrence Erlbaum.

Anderson, J.R. (1982). Acquisition of cognitive skill. *Psychological Review*, **4**, 369–406.

Anderson, J.R. (1983). *The architecture of cognition*. Cambridge, MA: Harvard University Press.

Anderson, J.R. (1985). *Cognitive psychology and its implications*. Second edition. New York: W.H. Freeman and Company.

Anderson, J.R. (1987). Skill acquisition: Compilation of weak-method problem solutions. *Psychological Review*, **94**, 192–210.

Annett, J. (1961). The role of knowledge of results in learning: A survey, Report No. 342–3. New York: US Naval Training Devices Center.

Annett, J. (1969). *Feedback and human behaviour*. Harmondsworth: Penguin.

Anzai, Y. and Simon, H.A. (1979). The theory of learning by doing. *Psychological Review*, **86**, 124–140.

Bainbridge, L. (1982). Ironies of automation. In Johannsen, G. and Rijnsdorp, J.E. (Eds) *Analysis, design and evaluation of man-machine systems*. Proceedings of the IFAC/IFIP/ IFORS/IEA Conference, Baden-Baden, Federal Republic of Germany.

Bainbridge, L. (1989). Development of skill, reduction of workload. In Bainbridge, L. and Quintanilla, S.A.R. (Eds) *Developing skills with information technology*. Chichester: John Wiley and Sons.

Bartlett, F.C. (1932). *Remembering*. Cambridge University Press.

Bilodeau, I. McD. (1966). Information feedback. In Bilodeau, E.A. (Ed.) *Acquisition of skill*. New York: Academic Press.

Bower, C.H., Black, J.B. and Turner, T.J. (1979). Scripts in memory for text. *Cognitive Psychology*, **11**, 177–220.

Broadbent, D.E. (1987). Structures and strategies: Where are we now? *Psychological Research*, **49**, 73–79.

Broadbent, D.E. (1990). Effective decisions and their verbal justification. *Philosophical Transactions of the Royal Society of London*, Series B, **327**, 493–50?

Bruner, J.S., Goodnow, J. and Austin, G. (1956). *A study of thinking*. New York: Wiley.

Bryan, W.L. and Harter, N. (1897). Studies in the physiology and psychology of telegraphic language. *Psychological Review*, **4**, 27–53.

Bryan, W.L. and Harter, N. (1899). Studies on the telegraphic language. *Psychological Review*, **6**, 345–375.

Card, S.K., Moran, T.P. and Newell, A. (1983). *The psychology of human–computer interaction*. Hillsdale, NJ: Lawrence Erlbaum.

Cheng, P.W. (1985). Restructuring versus automaticity: Alternative accounts of skill acquisition. *Psychological Review*, **92**, 414–423.

Chi, M.T.H., Glaser, R. and Farr, M. (Eds) (1988). *The nature of expertise*. Hillsdale, NJ: Lawrence Erlbaum.

Crossman, E.R.F.W. (1959). A theory of the acquisition of speed-skill. *Ergonomics*, **2**, 153–166.

De Groot, A.D. (1965). *Thought and choice in chess*. The Hague: Mouton.

De Groot, A.D. (1966). Perception and memory versus thought. In Kleinmuntz, B. (Ed.) *Problem solving*. New York: Wiley.

De Jong, R.J. (1957). The effects of increasing skill on cycle-time and its consequences for time-standards. *Ergonomics*, **1**, 51–60.

Department of Employment (1971). *Glossary of training terms*. 2nd edition. London: HMSO.

Ericsson, K.A. and Polson, P.G. (1988). A cognitive analysis of exceptional memory for restaurant orders. In Chi, M.T.H., Glaser, R. and Farr, M. (Eds) *The nature of expertise*. Hillsdale, NJ: Lawrence Erlbaum.

Fitts, P.M. (1962). Factors in complex skill training. In Glaser, R. (Ed.) *Training research and education*. University of Pittsburg. (Reprinted in 1965, New York: Wiley.)

Fitts, P.M. and Posner, M.I. (1967). *Human performance*. Belmont, CA: Brooks Cole.

Gentner, D.R. (1988). Expertise in typewriting. In Chi, M.T.H., Glaser, R. and Farr, M. (Eds) *The nature of expertise*. Hillsdale, NJ: Lawrence Erlbaum.

Goodstein, L.P. (Ed.) (1986). Training diagnostic skills for nuclear power plants. Final Report of the NKA Project LIT-4. Nordic Liaison Committee for Atomic Energy.

Hayes, N. and Broadbent, D.E. (1988). Two modes of learning for interactive tasks. *Cognition*, **28**, 249–277.

Herry, N. (1987). Errors in the execution of prescribed instructions. Design of process control work aids. In Rasmussen, J., Duncan, K.D. and Leplat, J. (Eds) *New technology and human error*. Chichester: John Wiley.

Holding, D.H. (1965). *Principles of training*. Oxford: Pergamon Press.

Hull, C.L. (1943). *Principles of behaviour*. New York: Appleton-Century.

Hunt, E. (1989). Cognitive science: Definition, status, and questions. *Annual Review of Psychology*, **40**, 603–629.

James, W. (1890). *The principles of psychology*. New York: Henry Holt.

Keele, S.W. (1968). Movement control in skilled motor performance. *Psychological Bulletin*, **70**, 387–403.

Keller, F.S. (1958). The phantom plateau. *Journal of Experimental Analysis of Behaviour*, **1**, 1–13.

Klemmer, E.T. (1962). Communication and human performance. *Human Factors*, **4**, 75–79.

Lesgold, A.M. (1984). Human skill in a computerized society: Complex skills and their acquisition. *Behaviour Research Methods, Instruments and Computers*, **16**(2), 79–87.

Lesgold, A.M., Rubinson, H., Feltovich, P., Glaser, P., Klopfer, D. and Wang, Y. (1988). Expertise in a complex skill: Diagnosing X-ray pictures. In Chi, M.T.H., Glaser, R. and Farr, M. (Eds) *The nature of expertise*. Hillsdale, NJ: Lawrence Erlbaum.

Logan, G.D. (1985). Skill and automaticity. Relations, implications and future directions. *Canadian Journal of Psychology*, **39**, 367–386.

Logan, G.D. (1988). Toward an instance theory of automatization. *Psychological Review*, **95**(4), 492–527.

Logie, R., Baddeley, A., Mané, A., Donchin, E. and Sheptak, R. (1989). Working memory in the acquisition of complex cognitive skills. *Acta Psychologica*, **71**, 53–87.

MacKay, D.G. (1982). The problems of flexibility, fluency, and speed–accuracy trade-off in skilled behaviour. *Psychological Review*, **89**(5), 483–506.

Miller, G.A., Galanter, E. and Pribram, K.H. (1960). *Plans and the structure of behaviour*. New York: Holt, Rinehart and Winston.

Moran, T.P. (1980). Compiling cognitive skill. AIP Memo 150, Xerox, Palo Alto Research Center.

Moray, N., Lootsteen, P. and Pajak, J. (1986). Acquisition of process control skills. *IEEE Transactions on Systems, Man, and Cybernetics*, **16**, 497–504.

Neeves, D.M. and Anderson, J.R. (1981). Knowledge compilation: Mechanisms for the automatization of cognitive skills. In Anderson, J.R. (Ed.) *Cognitive skills and their acquisition*. Hillsdale, NJ: Lawrence Erlbaum.

Neisser, U., Novick, R. and Lazar, R. (1963). Searching for ten targets simultaneously. *Perceptual and Motor Skills*, **17**, 955–961.

Newell, A. and Rosenbloom, A. (1981). Mechanisms of skill acquisition and the law of practice. In Anderson, J.R. (Ed.) *Cognitive skills and their acquisition*. Hillsdale, NJ: Lawrence Erlbaum.

Norman, D.A. (1981). Categorization of action slips. *Psychological Review*, **88**, 1–15.

Norman, D.A. (1986). Cognitive engineering. In Norman, D.A. and Draper, S.W. (Eds) *User-centered system design*. Hillsdale, NJ: Lawrence Erlbaum.

Norman, D.A. and Shallice, T. (1980). Attention to action: willed and automatic control of behaviour. Report 99. San Diego: University of California, San Diego.

Norros, L. and Sammatti, P. (1986). Nuclear power plant operator errors during simulator training. Research Report 446. Espoo: Technical Research Centre of Finland.

Pew, R.W. (1966). Acquisition of hierarchical control over the temporal organisation of a skill. *Journal of Experimental Psychology*, **71**, 764–771.

Pew, R.W., Miller, D.C. and Feehrer, C.E. (1981). Evaluation of proposed control room improvements through analysis of critical operator decisions. Final Report 891. Cambridge, MA: Bolt, Beranek and Newman.

Postman, L. (1947). The history and present status of the law of effect. *Psychological Bulletin*, **44**, 489–563.

Rabbitt, P.M.A. (1981). Sequential reactions. In Holding, D.H. (Ed.) *Human skills*. New York: Wiley.

Rasmussen, J. (1986). *Information processing and human–machine interaction: An approach to cognitive engineering*. Amsterdam: North Holland.

Reason, J. (1984a). Absent-mindedness and cognitive control. In Harris, J. and Morris, P. (Eds) *Everyday memory, actions and absent-mindedness*. London: Academic Press.

Reason, J. (1984b). Lapses of attention in everyday life. In Parasuraman, R. and Davies, D.R. (Eds) *Varieties of attention*. Orlando: Academic Press.

Reason, J. (1987a). A preliminary classification of mistakes. In Rasmussen, J., Duncan, K.D. and Leplat, J. (Eds) *New technology and human error*. Chichester: John Wiley.

Reason, J. (1987b). The psychology of mistakes: A brief review of planning failures. In Rasmussen, J., Duncan, K.D. and Leplat, J. (Eds) *New technology and human error*. Chichester: John Wiley.

Restle, F. and Greeno, J. (1970). *Introduction to mathematical psychology*. Reading, Ma: Addison-Wesley.

Rumelhart, D.E. and Norman, D.A. (1978). Accretion, tuning and restructuring. Three modes of learning. In Cotton, J.W. and Klatzky, R. (Eds) *Semantic factors in cognition*. Hillsdale, NJ: Lawrence Erlbaum.

Rumelhart, D.E. and Norman, D.A. (1981). Analogical processes in learning. In Anderson, J.R. (Ed.) *Cognitive skills and their acquisition*. Hillsdale, NJ: Lawrence Erlbaum.

Ryan, C. (1983). Reassessing the automaticity-control distinction: Item recognition as a paradigm case. *Psychological Review*. **90**, 171–178.

Ryle, G. (1949). *The concept of mind*. London: Hutchinson.

Schank, R.C. and Abelson, R. (1977). *Scripts, plans, goals and understanding*. Hillsdale, NJ: Lawrence Erlbaum.

Schmidt, R.A. (1975). A schema theory of discrete motor skill learning. *Psychological Review*, **82**(4), 225–260.

Schmidt, R.A. (1982a). *Motor control and learning*. Champaign, IL: Human Kinetics.

Schmidt, R.A. (1982b). The schema concept. In Kelso, J.A.S. (Ed.) *Human motor behaviour: An introduction*. Hillsdale, NJ: Lawrence Erlbaum.

Schneider, W. (1985). Training high-performance skills: Fallacies and guidelines. *Human Factors*, **27**(3), 285–300.

Schneider, W. and Shiffrin, R.M. (1977). Controlled and automatic human information processing: I. Detection, search and attention. *Psychological Review*, **84**, 1–66.

Seibel, R. (1963). Discrimination reaction time for a 1,023 alternative task. *Journal of Experimental Psychology*, **66**, 215–226.

Shannon, C.E. (1948). A mathematical theory of communication. *Bell System Technical Journal*, **27**, 379–423, 623–656.

Shapiro, D.C. and Schmidt, R.A. (1982). The schema theory: Recent evidence and developmental implications. In Kelso, J.A.S. and Clark, J.E. (Eds) *The development of movement control and co-ordination*. Chichester: Wiley.

Shiffrin, R.M. and Schneider, W. (1977). Controlled and automatic human information processing: II. Perceptual learning, automatic attending, and a general theory. *Psychological Review*, **84**, 127–190.

Shiffrin, R.M. and Dumais, S.T. (1981). The development of automatism. In Anderson, J.R. (Ed.) *Cognitive skills and their acquisiton*. Hillsdale, NJ: Lawrence Erlbaum.

Skinner, B.F. (1953). *Science and human behavior*. New York: The Macmillan Company.

Snoddy, G.S. (1926). Learning and stability. *Journal of Applied Psychology*, **10**, 1–36.

Stammers, R. and Patrick, J. (1975). *The psychology of training*. London: Methuen.

Taylor, D.W. (1943). Learning telegraphic code. *Psychological Bulletin*, **40**, 461–487.

Thorndike, E.L. (1898). Animal intelligence: An experimental study of the associative processes in animals. *Psychological Review, Monograph Supplement*, **2**, 8.

Thurstone, L.L. (1919). The learning curve equation. *Psychological Monographs*, **26**, 114.

Welford, A.T. (1968). *Fundamentals of skill*. London: Methuen.

White, B.Y. and Frederiksen, J.R. (1987). Qualitative models and intelligent learning environments. In Lawler, R.W. and Yazdani, M. (Eds) *Artificial intelligence and education, Volume 1: Learning environments and tutoring systems*. Norwood, NJ: Lawrence Erlbaum.

CHAPTER 3
Transfer and retention of skill

3.1 INTRODUCTION

This chapter discusses the topics of transfer and retention of skills. One feels distinctly uneasy telling people on the one hand that both of these topics are central to training and have been studied since the beginning of the century, and yet on the other hand, no strong theoretical ideas exist to integrate many diverse findings. Hence, whilst exhorting those in training to take greater notice of these topics, there is no coherent corpus of knowledge from which training principles flow. Perhaps this is unnecessarily pessimistic; the reader will be the judge.

We all believe that the skills and knowledge we possess affect how easily new skills are developed. Thus learning to hit a ball with a squash racquet is easier if one can already play tennis. Psychologists have studied this topic of transfer extensively throughout this century. Essentially it is believed that transfer, of a facilitating kind, will occur between tasks which require the same skills or skill components. This was proposed as long ago as 1901 by Thorndike and Woodworth who suggested that transfer depended upon the number of "identical elements" shared between two tasks. Understanding and predicting transfer therefore boiled down to analysing the similarities between tasks and the skills they required. How such similarity is defined and measured has been a major headache. Early in this century, following the behaviourist tradition, similarity between tasks was defined in terms of stimulus and response elements. Subsequently attempts have been made to examine similarity in terms of the intervening cognitive processes although how this is done has been influenced by the changing fashions in psychology.

Memory has been the most extensively studied area of psychology since Ebbinghaus found his famous "curve of forgetting". Most work has been directed toward developing a theoretical understanding of the structure and nature of memory, particularly for verbal materials. The majority of this work, until recently, has involved laboratory-based memory experiments which, as Annett (1977) pointed out, differ in significant ways from the retention of skills in everyday situations. Classically, memory experiments have used unfamiliar, sometimes non-meaningful, material and retention is assessed in a situation which is

75

intentionally devoid of helpful cues. The reverse is true of practical skills, parts of which are usually already in a person's repertoire and are therefore familiar and retention is usually required in a situation which is rich in cues for action. The literature concerning skill loss has been dominated by the retention of perceptual-motor skills, which was the dominant concern of experimental psychologists up to the 1960s. Whilst there are many new ideas concerning the *acquisition* of cognitive skills emanating from recent cognitive psychology, there is very little corresponding work on the retention of cognitive skills, particularly complex ones. What is known about the retention of well-learned, skilled performance is well established and has not seen any dramatic changes from studies carried out in the 1960s.

3.2 DEFINITIONS AND MEASURES OF TRANSFER

Transfer is sometimes referred to as "transfer of learning" or "transfer of training". The Department of Employment's *Glossary of Training Terms* (1971) defined transfer of training as that which:

> occurs whenever the existence of a previously established habit or *skill* has an influence upon the acquisition, performance or relearning of another habit or *skill*. "Positive transfer" occurs when the existence of the previous habit or skill facilitates learning the new one; "negative transfer" refers to the interference by a previously learned habit or *skill* on new learning (p. 32).

This definition emphasises that transfer, either positive or negative, takes place both during the *learning* of new skills and also the *performance* of old ones. Some errors, either slips or mistakes (discussed in Section 2.5), may be the result of the negative transfer from an existing skill to the *performance* of another one. One kind of slip is an intrusion error in which a procedure or "action unit" from one skill somehow becomes incorrectly triggered in the performance of another skill. For example, one starts driving to a new destination and then at a familiar junction one slips into the routine of driving to work instead. A well-known example of a mistake due to negative transfer was given in a study of problem solving by Luchins (1942) in which people incorrectly applied a "solution rule" to new problems because it had been successfully used with previous problems. Therefore transfer can occur in either the learning or performance of a skill and it can be either helpful (i.e. positive transfer) or a hindrance (i.e. negative transfer or interference). In some situations there will be no influence between the two skills or tasks, in which case there is zero transfer.

Two further distinctions are commonly made in the discussion of transfer; that between horizontal versus vertical transfer and another between general versus specific transfer. Our discussion so far has focused on horizontal transfer because transfer has been considered from one task to a second task. Vertical transfer is concerned with transfer *within* a task so that mastery of the whole task may be influenced by the transfer of certain subordinate or prerequisite skills. Making mathematical proofs depends on the component skills of reading and being able to interpret the meaning of various symbols. Hence vertical transfer is concerned with transfer from part to whole task training (Section 9.5) and is closely associated with the theoretical ideas of Gagné (Section 8.3). The difference between general and specific transfer, as the terms suggest, lies in the specificity of the transfer effect. General transfer is said to take place when one task affects learning or performance of a range of tasks. One example is the "warm-up" effect where a trainee who has performed one task will perform better on a second task in comparison to another trainee who has not "warmed-up" on that initial task. Another example of general transfer is the phenomenon of "learning how to learn" (Harlow, 1949), where people improve in their ability to learn new tasks after they have had experience or practice in dealing with similar tasks. How "learning strategies" support transfer from one learning situation to others is discussed in Chapter 10.

Transfer studies have used a variety of designs. Two of the most simple transfer designs are illustrated in Table 3.1. Design (a) represents a before and after design in which two matched groups 1 and 2 are compared in their change in performance between the test and retest on task B. If the change in performance for Group 2 is subtracted from the corresponding change for Group 1, we have an estimate of the transfer effect of prior training on task A. If performance by Group 1 at task B is faster or more accurate than that of Group 2, then positive transfer has occurred from task A. On the other hand if Group 1 is worse than Group 2 at task B, then negative transfer (or interference) has taken place from task A. Design (b) is similar to design (a) except that transfer is reflected in how easily Groups 1 and 2 *learn*, rather than perform, task B.

Various measures of transfer exist which have been discussed by Ellis (1965). The aim of training is to maximise the amount of positive transfer, say, from part of a task to the whole task or from training on an aircraft simulator to training in an actual plane. There are two types of measure which are important from a training perspective: a "savings" measure and a "first-shot" measure (Hammerton, 1967). The relevance

Table 3.1 Two simple transfer designs

(a) Transfer on performance			
Group 1	Test on transfer task B	Training on task A	Retest on transfer task B
Group 2	Test on transfer task B	Nothing	Retest on transfer task B
(b) Transfer on learning			
Group 1	Training on task A	Training on task B	
Group 2	Nothing	Training on task B	

of "savings" or "first-shot" measures will be dictated by the nature of the training situation. In pilot training the goal is to reduce the training hours needed in a real plane which are expensive and potentially dangerous. Therefore interest centres on any "savings" in these hours as a result of positive transfer from training in a simulated situation. In some situations training is less concerned with such "savings" than "first-shot" performance which may have to be as near perfect as possible, for example, in a lunar landing. Consequently, it is important for those concerned with transfer of training to select a transfer measure which is consistent with the aims of the training programme.

One of the most straightforward measures of "savings" is given below:

$$\% \text{ savings } = \frac{B_2 - B_1}{B_2} \times 100$$

where B_1 number of training sessions or hours to learn task B after training on task A. (This corresponds to Group 1 in the previous transfer design (b).)

B_2 number of training sessions or hours to learn task B with no prior training on task A. (This corresponds to Group 2 in the previous transfer design (b).)

Imagine that one was interested in how much transfer took place when a motorcyclist was to be trained to drive a car. If it took a motorcyclist 70 hours to be trained to drive a car in comparison to the normal 100 hours for a person with no such experience, then the percent savings is 30%. This means that 30 hours (or 30%) of training to drive a car is "saved" because of transfer from having learnt to ride a motorcycle. Whilst this formula for savings is simple, it is not entirely satisfactory, as Roscoe (1971) pointed out. It fails to take account of the "cost", in the widest sense, of the prior training, in this example, learning to ride a motorcycle. In other words how much does one have to pay for this transfer and is it cost-effective? In some training situations this cost is of no consequence. For example, trainees might already possess certain skills and the question is whether these skills facilitate the acquisition of the new ones to be trained. In contrast, if one is concerned with transfer from part of the task, possibly involving a simulator, to the whole task, then cost-effectiveness is an important issue. It is only cost-effective to train a person in a car simulator if the transfer savings to training in a real car are worth more than the cost of training in the simulator.

These questions have been examined with respect to pilot training where the cost of training using a simulator is considerably cheaper than using a real aircraft. A study by Povenmire and Roscoe (1973) illustrates these transfer issues. They were interested in the transfer effectiveness of a flight simulator (named the GAT-1 Link trainer) for training to fly the Piper Cherokee aeroplane. Four groups of trainees received 0, 3, 7, and 11 hours respectively of training in the flight simulator. Two measures of transfer were used, both of which reflected the number of training hours required in the aeroplane before being judged as competent. Increasing the number of hours in the flight simulator decreased the number of training hours required in the aeroplane, some of which were therefore "saved". However Povenmire and Roscoe concluded that the savings of the groups which spent 7 and 11 hours in the flight simulator were not worthwhile as indicated in their following assessment:

> Based on an hourly cost of $16 for GAT-1 instruction ($8 for the GAT-1 and $8 for the instructor) and $22 for the Cherokee ($14 and $8), ground [i.e. simulator] training could be continued profitably until the next hour would save less than 16/22 or 0.73 hour in flight ...
> ... that point occurred between the fourth and fifth hours of ground [i.e. simulator] instruction in this experiment (Povenmire and Roscoe, 1973, p. 540). (Square parentheses added.)

The cut-off point at which transfer is no longer cost-effective will vary according to the training situation. Roscoe (1971) suggested that there will be diminishing returns in transfer as the amount of training on a flight simulator increases. Hence the second hour of training in the simulator will contribute less than the first hour and so on. This hypothetical relationship between amount of training in the simulator and transfer is depicted in Figure 3.1. Percent transfer is a negatively accelerating curve which reaches 70% after 15 hours in simulator training.

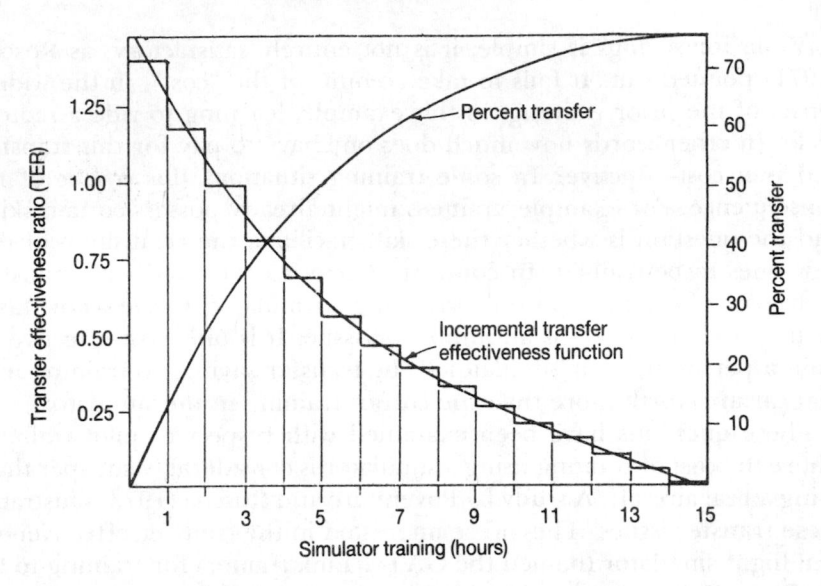

Figure 3.1   Two measures of transfer to flight training as a function of number of hours spent in simulator training. Based on hypothetical data (adapted from Roscoe, 1971).

What Roscoe termed the "incremental transfer effectiveness function" demonstrates that each subsequent hour of simulator training produces less transfer than the last. (This relationship is similar to the power law of practice, discussed in Chapter 2, which states that increasing the amount of training on the actual task will have diminishing returns in terms of subsequent performance improvement.) Notice that the first hour in simulator training is hypothesised to save more than one hour in flight training since the incremental transfer effectiveness ratio is more than one.

3.3   THE IMPORTANCE OF TRANSFER TO TRAINING

Our discussion so far has already suggested some ways in which transfer is important to training. Indeed training and transfer are inseparably linked as is evident from the following list of four training situations in which transfer is important.

1. Transfer of a trainee's existing skills and knowledge to the training of a new task

Any new training is affected by the transfer of a trainee's existing skills and knowledge. Old habits may be either helpful or a hindrance to the mastery of new ones. Questions concerning the amount and direction (i.e. positive or negative) of transfer can be asked of skills in the same or different domains. What transfer occurs from driving on the left of the road to learning to drive on the right? To what extent might positive transfer occur between the skills of a butcher and those required by a surgeon or between the skills of writing a letter and composing an essay? In the absence of good training material, a trainee may attempt to understand a new task by importing analogies or metaphors from different domains or using general problem-solving methods. This brings the dangers that the trainee will not appreciate those parts of an analogy which are relevant and those which are not or will fail to understand when and how general problem-solving methods should be adapted to support performance of the new task. Such risks are reduced if training programmes can somehow explicitly encourage the development and use of optimal "methods" for both learning and performance.

2. Transfer from part-task training to whole-task training

Jobs and tasks which require training may result in such an extensive training programme that it is necessary to break them down into part-task/part-job training. The overriding aim of any part-task training, irrespective of whether it involves simulation, computer-based training, training books etc., is to maximise the amount of positive transfer to the complete job or task. A major question is how tasks should be divided into parts so that these parts can be reassembled into performance of the whole task without causing the trainee any extra difficulties (see Section 9.5).

3. Transfer from training exercises to unsupported performance at the end of training

During training the task may be distorted or manipulated in some way to facilitate learning. For example, an important training principle is to provide the trainee with knowledge of results or feedback concerning aspects of performance. This information is additional to that which is normally available in performance of the task. Therefore training has to be designed to maximise positive transfer from supported performance during training to unsupported performance at the end of training. This might be achieved by "fading" the support given during training. If the task has been distorted in some other way (for example, in terms of its temporal characteristics) then the trainee may be given distortions of the task during training which become progressively closer approximations to the actual task. In this way positive transfer can be maximised by decreasing the difference between performance required during training and performance required at the end of training.

4. Transfer from the training environment to performance of a job or task in its natural context

Satisfactory levels of performance at the end of training do not guarantee that positive transfer will occur to performance of the job or task in the "real-world" situation. Much training takes place in an occupational context, and it is important that training results in positive transfer in performance of the job or task in the work situation. Unfortunately, assessment of this form of transfer is frequently missing from training evaluation studies.

In summary, transfer is important in different aspects of training. At the "input" side, a trainee's existing skills and knowledge influence how easily a new task is mastered. Transfer also occurs at the "output" side of training where a trainee has to transfer skills developed during training to performance in the real world. In between the "input" and "output" sides of training, transfer is important during training. Positive transfer has to be engineered between different training exercises and successful performance of the task at the end of training.

3.4 THEORETICAL APPROACHES TO TRANSFER

The original notion of transfer, dating back to the nineteenth century, was known as the doctrine of "formal discipline". It was believed that the quality of task performance was a reflection of underlying mental faculties (e.g. memory, observation, judgement). These faculties could be strengthened by training in tasks which required them. This philosophy was reflected in the educational curricula of that time in which subjects like Latin and mathematics were regarded as strengthening one's reasoning and memory faculties. Transfer, of a positive nature, was seen as widespread and occurred naturally when tasks were undertaken which exercised these basic faculties.

This formal discipline theory of transfer was attacked by Thorndike and Woodworth (1901) who argued that there was no substantial evidence in support of it. However, it has to be mentioned that some of the well-known studies (e.g. Thorndike, 1924) which supposedly refute the formal discipline theory are methodologically difficult to interpret. For example, Thorndike (1924) attempted to examine the transfer effects of studying different subjects at school by examining changes in intelligence over a one-year period. Such data are ambiguous for various methodological reasons. Nevertheless, Thorndike and Woodworth (1901) proposed that the determinant of transfer was the extent to which two tasks contained what they termed "identical elements". These identical elements were widely interpreted by behaviourist psychology as referring to stimuli and responses. However there are clues in the following quotation from Thorndike (1903) that a much more cognitive interpretation was intended:

> Chief amongst such identical elements of practical importance in education are associations including ideas about aims and ideas of method and general principles and associations involving elementary facts of experience such as length, colour, number, which are repeated again and again in differing combinations.
>
> By identical elements are meant mental processes ... (extract from Thorndike, 1903, cited by Grose and Birney, 1963, p. 2; italics added).

The theory of identical elements rejected any notion of underlying mental faculties. Instead transfer is determined by the extent to which two tasks share common methods, principles, procedures, associations and even give rise to the same attitudes. It is not entirely clear how "methods, principles, procedures and associations" were intended to be defined although the theory has some common sense appeal. It is argued that multiplication is easier to learn having mastered addition, since part of multiplication involves the procedures of addition. High positive transfer takes place in learning various foreign languages, e.g. between Spanish and Portuguese, because of the similar notations and grammatical constructions used in these two languages. Broadly, the identical elements approach to transfer can be broken down into two perspectives: one which interpreted these elements in terms of overt aspects of a task, i.e. the stimuli and responses, and a second which interpreted these elements more in terms of the cognitive or mental activities which a task required. This dichotomy is somewhat crude but illustrates the shift from a behaviourist approach to transfer to a more cognitive one which has taken place during this century.

Identical elements as stimuli and responses

Thorndike's theory of identical elements stated that the more identical elements occurring between two tasks, the more similar are the two tasks and therefore the more positive transfer predicted. As mentioned previously, in the absence of a psychology which discussed mental activities, similarity between tasks was originally identified in terms of the stimuli presented and the responses required. An illustrative study was carried out by Yum (1931). Visual patterns were presented and each one had to be linked by the person to a three letter word. Twenty-four hours later, 26 people attempted to recall these words. In one condition the original visual patterns were presented, whereas in the other four conditions, the visual patterns were varied in their degree of similarity to the original patterns (Figure 3.2), as rated by a panel of judges. The amount recalled was directly related to the degree of similarity of the test patterns to the original pattern. Thus there was greater positive transfer (in terms of *recall* rather than learning), the more similar the stimulus materials.

Table 3.2   Transfer as a function of stimulus similarity (Yum, 1931)

Degree of stimulus similarity	Percentage recalled (average)
Identity (i.e. same visual pattern)	84.62
1st degree similarity	64.53
2nd degree similarity	49.30
3rd degree similarity	45.30
4th degree similarity	36.32

As might be expected, this simple formulation of transfer turned out to be more complicated. A study by Gibson (1941), also using visual patterns, was important in demonstrating that the similarity of the responses, besides the similarity of stimuli, was important in determining transfer. The high positive transfer found by Yum, with highly similar stimulus materials disappeared when different, as opposed to identical, responses were required. This is supported by our everyday experiences when the opposite of our normal response to a situation is required such as in operating a new cooker or looking for traffic having switched from driving on one side of the road to the other. After

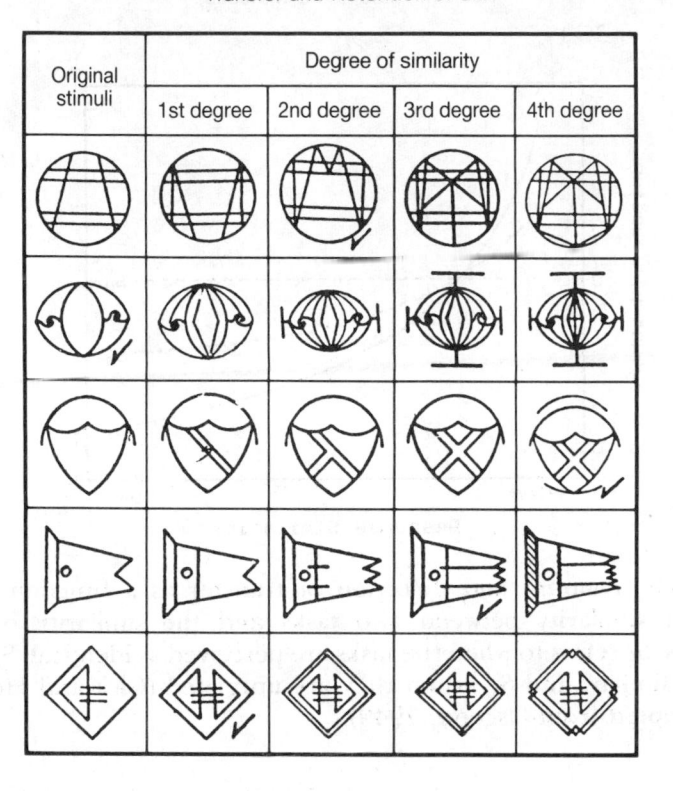

Figure 3.2 Transfer materials used by Yum, 1931.

Gibson's study, a great amount of research investigated transfer in the areas of verbal and motor learning in terms of the relationships between stimuli and responses.

Osgood (1949) attempted to integrate many diverse findings into his well-known empirical generalisations concerning transfer. Gick and Holyoak (1987) preserved Osgood's empirical relationships (as shown in Figure 3.3) but gave them a more contemporary interpretation. They emphasised that transfer depends upon the *perceived* similarity between the new and old situation (situation rather than stimuli). Also altering similarity to *perceived* similarity does acknowledge the influence of a person's perception, understanding etc. on transfer. Perceived similarity is influenced by both superficial and more fundamental differences between the training and transfer situations. How transfer varies as a function of this perceived similarity and also the similarity of the responses required is represented by Osgood's laws, which are preserved in Figure 3.3. When the situations are perceived as similar or identical

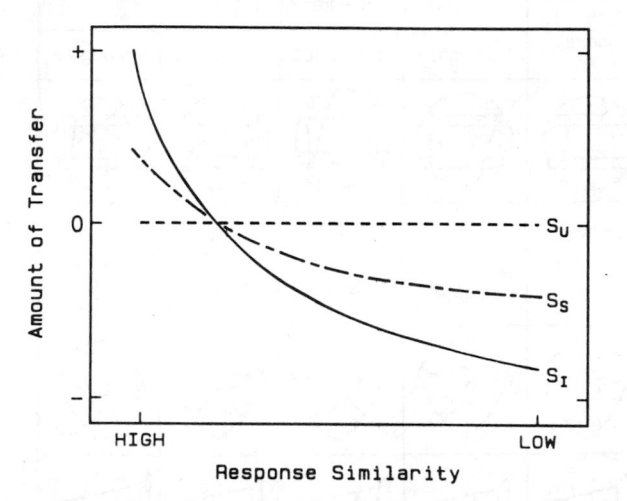

Figure 3.3   Amount and direction of transfer as a function of the perceived similarity between two tasks and the similarity of their responses. S_I refers to when the tasks are perceived as identical; S_S when they are similar; and S_U when they are unrelated (Gick and Holyoak, 1987, adapted from Osgood, 1949).

and the responses required are similar, then positive transfer takes place, whereas as the responses become less similar, then transfer becomes increasingly negative. When the situations are perceived as unrelated, even if they are not in objective terms, then no transfer will occur.

This formulation of transfer, derived from Osgood, is not entirely satisfactory. Firstly, characterising tasks in terms of similarity between stimuli/situations and responses is a simplification which ignores much of what we know about the nature of skilled performance (as discussed in Chapter 2). Similarity between tasks needs to be defined more in terms of the psychological nature of the skills required rather than more obvious, but potentially misleading, task characteristics. Secondly, various other factors, such as the degree of original learning, affect transfer but are not represented in Figure 3.3. Thirdly, some criticism has been made of the accuracy of the transfer predictions, particularly the predicted negative transfer effects which do not always occur (e.g. in the transfer of perceptual-motor skills, Bilodeau and Bilodeau, 1961).

Identical elements as cognitive elements

Two frequently cited studies by Judd (1908) and Hendrickson and Schroeder (1941) demonstrated what is usually referred to as "transfer of principles", but nowadays is equivalent to providing the trainee with a simple mental model from which action can be generated. In Judd's initial study the task of two groups of trainees was to hit a target under water using a small dart. In the initial sessions the target was under 12 inches of water and in later sessions, it was under only four inches of water. One group of trainees was given a theoretical explanation of the principle of refraction, whilst the other group was not. Whilst there was no difference in performance of the two groups in hitting the deeper target, the group which received the theoretical explanation of refraction was superior when the target was moved to its second shallower location. The reason, according to Judd, was that the theory enabled them to avoid applying their "twelve-inch habit to four inches of water". The study by Hendrickson and Schroeder (1941) replicated Judd's findings but extended them and their interpretation in two important respects. Using a gun to fire at targets submerged in two and six inches of water they found that: (a) trainees receiving a theoretical explanation of refraction showed some slight evidence of performance improvement even in hitting the initial target, although this appears to be not a statistically significant result; and (b) a group of trainees which received a slightly more extensive and relevant theoretical explanation performed even better on the second target. It appears that the theoretical explanation provided trainees with a useful mental model which was relevant to both tasks. This enabled aiming to be modified appropriately for the second target and positive transfer occurred from training with the first target. Some caution needs to be expressed in extrapolating from these findings. The theory-based material concerning principles of refraction was relatively simple and could be used quite easily by trainees in formulating their actions. In more complex tasks, training has to ensure that any theory-based training material is both valid (i.e. relevant to the task) and capable of being utilised by trainees (i.e. in Anderson's terms that task-specific procedures can be compiled). Sometimes, these requirements for theory-based training material can be met, as demonstrated in the training of fault-finding using a simulated chemical plant (Patrick and Haines, 1988). A group of trainees which received "theoretical" training in terms of a qualitative causal model of how the plant functioned was able to not only use this knowledge immediately in improving fault-finding but also transfer it to support fault-finding in a second, highly similar, plant.

The transfer theory of identical elements has received a considerable boost from Anderson (1987) who has provided his solution to the puzzle of what these "elements" exactly are. In Chapter 2, Anderson's theory of cognitive skill acquisition was discussed and it will be remembered that the building blocks of skilled performance (procedural knowledge in Anderson's terms) are rules of the IF ... THEN type. Anderson (1987) predicted that:

> there will be positive transfer between skills to the extent that the two skills involve the same productions [rules] (pp. 197–198; square parentheses added).

As Anderson acknowledged, there is a danger that observed transfer effects will result in post hoc analyses of tasks in terms of rules which accommodate these effects. To avoid this problem, some transfer studies were carried out of text editing (Singley and Anderson, 1985 and another study by the same authors cited by Anderson, 1987) since analyses of these tasks already existed. An analysis of the goal structure for text editing using the ED line editor when one word has to be substituted by another word resulted in the following seven rules. How these rules fit together is represented in Figure 3.4.

E0:   IF the goal is to edit a manuscript
    THEN set as subgoals
                1. To characterise the next edit to perform
                2. To perform the edit

E1:   IF the goal is to perform an edit
    THEN set as subgoals
                1. To locate the line
                2. To type the edit

E2:   IF the goal is to locate the target line
             and the current line is not the target line
    THEN increment the line

E3:   IF the goal is to locate the target line
             and the current line is the target line
    THEN POP success

E4:   IF the goal is to type an edit
    THEN set as subgoals
                1. To choose the arguments
                2. To type the command

E5:   IF the goal is to type the command
    THEN set as subgoals

1. To type the command name
2. To type the arguments

E6:   IF   the goal is to type the command name for substitution

    THEN   type S

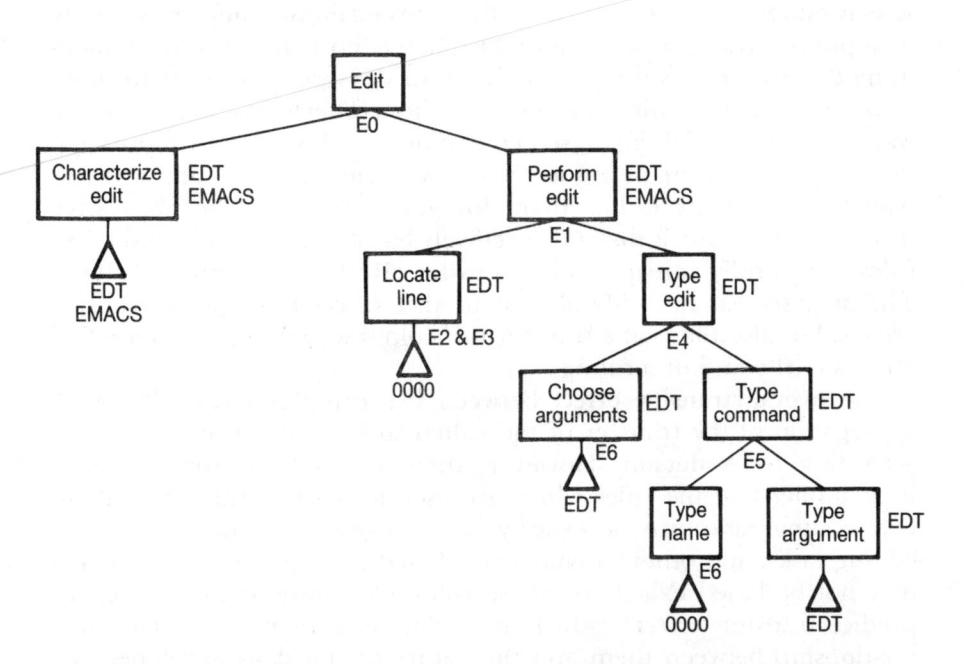

Figure 3.4 A representation of the hierarchy of goals for text editing using ED. E0–E6 refer to the rules on pp. 88–89. Goals and goal structures in common with EDT or EMACS are so labelled. Goal structures not in common with either are labelled 0000. A triangle represents a goal structure whose expansion is not represented (Anderson, 1987, p. 199).

In these studies, Singley and Anderson were interested in the transfer between three editors: ED and EDT which were line editors and EMACS which was a screen editor. Groups of trainees from a secretarial school had three hours training for six consecutive days. Each group experienced either one editor (EMACS for six days), two editors (ED or EDT for four days followed by EMACS for two days) or three editors (ED or EDT for two days, followed by EDT or ED for the next two days, followed by EMACS for the final two days). The predicted transfer effects can be understood from an examination of Figure 3.4. The

highest goals (rule E0) are common to all three editors, whilst only the
two line editors (ED and EDT) shared the remaining goal structure
(rules E1–E5), differing only with respect to how the command for
substitution is typed (rule E6) and how a line of text is located.
Therefore high positive transfer was expected from one line editor to
the other line editor, but less transfer from either line editor to the
screen editor. Results confirmed these predictions. There was nearly
total positive transfer between the two line editors. In contrast, trainees
using the line editors during the first four days were slower than those
who had practised with the screen editor. There was some positive
transfer from line editing to screen editing, but this was little more than
that of another group of trainees who had spent the initial four days just
typing edited texts rather than doing any editing. The impressive
feature of this study is that a theoretically based analysis of the tasks into
rules successfully anticipated the transfer effects of an empirical study.
The analysis was not only able to predict successfully global transfer
effects, but also that some transfer difficulties would arise between line
editors in the task of locating text.

The overall transfer effect between two complex tasks will be an
aggregation of the transfer of individual components, which are rules
according to Anderson. However, there is need for some caution
in assuming that the rules which are used to predict transfer in these
text editing tasks are necessarily psychological in nature. The text
editing tasks, and others, invite a rule-based description, although skill
may not be based exactly on these rules. Obviously, if these rules do
predict transfer effects, which they do, then there must be some
relationship between them and the nature of the skills developed for
these tasks.

This production-system or rule-based interpretation of Thorndike's
"identical elements" has also been made by Kieras and his co-workers in
order to understand transfer effects (e.g. Kieras and Bovair, 1986).
Transfer between procedures was a function of how many rules were
shared. Generally, it was found that the number of new rules in a
procedure to be learned was the best predictor of overall increase in
training time. A review of these and Anderson's studies is given by Gray
and Orasanu (1987). An interesting conclusion from Anderson's theory
is that transfer only occurs to the extent that there are identical rules in
procedural knowledge. When the same knowledge is used in different
ways, no transfer is predicted. Anderson's theory does not address the
question of how transfer takes place at low and intermediate levels of
skill before procedural knowledge is attained. Another point about this
rule-based approach to transfer is that it tends to convey the impression

that when identical rules exist, then transfer occurs easily and quite automatically. The existence of identical components is a necessary but not sufficient condition for transfer to take place. In the following section we will discuss why such transfer often fails to occur.

3.5 LACK OF POSITIVE TRANSFER BETWEEN COGNITIVE TASKS

Unfortunately, there is considerable evidence that positive transfer does not always occur between tasks, even when, from an "identical elements" perspective, it might be expected to do so. In other words, confirmation of identical elements between tasks, in whatever form, is a necessary but not sufficient condition for positive transfer to take place. This is important from a training perspective, since it means that even when one task can be performed competently, one cannot assume that performance on a second task requiring apparently the same skills will be improved.

Lack of positive transfer has been found primarily between cognitive tasks involving the transfer of both specific and general problem-solving methods and the transfer of factual knowledge between two situations. The disappointment and difficulties in producing positive transfer between cognitive tasks is a recurring theme in the two excellent volumes concerning *Thinking and Learning Skills* by Chipman, Segal and Glaser (1985) and Segal, Chipman and Glaser (1985). Learning, thinking and problem-solving skills which have been trained and are expected to generalise to a range of situations, often fail to do so. (Part of this debate involves the training and transfer of learning strategies, which is discussed in Chapter 10.) Also, sometimes transfer does not take place between two isomorphic problems (i.e. problems with the same structure) which require the same skills or strategies and only differ in terms of what appear to be superficial characteristics (e.g. Hayes and Simon, 1977; Brooke, Duncan and Cooper, 1980). The Brooke, Duncan and Cooper study used various fault-finding tasks and found that transfer between isomorphic problems depended upon whether trainees were alerted during training to the variety of transfer contexts to which their fault-finding skill was relevant. Bransford et al. (1989) discussed a similar problem of so-called "inert knowledge". Knowledge is said to be "inert" when it is relevant to a new task or situation but it is not activated or applied.

Two important reasons for this lack of transfer of cognitive skills are discussed below, together with the implications for training.

Lack of awareness by trainees

Trainees may be taught a procedure to apply to one task but may not be made aware of the range of tasks and associated circumstances in which the procedure should be used. It is therefore not surprising that such a procedure is not automatically transferred to a new situation. The trainee may not perceive the training and transfer situations as similar even when they are (Gick and Holyoak, 1987) and will therefore not select or access the relevant procedure. This point has been emphasised by Brown, Campione and Day (1981) who have criticised what they labelled "blind" training in which students are not informed why and when a procedure is relevant to task performance. There is evidence that when a trainee is so informed that positive transfer is more likely to occur to a different task requiring that same procedure. Campione and Armbruster (1985) summarised various training programmes designed to improve student's skills at learning from text passages and stated:

> We emphasise the need for "cognitive training with awareness" because the whole history of attempts to instill study and learning strategies in ineffectual learners attests to the futility of having students execute some strategy in the absence of concomitant understanding of why or how that activity works (p. 337).

Ironically in the development of skill, outlined in Chapter 2, a trainee becomes *less* aware of the nature of his skill as skill becomes more organised and automatised. Hence, even if training does stress the rationale underlying the use of a procedure and the range of situations to which it is applicable, the person may be unable to select and transfer a relevant procedure. This has led many to propose that people need to be trained in how to select, monitor and regulate their high level thought processes (i.e. metacognitive skills) which will mitigate against such problems.

Contextualised knowledge and skills

Closely related to the preceding point is the fact that, for whatever reason, knowledge and skills are highly context dependent. Because of this, it is very difficult for transfer to take place. In one sense one can argue that this is the result of a survival mechanism. The context of any new task evokes only a restricted range of strategies, procedures, skills etc., which a person might use. This is helpful in reducing the workload which would otherwise be unbearable. It enables the trained person to react fluently and quickly. Generally this works well. However, the disadvantage is that because a person's full repertoire of strategies etc., is not examined, then sometimes opportunities for transfer to a new task are missed.

Many argue that strategies and methods for performing tasks are in any case highly context specific and will therefore inevitably vary when applied to new situations (e.g. Hayes, 1985). This view is, of course, consistent with Anderson's view of cognitive skill acquisition in which specific procedures are developed for performing each new task. As these procedures become highly organised and automated, it is difficult for parts of them which are identical or similar to parts of other skills to be unravelled or unpacked successfully.

3.6 SOME PRINCIPLES FOR PROMOTING TRANSFER

In the preceding section, we discussed how transfer may be promoted by avoiding so-called "blind" training and informing the trainee of the "ifs" and "buts" surrounding what is learned and the boundaries of its applicability. In addition, there are other factors which have been cited as promoting transfer, some of which are discussed by Ellis (1965), Annett (1987) and Gick and Holyoak (1987).

1. Ensure that training objectives incorporate transfer requirements

In order to develop a training programme, training objectives need to be specified. (For a discussion see Chapter 4, particularly Section 4.5.) It is surprisingly easy to fail to incorporate transfer requirements in the specification of training objectives. Different transfer requirements can change dramatically both the nature of the skills to be trained and how training is to be designed. This is best explained with an example, taken from my own work concerned with the training of fault-finding skills. One major problem in this area concerns how to train people to deal with novel faults, i.e. faults which have not been encountered previously. As one considers this problem, it becomes evident that the nature of novelty can vary and this will affect the associated transfer requirements and therefore the training needed. There are at least three important ways in which a fault can be novel:

Case 1. It requires the same "method" to that developed in training to be applied to a new exemplar.

Case 2. It requires the same "methods" developed in training but these have to be reconfigured to deal with the novel fault.

Case 3. It requires a different "method" (or "methods") to that (those) developed in training.

The word "method" is used here to refer to any cognitive strategy, procedure or the like, used to diagnose the fault. The training implications of Cases 1–3 above are quite different. Case 1 presents the weakest form of novelty since the trainee has to be trained only to transfer or apply one "method" or fault-finding strategy to the novel fault. This "method", or strategy has to be identified by the trainer and it is then not a difficult matter to train a person to apply it successfully. Training for Case 1 faults only, assumes that the person will not encounter novel faults which cannot be diagnosed by application of this "method". Case 2 is a little more complex because the person has to use a variety of "methods" which have to be selected and assembled in an optimal fashion to diagnose this type of novel fault. The training implications therefore involve not only mastery of different methods, but practice at deciding how to select and assemble them in order to diagnose this more complex type of novel fault. Finally, faults in Case 3 are truly novel since they require the person to develop a new "method" (or "methods") for tackling them which is outside of that person's current repertoire. One might consider that this sort of training situation should never arise because the trainer will anticipate what "methods" might be needed. Unfortunately this is not always the case, for two reasons. Firstly, the sheer volume of potential faults in complex equipment or industrial plant makes it impossible to be certain that all necessary "methods" have been identified. Secondly, faults inevitably develop which were not anticipated by even the best designers and engineers and these may require different solutions to those which were anticipated. The training implications in Case 3 are quite daunting. The trainee has to be trained to detect when a fault cannot be diagnosed by already known "methods", such as those provided during training for Case 1 and Case 2 faults. Hence, somehow training has to enable a fault-finder to identify not only *when* an existing "method" is insufficient but also *how* to devise a new and more appropriate one. This sixty-four thousand dollar question is not only crucial for training people to solve these very difficult, novel faults but also applies to training for any sort of novel task, besides fault-finding, in which solutions cannot be predefined and therefore some innovation and improvisation is required. To the author's knowledge, training research has not so far tackled this challenge. The above example demonstrates that unless the transfer requirements of the trainee are specified adequately in the training objectives, then the resulting training programme might be quite inappropriate.

2. Increase task variability in training

Is transfer better when the trainee spends more time practising with one task or less time with a variety of tasks? The answer is that it depends on the criterion of training. Provision of a variety of tasks or examples during training improves transfer when this variety reflects what the trainee is expected to cope with after training. Thus if a person has to fly six types of aircraft, then training and subsequent transfer will be more successful the extent to which this variety is captured in the training programme. Some differences in flying these aircraft may be superficial, whilst others may be more fundamental, reflecting differences in procedure. Failure to capture any fundamental variations in a training programme will limit the extent of transfer.

The theoretical basis for increased variability improving transfer of training can be traced back to the notion of a schema. Psychologists have been interested in how we are able to apply our skills, often correctly, to examples of a task which have not been encountered previously. This is accomplished through the development of a "schema" which incorporates significant features or dimensions of a class of tasks. Thus we gradually build up a "schema" for what constitutes a dog, which enables us to classify new animals as being dogs or not. The trainee will develop a better and more sophisticated schema for dogs if a wide range of sizes (e.g. Pekinese to Great Dane), types of coat etc., are provided during training. In a similar way the visual discrimination of different types of aircraft and the detection of different ships using sonar is superior when training contains the widest variety of relevant examples. Schmidt's (1975) schema theory of motor learning, discussed in Section 2.4, predicts improved transfer when training involves a variety of movements which enables a more refined motor schema to be developed. Hence one is better able to throw a ball at a new target if one has been trained to throw balls at a variety of similar targets, even though this may not have included the new one. There is plenty of evidence to support the benefits of providing variability in the training of motor skills (e.g. Schmidt and Young, 1987).

3. Provide a high level of training

Another factor which has long been known to affect transfer is how well a task has been learned or how much training has been provided. Generally, when two tasks are similar in terms of "identical elements", positive transfer will increase as the amount of training on one task increases. With small amounts of training, negative transfer has sometimes been found (Mandler, 1962) presumably because the responses or skills required by the two tasks can be more easily muddled at this stage. Not surprisingly, therefore, both the amount and direction of transfer is closely related to the level of skill reached in both tasks.

In summary there are various factors which influence whether skills are transferred. Annett (1987) reviewed this topic in the context of how occupational training programmes might be devised to maximise what he termed "transferable skills". Four recommendations were made which summarise some of our discussion:

1. Ensure that the trainee is not simply capable of performing the skill to criterion level but also shows as much understanding of any principles and generalisations associated with the skill as is practically possible.
2. Use as many and as varied examples of the skill and the contexts in which it may be used as opportunity permits and if necessary create opportunities.
3. Ensure that the trainee is aware of the range of use of the skills he or she is expected to learn. The use of the record of achievement in this connection is recommended. [Record of achievement refers to some agreed, written statement of what skills have been mastered during training.]
4. Use training methods which encourage the trainee to take responsibility for his/her own learning. Appropriate methods include "guided discovery" and "expert scaffolding" in both of which the trainer supplies support, guidance and analysis rather than direction and correction (Annett, 1987, pp. 34–35; square parentheses added).

3.7 SKILL RETENTION

Training, transfer and retention of skills are closely related topics. Retention can be viewed as a special case of transfer, since it requires a trained person to transfer his or her skills to the same task after a period of time. From another perspective retention provides another, very important, criterion of training. In other words, training should not only produce adequate performance immediately after training but also after a subsequent period of no practice.

There are various practical situations in which the extent to which skills are retained is important. How well is procedural knowledge retained for use in emergency situations which, by definition, occur infrequently and yet are potentially costly? Can a doctor or an engineer in industry diagnose a problem which occurs very rarely and (s)he has not encountered for many years? How much refresher training is required by an operator of a nuclear power plant? Practical questions of this kind concerning the retention of skill have prompted a number of literature reviews of skill retention. The need for astronauts to retain skills associated with space missions, the duration of which was expected to increase, led to a review of the literature by Gardlin and Sitterley (1972). Evidently training for a lunar landing mission involved about 2200 training hours spread over a 44-week period, much of which was spent using spacecraft simulators. Maintaining skill levels during training and predicting how such skills would be retained were vital issues. A review by Annett (1977) re-examined the evidence concerning skill loss in the context of the provision of training for both employed and unemployed persons. The importance of retention of skill in military contexts has been emphasised by Hagman and Rose (1983) who provided a review of results from 13 studies of "real" military tasks including donning gas masks, visual aircraft recognition, machine-gun assembly/disassembly and testing pieces of equipment.

The findings from the Hagman and Rose review, and others, illustrate how difficult it is to make generalisations since retention varies with the nature of the task. In order to avoid such obvious statements, attempts have been made to identify categories of task, which have different retention characteristics. This trend was evident in the classic review of the retention of learned skills by Naylor and Briggs (1961) which used dichotomies of "discrete versus continuous" tasks, and "motor versus verbal" tasks to which can be added the distinction between "integrated versus non-integrated" tasks. There are two problems with this approach from an academic perspective. Firstly, comparison between these different types of task is often confounded by other factors which will themselves affect retention, e.g. performance measures, amount of training and "difficulty" of the task. Consequently, differences in retention characteristics may not reflect *intrinsic* differences between these types of task but rather the manner in which training was organised and performance measured. Secondly, it would be helpful to know which components of a skill are susceptible to forgetting rather than a global statement that the overall skill has been retained by a certain amount. For example, Swift (1905) examined two persons' retention of a ball tossing skill after one year. It was reported that there was some loss, but that relearning was remarkably rapid. One might ask what aspects of this skill degraded with no practice, which ones did not and how quickly different components were relearned.

A step in this direction was taken by a study by McKenna and Glendon (1985), cited by Baddeley (1990), which investigated the retention of the first-aid skill of cardio-pulmonary resuscitation after a period of up to three years. In this study three components of the skill were examined separately: the technique for inflating the lungs and pressing the chest; the performance and timing of the heart compression; and the diagnosis of the patient's consciousness, breathing and pulse rate. An overall rating of performance was made by an expert in terms of whether the patient would have been expected to live. The results in Figure 3.5 indicate the extent to which different components of this skill were forgotten. By the time three years had elapsed all of these components had decayed to such an extent that few, if any patients, who encountered the first-aid personnel used in this study, would have been expected to survive a heart attack. Further studies of this nature are needed which examine the different *psychological* components of tasks, such as planning, reasoning, decision-making etc. and in particular how and which components decay with no practice.

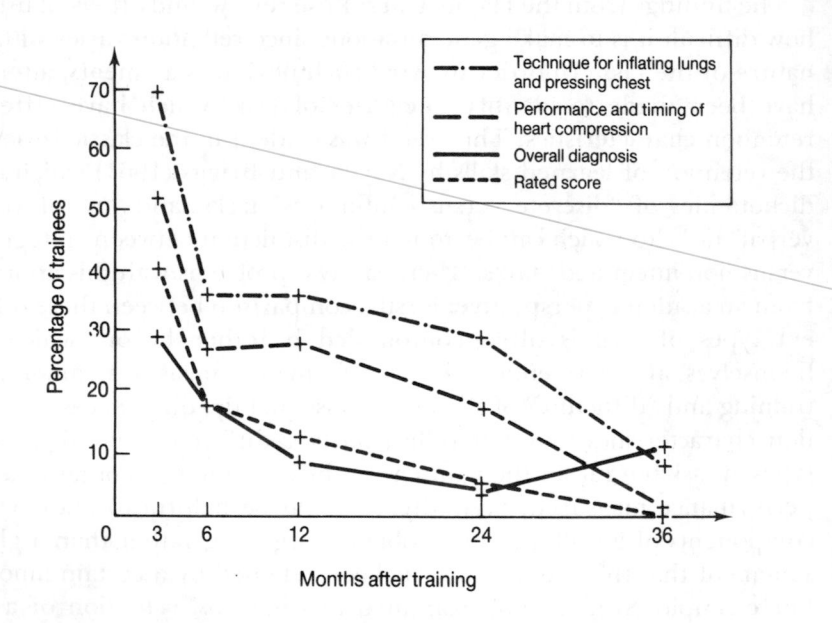

Figure 3.5 The effect of the duration of the retention period on the skill and subskills of resuscitation (McKenna and Glendon, 1985). The figure shows the percentage of trainees scoring at least 75% accuracy on the measures of CPR as a function of time after training.

Retention of perceptual-motor skills

Retention of perceptual-motor skills is classically viewed as almost perfect even, in some cases, after years of no practice. Driving, swimming and riding a bicycle are frequently quoted examples. These perceptual-motor tasks are described as "continuous" since the information given to the person performing the task is continuously changing, which requires a continuously adjustive response (e.g. in tracking a target with a gunnery sight). In contrast "discrete" tasks involve a series of steps, possibly in a procedure, such as turning a series of switches on and off.

The evidence concerning the retention of skill concerning continuous versus discrete tasks is clear-cut. For whatever reason, the former are extremely well remembered in contrast to the latter which are not. Fleishman and Parker (1962) reported the results from two studies which are representative of the high retention of continuous tasks, in this case a two-dimensional tracking task. A target dot was continuously displaced in the horizontal and vertical dimensions and the person was trained, over a six-week period, to keep the dot centred on the display. Retention intervals in Study 1 were 9, 14 and 24 months and those for Study 2 were 1, 5, 9 and 14 months. In Study 2 a little more training was provided in addition to practice with feedback. The results, represented in Figure 3.6, indicated that virtually no loss in proficiency occurred until 14 months. Even after two years the losses were so small that they were recovered during the first few minutes of retraining. Similar results have been found for other tasks of a continuous nature.

In contrast, procedural tasks are forgotten more quickly. Shields, Goldberg and Dressel (1979), cited by Hagman and Rose (1983), appeared to demonstrate that the more steps involved in a procedure to be remembered, the worse retention. Thus donning gas masks (15 steps) had a steeper decline in retention over a one year period than loading and firing a M203 grenade launcher (nine steps). An interesting and alarming subsidiary finding was that the steps which were forgotten most frequently were those which were not cued by previous steps or by the equipment itself. These included safety steps. Hence when taking a rifle to pieces and then reassembling it, soldiers would often forget the safety step of clearing the gun.

A study by Neumann and Ammons (1957) illustrates how quickly discrete tasks or procedures may be forgotten. People learned to "pair together" two sets of eight switches during 57 training sessions. Retention was examined after one minute, 20 minutes, two days, seven weeks and one year by splitting the 100 people into five groups of 20 in each.

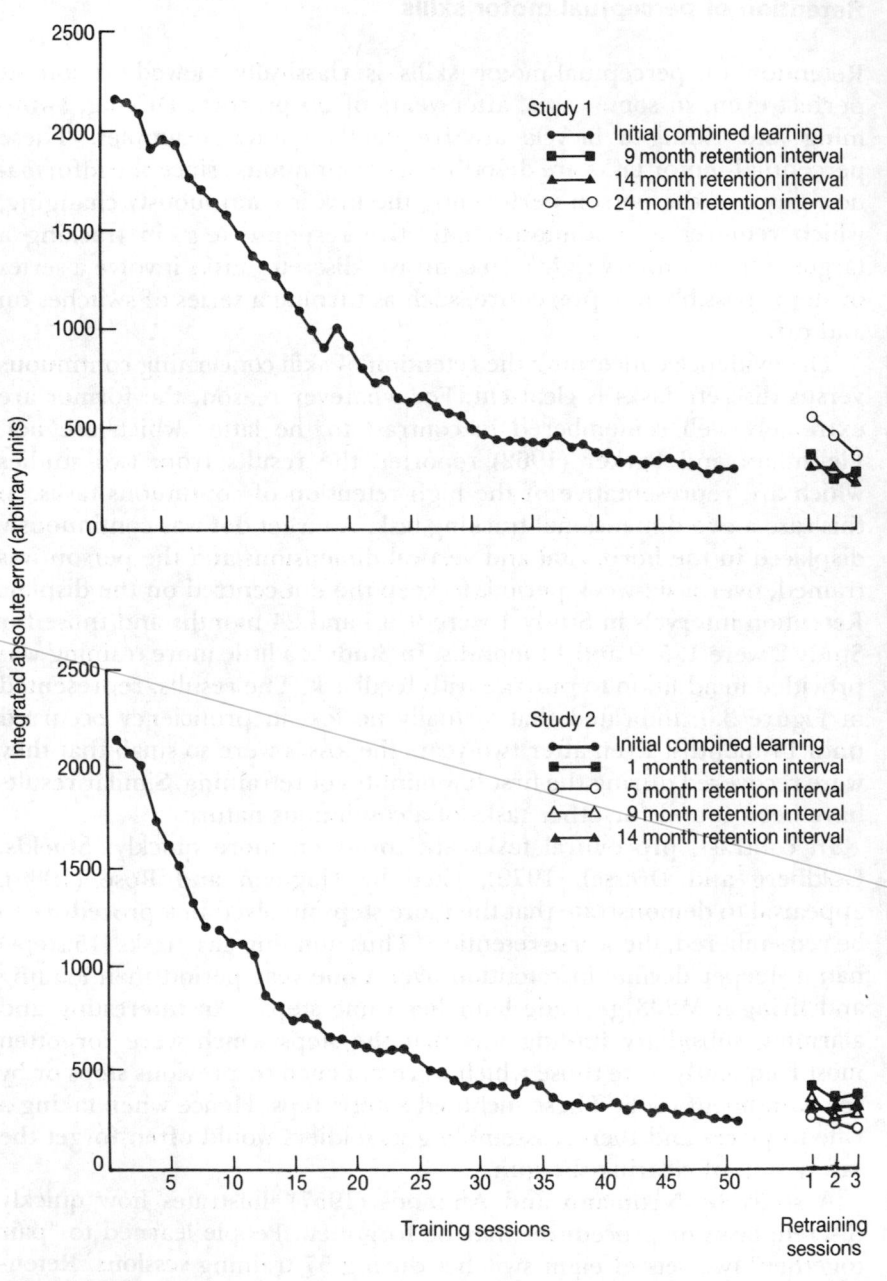

Figure 3.6 Performance of a tracking skill after periods of no practice (Fleishman and Parker, 1962).

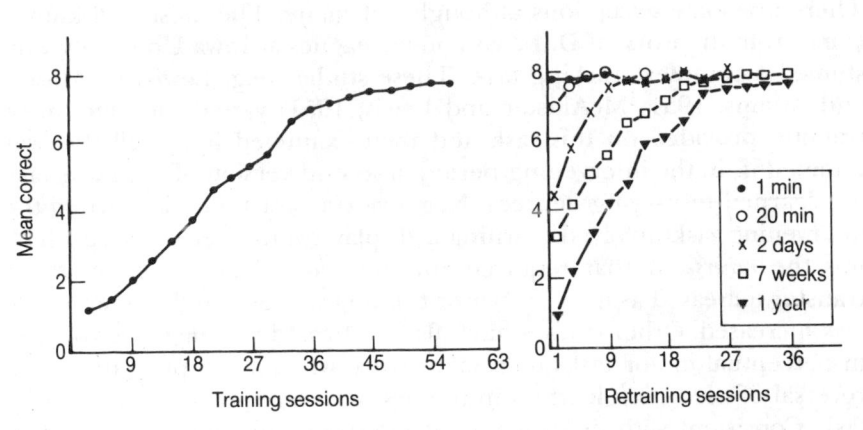

Figure 3.7 Retention of a procedural task (Neumann and Ammons, 1957).

Recall deteriorated with increasing retention interval (Figure 3.7). After one year, performance was equivalent to the level at the beginning of training, although it only took 36 retraining sessions to master the task again as opposed to the original 57 training sessions, thus indicating some "savings". A subsidiary, but very interesting, finding which emerged from this study was that people reported using different "methods" for learning the task which included using numbers, verbal–spatial labels, visualisation and movement patterns. Even though these reported methods may have been inaccurate and indeed were not linked to statistically significant performance differences, nevertheless it emphasises the danger in simplistic characterisations of tasks which do not reflect *how* they are performed. Performance of the "discrete" task used by Neumann and Ammons may have been supported by different types of skill. It is only after we understand the nature of skill supporting task performance, that it will be possible to progress in making useful generalisations concerning the retention characteristics of types of task.

Consistent with the high retention of continuous perceptual-motor tasks is the fact that these tasks do not generally suffer from negative transfer (or interference) from other similar ones. Adequate studies in this area are few and little progress has been made since studies in the 1950s. Bilodeau and Bilodeau (1961) summarised the findings by saying that interference effects in this area were more a matter of faith than fact. They concluded that:

> Negative transfer (a) is difficult to produce, (b) when produced obtains in small amounts, and (c) rapidly converts to positive transfer (p. 261).

There are some exceptions although not many. The most well-known come from the work of D. Lewis and colleagues at Iowa University who studied a complex tracking task. These studies (e.g. Lewis, McAllister and Adams, 1951; McAllister and Lewis, 1951) varied the amount of training provided on this task and then examined how well this was retained if, in the intervening period, a second version of the same task was learned to varying degrees. Negative transfer took place when the intervening task involved learning a display control relationship which was the *reverse* of that required for the original task. This negative transfer increased as the number of training sessions on the intervening task increased. Other studies have also confirmed that negative transfer in perceptual-motor tasks only takes place when a complete or partial reversal of the action learned in the first task is required by the second task. Consistent with the remarks of Bilodeau and Bilodeau is the fact that even in the study by Lewis, McAllister and Adams (1951), learning the intervening, reversed task was improved by learning the original task (i.e. positive transfer did take place).

Factors affecting retention of skill

It makes a reviewer's life a lot easier when there are not only a lot of reviews of a topic available, but they agree with each other. This is the case concerning generalisations about factors affecting the retention of skills. It has to be said, however, that these generalisations are not startling. In fact one is tempted to say that they are so blindingly obvious that they might be supplied by any person in the street. Three of these generalisations are discussed below.

1. Level of retention is positively related to the level of learning at the end of training. The best single predictor of retention is how well people have learned the task. Consequently, as Gardlin and Sitterley (1972) concluded, "the type of training which produces the highest level of performance will also produce the best initial retention test performance" (p. 14). Therefore any training variables which improve the level of performance at the end of training will also improve retention. The most potent variable is the amount of training which might be measured in terms of the number of training sessions or the amount of time devoted to training. The more training which is given before a period of "lay-off", the higher performance will be after this period. There is also evidence that "overtraining" will also help retention (see Section 9.8). By overtraining is meant that training continues even after an adequate level of performance has been reached by a trainee.

The *absolute* amount forgotten during a lay-off is not affected by the level of original learning, but by other factors such as the duration of the lay-off (e.g. Ammons et al., 1958). However, the *relative* amount forgotten does vary according to the level of original learning. In order to make this clear, imagine that two trainees, A and B, reached 90% and 60% levels of performance respectively by the end of training. Over the same retention period, both trainees might each "lose" 30%, resulting in recall levels of 60% and 30%. Hence the *absolute* amount lost is the same for each trainee so that the difference between the trainees in performance at the end of the retention period remains the same. In contrast their relative retention changes. The *relative* retention of trainee A is two-thirds (i.e. 60/90), whilst that of trainee B is one-half (i.e. 30/60) both of these figures being related to the level of performance at the end of training.

2. *Retention gets worse, the longer the retention interval.* Yes, not surprisingly, people forget more as the period of lay-off gets longer! This is consistently found and does not contradict our previous discussion that some sorts of skills are apparently forgotten more quickly than others (e.g. "discrete" as opposed to "continuous" tasks). The retention intervals which have been investigated range from less than one minute to 50 years! Indeed it is worth restating the amazing study reported by Hill (1957) which examined his own retention of a typing skill after 25 and 50 year periods during which, evidently, no practice took place. A summary is provided by Naylor and Briggs (1961):

> Hill (1957) reports data on retention for what appears to be the longest interval between original learning and relearning. In 1907 the author taught himself to type and in 1932 and in 1957 (25-year intervals) he relearned the skill to the original criterion with materials of equal difficulty for practice. No typing was performed by the author during either of the two retention periods. When the learning curves for all three sessions were compared, several things were noticeable. First, retention was quite persistent, with about 50 per cent retention after the first 25 years and 25 per cent retention at the end of 50 years. It should be noted that age effects, such as dexterity loss, probably also helped depress scores on the last retention task. In general, relearning was more rapid for both retention sessions than had been the original learning (p. 4).

3. *Rehearsal of a skill mitigates against skill loss during a lay-off.* If a trainee is provided with an opportunity to practise or rehearse a skill, this will reduce the amount of skill loss which would otherwise occur

(Annett, 1977; Gardlin and Sitterley, 1972). Again this is a rather obvious statement, and the benefits of rehearsal will depend upon how it is carried out and the nature of the task. Since procedural tasks are poorly retained in comparison to continuous ones, such as tracking, it is not surprising that rehearsal is particularly beneficial for them. This is to be expected if procedural tasks are largely verbally mediated, since rehearsal improves the retention of such verbal coding, which is otherwise easily forgotten. A study by Naylor and Briggs (1963) examined the retention of a procedural task which was rather like the check routine carried out on the flight deck of an aircraft before take-off. The task was somewhat unusual, since trainees had to learn not only to press the buttons in the correct sequence but to press each button at the correct time interval since the last one. Rehearsal was given for either the whole task, the sequential part of the task or the timing part of the task. Trainees were split into groups which were trained during days 1–5, had no practice during days 6–14, rehearsed the whole task or part of the task in days 15–19, had a further no practice period in days 20–29, and then had a retention test after 30 days. Rehearsal was of benefit in terms of reducing the number of errors of commission, although the groups which rehearsed the whole task were better than either of the part task rehearsal groups. It is to be expected that the less the rehearsal task resembles the actual task, the less benefit will be derived from such rehearsal. This is supported by the literature concerning the value of training using simulations, which is discussed in Chapter 12. One caveat which needs to be added is that this does not necessarily mean that rehearsal has to take place with the same task, rather that the trainee has to practise using a task which makes identical psychological requirements. Thus using a photograph or a cardboard mockup to rehearse a procedural task is just as effective as using the real equipment.

Provision of some sort of refresher training during periods of no practice is important in high cost performance situations. It is not possible to give a formula for calculating how much refresher training is necessary. Rather a pragmatic approach should be adopted, with performance levels being tested and extra training being supplied as necessary on a simulated version of the task. The question of how often refresher training should be supplied is closely related to the question of what the optimal intervals between any training sessions are. A discussion of the spacing of training sessions can be found in Section 9.7.

REFERENCES

Ammons, R.B., Farr, R.G., Bloch, E., Neumann, E., Dey, M., Marion, R. and Ammons, C.H. (1958). Long-term retention of perceptual-motor skills. *Journal of Experimental Psychology*, **55**, 318–328.

Anderson, J.R. (1987). Skill acquisition. Compilation of weak-method problem solutions. *Psychological Review*, **94**, 192–210.

Annett, J. (1977) *Skill loss. A review of the literature and recommendations for research.* Coventry: University of Warwick.

Annett, J. (1987). *Training in transferable skills. Final Report to Manpower Services Commission.* Coventry: University of Warwick.

Baddeley, A. (1990). *Human memory: Theory and practice.* Hove: Lawrence Erlbaum.

Bilodeau, E.A. and Bilodeau, I.M. (1961). Motor skills learning. *Annual Review of Psychology*, **12**, 243–280.

Bransford, J.D., Vye, N.J., Adams, L.T and Perfetto, G.A. (1989). Learning skills and the acquisition of knowledge. In Lesgold, A. and Glaser, R. (Eds). *Foundations for a psychology of education.* Hillsdale, NJ: Lawrence Erlbaum.

Brooke, J.B., Duncan, K.D. and Cooper, C. (1980). Interactive instruction in solving fault-finding problems – an experimental study. *International Journal of Man-Machine Studies*, **12**, 217–227.

Brown, A.L., Campione, J.C. and Day, J.D. (1981). Learning to learn: On training students to learn from texts. *Educational Researcher*, **10**, 14–21.

Campione, J.C. and Armbruster, B.B. (1985). Acquiring information from texts: An analysis of four approaches. In Segal, J.W., Chipman, S.F. and Glaser, R. (Eds). *Thinking and learning skills. Volume 1. Relating instruction to research.* Hillsdale. NJ: Lawrence Erlbaum.

Chipman, S.F., Segal, J.W. and Glaser, R. (Eds) (1985). *Thinking and learning skills. Volume 2. Research and open questions.* Hillsdale, NJ: Lawrence Erlbaum.

Department of Employment. (1971). *Glossary of training terms.* 2nd Edition. London: HMSO.

Ellis, H. (1965). *The transfer of learning.* New York: Macmillan.

Fleishman, E.A. and Parker, J.F. (1962). Factors in the retention and relearning of perceptual-motor skill. *Journal of Experimental Psychology*, **64**(3), 215–226.

Gardlin, G.R. and Sitterley, T.E. (1972). Degradation of learned skills – A review and annotated bibliography. Report Number D180–15080–1. Boeing Company.

Gibson, E.J. (1941). Retroactive inhibition as a function of the degree of generalisation between tasks. *Journal of Experimental Psychology*, **28**, 93–115.

Gick, M.L. and Holyoak, K.J. (1987). The cognitive basis of knowledge transfer. In Cormier, S.M. and Hagman, J.D. (Eds). *Transfer of learning: Contemporary research and applications.* New York: Academic Press.

Gray, W.D. and Orasanu, J.M. (1987). Transfer of cognitive skills. In Cormier, S.M. and Hagman, J.D. (Eds). *Transfer of learning: Contemporary research and applications.* New York: Academic Press.

Grose, R.F. and Birney, R.C. (Eds) (1963). *Transfer of learning.* New York: Van Nostrand.

Hagman, J.D. and Rose, A.M. (1983). Retention of military tasks: A review. *Human Factors*, **25**(2), 199–213.

Hammerton, M. (1967). Measures for the efficiency of simulators as training devices. *Ergonomics*, **10**, 63–65.

Harlow, H.F. (1949). The formation of learning sets. *Psychological Review*, **56**, 51–65.

Hayes, J.R. and Simon, H.A. (1977). Psychological differences among problem isomorphs. In Castellan, N. Jr., Pisoni, D. and Potts, G. (Eds). *Cognitive theory*. Volume II. Potomac, MD: Lawrence Erlbaum.

Hayes, J.R. (1985). Three problems in teaching general skills. In Chipman, S.F., Segal, J.W. and Glaser, R. (Eds). *Thinking and learning skills. Volume 1. Relating instruction to research*. Hillsdale NJ: Lawrence Erlbaum.

Hendrickson, G. and Schroeder, W.H. (1941). Transfer of training in learning to hit a submerged target. *Journal of Educational Psychology*, **32**, 205–213.

Hill, L.B. (1957). A second quarter century of delayed recall or relearning at eighty. *Journal of Educational Psychology*, **48**, 65–68.

Judd, C.H. (1908). The relation of special training to general intelligence. *Educational Review*, **36**, 28–42.

Kieras, D.E. and Bovair, S. (1986). The acquisition of procedures from text: A production system analysis of transfer of training. *Journal of Memory and Language*, **25**, 507–524.

Lewis, D., McAllister, D.E. and Adams, J.A. (1951). Facilitation and interference in performance on the Modified Mashburn Apparatus: I. The effects of varying the amount of original learning. *Journal of Experimental Psychology*, **41**, 247–260.

Luchins, A.S. (1942). Mechanization in problem solving: the effect of Einstellung. *Psychological Monographs*, **54**, 248.

Mandler, G. (1962). From association to structure. *Psychological Review*, **69**, 415–427.

McAllister, D.E. and Lewis, D. (1951). Facilitation and interference in performance on the Modified Mashburn Apparatus: II. The effects of varying the amount of interpolated learning. *Journal of Experimental Psychology*, **41**, 356–363.

McKenna, S.P. and Glendon, A.I. (1985). Occupational first aid training: Decay in cardiopulmonary resuscitation (CPR) skill. *Journal of Occupational Psychology*, **58**, 109–117.

Naylor, J.C. and Briggs, G.E. (1961). Long-term retention of learned skills: A review of the literature. ASD Technical Report 61–390. Ohio: Behavioural Sciences Laboratory, Wright-Patterson Air Force Base.

Naylor, J.C. and Briggs, G.E. (1963). Effect of rehearsal of temporal and spatial aspects on the long-term retention of a procedural skill. *Journal of Applied Psychology*, **47**(2), 120–126.

Neumann, E. and Ammons, R.B. (1957). Acquisition and long-term retention of a simple serial perceptual-motor skill. *Journal of Experimental Psychology*, **53**(3), 159–161.

Osgood, C.E. (1949). The similarity paradox in human learning: A resolution. *Psychological Review*, **56**, 132–143.

Patrick, J. and Haines, B. (1988). Training and transfer of fault-finding skill. *Ergonomics*, **31**, 193–210.

Povenmire, H.K. and Roscoe, S.N. (1973). Incremental transfer effectiveness of a ground-based general aviation trainer. *Human Factors*, **15**(6), 534–542.

Roscoe, S.N. (1971). Incremental transfer effectiveness. *Human Factors*, **13**(6), 561–567.

Schmidt, R.A. (1975). A schema theory of discrete motor skill learning. *Psychological Review*, **82**(4), 225–260.

Schmidt, R.A. and Young, D.E. (1987). Transfer of movement control in motor skill learning. In Cormier, S.M. and Hagman, J.D. (Eds). *Transfer of learning: Contemporary research and applications*. New York: Academic Press.

Segal, J.W., Chipman, S.F. and Glaser, R. (Eds) (1985). *Thinking and learning skills. Volume 1. Relating instruction to research*. Hillsdale, NJ: Lawrence Erlbaum.

Shields, J.L., Goldberg, S.L. and Dressel, J.D. (1979). Retention of basic soldiering skills. Research Report 1225. Alexandria, Va: US Army Research Institute for the Behavioral and Social Sciences.

Singley, M.K. and Anderson, J.R. (1985). The transfer of text-editing skill. *International Journal of Man-Machine Studies*, **22**, 403–423.

Swift, E.J. (1905). Memory of a complex skilful act. *American Journal of Psychology*, **16**, 131–133.

Thorndike, E.L. (1903). *Educational psychology*. New York: Leincke and Buechner.

Thorndike, E.L. (1924). Mental discipline in high-school studies. *Journal of Educational Psychology*, **15**, 1–22; 83–98.

Thorndike, E.L. and Woodworth, R.S. (1901). The influence of improvement in one mental function upon the efficiency of other functions. *Psychological Review*, **8**, 247–261; 384–395; 553–564.

Yum, K.S. (1931). An experimental test of the law of assimilation. *Journal of Experimental Psychology*, **14**, 68–82.

CHAPTER 4
Systems approaches to training

4.1 WHAT IS A SYSTEMS APPROACH?

There are two important aspects of a systems approach. Firstly, any functioning entity can be viewed as a system and defined in terms of its objectives or what it is attempting to achieve. A car, a university, or indeed training within an organisation can be viewed as a system with its own specific goals or objectives. Secondly, a system can be broken down into its subsystems and the interrelationships between them. These subsystems perform different functions which enable the system to achieve its objectives. For example, a car can be represented as a system whose overall objective is to achieve motion in a controllable fashion. This system can be divided into various subsystems, each of which performs a particular function, such as the braking subsystem and the fuel subsystem. All of these subsystems inter-relate in a specifiable manner to achieve the controllable movement of the car. Any change in the interrelationships between subsystems or the functions they perform can affect the operation of the system.

From this it follows that systems should be viewed hierarchically. A car is part of a road transport system which is in turn part of a transport system. Conversely, the braking subsystem of a car can be partitioned into its own subsystems which in turn can be further subdivided. Therefore use of the term "system" or "subsystem" is relative and depends upon one's perspective. It is not contradictory to speak of X as a system which can be divided into subsystems whilst also describing X as a subsystem of something else. The attraction of the systems approach is not in its rigour but in its generality and the perspective which it brings. It enables us to ask searching questions concerning what a system is trying to achieve and what functions have to be performed for this to happen. It also emphasises that it is important to analyse the inter-relationships between subsystems within a system. Subsystems may transfer information, mass, energy or control between each other and this transfer can take place in one or both directions. Transfer of information between two subsystems can enable them to be self-regulating. For example, an organisation is a system composed of various subsystems, including one concerned with training and another with recruitment/selection. If the training subsystem spends too much time or money in producing trained personnel, then this information may effect a change in the recruitment/selection subsystem.

A systems approach provides insights into the domain of training in two ways:

1. Training can be viewed as a system which interacts with other systems such as personnel selection and ergonomics. Whilst this book is primarily concerned with training it is important to remember that these other systems may also hold the solution to a particular occupational or educational problem. The interaction of training with other such systems will be considered briefly in Section 4.2.
2. The development of training can itself be viewed as a system and can be analysed into its subsystems and how they interact with each other. This enables us to identify different functions involved in developing training programmes. This has given rise to what are termed Instructional Systems Development (ISD) models, four of which are discussed in Section 4.3. The advantages and disadvantages of such an approach are considered in Section 4.4. Such models provide a useful introduction to the various activities involved in developing training materials. The psychological contributions to these different training functions are elaborated in later chapters of this book.

4.2 TRAINING AND RELATED SYSTEMS

The training system interacts with the systems concerned with ergonomics and personnel selection. All three provide potential solutions to a performance problem and therefore need to be considered. An ergonomic approach attempts to design or redesign the person's job or tasks such that their psychological requirements are reduced, possibly with an improved human–machine interface. Sometimes this is not feasible possibly due to investment in poorly designed equipment, and sadly the psychologist has to train people to cope with such problems. In some cases such training may be difficult and time-consuming and require extra training resources. In this situation, the types of errors and their associated consequences both before and after any ergonomic or training intervention need to be carefully weighed. Some errors may be tolerable, whilst others may be catastrophic. Hence there is a close relationship between ergonomics and training.

Changes in selection criteria also may offer a solution to a performance problem. Selecting people either with higher aptitudes or abilities or with previous training in related skills may improve job performance. This issue will be partly discussed in Section 4.3 since the nature of the trainees selected will affect both the content and design of training. It is often the case that some combination of the three approaches – ergonomic, selection and training – needs to be adopted to produce a viable solution. It is therefore inappropriate to consider training in isolation from other types of intervention.

The training system is only part of a larger system which might be a company or organisation. Training requires resources which in turn have to be justified in terms of projected benefits. The development of training in the workplace will face practical constraints besides the limitations of our psychological expertise in devising an optimal training situation. An excellent training programme may fail in an organisation because it takes too long to devise or is too costly. Existing simulators may have to be used for training even though they are out-of-date. In a difficult economic climate an organisation's training budget is often the first to suffer arguably because the effects of such reductions are less visible than other cuts. Indeed it is easy to underestimate the resources required for training as is evident from many evaluation studies.

The costs of training include:

(a) Buildings and land, e.g. rent, maintenance and depreciation.
(b) Capital equipment, e.g. maintenance and depreciation of training equipment, simulators.
(c) New materials required for training.
(d) Cost of trainees participating in training, e.g. salary, time.
(e) Costs of instructors, trainers and any administrative staff.
(f) Training development costs, e.g. development of intelligent computer-assisted instruction, training of trainers.
(g) External course fees.

The benefits of training include:

(a) Improved job performance, e.g. quality and quantity of production.
(b) Improved safety standards.
(c) Less absenteeism, higher job satisfaction and improved managerial and trainee attitudes.
(d) Indirect consequences of improved job performance include, e.g. increased sales and reduced need for servicing of products.

A similar perspective of training is given in Figure 4.1 from Annett (1968). Resources for training can be broadly divided into manpower and physical resources. These determine the nature of the trainees and instructors, what task will be used for training, the type of training

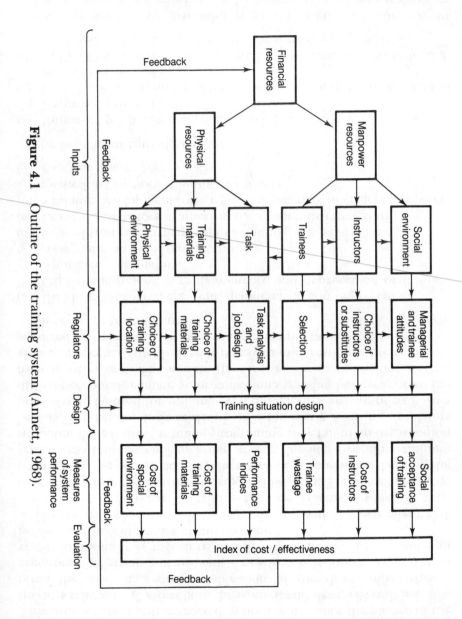

Figure 4.1 Outline of the training system (Annett, 1968).

materials and where training takes place. These, in turn, give rise to what Annett terms the "regulators" of the training system such as managerial and trainee attitudes, selection policy and choice of training location. Training is then designed and the effect of a training programme can be measured by indicators ranging from performance levels to costs and social acceptance of the training. Feedback from the evaluation phase will modify parts of the training system to improve its efficiency. Therefore the context of training is very important. The designer or manager of training is unlikely to have sufficient control over either the inputs or regulators of the training system and possibly even the measures of system performance. Consequently, training in the real world will be a compromise between a psychologically expedient design and the resources imposed or available for this purpose.

4.3 INSTRUCTIONAL SYSTEMS DEVELOPMENT (ISD) MODELS

A systems approach can identify different subsystems in the development of training, how they interrelate and the functions they perform. This has given rise to what are known as Instructional Systems Development (ISD) models. Distinctions made by these ISD models are *logical* in nature rather than *psychological* since the components of these models are specified in terms of their prescribed goals. There are many ISD models. Logan (1982) stated that Montemerlo and Tennyson (1976) found more than 100 manuals containing such models since 1951, whilst Andrews and Goodson (1980) identified over 60 such models.

The ISD approach is an attempt to analyse the development of training into a series of goals or decisions facing the training manager. Therefore ISD models can be used as job aids in the development of training. However, whilst these models specify *what* goals need to be achieved, they do not necessarily specify *how* these goals should be accomplished. For example, all models agree on the need to analyse a task and design a training programme although few are explicit about *how* this should be accomplished. These "how" decisions are essentially *psychological* in nature and are considerably more difficult than the specification of *what* has to be achieved. It should be noted, however, that some ISD models have been linked to psychological guidelines which can be used by the training manager.

Four ISD models are discussed below:

1. A model from Patrick (1980), adapted from Eckstrand (1964), which defines the major components in training development.
2. Interservices Procedures for Instructional Systems Development

(IPISD) (Branson et al., 1975; Branson, Wagner and Rayner, 1977) which was developed within the US military to improve the development of training material.
3. A model developed by Briggs and Wager (1981) in an educational context which proposes 15 stages in the design of instruction.
4. The Learning Systems Development (LSD) model (Patrick, Michael and Moore, 1986) developed within an industrial context and a hybrid of other models.

Adaptation of Eckstrand's (1964) training system

In Eckstrand's adapted training system (Figure 4.2), there are six major functions associated with the development of training. The first requirement is to identify some actual or potential problem or need within an organisation (1). This may be a result of the introduction of new equipment, staff redeployment, the development of new or more complex work or unacceptable levels of performance in terms of quality or quantity. We will assume that the optimal solution involves training or retraining personnel. It is then necessary to specify this need in terms of clear and unambiguous behavioural or performance objectives which form the goals of the training programme (3) (see Section 4.5). This in turn will enable appropriate criterion measures (6) to be developed which can be used to evaluate trainees' performance as "graduates" of the training programme.

Some analysis of the job or task has to be undertaken in order to define the training objectives (3) and to derive appropriate training content for these objectives to be met (4). This topic will be dealt with in Chapters 5–8. The final stage before running the training programme is the design of training in its widest sense (5). This covers the more important and "deep" design issues of structuring and sequencing the training materials and also the "surface" issues of how the training is delivered and presented. The psychologist therefore has to synthesise and bring to bear as many psychological principles as possible to the design of the training programme. Considerable ingenuity is required to engineer an effective training environment. The transition from training content to efficient training design has been acknowledged as notoriously difficult by many writers (e.g. Resnick, 1976; Wheaton et al., 1976). As a last resort some research may be needed to find the optimal training design. Finally, as can be seen in Figure 4.2, the trainees undergo training and emerge as "graduates" of the programme.

Any training development system should be capable of regulating itself by modifying and improving any of its subsystems. This can be achieved on the basis of feedback (7) which stems from an evaluation of the training programme via its "graduates". Amongst the most important evaluation indices is whether the trainees achieved the criterion performance. Feedback may result in modifications to the selection criteria, the training objectives, training content or any aspect of the design of the training programme. Indeed if trainees fail to develop an acceptable level of expertise, then it can be argued that it is the training development system which is at fault rather than those who receive training. Evaluation of training is discussed in Chapter 13. In this adaptation of Eckstrand's system, the personnel selection function (2) is represented in Figure 4.2. There are two reasons for this. Firstly, in the present industrial and economic climate the issue is not so much training or selection but selection for retraining (given the level of unemployment and the rapidly changing job demands). Secondly, this results in an important trade-off between selection and training. How do we decide which trainees to select for training if there is a pool of potential trainees? To answer this question it is necessary to estimate what might be termed their transferability to the new job (Patrick, 1980). Some

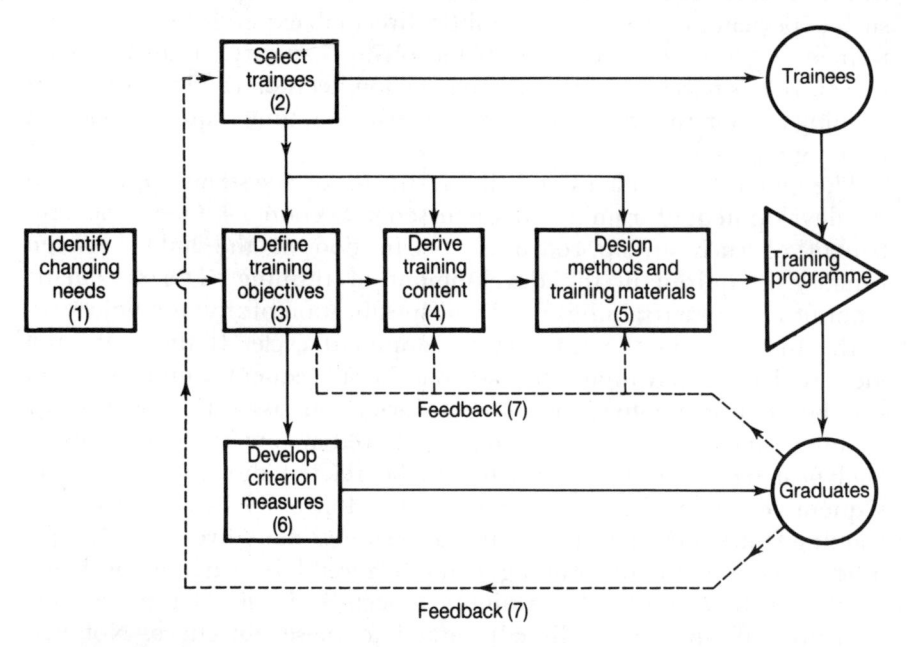

Figure 4.2 Relationships between training and selection decisions in the training system (Patrick 1980, adapted from Eckstrand, 1964).

indicators of transferability are concerned with extraneous factors in the work environment and the motivation and interests of the trainees, e.g. pay scales, status of job. Other aspects of transferability are more psychological in nature and relate to the interaction between the person's existing knowledge and skills and those which have to be acquired via the training programme. The selection decision affects both the objectives (3) and content (4) of training and its subsequent design (5).

Imagine that there are two potential trainees (A and B) for a new job. On a simple quantitative measure, trainee A already has competence in 75% of the new job's areas whereas trainee B has only 25%. Therefore trainee B has more training objectives and content to master than trainee A. However, it is not necessarily the case that trainee A has a higher transferability estimate than trainee B. Any statement of training need should also include some qualitative index of the psychological requirements imposed by the new job and the training conditions required. An examination of the 25% of the job to be mastered by trainee A might reveal the need for innovative problem-solving skills which trainee B might already have, albeit from a different context. In transferability terms, it might be cost-effective to select trainee B with such experience or capacities and little direct job experience rather than trainee A with no proven problem-solving capacity. Transferability therefore has to be estimated in the selection decision (2) by considering training costs in the widest sense of the term, e.g. time required to learn, training equipment etc.

The general advantages and disadvantages of a systems approach to the development of training are discussed in Section 4.4. One important benefit of such an approach is specification of the links between functions required in the development of training. The systematic identification of a (training) need and specification of training objectives is the first step in the training development cycle. If these are not identified accurately then it follows that the subsequent training content will be inappropriate. Therefore information associated with each training function not only has to be gathered systematically (e.g. using analytical techniques) but also has to be related directly to the subsequent activity in the development cycle. Hence needs, objectives and training content (1, 3 and 4, Figure 4.2) should map directly onto each other. Every piece of training content should be capable of being justified with respect to its training objective. Similarly the criterion measures (6) should be directly linked to these objectives. Not surprisingly, if such a modus operandi is not adopted, then training can easily become inappropriate. For example, training might be devised for a nonexistent task or training objectives may fail to represent a performance need.

Interservices Procedures for Instructional Systems Development (IPISD) (Branson et al., 1975)

The IPISD model is probably the most well-known and influential ISD model. It was developed in the context of US military training (Branson et al., 1975; Branson, Wagner and Rayner, 1977). The intention was to disseminate principles concerning the development of training which were considered to be common to different training problems and contexts. Eventually the model, which is detailed in five large manuals, was adopted by all of the American services. Since these references (given at the end of this chapter) are not immediately accessible, the interested reader will find summaries in Logan (1978, 1979).

The IPISD model (Figure 4.3) divides the development of training into five main phases: analyse, design, develop, implement and control. These are further divided into a total of 19 subphases. The executive summary describes the five phases as follows:

Phase 1, Analyse. Inputs, processes and outputs in Phase 1 are all based on job information. An inventory of job tasks is compiled and divided into two groups: tasks not selected for instruction and tasks selected for instruction. Performance standards for tasks selected for instruction are determined by interview or observation at job sites and verified by subject matter experts. The analysis of existing course documentation is done to determine if all or portions of the analysis phase and other phases have already been done by someone else following the ISD guidelines. As a final analysis phase step, the list of tasks selected for instruction is analysed for the most suitable instructional setting for each task.

Phase 2, Design. Beginning with Phase 2, the ISD model is concerned with designing instruction using the job analysis information from Phase 1. The first step is the conversion of each task selected for training into a terminal learning objective. Each terminal learning objective is then analysed to determine learning objectives and learning steps necessary for mastery of the terminal learning objective. Tests are designed to match the learning objectives. A sample of students is tested to ensure that their entry behaviours match the level of learning analysis. Finally, a sequence of instruction is designed for the learning objectives.

Phase 3, Develop. The instructional development phase begins with the classification of learning objectives by learning category so as to identify learning guidelines necessary for optimum learning to take place. Determining how instruction is to be packaged and presented to the student is accomplished through a media selection process which takes into account such factors as learning category and guideline, media characteristics, training setting criteria, and costs. Instructional management plans are

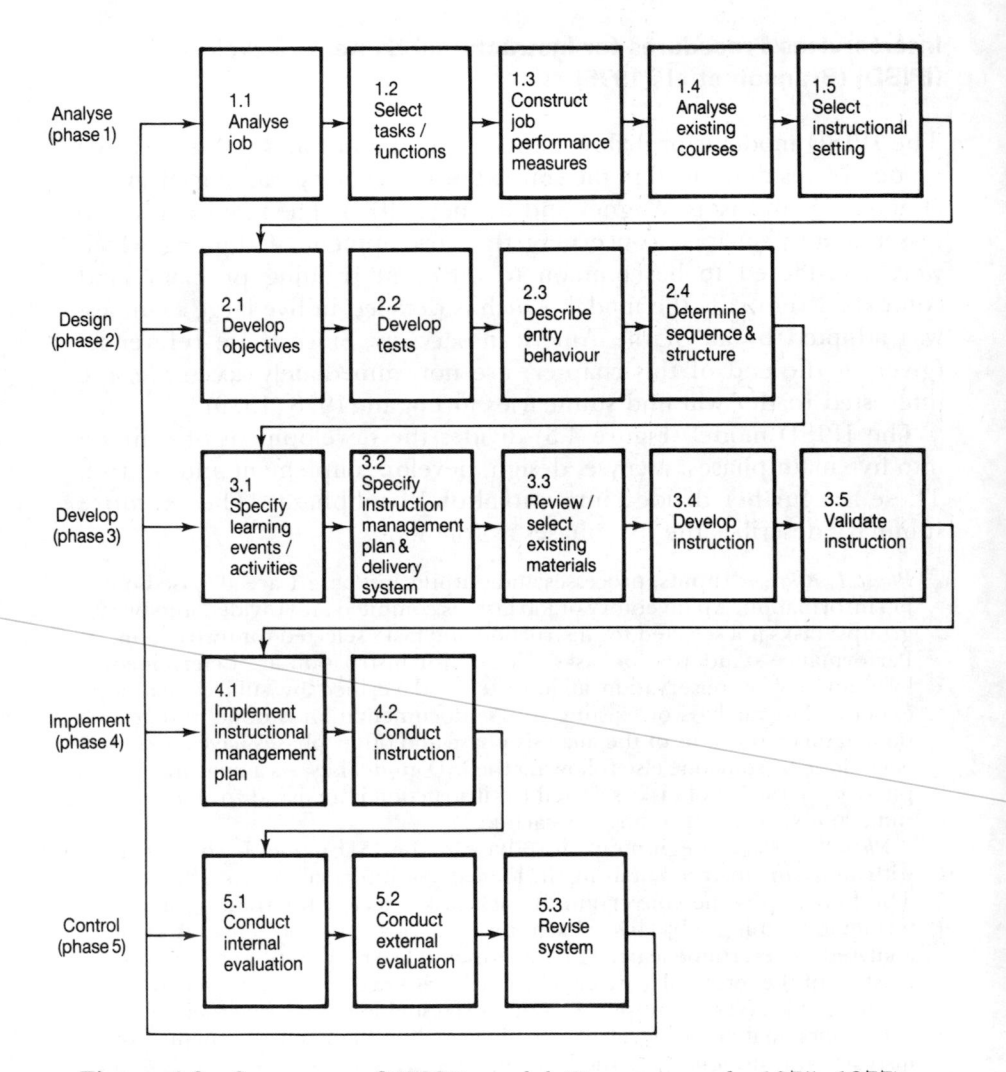

Figure 4.3 Summary of IPISD model (Branson et al., 1975, 1977).

developed to allocate and manage all resources for conducting instruction. Instructional materials are selected or developed and tried out. When materials have been validated on the basis of empirical data obtained from groups of typical students, the course is ready for implementation.

Phase 4, Implement. Staff training is required for the implementation of the instructional management plan and the instruction. Some key personnel must be trained to be managers in the specified management plan. The instructional staff must be trained to conduct the instruction and collect evaluative data on all of the instructional components. At the completion of each instructional cycle, management staff should be able to use the collected information to improve the instructional system.

Phase 5, Control. Evaluation and revision of instruction are carried out by personnel who preferably are neither the instructional designers nor the managers of the course under study. The first activity (internal evaluation) is the analysis of learner performance in the course to determine instances of deficient or irrelevant instruction. The evaluation team then suggests solutions for the problems. In the external evaluation, personnel assess job task performance on the job to determine the actual performance of course graduates and other job incumbents. All collected data, internal and external, can be used as quality control on instruction and as input to any phase of the system for revision (Branson et al., 1975, preface).

The IPISD model is more detailed than Eckstrand's adapted training system discussed previously. In the IPISD model the derivation of training content and the subsequent design of training is split into a further series of functions or stages which have to be performed by the training developer. The reader should not be alarmed at the apparent discrepancies amongst these two and other ISD models. Each model shares the same general goal, which is the development of effective training. However, the sizes into which this cake is cut varies as does the labelling of the pieces. The number of stages in a model depends upon the level of description used and the nomenclature varies with the training context and preference of the ISD designer. Differences between ISD models are more superficial than they might, at first, appear and therefore should not be treated dogmatically. Rather, ISD models should be viewed as providing a framework and series of useful prompts in the development of training.

A general criticism of the ISD approach is that whilst some generalisable stages in the development of training are specified (i.e. *what* has to be achieved), prescriptions concerning *how* these are to be accomplished are not as readily available. In order to proceduralise the development of training fully, it would be necessary to link techniques or procedures to each stage specified in an ISD model. Training programmes could then be developed by those unfamiliar with training, or indeed by automated devices. Considerable efforts have been made in this direction with the IPISD model, although they have met with limited success. Logan (1978, 1979), who is an enthusiast of the IPISD model, has carried out large scale surveys of which techniques or procedures (sometimes referred to as author aids) can be used for different functions in the IPISD model. Not surprisingly for some it is difficult to prescribe which technique or procedure should be used under what circumstances, whilst for others, very few techniques exist. Such techniques vary in terms of their reliability and validity and also in terms of whether they transfer between different training contexts. For example, it is possible to specify guidelines on how to write multiple choice questions which are reasonably generalisable. On the other hand, prescribing the design of a simulation for training is more problematic and will depend heavily upon the nature of the task to be trained.

Author aids for the IPISD model are described by Logan (1978, 1979) and O'Neil (1979a, b). This includes work by O'Neal, Faust and O'Neal (1979) who described a training course for authors of training materials which included classifying training objectives and designing the training of rules, concepts and procedures. Computerised aids which have been developed for functions 2.2 and 3.4 of the IPISD model (Figure 4.3) support the development of tests (e.g. in terms of reliability and validity) and training materials (e.g. in terms of reading level of audience, type of feedback provided). In a similar vein, Conoley and O'Neil (1979) discussed the construction of good and poor test items (e.g. multiple choice) and provided a set of guidelines for those developing such training materials. Taylor (1979) and Harris (1979) described computer-based systems which were designed to facilitate the design of training and the preparation of lessons.

These efforts to support training development are undoubtedly useful. They are nevertheless either limited to relatively small parts of the overall design process (e.g. test item development) or fail to cover important design issues in sufficient depth. It is not surprising that we cannot proceduralise the development of training, since a complete psychology of training does not yet exist. Consequently, it is important that the relevant knowledge base of psychology from which guidelines might be generated is understood by those involved in training. This is, of course, the raison d'etre for this book.

Briggs and Wager's (1981) ISD model

Briggs and Wager (1981) presented a model for training development which is couched more in the language of classroom teaching. The model consists of the following 15 functions or stages.

1. Assessment of needs, goals and priorities.
2. Assessment of resources, constraints and selection of a delivery system.

3. Identification of curriculum and course scope and sequence.
4. Determination of gross structure of courses.
5. Determination of sequence of unit and specific objectives.
6. Definition of performance objectives.
7. Analysis of objectives for sequencing of enablers.
8. Preparation of assessments of learner performance.
9. Designing lessons and materials:
   instructional events;
   media;
   prescriptions (utilising appropriate conditions of learning).
10. Development of media, materials, activities.
11. Formative evaluation.
12. Field tests and revision.
13. Instructor training.
14. Summative evaluation.
15. Diffusion and operational installation.

These functions or stages are listed in the approximate order in which they should be performed, although the authors noted that there will be iteration between most of them as materials are developed and finalised. Formative evaluation, stage 11, involves pilot testing of the materials in various ways which may lead to modification in the preceding stages. Despite the differences in nomenclature and number of stages between this model and the IPISD approach, both essentially cover the same ground. The IPISD model is more concerned with the occupational context of jobs and tasks, whereas Briggs and Wager's model emphasises the education context. Both models proceed from an assessment of training needs to a specification of objectives and to the subsequent design/development of training materials. Both models also emphasise that training materials should be evaluated both prior to and after the training programme.

Briggs and Wager (1981) have written a handbook whose chapters instruct the reader on different stages of their model.

Learning Systems Development (LSD) model (Patrick et al., 1986)

The LSD model has three phases: analyse, design/develop and implement/control. These phases are broken down into the tasks facing the training designer: five tasks in the analyse phase, four tasks in the design/develop phase and three tasks in the implement/control phase (see Figure 4.4). In addition the design and development phase,

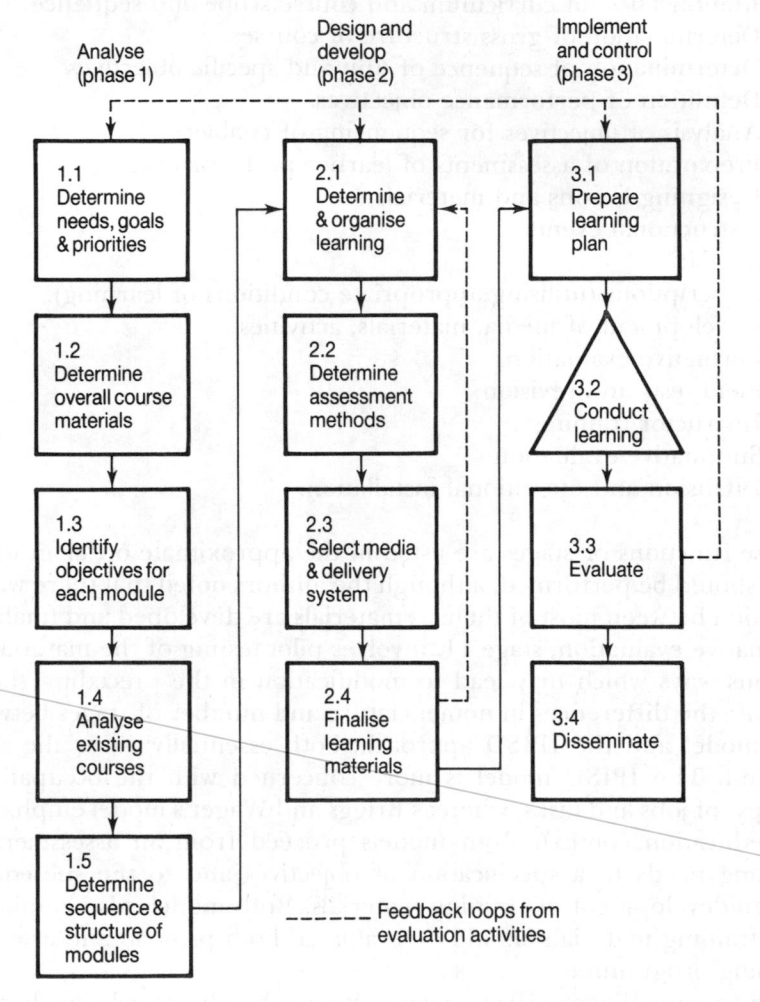

Figure 4.4 Learning Systems Development (LSD) model (Patrick et al., 1986).

involving four tasks, is further subdivided into a total of 14 subtasks. Each subtask in the design/develop phase has an associated set of guidelines for the practitioner which describe, for example, how to identify types of learning, structure the learning material and optimise presentation.

4.4   ADVANTAGES AND DISADVANTAGES OF ISD MODELS

Four ISD models have been reviewed in Section 4.3. The general nature of this systems approach to the development of training should now be evident and its overall benefits and shortcomings will now be addressed.

The advantages of an ISD approach are:

(a) *ISD models identify generalisable functions in the development of training.* An ISD model views the development of training as a system and breaks it down into subsystems and the functions they perform. Terminology varies and sometimes these subsystems are described as phases, stages, goals, functions, components or tasks. Irrespective of how they are labelled, the important point is that each function has to be performed in the development of *any* training pro-gramme. Hence ISD models claim to be general purpose or context independent.

(b) *ISD models are helpful to those unfamiliar with training development.* Any ISD model prescribes the functions involved in training develop-ment together with the sequence in which they should be carried out. Hence such a model can be an aid to those with little knowledge of how to develop training systematically.

(c) *ISD models are particularly useful to large-scale organisations.* In large military, educational or business establishments, there are many jobs which require training. As a result, various people may be involved in training development activities for even the same job. An ISD model not only enables a sensible division of labour to take place but also facilitates coordination of these training activities, since the output of one subsystem is the input to another. It is no coincidence that large military and educational organisations have been at the forefront of development of such ISD models.

(d) *Psychological principles can be appended.* The Briggs and Wager and LSD models discussed in Section 4.3 have psychological principles, techniques etc. directly linked to the different functions in the models. To a lesser extent this is true of the IPISD model. Such models therefore make it easier to organise and target relevant psychological findings with respect to the training functions to which they apply. It was mentioned in Chapter 1 that the chapters in this book reflect three major ISD functions: analysis (Chapters 5–8), design (Chapters 8–12) and evaluation (Chapter 13).

(e) *An ISD model can be used as an evaluation framework.* Training can be evaluated by not only examining the product(s) of training, but also the *process* of training development. Legitimate and revealing questions are: how many ISD functions were addressed explicitly in the development of this training programme? How were these functions accomplished and which, if any, techniques or psychological principles were involved? Consequently an ISD model can provide a framework for the evaluation of *how* training was developed.

The disadvantages of an ISD approach are:

(a) *It is an idealised, top-down view of training development.* ISD models arguably present a too idealistic perspective and obscure training development activities which are often idiosyncratic (e.g. Bunderson, 1977). Whilst moving from a specification of training needs and objectives to the design, development and evaluation functions is the rational approach, even those expert in training may deviate from this linear top-down sequence.

(b) *ISD models specify "what to do" rather than "how to do it".* As we discussed in Section 4.3, ISD models themselves do not provide detailed prescriptions or guidelines of how the training functions should be performed. They are skeletons without flesh.

In conclusion, it is evident from the above advantages and disadvantages that on balance, an ISD approach is of benefit. It is not suggested that any one model should be followed slavishly. Also the use of any model does not guarantee the development of good training. Nevertheless, an awareness of the functions involved in developing training and how they inter-relate provide an important framework for those engaged in devising training programmes.

4.5 TRAINING OBJECTIVES

The specification of training objectives is an important first step in the development of training, as we have seen from the various ISD models. Training objectives determine both the content and design of training and also what trained persons should be able to accomplish after training. A massive literature exists concerning the writing and use of different types of objective in the design of training (e.g. Davies, 1976; Tyler, 1950). Mager (1962) provided the classic account of developing objectives which, he argued, are primarily for communicating instructional intent. Objectives should have three components:

> *First,* identify the terminal behaviour by name; you can specify the kind of behaviour that will be accepted as evidence that the learner has achieved the objective.

Second, try to define the desired behaviour further by describing the important conditions under which the behaviour will be expected to occur.

Third, specify the criteria of acceptable performance by describing how well the learner must perform to be considered acceptable (Mager, 1962, p. 12).

An example provided by Mager of an objective is:

Given a DC motor of ten horsepower or less that contains a single malfunction, and given a standard kit of tools and references, the learner must be able to repair the motor within a period of 45 minutes (p. 39).

Mager therefore prescribed that objectives are tightly linked to performance requirements and should specify the actions which the trainee should be able to perform after training, the conditions under which these actions are to be performed and the standards of performance which must be met. Merrill (1983) has extended Mager's formulation for the specification of objectives by detailing generic forms of objectives for different types of learning in his Component Display Theory. This theory of instruction is discussed in Chapter 8.

Gagné and Briggs (1974) have proposed five components for writing objectives which overlap with those proposed by Mager and include specification of the situation, the object, the action, the tools and other constraints and the capability to be learned. Gagné and Briggs provided the following example of how a typist's task of copying a written letter can be specified by these five components:

Given a written longhand letter	(Situation)
executes	(The learned capability, a motor skill)
a copy	(Object)
by typing	(Action)
using an electric typewriter making one carbon of a one page letter	(Tools and other constraints)
(Gagné and Briggs, 1974, p. 81.)	

Such guidelines for writing adequate objectives are useful but do not guarantee good training. It is unfortunate that many courses concerned with training go little further than emphasising the role of objectives and the use of Mager's guidelines and fail to consider other equally important training issues. MacDonald-Ross (1973) criticised the excessive prominence given to behavioural objectives in the development of training. Firstly, as MacDonald-Ross asked, what are the origins of such objectives? How are they generated and selected as being relevant to a training programme? Such questions are difficult to answer systematically, although some analysis techniques (e.g. Hierarchical Task Analysis,

Chapter 6) arguably provide an answer. Naturally, performance objectives for a training programme should correspond as closely as possible to those which occur in performance of the real task or job. Secondly, objectives depend upon the use of verbs to describe performance. These should be concrete (Duncan, 1972) and action-oriented (Gagné and Briggs, 1974). This will reduce the ambiguity inherent in such verbs as "to know" or "to understand", although, of course, ambiguity can never be totally eliminated. It is recommended therefore that when performance objectives are being developed during the analysis of a task or job, a set of action verbs should be defined. Such an approach was adopted by Frederickson and Freer (1978) in a study of the basic electronic skills of maintenance personnel. They provided a list of twelve action verbs which make distinctions in maintenance functions with associated definitions. This at least restricts the room for ambiguity. For example:

Inspect: To determine the serviceability of an item by examining its physical, mechanical and/or electrical characteristics and comparing these measurements with established standards.

Adjust: To bring an operating characteristic of an item into prescribed limits by setting variable controls to the specific, proper or exact positions (Frederickson and Freer, 1978, p. II–6).

In our discussion of ISD models, we found that training functions were specified in terms of goals without the means of achieving them necessarily being made explicit. A similar criticism can be made of behavioural objectives. If objectives are associated with simple perceptual-motor tasks, this may present less of a problem since there may be few alternative methods which the trainee can use to achieve such objectives. On the other hand, when these objectives refer to complex and/or cognitive activities, the number of different strategies for achieving them will increase. For example, diagnosing faults in a car engine might involve pattern matching of symptoms, use of an algorithm, use of heuristics or qualitative reasoning from first principles concerning the cause and effect relationships of variables (e.g. fuel, electricity) used in the operation of the car. The psychological demands of this task and also the necessary training will vary immensely depending upon which strategy or combination of strategies the fault-finder has to master to achieve the objective of fault-finding. Consequently, the use of training objectives needs to be linked to some psychological analysis of the nature of the task which is to be trained. These issues are explored in Chapters 7 and 8.

The objectives of training affect both the content and design of

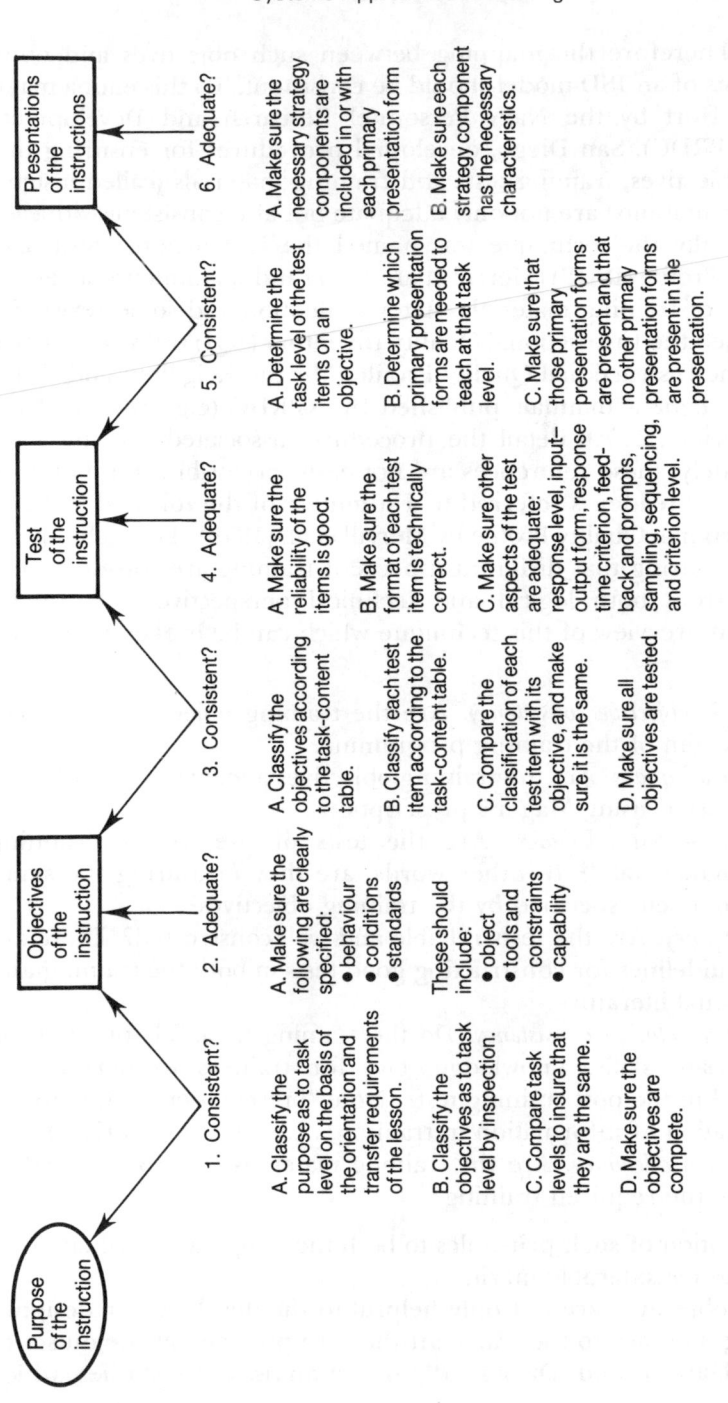

Figure 4.5 A summary of the aspects of instructional quality analysed by the Instructional Quality Profile (Merrill et al., 1979).

training. Therefore the mapping between such objectives and other components of an ISD model should be consistent. To this end, a major research effort by the Navy Personnel Research and Development Center (NPRDC), San Diego, developed procedures for ensuring that training objectives, training tests and training materials (called instructional presentations) are not only adequate but also consistent with each other. Initially the technique was named the Instructional Strategies Diagnostic Profile (ISDP) (Merrill et al., 1977) and was aimed at assessing the quality of training materials. After evaluation and some revision it was renamed the Instructional Quality Inventory (IQI) (Ellis et al., 1978) and also the Instructional Quality Profile (Merrill, Reigeluth and Faust, 1979). Subsequent manuals published by NPRDC (e.g. Ellis, Wulfeck and Fredericks, 1979) detail the procedures associated with the IQI. Unfortunately, these references are not easily accessible and therefore the interested reader is referred to a summary of the role and scope of the Instructional Quality Profile by Merrill et al. (1979). The technique is aimed at ensuring that different aspects of training are consistent and adequate from both logical and technical perspectives. Figure 4.5 provides an overview of this technique which can be broken down into six areas:

1. *Purpose – objective consistency.* Are the training objectives consistent with the aim of the training programme?
2. *Objective adequacy.* Are the training objectives adequately stated? This can be tested using Mager's prescriptions.
3. *Objective – test adequacy.* Are the tests of pre- or post-training performance valid? In other words, are they measuring the skills, knowledge, etc. specified by the training objectives?
4. *Test adequacy.* Are the tests reliable and well constructed? There are many guidelines for constructing good tests in both the training and educational literature.
5. *Test – presentation consistency.* Do the training materials provide the appropriate skills, knowledge, etc. for trainees to perform as required in the post-training test? (Note "presentation" refers to the presentation of information in training, i.e. training materials.)
6. *Presentation adequacy.* Are the training materials well constructed to promote the required training?

The application of such principles to both the design and evaluation of training has considerable merit.

Finally, objectives are not only helpful to the developer or designer of training, but also to the trainee if they are provided at the outset of training. Hartley and Davies (1976) summarised 40 studies which evaluated the improvement in learning by giving trainees behavioural objectives prior to training. They concluded that, despite methodological differences and a lack of agreement on the level of detail of such objectives between evaluation studies, it is beneficial to provide the trainee with objectives before training. This, and other pretraining strategies are discussed in Chapter 9.

REFERENCES

Andrews, D.II. and Goodson, L.A. (1980). A comparative analysis of models of instructional design. *Journal of Instructional Development*, **3**, 2–16.

Annett, J. (1968). A systems approach. In *Planning industrial training*. London: National Institute of Adult Education.

Branson, R.K., Rayner, G.T., Cox, L., Furman, J.P., King, F.J. and Hannum, W.H. (1975). Interservice procedures for instructional systems development: Executive summary and model. Tallahassee, FL: Center for Educational Technology, Florida State University. Distributed by Defense Technical Information Center, Alexandria, VA. (Phases 1, 2, 3, 4 and 5 of Interservice procedures for instructional systems development are ED 122 018–022 respectively – same publisher and authors.)

Branson, R.K., Wagner, B.M. and Rayner, G.T. (1977). Interservice procedures for instructional systems development: Task V Final Report. Tallahassee, FL: Center for Educational Technology, Florida State University. (ED 164 745).

Briggs, L.J. and Wager, W.W. (1981). *Handbook of procedures for the design of instruction*. 2nd edition. Englewood Cliffs, NJ: Educational Technology Publications.

Bunderson, C.V. (1977). Analysis of needs and goals for author training and production management systems. Technical Report 1, MDA-903-76-C-0216, San Diego, CA: Courseware Inc.

Conoley, J.C. and O'Neil, H.F. Jr (1979). A primer for developing test items. In O'Neil, H.F. Jr (Ed.) *Procedures for instructional systems development*. New York: Academic Press.

Davies, I.K. (1976). *Objectives in curriculum design*. London: McGraw Hill.

Duncan, K.D. (1972). Strategies for analysis of the task. In Hartley, J. (Ed.) *Strategies for programmed instruction: an educational technology*. London: Butterworth.

Eckstrand, G.A. (1964). Current status of the technology of training. Report AMRL-TDR-64-86. Wright-Patterson Air Force Base Aerospace Medical Laboratories.

Ellis, J.A., Wulfeck II, W.H., Merrill, M.D., Richards, R.E., Schmidt, R.V. and Wood, N.D. (1978). Interim training manual for the Instructional Quality Inventory. NPRDC Technical Note 78–5. San Diego, CA: Navy Personnel Research and Development Center.

Ellis, J.A., Wulfeck, II, W.H. and Fredericks, P.S. (1979). The Instructional Quality Inventory II. Users manual. NPRDC SR 79–24. San Diego, CA: Navy Personnel Research and Development Center.

Frederickson, E.W. and Freer, D.R. (1978). Basic electronics skills and knowledge. Research Note 79–5. Alexandria, VA: US Army Research Institute.

Gagné, R.M. and Briggs, L.J. (1974). *Principles of instructional design*. New York: Holt, Rinehart and Winston.

Harris, W.P. (1979). An authoring system for on-the-job environments. In O'Neil, H.F. Jr (Ed.) *Issues in instructional systems development*. New York: Academic Press.

Hartley, J. and Davies, I.K. (1976). Preinstructional strategies: the role of pretexts, behavioural objectives, overviews and advance organisers. *Review of Educational Research*, **46** (2), 239–265.

Logan, R.S. (1978). An instructional systems development approach for learning strategies. In O'Neil, H.F. Jr (Ed.) *Learning strategies*. New York: Academic Press.

Logan, R.S. (1979). A state of the art assessment of instructional systems development. In O'Neil, H.F. Jr (Ed.) *Issues in instructional systems development*. New York: Academic Press.

Logan, R.S. (1982). *Instructional systems development – an international view of theory and practice*. New York: Academic Press.

MacDonald-Ross, M. (1973). Behavioural objectives – a critical review. *Instructional Science*, **2**, 1–52.

Mager, R.F. (1962). *Preparing instructional objectives*. Palo Alto: Fearon.

Merrill, M.D. (1983). Component display theory. In Reigeluth, C.M. (Ed.) *Instructional design theories and models: An overview of their current status*. Hillsdale, NJ: Lawrence Erlbaum.

Merrill, M.D., Reigeluth, C.M. and Faust, G.W. (1979). The instructional quality profile: a curriculum evaluation and design tool. In O'Neil, H.F. Jr (Ed.) *Procedures for instructional systems development*. New York: Academic Press.

Merrill, M.D., Richards, R.E., Schmidt, R.V. and Wood, N.D. (1977). Interim training manual for the Instructional Strategy Diagrammatic Profile. NPRDC Report 77–14. San Diego, CA: Navy Personnel Research and Development Center.

Montemerlo, M.D. and Tennyson, M.E. (1976). Instructional systems development. Conceptual analysis and comprehensive bibliography. Report No. NTEC-14-257. Orlando, FL: Naval Training Equipment Center. (NTIS AD A024 526).

O'Neal, H.L., Faust, G.W. and O'Neal, A.F. (1979). An author training course. In O'Neil, H.F. Jr (Ed.) *Procedures for instructional systems development*. New York: Academic Press.

O'Neil, H.F.Jr. (Ed) (1979a). *Issues in instructional systems development*. New York: Academic Press.

O'Neil, H.F. Jr (Ed.) (1979b). *Procedures for instructional systems development*. New York: Academic Press.

Patrick, J. (1980). Job analysis, training and transferability: Some theoretical and practical issues. In Duncan, K.D., Gruneberg, M.M. and Wallis, D. (Eds) *Changes in working life*. Chichester: Wiley.

Patrick, J., Michael, I. and Moore, A. (1986). *Designing for learning – Some guidelines*. Birmingham: Occupation Services Ltd.

Resnick, L.B. (1976). Task analysis in instruction. In Klahr, D. (Ed.) *Cognition and instruction*. Chichester: Wiley.

Taylor, S.S. (1979) CREATE: A computer-based authoring curriculum. In O'Neil, H.F. Jr (Ed.) *Issues in instructional systems development*. New York: Academic Press.

Tyler, R.W. (1950) *Basic principles of curriculum and instruction*. University of Chicago Press.

Wheaton, G., Rose, A.M., Fingerman, P., Karotkin, A.L. and Holding, D.H. (1976). Evaluation of the effectiveness of training devices: literature review and preliminary model. Research Memorandum, 76–6. Washington: US Army Research Institute for the Behavioural and Social Sciences.

CHAPTER 5

Analysis: general methodological issues

Some systematic analysis of the task (or job) is a prerequisite for the development of effective training. The initial stages in all of the Instructional Systems Development (ISD) models, discussed in Chapter 4, were concerned with analysis. Analysis contributes to the following training functions:

identification of training needs;
specification of training objectives;
identification of training content;
design of training programme.

The content of training has to cover all of the activities of a task or job which are problematic, hence enabling the training objectives to be met. In order to design training, it is necessary for some analysis to identify the nature of the psychological requirements (e.g. information processing) placed upon the trainee whilst performing the task. Because of these different functions which analysis fulfils, it is necessary to use more than one form of analysis in the development of training.

One aim of analysis is to prevent armchair theorising about what should go into a training programme. Perception of the activities or features of a task can easily be biased or distorted unless some systematic analysis is carried out. For example, one might assume, unwisely, that a job title is indicative of job content. However, job titles develop for historical or idiosyncratic reasons and are invariably poor indicators of the tasks involved in a job. People with different job titles may have many tasks in common. Conversely, those with identical job titles may perform mostly different tasks. From a training perspective, the goal of analysis is to provide information about tasks or a job in as objective a manner as possible.

Nobody would disagree with these sentiments. However, the gospel that good training is founded on good analysis has not penetrated far into industrial and educational practice. For example, a national survey in the UK involving a representative sample of 665 employers of computer personnel was carried out to assess training practice in this important and rapidly changing industry (Spurgeon, Michael and Patrick, 1984). The jobs of interest were those of programmer, systems analyst and analyst programmer. Training provision was alarmingly poor and a significant fact which emerged was that less than one-fifth of the sample had carried out any formal analysis, let alone updating such analysis as a consequence of the rapidly changing nature of such jobs.

One reason for the lack of analysis by training practitioners lies in the perceived cost–benefit relationship. Formal analyses are perceived as expensive in terms of both time and money, whilst their benefits are difficult to predict and quantify. A second reason (or perhaps rationalisation) is that the practitioner is confronted with a multitude of analysis techniques with a bewildering array of titles and jargon terms. This is partly because analysis of a task or job is also required in other areas of occupational/industrial psychology besides training such as selection, vocational guidance, career planning and development, performance appraisal, job design and job evaluation. Hence techniques and terminology proliferate. Terms such as task, skills, job, ability, performance and cognitive can each be linked with the word "analysis". Terms are often used interchangeably. Some analysis techniques claim to be multipurpose, whilst others are dedicated to one purpose such as training or selection. Also the developer of one type of analysis tends to advocate it as a panacea. It is therefore unsurprising that genuine confusion exists concerning the differences between techniques and which ones to use.

Before we consider in detail different techniques in Chapter 6, it is important to attempt to unravel the mysteries of how techniques differ. This will enable superficial differences in terminology to be distinguished from more fundamental differences in method. In order to do this we have to ask two basic questions. What is meant by analysis? How is it achieved or carried out? In answering these questions, it is helpful to distinguish some dimensions along which analyses differ. Sections 5.1 and 5.2 are devoted to these methodological considerations which will hopefully provide the reader with a framework for understanding this difficult but vital topic. Subsequently, in Section 5.3, issues concerning the reliability, validity and utility of any analysis are addressed.

The most important dimension in any analysis of a job or task is the nature of the descriptive terms which are used. These can be broadly dichotomised as either task-oriented (nonpsychological) or person-oriented (psychological). These distinctions are discussed in Section 5.2. Both types of description are necessary for training purposes although a major problem exists concerning how they can be linked systematically. Chapter 6 describes four task-oriented approaches which are particularly useful in the context of training. Chapter 7 discusses different person-oriented or psychological approaches to analysis which involve: information processing taxonomies; traditional ability-type frameworks; and more ad hoc cognitive analyses involving what is now labelled knowledge representation. Section 8.1 discusses the use of taxonomies of learning and their ramifications for both analysis of tasks and training design.

5.1   THE PROCESS AND PRODUCTS OF ANALYSIS

The term analysis is used in a broad sense. In this book, the term not only encompasses the application of recognised techniques or methods of, e.g. job, task and skills analysis by occupational and industrial psychologists but also the use of less formal methods to describe cognitive phemonena. The former analysis techniques have a similar status to psychometric instruments, whereas the latter typically involve more ad hoc and less explicit methods.

A common feature of any type of analysis, in this broad sense, is that information concerning a subject matter is selected, abstracted and classified. The manner in which this translation process is achieved enables one to differentiate between types of analysis. This view emphasises the differences in the *process* of analysis in addition to the differences in its *product*. Such a perspective is similar to that put forward by Stevens (1946) concerning the measurement problem. He argued that measurement involved modelling and abstracting aspects of a phenomenon. Therefore the manner in which numbers are assigned to objects affects the legitimacy of subsequent operations and how the results of these operations relate to the phenomenon originally measured. Similarly analysis or description of a subject matter can be seen as a construction process which is influenced by both the prejudices of the analyst and the assumptions and structure of the analysis itself.

The aim of any analysis is to determine certain products. Hence an analysis concerned with training might specify products such as the objectives or activities of a task. However, the view that analysis is an abstraction and classification process suggests that different processes will result in different products being identified. This may sound commonsense, but it is often forgotten by those engaged in analysis. Different types of analysis (involving different processes) will come up with different results (or products) even when analysing the *same* task. For example, one analysis of a production technician's job might identify that one task objective is to "establish final product and production specifications", whilst another type of analysis might indicate that this task involves a high level of decision-making and problem-solving skill. It is nonsense to ask which analysis is correct. Assuming that both are equally reliable, then their different processes result in different products, which in this case provide complementary information for the trainer.

If empirical comfirmation of this is needed, a study by Cornelius, Carron and Collins (1979) illustrated the effect of different types of analysis in the context of job classification. Seven jobs performed by foremen in a chemical processing plant were analysed by three types of analysis. These analyses identified: task activities; inferred abilities; and what were termed "worker-oriented" statements using the Position Analysis Questionnaire (PAQ) developed by McCormick and colleagues. (PAQ is discussed in Section 7.1, pp. 220–225.) The products of these three analyses were subjected to the same hierarchical clustering procedure. Not surprisingly it was found that the job clusters which were identified varied according to the type of analysis used. In other words, the type of analysis affected the results obtained. Therefore selection of an appropriate type of analysis is a serious issue.

The reader may still be curious as to why such obvious and yet esoteric distinctions between process and product are of significance to training. Here are three reasons:

(a) The analyst might be unaware of the assumptions or decisions being made concerning how the analysis takes place particularly if no formal method is being used. This may be dangerous if the analyst believes that some phenomenon can be described in a particular form (e.g. a set of IF...THEN rules) which can become a self-fulfilling prophecy. Whether or not the phenomenon can be more completely or usefully described in other terms is then overlooked. Unfortunately in training, as in other areas of applied psychology, alternative analyses of the same subject matter are rarely conducted and then compared.

(b) It is almost impossible to translate the product of one analysis into that from another analysis with any degree of confidence. This point is well made in the following quotation from Wheaton (1968):

> When a specific application dictates classification a unique system will be required. For each new content area, a different classification will be necessary. Establishing a function to effectively translate one system of classification into another, in the attempt to synthesise, interrelate and integrate data would be difficult if not impossible (pp. 11, 12).

This does produce a problem because at least two types of analysis are required for training: one is task-oriented, whilst the other is psychological in nature. It is not possible to derive one type of information from the other or to link them systematically, for the reason given by Wheaton. This issue bedevils the general area of job analysis and classification (e.g. Dunnette, 1976; Prien, 1977) and also the use of analysis techniques for training purposes (Patrick, 1980).

(c) A major debate within both industrial and educational contexts concerns the extent to which skills are context-free or context-specific (Annett, 1987; Chipman, Segal and Glaser, 1985; Segal, Chipman and Glaser, 1985). (Context-free is an unfortunate term, since such a state is impossible. However, the term is meant to indicate that some skills transfer between different contexts and are therefore less context-dependent.) This debate has ramifications for how skills are trained, particularly if transfer has to be facilitated to a range of situations. Arguably, much of this debate depends upon how such skills are analysed in the first place. One analysis can emphasise the common elements between two tasks, whilst another can focus on their unique requirements. As soon as we analyse or classify such skills, we are abstracting particular features and imposing the methodological assumptions associated with a particular form of analysis. Similar problems have plagued other areas of psychology, such as the study of individual differences and the nature of intelligence. On the one hand, Thurstone (1938) proposed that intelligence comprised seven separate abilities, whilst on the other hand, Spearman found an underlying general factor (g). Much of this debate rested upon the type of factor analysis used with its associated statistical process and assumptions.

5.2   DIMENSIONS OF ANALYSIS

Six dimensions along which analyses differ are:

(a) purpose of analysis;
(b) nomenclature;
(c) subject matter;
(d) descriptive terms;
(e) structuring and classification procedures;
(f) data sources and collection methods.

Each of these is discussed below. The identification of these dimensions has been influenced by the insightful ideas of Wheaton (1968) concerning the development of taxonomies of human performance. These ideas have been taken up by others including Fleishman and Quaintance

(1984) in their useful review of taxonomies of performance and Pearlman (1980) in a review of job classification with respect to issues in personnel selection.

Many variations are possible for *each* dimension of analysis. Consequently there are many ways of performing an analysis which accounts for the vast number of task and job analysis methods in the literature.

Purpose of analysis

Analyses are performed for many purposes. Blum and Naylor (1968) quoted a survey by Zerga (1943) of some 401 articles which distinguished the following 20 uses of job analysis:

1. Job grading and classification.
2. Wage setting and standardisation.
3. Provision of hiring specifications.
4. Clarification of job duties and responsibilities.
5. Transfers and promotions.
6. Adjustment of grievances.
7. Establishment of a common understanding between various levels of workers and management.
8. Defining and outlining promotional steps.
9. Investigating accidents.
10. Indicating faulty work procedures or duplication of effort.
11. Maintaining, generating and adjusting machinery.
12. Time and motion studies.
13. Defining limits of authority.
14. Indicating cases of individual merit.
15. Indicating causes of personal failure.
16. Education and training.
17. Facilitating job placement.
18. Studies of health and fatigue.
19. Scientific guidance.
20. Determining jobs suitable for occupational therapy.

Some job analysis techniques are multipurpose and aim to solve a variety of personnel problems including selection, job evaluation, vocational guidance, manpower planning and training. Some of them are linked to wide-ranging job classification systems. An example is Functional Job Analysis (Fine and Heinz, 1958), part of which has been incorporated into the Dictionary of Occupational Titles (DOT) which is a classification of types of job in the United States economy. Part of DOT involves dividing a worker's function into three functional levels consisting of activities with respect to data, people and things. In each of these three areas a hierarchy of activities exists such that the higher ones subsume the lower ones. For example with respect to data, one might be synthesising, coordinating, analysing, computing, copying or comparing, proceeding from the highest to the lowest activities. Another multi-purpose technique is Smith's (1973) Generic Skills which suggests that work can be analysed into basic categories such as mathematics, communication, reasoning, interpersonal and manipulative skills. These can be further subdivided into various job elements.

It is doubtful whether such broad-based multi-purpose analysis techniques can provide the detailed information required for training purposes. Despite considerable effort to define job categories rigorously, it is inevitable that in the process of analysis a considerable amount of important information is lost which cannot easily be retrieved without a re-examination of the job. It is not surprising, therefore, that multi-purpose analysis techniques will be less effective for training than a technique specifically designed for such a purpose. One analysis technique specifically oriented towards training is Hierarchical Task Analysis (Annett and Duncan, 1967) which is discussed in detail in Section 6.1.

Nomenclature

Considerable differences exist in terminology. Let us first of all examine what is meant by such basic terms as "job" and "task" which are frequently referred to in training. There is consensus that the term "job" is at the higher level and refers to all the tasks which occur within a person's prescribed duties of employment. In discussion of the IPISD model, Branson et al. (1975) defined a task as:

> the lowest level of behaviour in a job that describes the performance of a meaningful function in the job under consideration (p. 171).

Therefore for training purposes the terms "job", "task" and "subtask" are typically related in the manner outlined in Figure 5.1.

An important aspect of a task is that it is goal oriented, as the following definition by R.B. Miller illustrates:

> A task is any set of activities occurring at about the same time sharing the same common purpose that is recognisable by the task performer.

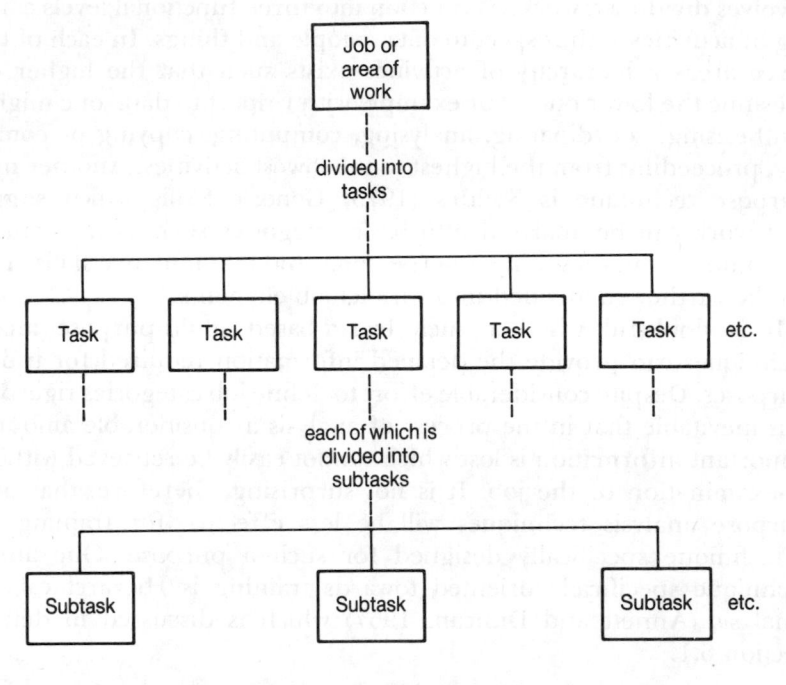

Figure 5.1 Typical terminology for analysing a job or area of activity.

Wheaton (1968) distinguished two dimensions along which even definitions of tasks differ. The first of these involves the scope or breadth of
the definition with respect to the environment under consideration. For
example, a task may span a wide range of activities which are involved in
a job, whilst at the other extreme it might focus on the analogical
reasoning items within a classical intelligence test such as those studied
by Sternberg (1977). The second dimension is whether a task is viewed
as having some objective reality, or whether it can only be subjectively
defined with respect to the perceptions and values of the person who
performs it.

Let us examine some of the terms which imply some form of analysis.
Within industrial or occupational psychology the terms job analysis, task
analysis and skills analysis are sometimes used interchangeably. More
recently in connection with the analysis of cognitive tasks we speak of
cognitive task analysis (e.g. Means and Gott, 1988) or knowledge
representation (e.g. Ringland and Duce, 1988).

Job analysis is probably the most commonly used term in industry. It is
a broad term, used in various branches of occupational psychology, to

refer to any systematic breakdown of a job in the work situation. Many job analysis methods exist. The Department of Employment's *Glossary of Training Terms* (1971) defines job analysis as:

> The process of examining a *job* in detail in order to identify its component *tasks*. The detail and approach may vary according to the purpose for which the job is being analysed e.g. *training*, equipment design, work lay-out (p. 14).

The term skills analysis is used in at least three ways. As mentioned above, it can be a synonym for job analysis. Secondly, the term can indicate the use of a skill taxonomy. Such an approach assumes that performance is dependent upon a set of basic skills. An example is the taxonomy of Generic Skills by Smith (1973) which, as mentioned earlier, includes mathematics, communication, reasoning, interpersonal and manipulative skills. Thirdly, skills analysis can refer to a particular technique devised by Seymour (1966) which records detailed movements in perceptual-motor tasks. The cues used by an operator for both input and feedback are noted together with the nature of the action and the limb involved. An example of this type of analysis is given in Figure 5.2, which details how a butcher should prepare one particular cut of meat. Timings are given for each action together with how the action should be performed, i.e. left and right hand and the position of the fingers and thumb. Cues to be attended to by the trainee are also listed.

The term task analysis is less varied in usage and generally refers to analyses which have applications in training. This is exemplified by the definition of task analysis by Annett et al. (1971):

> ... task analysis is ... the process of collecting information necessary to reach decisions about what to train, how to train, even how well to train and perhaps how much to spend on training. In short task analysis should lead *directly* to a training design specifying not only what is usually called "course content" but also the output or criterion performance and the method or methods of training by which this can be achieved (p. 1).

This definition is ambitious since it suggests that task analysis should not only describe behaviour but should also provide the basis for the design of a training programme. This is beyond the capability of most analysis techniques and at best they provide only global suggestions concerning training design as we will discover in Chapter 8.

INSTRUCTION SCHEDULE

Look-up Joint: 120 N/sec Section: Meat Preparation
Slice Joint: 23 N/sec   Operation: Look-up and Slice Shoulder Off Cut   Sub-Joints: Two
Joint to Band: 3.9 N/sec Requirements: 9"/11" Fluted Blade: Shoulder Off Cut; 4 gallon tins; 1 Skip   Photograph No. 6

No.	N/sec	Description	Left hand	Attention points	Right hand
1	3.9	Place on table fatter side downwards	Reach to gallon tin and grasp joint to be picked up. Body turn and carry to table placing wider end nearest body	Eyes to gallon tin. Only one shoulder off cut $\frac{1,2,3,4}{T}$ lift. Differentiate. Body turn	Retain grasp on knife
2	35	Take out two sub-joints	Grasp sub-joint $\frac{1,2,3,4}{T}$ and pull away from main joint. Hold sub-joint 1, 2, 3, 4 with fingers arched and gripping. Repeat for other sub-joint	Use tip of knife. Eyes on seam. Fingers on top but behind knife	Reference knife movements and angles No. IV
3	42	Look-up triangular one	Skin and fat grasped $\frac{1,2}{T}$. Grasp joint $\frac{1,2,3,4}{T}$	Body turn. Check correct tin. Hold in position for slicing	As per knife movements and angles No. II. As per I (b)
4	6	Take out all visible fat (if boned out correctly, only fat will now remain)	Hold fat $\frac{1,2,3,4}{T}$ and pull away Fat to tin	Small fat take out towards L.H. side of body. Body turn, eyes check correct tin	As per II
5	23	Remove all loose small fat and skin from second sub-joint (spiral)	Lift skin $\frac{1,2,3,4}{T}$ and pull upwards Hold gristle $\frac{1,2,3,4}{T}$ and pull away from body and direction knife is moving	Knife cuts close to meat. L.H. is behind knife. Eyes control R.H. movements Eyes check for any further gristle	As per II. As per II for removing top gristle. Retain grasp on knife

Figure 5.2 Skills analysis of a butcher's actions in preparing one type of joint (Seymour, 1966).

Subject matter

More significant than terminology is the nature of the subject matter to be analysed. An important dichotomy made by many writers in different guises is that between an analysis which is psychological and one which is not. Both are needed for training purposes. Miller (1962) distinguished between task description and task analysis. The former is concerned with describing the goals of behaviour, whilst the latter is a specification of the psychological demands which the task imposes on the person performing it. (In this book the term task analysis is used to cover both meanings.) Others have made essentially the same point in a different way. Leplat, in various publications (e.g. Leplat, 1987) contrasted the "prescribed" task which is defined by some organisation or outside agent with the "real" task, which is how the person actually carries out the task. These are quite different. Similarly, it is possible to perform a rational or logical analysis of how a task should be carried out although this may differ markedly from actual performance. For example, Johnson-Laird (1985) concluded that how a person deals with complex cognitive tasks involving for example, inference, reasoning or problem solving is quite different from so-called rational analyses. Psychology can point to many instances in which cognitive behaviour deviates from some supposedly "rational" or "ideal" method. Visser (1988) studied the manner in which programmable controllers were designed. A top-down hierarchical planning activity represented the rational approach although this failed to capture how the "real" task was tackled. We must therefore be careful to determine whether the subject matter to be analysed is psychological or not.

Any psychological analysis involves *inference* from observable behaviour. It is therefore hypothetical in nature and should be treated as such. When no formal technique is used, this inference depends upon the ingenuity of the analyst or psychologist. (Such issues of knowledge elicitation for cognitive tasks are dealt with later in this chapter, pp. 154–156.) This inference may be less apparent when a formal set of descriptive terms is provided together with a method for data collection (e.g. task analysis using a questionnaire format). However, the inference still has to be made although the responsibility for making it is shifted from the analyst to the person, e.g. filling out the questionnaire, using the descriptive terms provided.

In summary, a plethora of different terms is used to refer to some form of analysis of a task or subject matter. These superficial differences in terminology should not obscure the more fundamental differences between analyses. An analysis may be of psychological subject matter as opposed to a rational, logical or ideal analysis of how a task should be performed. Further, analysis may be guided by a formal method which is explicit, or it may be ad hoc and implicit. A common feature of any analysis is that a process of abstraction is involved in the description and organisation of subject matter in a fashion which suits the analyst's purpose.

Descriptive terms

The heart of any analysis is how it describes its subject matter and the constructs and categories used for this purpose. This dimension is explicit in any analysis. The descriptive terms can be viewed as providing the building blocks for developing a model of a subject matter. As Morgan (1972) pointed out in a useful and little-known review of job classification, various types of descriptive term can be used to describe a job or task. An analysis may be concerned with the content of a job, the context in which it is performed or the requirements of the person performing it.

In our previous discussion we noted that a major distinction exists between an analysis which focuses on psychological subject matter and one which does not. Not surprisingly different types of descriptor are associated with these different analyses. Hence some analyses use *task-oriented* descriptors whilst others use *person-oriented* ones, the latter being psychological in nature (Patrick, 1980). (A similar distinction has been made by Prien and Ronan, 1971.) Patrick (1980) defined the difference as follows:

> Task-oriented descriptions concern the goal of performance, the equipment or conditions in the work situation or the observable activities associated with a task. Person-oriented descriptors relate to the cognitive capacities used or required by the person performing the job. For example, the description of a task associated with the job of a production technician in industry as "establish the machine conditions for operating" would be task-oriented. On the other hand a description of the same situation in terms of the abilities, skills, aptitudes or capacities required by the technician for efficient performance would be person-oriented (p. 56).

Similar distinctions have been made by Wheaton (1968), Fleishman (1975, 1978) and Fleishman and Quaintance (1984) who have defined four possible conceptual bases for the classification of performance. Two of these, named the behaviour and ability requirements approaches, use person-oriented descriptors whilst the other two, named the behaviour description and task characteristic approaches, use task-oriented ones. Task-oriented descriptions or analyses are necessary in order to derive the needs, objectives and content of a training programme. On the other hand, it is necessary to describe the psychological requirements of the task in order to: select potential trainees with the necessary qualities; design training in a psychologically expedient fashion; and analyse the skills involved in task performance. Since both types of description are required for training (and other personnel functions) it is not surprising that considerable discussion has focused upon how these different types of description can be linked systematically. One solution, which is far from ideal, is to link them by human judgement (and preferably by a psychologist who is familiar with the task!). Another solution is to statistically associate the two types of descriptor. This latter approach has been taken up by Fleishman and colleagues and is discussed in Section 7.2. For a detailed account of these and related issues the reader should consult Dunnette (1976) and Peterson and Bownas (1982).

Let us briefly review some of the descriptors used by different analysis techniques. Those listed in Table 5.1 are discussed in this book.

Table 5.1   Different approaches to the analysis of tasks

Task-oriented approaches to analysis (Chapter 6)
1. Hierarchical Task Analysis (Annett and Duncan, 1967)
2. Critical Incident Technique (Flanagan, 1954)
3. Task inventories
    USAF Task Taxonomy (Christal, 1974)
    Work Performance Survey System (Gael, 1983)
4. Trainability and work sample testing

Person-oriented/psychological approaches to analysis (Chapter 7)
1. Information processing
    Task Functions (Miller, 1974)
    Information Theoretic Approach (e.g. Levine and Teichner, 1973)
2. Ability requirements
    Fleishman's 11 psychomotor abilities (1964)
    Guilford's Structure of Intellect Model (1956)
3. Knowledge representation
4. Types of learning (Section 8.3)
    Intellectual Skills and Cognitive Strategies (Gagné, e.g. 1977)
    Component Display Theory (Merrill, 1983)

Task-oriented analyses for training are covered in Chapter 6. The majority of forms of analysis for training purposes use the term task analysis and as one would expect use task-oriented data. This is because the main concern has been to determine accurately the content of training. Smith (1964) is typical in describing how a job can be broken down into a series of tasks and subtasks. Hierarchical Task Analysis, developed by Annett and Duncan (1967) at the University of Hull, uses operations (defined by the objectives of performance) and plans (the manner in which operations are organised) as the task-oriented descriptors. It is particularly suited both to deriving training content and also to specifying training objectives (Section 6.1). Flanagan (1954) used task-oriented data in his well-known Critical Incident Technique which records job behaviour which has a significant effect on satisfactory or unsatisfactory performance of the job. It is useful in identifying some training needs (Section 6.2). Another approach is to use a task inventory involving a few hundred or even a few thousand task statements to analyse the jobs in either an occupational area or an organisation (Section 6.3). The task inventory may be used to monitor and contrast the content of jobs for various personnel purposes, including training. The prime example of such an approach was in the United States Air Force during the 1960s and afterwards (e.g. Christal, 1972, 1974). Finally, trainability testing is a means of selecting people for training by evaluating performance and/or learning on a sample of job behaviour (Section 6.4). This approach also uses task-oriented data.

Four psychological approaches to analysis are discussed in Chapter 7 (see Table 5.1). The information processing approach (Section 7.1) uses descriptive terms which fall into the input–processing–output framework. Examples are Miller's (1974) set of task functions and Levine and Teichner's (1973) information theoretic approach. In contrast the traditional "abilities/aptitudes" approach (Section 7.2) has grown out of the study of individual differences and psychometrics. It is based on the belief that people can be described as possessing relatively enduring traits and abilities. The literature pertaining to the information processing and abilities/aptitudes approaches has remained separate although these two approaches are rather two sides of the same coin.

More recently, cognitive science has been concerned with knowledge representation influenced by the desire to capture expertise and incorporate it into some artificial form. Descriptors used are more ad hoc and microscopic (i.e. pertaining to smaller units of performance) than those in the previous approaches discussed. Such descriptors are derived from cognitive psychology and some are discussed in Section 7.3.

A final approach to person-oriented description is to categorise the type(s) of learning involved in a task (Section 8.3). Each type of learning makes different psychological requirements of the trainee. This perspective was pioneered by Gagné in many publications from the early 1970s onwards. The reason that his ideas are especially relevant to training is that each type of learning requires different learning or training conditions. Further, some types of what he terms "intellectual" skill should be mastered before others which, therefore, has implications for the sequence of training materials. More recently, Merrill has elaborated his Component Display Theory (CDT), which is a rapprochement between some of Gagne's ideas and the specification of training objectives.

In summary, the most important dimension of any analysis is the nature of the descriptive terms used to analyse the subject matter. A major distinction can be drawn between task-oriented (nonpsychological) and person-oriented (psychological) descriptors. Training requires both types of descriptor although most analyses for training purposes have focused on task-oriented data.

Structuring and classification procedures

Most analyses structure or classify the descriptive terms in some manner. This may take place on the basis of theoretical or practical distinctions or some statistical methodology.

Analyses which use the information processing or abilities approaches can capitalise on the psychological distinctions within these paradigms to cluster and categorise items. For example, the Position Analysis Questionnaire (PAQ) Form B (McCormick, Jeanneret and Mecham, 1969) has 194 job elements which are organised into six dimensions. The first three dimensions cover the information-processing categories of information input, mental processes and work output. Alternatively, analyses using task-oriented data may use some functional or practical headings which relate to the domain in question. For example, Wirstad (1988) divided the knowledge required by nuclear power plant operators into 13 categories such as knowledge of safety regulations, reactor core knowledge, and knowledge of displays and controls in the control room. A disadvantage of structuring the analysis in this way is that material which is psychologically similar may remain separate because of the practical categories imposed. On the other hand, such categories are sometimes the only way of making sense of large domains of knowledge which have to be taught.

Descriptors may be quantified. If they are, then some structuring or classification can take place on a statistical basis. Quantification of descriptors may involve various scales, the most popular being the frequency of occurrence, the importance and the criticality of a task. Choice of scale(s) to be used is a difficult issue. Christal (1974) argued that a seven-point scale of relative time spent was more meaningful to job incumbents completing his task inventory. It also had statistical advantages. Associated with Christal's task inventory is the Comprehensive Occupational Data Analysis Programs (CODAP) developed by the United States Air Force. This suite of programs performs various functions such as producing a job description; listing the differences in work patterns of two specified groups; and identifying types of job existing in a specified occupational area using cluster analysis.

McCormick used factor analysis to derive various job dimensions and the loadings of job elements on these dimensions for the Position Analysis Questionnaire. This is discussed further on pp. 220–225. Multivariate statistical techniques such as cluster analysis, factor analysis and profile analysis are helpful in reducing the data associated with large scale analysis work. Nevertheless all of these techniques make a variety of statistical assumptions which require careful consideration (see Harvey, 1986 for a discussion). There is no guarantee that the derived dimensions of jobs or tasks have psychological validity, irrespective of the statistical sophistication of any analysis.

Data sources and collection methods

Any analysis requires an information source and a method of extracting information from that source. Both of these are subject to bias or distortion although it is often impossible to disentangle the contribution of each. The source of information might be a job incumbent who may exaggerate some aspects of his or her job. This may result in elevated ratings of a task or job item. Alternatively, the observational method may fail to identify all of the aspects of a job, due to unrepresentative sampling. No source of information or method of data collection is immune from error. Questions concerning the reliability and validity of analysis are just as relevant to any task analysis as they are to the use of a psychometric test of ability. These questions are addressed in Section 5.3. There are no easy solutions. It is not possible to identify one source of information or one data collection method as being consistently more reliable or valid than any other. Perhaps the best advice that can be given to the analyst is to use a variety of sources and methods and to strive to corroborate information, rather than relying on only one source or one method of data collection.

There are many sources of information for an analysis of a task or job. Four of the most common are:

1. A person performing, or knowledgeable about the task.
2. Existing documentation.

3. Simulation.
4. Experiment.

1. A person performing, or knowledgeable about the task.   The activities of the person carrying out the task are a valuable source of information for the analyst. Alternatively, the views of a person knowledgeable about the nature of the task can be useful. Such a person may be the job incumbent, his or her supervisor, some designated "expert" or indeed the trainer. Such familiarity and knowledge of the task will vary according to that person's experience, the amount of time spent with this task and the person's level of involvement. All of these factors should be taken into account by the analyst.

2. Existing documentation.   This includes previous task analyses or job descriptions, operating manuals, maintenance guides and existing training materials. Existing documentation provides the analyst with an introduction both to the task domain and to the nature of the task to be analysed. Such documentation should be treated with caution and scepticism. Existing job descriptions may be out of date, incomplete and most probably were produced for some other purpose, such as job evaluation. Existing training materials may not have been produced by any systematic process, whilst operating manuals or management procedures may bear little relationship to how the tasks are actually performed. Therefore on the one hand, such documentation may be inaccurate and lead to erroneous expectations prior to analysis. On the other hand, such documentation can familiarise the analyst with the domain and provide a source of questions and hypotheses about the job during the initial pilot phase and before a more formal analysis takes place.

3. Simulation.   Simulation is not only useful as a means of training but can also be a source of information to the analyst. Simulation can take many forms. These include a person using a simulated car or aircraft; an operator studying a symbolic display of a nuclear plant on a VDU or a photograph; a problem-solver doing some paper and pencil exercises; and some simulated social or management behaviours relevant to particular job situations. Such simulations are primarily used to *generate* information for the analyst, although a secondary function can be to *validate* information. In this latter role, simulation is used to verify that information concerning the performance of a task, e.g. a procedure for diagnosing a fault, is accurate and does work.
Simulations may be necessary as a source of information for various

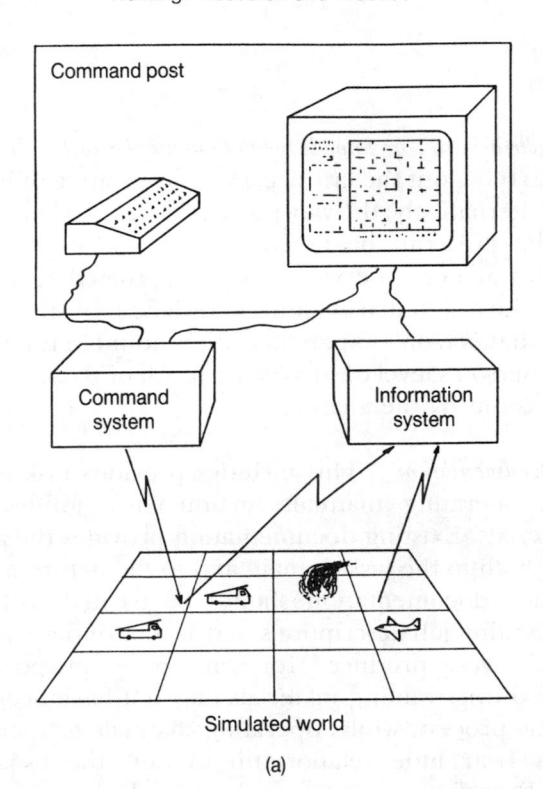

Simulated world

(a)

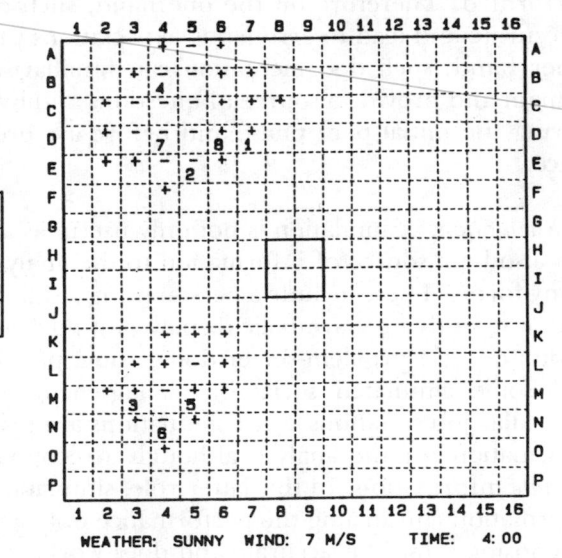

(b)

reasons. Firstly, the only means of analysing new tasks which do not yet exist is by using some form of simulation. At one extreme this might involve the use of a simulated space vehicle for a lunar landing to a mental simulation of how the task is to be performed. Secondly, some tasks might be either too dangerous to analyse in the real situation or too difficult to analyse retrospectively. For example, in a study of air traffic control, Leplat and Bisseret (1966) presented simulated situations and analysed the strategies which were used by the controllers. Brehmer (1987) described a Dynamic Environmental Simulation System (DESSY) which simulated the dynamic decision-making problems involved in fire-fighting and control. The simulation was used to analyse the decision-making of fire chiefs. The layout of the system is given in Figure 5.3. Brehmer described the simulation as follows:

> DESSY simulates the decision problems facing a fire chief who obtains information about forest fires from a reconnaissance place. The information is displayed on a graphics terminal in front of him. Fires are reported accurately and without delay by the plane. When a fire breaks out the fire chief can send his fire-fighting units to the fire by means of one of two commands: either an unconditional command to go to a given place regardless of whether a fire is encountered en route; or by a command which enables the fire-fighting unit to move towards a given location and start fighting those fires they may meet on their way to this location. The fire-fighting units report back to the fire chief about their location and the results of their actions but these reports may be delayed. As the fire chief is fighting one fire, a new fire might start. The fires spread according to weather conditions such as direction of the wind. In fighting the fire he has two goals. The one with the highest priority is to prevent the fire from reaching the base where he himself is located. The second goal is to minimise the area that is burned down (pp. 115, 116).

Figure 5.3 (a) Schematic representation of the main features of the simulated fire fighting situation together with the fire chief's monitor and keyboard (adapted from Brehmer, 1987). (b) Information displayed to the fire chief on the monitor in Figure 5.2a. The plus signs indicate fire, the minus signs indicate fire that has been put out, the numbers indicate the location of fire-fighting units and the square in the middle is the base which must be protected. The weather report is given under the display and the displays to the left give information about action of the units, when they reported and what commands have been issued and at what time (Brehmer, 1987).

Such simulations are useful in the analysis of complex cognitive tasks which otherwise might be inaccessible. With ingenuity the simulation can be designed to externalise the covert cognitive processes of the performer. Dorner (1987) developed a computer simulation of the social, psychological, economic and ecological relations of a small city named Lohhausen, which had 3500 residents. A person acted as mayor and "controlled" the fate of the city by his/her actions in the simulation. Therefore the simulation provided a means of studying the cognitive deficiencies occurring at various stages of the task, including goal planning, accumulating and restructuring information and planning and implementing action. Inappropriate analogies were often used in coping with this complex situation and the planning stage frequently neglected side effects and long-term consequences of proposed actions.

Despite these advantages for simulation as a source of information for analysis, some caution is necessary. A simulation is a representation of a task and as such necessarily omits some features of the real situation. It is important that the situation being analysed is not significantly changed by the features omitted in the simulation. This is in fact very difficult to be certain about. For example the stress missing from Brehmer's fire-fighting simulation may be a significant factor which affects decision making. It is for this reason that in some potentially high-risk performance situations information derived in this fashion can only be validated by a highly realistic simulation and ultimately by performance in the real situation. Simulation is discussed further in Chapter 12.

4. Experiment. An experiment can be carried out in a laboratory or a field setting. It is usually employed with a simulated task, where the analyst is not just content to describe performance but wishes to determine systematically the effect of some variable(s) on performance. For example, Reiersen, Baker and Marshall (1988) used such an approach in evaluating the effect of an advanced alarm system for nuclear power plants on operators' performance. This sort of experimental study can provide valuable insights into the nature of performance (e.g. errors) under different conditions. Such experiments usually face a difficult dilemma. On the one hand, the experimental situation has to be sufficiently representative and realistic of the "real" situation, which means that it is difficult to control the effect of many factors which threaten the validity of the experiment's design. On the other hand, a simpler or less realistic task which is examined in a laboratory setting can enable the effect of different variables to be disentangled more easily, although the findings may not generalise to the real situation. The knack is to find the appropriate compromise. Because experiments are carried out not only to analyse task performance, but also to analyse the effect of training on that performance, this topic is discussed further in the context of the evaluation of training, Chapter 13, pp. 534–540. This discussion covers the validity of experimental designs in both laboratory and field settings.

Five common methods of data collection are:

1. Observation.
2. Interview.
3. Questionnaire.
4. Diary.
5. Verbal report.

1. Observation.   The analyst might observe the activities of a "representative" job incumbent. This can range from simple note-taking of what happens when, to some form of video recording. Continual observation may be necessary for some tasks, whilst activity sampling may be sufficient for others. The analyst's role may be concealed or explicit and the analyst may "participate" in varying degrees in the situation which is being observed. For a summary of the "participant observation" literature plus an account of the types of errors associated with observation, the reader should consult Bouchard (1976).

The advantage of observation is that the analyst has direct access to the job and does not have to rely on the fallible recall and verbal report of another person. In addition, observation of a task in the context of the overall work situation means that other important factors are less likely to be overlooked. The disadvantages of the observational method are that it is time-consuming and that the observation itself may change or interfere with the very activities which are to be observed.

2. Interview.   The analyst may question the person who performs the task either during task performance or afterwards, possibly away from the work situation. Such an interview can take many forms. It might be totally structured, in which case the job incumbent is asked standard questions and provided with a specified set of terms with which to reply. Semi-structured interviews involve a prepared set of questions pertaining to a job and can probe areas which are problematic. At the other extreme, the interview can be totally unstructured. In eliciting information for training purposes the analyst/interviewer will generally have an initial set of issues to cover, although others may arise in the course of the interview. Therefore, a semi-structured format is to be preferred and it is a good idea to have at least a second interview with the same person. In this way the analyst has time to identify and structure the information provided, recheck its reliability and subsequently have any remaining questions answered.

Typically, the interview is between the analyst and the job incumbent. However, on occasions, more than one analyst may be used or more than one job incumbent may participate in a group interview and discussion. Sometimes a panel of experts might be gathered together. This is particularly helpful for disentangling and agreeing on parts of a job which are difficult to analyse, although such a situation should be handled with care and good preparation. McCormick (1979) provided a set of practical guidelines for interviewing in the context of job analysis, which are based upon the suggestions of Kuriloff, Yoder and Stone (1975) and the *Handbook for Analysing Jobs* (1972) issued by the US Employment Service. The interview has received a great deal of attention from occupational and industrial psychologists with respect to its reliability and validity. This has been primarily in the context of the employment interview which is used for personnel selection (for a review of this literature see Arvey and Campion, 1982). Many of the biases found when the interviewer is in such a decision-making role do not apply when interviewing is concerned with job or task analysis. On the other hand, this literature does emphasise that an interview is a delicate interaction which can easily be affected by the attitudes, expectations and stereotypes of both interviewer and interviewee. Cognisant of these potential problems, there is agreement that interviewing skills should be developed by training (see Arvey and Campion, 1982; Bouchard, 1976).

3. Questionnaire. Many job analyses are embodied in questionnaires which are distributed by post to respondents. For example, variation in the content of technician's jobs might be examined by a questionnaire in the form of either a task inventory or a job analysis technique such as McCormick's Position Analysis Questionnaire. It should be remembered when deciding whether to use a questionnaire that some job incumbents may be unfamiliar with its literary demands, especially if open-ended questions are involved. Also, a questionnaire depends upon the memory of the person being questioned. The design of questionnaires has received considerable attention and has focused on the provision of clear instructions, questions which are unambiguous and rating scales which are relevant. The reader should consult Oppenheim (1982) and Schuman and Presser (1981) for a detailed treatment of these issues. Twenty questions are provided in Table 5.2, adapted from Bouchard

Table 5.2 Twenty questions relating to the design of a questionnaire (adapted from Bouchard, 1976)

1. Is the question necessary and directly related to the analyst's purpose?
2. Is the questionnaire repetitive?
3. Could the answer be obtained more easily elsewhere — by simple observation or from records?
4. Does the question contain more than one idea? Is it double-barrelled or ambiguous?
5. Is the question adequate as it stands or should complementary questions or information be given?
6. Should the respondent have the necessary knowledge to answer the question?
7. Will the question embarrass the respondent?
8. Could the question be made more specific or concrete?
9. Is the question clear?
10. Does the respondent need to consult other records etc. to answer the question?
11. Is the question too indirect?
12. Is the response format adequate from a theoretical point of view and from the respondent's point of view?
13. Are precoded answers given, since they will yield more accurate answers than open-ended questions?
14. Is the questionnaire susceptible to an order effect?
15. Can the items be arranged so that particular answers preclude the need to answer others?
16. Is an item likely to bias those following it?
17. Is the ordering of the questions natural or reasonable?
18. Does the sequence of questions maintain motivation?
19. Are the opening few questions appropriate?
20. Will the respondent be able to read and understand the questions?

(1976), which should be considered in the formulation and sequencing of questions. In addition, considerable work has focused on the errors and distortions associated with rating job behaviour (e.g. Borman, 1983, for a review of the rating of work performance in organisations).

4. Diary. This method requires job incumbents to record their daily activities typically over a period of a few days or weeks. Entries can either be in the incumbent's own words, or some coding of tasks and activities may be provided which will facilitate subsequent analysis. Entries are usually made throughout the day as activities change. In this way accuracy is maintained, although recording can be time-consuming and therefore disruptive to normal task performance.

5. *Verbal report.* One important means of collecting information about a task is for the person who performs it to report verbally about how the task is carried out. This is valuable for complex tasks, particularly of a cognitive nature, where a person's activities provide insufficient clues about the nature of the skill or expertise involved. Verbal report (as opposed to interview, discussion) is a term used where the aim is to elicit information about the person's cognitive activities in performing the task; hence the recent use of the term "knowledge elicitation". Verbal reports can be elicited from the task performer or perhaps an "expert", in a real or simulated situation, during or after performance of the task. They have been used extensively to analyse both the reasoning processes of operators who control complex industrial manufacturing processes and the problem-solving of technical personnel who diagnose faults in equipment.

Given that behaviourism banished the use of introspection many decades ago, psychology has been slow to capitalise upon verbal reports as a potentially rich source of information about how a task is performed. However, the debate concerning their reliability and validity was revived in the late 1970s. This debate is not straightforward and much has been written. Any analyst making use of verbal report in order to identify the thinking and reasoning processes involved in performance of a task is well advised to consult the literature. Fortunately, some useful summaries and overviews have been provided by Bainbridge (1979, 1990), Leplat (1986) and Leplat and Hoc (1981).

An article by Nisbett and Wilson (1977) suggested that retrospective verbal reports are likely to be unreliable and biased indicators of a person's behaviour. They argued that people tended to theorise about their previous cognitive processes, sometimes rationalising, and that the resulting verbalisations departed from reality. Subsequently, Ericsson and Simon (1980, 1984) provided a comprehensive theoretical discussion of this topic. They criticised the methodology used in many of the experiments cited by Nisbett and Wilson and argued that the validity of verbal reports depends upon the circumstances in which they are elicited. They viewed verbal reports as data which in certain situations can provide insights into how a person carries out a task. They distinguished between concurrent ("think aloud") and retrospective verbal reports and discussed them with respect to two factors:

(a) whether the information to be verbalised by the person was in a verbal form;
(b) whether this information was available in short-term memory or had to be retrieved from long-term memory.

The first possible problem is that a person's procedural knowledge or skill may not be accessible by verbal report, even if that person wishes it to be. It may not be in verbal form and it may not be capable of being translated adequately into such a form. Various writers (e.g. Hayes and Broadbent, 1988) have contrasted "implicit" knowledge which cannot be articulated by the performer adequately and "explicit" knowledge which can. The accuracy of verbal reports is affected adversely, the greater the extent of any intermediate cognitive activities needed to recode the knowledge/skill in order to produce the verbal report. Indeed, if these transformations are considerable in concurrent verbal reporting, then they will interfere with performance of the actual task. The second factor is concerned with whether the information to be verbalised is available in short-term memory. If it is not, then various distortions can occur in verbal reports, such as when there is a long time interval between task performance and retrospective verbalisation. Also the kind of instructions given to a person who has to "think aloud" whilst performing a task can create difficulties if they require that person to do anything more than just verbalise information that would naturally be in short-term memory during execution of the task.

In sum, it is possible to use verbal reports to make useful inferences about the cognitive activities involved in carrying out a task, although great care has to be taken in the circumstances in which they are collected. Requiring a person to produce a verbal report is itself a cognitive task which is affected by the nature of the cognitive activities and also constrained by the form of the report, not least of which is its serial nature. The "safest" type of verbal report is one which is generated concurrently with performance and concerns information which is already in verbal form and is available in short-term memory. It is even better when the verbal report is used as a means of elucidating the reasoning behind a series of actions made by a person, and the nature of the actions can be observed and used to corroborate the verbal report.

After verbal reports have been collected they have to be analysed in a reliable fashion. Analysis is a complex iterative process which partly involves categorising the different cognitive processes implied in the reports. In order to do this, there is a need at the first stage for analysts with sufficient knowledge of the domain to develop useful categories and at the second stage for another set of analysts to apply these categories in coding the verbal reports. The outputs at both stages need to be checked for consistency.

5.3   RELIABILITY, VALIDITY AND UTILITY

In the previous section, six dimensions along which analyses differ were discussed. All of these, except for terminology, determine the type of analysis which is carried out and influence the results found. Many variants exist for these dimensions which explains why so many types of analysis are available. Having carried out a job or task analysis, it is reasonable to ask: how reliable is it? How accurate is it? Is it useful for training purposes? These questions cover the criteria of *reliability*, *validity* and *utility* which should be asked of any type of analysis. For a basic introduction to these issues, the reader should consult Chapanis (1959) and Blum and Naylor (1968). Historically, issues of reliability and validity have been closely associated with the development and use of psychometric instruments which measure, for example, abilities or aptitudes. However, such criteria are just as important and relevant to any analysis of a task not least because error has serious consequences for the development of an appropriate training programme. Training needs, training objectives and training content will be incorrect if an analysis is inaccurate. It is therefore surprising that the reliability, validity and utility of analyses have received little sustained attention in comparison to the development of tests and measures in the area of psychometrics. One exception to this is the use of job analysis for selection purposes, where concepts of fairness and validity are important in both American and British legislation. A great deal of research has been concerned with the validity of different data collection methods, including the errors associated with rating scales when used for selection purposes. Unfortunately, there have been no parallel developments in the training context.

Reliability

Reliability of analysis refers to the consistency of the job or task analysis. There are two main types of reliability or consistency: retest reliability and inter-rater agreement. The consistency of two analyses of the same subject matter involving the same analyst, respondents etc. on *different occasions* is referred to as retest reliability. If the analyses are quantified in some way then a retest reliability coefficient can be calculated. Such correlation coefficients vary between +1.0 (perfect agreement) to zero (no relationship) to −1.0 (perfect disagreement). The second type of reliability concerns the extent to which there is consistency or agreement between *different persons* involved in the same analysis. The degree of agreement (or disagreement) between different analysts of the same job can be calculated and also that between different supervisors or job incumbents who rate aspects of the job. This is known as inter-rater agreement and again is typically measured by a correlation coefficient. Even when it is not possible to quantify the description of a task or job element, it is still possible to devise some simple measure which indicates the consistency of the analysis. For example, calculating the percentage of identical tasks between two analyses would be a useful initial step and undoubtedly more sophisticated measures of reliability could be devised.

Three important methodological points concerning reliability are frequently overlooked:

(a) Correlation coefficients concerned with reliability (except intraclass correlation) do not indicate the *difference* in level of performance between two analyses. For example, imagine that we calculate the retest reliability of two analyses of a job covering 10 tasks, each rated for frequency of occurrence. Hypothetical data are presented in Table 5.3. Tasks which are rated highest in the first analysis are also rated highest in the retest. The same applies to tasks with lower ratings. These two analyses have a perfect retest reliability with a correlation of +1.0. However, the ratings in the retest are consistently higher than those in the original analysis. There is a significant difference between the analyses of one point on the rating scale for

Table 5.3   Test–retest ratings of frequency of occurrence of 10 tasks in a job

Task	Test	Retest
A	1	2
B	0	1
C	4	5
D	6	7
E	2	3
F	1	2
G	0	1
H	0	1
I	2	3
J	4	5

each task even though there is perfect reliability between the two analyses with a correlation of $+1.0$. In some circumstances such a difference will affect subsequent training decisions. Therefore when differences in level of performance are important, correlations are not appropriate indicators.

(b) Reliabilities are easily exaggerated when job analysis instruments using a prespecified number of tasks or job elements are employed. The reason for this is that inevitably a significant number of these tasks will not be relevant to the job under consideration. Hence ratings of zero will indicate apparent agreement and the reliability calculated will be higher than it should be. This interpretation is supported by a study by Harvey and Hayes (1986) which examined the Position Analysis Questionnaire (PAQ). (For a discussion of PAQ, see Section 7.1.) In a Monte Carlo simulated study using the 194 items of PAQ, they investigated the effect of varying both the number of items which did not apply in the analysis and the number of raters on estimates of inter-rater reliability. In addition they derived the worst case scenario by assuming that raters responded in random disagreement to the items or tasks which did apply to the job. They demonstrated that with only 30 items which did not apply, it was possible to find inter-rater correlations of about 0.5 even when the responses on the remaining items were randomly generated. Therefore the apparent agreement on the items which did not apply masked the disagreement on the remaining items. This effect got worse as the number of items which did not apply in the analysis increased. When there were 100 such items, the reliabilities ranged between 0.52 and 0.75. This study emphasises that the calculation and interpretation of reliability is not straightforward for analyses which involve a fixed number of job elements. A considerable literature exists on this topic in scattered journal articles and the reader is advised to proceed with caution in this area.

(c) Studies only investigate reliability in a gross fashion. In Section 5.2 we discussed how analyses vary in terms of, e.g. descriptive terms, classification procedures and data collection methods. Ideally, the contribution of each of these dimensions to reliability should be assessed. Unfortunately, such fine grained studies have not been the trend in the literature. Generally, if reliability is calculated at all, only an overall reliability figure is produced rather than identifying how reliability varies with subtle changes in how the analysis is carried out.

Reliability is an under researched topic in the context of task analysis. There are reasons for this. It is practically difficult and time-consuming to reanalyse jobs. Similarly, calculations of inter-rater reliability are difficult and depend upon sufficient raters being available. Some of the reliabilities associated with different analysis techniques are discussed below. This is not an exhaustive account, but is intended to give the reader a flavour of work in this area.

The retest reliabilities of task or job inventories which use frequency of task performance and length of task time as rating scales are in the region of 0.70 according to Morsch (1964). Studies by McCormick and Ammerman (1960), Birt (1968) and Cragun and McCormick (1967) indicated a range of reliabilities between 0.35 and 0.87. Frequency of task occurrence is more reliably reported than the relative proportion of time spent on different tasks which is in turn more reliably reported than the difficulty of a task. Christal (1971), cited by McCormick (1979), is concerned with what he termed the "stability" of responses to his task inventory used in the United States Air Force. Reliability was investigated by splitting the task inventory data covering 35 jobs in 10 career areas randomly into two halves ($n=9822$). The responses between the two halves were correlated for each of two measures: the percentage of the group performing the task and the percentage of time spent by the total group on a task. The median correlations were 0.98 and 0.97 respectively for these two measures, indicating a high level of reliability. It should be remembered, however, that reliability will inevitably increase with the number of tasks being assessed and a large number of tasks was involved in this study.

The Position Analysis Questionnaire (PAQ) and various versions of it have been the subject of both retest and inter-rater reliability studies. Taylor (1978) and Taylor and Colbert (1978) carried out retest studies with PAQ after a period of 90 days. Taylor (1978) reported a median retest reliability across the 27 component dimensions of PAQ of 0.69, whilst Taylor and Colbert (1978) found an average retest reliability for items of PAQ of 0.78 based on 427 pairs of ratings. The average retest reliability after six weeks for job elements in a modified and anglicised version of PAQ was 0.76 (Patrick and Moore, 1985). In this study, no differences were found in retest reliability between supervisors and job incumbents. The evidence concerning inter-rater agreement associated with use of the PAQ is complex and much of the evidence is summarised in Patrick and Moore (1985).

The *Dictionary of Occupational Titles* (DOT) provides job-related information which is widely used in the US. In its fourth edition (US Department of Labor, 1977) it provides ratings on 46 characteristics for 12,099 occupations. These characteristics cover the complexity of the tasks in that occupation, and their associated requirements in terms of training requirements, interests, aptitudes and temperament, physical demands and working conditions. Cain and Green (1983) were concerned with the reliability of ratings of these characteristics. They used 24 job descriptions from the service and manufacturing sectors and had 42 job analysts in seven centres rate each of the job descriptions in terms of a subset of 20 of those characteristics. Generally, there was considerable variation in the reliabilities. Reliability was affected by both the nature of the characteristic being assessed and whether the jobs were in the service or manufacturing sectors, the former being less reliably assessed.

All of this evidence suggests that reliability will vary considerably according to the type of measure used and the type of analysis under consideration. Unfortunately, the analyst is unlikely to find a reliability figure corresponding to a form of analysis which (s)he has in mind. This implies that each task or job analysis performed should be accompanied by a reliability study. This advice will undoubtedly be poorly received by practitioners who argue that systematic job analysis is already too time-consuming. However, if we are to take the issue of reliability seriously, there is little alternative until general guidelines can be derived from a greater body of research evidence.

Validity

An analysis may be reliable, but this does not guarantee that it has validity. Validity is concerned with whether the analysis is an accurate reflection of a job or task. Some sources of invalidity have been discussed in relation to data collection sources and methods (Section 5.2). For example, direct observation may fail to capture all of the tasks performed or may itself affect task performance. How then can validity be measured? This question involves what is known as the criterion problem. What yardstick or criterion can be used, against which an analysis can be compared or validated? No totally objective solution exists and the criterion problem is a major headache not only for task analysis, but also for all validity studies in the area of psychometrics.

One approach to validity has been to compare results between two analyses which use different data sources or data collection methods. The rationale is that if the results are similar, then it is more likely that they are valid. The alternative explanation is that both analyses are subject to the same distortion or error, which is unlikely, although not impossible. Hence the responses obtained from job incumbents about a job might be compared with those from their supervisors. Similarly, different types of observation or interview method might be employed. Studies of this nature are all too few.

Another approach to validity has been to investigate the accuracy of different types of assessment about a task. Accuracy or validity is measured by comparing the assessment either against the actual figure, if this can be obtained, or against a criterion which is presumed to be close to the actual figure. Klemmer and Snyder (1972) evaluated the accuracy of workers' self-reports of activities in their jobs. They found considerable variation in the accuracy of workers" estimates when compared against actual job behaviours derived by random activity sampling. Time spent in conversation was underestimated, whereas time involved in reading and writing was overestimated. Hartley et al. (1977) investigated the accuracy of workers' self reports of three aspects of their work: the tasks involved, the relative time spent on these tasks and the absolute time spent on them. They studied 36 workers from two legal aid organisations who were described as falling into the categories of "principals", "administrative secretary" and "correspondence secretary". Workers' estimates were collected by means of a card-sorting task involving the activities identified below and also a questionnaire covering workers' activities. The criterion measure of validity was derived from an observational activity sampling of each worker's job behaviour at 30 second intervals on one day. Two independent observers coded each worker's activity using the following major categories, some of which were further subdivided:

Calculating
Dictating
Don't know
Face-to-face conversation
Filing
Maintenance
Moving about
One-way communication, active (e.g. speaking before a group)
One-way communication, passive (e.g. listening to a lecture)
Other telecommunications (all telecommunications media except telephone)
Pause (apparent inactivity, as when thinking)
Personal (e.g. coffee breaks)
Reading
Searching
Tending (monitoring the operation of machines)
Telephone

Transition (a change from one activity to another)
Typing
Waiting
Writing

The authors reported that the agreement between observers on the activities within these categories ranged from 70% to 90% with a mean of 82.8%. Accuracy was then assessed by comparing workers' self-report estimates with those made by the independent observers. The results indicated that workers accurately identified between 85% and 92% of the tasks involved in their jobs. An assessment was made of the accuracy of the relative amount of time which workers reported spending on these activities. The average correlation between the "actual" and estimated rank order of time spent on different activities was 0.58 and 0.66 for the two legal aid organisations. Finally, it was found that workers were quite inaccurate at estimating the absolute amount of time spent on the various tasks. The authors sum up their results by pointing out that the accuracy of self-report decreases as the level of measurement associated with self-report increases. Hence the identification of activities involved in a job is most accurate, as this uses a nominal scale of measurement. Identification of relative time spent on these activities is less accurately reported (an ordinal scale), whilst identification of absolute time spent is quite inaccurate (a ratio scale).

The Hartley et al. study is a step towards developing guidelines concerning the validity of different types of self-report data. Inevitably, criticisms can be made of this study (and any other carried out on this important but difficult topic). The extent to which the criterion measure itself was an "objective" measure of activities in the jobs is questionable. In addition, the activity categories were wide-ranging and arguably, workers needed training not only in using them, but also more generally, in the use of self-report techniques. A further question concerns the extent to which such findings generalise to other jobs involving tasks of a different nature. Further research of this nature is needed so that recommendations can be made to practitioners concerning the validity of different types of task and job analysis.

Utility

From a training perspective, it is important that any task analysis is useful in the development of a successful training programme. Reliability and validity are prerequisites, but they do not ensure that any analysis has utility. R.B. Miller, in various publications, has emphasised the importance of utility over other criteria. However, assessment of the contribution of any task analysis to a successful training programme is difficult, since many other factors, for example, the design of training, also affect such an outcome. What is needed is research which compares types of analysis using different indicators of utility.

One of the few studies to have adopted such an approach is by Levine, Ash and Bennett (1980), although it was carried out in the context of personnel selection rather than training. Despite the limitations of the study, acknowledged by the authors themselves, it is illustrative of the type of research needed in this area. Four job analysis techniques were compared: the Critical Incident Technique (Flanagan, 1954; see Section 6.2); the Job Elements Method (Primoff, 1975); the Position Analysis Questionnaire; and task analysis, as advocated by the US Department of Labor (1972) in which jobs were broken down into tasks and then rated on various scales. The researchers applied each of these four analyses to four jobs to produce a total of 16 job analyses. Sixty-four persons, mostly engaged in the area of personnel selection, then rated these analyses in terms of adequacy, utility etc. An impressive feature of the study was that utility was also judged by requiring the participants to generate what was termed an "examination plan" to select a person for the job in question. Examination plans were evaluated by the participants, by occupational experts and by the researchers who analysed the content of these examination plans. The results are not straightforward. Some limitations of the study included the differential familiarity of the participants with the analysis methods, the limited range of jobs and the use of PAQ with job experts rather than workers and their supervisors. However, the results indicated that PAQ was the least costly analysis method, although it was viewed less favourably by participants. The Critical Incident Technique was the most costly, but resulted in higher quality examination plans than those devised by other analysis methods. The authors, somewhat surprisingly, found that the different analysis techniques had relatively little impact on either the content of the examination plans or the costs of developing them. Of course, such findings may change in a training context, where more detailed objectives and content have to be derived for a training programme.

The utility of an analysis can sometimes be judged with respect to whether it enables the analyst to make some useful prediction, a sort of predictive validity. A prime example of this approach is given by Card, Moran and Newell (1983) who studied routine cognitive tasks which occur in human–computer interaction. They developed an analysis or model of user behaviour called GOMS. This acronym stands for Goals and subgoals of the user; *O*perators which are elementary perceptual, motor or cognitive acts; *M*ethods which are procedures for achieving goals; and *S*election rules, which are necessary when more than one method exists for achieving a goal. This approach was used to analyse the demands of various text editors and the analyses were impressively predictive of both speed and usability of different text editors.

REFERENCES

Annett, J. (1987). Training in transferable skills. Final report submitted to Manpower Services Commission. Coventry: University of Warwick.

Annett, J. and Duncan, K.D. (1967). Task analysis and training design. *Occupational Psychology*, **41**, 211–221.

Annett, J., Duncan, K.D., Stammers, R.B. and Gray, M.J. (1971). *Task analysis*. Training Information No 6. London: HMSO.

Arvey, R.D. and Campion, J.E. (1982). The employment interview. A summary and review of recent research. *Personnel Psychology*, **35**, 281–322.

Bainbridge, L. (1979). Verbal reports as evidence of the process operator's knowledge. *International Journal of Man-Machine Studies*, **11**, 411–436.

Bainbridge, L. (1990). Verbal protocol analysis. In Wilson, J.R. and Corlett, E.N. (Eds) *Evaluation of human work: A practical ergonomics methodology*. London: Taylor and Francis.

Birt, J.A. (1968). The effect of the consistency of job inventory information upon simulated airmen reassignment. Unpublished PhD thesis. Lafayette, Indiana: Purdue University.

Blum, M.L. and Naylor, J.C. (1968). *Industrial psychology*. New York: Harper & Row.

Borman, W.C. (1983). Implications of personality theory and research for the rating of work performance in organisations. In Landy, F., Zedeck, S. and Cleveland, J. (Eds) *Performance measurement and theory*. Hillsdale, NJ: Lawrence Erlbaum.

Bouchard, T.S. Jr (1976). Field research methods: Interviewing, questionnaires, participant observation, systematic observation, unobtrusive measures. In Dunnette, M.D. (Ed.) *Handbook of industrial and organisational psychology*. Chicago: Rand McNally. (Reprinted New York: Wiley.)

Branson, R.K., Rayner, G.T., Cox, L., Furman, J.P., King, F.J. and Hannum, W.H. (1975). Interservice procedures for instructional systems development: Executive summary and model. Tallahassee, FL: Center for Educational Technology, Florida State University. Distributed by Defense Technical Information Center, Alexandria, VA. (Phases 1, 2, 3, 4 and 5 of Interservice procedures for instructional systems development are ED 122 018–022 respectively – same publisher and authors.)

Brehmer, B. (1987). Development of mental models for decision in technological systems. In Rasmussen, J., Duncan, K. and Leplat, J. (Eds) *New technology and human error*. Chichester: Wiley.

Cain, P.S. and Green, B.F.(1983). Reliabilities of selected ratings available from the Dictionary of Occupational Titles. *Journal of Applied Psychology*, **68**(1), 155–165.

Card, S.K., Moran, T.P. and Newell, A. (1983). *The psychology of human–computer interaction*. Hillsdale, NJ: Lawrence Erlbaum.

Chapanis, A. (1959). *Research techniques in human engineering*. Baltimore: John Hopkins Press.

Chipman, S.F., Segal, J.W. and Glaser, R. (Eds) (1985). *Thinking and learning skills, Volume 2, Research and open questions*. Hillsdale, NJ: Lawrence Erlbaum.

Christal, R.E. (1971). Stability of consolidated job descriptions based on task inventory survey information. Report AFHRL-TR-71–48. Texas: Personnel Research Division, Lackland Air Force Base.

Christal, R.E. (1972). New directions in the Air Force occupational research program. USAF, AFHRL. Texas: Personnel Research Division, Lackland Air Force Base.

Christal, R.E. (1974). The United States Air Force occupational research project. Technical Report AFHRL-TR-73–75. Texas: Air Force Human Resources Laboratory, Occupation Research Division.

Cornelius, E.T. III, Carron, T.J. and Collins, M.N. (1979). Job analysis models and job classification. *Personnel Psychology*, **32**, 693–708.

Cragun, J.R. and McCormick, E.J. (1967). Job inventory information: Task and scale reliabilities and scale interrelationships. Report PRL-TR-67–15. Texas: Personnel Research Laboratory, Aerospace Medical Division, Lackland Air Force Base.

Dorner, D. (1987). On the difficulties people have in dealing with complexity. In Rasmussen, J., Duncan, K. and Leplat, J. (Eds) *New technology and human error*. Chichester: Wiley.

Dunnette, M.D. (1976). Aptitudes, abilities and skills. In Dunnette, M.D. (Ed.) *Handbook of industrial and organisational psychology*. Chicago: Rand McNally. (1983 reprinted New York: Wiley).

Ericsson, K.A. and Simon, H.A. (1980). Verbal reports as data. *Psychological Review*, **87**(3), 215–251.

Ericsson, K.A. and Simon, H.A. (1984). *Protocol analysis: Verbal reports as data*. Cambridge, MA: MIT Press.

Fine, S.A. and Heinz, C.A. (1958). The functional occupational classification structure. *Personnel and Guidance Journal*, **37**, 180–192.

Flanagan, J.C. (1954). The Critical Incident Technique. *Psychological Bulletin*, **51**, 327–358.

Fleishman, E.A. (1964). *The structure and measurement of physical fitness*. Englewood Cliffs, NJ: Prentice-Hall.

Fleishman, E.A. (1975). Toward a taxonomy of performance. *American Psychologist*, **30**, 1127–1149.

Fleishman, E.A. (1978). Relating individual differences to the dimensions of human tasks, *Ergonomics*, **21**(12), 1007–1019.

Fleishman, E. and Quaintance, M.F. (1984). *Taxonomies of human performance*. Orlando, FL: Academic Press.

Gael, S. (1983). *Job analysis. A guide to assessing work activities*. San Francisco: Jossey-Bass.

Gagné, R.M. (1977). *The conditions of learning*. 3rd edition. New York: Holt, Rinehart and Winston.

Guilford, J.P. (1956). The structure of intellect. *Psychological Bulletin*, **53**, 267–293.

Hartley, C., Brecht, M., Pagerey, P., Weeks, G., Chapanis, A. and Hoecker, D. (1977). Subjective time estimates of work tasks by office workers. *Journal of Occupational Psychology*, **50**, 23–43.

Harvey, R.J. (1986). Quantitative approaches to job classification. A review and critique. *Personnel Psychology*, **39**, 267–289.

Harvey, R.J. and Hayes, T.L. (1986) Monte Carlo baselines for interrater reliability correlations using the Position Analysis Questionnaire. *Personnel Psychology*, **39**, 345–357.

Hayes, N. and Broadbent, D.E. (1988). Two modes of learning for interactive tasks. *Cognition*, **28**, 249–277.

Johnson-Laird, P.N. (1985). Logical thinking: Does it occur in daily life? Can it be taught?

In Chipman, S.F., Segal, J.W. and Glaser, R. (Eds) *Thinking and learning skills, Volume 2, Research and open questions*. Hillsdale, NJ: Lawrence Erlbaum.

Klemmer, E.T. and Snyder, F.W. (1972). Measurement of the time spent communicating. *Journal of Communication*, **22**, 142–158.

Kuriloff, A.H., Yoder, D. and Stone, C.H. (1975). Training guide for observing and interviewing in marine corps task analysis. Evaluation of the marine corps task analysis program. Technical Report No 2. Los Angeles: California State University.

Leplat, J. (1986). The elicitation of expert knowledge. In Hollnagel, E., Mancini, G. and Woods, D.D. (Eds) *Intelligent decision support in process environments*. Heidelberg: Springer-Verlag.

Leplat, J. (1987). Methodology of task analysis and design. Paper presented to European Methodologies in Work and Organisational Psychology Symposium, Hungary, May.

Leplat, J. and Bisseret, A. (1966). Analysis of the processes involved in the treatment of information by the air traffic controller. *The Controller*, **5**, 13–22.

Leplat, J. and Hoc, J.M. (1981). Subsequent verbalization in the study of cognitive processes. *Ergonomics*, **24**(10), 743–755.

Levine, E.L., Ash, R.A. and Bennett, N. (1980). Exploratory comparative study of four job analysis methods. *Journal of Applied Psychology*, **65**(5), 524–535.

Levine, J.M. and Teichner, W.H. (1973). Development of a taxonomy of human performance: An information theoretic approach. JSAS Catalogue of Selected Documents in Psychology, **3**, 28.

McCormick, E.J. (1979). *Job analyses: Methods and applications*. New York: Amacom.

McCormick, E.J. and Ammerman, H.L. (1960). Development of worker activity check lists for use in occupational analysis. Report WADD-TR-60–77. Lackland Air Force Base. Texas: Personnel Laboratory, Wright Air Development Division.

McCormick, E.J., Jeanneret, P.R. and Mecham, R.C. (1969). A study of job characteristics and job dimensions as based on the Position Analysis Questionnaire. Report No. 6. Purdue, Lafayette: Occupational Research Centre, Purdue University.

Means, B. and Gott, S.P. (1988). Cognitive task analysis as a basis for tutor development: Articulating abstract knowledge representations. In Psotka, J., Massey, L.D. and Mutter, S.A. (Eds) *Intelligent tutoring systems: Lessons learned*. Hillsdale, NJ: Lawrence Erlbaum.

Merrill, M.D. (1983). Component display theory. In Reigeluth, C.M. (Ed.) *Instructional design theories and models: An overview of their current status*. Hillsdale, NJ: Lawrence Erlbaum.

Miller, R.B. (1962). Task description and analysis. In Gagné, R.M. (Ed.) *Psychological principles in system development*. New York: Holt, Rinehart and Winston.

Miller, R.B. (1974). A method for determining task strategies. Technical Report AFHRL-TR-74–26. American Institute for Research.

Morgan, T. (1972). Occupational description and classification. Report RE-D-19. UK: Air Transport and Travel Industry Training Board.

Morsch, J.E. (1964). Job analysis in the United States Air Force. *Personnel Psychology*, **17**, 1–17.

Nisbett, R.E. and Wilson, T.D. (1977). Telling more than we know: verbal reports on mental processes. *Psychological Review*, **84**, 231–259.

Oppenheim, A.N. (1982). *Questionnaire design and attitude measurement*. London: Heinemann.

Patrick, J. (1980). Job analysis, training and transferability: Some theoretical and practical issues. In Duncan, K.D., Gruneberg, M.M. and Wallis, D. (Eds) *Changes in working life*. Chichester: Wiley.

Patrick, J. and Moore, A.K. (1985). Development and reliability of a job analysis technique. *Journal of Occupational Psychology*, **58**, 149–158.

Pearlman, K. (1980). Job families: A review and discussion of their implications for personnel selection. *Psychological Bulletin*, **87**(1), 1–28.

Peterson, N.G. and Bownas, D.A. (1982). Skills, task structure and performance acquisition. In Dunnette, M.D. and Fleishman, E.A. (Eds) *Volume 1. Human capability assessment*. Hillsdale, NJ: Lawrence Erlbaum.

Prien, E.P. (1977). The function of job analysis in content validation. *Personnel Psychology*, **30**, 167–174.

Prien, E. and Ronan, W.W. (1971). Job analysis: A review of research findings. *Personnel Psychology*, **24**(3), 372–396.

Primoff, E.S. (1975) How to prepare and conduct job element examinations. Report TS-75-1. Washington: Research Section Personnel Research and Development Center, US Civil Service Commission.

Reiersen, C.S., Baker, S.M. and Marshall, E.C. (1988). An experimental evaluation of an advanced alarm system for nuclear power plants – a comparative study. In Patrick, J. and Duncan, K.D. (Eds) *Training, decision making and control*. Amsterdam: Elsevier.

Ringland, G.A. and Duce, D.A. (Eds) (1988). *Approaches to knowledge representation: An introduction*. Chichester: Wiley.

Schuman, H. and Presser, S. (1981). *Questions and answers in attitude surveys*. New York: Academic Press.

Segal, J.W., Chipman, S.F. and Glaser, R. (Eds) (1985). *Thinking and learning skills, Volume 1, Relating instruction to research*. Hillsdale, NJ: Lawrence Erlbaum.

Seymour, W.D. (1966). *Industrial skills*. London: Pitman.

Smith, A.D.W. (1973). General skills in the reasoning and interpersonal domain. Prince Albert, Saskatchewan: Training Research and Development Station.

Smith, R.G. (1964). The development of training objectives. Research Bulletin II, HUMRRO, George Washington University.

Spurgeon P., Michael, I. and Patrick, J. (1984). *Training and selection of computer personnel*. Research and Development No.18. Sheffield: Manpower Services Commission.

Sternberg, R.J. (1977). Component processes in analogical reasoning. *Psychological Review*, **84**, 353–378.

Stevens, S.S. (1946). On the theory of scales of measurement. *Science*, **103**, 677–680.

Taylor, L.R. (1978). Empiricaly derived job families as a foundation for the study of validity generalisation. Study I. The construction of job families based on the component and overall dimensions of the PAQ. *Personnel Psychology*, **31**, 325–340.

Taylor, L.R. and Colbert, G.A. (1978). Empirically derived job families as a foundation for the study of validity generalisation. Study II. The construction of job families based on the company specific PAQ job dimensions. *Personnel Psychology*, **31**, 341–353.

Thurstone, L.L. (1938). Primary mental abilities. *Psychometric Monographs*, No 1.

US Department of Labor (1972). *Handbook for analysing jobs*. Manpower Administration, Washington DC, US Government Printing Office.

US Department of Labor (1977). *Dictionary of Occupational Titles*. 4th edition.

Visser, W. (1988). Giving up a hierarchical plan in a design activity. Research Report 814. Rocquencourt: Institut National de Recherche en Informatique et en Automatique.

Wheaton, G. (1968). Development of a taxonomy of human performance: A review of classificatory systems relating to tasks and performance, Technical Report 1. Washington: American Institute for Research.

Wirstad, J. (1988). On knowledge structures for process operators. In Goodstein, L.P., Anderson, H.B. and Olsen, S.E. (Eds) *Tasks, errors and mental models*. London: Taylor and Francis.

Zerga, J.E. (1943). Job analysis. A resume and bibliography. *Journal of Applied Psychology*, **27**, 249–267.

CHAPTER 6
Task-oriented analysis

In Chapter 5, we distinguished between task-oriented and person-oriented types of analysis. The latter are psychological in nature whilst the former are not. Task-oriented analyses of a job or task make important contributions to the development of training. In this chapter, we will consider four task-oriented approaches. Discussion of each will cover its relevance to training, how it works, examples of its application, a summary of its advantages and disadvantages plus major references to it. The four task-oriented approaches are:

(a) Hierarchical Task Analysis.
(b) Critical Incident Technique.
(c) Task inventories.
(d) Trainability analyses.

6.1 HIERARCHICAL TASK ANALYSIS

A variety of task analysis techniques were developed in the 1950s and 1960s, which break down a task into a series of subtasks. One of these is named Hierarchical Task Analysis (HTA) and was developed by Annett and Duncan (1967). It has been described in detail by Annett et al. (1971), Duncan (1972) and more recently by Shepherd (1985). Patrick, Spurgeon and Shepherd (1986) have produced a guide to HTA and related forms of analysis for practitioners.

Hierarchical Task Analysis is well suited to the development of training materials and can be used for identifying training needs, specifying training objectives and elaborating training content. As its name suggests, the analysis utilises task-oriented descriptions to decompose a job or task into a hierarchical array of subtasks. It provides a logical rather than a psychological analysis of a task.

Features of Hierarchical Task Analysis

There are four main features of HTA: hierarchical breakdown, operations, criteria for stopping the analysis and plans. Each of these is discussed below.

169

1. Hierarchical breakdown. The analysis begins by specifying a general task and then progressively breaks it down into a series of subtasks which logically comprise and exhaust the higher level task. Subtasks in turn can be broken down into their constituent subsubtasks and this decomposition can be repeated a number of times. The analysis therefore proceeds from the general to the specific with lower level tasks being the logical expansion of higher order ones.

2. Operations. Formally, Annett et al. (1971) proposed that the units of analysis are termed "operations". Operations are defined as "any unit of behaviour, no matter how long or short its duration and no matter how simple or complex its structure which can be defined in terms of its objective". This emphasis on the objective of a task is important and convenient for training purposes. There is a danger that an analyst will concentrate on the activities of a task rather than viewing them as a means of achieving an objective or goal. Only after goals have been specified, is it sensible to consider the activities or different methods of achieving them. Also, since HTA specifies tasks in terms of objectives, these can be directly translated into the training needs and training objectives which have to be met by a training programme. The manner in which training objectives should be specified is discussed in Section 4.5. These prescriptions can also be applied to the specification of operations within HTA.

Hence tasks are described as operations which are broken down into suboperations which in turn may be further subdivided. There is no fixed number of levels of analysis. This aspect of HTA is one of its claimed advantages over techniques which use either a single level of analysis throughout, or a fixed set of job items or a fixed number of levels of analysis (e.g. tasks, activities and elements). Flexibility in the level of analysis enables the discriminatory power to vary as required, a feature which is absent when the same items or levels of analysis are prescribed prior to the analysis. In HTA the level of analysis is guided by the $P \times C$ criterion for stopping, which is discussed below.

In theory, the concept of an operation can be applied to any task and hierarchical descriptions can be developed with varying amounts of detail dependent upon the context and purpose of the analysis. An example is given in Figure 6.1 which is from a study by Patrick et al. (1980) of the analysis of a production technician's job concerned with injection moulding in the plastics processing industry. The overall job was broken down into three superordinate operations or tasks, numbered 1–3 in Figure 6.1(a). Each of these was analysed further, to give a more extensive hierarchical breakdown of the tasks involved, as in

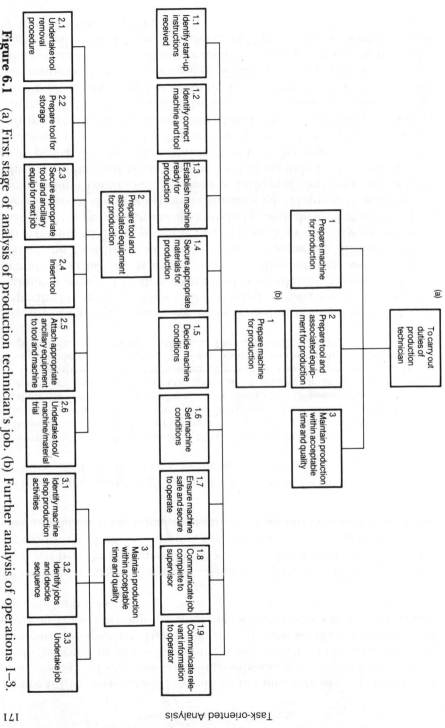

Figure 6.1 (a) First stage of analysis of production technician's job. (b) Further analysis of operations 1–3.

Figure 6.1(b). Hence task 1 is subdivided into subtasks 1.1–1.9, task 2 into subtasks 2.1–2.6 and task 3 into subtasks 3.1–3.3. Such an analysis could proceed to absurdly minute levels which would have no consequence for training. Hence the next feature of HTA which we will consider is the criterion for stopping, which specifies how detailed any analysis should be.

3. Criterion for stopping analysis.   Annett and Duncan (1967) proposed what has become known as the "$P \times C$ rule" for deciding when further redescription of an operation is not necessary. They suggested that as each operation is identified, two questions should be asked of it by the analyst:

1. What is the probability P without training of inadequate performance?
2. What would be the costs C to the system of inadequate performance?

> If the best available estimates of these values, or rather if their product is unacceptable, then the performance in question is redescribed in more detail i.e. broken down into subordinate operations and each of these is then submitted in turn to the same decision rule. In some cases it will be necessary to redescribe several times in increasing detail, in others not. The analysis ceases, either when the values specified in the rule are acceptable to the system, or when training requirements for adequate performance are clear (Annett and Duncan, 1967, p. 212).

The first question, posed above, is concerned with the probability P that a specified target population will perform the operation unsatisfactorily without training. In other words will a simple instruction to do the operation suffice or is more detail, i.e. further analysis necessary? Hence the probability of failure P incorporates the difficulty which performance of a task presents to a person. This will vary according to that person's previous training, knowledge and ability. Let us return to the analysis of the production technician's job (Figure 6.1). Subtask 1.6 "set machine conditions" involved a variety of decisions and actions which an untrained person would find impossible to do. Therefore a high probability of failure exists. Further, the nature of a training solution was not evident to the analyst and therefore the task had to be further broken down. On the other hand, subtask 1.2 "identify correct machine and tool" was straightforward and at most the trainee had to learn a set of simple discriminations. In HTA the process of redescription continues until the probability of failure is acceptable or a training solution can be envisaged by the analyst. The analysis will therefore be more detailed, the less the experience or ability of the person who has to be trained to perform the task.

The second question concerns the cost C, in the widest sense of the word, of inadequate performance of the task. Designing a training programme for some tasks may cost more than poor performance of the task costs in terms of lost production and inefficiency. On the other hand, some critical tasks have unacceptably high costs if performed inadequately. For example, a task in the production technicians job was to "prepare machine for tool removal". Inadequate performance could result in serious damage to the tool and/or machine causing considerable financial loss together with wasted production. Further examples might be cited from the operation of nuclear or chemical processing plants in which consequences of inadequate performance can sometimes be catastrophic.

The decision rule concerning redescription is to combine P and C in a multiplicative manner i.e. $P \times C$. In short-hand this rule states:

If $P \times C$ is unacceptable,
Then continue the analysis or redescription of the task,
Unless a training programme can be designed which would then make $P \times C$ acceptable.

This rule emphasises that the training context is important, since it will determine both what is acceptable and also the resources available for the development of a training solution. The multiplicative rule means that if either P or C is at or near zero, then their product will also be at or near zero. Application of this rule is designed to indicate which operations are problematic, thus requiring further analysis.

The $P \times C$ rule suggests that P and C can be measured precisely. As Duncan (1972) and Shepherd (1985) pointed out, accurate estimation of these parameters is rarely feasible and is a subjective matter. Very often the best that can be achieved is a gross judgement which dichotomises the probability or costs of inadequate performance as satisfactory or not. Hence, whilst the rule smacks of precision and objectivity, both are rarely attainable.

One form of hierarchical task analysis has been labelled Overview Task Analysis by Patrick et al. (1980). Its main feature is that it is intended to facilitate comparison of task content between jobs with the same or similar job titles in a particular industrial sector. Consequently, it uses a stopping rule of redescription which specifies that the tasks are *generalisable* between different companies or organisations in the same industry. Such an approach was used to analyse the tasks of computer personnel within three companies, each representing a different sector of the computing industry: employers, manufacturers and services. Some of the tasks which refer to the job of "programmer" in each of

Table 6.1 Some of the tasks and subtasks performed by "programmers" from different types of company (Patrick et al., 1986)

Subtasks	A Service company	B User company	C Manufacturing company
1. To determine computing requirements re. business needs			
1.1.1 Collect information	×	×	√
1.1.3 Determine design methods and techniques			
1.1.4.2 Estimate programming time needed	×	×	√
1.1.4.3 Estimate machine time needed	×	×	√
1.1.4.4 Specify hardware requirements	×	×	√
2. To design systems to meet requirements			
2.2.4 Agree work schedule and resources	×	×	√
2.3.1 Finalise design methods and techniques	×	×	√
2.3.2 Finalise system specifications	×	×	√
2.3.3.1 Specify preliminary information	×	√	√
2.3.3.2 Outline aims of system	×	√	√
2.3.3.3 Describe system	×	√	√
2.3.3.4 Specify changeover procedure	×	√	√
2.3.3.5 Describe equipment utilisation	×	√	×
2.3.3.6 Prepare source document specifications	×	√	×

2.3.3.9	Describe systems test data	×	✓	×	✓	✓
2.3.3.10	Prepare program descriptions	×	✓	✓	✓	✓
2.3.4.2	Design and code programs	✓	✓	✓	✓	✓
2.3.4.3	Maintain documentation	×	✓	×	✓	✓
2.3.5	Prepare operating instructions for systems	×	✓	✓	×	✓
2.4.2.1	Prepare test data/files for program testing	✓	✓	✓	✓	×
2.4.2.2	Run program tests	✓	✓	✓	✓	×
2.4.2.3	Diagnose and correct program errors	✓	✓	✓	✓	✓
3.	**To implement new systems**					
3.3	Deliver systems to customers	✓	✓	×	✓	×
3.4	Carry out file conversion	✓	✓	×	✓	×
3.5	Carry out trial running and consolidation	×	✓	✓	✓	✓
3.6	Provide necessary presentations to user management, users and other relevant staff	✓	×	×	×	×
3.7	Train user departments	✓	×	×	×	×
4.	**To maintain existing systems**					
4.2.3	Identify program faults	✓	✓	✓	✓	×
4.3	Correct faults	✓	✓	✓	✓	×
4.4	Modify system in accordance with need	✓	×	✓	×	×
4.5	Provide system users with advice/assistance as required	✓	✓	✓	✓	×

√: subtask performed; ×: subtask not performed.

these sectors of the industry are given in Table 6.1. In this application, the hierarchical array of tasks is being used as a checklist or task inventory and appropriate scales could be appended if required. The tasks performed by the programmers indicate that different training programmes are needed for each job despite sharing the same job title. There are only four subtasks which are common to programmers' jobs in all three companies. There are 10 common subtasks between programmers in B and C. Programmers in A are different in two respects. Firstly, they do not produce program specifications and secondly they modify systems (subtask 4.4) and provide users with advice (subtask 4.5). Programmers in C carry out subtask 1 whereas those in A and B do not.

4. Plans.   By now the discerning reader will have noticed that there is an important feature missing in our discussion of HTA so far. The clue lies in the statement that one of the rules of HTA is that a task is broken down into its constituent subtasks which must be *logically* equivalent to it. This is not the case unless in addition to a series of subtasks, there is a means of stating how these fit together. Hence a "plan" has to be identi- fied which is a necessary complement to the description of "operations". A plan specifies when and in which sequence the operations (or tasks) should be performed. A skilled person is not only competent at each subtask but is also able to orchestrate the execution of subtasks as appropriate. However, a "plan" identified during HTA is not necessarily psychological in nature (although it may be) as the breakdown of a task into subtasks is only guided by their logical equivalence.

Let us illustrate the importance of specifying a plan with an everyday example of analysing the task of making an omelette. One of the tasks in the analysis is: "Add mixture, control and terminate cooking", which can be broken down into the following subtasks:

put butter/oil in pan;
pour mixture into pan;
inspect omelette;
adjust heat;
adjust omelette;
turn heat off.

One might argue that the key to a successful omelette, which will distinguish a good cook from a novice, is a plan which details *which* of these subtasks to perform *when*. The subtasks themselves are not intrinsically difficult. The plan will state that the first subtask is to "put butter/oil in pan" followed by "adjust heat", until the butter turns slightly brown and the pan is sufficiently hot. The next subtask to be performed is "pour mixture into pan". The remainder of the plan would specify the order and conditions for moving between the three remaining subtasks:

inspect omelette;
adjust heat;
adjust omelette.

The remaining part of this plan is very difficult if not impossible to state verbally. The difficulty lies in describing the visual cues differentiating the various stages of omelette cooking; the predicted relationship between adjustments in heat, position of the omelette and its cooked status; and the timing and iterative nature of the cook's interventions, with some subtasks being performed in parallel. In this situation, if a plan is not specifiable, then the only solution is to provide the trainee with sufficient training or experience with the task until such a plan is developed and internalised, even though it cannot be made verbally explicit.

Various types of plan exist. Some plans are straightforward and involve invariant sequences or procedures such as "do subtask 1, then do subtask 2, then do subtask 3 etc". These are characteristic of the start-up or shut-down procedures of machines, plant or equipment. Such fixed procedures are often automated. If they are not, it is straightforward to enable the trainee to master such plans. Other plans involve different tasks being performed at the same time, as in our omelette example above. In some analyses, no fixed order of performance may exist. For example, a traffic warden does various tasks such as "giving parking tickets", "directing traffic", "giving directions to traffic" etc. There is an order of priorities for these tasks which needs to be made explicit, although there is no predetermined sequence for them which is intrinsic to the job of a traffic warden. The traffic warden will, however, have to be trained in a task concerned with "determining which is the highest priority task to do next".

Some tasks involve complex plans which involve decisions, the answers to which will dictate the sequence of operations to be followed. Such a plan may be represented in the form of a decision tree or algorithm which specifies the rules or conditions under which operations are executed. An example is provided in Figure 6.2, which presents a simple algorithm for locating faults in an industrial process of radiator welding. In some situations an operation from such a decision tree might be further broken down into another series of operations and sequencing rules.

It might be argued that the tasks which will remain in industry for

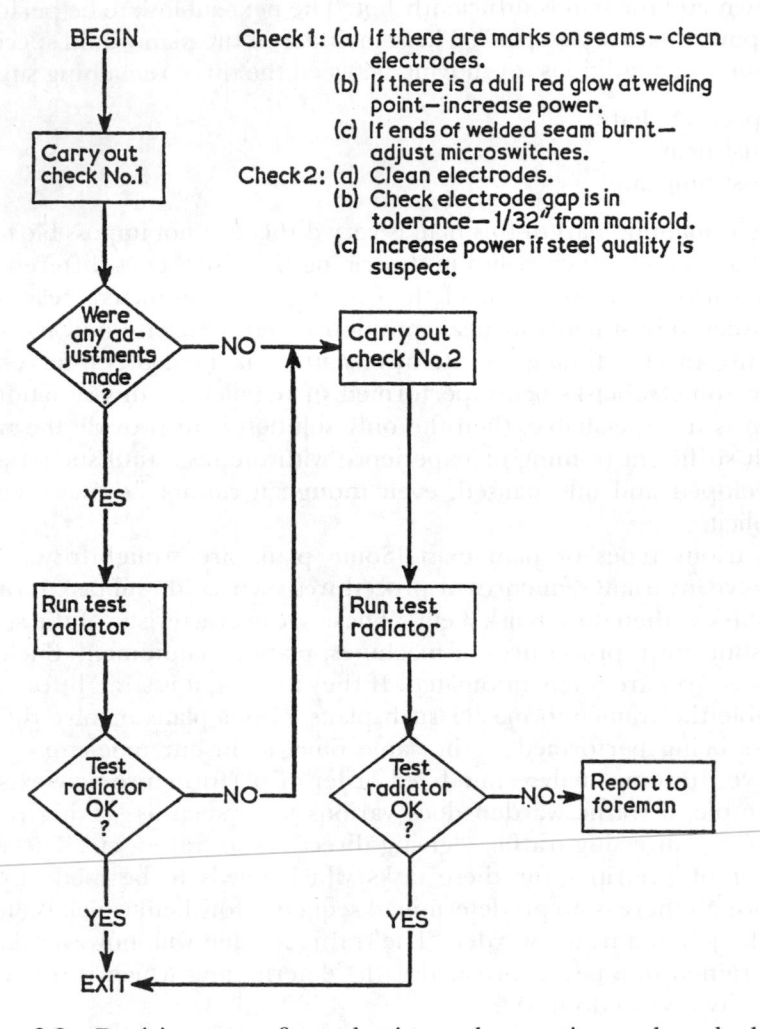

BEGIN

Check 1: (a) If there are marks on seams – clean electrodes.
(b) If there is a dull red glow at welding point – increase power.
(c) If ends of welded seam burnt – adjust microswitches.

Check 2: (a) Clean electrodes.
(b) Check electrode gap is in tolerance – 1/32″ from manifold.
(c) Increase power if steel quality is suspect.

Carry out check No.1

Were any ad- justments made ? —NO→ Carry out check No.2

YES

Run test radiator

Run test radiator

Test radiator OK ? —NO→

Test radiator OK ? —NO→ Report to foreman

YES

YES

EXIT ←

Figure 6.2 Decision tree for selecting suboperations when leaking radiators are reported (Annett et al., 1971).

humans to perform, after automation, will make greater cognitive demands and therefore the specification of plans or strategies will become even more important in the development of effective training. Shepherd and Duncan (1980) described such a complex task in which a "controller" of a chlorine plant has to "balance" production of gas from various units with its consumption. The primary problem in the task analysis was to identify and specify the plans and subplans involved in this complex decision-making task. These could not be immediately inferred by the analyst or verbalised by the skilled controllers.

Documenting and recording the analysis

In the previous section we discussed the four main features of HTA: hierarchical breakdown, operations, criteria for stopping the analysis and plans. Some examples of partial analyses have been presented in our discussion so far, although the format for documenting the task analysis has not been addressed explicitly. This is because whilst documentation techniques are important, the goals and underlying structure of the analysis are more important than the format in which it is presented. Some form of documentation is needed to record, revise and communicate the task analysis. The process of analysis will involve many revisions. It is useful to develop a systematic means of numbering tasks, subtasks and plans particularly in large analyses. Guidelines concerning documentation are given in Annett et al. (1971), Duncan (1972) and more recently in Patrick et al. (1986).

There are two main methods for documenting a task analysis:

(a) Hierarchical diagrams.
(b) Tables.

1. Hierarchical diagrams.   These can be used to document tasks, subtasks and plans. An example concerning the analysis of a task in the chemical processing industry is represented in Figure 6.3. There are a number of points to note:

(a) Subtasks which do not require further analyses are underlined.
(b) The numbering system for tasks extends an additional digit for each level of subtasks specified.
(c) A superordinate task is broken down into its constituent subtasks and plan. Hence plan 1 refers to how the subtasks 1.1–1.5 of task 1 are sequenced etc.

2. Tables.   The hierarchical diagram is useful for showing the task structure but is limited in the amount of information that can be conveniently recorded. It is therefore recommended that it is used in conjunction with a table in which the task, subtasks together with notes concerning the nature of training can also be recorded.

Originally, Annett et al. (1971) proposed that the tabular format should be as that illustrated in Figure 6.4 which contains an extract from

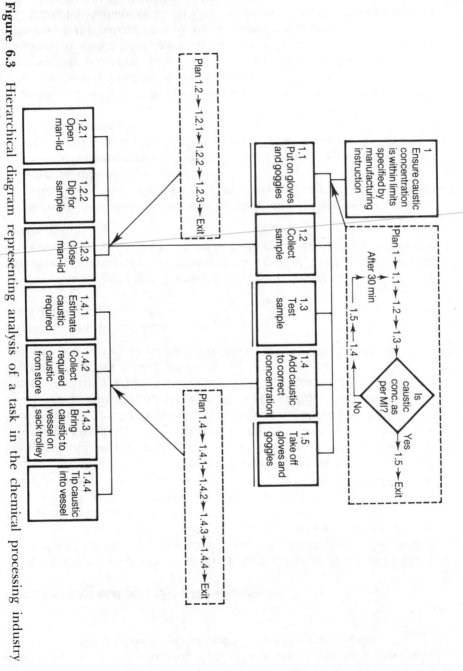

Figure 6.3 Hierarchical diagram representing analysis of a task in the chemical processing industry (Patrick et al., 1986).

No.	Description of operation and training notes	I/F	A	Redescribed
1	Fence with the sabre. [R.] Convention means an invariant order 1.1 to 1.3. Score a hit on the target of the opponent without getting hit oneself within the rules. Must learn the convention – possibly fencing films.	–	x	1.1–1.3
1.1	Attack the opponet. [R.] Invariant order 1.1.1 to 1.1.3 although 1.1.1 (the grip) is maintained throughout the fight. The target is anywhere above the waist of the opponent including the arms. Once indicated this should be clear; may be helped by colouring the target area.	–	x	1.1.1–1.1.3
1.2	Defend an opponent's attack. [R.] Always 1.2.1 but defence may be either evasion (1.2.2) or by parrying (1.2.3) [I.] The choice of alternative depends on the amount of pressure in the fight and upon the strengths and weaknesses of the opponent and is thus specific to each fight. Evasion should not be encouraged because it does not earn the right to attack.	x	x	1.2.1–1.2.3
1.3	Reply to opponent's attack. [R.] Operation 1.3.1 and 1.3.2 are wholly time shared but the type of hit (1.3.2) will vary from one riposte to another. All ripostes follow a parry by the rules of fencing.	–	x	1.3.1–1.3.2

Figure 6.4 Extract from a task analysis of fencing (Stammers and Patrick, 1975).

an analysis of fencing. The first column refers to the task number. The second column contains a statement of the task, rules R which sequence subtasks (i.e. plans) and notes concerning possible training solutions. In addition Annett et al. proposed that one should consider any input I, action A and feedback F difficulties associated with a task which should also be recorded as in Figure 6.4. As Shepherd (1985) pointed out, the I–A–F taxonomy is most useful for tasks involving the control of physical action and it is less appropriate for more cognitively oriented tasks. The final columns in the tabular format are concerned with identifying any difficulties associated with a task together with the reference numbers of any further redescription of that task. Shepherd (1976) proposed some changes to this tabular format, notably that plans are given greater emphasis. The same analysis of the task in the chemical processing industry represented by a hierarchical diagram in Figure 6.3 is given in this revised tabular format in Figure 6.5.

Super-ordinate	Subtask or plan	Notes
1	Ensure caustic concentration is within limits specified by manufacturing instructions	The 'notes' are, at this stage merely suggestions that the analyst is making to improve subtasks. They may be taken up during instruction or they may be suggestions to a plant manager for modifying the task.
	P1→ 1.1→ 1.2→ 1.3→ After 30 mins ← 1.5 ← 1.4 ← (Is conc. as per M.I.? Yes → 1.5 → Exit / No)	
	1.1 Put on gloves and goggles //	Emphasise the dangers of handling caustic without proper protection.
	1.2 Collect sample	Instruct using laboratory training materials.
	1.3 Test sample //	Show correct way of removing gloves without bare hands comming into contact with caustic.
	1.4 Add caustic to correct concentration	
	1.5 Take off gloves and goggles //	
1.2	Collect sample	Emphasise safety equipment throughout. Make sure men practise with full equipment.
	P1.2→ 1.2.1→ 1.2.2→ 1.2.3→ Exit	
	1.2.1 Open man-lid //	
	1.2.2 Dip for sample //	
	1.2.3 Close man-lid //	
1.4	Add caustic to correct concentration	Can tables be prepared to help men more accurately estimate caustic requirements in the light of the test result?
	1.4 → 1.4.1 → 1.4.2 → 1.4.3 → 1.4.4 → Exit	Emphasise correct lifting procedures.
	1.4.1 Estimate caustic required	The procedure for tipping caustic seems rather unsatisfactory. Men soon get fed up with using the scoop provided and try to manipulate the whole sack. Dealing with a heavy shifting load is likely to lead to spillages. The awkward posture required may lead to injury. The procedure for transporting and charging caustic may need revising. A rigid vessel suitable for lifting and tipping by two men should be investigated.
	1.4.2 Collect required caustic from store //	
	1.4.3 Bring caustic to vessel on sack trolley //	
	1.4.4 Tip caustic into vessel //	

Figure 6.5 Table representing the same analysis of a task in the chemical processing industry as Figure 6.3 (Patrick et al., 1986).

Advantages and disadvantages of Hierarchical Task Analysis

HTA has the following advantages:

(a) *Flexible and economic in level of analysis.* HTA does not have a fixed number of levels of analysis. A predetermined level of analysis will provide the analyst with either too much or too little discriminatory power. The $P \times C$ stopping rule of HTA enables the analysis to cease at an appropriate level for the training problem under consideration.
(b) *General applicability.* It is not restricted by the nature of the tasks which it can analyse. In this sense it might be said to be context-independent and can be applied to the analysis of sports, industrial and management activities as well as to tasks with various psychological demands (e.g. cognitive, social, perceptual-motor). Its only requirement is that tasks can be stated in terms of goals.
(c) *Tasks can be translated into training needs and objectives.* Specification of a task in terms of the goal or objective of performance means that unsatisfactory performance can be directly translated into the training needs and objectives of a training programme.
(d) *Logically exhaustive.* With some task analyses, it is easy to overlook a task or tasks in the analysis. The danger of this is reduced with HTA since its rule of decomposition requires the analyst to check that each set of subordinate operations together with its plan, is logically equivalent to the superordinate task. The skill of the analyst will determine whether this criterion is met.
(e) *An analysis provides the framework for training content.* The tasks identified by HTA and their inter-relationships provide the skeleton for a subsequent training programme on which the flesh of detailed task activities has to be hung.

The disadvantages of HTA are:

(a) *It is difficult.* Various features of HTA make it not a straightforward technique to use. Carrying out HTA is itself a complex cognitive task. The rule of logical decomposition is difficult as is the specification of plans for complex tasks. Analysts require considerable training and even afterwards, errors are to be expected. Also, as has previously been noted, the $P \times C$ stopping rule is usually difficult to quantify except in a gross subjective manner.
(b) *Technique and the role of the analyst.* It is not clear the extent to which HTA is a technique since it relies heavily on the skill and ingenuity of the analyst. Reliability has not been investigated and different analysts may produce different analyses. The extent to which this

affects subsequent training decisions needs investigation. These issues are particularly pertinent to the analysis of complex tasks such as problem-solving and decision-making, in which few external referents of behaviour may be available for the analyst to observe. Perhaps HTA should be viewed as providing the analyst with a set of guidelines, rather than being a rigid analysis technique. Several studies have demonstrated its utility.

6.2 CRITICAL INCIDENT TECHNIQUE

This famous technique was developed by Flanagan and colleagues in the Aviation Psychology Programme of the United States Army Air Forces in the Second World War. One of the most useful sources is Flanagan's original careful description of the method (Flanagan, 1954). He characterised the technique not as a rigid method, but as a collection of procedures and principles. He described the following five steps in the Critical Incident Technique:

1. Determination of the general aim and objectives of the activity i.e. job, task to be investigated.
2. Preparation of plans and specifications for collecting factual incidents about the activity including instructions to observers.
3. Collection of the incidents from interviews, observation etc.
4. Analysis of the incidents including developing categories of incidents.
5. Interpreting and reporting.

Each of these steps is elaborated by Flanagan with the goal being to optimise the objectivity and utility of the data. Critical incidents are defined as "extreme behaviour, either outstandingly effective or ineffective with respect to attaining the general aims of the activity" (Flanagan, 1954, p. 338). The nature of critical incidents and how they are observed is further described by Flanagan and reproduced in Table 6.2. He argued that extreme behaviours are particularly significant and can be more accurately identified by observation. During data collection (step 3 above) an important consideration is the number of incidents required. This will depend on the complexity of the job or task and varies between a few hundred and a couple of thousand. To ensure adequate coverage, one criterion proposed by Flanagan is to stop collecting critical incidents when only two or three of 100 new ones are providing additional information.

Two illustrative studies of the use of the Critical Incident Technique are those by Kay (1959) and Kirchner and Dunnette (1957), which

Table 6.2 Guidelines about the use of observation in the Critical Incident Technique (Flanagan, 1954)

1 *The situations observed*. The first necessary specification is a delimitation of the situations to be observed. This specification must include information about the place, the persons, the conditions, and the activities. Such specifications are rather easily defined in many instances. For example, such brief specifications as observations of "the behavior in classrooms of regularly employed teachers in a specified high school while instructing students during class periods," constitute a fairly adequate definition of a situation of this type.

In complex situations it is probably essential not only that the specifications with respect to the situation be relatively complete and specific, but also that practical examples be provided to assist the observer in deciding in an objective fashion whether or not a specific behavior should be observed and recorded.

2 *Relevance to the general aim*. After the decision has been made that a particular situation is an appropriate one for making observations, the next step is to decide whether or not a specific behavior which is observed is relevant to the general aim of the activity as defined in the section above. For example, if the general aim of the activity was defined as sustained high quality and quantity of production, it might be difficult to decide whether or not to include an action such as encouraging an unusually effective subordinate to get training that would assist him in developing his ability in an avocational or recreational activity not related to his work. In this case, it might be specified that any action which either directly or indirectly could be expected over a long period of time to have a significant effect on the general aim should be included. If it could not be predicted with some confidence whether this effect would be good or bad, it should probably not be considered.

The extent of detail required to obtain objectivity with respect to this type of decision depends to a considerable degree on the background and experiences of the observers with respect to this activity. For example, supervisors with substantial experience in a particular company can be expected to agree on whether or not a particular behavior is relevant to the attainment of the general aim. On the other hand, if outside observers were to be used, it would probably be necessary to specify in considerable detail the activities that can be expected to have an effect on the general aim.

3 *Extent of effect on the general aim*. The remaining decision that the observer must make is how important an effect the observed incident has on the general aim. It is necessary to specify two points on the scale of importance: (*a*) a level of positive contributions to the general aim in specific terms, preferably including a concrete example, and (*b*) the corresponding level of negative effect on the general aim expressed in similar terms.

A definition which has been found useful is that an incident is critical if it makes a "significant" contribution, either positively or negatively, to the general aim of the activity. The definition of "significant" will depend on the nature of the activity. If the general aim of the activity is in terms of production, a significant contribution might be one which caused, or might have caused, an appreciable change in the daily production of the department either in the form of an increase or a decrease.

In certain specific situations, it might be desirable and possible to set up a quantitative criterion such as saving or wasting 15 minutes of an average worker's production. In some situations, a definition of significance might be set up in terms of dollars saved or lost both directly or indirectly.

Actions which influence the attitudes of others are more difficult to evaluate objectively. Perhaps the best we might be able to do is to state it in terms of a probability estimate. For example, one such criterion might be that the minimum critical level would be an action that would have an influence such that at least one person in ten might change his vote on an issue of importance to the company.

4 *Persons to make the observations.* One additional set of specifications refers to the selection and training of the observers who are to make and report the judgments outlined in the steps above.

Wherever possible, the observers should be selected on the basis of their familiarity with the activity. Special consideration should be given to observers who have made numerous observations on persons engaged in the activity. Thus, for most jobs, by far the best observers are supervisors whose responsibility it is to see that the particular job being studied is done. However, in some cases very useful observations can be contributed by consumers of the products and services of the activity. For example, for a study of effective sales activities, the customers may have valuable data to contribute. For a study of effective parental activity, the children may be able to make valuable contributions.

In addition to careful selection of the persons to make observations, attention should be given to their training. Minimal training should include a review of the nature of the general aim of the activity and a study of the specifications and definitions for the judgments they will be required to make. Where the situation is complex or the observers are not thoroughly familiar with the activity, supervised practice in applying these definitions should be provided. This can be done by preparing descriptions of observations and asking the observers to make judgments about these materials. Their judgments can be immediately confirmed or corrected during such supervised practice periods.

In the chart is shown a form for use in developing specifications regarding observations. The use of this form in making plans for the collection of critical incidents or other types of observational data should aid in objectifying these specifications.

Specifications regarding observations

---

1. Persons to make the observations.
    a. Knowledge concerning the activity
    b. Relation to those observed
    c. Training requirements
2. Groups to be observed
    a. General description
    b. Location
    c. Persons
    d. Times
    e. Conditions
3. Behaviours to be observed
    a. General type of activity
    b. Specific behaviours
    c. Criteria of relevance to general aim
    d. Criteria of importance to general aim (critical points)

Chart indicating specifications regarding observations

analysed the activities of foremen and salespersons respectively. In the Kay study, 691 incidents were collected from interviews with 49 supervisory and 25 nonsupervisory staff in the Submarine Cable Division of the Simplex Wire and Cable Company. In the Kirchner and Dunnette study, 85 sales managers from the Minnesota Mining and Manufacturing Company were sent critical incident record forms from which 135

Table 6.3 Examples of critical incidents and categories of performance from two studies

Critical incidents	Kirchner and Dunnette (1957): Salespersons	Kay (1959): Foremen
Effective performance	"A salesman driving down the street saw a truck containing equipment for which company products might be used. He followed the truck to find the delivery point, made a call on this account, which was a new one and obtained an order."	"Aware that a change in set-up was scheduled for the next day, a foreman checked a machine, noted a missing part and ordered it."
Ineffective performance	"A salesman received a complaint from a customer about the quality of a particular type of tape. He failed to look into the matter or write up a formal complaint. The defective tape was returned to the jobber or to the retailer and no credit was issued to the jobber or to the retailer involved. While the account was not lost, the customer was dissatisfied for a long time."	"A foreman failed to notify the relief shift foreman that a machine was in need of repair before it could be operated again."
Critical categories or areas of activity	1. Following-up: complaints, requests, orders and leads 2. Planning ahead 3. Communicating all necessary information to sales managers 4. Communicating truthful information to managers and customers 5. Carrying out promises 6. Persisting on tough accounts 7. Pointing out uses for other company products besides the salesman's own line 8. Using new sales techniques and methods 9. Preventing price-cutting by dealers and customers 10. Initiating new selling ideas 11. Knowing customer requirements 12. Defending company policies 13. Calling on all accounts 14. Helping customers with equipment and displays 15. Showing nonpassive attitude	*Competence in administrative matters* 1. Planning operations 2. Following instructions 3. Attention to details 4. Adherence to company policy 5. Selection of work for active supervision 6. Willingness to assume responsibility 7. Tact and discretion *Competence in supervising subordinates* 8. Development of subordinates 9. Correction of undesirable behaviour 10. Giving credit where due 11. Equality of treatment 12. Concern for employee's welfare 13. Keeping subordinates informed *Relations with equals and superiors* 14. Adherence to chain of authority 15. Acceptance of criticism and suggestions 16. Communication with equals and superiors

incidents were reported; 96 of these were deemed usable, out of which 61 were instances of effective performance while 35 concerned non-effective performance. Examples of critical incidents from each study are given in Table 6.3. The next step of the analysis involved organising the incidents into various categories. There are no guidelines for how this should be accomplished. In the study by Kay, the 691 incidents were divided into three main categories concerning competence in administrative matters, competence in supervising subordinates and relations with equals and superiors. These categories were subdivided further into a total of 16 areas of activity which are detailed in Table 6.3. The critical incidents associated with salespersons activities from the Kirchner and Dunnette study were organised into 15 categories which the authors expected would generalise to other salespersons jobs in different contexts (see Table 6.3). Such categories together with their associated critical incidents begin to delineate the behaviour of an effective foreman or salesperson. Consequently, often a checklist or questionnaire is devised from this information which can be used to appraise the performance of job incumbents. This material can also be used to specify some behaviours which need to be trained.

Dunnette (1976) found a combination of the Critical Incident Technique with Behaviour Observation Scaling (BOS) useful in deriving the behavioural requirements of jobs. The methodology has been applied to a variety of jobs including department managers in retail stores (Campbell et al., 1973), first line supervisors in a large insurance company (Borman, 1973), clerical personnel (Palef and Stewart, 1971), and production foremen in car assembly plants (Hellervik, Dunnette and Arvey, 1971). Job behaviours are elicited from the observations of those familiar with a job using four to six workshop sessions. Subsequently, job categories or dimensions are devised and incidents assigned to them.

Advantages and disadvantages

The advantages of the Critical Incident Technique are:

(a) *Identification of important task components.* By definition the technique should identify parts of a task or job which are important and therefore form part of a training programme.
(b) *Identification of training needs.* A corollary of the previous point is that those components which are judged as critical because performance was ineffective automatically become the needs of a training programme.

Its disadvantages are:

(a) *Incompleteness.* The components identified are not exhaustive. Any training programme will require details of other components of the task or job which are not judged as critical, but still require inclusion in order for the content of training to be exhaustive.

(b) *Expert analysts are required.* As HTA, the Critical Incident Technique is not as straightforward and easy to apply as might appear at first sight. Definition of what constitutes a critical incident or effective/ineffective behaviour requires careful definition. Further, trained observers are needed who sample adequately the different activities involved in a job or task.

6.3 TASK INVENTORIES

Task inventories or task banks are used to analyse work in a range of jobs in a specific context or organisation. They consist of a list of tasks or task statements which are rated by those familiar with a job (typically job incumbents) using such scales as applicability, difficulty, time spent, etc. In essence a task inventory is a similar type of analysis technique as a job analysis questionnaire, for example, McCormick's Position Analysis Questionnaire. However, there are two main differences. Firstly, a task inventory is more specifically targeted at a range of jobs in a particular context (e.g. jobs in the US Air Force). Therefore, different task inventories exist which have been developed for different contexts and applications. Secondly, task inventories include a few hundred up to even a few thousand task statements. Not surprisingly the high development costs of task inventories have to be justified not only by an increase in the quality of job related information obtained but also by the continued use of such an inventory over several years.

A well-known task inventory was developed in the US Air Force from the early 1960s onwards (e.g. Christal, 1972, 1974; Morsch and Archer, 1967; Morsch, Madden and Christal, 1961). An example of some task statements from the task inventory for the airman supply career field is given in Table 6.4. Task statements are organised under broader duties.

Task inventories have been used in various contexts: Hemphill (1960), cited by Morgan (1972), used a 594 item inventory to analyse the content of managerial jobs; Patrick, Spurgeon and Sparrow (1982) developed a list of 1047 system components in conjunction with 12 maintenance actions to survey the training requirements of instrument technicians. Gael (1983) used a task inventory approach named the Work Performance Survey System (WPSS), which was developed at the American Telephone and Telegraph Company.

Table 6.4 Examples of duty and task statements from the Job Inventory for the Airman Supply Career Field (cited by Morgan, 1972)

Duty A	*Organising and Planning*
Tasks 1	Recommend policy revisions
2	Develop or revise the organisation of the section
3	Determine personnel requirements
Duty E	*Supervising Performance of Work*
Tasks 1	Supervise identifying and determining condition and status of property items (ref. Duty F)
2	Supervise resolving supply inspection problems (ref. Duty G)
Duty G	*Resolving Supply Inspection Problems*
Tasks 1	Request identification information for property that cannot be identified
2	Recommend assignment of issue codes and disposition of unidentified property items
3	Consult with technical specialists regarding the condition and status of property items received

Table 6.5

Task title		1	2	3	4
A10	Develop and improve work methods and procedures	53.55	0.91	0.49	63.84
A5	Assure the availability of equipment and supplies	42.64	1.06	0.45	67.57
A21	Plan reports for the section	32.99	0.99	0.33	79.45

1: Cumulative sum of average percent time spent by all members.
2: Average percent time spent by all members.
3: Average percent time spent by members performing.
4: Percent members performing.

Typically, task inventories are used for wide-ranging personnel purposes, which include the development of job descriptions and training needs, comparison of jobs and training content, monitoring of changing job content and job evaluation. One appealing feature of the task inventory approach is that the resulting data can be stored and manipulated by computer-based statistical packages. The Comprehensive Occupational Data Analysis Programs (CODAP) were developed to analyse the task inventory used by the US Air Force. These programs perform both simple and complex manipulations of task statements

Table 6.6 A summary of the maintenance actions undertaken by instrument technicians (Patrick et al., 1982)

Instrument technician maintenance actions	Systems component group
Design (or modify)	Relays Vacuum gauges Valve operating devices Valves
Calibrate	Converters Counters
Design (or modify), diagnose	Temperature controllers Temperature instrumentation
Build, calibrate	Resistors
Calibrate, diagnose	Switches
Design (or modify), calibrate, diagnose	Timers
Calibrate, adjust, test	Clocks
Design (or modify), build, calibrate, diagnose	Chart recorders Magnetic recorders
Design (or modify), calibrate, diagnose, adjust	Pump accessories Pumps
Design (or modify) build, calibrate, diagnose, adjust	Programmable controllers Programmers
Design (or modify), build, calibrate, diagnose, repair	Semi-conductor devices
Diagnose, adjust, test, repair, use	Electric calibrators Electric meters
Design (or modify), build, calibrate, diagnose, adjust, repair	Power supplies
Design (or modify), build, install, calibrate, diagnose, adjust, repair	Pressure and vacuum system hardware Pressure controllers Pressure gauges Pressure transducers

rated on a relative time spent scale. (Christal, 1974, argued that relative time spent was the most appropriate and reliable measure of task performance.) These analyses included the calculation of inter-rater agreement, correlations, regression and different types of averaging and the clustering of individuals and groups of individuals. For example, the output of part of the job description for journeyman medical laboratory specialist ($N=394$) details the percentage of group members performing the task, the average percentage of time spent by members performing it and the average percentage time spent by all members etc. A sample output is given in Table 6.5.

The task inventory developed by Patrick et al. (1982) was designed to analyse the training requirements of instrument personnel in the cement and cement products industry. A checklist of 1047 system components was identified in collaboration with experts from the industry. Twelve maintenance actions were defined which might apply to the maintenance of each system component. These extended the maintenance distinctions proposed by Frederickson and Freer (1978), and were: design (or modify), build, install, calibrate, inspect, diagnose, adjust, replace, test, service, repair and apply. The task inventory was given to experts who rated the different maintenance actions performed by instrument personnel in the different sectors of the industry (e.g. precast concrete, gypsum, cement, asbestos-cement). It was then possible to identify the varying training requirements of different instrument personnel. Differences existed in both the system components used and the type of maintenance action required. An example of a consolidated description of the maintenance actions of an instrument technician in the cement industry is given in Table 6.6.

The development of task inventories

Various guidelines are available concerning the development of task inventories (Gael, 1983; McCormick, 1979; Melching and Borcher, 1973; Morsch and Archer, 1967) although as McCormick observed guidelines tend to specify *what* has to be accomplished rather than *how* to do it. McCormick discussed nine steps in the development of a task inventory:

1. Define scope of performance situation.
2. Locate written sources of activity statements.
3. Develop preliminary inventory.
4. Review preliminary inventory.
5. Prepare revised draft of inventory.
6. Select scales to be used.
7. Administer a pilot inventory.
8. Print inventory.
9. Administer inventory.

The process of development is iterative. Task statements and their accompanying rating scales are developed and reviewed with respect to their clarity, accuracy and coverage of activities in the area to be sampled. Our prescriptions concerning the development of training objectives (Section 4.5) can also be applied to the development of task statements in an inventory. One issue that is notoriously problematic is the level of description used to describe a task. On the one hand, global task statements will not be useful for training purposes, whilst statements of the type "push lever X" will produce an absurdly large and unmanageable task inventory. The level of description should be dictated by the range of jobs to be covered and the applications of the task inventory data. It is imperative that careful consideration is given to these issues before the inventory is developed, since level of description cannot be modified subsequently without a further development process, which will be costly. A second issue, which is not easily resolved, is the rating scale to be used with the task statement, such as relative time spent, applicability, frequency of occurrence. An applicability scale is often useful, although the selection of other scales depends upon their psychometric aspects and their relative merits to the applications envisaged.

The reader should conclude that there are no precise technical guidelines for developing task inventories. Care and common sense should suffice.

Advantages and disadvantages of task inventories

The advantages are:

(a) *Identification of training needs.* It is possible to identify similarities and differences in training needs for different jobs or groups of jobs. The task statements will provide information which can be translated into training objectives and elaborated into training content.

(b) *Easy storage, manipulation and analysis of task inventory data.* Task inventory statements can be presented and analysed by computer. This provides various advantages. Given the large number of task statements in such inventories, they are ideally suited to the manipulation and processing power of statistical packages. Different analyses can be carried out on the same data. Also a company or organisation is readily able to readminister and reanalyse a task inventory in order to monitor, for example, changing training requirements as a consequence of technological change. Job descriptions can be updated easily.

The disadvantages are:

(a) *High development costs*. It has been stated that the high cost of development of a task inventory has to be justified on the basis of its range of applications to jobs in a sector of industry, or one large organisation. In addition, use of the same task inventory is necessary for at least a five year period, in order to repay development costs.

(b) *Level of description of task statements*. A task inventory has one level of description as defined by its task statements. This level of description will not provide optimal discriminatory power for all applications.

(c) *Revision of task inventory*. Inevitably, some task statements will change or become obsolete and new ones will be required. This necessitates revision on a regular basis, with all of the accompanying checks for reliability, validity and utility. Such revisions are difficult and costly.

6.4 WORK SAMPLING AND TRAINABILITY TESTING

Training is expensive and training resources are always limited. Therefore predicting a person's success in training and subsequent job proficiency is an important training issue. How this might be achieved has been the subject of much debate. There has been dissatisfaction with the predictive validity of aptitude tests which are low and in the region of 0.30 (Ghiselli, 1966). The search for an alternative approach was stimulated by the suggestion that higher validities might be achieved if the measures being used as predictors were as similar as possible to criterion behaviour, i.e. to training or job performance (Wernimont and Campbell, 1968). Similarly, Asher and Sciarrino (1974) argued that prediction will increase with, what they termed, the point-to-point correspondence between the predictor and criterion space. In other words, prediction will improve as the number of common elements between the trainability assessment and the criterion to be predicted increases.

Work sample tests and trainability tests have been developed in which a sample of job or task behaviours are administered to potential trainees or job incumbents. These tests involve a sample of task elements or behaviours which occur in performance of the actual task or job. The distinguishing feature between a work sample and a trainability test is that the latter additionally involves some training on these task elements. Typically performance in a trainability test is assessed during or at the end of a mini-training period. Unfortunately, in the literature this distinction is often not reflected in the terms used. For example, some tests which are referred to as work sample tests are sometimes administered during training (e.g. Gordon, 1967; Gordon and Kleiman, 1976).

From a training perspective the main interest of this work is to assess trainability, i.e. to select people who will most benefit from training. This will reduce training costs and also avoid the difficulty of rejecting individuals who are unsuccessful in training (although with a properly designed training programme the latter should not happen). Alternatively different training programmes may be required for those who differ in their trainability estimates. In this way more resources can be directed at those who most require them. Hence training can be tailored more to the needs of individual trainees.

The criterion of trainability is the trainee's success as judged either by an assessment at the end of the full training programme or by performance of the actual job. Both can be measured in various ways including results from training assessments, instructors' ratings, supervisors' evaluation of job proficiency and labour turnover. In a review of the literature, Asher and Sciarrino (1974) compared *motor* and *verbal* work sample tests in predicting success in training and job proficiency. A motor work sample was defined as involving some physical manipulation whereas a verbal one covered "people-oriented or language-oriented" issues. The authors summarised their findings as follows:

1. When job proficiency was the criterion, realistic motor work sample tests had the highest validity coefficients second only to biographical information. Verbal work sample tests were not as high as the motor but they were in the top half of the predictors.
2. When the criterion was success in training, verbal work sample tests were more powerful in predicting success in training than in forecasting job proficiency. Verbal work sample tests had substantially more significant validity coefficients than the motor when there was a training criterion (Asher and Sciarrino, 1974, p. 529).

The superiority of verbal work samples in predicting training success is illustrated in Figure 6.6. Robertson and Kandola (1982) suggested that the distinction between verbal and motor work sample tests made by Asher and Sciarrino was somewhat crude. They proposed four categories of work sample: psychomotor (the same as Asher and Sciarrino's motor category); individual decision-making; job-related knowledge; and group decision-making. They analysed the correlations between the type of work sample test and different criteria of trainability using data from over 60 studies. Four criteria of trainability were job performance, job progress, success at training and another, typically larger, work sample test. The results (Table 6.7), indicated that job-related information was a reasonably good predictor of success in training (median = 0.50), whereas psychomotor tests had the highest correlation with job performance (median = 0.44). (It should be remembered that a correlation of 0.50 indicates that only 25% of the variation in performance of the criterion can be predicted by the work sample test.)

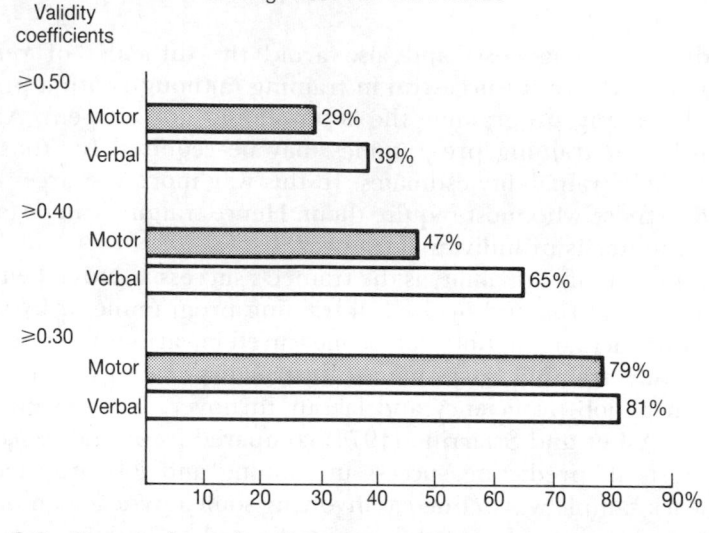

Figure 6.6 Proportion of validity coefficients for motor versus verbal work samples when the criterion was success in training (Asher and Sciarrino, 1974).

Table 6.7 The relationships between different work sample tests and different criteria. From a review by Robertson and Kandola, (1982)

	Type of criterion			
Type of test	Job performance	Job progress	Training	Work sample
Psychomotor				
Median	0.44	–	0.38	0.49
Number of coefficients	16	–	52	10
Job-related information				
Median	0.21	–	0.50	–
Number of coefficients	11	–	14	–
Situational decision-making				
Median	0.28	0.28	0.25	0.75
Number of coefficients	26	11	9	7
Group discussion				
Median	0.35	0.33	–	–
Number of coefficients	10	16	–	–

In the UK, a number of studies have been concerned with what has been termed trainability testing. These have been reviewed by Robertson and Downs (1979). The initial impetus for these studies was an increasing number of redundancies in the late 1960s and 1970s, rapid technological change and the need to predict whether older trainees (i.e. defined as over 35 years of age!) would benefit from retraining. Studies of trainability testing summarised by Robertson and Downs (1979), are listed in Table 6.8. All of the jobs for which trainability tests were devised fell into the psychomotor category. For example, trainability tests for the jobs of carpentry and electronic assembly involved making half-lap T joints and soldering joints respectively. The time between trainability testing and measurement of training success varied from a few days to six months. The criterion of training success involved either errors during performance or instructor ratings or both. Out of 21 correlations between trainability score and error measures, 13 were statistically significant although only three of these were greater than 0.5 (Table 6.8). Out of 24 correlations between trainability score and rating of training success, 20 were significant, of which ten were over 0.5 (Table 6.8). The trainability tests were therefore more predictive of rated success in training than errors committed during training. More recently, Robertson and Downs (1989) have reported, using meta-analysis procedures, that the predictive validity of trainability studies decreases as the interval after training increases, particularly when this is more than one year.

In the US the same approach has been used by Siegel and colleagues and named "miniature job training" (e.g. Seigel, 1983; Seigel and Bergman, 1975; Siegel and Wiesen, 1977). The study by Siegel (1983) illustrates the miniature job training approach and also some of the problems facing studies of trainability. One thousand and thirty-four male personnel who had enlisted at the Apprentice School, Naval Training Center, San Diego during 1978 were used in the study. Nine miniature job training and evaluation situations were developed which had a "high degree of correspondence with actual tasks of Navy personnel". These training/test situations were:

(a) Reading the course of two ships.
(b) Understanding and troubleshooting a simulated electronic chemical pumping system.
(c) Identifying the name and use of objects.
(d) Time sharing between a vigilance task and a pipe assembly task.
(e) Inspecting and sorting good and defective items.
(f) Recording ships speeds and headings.
(g) Working in groups.
(h) Working with an orthographic drawing to produce an object.
(i) Relating diagrams with objects.

These tests were group administered to naval ratings who were seamen, firemen and airmen. Success in the job was evaluated after nine and 18

Table 6.8 A review of results from trainability test studies (Robertson and Downs, 1979)

Job	Test piece	Criterion	Follow-up period	No. in study[a]	Correlation coefficients TT and criterion		Comments and additional points	Reference
					Error	Rating		
Carpentry	Half lap T joint	Training success	6 mo	228	—	—	Predicted well for men 35 yr. or more, $\chi^2 = 51.83$***	Downs (1968)
Welding (electric arc)	Six straight runs on mild steel	Training success	26 wk	112	—	—	Predicted well for men 35 yr. or more, $\chi^2 = 20.51$***	Downs (1968)
Sewing machining	Joining two pieces to make an open bag Three identical bags Overlock machine	Training success	6 wk	82	0.31**	0.51***	No significant differences between overseas and British applicants	Downs (1970)
Sewing machining	Joining two pieces to make an open bag Three identical bags Lockstitch machine	Training success	4 wk	73	0.33**	0.56***	Ninety-one applicants given the test on two different machines, overlock and lockstitch; both rating and error scores correlated beyond 0.001 level	Downs (1973)
		On-the-job success	13 wk	65	0.36**	0.69***		
		On-the-job success	26 wk	55	0.21	0.45***		
Sewing machining	Joining pieces of cloth Lockstitch machine Overlock machine Linking machine	Assessment by instructors of trainees' speed, quality, adaptability, and attitude	4 wk	(1134) 46 77 38	— — —	0.39** 0.48*** 0.78***	Applicants with low scores less likely to turn up for training and more likely to leave in first month	Knitting, Lace and Net Industry Training Board, (1976).
Fork truck operating	Drive truck round a drum and pick up a pallet; place pallet in marked area and reverse truck back round drum to start	Error score on operating test at end of training	3/5 days	(164)			Predictive for young and old Previous experience of car driving not significantly related to TT or criteria	Downs (1972)

Trade	Task	Criterion	Time	n	Correlation		Notes	Reference
					...memory component in TT			
	Quality				0.26	0.37**		
	Speed				0.03	0.30		
	On the job:							
	Speed		6 wk	57	0.23	0.49**		
	Quality				0.00	0.20		
	Versatility				0.21	0.37*		
Dentistry	Cavity preparation in casein teeth	Test piece after operative techniques course and exam	6 mo	42	0.61***	0.52***	Research being replicated	Deubert et al. (1975)
Metal using sheet	Marking out a metal sheet	Phase tests	3 mo	51	0.43**	0.09	No significant correlations after 1 yr (n = 20)	Smith and Downs (1975)
Fitting	Cutting metal shape accurately	Phase tests	3 mo	34	0.38*	0.38*	No significant correlations after 1 yr (n = 19)	Smith and Downs (1975)
Electrical work	Wiring a circuit	Phase test	3 mo	49	0.45**	0.42**	No significant correlations after 1 yr (n = 8)	Smith and Downs (1975)
Welding (electric arc)	Single run on mild steel	Training success	3 wk	33	0.02	0.32	Data from long follow-up period being collected	Robertson (1978)
Carpentry	Half-lap T joint	Training success	3 wk	26	0.42*	0.81***	Data from longer follow-up period being collected	Robertson (1978)
Brick laying	Laying bricks in missing section of partly built wall	Training success	3 wk	37	0.43**	0.35*	Data from longer follow-up period being collected	Robertson (1978)
Center lathe turning	Set up machine and produce small component	Training success	3 wk	40	0.46**	0.63***	Data from longer follow-up period being collected	Robertson (1978)
Capstan operating	Set up machine and produce small component	Training success	3 wk	34	0.38*	0.62***	Data from longer follow-up period being collected	Robertson (1978)

[a] Numbers in parentheses are the numbers in total study; numbers immediately below them are for single site.

* $p < 0.05$

** $p < 0.01$

*** $p < 0.001$

months by supervisors who rated 34 tasks (derived from standard in-service job descriptions) on a seven-point scale. Not surprisingly return rates were low: 39% and 29% for the nine and 18 month evaluations respectively. In the first follow-up both a total measure and five out of nine of the miniature job training tests correlated significantly with supervisory ratings for both seamen and firemen. In the second follow-up both a total measure and six out of nine and two out of nine tests were correlated significantly with ratings for seamen and firemen respectively. However, the correlations were modest, having medians of 0.14 and 0.24 in the first follow-up study and 0.18 and 0.17 in the second. As Siegel suggested, because only low-aptitude personnel were used, this may have restricted the range of scores and possibly depressed the correlations. In addition, the reliability and validity of supervisors ratings may have been a significant problem as no training was provided in making such ratings. (In another study, Siegel, 1978, examined inter-examiner reliability and validity with encouraging results.) Another criticism of Siegel's study is that the test battery which was given to seamen, firemen and airmen was later reported not to be applicable to the work performed by airmen. An important requirement of any work sample or trainability test is that it is derived from the actual job and this should be guaranteed by a systematic task analysis. It is both unfortunate and surprising that not only Siegel's study but also the majority of studies of work sample and trainability testing have not used any analysis techniques.

The work sample, trainability and miniature job training approach has demonstrated modest but encouraging results. However, such assessments have been performed primarily for jobs and tasks of a psychomotor nature. One criticism is that even in these situations, no systematic guidelines have been developed which indicate how to: (a) carry out a job or task analysis and (b) select parts of the analysis to form the basis of the trainability test. Both of these important activities are carried out subjectively, which is unsatisfactory. In tasks with large cognitive components, these problems will become more acute, as it will be less possible to develop an appropriate test intuitively based on a sample of the job or task, as say in a bricklayer's job. How does one analyse and select parts of a complex fault-finding task in order to develop a trainability test? This question also raises two theoretical issues. The first is that presumably the trainability test which is developed has to be as representative as possible of the different psychological requirements of the task (or job). The extent to which it is not so, will be reflected in reduced predictive power. A work sample or trainability test can be viewed as providing the trainee with a simulation of part of the task. This simulation necessarily omits certain features of the task. How to decide which features to omit and which ones to include is a major problem, not only in the development of trainability tests but also in the development of simulations for training purposes (see pp. 489–491). The second issue is that different abilities are required at different stages of learning a task or a sample of it. Fleishman and Hempel (1955) demonstrated that general abilities are important early in learning a task, whereas task-specific factors are important later. Hence the time at which trainability is assessed during training is critical and will determine which abilities are tested. Trainees may therefore vary in their trainability assessments according to when these assessments were made. Whilst the trainability approach has some appeal, further research and development is needed in order for the assessment of trainability to become standard practice, even for training the more traditional perceptual-motor skills.

Attitudinal effects

An important and neglected issue in training is the attitudes of the trainees and their expectations concerning the job or task to be performed. The attitudes of trainees will affect performance both during training and subsequently in the job whilst attitudes in turn will be influenced by the experiences gained during training and in the job.

There is some evidence that a subsidiary effect of assessing trainability is an improvement in trainees' attitudes, motivation etc. Some relevant studies have been summarised by Robertson and Kandola (1982). They cited a study by Cascio and Phillips (1979) in which applicants for promotion who were selected by work sample tests had fewer complaints than those selected by conventional tests. In addition, it was claimed that there was a considerable reduction in turnover which coincided with the introduction of work sample tests. Such tests may provide the trainee with more realistic expectations concerning a job and therefore avoid subsequent disappointment which may lead to resignation. This is consistent with evidence that realistic job previews reduce subsequent turnover (Ilgen and Seely, 1974; Wanous, 1977).

Gordon and Kleiman (1976) compared work sample tests with an intelligence test in predicting trainability for basic police work. The criterion of trainability was the total of each recruits' score on various graded exercises administered during a 20 week induction training course. Interest centred upon one general test of a recruits "ability to become oriented towards law enforcement" which was administered after two weeks of the training programme. Prediction of trainability was better with this work sample measure than with the Otis–Lennon Mental Ability Test. The authors suggested that the face validity of the work sample tests may have provided encouragement for those who were interested in and motivated to perform the job, hence producing a higher validity coefficient.

REFERENCES

Annett, J. and Duncan, K.D. (1967). Task analysis and training design. *Occupational Psychology*, **41**, 211–221.

Annett, J., Duncan, K.D., Stammers, R.B. and Gray, M.J. (1971). *Task analysis*. Training Information No 6. London: HMSO.

Asher, J.J. and Sciarrino, J.A. (1974). Realistic work sample tests: A review. *Personnel Psychology*, **27**, 519–533.

Borman, W.C. (1973). *First line supervisor validation study*. Minneapolis: Personnel Decisions Inc.

Campbell, J.P., Dunnette, M.D., Arvey, R.D. and Hellervik, L.W. (1973). The development and evaluation of behaviourally based rating scales. *Journal of Applied Psychology*, **57**, 15–22.

Cascio, W.F. and Phillips, N.F. (1979). Performance testing. A rose among thorns? *Personnel Psychology*, **32**, 751–766.

Christal, R.E. (1972). New directions in the Air Force occupational research program. USAF, AFHRL. Texas: Personnel Research Division, Lackland Air Force Base.

Christal, R.E. (1974). The United States Air Force occupational research project. Technical Report AFHRL-TR-73–75. Texas: Airforce Human Resources Laboratory, Occupational Research Division.

Deubert, L.W., Smith, M.C., Downs S., Jenkins, L.C.B. and Berry, D.C. (1975). The selection of dental students: A pilot study of an assessment of manual ability by practical tests. *British Dental Journal*, **139**, 357–361.

Downs, S. (1968). Selecting the older trainee. A pilot study of trainability tests. *National Institute of Industrial Psychology Bulletin*, 19–26.

Downs, S. (1970). Predicting training potential. *Personnel Management*, **2**, 26–28.

Downs, S. (1972). Trainability assessments: Fork truck operators. Research Paper SL4. Cambridge: Industrial Training Research Unit.

Downs, S. (1973). Trainability assessments: Sewing machinists. Research Paper SL6. Cambridge: Industrial Training Research Unit.

Duncan, K.D. (1972). Strategies for analysis of the task. In Hartley, J. (Ed.) *Strategies for programmed instruction: An educational technology*. London: Butterworths.

Dunnette, M.D. (1976). Aptitudes, abilities, and skills. In Dunnette, M.D. (Ed.) *Handbook of industrial and organizational psychology*. Chicago: Rand McNally (Reprinted in 1983 by Wiley.)

Flanagan, J.C. (1954). The critical incident technique. *Psychological Bulletin*, **51**, 327–358.

Fleishman, E.A. and Hempel, W.E. Jr (1955). The relation between abilities and improvement with practice in a visual discrimination reaction task. *Journal of Experimental Psychology*, **49**, 301–312.

Frederickson, E.W. and Freer, D.R. (1978). Basic electronics skills and knowledge. Research Note 79–5. Alexandria, VA: US Army Research Institute.

Gael, S. (1983). *Job analysis. A guide to assessing work activities.* San Francisco: Jossey-Bass.

Ghiselli, E.E. (1966). *The validity of occupational aptitude tests.* New York: John Wiley and Sons.

Gordon, L.V. (1967). Clinical psychometric and work-sample approaches in the prediction of success in Peace Corps training. *Journal of Applied Psychology,* **51**(2), 111–119.

Gordon, M.E. and Kleiman, L.S. (1976). The prediction of trainability using a work sample test and an aptitude test: A direct comparison. *Personnel Psychology,* **29**, 243–253.

Hellervik, L.W., Dunnette, M.D. and Arvey, R.D. (1971). *Development and pretesting of behaviourally defined job performance measures for foremen in Ford Motor Company's transmission and chassis and automative assembly divisions.* Minneapolis: Personnel Decisions Inc.

Hemphill, J.K. (1960). *Dimensions of executive positions.* Research Monograph 89. Ohio: The Ohio State University, Bureau of Business Research.

Ilgen, D.R. and Seely, W. (1974). Realistic expectations as an aid in reducing voluntary resignations. *Journal of Applied Psychology,* **59**, 452–455.

Kay, B.R. (1959). Key factors in effective foreman behaviour. *Personnel,* **36**, 25–31.

Kirchner, W.K. and Dunnette, M.D. (1957). Identifying the critical factors in successful salesmanship. *Personnel,* **34**, 54–59.

Knitting, Lace and Net Industry Training Board (1976). Validation of trainability tests: Report on 1973/5 research project. Nottingham: Knitting, Lace and Net Industry Training Board.

McCormick, E.J. (1979). *Job analyses: Methods and applications.* New York: Amacom.

Melching, M.H. and Borcher, S.D. (1973). Procedures for constructing and using task inventories. Center for Vocational and Technical Education. Research and Development Series No. 91. Columbus, Ohio: The Ohio State University.

Morgan, T. (1972). Occupational description and classification. Report RE-D-19. UK: Air Transport and Travel Industry Training Board.

Morsch, J.E. and Archer, W.B. (1967). Procedural guide for conducting occupational surveys in the United States Air Force. Technical Report PRL-TR-67–11, Lackland Air Force Base, Texas: US Air Force.

Morsch, J.E., Madden, J.M. and Christal, R.E. (1961). Job analysis in the United States Air Force. Technical Report WADD-TR-61–113. Lackland Air Force Base, Texas: US Air Force.

Palef, S. and Stewart, C.P. (1971). Development of a rating scale. *Studies in Personnel Psychology,* **3**, 7–20.

Patrick, J., Spurgeon, P., Barwell, F. and Sparrow, J. (1980). Grouping of skills – redeployment by upgrading to technicians. Phase III. Report submitted to the Training Services Division of the Manpower Services Commission.

Patrick, J., Spurgeon, P. and Shepherd, A. (1986). *A guide to task analysis: Applications of hierarchical methods.* Birmingham: Occupational Services Ltd.

Patrick, J., Spurgeon, P. and Sparrow J. (1982). The selection and training requirements of instrumentation personnel in the context of technological change. Report submitted to the Ceramics, Glass and Mineral Products Industry Training Board. Birmingham: Applied Psychology Department, University of Aston in Birmingham.

Robertson, I.T. (1978). A job learning approach to the prediction of performance: An attempt to examine the value of trainability tests. Paper presented at the Annual Occupational Psychology Conference of the British Psychological Society. Cambridge. January.

Robertson, I.T. and Downs, S. (1979). Learning and the prediction of performance:

Development of trainability testing in the United Kingdom. *Journal of Applied Psychology*, **64**(1), 42–50.

Robertson, I.T. and Downs, S. (1989). Work-sample tests of trainability: A meta-analysis. *Journal of Applied Psychology*, **74**, 402–410.

Robertson, I.T. and Kandola, R.S. (1982). Work sample tests: Validity, adverse impact and applicant reaction. *Journal of Occupational Psychology*, **55**, 171–183.

Shepherd, A. (1976). An improved tabular format for task analysis. *Journal of Occupational Psychology*, **49**, 93–104.

Shepherd, A. (1985). Hierarchical task analysis and training decisions. *Programmed Learning and Educational Technology*, **22**(3), 162–176.

Shepherd, A and Duncan, K.D. (1980). Analysing a complex planning task. In Duncan, K.D., Gruneberg, M.M. and Wallis, D. (Eds) *Changes in working life*. Chichester: John Wiley.

Siegel, A.I. (1978). Miniature job training and evaluation as a selection/classification device. *Human Factors*, **20**(2), 189–200.

Siegel, A.I. (1983). The miniature job training and evaluation approach: Additional findings. *Personnel Psychology*, **36**, 41–56.

Siegel, A.I. and Bergman, B.A. (1975). A job learning approach to performance prediction. *Personnel Psychology*, **28**, 325–339.

Siegel, A.I. and Wiesen, J.P. (1977). Experimental procedures for the classification of Naval Personnel. NPRDCTR-77-3. San Diego: Navy Personnel Research and Development Center.

Smith, M.C. (1972). Trainability assessment: Electronic assemblers. Research Paper SL5. Cambridge: Industrial Training Research Unit.

Smith, M.C. and Downs, S. (1975). Trainability assessments for apprentice selection in shipbuilding. *Journal of Occupational Psychology*, **48**, 39–43.

Stammers, R. and Patrick, J. (1975). *The psychology of training*. London: Methuen.

Wanous, J.P. (1977). Organizational entry: Newcomers moving from outside to inside. *Psychological Bulletin*, **84**, 601–618.

Wernimont, P.F. and Campbell, J. (1968). Signs, samples and criteria. *Journal of Applied Psychology*, **52**, 372–376.

CHAPTER 7
Psychological approaches to analysis

The development of a training programme requires some psychological analysis of the job or task to be trained. Such an analysis can serve various purposes. It can be used to select people for training; identify psychological features of tasks which have implications for training design; and identify the skill or expertise which needs to be developed by appropriate training content.

The basis of most psychological analyses is the use of a classification scheme or taxonomy which categorises aspects of the task. The development of such taxonomies has a long tradition in psychology. Different taxonomies have been developed for various purposes although only a few of these have been directed towards training. For a discussion of the general principles underlying taxonomies and a description of some of those included in this chapter, the reader should consult Fleishman and Quaintance (1984).

Taxonomies are evaluated against several criteria. R.B. Miller argued that the most important criterion was a taxonomy's utility. Hence we should not be impressed by the elegance of a taxonomy but rather by how relevant and useful it is for training purposes. In a review of taxonomies for training, Annett and Duncan (1967) suggested three further criteria: taxonomic categories should be mutually exclusive, exhaustive and each should have different training implications. Duncan (1972) pointed out that the criterion of exclusiveness is approached by the careful formal definition of categories whilst the criterion of exhaustiveness is either examined by massive surveys of tasks in the literature or by inclusion of a catch-all category. The remaining criterion that categories should have differential training implications is the most important and problematic. Taxonomies of different types of learning have the strongest claim that their categories lead to different training recommendations. These include Gagné's well-known taxonomy of intellectual skills and Merrill's Component Display Theory, both of which are discussed in Section 8.3. With other taxonomies, it is left to the analyst's ingenuity to develop sensible training recommendations on the basis of the categories distinguished.

One of the most influential and famous taxonomies was developed by Bloom and colleagues in *A Taxonomy of Educational Objectives, Handbook 1:*

Cognitive Domain (Bloom, 1956) and *A Taxonomy of Educational Objectives, Handbook II: Affective Domain* (Krathwohl, Bloom and Masia, 1964). The taxonomy was divided into three domains. The cognitive domain

> includes those objectives which deal with the recall or recognition of knowledge and the development of intellectual abilities and skills (Bloom, 1956, p. 7).

The affective domain

> includes objectives which describe changes in interest, attitudes, and values, and the development of appreciations and adequate adjustment (p. 7).

The psychomotor domain

> is the manipulative or motor-skill area (p. 7).

The categories for the psychomotor domain were devised subsequently by Harrow (1972). The goal of Bloom's taxonomy was to help curriculum developers to specify objectives "so that it becomes easier to plan learning experiences and prepare evaluation devices". The taxonomy certainly led to increased discussion of what is and should be covered by education and how this might be tested.

Bloom's cognitive domain is divided into two parts: knowledge, and intellectual abilities and skills (Table 7.1). This distinction is similar to the more recent one made by Anderson (1980), between declarative and procedural knowledge. Each of the six categories in the cognitive domain is defined with examples, illustrative objectives and test items. The meaning of some categories is ambiguous. For example, "application" is defined as "the use of abstractions in particular and concrete situations". Bloom proceeded to suggest that "application" involves the use of an abstraction to solve a problem correctly. Such definitions are not easy to interpret. Also critics have argued that there are gaps and overlap between the categories (e.g. Gagné, 1965; Rowntree, 1977). Bloom argued that the categories were arranged in a hierarchical manner from knowledge (lowest) to evaluation (highest). Higher order categories subsumed lower order ones such that, for example, category 2 (comprehension) involves categories 1 and 2 whilst category 3 (application) involves categories 1, 2 and 3, etc. Two dimensions which were claimed to underpin this hierarchical ordering were "simple to complex" and "concrete to abstract".

This chapter and Section 8.3 deal with different psychological approaches to analysis of a task or subject matter. Three types of taxonomy are discussed, which cover information processing (Section

Table 7.1 Categories in the cognitive domain (adapted from Bloom, 1956)

Knowledge
1. Knowledge
   1.1 Knowledge of specifics
      1.1.1 Knowledge of terminology
      1.1.2 Knowledge of specific facts
   1.2 Knowledge of ways and means of dealing with specifics
      1.2.1 Knowledge of conventions
      1.2.2 Knowledge of trends and sequences
      1.2.3 Knowledge of classifications and categories
      1.2.4 Knowledge of criteria
      1.2.5 Knowledge of methodology
   1.3 Knowledge of the universals and abstractions in a field
      1.3.1 Knowledge of principles and generalisations
      1.3.2 Knowledge of theories and structures

Intellectual Abilities and Skills
2. Comprehension
   2.1 Translation
   2.2 Interpretation
   2.3 Extrapolation
3. Application
4. Analysis
   4.1 Analysis of elements
   4.2 Analysis of relationships
   4.3 Analysis of organisational principles
5. Synthesis
   5.1 Production of a unique communication
   5.2 Production of a plan or proposed set of operations
   5.3 Derivation of a set of abstract relations
6. Evaluation
   6.1 Judgements in terms of internal evidence
   6.2 Judgements in terms of external criteria

7.1), ability requirements (Section 7.2) and types of learning (Section 8.3). More recently analyses of expertise, particularly in work situations, have been carried out by cognitive psychologists. These are subsumed under the label of "representation" (i.e. knowledge representation). Typically, these analyses are more ad hoc but more detailed than those which involve the use of standard taxonomies. This topic is discussed, with examples, in Section 7.3.

Studies concerning information processing and ability approaches to human performance are rooted in different areas of psychology. The information processing approach is associated with cognitive (formerly experimental) psychology, whilst the ability requirements approach is associated with the study of individual differences. Two major differences between these two approaches are the units of analysis used and the mechanisms proposed to explain performance. The information processing approach focuses on cognitive processes and is more fine-grained, whereas the ability requirements approach is typically more global, since it examines the requirements of various tasks in the wider job context. The former approach explains performance in terms of learning and transfer mechanisms whereas the latter emphasises the mediation of a person's abilities, aptitudes and interests.

These two perspectives are more closely linked than might be supposed. Two insightful papers by Ferguson, written over 30 years ago, discuss the relationship between the concepts of learning, transfer and ability in psychological terms (Ferguson, 1954, 1956). He points out that training studies are concerned with changes in "ability" to perform certain tasks, although this term normally refers to relatively stable performance on standard psychological tests. Ferguson noted that an ability can be viewed as a manifestation of a previously overlearned behaviour which has reached the limit of improvement. Hence in training situations, ability refers to the fact that some prior overlearned pattern of behaviour may transfer positively or negatively to task performance. Therefore, a person with a high ability has a "transfer potential" to move successfully between similar tasks, compared with a person who is low in that ability. Thus abilities can be viewed as a means of identifying transfer potential. A training situation is itself a specific case of transfer where the trainee adapts previously learned skills, some of which will be described by the trainee's pattern of abilities.

Sternberg's work (e.g. 1977) has also emphasised the close relationship between abilities and information processing approaches. He has examined the different information-processing components which contribute to the speed of performing items in conventional intelligence tests such as analogies. A rapprochement between these two approaches is a major step forward in psychology and emphasises that they represent different but complementary psychological approaches to the analysis of a task.

7.1 INFORMATION-PROCESSING APPROACHES

The information-processing paradigm distinguishes between psychological processes occurring during the input, processing and output of information. During analysis of a task, information-processing distinctions can be used to identify the psychological demands of a task, i.e. where performance is likely to be difficult. Performance of a task may make demands at the input, processing or output stages or indeed any combination of them.

A recent study by Reinartz and Reinartz (1989) analysed the nature of operators' activities during simulated nuclear power plant incidents. Retrospective verbal reports were collected during a replay of a team of operators' recorded activities during the simulated incidents. Twenty-three categories were used to classify the overt activities of the operator, (three of these relating to team activities), and an attempt was made to identify the cognitive processes associated with them (see Table 7.2). Many of these cognitive processes fall within the input–processing–output paradigm as illustrated in Table 7.2.

Various information-processing schemes are available to help differentiate cognitive activities. Whilst it is unlikely that any one of these provides the optimal type and level of description for any one analysis, they provide useful starting points. Levine and Teichner (1973) provided an information-theoretic approach which conceptualises the task as a transfer of information between an input and an output which is subject to constraints. These constraints are divided into

> (1) the nature of the constraints that are imposed by the tasks or the restrictions placed on the random sampling of stimulus and response events at the source and at the receiver; (2) the location of the constraint, whether on the input (source) or on the output (receiver); (3) the amount and form of informational redundancy in the stimulus and/or response ensemble; and (4) the relationship between the amount of information in the input and the amount of information in the output (Fleishman and Quaintance, 1984, p. 246).

Some information processing approaches involve the use of a questionnaire which requests information concerning job elements which fall into the input–processing–output paradigm. In this tradition is the Occupation Analysis Inventory (OAI) developed by Cunningham and colleagues (e.g. Cunningham et al., 1983) which has 617 "work elements", some of a technological nature. Similarly, McCormick and colleagues developed the Position Analysis Questionnaire (PAQ) which contains 194 "job elements" many of which reflect an information-processing approach.

Table 7.2 Relating cognitive processes to overt behaviour (Reinartz and Reinartz, 1989)

Cognitive processes	Overt behaviour
Data/information collecting	
Activation	Responding to alarm
Orienting response	
Information seeking	Monitoring
Active attention or hypothesis	Checking
testing	Searching in operating handbook
Incidentally noticing	Requesting status reports*
Information processing	
Identification of system state	Assessment of state*
Interpretation	Monitoring
Evaluation	Checking
Situation assessment	Making a prediction*
Conscious problem solving	Exchange of knowledge*
Knowledge or belief about process state	
Hypothesis and test	
Planning and strategy	
Goal selection	Assessment of state*
Procedure selection	Making a guess*
Generation, evaluation and	Making a suggestion*
selection of alternatives	Searching in operating handbook
Recursion	Making a decision
Working memory and multiple gaols	
Actions	
Execution	Manual action
Execution and monitoring	Manual action suspended
Feedback	Manual action resumed
	Recording plant status
	Checking
	Monitoring
	Carrying out instructions
Team specific: Information distribution, task allocation and management	
Working memory of colleagues'	Bring something to colleague's
goals, priorities and activities	attention*
Evaluation of team value of	Requesting status reports*
information and knowledge	Passing on information*
Periodic newscasting of own goals,	Exchange of knowledge*
priorities and activities	Giving an explanation*
	Making a decision
	Making a suggestion*
	Making a guess*
	Giving instructions*
	Carrying out instructions
	Checking the implementation of
	an instruction

* Those functions which were either totally or predominantly verbal exchanges

Four information-processing approaches are discussed in more detail below:

(a) Miller's 25 Task Functions.
(b) Altman's Motivational, Behavioural and Contextual Domains.
(c) McCormick's Position Analysis Questionnaire.
(d) Sternberg's Componential Metatheory (Sternberg, 1980).

Miller's 25 task functions

R.B. Miller's publications began in the 1950s and they were concerned primarily with problems of task analysis and training. Many of the ideas in his early publications led to the emergence of training as an important area of applied psychology and also profoundly influenced the direction of research into training. Unfortunately, whilst his work remains a rich source of ideas, much has not been tested systematically or translated into guidelines for practitioners. Most of his publications are in technical reports which are not easily accessible. A summary of his work can be found in Fleishman and Quaintance (1984).

Miller (1973), cited by Fleishman and Quaintance (1984), suggested that information about a task can be categorised into four dimensions:

1. *Task content.* This refers to the subject matter of the task and will vary from task to task. Miller was uncertain whether it was possible to differentiate task structure from task content or distinguish between different types of content by factor analytic methods.
2. *Task environment.* This includes the physiological and psychological states of the operator (e.g. stress) and the conditions imposed by all the activities associated with the task (e.g. time sharing).
3. *Level of learning.* Different abilities are required at different stages of practice and qualitative changes occur during practice which have consequences for the design of training (see pp. 39–70 and pp. 241–245). Types of task function (the fourth dimension below) will therefore interact with level of learning.
4. *Task functions.* These are defined by a set of 25 terms, falling into an information processing approach which can be used to describe the cognitive processes occurring during performance of a task (Miller, 1974).

The fourth dimension, regarding task function, has been the subject of sustained interest and development by Miller. Miller (1967) presented an early version of a taxonomy of task functions by asking the question:

what functions would have to be built into a robot to make him behave like a human performing a particular task? In reply he listed eight categories: a concept of purpose, a scanning function, identification of relevant cues, interpretation of cues, short-term memory, long-term memory, decision-making and problem solving and effector response. These categories fit into an input–processing–output paradigm except of course the concept of purpose which he noted would be most difficult to design into a robot. The other categories draw attention to the types of activity involved in performance of a task and the nature of the psychological demands placed on the performer. Eventually, Miller (1974) expanded his scheme to 25 categories which are listed in Table 7.3 with short titles and some further explanation where this is helpful.

Table 7.3   Index of information-processing terms and selected definitions (adapted from Miller, 1974)

MESSAGE	A collection of symbols sent as a meaningful statement. A task message is some collection of signs and symbols which have a meaning to the recipient – that is, have some potential reference to a task action or a context for action. A message is not a function but the unit of information
INPUT SELECT	Selecting what to pay attention to next
FILTER	Straining out what does not matter. Filtering consists of procedures which reduce or eliminate irrelevance and disturbance from messages and message contexts
QUEUE TO CHANNEL	Lining up to get through the gate. These are rules and operations for organising random message arrivals into "waiting lines" so that messages that belong together are grouped together. Restated it is sequencing things to be attended to
DETECT	Is something there?
SEARCH	Looking for something. Search is a form of scan where the identity of the sought object is known. The object may be hidden in a heterogeneous field

– like the needle in the haystack – or it may have to be discriminated from a field of similar objects – such as a face in a crowd

IDENTIFY

What is it and what is its name? One form of identification is the characterising of a message by type of source. A more common usage is the recognition of an object or entity and the application of a label to it

CODE

Translating the same thing from one code to another. Coding is defined as the rules for translating messages in one symbolic form to another symbolic form presumably without loss of information content

INTERPRET

What does it mean?

CATEGORISE

Defining and naming a group of things. Categorisation consists of the rules and operations for classifying objects, phenomena, data or intelligence according to some one or more shared attributes, purposes or implications. The process overlaps identification and interpretation and memory

TRANSMIT

Moving something from one place to another

STORE (LONG-TERM MEMORY)

Keeping something intact for future use

SHORT-TERM MEMORY

Holding something temporarily. Short-term memory, more appropriately called "working memory" may be defined as the rules and facilities for holding in temporary storage messages or parts of messages for use at later times during a task cycle or duty cycle or for combining with other information during the cycle

COUNT

Keeping track of how many

DECIDE/SELECT   Choosing a response to fit the situation. Deciding, by a loose definition, is the choice of a response alternative in a conditional situation. The nature of the choice-making has many variations, ranging from binary choice to either of two unambiguous signals to intuitive decision-making at strategic levels of response

PLAN   Matching resources over time to expectations of needs. This is an important subset of decision-making. It is defined as the rules and facilities for predicting what future sets of conditions will occur and what responses to make to them, and in what order, so that given goals are likely to be achieved. It is the construction of an action path through a set of anticipated circumstances towards an intended goal state. Planning may also be defined as the matching of a set of requirements to a selected set of resources according to a temporal sequence

TEST   Is it what it should be? Testing consists of the rules and procedures for deciding on the integrity or acceptability of a signal, message or mechanism

CONTROL   Changing an action according to plan. Physical control is the process of changing the direction, rate, or magnitude of a physical force that may be acting on objects, processes or symbols. The stimulus may be embedded in a fixed serial order or it may consist of feedback test signals. Symbolic control is found in the source of instruction stating what will be done next with what facility

EDIT   Arranging/correcting things according to rule. Editing is applying rules for arranging and symbolising information in messages according to prescribed formats. An example is a customer giving an order in narrative prose which the clerk translates into the content on an office order form

DISPLAY   Showing something that makes sense. In terms of human tasks "displaying" is the arrangement of messages into formats and symbol patterns for human perception and interpretation – structuring an intended meaning into a communicable representation

ADAPT/LEARN   Making and remembering new responses to a repeat situation. Learning consists of structural modification of the behaviour of a system as the result of experience where the behaviour change carries over from one cycle of operation to another

PURGE   Getting rid of dead stuff. The purge function is made up of rules for eliminating unwanted information. The concept of purge in terms of erasure seems inapplicable to humans. It does have applicability to the problem of the intrusion of responses that are incorrect in a new context

RESET   Getting ready for some different action. In automatic systems, a reset may consist of emptying a counter of contents and returning to zero or purging a program no longer needed from foreground memory; or erasing working data no longer required. The second step in a reset is that of initiating the system for a new task; readying it with different programs and working data. Similar processes occur in the human when terminating a task cycle or shifting from one task to another

GOAL IMAGE   A picture of a task well done. The operator's goal image embodies criteria for terminating a task or segment of work or mission, and terminating it with an experience of some degree of success or failure. The goal image is a mental picture of the conditions that should obtain when a task cycle is completed

---

Miller referred to these task functions as a system vocabulary as he envisaged that they were applicable to both human and nonhuman performance of tasks. Miller acknowledged that application of his taxonomy would depend upon the judgement of an analyst (who was hopefully trained) and that inevitably there would be some ambiguity in the assignment of these psychological categories to task performance. He recommended that the taxonomy be used during analysis of any task. Section 6.1 discusses how Hierarchical Task Analysis progressively redescribes a task into a hierarchical array of subtasks each with an associated plan. Miller's taxonomy could be applied to lower levels of this hierarchy in order to identify the psychological demands of a task and where difficulties are likely to arise. It might be argued that most of the task functions are at least minimally involved in the performance of any task. Therefore the analyst's objective is to identify which task functions are particularly important and problematic in performance of the tasks to be trained. For example, task 1 might depend upon functions A, B, D and E whilst task 2 might use functions B, C and F. For each task to be analysed it is sensible if the relevance of the task functions is considered in the order presented in Table 7.3, since this reflects the input–processing–output sequence. Also, as noted above, the degree to which these functions are involved is likely to vary as a result of the stage of training or level of learning.

Miller's ideas go further than just an identification of task functions. He argued that different functions have different training implications and will therefore form the basis of separate training exercises. However, this link between task functions and their associated training methods is weak and was not made sufficiently explicit. One reason is that it is difficult to specify a training solution which is generalisable such that it applies to a task function irrespective of the specific content or context of the task. Miller (1974) attempted to overcome this problem by introducing the notion of "work strategies" which were defined either as techniques for maximising the information – processing of the performer or the strategies for coping with the demands of the task in the work environment. An attempt was made to identify work strategies for each of the 25 task functions. However, further development work is needed before this approach can be used. As an aside it should be noted that these strategies provide a basis for distinguishing between skilled and unskilled performance with respect to each task function. Some of the best described work strategies are related to the INPUT SELECT function which concerns what is noticed next or paid attention to. These strategies are:

1. Having a mental map of the task cycle and mission well enough in mind that one can 'tag' messages for context outside those of the moment.
2. On occasion, deliberately interrupting preoccupations of the moment to examine overall status, and, thereby possibly modifying criteria of message relevance.

3. Learning that rapidly changing variables require more frequent sampling priority.
4. Remembering to relate status messages to strategic (longer-term) goals, as well as to tactical (short-term) goals.
5. Standardising the maximum intervals when any message source will be sampled.
6. Scanning messages in advance of having to respond to them.
7. Sampling frequently when a resource of uncertain capability is used.
8. Collecting and grouping messages that build up the 'complete' context for a response of large commitment.
9. Giving special priority to garbled messages.

It is of course possible to program training exercises in such a way that the operator is forced to acquire these strategies to compensate for the liabilities he acquires in processing 'normal' messages and normal message sequences. But the operator must acquire sufficient facility with the normal operations that he has enough attention left over for coping with these interruptions to the ordinary flow of events (Miller, 1974, p. 11).

In considering strategies for task performance, Miller (1975) introduced the notion of "task formats" which is similar to the psychological concept of a script or a schema. Formats provide the performer with a means of organising and assimilating information in a form which supports normal performance. However such formats or predispositions also lead to errors when some change in format is required by a new task or by an alteration in an old task. This is evident in Miller's discussion of the EDIT task function (see Table 7.3 for a definition), which was as follows:

Task strategies should aim to provide the editor, insofar as feasible, a structure of output that is compatible with input structure, and its variations. Thus, the waiter in a restaurant offers a menu in which classes of items are listed in the same order in which he sets down the order to the chef. Again where feasible, the editor should be enabled to cope with exceptional conditions not anticipated by his format; this may consist at least of a cell for entering a 'comment'. It is usually difficult for an operator to apply a number of rules at the same time, so he should be taught to sequence (where feasible) the classes of information to which editing rules are applied. Thus, editing a text for the meaning of its content makes it difficult to edit for typographical errors and vice versa. Separate passes with different 'set' (rule prepotency) should be made. If editing time is at a premium, the sequence should be privatized from the most important aspect of editing to the least important according to the recipient's criteria of importance (Miller, 1974, p. 22).

Such notions are familiar ones in cognitive psychology. It is unfortunate that Miller's approach was not pursued sufficiently so that his 25 task functions could be directly linked to both the literature in cognitive psychology, measurement in the work situation, and training solutions with detailed examples. Also to some extent his work can be criticised by the criterion which he himself advocated as being of prime importance: that of utility. To the author's best knowledge, the utility of his list of task functions remains to be demonstrated by research studies in training. Nevertheless some of his ideas into the problems of task analysis were insightful and greatly influenced those working in this area of training.

Altman's motivational, behavioural and contextual domains

Altman (1976) was concerned with the "transferability" of vocational skills and implications for the design of educational programmes. He lamented that confidence in such programmes came from "blind faith, broad subjective impressions, and occasional anecdote" (p. 38) rather than from any systematic analysis of the requirements of the workplace. Like Bloom, he adopted a top-down approach to analysis and divided performance at work into three domains:

> The MOTIVATIONAL domain is concerned with the interests, attitudes, goals and reinforcers which guide the individual's actions.
>
> The BEHAVIOURAL domain is concerned with the sequence and array of processes through which an individual arrives at measurable end performance having practical utility.
>
> The CONTEXTUAL domain is concerned with the performance requirements imposed by the environment as well as the organisational, information, and physical support provided (Altman, 1976, p. 1).

Altman warned that our knowledge within each domain is rudimentary, making it difficult to be strongly prescriptive. The distinctions which Altman made within the motivational and behavioural domains were laudably justified on the basis of the available theoretical and empirical evidence at that time. The behavioural domain is made up of five interacting stages which are consistent with an information processing perspective. These stages are represented in Figure 7.1. Each stage is further sub-divided. For example, intellectual processing takes ideas from other taxonomies such as Bloom's and Gagné's and distinguishes between the following seven types of major intellectual process:

1. Perceptual transfer – "the application of relatively fixed routines for translating perceptual input into response instructions" (Altman, 1976, p. 26).
2. Conceptual processes – "the classification of perceptions as belonging within a particular category where objective characteristics of perceptions within a class may be widely dissimilar" (p. 26).
3. Principle processes – "the delineation and application of relationships among classes of elements (concepts)" (p. 26).

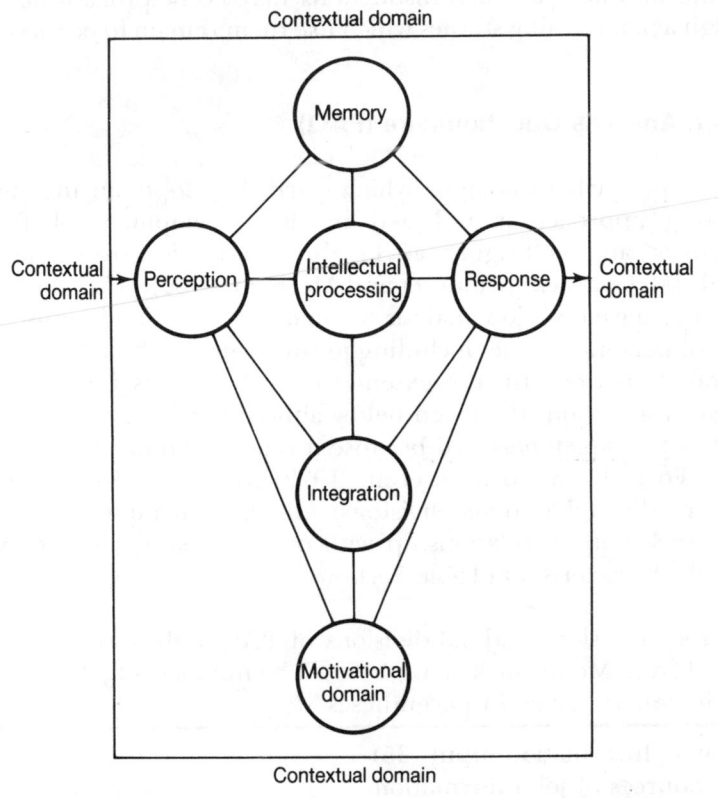

Figure 7.1 Five stages in the behavioural domain and their relationships with the motivational and contextual domains (from Altman, 1976).

4. Discovery – "the generation of new concepts and/or principles which can at least retrospectively, be derived directly from available perceptions and remembered data" (p. 27).
5. Invention – "the development of hypothetical constructs concerning concepts and/or their relationships which cannot be directly observed and which cannot be directly derived using established rules" (p. 27).
6. Formulation – "taking the results of any of the intellectual skills delineated above and structuring them in a suitable form for: pre-response evaluation and post-evaluation instruction to the response mechanism" (pp. 27, 28).
7. Evaluation – "the application of pre-response criteria to formulated output of intellectual processing" (p. 28).

During task analysis such distinctions may be helpful to the analyst although again training studies which use them remain to be carried out.

Position Analysis Questionnaire (PAQ)

A third approach to analysis which partially adopts an information-processing approach is reflected in the development of PAQ by McCormick and colleagues at Purdue University from the 1960s onwards (McCormick, Jeanneret and Mecham, 1969, 1972). The overall aim was to develop a job analysis technique which could be used for a variety of personnel issues including job evaluation, job classification and selection. It is doubtful the extent to which it is useful for training purposes for reasons discussed below although it is described here for the sake of completeness and because it is a well-known technique.

PAQ, Form B (McCormick et al., 1972) comprises 194 job elements which are divided into six divisions: information input, mental processes, work output, relationship with other workers, job context and other job characteristics (Table 7.4).

Table 7.4 Divisions and subdivisions of PAQ with selected examples (adapted from McCormick et al., 1969). The numbers of job elements in each division are given in parentheses

---

Division 1: Information input (35)
  1.1 Sources of job information
      1.1.1 Visual sources of job information (14)
          Example, item 1: written materials (books, reports, office notes, articles, job instructions, signs, etc.) (assessed on a six point extent of use scale)
      1.1.2 Non-visual sources of job information (5)
  1.2 Sensory and perceptual processes (8)
  1.3 Estimation activities (8)

Division 2: Mental processes (14)
  2.1 Decision-making, reasoning and planning/scheduling (3)
     Example, item 37: Reasoning in problem solving (indicate, using the code below, the level of reasoning that is required of the worker in applying his knowledge, experience, and judgement to problems)

     Code   Level of reasoning in problem-solving
     1.   Low (use of common sense to carry out simple, or relatively

uninvolved instructions, for example, janitor, delivery-man, hod carrier, etc.)

2.   Below average (use of some training and/or experience to select from a limited number of solutions the most appropriate action or procedure in performing the job, for example, sales clek, postman, electrician apprentice, keypunch operator, etc.)

3.   Average (use of relevant principles to solve practical problems and to deal with a variety of concrete variables in situations where only limited standardization exists, for example, draftsman, carpenter, farmer, etc.)

4.   Above average (use of logic or scientific thinking to define problems, collect information, establish facts and draw valid conclusions, for example, mechanical engineer, personnel director, manager of a "chain" store, etc.)

5.   High (use of principles of logical or scientific thinking to solve a wide range of intellectual and practical problems, for example, research chemist, nuclear engineer, corporate president or manager of a large branch or plant, etc.)

2.2   Information-processing activities (6)
2.3   Use of learned information (5)

Division 3: Work output (49)
  3.1   Use of devices and equipment
      3.1.1   Hand-held tools or instruments (6)
      3.1.2   Other hand-held devices (5)
      3.1.3   Stationary devices (1)
      3.1.4   Control devices (8)
      3.1.5   Transportation and mobile equipment (8)
  3.2   Manual activities (7)
  3.3   Activities of the entire body (2)
      Example, item 85: highly skilled body coordination (activities involving extensive, and often highly learned coordination activities of the whole body, for example, athletics, dancing, etc.) (assessed on a six point scale of importance)
  3.4   Level of physical exertion (1)
  3.5   Body position/postures (5)
  3.6   Manipulation/coordination activities (6)

Division 4: Relationships with other workers (36)
  4.1   Communications
      4.1.1   Oral (8)
          Example, item 99: advising (dealing with individuals in

order to counsel and/or guide them with regard to problems that may be resolved by legal, financial, scientific, technical, clinical, spiritual, and/or other professional principles) (assessed on a six point scale of importance)

4.1.2 Written (1)

4.1.3 Other communications (2)

4.2 Miscellaneous interpersonal relationships (2)

4.3 Amount of job required personal contact (1)

4.4 Types of job required personal contact (15)

4.5 Supervision and coordination

    4.5.1 Supervision/direction given (3)

    4.5.2 Other organisational activities (3)

    4.5.3 Supervision received (1)

Division 5: Job environment and work situation (19)

5.1 Physical working conditions

    5.1.1 Outdoor environment (1)

    5.1.2 Indoor temperatures (2)

    5.1.3 Other physical working conditions (6)

5.2 Physical hazards (4)

5.3 Personal and social aspects (6)

Example, item 50: Interpersonal conflict situations (job situations in which there are virtually inevitable differences in objectives, opinions, or viewpoints between the worker and other persons or groups of persons, and which may "set the stage" for conflict, for example, persons involved in labour negotiations, supervisors who must enforce an unpopular policy, etc.) (assessed on a six point importance scale)

Division 6: Other job characteristics (41)

6.1 Apparel worn (6)

Example, item 155: Specific uniform/apparel (nurse, doorman, bus driver, etc.) (assessed on a dichotomous applicability scale)

6.2 Licensing (1)

6.3 Work schedule

    6.3.1 Continuity of work (2)

    6.3.2 Regularity of working hours (3)

    6.3.3 Day–night schedule (3)

6.4 Job demands (14)

6.5 Responsibility (3)

6.6 Job structure (1)

6.7 Criticability of position (1)

6.8 Pay/income (7)

The instrument has most discriminatory power for blue-collar skilled and semi-skilled manual jobs as reflected by the number of items in the divisions concerned with work output and relationships with other workers. Relatively few job elements are concerned with decision-making and intellectual processes. A variety of scales is used to assess job elements: applicability, extent of use, importance to the job, amount of time, possibility of occurrence and special codes as, for example, item 37 in Table 7.4, which is concerned with decision making, reasoning and planning. It is not clear why so many different scales are used. Additionally, they make subsequent statistical analysis problematic particularly for any analysis involving comparison between items. Issues concerning the reliability of PAQ are discussed in Section 5.3, pp. 158–159.

Various studies have been carried out to identify the general dimensions of jobs derived from the job elements in PAQ. Elements within each of the six divisions have been subjected to principal components analysis. The results of three studies were broadly similar. The first study analysed 536 jobs and identified 27 factors (McCormick, Jeanneret and Mecham, 1969). The second study was carried out by Marquardt and McCormick (1974) and identified 31 factors using a sample of 3700 jobs (see Table 7.5). The third study found 32 factors from a sample of 2200 jobs (McCormick, Mecham and Jeanneret, 1977). McCormick preferred the latter study which he argued was more representative in its range of jobs.

A series of studies has linked the job elements of PAQ with their associated human attributes (Marquardt, 1972; Mecham and McCormick, 1969). This link was made from the ratings of industrial psychologists who were given a list of the definitions of 76 human attributes (44 of an aptitude nature and 32 of an "interest or temperament" nature) and asked to estimate the relevance of each attribute to each of the job elements. The study by Marquardt (1972) found that using 8–10 raters produced good levels of reliability for the contribution of each attribute to performance of each job element. One exception was attribute 58 which was defined as "working alone" which only had an intraclass correlation coefficient of 0.043. Generally the attributes of an aptitude nature were rated more reliably than those of an interest or temperament nature. The overall aim of this work was to specify the relative contribution of different human attributes to performance of different jobs. Hence, given the relative weightings of attributes to job elements together with an analysis of the job elements required in a job, it would be a simple matter to calculate the relative contribution of human attributes to that job. The idea behind this work was presumably that a standard set of tests could be developed to measure these attributes. It

Table 7.5 Job dimensions, relating to PAQ divisions, derived by principal components analysis (Marquardt and McCormick, 1974)

PAQ division	Dimension title
1. Information input	1. Perceptual interpretation
	2. Evaluation of sensory input
	3. Visual input from devices/materials
	4. Input from representational sources
	5. Environmental awareness
2. Mental processes	6. Decision-making
	7. Information-processing
3. Work input	8. Manual/control activities
	9. Physical coordination in control/related activities
	10. General body activity
	11. Manipulating/handling activities
	12. Adjusting/operating machines/equipment
	13. Skilled/technical activities
	14. Use of miscellaneous equipment/devices
4. Relationships with other persons	15. Interchange of ideas/judgements/related information
	16. Supervisory/staff activities
	17. Public/related personal contact
	18. Communicating instructions/directions/related job information
	19. General personal contact
	20. Job-related communications
5. Job content	21. Potentially stressful/unpleasant environment
	22. Potentially hazardous job situations
	23. Personally demanding situations
6. Other job characteristics	24. Attentive job demands
	25. Vigilant/discriminating work activities
	26. Structured versus unstructured work activities
	27. Regular versus irregular work activities
	28. Work/protective versus business clothing
	29. Specific versus nonspecific clothing
	30. Continuity of work load
	31. (Unnamed)

would then be possible to link a job analysis directly to a selection procedure which tested applicants for the types of attributes required by the job under consideration. This approach has not been developed further. One reason is that the job elements of PAQ are already global descriptions of performance in a job. Attempting to build a bridge between these job elements and inferred abilities which is applicable irrespective of job content and context is exceedingly difficult. Even though reliability has been demonstrated, the validity of the attributes is more difficult and remains to be examined.

Whilst the job elements of PAQ have been used for various wide-ranging personnel issues, it is doubtful whether they are useful for training purposes. The reason for this is that the job analysis information is too global and not sufficiently fine-grained. One has to remember that the rating of a job element applies to *all* of the tasks being performed by a job incumbent. The utility of such a rating is not only questionable because of its accuracy, but also because it is not possible to disentangle the information processing demands of individual tasks within the job. From a training perspective it is desirable to associate *each* task with its information processing requirements.

Advantages and disadvantages of information processing taxonomies

The advantages of using an information processing taxonomy to identify the psychological aspects of a task are:

(a) *Information processing terms are comprehensive.* These taxonomies cover all aspects of performance, i.e. input, decision making and output. To be weighed against this advantage is the variability in the number of categories used by taxonomies. For example, Miller distinguished 25 task functions, whereas Altman identified five categories in his behavioural domain. Taxonomies therefore vary in their discriminative power.

(b) *Information processing terms are context independent.* By definition, use of such a taxonomy enables the analyst to compare and contrast the psychological aspects of different tasks using a common vocabulary which does not depend upon the particular job content or context.

(c) *Distinctions are theoretically based.* Some comfort should be taken from the fact that information processing distinctions form part of a theoretical approach in psychology. Different theorists might disagree over whether more or fewer distinctions should be made, but

at least they provide some a priori basis for a psychological analysis
of a task. Recently, there seems to have been a proliferation of
cognitive analyses which use ad hoc distinctions, some of which are
partial reinventions of information processing taxonomies. Even
though it is not possible or appropriate to decide which *one*
taxonomy should be used, such theoretically based taxonomies
represent a sensible starting point for a psychological analysis.

The disadvantages of the information processing approach are:

(a) *The changing nature of psychology*. Taxonomies reflect the psychology
at the time of their development. It is therefore inevitable that more
recent psychological perspectives might wish to add or modify
information processing categories.
(b) *The lack of dynamic integration*. Typically a task is described as
having various information processing characteristics: e.g. short-
term memory, perceptual interpretation etc. This type of analysis
produces a list of information processing activities, but fails to
identify how these interact during task performance.
(c) *The lack of higher-order cognitive processes*. The three information-
processing taxonomies discussed previously suggest that it is sufficient
to break down performance into a series of discrete lower-level
information-processing components. This is misleading. In skilled
performance such components are controlled by higher-order
executive processes which also need to be identified (Section 2.5).
As we have discussed in Chapter 2, one hallmark of skilled performance is its flexibility such that different methods or strategies
can be used to achieve the same goal. Therefore important questions
include the extent to which the performer is aware of the method
selected; why that method is selected and how performance is
monitored. These questions lead one to ask how higher-order
control processes operate, which is an important part of any complete
psychological analysis. This is discussed further in the following
section.

Recent developments in cognitive psychology

Two points emerge from more recent developments in cognitive
psychology which relate to our discussion of psychological approaches to
analysis and information-processing approaches in particular. First,
taxonomies of cognitive processes have been proposed by Sternberg
(1980) and Feuerstein (1980) which do acknowledge the role of higher-
order processes. Second, the traditional gulf between the information-

processing and ability requirements approaches is becoming more blurred.

Sternberg has taken a new look at intellectual ability by using an information-processing theory to break it down into its components. His early work was concerned with the component processes involved in analogical reasoning items and therefore what such items measured in conventional intelligence tests (Sternberg, 1977). He developed methods for estimating the contribution and speed of component processes such as inference (the relationship between the first two items of the analogy), mapping (the higher-order rule which connects the first half of the analogy to the second) and application (the relationship inferred from the first half and applied to the second of the analogy). Sternberg (1980) subsequently distinguished three types of component which are involved in intellectual functioning:

(a) *Performance components* which are "processes used in the execution of strategies for task performance" (Sternberg, 1985, p. 226). Performance components have been identified for inductive reasoning, although Sternberg suggested that generally components can be grouped into four stages of strategy execution: (1) encoding the elements of a problem; (2) combining these elements into a potential solution; (3) evaluating the potential solution against others; (4) responding.

(b) *Metacomponents* refer to executive processes used in complex cognitive tasks such as problem-solving. These higher-order processes help us to recognise the nature of the problem; select lower-order performance components for the solution; determine how to combine the performance components; allocate processing resources; and keep track of task performance.

(c) *Knowledge acquisition, transfer and retention components* are processes involved in learning new information, transferring knowledge or skills from one situation to another and retrieving information which has been learned.

Sternberg's performance components are based on an analysis of reasoning tasks and others remain to be identified for other types of task. Of particular interest are his metacomponents which refer to higher-order processes which are important in many tasks besides problem-solving such as reading, writing and learning itself. These have been labelled "metacognitive" skills, since they imply some monitoring of the cognitive processes involved in task performance. Such metacognitive skills are absent in R.B. Miller's taxonomy of information-processing functions and are not addressed in job analysis techniques such as PAQ, where only a few items refer, for example, to decision-making and reasoning, albeit in a global manner. Any psychological analysis of a task should attempt to articulate these higher-order skills besides identifying the more straightforward lower-order components. Unfortunately, this exhortation cannot be accompanied by guidelines of how this might be achieved.

Whether these higher-order cognitive skills are specific to particular tasks, or whether they are general and can be trained to transfer between different tasks is an old question which has been the subject of much recent debate (e.g. Chipman, Segal and Glaser, 1985; Segal, Chipman and Glaser, 1985). This question raises fundamental theoretical and practical issues about the nature of training and transfer and how educational experiences should be organised. Resnick (1987) has provided an eloquent review of these problems in the context of how education might encourage the development of higher-order thinking and reasoning processes.

Feuerstein (1980) has also adopted an information-processing approach in his instrumental enrichment programme (for overviews see Bransford et al., 1985; Sternberg, 1985). This programme was aimed at helping adolescents overcome what Feuerstein believed to be deficiencies in problem-solving skills which restricted potential cognitive development. These "deficient cognitive functions" fall into impairments at the input phase, elaborational phase and output phase. These include, for example, lack of accuracy in data gathering (input), inability to select relevant cues (elaboration) and lack of verbal tools for communicating a solution (output). Feuerstein's instrumental enrichment programme and Sternberg's componential training programme (Sternberg, 1985; 1986) are concerned with training the cognitive components or processes underlying intelligence. Consequently, both Feuerstein's and Sternberg's work are examples of sophisticated psychological analyses of tasks based in the information-processing tradition. These analyses are used for the subsequent development of a training programme. The information-processing categories include higher-order skills, unlike Miller's taxonomy, and are elaborated in the context of specific tasks which individuals are trained to perform. For further details the reader should consult Feuerstein (1980) and Sternberg (1985, 1986) whilst Bransford et al. (1985) provided some insightful comments on the instrumental enrichment programme.

7.2 ABILITY REQUIREMENTS

Another psychological approach to analysis is to focus on the sorts of abilities required by the person performing the task. Tasks are therefore analysed and compared in terms of the ability requirements of the performer, rather than the information-processing demands of the task. The appeal of this approach is obvious. If abilities can be operationally defined, they can be measured and tests devised. It is then possible to evaluate the extent to which individual trainees possess the necessary abilities for performing a task or job. In an ideal situation, only trainees with the necessary abilities to perform the task would be selected for training, which means that the resources required for training are minimised.

This apparently simple approach is more problematic than might appear at first sight. A major problem is *how* to determine which abilities are required to perform the task(s) in a job. Two possibilities exist. On the one hand the trainer, preferably a qualified psychologist, *infers* the abilities required from a task analysis of the sort discussed in Chapter 6. Such judgements are inevitably prone to error and whilst reliability can be improved by increasing the number of people making such judgements, validity is a major problem. The other option is that the trainer carries out an empirical study which statistically links measures of ability to performance of the task(s). Hence a battery of ability measures is administered to job incumbents and the results are then correlated with job performance. Those which are most predictive are used subsequently for the selection of trainees. This approach is more systematic than the former but requires considerable resources which would be difficult to justify unless the job was particularly difficult to train. Irrespective of which approach is adopted, the trainer is still confronted with the problem of selecting a taxonomy of abilities to use. Much will depend upon the ingenuity or skill of the applied psychologist in selecting a taxonomy which distinguishes between abilities which at least have a prima facie case of being involved in the job in question.

Some taxonomies of cognitive and psychomotor ability are described below. In addition, evidence is reviewed that ability requirements change during the training of a task and also that slight modifications in the nature of the task can produce considerable changes in ability requirements.

Traditional ability taxonomies

A great amount of research during this century has investigated human abilities and aptitudes in the areas of differential psychology or individual differences (e.g. Cronbach, 1970). The relationship between abilities and jobs has been reviewed by Dunnette (1976) and Fleishman and Quaintance (1984). The assumption is that people can be described as possessing relatively stable or enduring abilities which influence task performance. Some abilities are general and affect the performance of many tasks (e.g. intelligence, verbal ability), whilst others are task specific. Cognitive or intellectual abilities are distinguished from motor (or psychomotor) ones. Before describing some well-known taxonomies, let us pause to consider what abilities are and how they are identified.

It is easy to conceptualise a person's abilities as fixed and measurable, analogous to our physical dimensions which are measured when we need a new suit or dress. However, this analogy is very misleading. Height, waist, arm length are physical dimensions, whereas verbal, spatial or other abilities are hypothetical constructs devised by psychologists for explaining variations in performance on different tasks. It is illuminating to describe how abilities are inferred. A large battery of tests is administered to a set of individuals and their scores on each pair of tests is correlated. Next the correlations are subjected to statistical techniques such as factor analysis (involving various statistical assumptions), which extract a smaller number of "factors" which supposedly underlie performance on the tests. Tests which are strongly positively or negatively correlated are influenced by the same factors, whereas those which are uncorrelated are subject to different factors. These factors are interpreted and labelled as different abilities and the contribution of different abilities to each test can be calculated. Techniques are available for developing standardised tests which measure one or more specified abilities. This whole process involves inference and the use of statistical methods, with their accompanying assumptions, in order to construct "abilities" which explain the common statistical variation in the performance of different tests or tasks.

Another major problem with the abilities approach is that many different taxonomies exist even within the same area. For example, as Sternberg (1985) noted, the number of factors proposed to explain human intelligence varies between 1 and 150! Consequently, some factors, such as Spearman's g, are very general factors whilst others such as Thurstone's seven "primary mental abilities" are more specific. The number of factors is not only influenced by theoretical assumptions, but also by the type of factor analysis used. Hence the number of factors in an area varies, as does their level of description, which ranges from gross to fine-grained. It should be apparent by now that it is not a matter of which taxonomy is correct, but which is most useful.

Cognitive abilities. Reviews of taxonomies of cognitive abilities have been provided by Dunnette (1976), Ekstrom (1979), Fleishman and Quaintance (1984) and Sternberg (1985).

Spearman (1927) proposed a two factor theory of intelligence in which intelligence comprised a general factor, *g*, which affects performance on all intellectual tasks and specific factors which are only relevant to individual tasks. In contrast, Thurstone (1938) denied the existence of *g* and suggested that intelligence was founded on seven primary mental abilities: spatial ability, perceptual speed, numerical ability, verbal meaning, memory, verbal fluency and inductive reasoning. Vernon (1971) provided a hierarchical model of human intelligence. General intelligence, *g*, is divided into two groups of factors: practical/mechanical and verbal/educational, both of which are further subdivided.

The debate concerning the number and nature of cognitive abilities has been long and energetic. In 1963 the Educational Testing Service (ETS) attempted to overcome this confusion by identifying 24 factors with a list of reference tests to measure them (French, Ekstrom and Price, 1963). In the light of a review of these 24 factors by Ekstrom (1973) a decade later, Dunnette (1976) suggested that an abbreviated set of 10 factors be used. Further work at the Educational Testing Service suggested that three further factors should be added: verbal closure, figural fluency and visual memory. Peterson and Bownas (1982) listed the resulting 12 cognitive factors, all of which have two or three associated tests developed and distributed by ETS. It should be noted that figural fluency was added to the more general fluency category which also includes associative, expressional, ideational and word fluency. Below is a list of the 12 cognitive factors taken from Peterson and Bownas, most of which is in turn a summary from Dunnette (1976). The factors are:

1. *Flexibility and speed of closure*: the ability to "hold in mind" a particular visual percept and find it embedded in distracting material; and the ability to "take in" a perceptual field as a whole, to fill in unseen portions with likely material and thus to coalesce somewhat disparate parts into a visual percept.
2. *Fluency*: a combination of five different fluencies: associative, producing words from a restricted area of meaning; expressional, supplying proper verbal expressions for ideas already stated or

finding a suitable expression that would fit a given semantic frame of reference; ideational fluency, quickly producing ideas and examples of an idea about a stated condition or object; word fluency, producing isolated words that contain one or more structural, essentially phonetic, restrictions without reference to the meaning of the words; figural fluency, producing a response quickly by drawing a number of examples, elaborations or restructurings based on a given visual or descriptive stimulus.

3. *Inductive reasoning*: ability in forming and testing hypotheses directed at finding a relationship among elements and applying the principle to identifying an element fitting the relationship.
4. *Associative (rote) memory*: ability to remember bits of unrelated material.
5. *Span memory*: ability to recall perfectly for immediate reproduction a series of items after only one presentation of the series.
6. *Number facility*: ability to manipulate numbers in arithmetical operations rapidly, facility in performing elementary arithmetical operations (typically under speed conditions).
7. *Perceptual speed*: speed in finding figures, making comparisons and carrying out other very simple tasks involving visual perception.
8. *Syllogistic (deductive) reasoning*: ability to reason from stated premises to their necessary conclusion; ability in formal reasoning from stated premises to rule out nonpermissible combinations and thus arrive at necessary conclusions.
9. *Spatial orientation and visualisation*: ability to perceive spatial patterns or to maintain orientation with respect to objects in space and the ability to manipulate or transform the image of spatial patterns into other visual arrangements.
10. *Verbal comprehension:* knowledge of words and their meaning as well as the application of this knowledge in understanding connected discourse.
11. *Verbal closure*: the ability to solve problems requiring the identification of words, when some of the letters are missing, disarranged or mixed with other letters.
12. *Visual memory*: the ability to remember the configuration, location and orientation of figural material.

The largest number of cognitive abilities has been formulated in the Structure of Intellect model devised by Guilford over a period of three decades of research (e.g. Guilford, 1956, 1967, 1982). He viewed intellectual abilities as being organised along three dimensions: operations, contents and products. *Operations* refer to basic psychological processes which operate on some *content* or kind of material to produce some *products* which represent the forms that information takes whilst being processed. Each of these dimensions can vary, as depicted in the Structure of Intellect model represented in Figure 7.2. Originally,

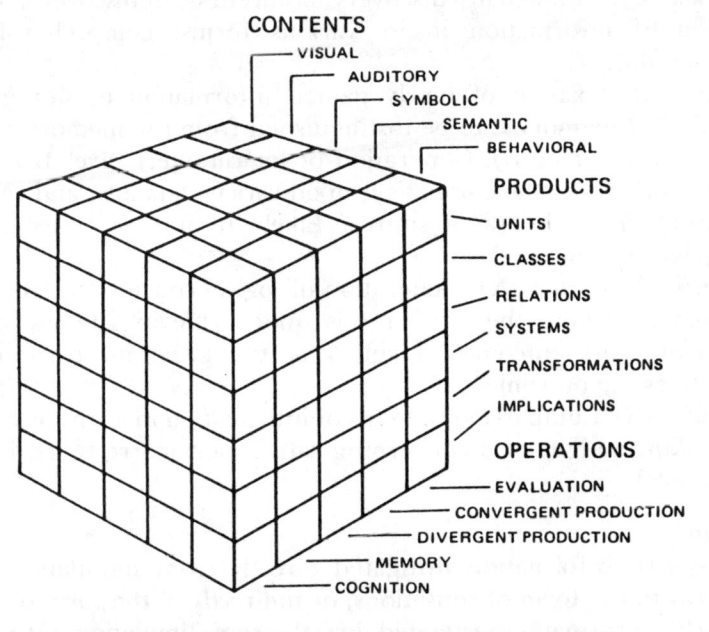

Figure 7.2   Structure of Intellect model (Guilford, 1977).

Guilford (1967) proposed four types of content which could be combined with five operations and six products, resulting in 120 distinct cognitive factors or cells in the model. This number of factors was increased to 150 by Guilford (1982), with the figural relations content being split into visual and auditory content (see Table 7.6). Tests have been devised to measure the factors and Guilford claimed to have identified the existence of over two-thirds of them.

Such a scheme has not been without its critics. Many of the criticisms are summarised by Dunnette (1976):

(a) There is some dispute over the existence of some factors, due to the manner in which the factor analysis was conducted, particularly the use of subjective rotation methods. Whilst this is true, one might argue that there are many assumptions and subjective issues which are intrinsic to factor analysis even when it is being used as a confirmatory technique.

Table 7.6 Definitions of the operations, contents and products in Guildford's Structure of Intellect model (from Fleishman and Quaintance, 1984)

Operations

Cognition (C). Immediate discovery, awareness, rediscovery, or recognition of information in its various forms; comprehension, or understanding

Memory (M). Fixation of newly gained information in storage. The operation of memory is to be distinguished from the memory store

Divergent Production (D). Generation of logical alternatives from given information, where the emphasis is upon variety, quantity, and relevance of output from the same source. Likely to involve transfer recall (instigated by new cues)

Convergent Production (N). Generation of logical conclusions from given information, where the emphasis is upon achieving unique or conventionally best outcomes. Likely that the given information fully determines the outcome

Evaluation (E). Comparison of items of information in terms of variables and making judgements concerning satisfaction (correctness, identity, consistency)

Contents

Auditory (A). Information instigated directly from stimulation of the inner ear in the form of sensations, or indirectly in the form of images

Visual (V). Information instigated directly from stimulation of the eye in the form of sensations, or indirectly in the form of images

Symbolic (S). Pertaining to information in the form of denotative signs having no significance in and of themselves, such as letters, numbers, musical notations, codes, and words (as ordered letter combinations)

Semantic (M). Pertaining to information in the form of conceptions or mental constructs to which words are often applied. Most notable in verbal thinking and verbal communication, but not necessarily dependent upon words. Meaningful pictures also convey semantic information

Behavioural (B). Pertaining to information, essentially nonfigural and nonverbal, involved in human interactions, in which the attitudes, needs, desires, moods, intentions, and thoughts of others and of ourselves are involved

Products

Units (U). Relatively segregated or circumscribed items or "chunks" of information having the character of a "thing". May be close to Gestalt psychology's "figure on a ground"

Classes (C). Conceptions underlying sets of items of information grouped by virtue of their common properties

Relations (R). Connections between items of information based upon variables or points of contact that apply to them. Relational connections are more definable than implicational connections

Systems (S). Organised or structured aggregates of items of information; complexes of inter-related or interacting parts

Transformations (T). Changes of various kinds (redefinitions, shifts, transitions, or modifications) in existing information

Implications (I). Circumstantial connections between items of information, as by virtue of contiguity or any condition that promotes "belongingness"

(b) Some factors might be interpreted as conventional abilities, e.g. the different operations requiring a semantic content might be judged to be tapping the traditional verbal aptitude factor.

(c) Dunnette, writing in 1976, reserved his most damning criticism for the lack of application of the model, remarking that it "has been internally oriented, making little or no contact with the real world of human work performance". This judgement on balance is a fair one, since there has not been a reciprocal relationship between theoretical development and practical application. There are some signs of use of the model in the development of curricula in child education (Meeker, 1981).

Guilford's model should be viewed as a rich source of hypotheses concerning the nature of intellectual activities. Even though it is treated here as an example of an ability requirements approach, it does distinguish between different cognitive activities. It differentiates three important dimensions of intellectual functioning which are relevant in the analysis of task performance. Whilst the cells in Guilford's model are claimed to be logically independent, it is likely that a variety of factors will be linked in the psychological analysis of any one task. Because of the technical complexities of the distinctions between the different operations, contents and products (Table 7.6), it is not possible to infer or guess easily which factors may be involved in particular tasks. Strictly speaking, the only systematic means of analysis is to administer a battery of reference tests for the factors devised by Guilford in order to identify their contribution to task performance.

Motor abilities. Despite the shift in society away from tasks requiring motor skills, especially in industry, there are many areas in which these tasks remain important, e.g. in sports, musical and some military activities. There is often a need for some physical manipulation of objects involving coordination of fingers, arms, legs etc. In physical education, research has examined whether performance at various sports is determined by either a general (motor) factor or specific abilities. The search for a general factor, comparable to general intelligence, has not been successful and different tasks have been found to comprise unique patterns of motor abilities. Even tests of supposedly the same ability often reveal surprisingly low intercorrelations. For example, Scott (1955) found few intercorrelations in a battery of 28 tests of proprioceptive ability. (This ability involves the discrimination of bodily position, movement of bodily parts plus discrimination of their rate and direction.)

The most extensive work in the area of motor abilities has been carried out by Fleishman and his associates spanning the period from the mid-1950s to the present day. His work depends upon the factor analytic approach to identify motor abilities. A large battery of tasks are administered to a large number of subjects and different abilities are postulated to explain the common statistical variation in performance of the tasks. Over the years, Fleishman's taxonomy has been revised and extended. His early work (e.g. Fleishman, 1964) identified 11 psychomotor factors together with nine physical proficiency factors which are elaborated in Table 7.7. Subsequently, Fleishman expanded his

Table 7.7 Fleishman's psychomotor and physical proficiency factors (from Fleishman and Quaintance, 1984)

Psychomotor factors

Control precision. The ability to make fine, highly controlled muscular movements required to adjust the position of a control mechanism. Examples of control mechanisms are joy sticks, levers, pedals, and rudders. A series of adjustments may be required, but they need not be performed simultaneously. This ability is most critical where adjustments must be rapid, but precise. Adjustments are made to visual stimuli and involve the use of a single limb, either arm–hand or leg
    Examples: Rotary Pursuit Test; operate a joy stick to steer an aircraft

Multilimb coordination. The ability to coordinate the movement of a number of limbs simultaneously. Best measured by devices involving multiple controls. (Hands, feet, or hands and feet)
    Examples: Complex Coordination Test; operate a bulldozer

Response orientation. This factor is general to visual discrimination tasks. These tasks involve rapid recognition of the direction (north, south, east, west) indicated by a particular visual stimulus (e.g. an arrow) followed by the appropriate motor response chosen from several alternatives. The response may be simple or complex (push a button and pull a switch versus push a button). This ability appears to be most critical when the conditions are highly speeded

Example: flip different switches in response to different coloured lights appearing on a display panel

Reaction time. This ability represents the speed with which the individual can provide a single motor response to a single stimulus when it appears. It is independent of the mode of presentation (auditory or visual) and also of the type of motor response required. Response cannot involve alternative choices

Example: depress a button as soon as possible after hearing a buzzer.

Speed of arm movement. The speed with which an individual can make a gross, discrete arm movement where accuracy is minimised. There is ample evidence that this ability is independent of reaction time

Example: move a series of control levers to new positions in rapid succession

Rate control. Involves the timing of continuous anticipatory motor adjustments relative to changes in speed and/or direction of a continuously moving target or object. Actual motor response to change (rather than verbal estimate) is necessary. Extends to tasks involving compensatory as well as following pursuit and to those involving responses to changes in rate.

Example: track a moving target by keeping a circle around a dot which changes in speed and direction of movement

Manual dexterity. The ability to make skilful, well directed arm–hand movements in manipulating fairly large objects under speeded conditions

Examples: Minnesota Rate of Manipulation Test; use hand tools to assemble an aircraft engine

Finger Dexterity. The ability to make skilful, controlled manipulations of objects small enough to be handled with the fingers

Examples: Purdue Pegboard Test; assemble peg, washer, and collar units and insert them in small holes

Arm-hand steadiness. The ability to make precise arm–hand positioning movements in which strength and speed are minimised. It extends to

tasks that require steadiness during movement as well as those that require a minimum of tremor while maintaining a static arm position
   Examples: Arm Tremor Test; perform retinal surgery

Wrist-finger speed. The ability to make rapid pendular (back and forth) and/or rotary wrist movements in which accuracy is not critical
   Example: Tapping Test

Aiming. The ability to make highly accurate, restricted hand movements requiring precise eye–hand coordination
   Example: Make a dot in a series of very small circles on a printed test

---

Physical proficiency factors

Extent flexibility. The ability to extend or stretch the body. Tests that load on this factor require stretching of the trunk and back muscles as far as possible, without speed, either laterally, forward, or backward
   Example: Twist as far around as possible, touching the scale on the wall

Dynamic flexibility. Common to tasks that require rapid and repeated trunk and/or limb movements. Emphasises both speed and flexibility
   Example: Without moving your feet, bend and touch a spot on the floor, stand up, twist, and touch a spot on the wall behind as rapidly as possible

Explosive strength. Common to tasks that require expenditure of a maximum of energy in one or a series of explosive acts. This factor emphasises the mobilisation of energy for a burst of effort, rather than continuous strain, stress, or repeated exertion of muscles
   Examples: broad jump; sprint 50 yards

Static strength. Common to tasks that require the exertion of maximum strength against a fairly immovable external object, even for a brief period. It is general to different muscle groups (hand, arm, back, shoulder, leg) and to different kinds of tasks
   Examples: squeeze a grip dynamometer as hard as possible; lift heavy objects

Dynamic strength. The ability to exert muscular force repeatedly or continuously over time. It represents muscular endurance and emphasises the resistance of the muscles to fatigue. Tests loading on this factor tend to emphasise the power of the muscles to propel, support, or move the body repeatedly or to support it for prolonged periods
   Examples: pull-ups; scale a wall

Trunk strength. This is a second, more limited, dynamic strength factor specific to the trunk muscles, particularly the abdominal muscles

Examples: leg-lifts; sit-ups

Gross body coordination. The ability to perform movements simultaneously that involve the entire body.

Example: holding the ends of a short rope in each hand, jump over the rope without tripping, falling or releasing the rope

Gross body equilibrium. The ability to maintain or regain body balance, especially in situations in which equilibrium is threatened or temporarily lost

Example: walk a narrow rail without falling off

Stamina (cardiovascular endurance). The ability to exert sustained physical effort involving the cardiovascular system

Examples: run a distance of one mile as fast as you can; extinguish a building fire

---

taxonomy to cover abilities outside of the motor area since the appeal of a universally agreed and unambiguous set of abilities is obvious. Theologus, Romashko and Fleishman (1973) added factors from Guilford's and Ekstrom's work to identify 48 abilities which were reduced subsequently to 37 abilities by elimination and condensation. Further abilities were added from the sensory-perceptual domain, particularly for vision and audition bringing the count to 52 factors as defined in the Manual for the Ability Requirement Scales (MARS). These are detailed in Fleishman and Quaintance (1984) which is also a good source for the reliability studies carried out during these successive refinements.

Considerable effort was made by Fleishman to enable these ability distinctions to be useful in measuring the requirements of jobs. Two developments are noteworthy in this connection. Firstly, seven point rating scales were developed which provided definitions and examples of tasks which would be placed at points on the scale. For example, with respect to manual dexterity, "performing open heart surgery" was rated 7, "turning the pages of a book" was rated just over 1 and "making a good basketball shot with one hand" was rated in the middle of the scale. Fleishman and Quaintance (1984) summarised the findings from studies aimed at improving the reliability of such scales. They concluded that experience of the task is not a prerequisite for using such scales and that such ratings did not need any specific expertise in psychological assessment.

A second development was aimed at providing analysts with some decision support in estimating which abilities are likely to be involved in different tasks (Fleishman and Stephenson, 1970; Mallamad, Levine and Fleishman, 1980). Decision charts or algorithms were developed in order to enable the analyst to identify the ability requirements of tasks and presumably avoid some of the "false positives" which occur if only a set of rating scales are available. An example of part of such a decision chart is given in Figure 7.3.

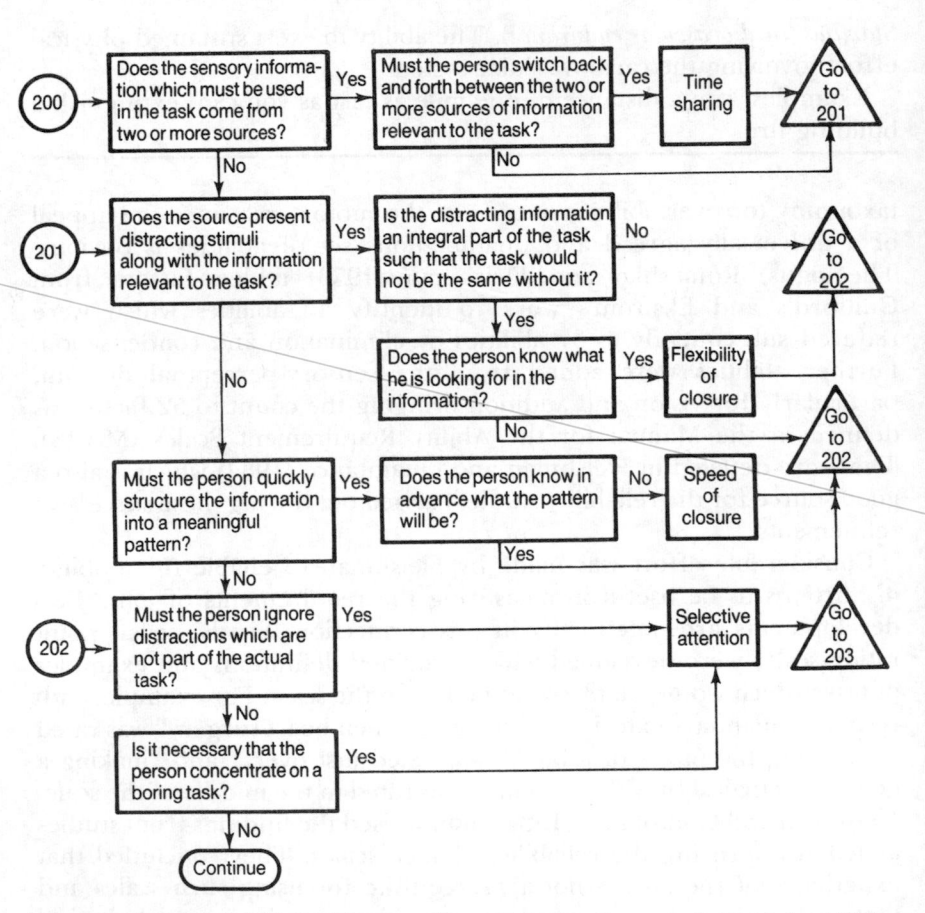

Figure 7.3 Decision aid for identifying some perceptual abilities (Mallamad et al., 1980).

Changing ability requirements during training

Significant findings from a training perspective are that ability requirements change as a function of the stage of training (e.g. Dunham,
Guilford and Hoepfner, 1968) and a task specific ability becomes more
important with increased levels of proficiency (e.g. Fleishman and
Fruchter, 1960). These findings are illustrated in a classic study by
Fleishman and Hempel (1955) which examined learning of a visual
discrimination reaction time task. The contributions of different abilities
were determined from the correlations at different stages of training
between task performance and a battery of reference ability tasks. In
Figure 7.4 it can be seen that verbal and spatial factors are decreasingly
important with practice whilst the influence of a task specific factor
increases.

Fleishman and Rich (1963) investigated acquisition of a two-hand
coordination task in which a "target" had to be tracked by manipulation
of two handles which affected movement of the cursor in the horizontal

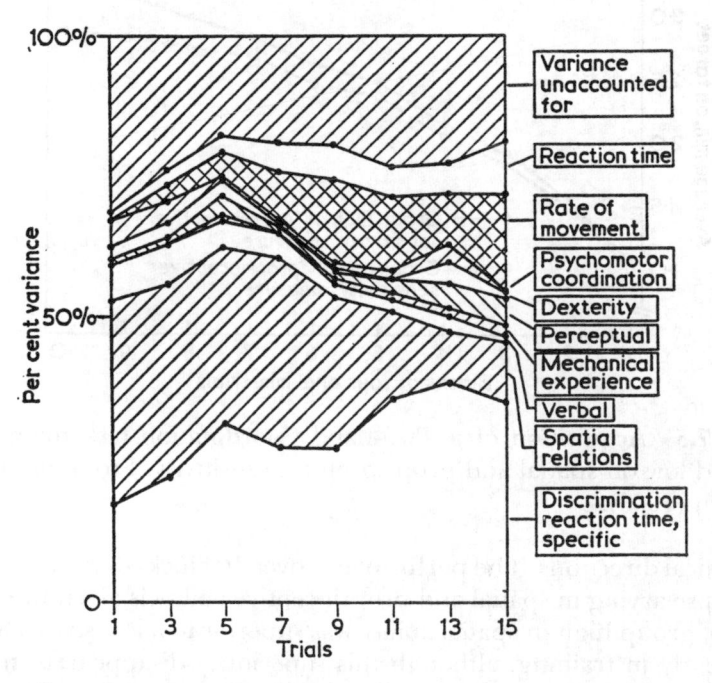

Figure 7.4 Percentage of variance represented by each factor at
different stages of training on the Discrimination Reaction Time Task
(after Fleishman and Hempel, 1955).

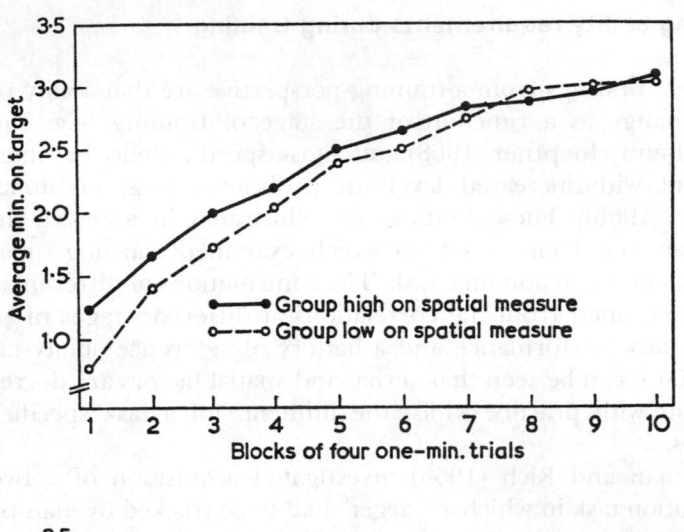

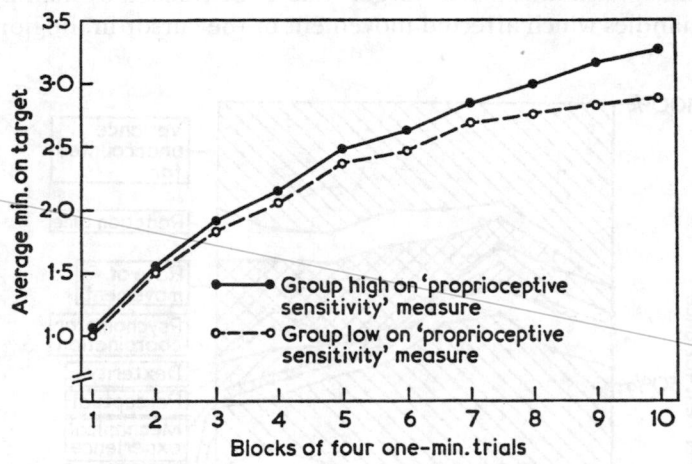

Figure 7.5 Acquisition of a Two-hand Coordination task for groups high and low on spatial and proprioceptive sensitivity. From Fleishman and Rich (1963).

and vertical directions. The performance over 10 blocks of training trials of groups varying in spatial and proprioceptive ability is given in Figure 7.5. The group high in spatial ability was superior to a low spatial ability group early in training, although this superiority disappeared in later stages of training. Conversely, there was no difference in performance between groups of high and low proprioceptive ability early in training, although there was a gradual divergence later in favour of the high proprioceptive ability group. These findings are consistent with some of the theories of skill acquisition, discussed in Chapter 2, which suggest that exteroceptive sources of feedback are more important in the initial stages of skill acquisition, whilst proprioceptive cues are important in later learning. However, one must be cautious in this interpretation of the Fleishman and Rich study, since the differences in performance between groups of different levels of ability does not necessarily indicate that this was due to differential utilisation of the feedback cues relating to these abilities. Further, the criterion of proprioceptive ability involved discrimination between lifted weights which is only one of a number of possible tests of proprioceptive ability.

The fact that ability requirements change at different levels of training is not inconsistent with the various qualitative changes occurring in skill development, discussed in Chapter 2. The implication for training is that one should be careful *when* the ability requirements of a task or job are assessed. Since one is interested in post-training levels of performance, it might be argued that assessment should be made at this time. On the other hand, if other abilities are needed at earlier stages of training then these are just as necessary for the trainee. Parker and Fleishman (1961) used information about the varying contribution of abilities required during training of an aeronautical tracking task in order to improve the nature of the training programme. They capitalised upon an analysis which revealed that spatial orientation had a decreasing contribution as training progressed, whilst the reverse held for multi-limb coordination. Consequently, one training condition received, in addition to standard training, instructions about how to perform the task which took account of the contribution of these two abilities and at what stage of training they were required. This training condition learned at a faster rate and reached a higher level of proficiency than the standard training condition. Interpretation of such a study is difficult because in order to be certain that it was analysis of the ability requirements which improved training, it is necessary to use other equally "detailed" training conditions derived from other types of analysis. It might be that any detailed task analysis combined with some knowledge of psychology would have led to the design of an equally successful training condition, thus by-passing the need to invoke the notion of abilities. It is also likely that any training programme will itself influence the pattern of abilities required.

The observation that the contribution of a task specific ability increases with training is a general finding. This result exposes the limitation of using measures of ability as predictors of performance or the basis for personnel selection techniques. It suggests that tests which involve real samples of a task, if suitably constructed, will be better at predicting task performance and therefore of use in personnel selection. Such a philosophy is reflected in the use of work sample, trainability and miniature job performance tests, which are reviewed in Section 6.4.

An additional problem is that ability requirements are sensitive to slight changes in the task. Fleishman (1978) reported studies in auditory detection, problem-solving and concept formation, in which characteristics of the task were manipulated and concomitant changes in ability requirements were produced. For example, signal duration and signal-to-noise ratio were manipulated in an auditory detection task. Subjects received a battery of reference tests which measured perceptual and memory abilities and then performed the various detection tasks. Factor analysis revealed that the contribution of particular abilities (e.g. auditory perceptual) varied with relatively small changes in the task.

Advantages and disadvantages of an ability requirements approach

The advantages are:

(a) *Abilities are associated with standardised tests.* Tests are available which provide an operational and systematic means of measuring different abilities.
(b) *Ability requirements of tasks can be matched to the trainee's abilities.* The main attraction is that by identifying ability requirements, the selection of trainees can be improved, hence reducing the training resources required.

The disadvantages of the ability requirements approach are:

(a) *The difficulty of identifying which abilities are involved in task performance.* The trainer is faced with a dilemma. On the one hand, the abilities involved in task performance can be inferred, for example, by using rating scales and/or the supposed expertise of psychologists. Both are prone to error. Alternatively, a battery of reference ability tests can be administered and scores correlated with task performance. Abilities can then be identified through factor analytic methods. This solution is more systematic but requires a large investment of resources. Such resources are only likely to be available when either the tasks are problematic (e.g. poor performance leading to catastrophic or costly consequences), or the tasks are unlikely to change over a long period of time and therefore high investment can be justified.

(b) *Abilities are less relevant to training decisions.* Some argue that when making training decisions there is no need to invoke the concept of abilities, which raises difficulties of definition, the use of factor analytic methods etc. Ability requirements do not help with devising training content and whilst, in principle, training design should be tailored to accommodate them, in practice this is difficult. Ability requirements have to be linked to parts of the task (e.g. subtasks, component processes) before the trainer can use them in the design of training.

7.3 KNOWLEDGE REPRESENTATION

The reader will be aware that whilst the taxonomies reviewed in the preceding sections of this chapter are useful during the analysis of a task, they do not provide a complete psychological description. Skill or expertise, particularly in complex tasks involving reasoning or problem solving, will not be captured adequately by distinctions in the information processing demands or ability requirements of the tasks. There is no panacea for the analysis of complex skill. This is not surprising, since our understanding of what constitutes complex skill is still in its infancy. For a few decades, cognitive psychology has explored different constructs in order to understand the characteristics of skilled performance. Unfortunately, this exploration has rarely included comparison of different ways of analysing the skill involved in the *same* task. Hence it is not possible to draw any firm conclusions about the optimal means of analysing skill. Few generalisations or guidelines concerning analysis have emerged which are of use to practitioners in devising training programmes for complex skills. This trend is reflected in the comment by Glaser and Bassok (1989) in their review of learning theory and instruction that:

> The design of instruction in the studies we have reviewed relies more on models of competent performances in specified areas of knowledge and skill than on models of how this performance is acquired (p. 662).

This problem is exacerbated by the fact that cognitive psychology has not, until recently, linked analyses of skill and expertise with training studies. An acid test of any analysis or description of cognitive behaviour is whether it can be used successfully to pass on such expertise to others via the development of a training programme. Alas, such studies are rare.

This section will provide a flavour of work concerned with the analysis of complex skill. Two areas in which considerable effort has been made in the context of solving applied problems are human–computer inter-action (e.g. Norman and Draper, 1986; Wilson et al., 1988) and process control (e.g. Bainbridge, 1988; Rasmussen, 1986). Two conclusions can be drawn from many diverse studies in these and other areas. First, analyses which focus on the goals of performance provide a useful framework from which more detailed cognitive descriptions can be produced. Second, analysis of complex skill requires considerable improvisation and skill on the part of the analyst. Some examples of such analyses are discussed later in this chapter. Beforehand, it is worth considering briefly some of the problems surrounding cognitive analyses which will hopefully serve as warnings to the incautious analyst.

Some problems in analysing cognitive tasks

Three significant problems in the analysis of cognitive skill are:

1. Identifying the many types of knowledge involved.
2. Determining alternative representations of the same knowledge.
3. Assembling types of knowledge and their representations into a complete and coherent model of expert performance.

Each of these problems will be discussed in turn.

1. Types of knowledge. There are many types of knowledge which underpin performance of a complex task. In order to produce a complete analysis, all of these have to be identified, described and assembled into a coherent whole. To use Anderson's terms, this will involve distinguishing between types of declarative and procedural knowledge (see Chapter 2, pp. 49–54). Put simply, declarative know-ledge is concerned with factual knowledge in a domain which is gradually assembled into procedural knowledge which consists of a set of rules of the if...then type which support skilled performance. Declarative and procedural knowledge can each be divided into many different varieties which depend upon the nature of the domain being analysed and the psychological constructs or descriptors preferred. For example Mayer, Larkin and Kadane (1984) distinguished between four types of knowledge required in solving an algebra story problem, which they termed factual and linguistic, schematic, strategic and algorithmic.

Let us illustrate the complexity of types of knowledge which underlie performance with an example from Bainbridge (1989). Bainbridge (1988, 1989) was interested in the types of knowledge required by a process control operator. Figure 7.6 illustrates some of the knowledge required by one small part of the process, namely a pump. A pump is a component of a "parts-of" hierarchy concerned with the physical structure of a plant such that a pump is part of a larger component of the process and yet a pump also has its own parts such as a means of pump control. A pump control has a valve or setting which affects the speed of the pump, which in turn determines the flow rate. Flow rate is itself only part of many other variables or functions which have to be controlled by the operator in order, for example, to maintain the function of a distillation column or a heat exchanger. The pump is also a member of the general category "pump", members of which share common features known by the operator. During control of the process the operator has various goals which can also be represented as a parts-of hierarchy. Higher-order goals will dictate the flow rate required which will be monitored by a lower-level goal, such that if this is not satisfactory, the operator will decide how to change the setting. As Bainbridge noted, the relationships between these different hierarchies are not straightforward mappings and even Figure 7.6 does not capture all of the knowledge involved. For example, the operator will be

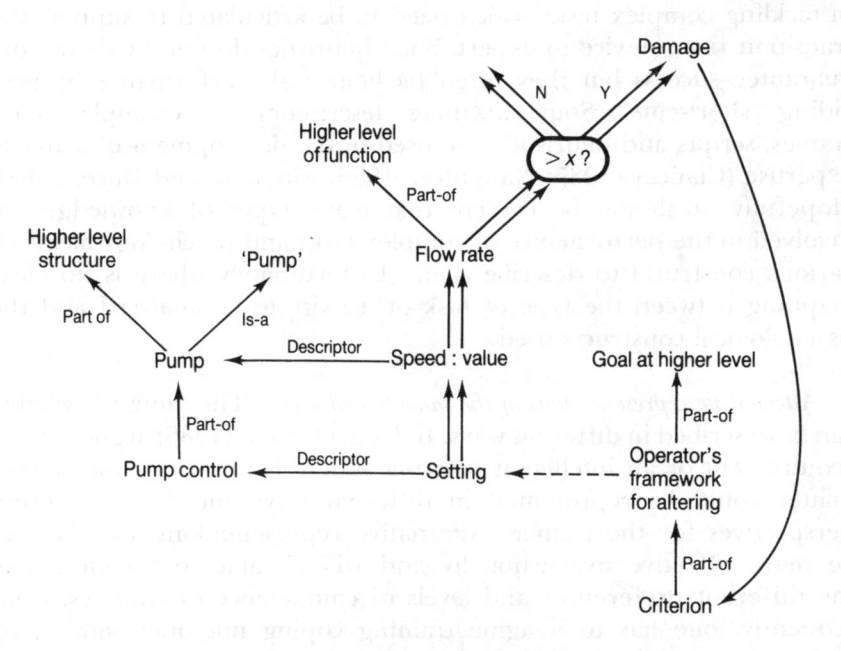

Figure 7.6 Some of the links in the knowledge structure about a small part of a complex process (Bainbridge, 1989). (Double line indicates cause–effect relation.)

influenced by past, present and predicted future states of the process, together with his memory of important states and patterns of variables.

Cognitive psychology has developed many constructs to describe knowledge representation some of which are reviewed by Evans (1988) and Sage and Lagomasino (1984). In procedural knowledge the notion of a schema is important at explaining how experiences are organised in memory, how new information is assimilated and how actions are organised in familiar situations. The notion of a schema originates from the classic work of Bartlett (1932) concerning memory and is closely related to the concepts of frames (Minsky, 1975) and scripts (Schank and Abelson, 1977). Others have emphasised that the acquisition of rules of the if...then type characterise performance of complex cognitive tasks involving reasoning and problem-solving. Recently, there has been much talk of "mental models", which has been provoked by two publications on this topic by Gentner and Stevens (1983) and Johnson-Laird (1983). The term "mental model" is used in a variety of ways (Evans, 1988; Rouse and Morris, 1986) ranging from the simulation of a cognitive activity to something resembling the notion of a schema. Other analyses have emphasised that experts use "rules of thumb" or heuristics in tackling complex tasks which need to be articulated to support the transition from novice to expert. Such heuristics do not, by definition, guarantee success but they often facilitate task performance by providing "short-cuts". Some of these descriptors, for example, rules, frames, scripts and heuristics, are used in the development of artificial expertise (Clancey, 1985; Naughton, 1986; Ringland and Duce, 1988). Hopefully, it should be evident that many types of knowledge are involved in the performance of complex tasks and psychology has used various constructs to describe them. Unfortunately, there is no clear mapping between the type of task or activity to be analysed and the psychological constructs used.

2. *Alternative representations of the same knowledge.* The same knowledge can be described in different ways. Indeed, Ohlsson (1986) argued that a requirement of an intelligent tutoring system is that the same subject matter could be represented in different ways and from different perspectives for the trainee. Alternative representations are likely to be more effective instructionally and will be able to accommodate the different preferences and levels of competence of trainees. Consequently, one has to imagine training coping not only with many different types of knowledge, but also with a number of representations of that same knowledge. (It should be noted that different representations of the same knowledge can only be approximately

equivalent in content, since as Leplat (1985) pointed out, "it is difficult to dissociate knowledge from the expression of this knowledge".)

This results in a need to be able to select between alternative representations of the same knowledge. For example, Bainbridge (1988) distinguished between predicate-type (language like) and pattern-type (diagrammatic) representations of the same knowledge. She commented that whilst pattern representations may be more efficient at "specifying the values of attributes like spatial proximity, shape, colour and intensity and for showing interconnections" (p. 82), they also require inference by the observer who has to share in the diagram designer's conventions and assumptions. In a similar vein, Bainbridge (1986) discussed what a "good" model of a nuclear power plant operator should contain.

3. Assembling an expert model.   Analysis of a cognitive task should result in a model of how an expert performs the task, together with the many types of knowledge involved and their associated representations. This presents formidable difficulties.

First, we know that an expert has the ability to switch between different types of knowledge and use them almost simultaneously during performance of the same cognitive task. This is illustrated in the following example given by Singleton (1989):

> Consider for example the maintenance engineer operating as a diagnostician. He will look at a piece of equipment to try to detect signs which indicate what is wrong. Is there a gap or a hole which indicates a leak? Is there a part which is too hot? Most of this information comes not so much from what is happening but from what is not happening. Basically the thing is not working as it should, the outputs are not as they should be so he will probably begin by checking that the inputs are present, that is the electric power or fuel or other materials are available. He will then envisage the designed chain of events between input and output and look for the hiatus, he may do this by rules, by a pictorial model or by a model involving some symbolism such as expected voltage levels. He will shift very rapidly between different representations of the equipment; the thing itself, his maintenance instructions, the manual, the drawings of the system, verbal discussion with a colleague, his recollection of what has happened to it in the past and so on. He may think in terms of bits of equipment, flows of material, flows of energy or flows of information. He will shift through levels of generality and levels of abstraction until he has formulated an hypothesis which takes the form of "if I do this – that should happen". He will perform an action and check its results. There are many interesting facets of this complex diagnostic process and three are worthy of re-emphasis: firstly most of his information comes not from positive signals, stimuli or cues but from their absence, secondly he is relying on a hybrid model – a mixture of rules, mental pictures and symbolism, thirdly it all happens without very much conscious guidance –

one mental or physical event leads to another and each event in the chain plays its part before handing over to the next one (pp. 86–87).

Rasmussen and Lind (1981) provided some handle on this sort of problem in their discussion of the human operator in complex technical systems. They identified two dimensions which can be used to map types and levels of knowledge involved in performance. They were particularly concerned with supervisory and diagnostic skills in process control contexts. One dimension refers to the size of the unit under consideration, which can vary from the overall system to a subsystem, such as a major piece of equipment, to a small component. This was termed the dimension of "aggregation". The second dimension was originally labelled "abstraction" by Rasmussen and Lind (1981), although it was subsequently explained in terms of "means–ends" in later publications (e.g. Rasmussen, 1986). There are five levels of abstraction which represent the functional properties of a system:

1. *System purpose* relates to the objectives of the system, constraints imposed and input/output relationships.
2. *Abstract function* refers to representing the function of the system in terms of, for example, information or mass energy flows.
3. *Generalised function* includes description in terms of standard functions and processes such as feedback loops, heat transfer, etc.
4. *Physical function* covers the mechanical, electrical or chemical processes of the system or its parts.
5. *Physical form* is the actual physical appearance and configuration of the system and its parts.

Rasmussen (1986) provided three examples of application of this "means–ends" dimension which illustrate the differences between these levels of function for a washing machine, a manufacturing plant and a computer system. The important point is that a performer moves between different levels during performance of a task. This will be determined by the nature of the task. Different types of knowledge are required to support performance at each level. It is possible to combine the dimensions of "aggregation" and "means–ends" to chart the progression of cognitive behaviour during execution of a task. An example is provided by Rasmussen (1985) in which the focus of attention of a person troubleshooting a computer system is mapped onto both dimensions (Figure 7.7). In this example there is a clear temporal sequence of search activities which either have some observable behaviours or can be articulated by the troubleshooter. Such fluctuations in type and level of knowledge will also occur in cognitive activities spanning very short time

Table 7.8 Examples of descriptions in the means–ends abstraction hierarchy (Rasmussen, 1986)

Washing machine	Manufacturing plant	Computer system
Purpose		
Washing specifications	Market relations	Decision flow graphs in
Energy waste	Supply sources	problem terms
requirements	Energy and waste	
	constraints	
	Safety requirements	
Abstract function		
Energy, water and	Flow of energy and	Information flow
detergent flow	mass, products,	Operations in boolean
topology	monetary values	logic terms, truth
	Mass, energy balances	tables
	Information flow	Symbolic algebraic
	structure in system	functions and
	and organisation	operations
Generic function		
Washing, draining,	Production, assembly,	Memories and registers
drying	maintenance	Amplification,
Heating, temperature	Heat removal,	analog integration
control	combustion, power	and summation
	supply	Feedback loops, power
	Feedback loops	supply
Physical function		
Mechanical drum	Physical functioning	Electrical function of
drive	of equipment and	circuitry
Pump and valve	machinery	Mechanical function of
function	Equipment	input–output
Electrical/gas heating	specifications and	equipment
circuit	characteristics	
	Office and workshop	
	activities	
Physical form		
Configuration and	Form, weight, colour	Physical anatomy
weight, size	of parts and	Form and location of
"Style" and colour	components	components
	Their location and	
	anatomical relation	
	Building layout and	
	appearance	

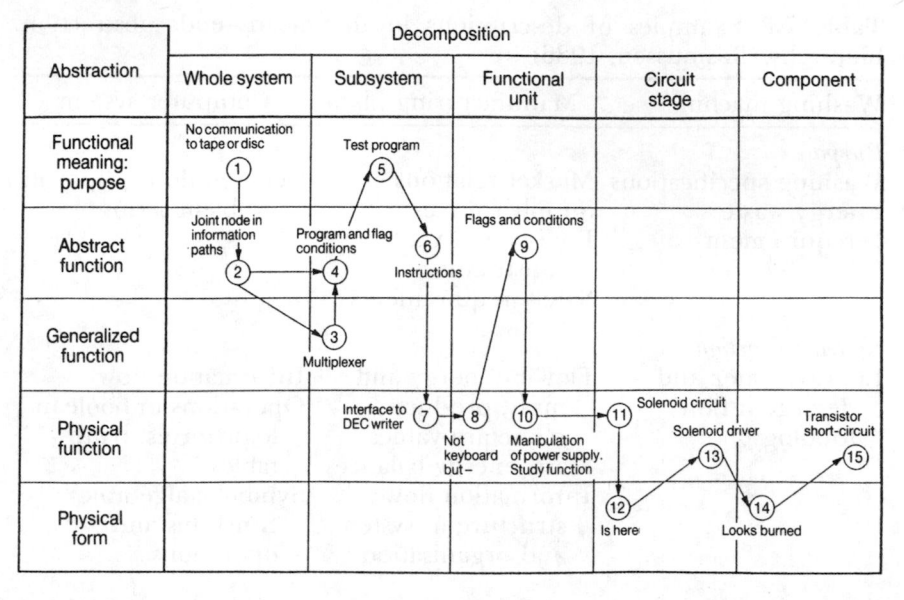

Figure 7.7   The focus of a computer troubleshooter's attention varying with respect to the part–whole dimension and to the level of abstraction during performance of a diagnostic task (Rasmussen, 1986).

periods with no corresponding observable behaviours. Uncovering such changes poses a major challenge for any analyst.

To return to the argument, it is evident that many types of knowledge are required and experts switch rapidly between different types and levels of knowledge. Complex tasks involve knowledge of goals, strategies, rules and facts together with the links between them. A goal may be linked to different methods of achieving it whilst an item may link to different types of declarative knowledge, as in the example from Bainbridge in Figure 7.6. Even though mapping in this way is exceedingly complex, it is essentially static and fails to take account of the control and memory processes which make it dynamic. Dependent upon the type of task, level of expertise and the performance constraints, control may be automatic or attention-based. In the latter case working memory will impose limitations on the nature of the reasoning or problem solving activities engaged in. The reader should now be in no doubt that it is currently beyond the scope of psychology to understand how such mechanisms operate on a multitude of fragments of knowledge which interact in ways that are barely specifiable. Hence for these and other reasons summarised above it is not possible to perform a full and coherent psychological analysis of a complex task. This will only be possible when psychology has advanced further. Anderson (1988) came to a similar conclusion in discussing how to devise the expert module for intelligent tutoring systems saying that:

> The range of tasks for which accurate student models can be reasonably produced is relatively narrow and consists of tasks which are algorithmically tractable and do not involve a great deal of general world knowledge. A prime example is calculus. To understand human expertise more generally will involve a great deal more empirical and simulation research (p. 48).

Top-down, bottom-up and mixed approaches

If, for all the reasons discussed, a complete analysis of complex skills is not possible, then how do we proceed? Inevitably, some compromises and intuitive leaps are necessary.

A distinction can be drawn between top-down, bottom-up and mixed approaches to analysis. Proceeding in a purely bottom-up manner presents insurmountable problems of how a lot of microscopic analyses are assembled into a whole. On the other hand, a top-down approach uses initially high-level descriptions to break down cognitive activities into more manageable chunks which can then be subjected to detailed examination. It will be argued that an intelligent mixture of these two approaches is the optimal solution.

Goal-oriented models and analyses

Identifying what the goals of the performer should be provides a powerful start to the analysis of a complex task, particularly when training has to be developed. The goals and subgoals which are necessary to perform the task are significant because from them flow the different types of knowledge needed to achieve them. Goals are accomplished by different methods or strategies, which in turn have their own knowledge requirements. A similar argument of how to analyse complex tasks has been put forward recently by Woods and Hollnagel (1987).

Various models of complex cognitive activities have been proposed, which are specified in terms of the goals of the task performer. Goals are often described in terms which generalise to tasks of the same type. For example, Bransford and Stein (1984) proposed IDEAL as a model for problem solving or intellectual type tasks. IDEAL is split into five goals or substages: *i*dentifying the problem, *d*efining and representing the problem, *exploring* possible solution strategies, *acting* on these strategies and *looking* back and evaluating the effect of these strategies. A logical, rational sequence is from I to L, although actual performance, even of experts, may deviate from this.

More recently, Norman (1986) has provided a similar approach in what he termed a "theory of action" which is designed to understand stages of user activity in the context of human–computer interaction. Whilst Norman spoke of stages, these in essence are the subgoals which a performer has to achieve in order to fulfil the overall goal of satisfactory performance of the task. Norman proposed seven stages or subgoals of user activity with respect to a task:

1. Establishing the goal.
2. Forming the intention.
3. Specifying the action sequence.
4. Executing the action.
5. Perceiving the system state.
6. Interpreting the state.
7. Evaluating the system state with respect to the goals and intentions.

Norman pointed out that real activities do not always progress from stages one to seven. Sometimes stages are omitted or repeated. Norman provided an example of the use of this analysis in understanding the interaction with a word-processor of somebody who wished to reformat a letter (see Figure 7.8).

> Consider the example of someone who has written a letter on a computer word-processing system. The overall goal is to convey a message to the intended recipient. Along the way, the person prints a draft of the letter. Suppose the person decides that the draft, shown in Figure 7.8A doesn't look right. The person, therefore establishes the intention "Improve the appearance of the letter". Call this first intention *intention 1*. Note that this intention gives little hint of how the task is to be accomplished. As a result, some problem solving is required, perhaps ending with *intention 2*: "Change the indented paragraphs to block paragraphs". To do this requires *intention 3*: "Change the occurrences of .*pp* in the source code for the letter to .*sp*" This in turn requires the person to generate an action sequence appropriate for the text editor, and then, finally, to execute the actions on the computer keyboard. Now, to evaluate the results of the operation requires still further operations, including generation of a fourth intention, *intention 4*: "Format the file" (in order to see whether *intention 2* and *intention 1* were satisfied). The entire sequence of stages is shown in Figure 7.8B. The final product, the reformatted letter, is shown in Figure 7.8C. Even intentions that appear to be quite simple (eg *intention 1*: "Improve the appearance of the letter") lead to numerous subintentions. The intermediary stages may require generating some new subintentions (Norman, 1986, p. 43).

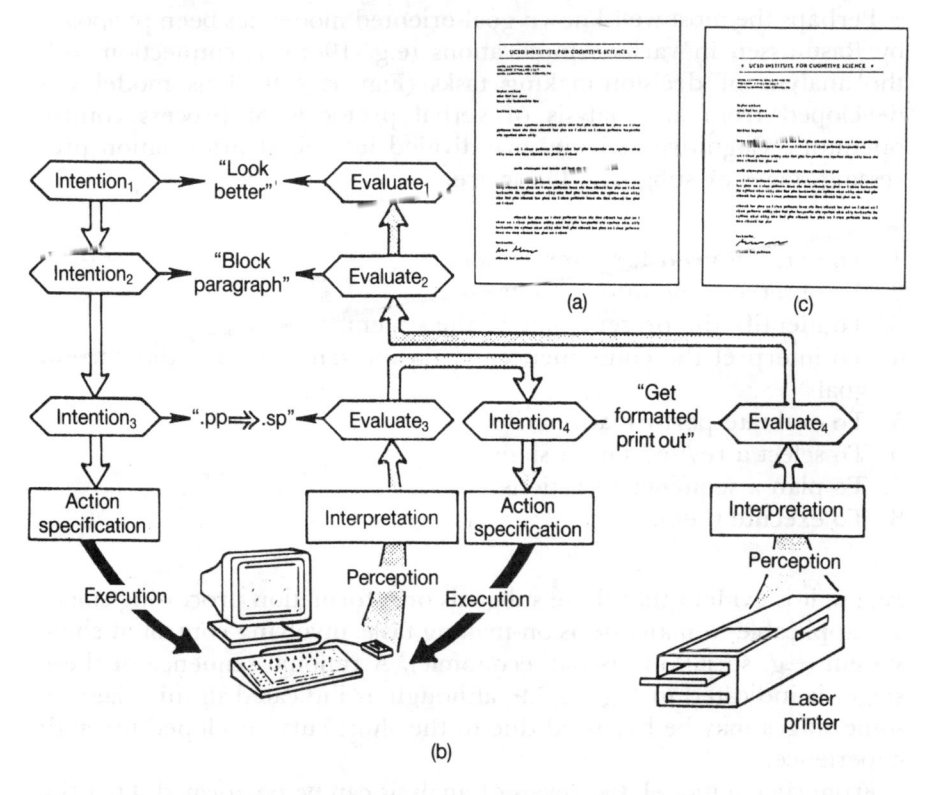

Figure 7.8 Sequence of stages in typical task. (a) The starting point. The letter doesn't look "right", so the initial intention is to "improve the appearance of the letter". (b) The sequence of stages necessary to make the appropriate changes to the source file of the manuscript, then to get a printed, formatted copy of the letter and finally, to evaluate the outcome against the several levels of intentions. (c) The final product, the reformatted letter (Norman, 1986).

The stages in Norman's user activities can be viewed as subgoals associated with performing a task. (The first subgoal is to establish a goal!). In this sense it is similar to the output from Hierarchical Task Analysis discussed in Chapter 6, except that these subgoals generalise to many tasks and are less context dependent. During analysis of a human–computer interaction task, these subgoals could usefully be examined in order to specify the methods and associated knowledge which is needed to accomplish them. This will begin to specify the training content for a person who has to master this task.

Perhaps the most well-known goal-oriented model has been proposed by Rasmussen in various publications (e.g. 1986) in connection with the analysis of decision-making tasks (Figure 7.9). This model was developed from an analysis of verbal protocols of process control operators. Cognitive activities are divided into eight information processing stages or subgoals. These are:

1. To detect a need for intervention.
2. To observe some information.
3. To identify the present state of the system.
4. To interpret the consequences of the present state for the current goal.
5. To evaluate performance criteria.
6. To select a revised target state.
7. To plan a sequence of actions.
8. To execute them.

Again, it is evident that these subgoals or information processing stages are applicable to many decision-making tasks involving control of some system (e.g. social, industrial, economic). A rational sequence of these stages is indicated in Figure 7.9, although as indicated in this diagram some stages may be bypassed due to the short-cuts developed through experience.

From such a model, two levels of analysis can be performed. First the model can be used to chart the performer's knowledge in terms of use of subgoals and their inter-relationships. This represents a high-level analysis of that person's strategy. Novices might be trained to follow the rational sequence initially, but with increasing expertise, training might be provided concerning which short-cuts are feasible and when they should be used. Patterns of errors at this macroscopic level will be informative and indicate training needs concerning the selection of goals. Second, a lower level of analysis can investigate the methods or strategies for achieving these subgoals. For example, how does one interpret the consequences of the current state of the system for the task in hand and how does one plan a sequence of actions to change the state of the system? As these types of questions are answered, it is possible to infer more accurately the processing demands and knowledge requirements of the performer for which training has to be devised. Samurcay and Rogalski (1988) used Rasmussen's model to analyse the cognitive activities in a tactical reasoning task and to structure a training solution. A most interesting analysis of the decision-making processes of nuclear

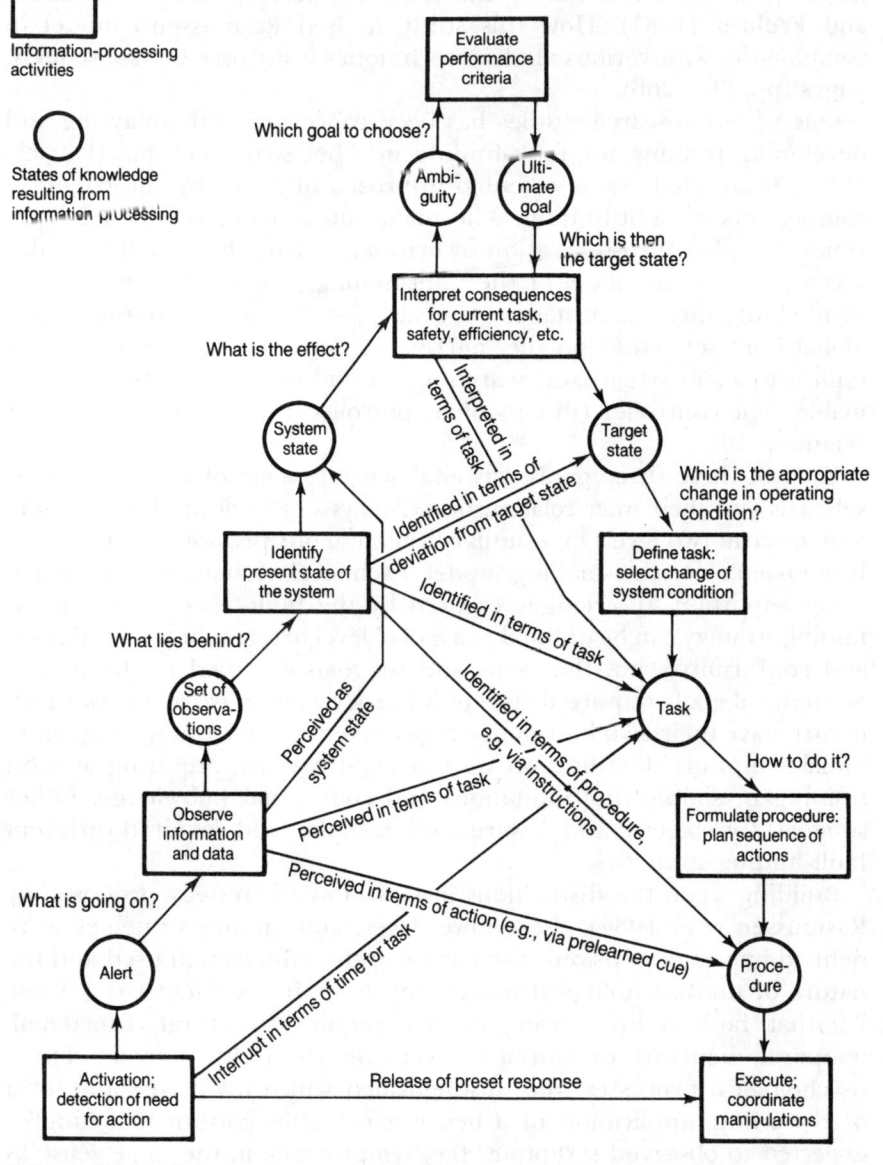

Figure 7.9 Schematic map of the sequence of cognitive processes involved in a control decision. Rational, causal reasoning connects the "states of knowledge" in the basic sequence. Stereotyped processes can bypass intermediate stages. (Rasmussen, 1986 adapted from Rasmussen, 1976.)

power plant operators during incidents was performed by Pew, Miller and Feehrer (1981). How this study utilised Rasmussen's model in combination with various analysis techniques is discussed in subsequent pages (pp. 261–266).

One of our research studies has been concerned with analysing and developing training for fault-finding in a hot strip steel mill (Patrick, 1989). It adopted a goal-oriented approach in analysing the cognitive components of fault-finding. The main output from various analyses, which included the observation of errors in solving hypothetical faults, was a prescriptive model of the fault-finding process. This model was divided into three main stages (or goals): initial symptom identification, global fault set reduction (i.e. narrowing down the area in which the fault is to a subsystem) and searching within the appropriate program-mable logic controller (PLC) which controlled this part of the process (Figure 7.10).

Each of these three goals was analysed into a set of context specific subgoals and their inter-relationships. Analysis of fault-finding strategies took place at two levels in a similar fashion to our previous discussion of Rasmussen's decision-making model. Each level of analysis determined some important knowledge required by the fault-finder. First, fault-finding strategy can be defined at a global level in terms of knowledge of, and conformity with, the goals and subgoals specified in the model. Second, subgoals require different lower-level cognitive activities which in turn have their own knowledge requirements. Some of the subgoals in initial symptom identification were straightforward, requiring at most training in simple discriminations and conceptual knowledge. Other subgoals for stages 2 and 3 were more complex and required different fault-finding strategies.

Building upon the distinctions in fault-finding strategy proposed by Rasmussen (e.g. 1984), these lower-level fault-finding strategies were defined by two dimensions: the nature of the information used and the nature of the psychological process involved. It is evident from Table 7.9 that fault-finding strategies may require structural, functional, temporal, heuristic or causal information from the domain. Three psychological processes were distinguished which involved some form of reasoning, application of a heuristic/rule and pattern matching of expected to observed symptoms (i.e. symptomatic in the same sense as that defined by Rasmussen, 1984). Each of these processes can utilise any one or more types of information. Thus it is possible to have a strategy which involves either application of a functional heuristic or reasoning based upon relationships between system variables. Goals 9, 13 and 18 in the model (Figure 7.10) are particularly significant, since they require

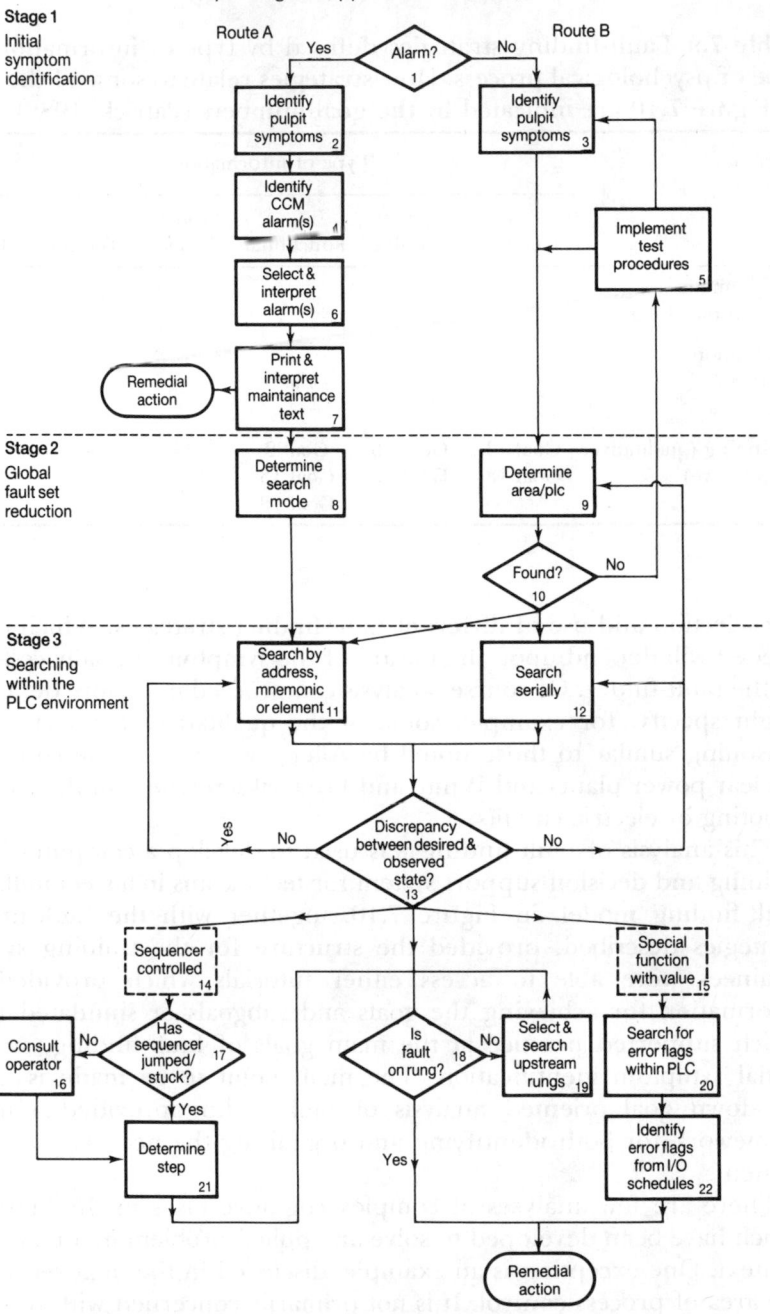

Figure 7.10 A model of fault-finding in the reversing rougher and coilbox of a hot strip steel mill (Patrick, 1989).

Table 7.9 Fault-finding strategies defined by type of information and type of psychological process. How strategies relate to some of the goals in Figure 7.10 are indicated by the goal numbers (Patrick, 1989)

Type of process	Type of information					
	Structural	System variable	Functional	Probab-alistic	Temporal	Other
Symptomatic /pattern matching						
Application of heuristic/ rule			Goal 9			Goal 9
Reasoning (qualitative, quantitative)	Goal 13 Goal 18	Goal 13 Goal 18	Goal 9 Goal 13 Goal 18		Goal 9	

the selection and use of different fault-finding strategies. Which one is needed will depend upon the nature of the symptoms initially collected by the fault-finder. Of course, analysis can proceed into more detail and might specify, for example, some of the qualitative causal chains of reasoning similar to those noted by Allengry (1987) in the control of nuclear power plants and White and Frederiksen (1987) in the troubleshooting of electric circuits.

This analysis of fault-finding was used to develop a computer-based training and decision support system for technicians in a steel mill. The fault-finding model, in Figure 7.10, together with the fault-finding strategies described, provided the structure for the training system. Trainees were able to access either tutorials which provided the information for achieving the goals and subgoals or simulated faults which supported practice at the main goals of fault-finding, such as initial symptom identification. The main point to be made is that a top-down goal oriented analysis of fault-finding provided a useful framework for both identifying and organising the necessary training content.

There are few analyses of complex cognitive tasks in the literature which have been developed to solve an applied problem in a real world context. One exception is an example, discussed in the next section, in the area of process control. It is not primarily concerned with training, although for various reasons it is a good illustration of how analyses of complex cognitive tasks can be carried out.

Decision-making of nuclear power plant operators (Pew, Miller and Feehrer, 1981)

One of the most impressive analyses of a complex cognitive task was performed by Pew, Miller and Feehrer (1981) in a study of the decision-making of nuclear power plant operators during off-normal incidents. A number of different types of analysis were necessary which involved considerable improvisation. Two particular strengths of the study were: (1) at each stage of the study both the process and products of each analysis were made explicit, and (2) the results from the different analyses were integrated in order to serve the overall aims of the investigation. The aims of the study were to develop an appropriate framework and methodology for such an analysis, to use this to evaluate the decision-making involved in four nuclear incidents and to evaluate the potential effect of changes in control room layout, computerised support and training. The study is exceedingly detailed and it is only possible here to give an outline of the analyses performed.

The study used both top-down and bottom-up approaches to analysis. The first part of the analysis was top-down and used Rasmussen's decision-making model with some minor modifications. Each of the eight stages of the model was extended to include sources of error. These were represented in so-called Murphy diagrams, so named after the originator of the law that "if anything can possibly go wrong, it will"! These errors are defined in a way which is specific to the context of the study. The Murphy diagram for identification of system state is given in Figure 7.11. There are two possible outcomes for the activity: success (S) or failure (F). Proximal sources refer mainly to any misconceptions of the operators at the end of this activity (i.e. identification of system state), whilst distal sources primarily cover some of the possible reasons for these misconceptions.

The decision-making to be analysed concerned four incidents in 1979: a steam tube rupture at Prairie Island; an excessive cooldown at North Anna; a loss of instrumentation followed by excessive cooldown at Oconee; and a loss of feedwater at Oyster Creek. Time lines of decision-making were developed for each incident using various data collection methods such as retrospective interviews and documentation in order to describe operator decisions. The time lines were designed to identify not only actual decisions but also associated beliefs, expectations, etc. For this purpose 10 categories were developed which included time, available information, event signalled, knowledge and/or belief state, intention, expectation and decision/action. From these time lines, a total of 17 decisions was judged as critical between the four incidents

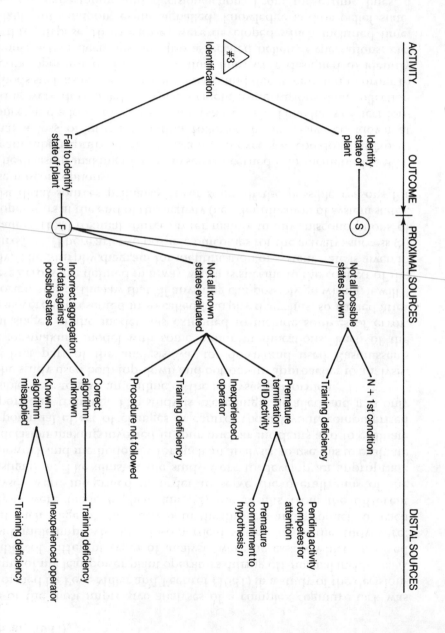

Figure 7.11 Murphy diagram for identification of system state, from a study by Pew, Miller and Feehrer (1981).

Table 7.10 Decision/action analysis and time line for the first critical decision ("initial diagnosis") in the Prairie Island incident (Pew, Miller and Feehrer, 1981)

Time	Available Info. or stimulus (info./loc.)	Event signalled	Knowledge and/or belief state components	Intention	Expectation	Decision/action	Source for D/A	Immediate feedback	Comments
1414	Hi-rad. alarm annunciator on IR15 air ejector	Discharge produces false alarms (steam generator) Not a full scale indication at this time	Occasional spiking produces false indications	Monitor for further indications	If not a false alarm, IR15 will alarm again	Annunciator turned off	Knowledge of false alarm possibilities and SOP for this type of normal alarm indication	Annunciator turned off. Rad. monitor returns to normal	Appropriate action in view of spiking properties and absence of other indications
≈1418	Hi-rad. alarm annunciator on IR15 air ejector	Discharge produces false alarms (steam generator)	Occasional spiking for further indications but 2 FA's may be unlikely; does not look like "typical spike"	Monitor closely for further indications	If not an FA, IR15 will alarm again	Annunciator turned off	Knowledge of FA possibilities and SOP for this type of alarm return toward normal	Annunciator off. Appropriate action in view of FA possibilities and absence of indications normal	Appropriate action in view of FA possibilities
≈1419	Hi-rad. alarm annunciator on IR15 air ejector	Discharge from secondary-current full-scale deflection suggests real leak	2 prior alarms and detector deflection suggests which would produce alarm	Verify that detector does not monitor, then monitor indication is correct	If no water on detector, then indication is correct	Dispatch operator to check for water on detector Verify trains Call Health Physics to obtain sample	SOP	Rad. monitor remains at full scale Next indication occurs before report of operator on detector	Appropriate action given prior alarms and full scale deflection
1420	Overtemp. ΔT Decreasing on Turbine pressure Turbine run-back alarm	Air rad. alarms, decreasing pzr level and pressure; Begin determination of which SG because of loss of primary coolant in SG	Air rad. alarms, decreasing pzr level and pressure; symptoms now suggest an SG tube is leaking	Monitor per level Pzr level and pressure; continue to fall	Pzr level and pressure will continue to fall because of loss of coolant in SG	Monitor level and pressure Dispatch operator to line up ventilation Check Health Physics	EOP – "Hi — Activity in secondary"		Appropriate actions given plant indications and beliefs
				Minimise effect on grid of reactor trip	Reactor trip on event of low pzr pressure	Notify grid controller of planned load reduction Commence load reduction	SOP in event of load reduction	Load indicators	Operators had recent simulator training on ST ruptures
≈1421	Feed flow—steam flow mismatch in SG "A"	Augmented Air rad. alarms, rapid pzr level and pressure decrease and mismatch unequivocally confirm rupture, probably in SG "A"				Reactor trip on low pzr pressure Automatic safety injection if no manual action taken	EOP in event of planned load power shutdown	Load indicators	Appropriate action; preferred action to sudden pulloff from grid following reactor trip

(method not specified), each of which was then subjected to a more detailed decision/action analysis. Each decision/action analysis involved 14 new categories which attempted to identify the wider circumstances relating to each decision such as purpose, action, preceding activities, input and output information, knowledge required and accessibility of control. To provide a flavour of the detail of these analyses, the decision/action analysis together with its time line for the first critical decision (diagnosis) in the Prairie Island incident are given in Table 7.10. This covers the time period between 14:14 and 14:21 hours on 2 October 1979.

A panel of experts assessed the decision/action analyses and the time lines for the 17 critical decisions. Therefore a link between these decisions and the potential impact of changes in training, decision support etc., was made via the ratings of these experts. Not surprisingly these ratings varied considerably.

Finally, components of the 17 critical decisions were then mapped onto the eight information processing stages of Rasmussen's model and the sources of error identified in the Murphy diagrams used in the initial top-down part of the analysis. Thus for the Prairie Island incident the key decision aspects for each of the five decisions judged as critical in this incident are summarised in Table 7.11. A profile of the critical decisions and whether or not they were successful was developed pooling data from the four incidents. The eight decision-making aspects are represented in Figure 7.12 in terms of their overall frequency and how often they were judged as unsuccessful.

Two suggestions which emerged from the analysis of the Prairie Island incident were a need to reduce the number of instruments giving false alarms and a need to reduce the time required for data collection activities by the use of some decision support system. The overall conclusion from the study was that whilst training and better procedures might help decision-making, better support for the detection and correction of errors by computer decision aids was important. Time stress was identified as a major factor in inefficient decision-making.

Pew et al.'s study therefore used a variety of types of analysis, including both top-down and bottom-up approaches. Considerable methodological improvisation and innovation were required. Inevitably, criticisms can be levelled at parts of the analysis such as retrospective interviews and expert ratings. However, one of the reasons that this study has been outlined is that it analyses a complex cognitive task with a series of carefully conducted and integrated analyses. No previous guidelines existed on how to analyse such cognitive activities. In addition, the analyses integrated the context specific decision-making

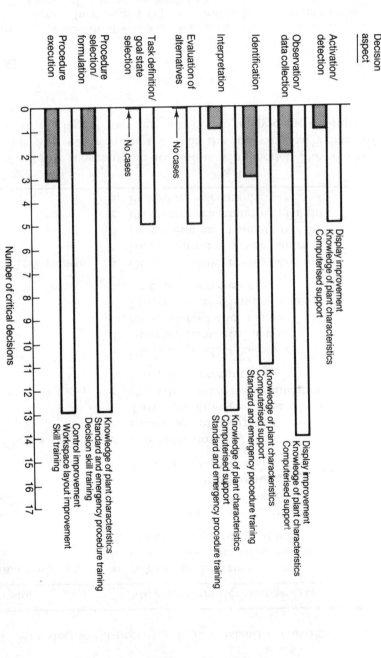

Figure 7.12 A summary of the number and type of decision aspects in 17 critical decisions involved in four nuclear power plant incidents (Pew et al., 1981). The unshaded bar in each pair represents overall frequency, whilst the shaded bar represents frequency of errors for each decision aspect. The three improvements judged to have the greatest potential impact on each decision aspect are listed beside each pair of bars.

Table 7.11 Key decision aspects for Prairie Island event (Pew et al., 1981)

Critical decision	Most relevant decision aspects
1. Initial diagnosis	a. Activation/detection b. Observation/data collection d. Interpretation of situation
2. Allow SI to occur automatically	b. Observation/data collection d. Interpretation of situation e. Evaluation of alternatives f. Task definition/goal state selection
3. Shut off RCPs	d. Interpretation e. Evaluation of alternatives f. Task definition/goal state selection g. Procedure selection/formulation h. Procedure execution
4. Close MSIV	b. Observation/data collection d. Interpretation of situation e. Evaluation of alternatives g. Procedure selection/formulation h. Procedure execution
5. Turn off HPI pumps	b. Observation/data collection c. Identification of system state d. Interpretation of situation g. Procedure selection/formulation h. Procedure execution

components within a generalisable decision making model. The conclusion from this and other studies is that the analyst clearly has to improvise in an intelligent manner in order to analyse such complex subject matter.

REFERENCES

Allengry, P. (1987). The analysis of knowledge representation of nuclear power plant control room operators. In Bullinger, H.J. and Shackel, B. (Eds) *Human–computer interaction – 'INTERACT' 87*. Amsterdam: North Holland.

Altman, J.W. (1976). Transferability of vocational skills: Review of literature and research information. Series No. 103. Ohio: Centre for Vocational Education.

Anderson, J.R. (1980). *Cognitive psychology and its implications*. San Francisco: W.H. Freeman and Company.

Anderson, J.R. (1988). The expert module. In Polson, M.C. and Richardson, J.J. (Eds) *Foundations of intelligent tutoring systems*. Hillsdale, NJ: Lawrence Erlbaum.

Annett, J. and Duncan K.D. (1967). Task analysis and training design. *Occupational Psychology*, **41**, 211–221.

Bainbridge, L. (1986). What should a good model of the NPP operator contain? In *Proceedings of the International Topical Meeting on Advances in Human Factors in Nuclear Power Systems*, American Nuclear Society, Knoxville, Tennessee, April.

Bainbridge, L. (1988). Types of representation. In Goodstein, L.P., Anderson, H.B. and Olsen, S.E. (Eds) *Tasks, errors and mental models*. London: Taylor and Francis.

Bainbridge, L. (1989). Multi-plexed VDT display system: A framework for good practice. In Weir, G.R.S. (Ed.) *HCI and complex systems*. London: Academic Press.

Bartlett, F.C. (1932). *Remembering*. Cambridge University Press.

Bloom, B.S. (Ed.) (1956). *A taxonomy of educational objectives. Handbook 1: Cognitive domain*. New York: McKay. (Reprinted in 1972 by Longman.)

Bransford, J.D., Arbitman-Smith, R., Stein, B.S. and Vye, N.J. (1985). Improving thinking and learning skills: An analysis of three approaches. In, Segal, J.W., Chipman, S.F. and Glaser, R. (Eds) *Thinking and learning skills: Volume 1. Relating instruction to research*. Hillsdale, NJ: Lawrence Erlbaum.

Bransford, J.D. and Stein, B.S. (1984). *The ideal problem solver. A guide for improving thinking, learning and creativity*. New York: Plenum.

Chipman, S.F., Segal, J.W. and Glaser, R. (1985) (Eds). *Thinking and learning skills, Volume 2, Research and open questions*. Hillsdale, NJ: Lawrence Erlbaum.

Clancey (1985). Heuristic classification. *Artificial Intelligence*, **27**, 289–350.

Cronbach, L.J. (1970). *Essentials of psychological testing*. 3rd edition. New York: Harper and Row.

Cunningham, J.W., Boese, R.R., Neeb, R.W. and Pass, J.J. (1983). Systematically derived work dimensions. Factor analyses of the Occupational Analysis Inventory. *Journal of Applied Psychology*, **68**, 232–252.

Duncan K.D. (1972). Strategies for analysis of the task. In Hartley, J. (Ed.) *Strategies for programmed instruction: An educational technology*. London: Butterworths.

Dunham, J., Guilford, J. and Hoepfner, R. (1968). Multivariate approaches to discovering the intellectual components of concept learning. *Psychological Review*, **75**, 206–221.

Dunnette, M.D. (1976). Aptitudes, abilities and skills. In Dunnette, M.D. (Ed.) *Handbook of industrial and organisational psychology*. Chicago: Rand McNally.

Ekstrom, R.B. (1973). Cognitive factors: Some recent literature. Technical Report No. 2. ONR Contract N00024–71–C-0227, NR 150–329. Princeton: Educational Testing Service.

Evans, J.S.B.T. (1988). The knowledge elicitation problem: A psychological perspective. *Behaviour and Information Technology*, **7**(2), 111–130.

Ferguson, G.A. (1954). On learning and human ability. *Canadian Journal of Psychology*, **8**, 95–112.

Ferguson, G.A. (1956). On transfer and the abilities of man. *Canadian Journal of Psychology*, **10**, 121–131.

Feuerstein, R. (1980). *Instrumental enrichments: An intervention program for cognitive modifiability*. Baltimore: University Park Press.

Fleishman, E.A. (1964). *The structure and measurement of physical fitness*. Englewood Cliffs, NJ: Prentice-Hall.

Fleishman, E.A. (1978). Relating individual differences to the dimensions of human tasks. *Ergonomics*, **21**(12), 1007–1019.

Fleishman, E.A. and Fruchter, B. (1960). Factor structure and predictability of successive stages of learning Morse Code. *Journal of Applied Psychology*, **44**, 97–101.

Fleishman E.A. and Hempel, W.E. Jr (1955). The relation between abilities and improvement with practice in a visual discrimination reaction task. *Journal of Experimental Psychology*, **49**, 301–312.

Fleishman, E.A. and Quaintance, M.F. (1984). *Taxonomies of human performance*. Orlando, FL: Academic Press.

Fleishman, E.A. and Rich, S (1963). Role of kinesthetic and spatial-visual abilities in perceptual-motor learning. *Journal of Experimental Psychology*, **66**, 6–11.

Fleishman, E.A. and Stephenson, R.W. (1970). Development of a taxonomy of human performance: A review of the third year's progress. *JSAS Catalog of Selected Documents in Psychology*, **48**, 1–68 (No. 113).

French, J.W., Ekstrom, R.B. and Price, L.A. (1963). *Kit of reference tests for cognitive factors*. Princeton: Educational Testing Service.

Gagne, R.M. (1965). *The conditions of learning*. New York: Holt, Rinehart and Winston.

Gentner, D. and Stevens, A.L. (Eds) (1983). *Mental models*. Hillsdale, NJ: Lawrence Erlbaum.

Glaser R. and Bassok, M. (1989). Learning theory and the study of instruction. *Annual Review of Psychology*, **40**, 631–666.

Guilford, J.P. (1956). The structure of intellect. *Psychological Bulletin*, **53**, 267–293.

Guilford, J.P. (1967). *The nature of human intelligence*. New York: McGraw-Hill.

Guilford, J.P. (1977). *Way beyond the IQ*. Buffalo, NY: Creative Education Foundation.

Guilford, J.P. (1982). Cognitive psychology's ambiguities: Some suggested remedies. *Psychological Review*, **89**, 48–59.

Harrow, A.J. (1972). *A taxonomy of the psychomotor domain: A guide for developing behavioural objectives*. New York: McKay.

Johnson-Laird, P. (1983). *Mental models*. Cambridge, MA: Harvard University Press.

Krathwohl, D.R., Bloom, B.S. and Masia, B.B. (1964). *Taxonomy of educational objectives: Handbook II: Affective domain*. New York: McKay. (Reprinted in 1972 by Longman.)

Leplat, J. (1985). The elicitation of expert knowledge. *Proceedings of Nato ASI Intelligent Decision Aids in Process Environments*, Pisa, September.

Levine, J.M. and Teichner, W.H. (1973). Development of a taxonomy of human performance: An information-theoretic approach. *JSAS Catalogue of Selected Documents in Psychology*, **3**, 28 (Ms No. 325).

Mallamad, S.M., Levine, J.M. and Fleishman, E.A. (1980). Identifying ability requirements by decision flow diagrams. *Human Factors*, **22**, 57–68.

Marquardt, L.D. (1972). The rated attribute requirements of job elements in a structured job analysis questionnaire – The Position Analysis Questionnaire. M.Sc. Thesis. Lafayette, Indiana: Purdue University.

Marquardt, L.D. and McCormick, E.J. (1974). The job dimensions underlying the job elements of the Position Analysis Questionnaire (PAQ). Report No. 4. Lafayette, Indiana: Occupational Research Center, Department of Psychological Science, Purdue University.

Mayer, R.E., Larkin, T.H. and Kadane, J.B. (1984). A cognitive analysis of mathematical problem-solving ability. In Sternberg, R.J. (Ed.) *Advances in the psychology of human intelligence*. Volume 2. Hillsdale, NJ: Lawrence Erlbaum.

McCormick, E.J., Jeanneret, P.R. and Mecham, R.C. (1969). A study of job characteristics and job dimensions as based on the Position Analysis Questionnaire. Report No. 6. Lafayette, IN: Occupational Research Centre, Purdue University.

McCormick, E.J., Jeanneret, P.R. & Mecham, R.C. (1972). A study of job characteristics and job dimensions as based on the Position Analysis Questionnaire (PAQ). *Journal of Applied Psychology*, **56**, 347–368.

McCormick, E.J., Mecham, R.C. and Jeanneret, P.R. (1977). Technical manual for the Position Analysis Questionnaire (PAQ) (System II). Logan, UT: PAQ Services.

Mecham, R.C. and McCormick, E.J. (1969). The rated attribute requirements of job elements in the Position Analysis Questionnaire (prepared for the Office of Naval Research Under Contract – Nonr-1100(28). Report No. 1. Lafayette, IN: Occupational Research Centre, Purdue University.

Meeker, M. (1981). The SOI Institute based on Guilford's 'Structure of Intellect' model. *Education*, **101**, 302–309.

Miller, R.B. (1967). Task taxonomy: science or technology. *Ergonomics*, **10**, 167–176.

Miller, R.B. (1973). Development of a taxonomy of human performance. Design of a systems task vocabulary. *JSAS Catalog of Selected Documents in Psychology*, **3**, 29–30 (No. 327).

Miller, R.B. (1974). A method for determining task strategies. Technical Report AFHRL-TR-74–26. Alexandria: American Institute for Research.

Miller, R.B. (1975). Task formats in human performance. Unpublished manuscript. From R.B. Miller, Colonial House, South Rd, Poughkeepsie, NY, 12601.

Minsky, M. (1975). A framework for representing knowledge. In Winston, P. (Ed.) *The psychology of computer vision*. New York: McGraw-Hill.

Naughton, J. (1986). *Artificial intelligence: Applications to training*. A Research Study by the Open University for the Training Technology Section of the Manpower Services Commission. Sheffield: HMSO.

Norman, D.A. (1986). Cognitive engineering. In Norman, D.A. and Draper, S.W. (Eds) *User centered system design*. Hillsdale, NJ: Lawrence Erlbaum.

Norman, D.A. and Draper, S.W. (Eds) (1986). *User centered design*. Hillsdale, NJ: Lawrence Erlbaum.

Ohlsson, S. (1986). Some principles of intelligent tutoring. *Instructional Science*, **14**, 293–326.

Parker, J.F. Jr and Fleishman, E.A. (1961). Use of analytical information concerning task requirements to measure the effectiveness of skill training. *Journal of Applied Psychology*, **45**, 295–302.

Patrick, J. (1989). Representation of fault-finding in complex industrial contexts. In Proceedings of the Second European Meeting on Cognitive Science Approaches in Process Control (pp. 269–281). Siena: University of Siena.

Peterson N.G. and Bownas, D.A. (1982). Skills, task structure and performance acquisition. In Dunnette, M.D. and Fleishman, E.A. (Eds) *Volume 1. Human capability assessment*. NJ: Lawrence Erlbaum.

Pew, R.W., Miller, D.C. and Feehrer, C.E. (1981). Evaluation of proposed control room improvements through analysis of critical operator decisions. EPRI NP-1982. Palo Alto, CA: Electric Power Research Institute.

Rasmussen, J. (1984). Strategies for state identification and diagnosis in supervisory control tasks and design of computer-based support systems. In Rouse, W.B. (Ed.) *Advances in man–machine systems research*, Volume 1, pp. 139–193. J.A.I. Press.

Rasmussen, J. (1985). The role of hierarchical knowledge representation in decision making and system management. *IEEE Transactions on Systems, Man and Cybernetics*, **SMC-15**, 2.

Rasmussen, J. (1986). *Information processing and human–machine interaction: An approach to cognitive engineering*. Amsterdam: North Holland.

Rasmussen, J. and Lind, M. (1981). Coping with complexity. *Riso-M-2293*, Riso National Laboratory, Roskilde, Denmark.

Reinartz, S.J. and Reinartz, G. (1989). Verbal communication in collective control of simulated nuclear power plant incidents. In *Proceedings of the 2nd European Meeting on Cognitive Science Approaches to Process Control*, pp. 195–203. Siena: University of Siena.

Resnick, L.B. (1987). *Education and learning to think*. Washington, DC: National Academy Press.

Ringland, G.A. and Duce, D.A. (Eds) (1988). *Approaches to knowledge representation: An introduction*. Chichester: Wiley.

Rouse, W.B. and Morris, N.M. (1986). On looking into the black box: Prospects and limits in the search for mental models. *Psychological Bulletin*, **100**(3), 349–363.

Rowntree, D. (1977). *Educational technology in curriculum development*. London: Harper and Row.

Sage, A.P. and Lagomasino, A. (1984). Knowledge representation and man–machine dialogue. *Advances in Man-Machine System Research*, **1**, 223–260.

Samurcay, R. and Rogalski, L. (1988). Analyses of operator's cognitive activities in learning and using a method for decision making in public safety. In Patrick, J. and Duncan, K.D. (Eds) *Training, human decision making and control*. Amsterdam: Elsevier.

Schank, R.C. and Abelson, R.P. (1977). *Scripts, plans, goals and understanding*. Hillsdale, NJ: Lawrence Erlbaum.

Scott, M.G. (1955). The measurement of kinesthesis. *The Research Quarterly*, **26**, 324–341.

Segal, J.W., Chipman, S.F. and Glaser, R. (Eds) (1985). *Thinking and learning skills, volume 1, Relating instruction to research*. Hillsdale, NJ: Lawrence Erlbaum.

Singleton, W.T. (1989). *The mind at work. Psychological ergonomics*. Cambridge University Press.

Spearman, C. (1927). *The abilities of man*. New York: Macmillan.

Sternberg, R.J. (1977). Component processes in analogical reasoning. *Psychological Review*, **84**, 353–378.

Sternberg, R.J. (1980). Sketch of a componential subtheory of human intelligence. *Behavioural and Brain Sciences*, **3**, 573–614.

Sternberg, R.J. (1985). Instrumental and componential approaches to the nature and training of intelligence. In Chipman, S.F., Segal, J.W. and Glaser, R. (Eds) *Thinking and learning skills, Volume 2, Research and open questions*. Hillsdale, NJ: Lawrence Erlbaum.

Sternberg, R.J. (1986). *Intelligence applied*. New York: Harcourt Brace Jovanovich.

Theologus, C.C., Romashko, T. and Fleishman, E.A. (1973). Developments of a taxonomy of human performance: A feasibility study of ability dimensions for classifying human tasks. *JSAS Catalog of Selected Documents in Psychology*, **3**, 25–26 (Ms. No. 321).

Thurstone, L.L. (1938). Primary mental abilities. *Psychometric Monographs*, No. 4.

Vernon, P.E. (1971). *The structure of human abilities*. London: Methuen.

White, B.Y. and Frederiksen, J.R. (1987). Qualitative models and intelligent learning environments. In Lawler, R.W. and Yazdani, M. (Eds). *Artificial intelligence and education, Volume 1, Learning environments and tutoring systems*. Hillsdale, NJ: Lawrence Erlbaum.

Wilson, W.D., Barnard, P.J. Green, T.R.G. and Maclean, A. (1988). Knowledge-based task analysis for human–computer systems. In Van der Veer, G.C., Green, T.R.G., Hoc, J.-M. and Murray, D.M. (Eds) *Working with computers: Theory versus outcome*. London: Academic Press.

Woods, D.D. and Hollnagel, E. (1987). Mapping cognitive demands in complex problem solving worlds. *International Journal of Man-Machine Studies*, **26**, 257–275.

CHAPTER 8
Training design: introduction and theories

8.1 GENERAL INTRODUCTION

As an introduction to the topic of training design, three basic questions will be addressed which concern the importance, nature and difficulty of training design. In addition, an overview will be given of how the content of Chapters 8–12 contributes to the design of training.

How important is the design of training?

The importance of training design can be gauged from the various Instructional Systems Development (ISD) models discussed in Chapter 4. Design of training follows an analysis of the tasks to be trained. It translates the content of training, which has been derived by some form of analysis, into an effective training programme. For example, the analysis phase in the IPISD model is followed by two phases of design and development which precede the implementation of training. Both of these phases are subsumed by the term training design as used here. Unfortunately, there is a widespread belief that after the content of training has been identified, it is a straightforward matter of "giving" the trainee this information in the same manner in which a patient swallows a pill. Given the limitations of the human as an information processor, how this information is structured and presented in a manner which facilitates learning is exceedingly important.

A further indication of the importance of training design is the large number of books and journals devoted to this topic spanning the areas of education, training and instruction.

What are the components of training design?

Training design covers all of the activities associated with translating training content into a training programme. These activities include:

providing pretraining;

organising and sequencing different types of training content;
selecting between different training methods for presenting information;
designing the sequence in which subskills are to be learned;
providing sufficient support to the trainee in terms of advice, explanation and feedback on progress;
ensuring that appropriate cognitive/learning strategies are activated
during training; and
assessing level of performance.

To bring some order to this list of issues, let us consider the
framework for training design which is proposed in Figure 8.1. There are
three main components or inputs to a fully designed training programme:

1. Training content.
2. Training methods and strategies.
3. Trainee characteristics.

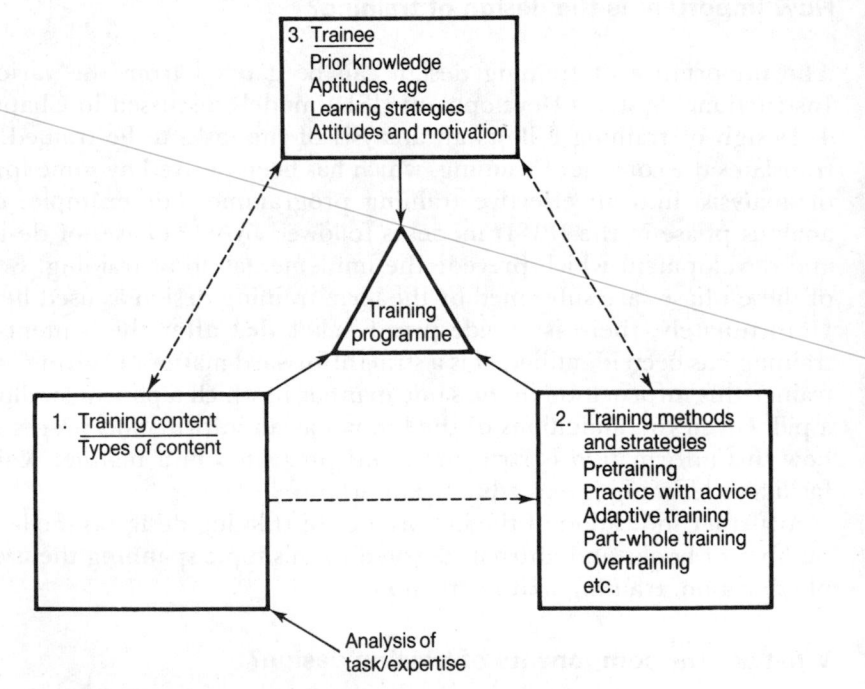

Figure 8.1 Three components in the design of training. All three
components have inputs to a training programme. Training content is
derived by some analysis of the task/expertise. The dotted lines represent the interactions between the three components.

Each component needs to be considered, although theories and principles of training design differ in which components they empha-sise. This framework is not only useful for mapping out the content of Chapters 8–12, but also for charting the changing perspectives of the psychology of training. Each of these components will be discussed together with their interactions (represented by dotted lines in Figure 8.1).

The first component in our framework is *training content* which forms the basis of the training programme which has to be mastered by the trainee. The training content which is identified by some analysis, as discussed in Chapters 5–7, will inevitably have some structure and sequence, although this may be changed in order to design an effective training programme. Training content has to be sequenced and broken up into manageable learning chunks according to various design methods and strategies. The amount and nature of training content will depend upon the training situation. At one extreme, a trainee might have to learn either a list of numerical codes or the functions of different keys on a word-processor. At the other extreme, a trainee might have to undergo a wide-ranging training programme in order to develop a technical understanding of nuclear power plants and their operating procedures. In this latter situation, training has to cover many types of knowledge.

The second component of training design is the *training methods and strategies* which organise and supplement this training content into a fully designed training programme. These are equivalent to what Reigeluth (1983) defined as "organisational instructional methods or strategies". These training methods are a mixed bag of principles and variables taken from psychological studies of learning and training which are sufficiently strong as to require the training designer's attention. They include the traditional issues of how to sequence and structure training content and the nature of the learning events and advice provided to trainees. Training methods and strategies can be distinguished in different ways and at different levels. Training strategies can be clas-sified by the phase of training to which they apply, i.e. before, during and at the end of training. Thus the decision to provide pretraining is an overall training strategy which can be implemented by the use of different methods. Similarly, there are at least three major methods of providing information to the trainee during training. Firstly, the provi-sion of some practice coupled with advice is a successful training method for many skills. Secondly, a demonstration of what is required can be given, as in the case of behaviour role-modelling in which a trainee imitates the role play of a model. Thirdly, the trainee may be prompted or cued with respect to when or what type of response is required in certain situations. These three methods differ fundamentally in *how* information is provided to the trainee. There is no reason why all of these strategies and methods of training might not be used within the same training programme. Thus a trainee might be given some pretraining followed by a demonstration of a role play situation which then has to be practised with advice provided by the trainer.

The author has omitted from training methods and strategies any reference to the media by which training is given (these are termed "delivery" strategies by Reigeluth, 1983). A great deal has been written about selecting the appropriate media (e.g. television, lecture, text, seminar, tutorial) and these are often elevated to the status of different methods. This is misleading, since these are only superficial characteristics from a training design perspective. Whilst media inevitably place some constraints upon the design of training, they do not prescribe any fundamental organisation of the training materials, interaction process etc. Hence a tutorial might provide good or poor training depending upon the nature of the interactions between the tutor and trainee and the quality of the explanations provided. Unfortunately, many studies of supposedly different methods of training confound media differences with the organisation and structure of the training materials. For discussions of the general advantages and disadvantages of different media, the reader should consult Briggs and Wager (1981) and Romiszowski (1974, 1986, 1988).

The third component in our framework of training design is the *trainee* (Figure 8.1). This component has had a distinctly patchy exposure in the training literature. The knowledge and skills of the trainee not only affect *what* has to be trained (i.e. the training content) but also *how* information in a training programme is understood and assimilated. Traditionally, individual difference variables such as age and IQ were of interest, whereas more recently the learning strategies which the trainee brings to bear upon the training materials have been investigated. Much-neglected design variables are the trainee's motivation and attitudes, which have a strong influence on the success of any training programme.

The prominence given to these three components of training design has varied with changes in psychology over the past 60 years. Behaviourism believed that learning was "effected" as a result of the principles of reinforcement. Consequently, training was concerned with the organisation of a task and its learning conditions, such that the correct behaviour was elicited from trainees and then reinforced. The trainee was essentially a passive recipient of information provided by a training programme. Learning supposedly occurred automatically under the appropriate behavioural conditions. Hence the trainee and training content components of training design were virtually ignored during this era. The early work of Gagné represented a reaction to this approach by pointing out that different types of training content required different training conditions. An enduring consequence of the behavioural approach has been recognition of the importance of providing the trainee with practice and feedback in order to learn a task. Since perceptual-motor skills were of dominant interest before and for some years after the Second World War, many studies in training design investigated the efficiency of different practice regimes and the optimal means of providing advice or feedback to the trainee. This was done with little reference to the cognitive processes involved, since such skills had observable components which could be demonstrated by trainers and practised by trainees. Such an approach is less feasible for the cognitive skills of concern today.

In the late 1960s and in the 1970s, studies were carried out under the heading of "Aptitude-Treatment Interaction" (ATI) research. These studies attempted to demonstrate that the effectiveness of different training methods depended upon trainee variables, such as IQ, anxiety etc. Despite a considerable research effort, this approach met with only limited success in terms of the robustness and generality of the findings which emerged.

More recently, cognitive psychology has analysed the activities of the trainee both during training and during subsequent performance of the task in a more fine-grained manner. The trainee is seen as searching for and constructing meaning as a consequence of not only his/her own mental models and strategies, but also the nature of the training content and the manner in which it is designed in the training programme. There is much subtle interplay between the three components of training design (Figure 8.1). This led Rigney (1978) to suggest that training should be more directly concerned with ensuring that appropriate cognitive strategies are generated by trainees. This, he argued, can be achieved by the development of "orienting tasks" which induce the trainee to adopt and develop the necessary cognitive strategies. One example of this approach is in training what are known as "learning strategies" which improve the learning and retention of primarily textual material. As we will find out in Chapter 10, even this approach has some difficulties.

There are no texts which chart these changing approaches to training design as a consequence of changes in psychological perspective. One strategy the reader might adopt is to consult the reviews of training or instructional psychology published in the *Annual Review of Psychology* for the last 20 years, in particular Campbell (1971), Glaser and Resnick (1972), McKeachie (1974), Wittrock and Lumsdaine (1977), Goldstein (1980), Resnick (1981), Gagné and Dick (1983), Wexley (1984), Pintrich et al. (1986) and Glaser and Bassok (1989). These are useful reviews and the studies cited not only reflect the reviewer's interests but also the training topics of interest at that time.

How difficult is training design?

By now the reader should be in no doubt as to the answer to this question. The transition from training content to a fully designed training programme has been recognised as notoriously difficult (e.g. Duncan, 1972; Resnick, 1976). Different components of training design are emphasised by different theoretical approaches and studies. No comprehensive and coherent set of principles of training design yet exists which indicates how the three components of training design in Figure 8.1 should be accommodated in any specific training situation. Nevertheless, there are many variables which are of use to practitioners in designing training programmes.

One potential strategy for advancing our understanding of training design is to present the same training problem to different investigators. Just such an approach has been taken in two recent publications. Reigeluth (1987a) asked eight people with different theoretical perspectives of training design to develop outline "lessons" for the same task. The task involved learning about different lenses, focal length and the use of an optical microscope. The resulting lessons varied considerably between the theoretical approaches. Snelbecker (1987), commenting on these lessons, pointed out that it was likely that different training materials would have resulted even from different designers using the *same* theoretical approach.

A more research-oriented venture is reported by Donchin (1989) in which the same task and general instructions of how to proceed were given to researchers each of whom investigated a different aspect of training design. The task was a "space fortress game" which was selected because it was not only complex and dynamic but it also enabled motor, visual monitoring and memory components to be varied independently. Issues which were explored included the role of working memory (Logie et al., 1989), decomposition into subskills and part-task training (Frederiksen and White, 1989), and adaptive training (Mané, Adams and Donchin, 1989). Whilst all of the studies in the project were in one sense complementary, it is difficult to envisage one optimal training design emerging from them.

Overview of Chapters 8–12

Chapters 8–12 are concerned with different aspects of training design. They vary in their emphasis on the three components of training design namely: training content, training methods and strategies, and trainee characteristics (see Figure 8.1).

Theories of training design are discussed in Section 8.2. The coverage of theories is not exhaustive and those discussed are selected either because they make substantial contributions to this topic or because they provide contrasting views on training design. Gagné's theoretical formulations and Merrill's Component Display Theory focus on the link between types of training content and methods of training. In contrast, Keller's theory concentrates on the importance of arousing and maintaining the trainee's motivation. Landa's Algo-heuristic Theory of instruction and Collins' and Stevens' Inquiry method are cognitively oriented theories of training design. The former emphasises the importance of enabling the trainee to discover the rules and heuristics which underlie expert performance. The latter illustrates the delicate inter-relationships between the trainee, the training content and the training method which occur during a Socratic dialogue.

Chapter 9 is concerned with training methods and strategies, including pretraining methods; practice with different types of advice; guidance and modelling; cueing and prompting methods; adaptive training; part versus whole training; and overtraining. Two further chapters, concerned with training design, consider: the trainees characteristics (Chapter 10); the role of the computer in training (Chapter 11), and the use of simulation (Chapter 12).

8.2 THEORETICAL PERSPECTIVES

Design of training is a major activity in the development of training programmes. Typically the term "instructional design" is used in the literature instead of training design and this term covers both training and education contexts. Theories of training design place different emphasis on the three components: the training content, the design methods and strategies, and the characteristics of the trainee. In the following quotation, Bruner (1966) stresses the importance of all three components for a theory of instruction. Also, training should be concerned with the development of cognitive processes, not just the acquisition of a body of knowledge.

> Finally, a theory of instruction seeks to take account of the fact that a curriculum reflects not only the nature of knowledge itself but also the nature of the knower and of the knowledge-getting process. It is the enterprise par excellence where the line between subject matter and method grows necessarily indistinct. A body of knowledge, enshrined in a university faculty and embodied in a series of authoritative volumes, is the result of much prior intellectual activity. To instruct someone in these disciplines is not a matter of getting him to commit results to mind. Rather, it is to teach him to participate in the process that makes possible the establishment of knowledge. We teach a subject not to produce little living libraries on that subject, but rather to get a student to think mathematically for himself, to consider matters as an historian does, to take part in the process of knowledge-getting. Knowing is a process, not a product (Bruner, 1966, p. 72).

Unfortunately, theories of training design are scattered throughout a variety of books and journal publications. One of the best introductions to this topic is given by Reigeluth (1983) which describes eight theoretical perspectives, six of which are discussed in this book. These eight are: the Gagné–Briggs (1979) model of instruction which not only identifies different types of learning but also focuses on nine training design "events" (see Section 8.3); a behavioural approach which emphasises the role of practice (Gropper, 1974, 1975, 1983); the Algo-heuristic Theory of instruction proposed by the Russian psychologist, Lev Landa (1974, 1976, 1983) (see Section 8.4); Structural Learning Theory put forward by Scandura in many publications which emphasises the role of rule learning (e.g. Scandura, 1973, 1983; Scandura and Brainerd, 1978); a Theory of Inquiry Teaching which refers to a Socratic dialogue between trainer and trainee (Collins and Stevens, 1982, 1983) (see Section 8.4); Component Display Theory (CDT) described by Merrill (1983, 1987) and summarised in Section 8.3; the Elaboration Theory of Instruction which builds upon Ausubel's ideas of advance organisers (Reigeluth et al., 1980; Reigeluth and Stein, 1983; Reigeluth, 1987b) and is discussed in Section 9.2; and motivational aspects of training design discussed by Keller (1983), subsequently revised into the ARCS model of motivational design (Keller and Kopp, 1987), and discussed in Section 8.4. This list of theories is by no means exhaustive. Other significant theoretical contributions to training design have come from Skinner, Bruner, Ausubel, Glaser, Gilbert, Pask and many others. Gagné and Dick (1983) have provided a summary of different theoretical perspectives.

There have been many attempts to distil theoretical ideas concerning training design into guidelines for practitioners (e.g. Dick and Carey,

1985; Romiszowski, 1981, 1984, 1986 and 1988). Briggs and Wager (1981) produced a self-instructional guide for the development of classroom instruction which incorporated many of the ideas of Gagné and Briggs.

The status and nature of instruction or instructional design theory has been considered by Bruner (1966), Glaser (1976) and Reigeluth (1983). Dewey (1900) pinpointed the need for a "linking science" between learning theory and educational practice. Instructional theory, at least in principle, provides such a linking science since it relates changes in the three components of training design (Figure 8.1) to changes in the rate or amount of learning. Bruner (1966) in his essay "Notes on a Theory of Instruction" pointed out that a theory of instruction was prescriptive "in the sense that it sets forth rules concerning the most effective way of achieving knowledge or skill" (p. 40). Bruner went on to suggest that there were four major components in a theory of instruction:

1. "The experiences which most effectively implant in the individual a predisposition toward learning – learning in general or a particular type of learning" (pp. 40–41).
2. "The ways in which a body of knowledge should be structured so that it can be most readily grasped by the learner" (p. 41).
3. "The most effective sequences in which to present the materials to be learned" (p. 41).
4. "The nature and pacing of rewards and punishments in the process of learning and teaching" (p. 41).

Predispositions, the first component above, include cultural, motivational and personal factors. Components two and three are straightforward from their description above whilst the fourth belies Bruner's understanding of much of the literature concerned with knowledge of results. Critical issues include the nature and timing of knowledge of results provided to the trainee and how this support is gradually faded such that it does not become a crutch to performance. Bruner emphasised the cognitive interplay between teacher and student and called for more attention to be paid to this *process* rather than the more obvious *products* of teaching.

Glaser (1976) specified four components in a psychology of instruction:

(a) Analysis of the competence, the state of knowledge and skill to be achieved.
(b) Description of the initial state with which the learner begins;
(c) Conditions that can be implemented to bring about change from the initial state of the learner to the state described as competence;
(d) Assessment procedures for determining the immediate and long-range

outcomes of the conditions that are put into effect to implement
change from the initial state of competence to further development
(Glaser, 1976, p. 8).

Glaser's components are more wide-ranging than Bruner's, since the
role of analysis is mentioned together with assessment of both immediate
and long-term changes in competence. Analysis is outside the definition
of training design used in this book, although it does produce training
content, which is one of the three components in the framework of
training design (see Section 8.1). In Glaser's terms, instruction supports
and encourages the translation process from novice to expert by
providing various training conditions and manipulations. Specifying
what these are is the main thrust of Chapters 8 and 9.

One dimension of training design which has been the subject of much
debate amongst theorists is whether instruction should be of an expository or discovery nature. In expository instruction the training content,
whatever it may be, is presented to the trainee, who then attempts to
digest it and then typically practises using it in some manner. In contrast,
the discovery method suggests that the trainee is active in discovering
the appropriate answers in more of a trial and error fashion. In simple
terms, expository versus discovery learning is the difference between
being told and finding out for oneself. However, the term "discovery
learning" has been ambiguous for many reasons. One is that it is not
clear whether one is concerned with learning *by* discovery or with
learning *to* discover (Rowntree, 1988), or sometimes a mixture of both.
Such uncertainty can be resolved by reference to the training objectives.
If some relatively restricted training content has to be mastered, then it
is unlikely that a discovery method will be more effective since it will
inevitably take more training time. Thus the philosophy in the so-called
RULEG approach to rule-learning developed by Evans, Homme and
Glaser (1962) is expository in nature. The trainee is presented with a
statement of the rule which has to be mastered together with a variety of
examples which demonstrate it. This is typically followed by practice in
application of the rule to novel examples. In contrast, in the discovery
method for rule learning, named EGRUL, the trainee is presented with
a range of examples which demonstrate the rule which has to be
discovered. Again, this is followed by practice in application of the rule
to novel examples. If the training objective is to learn to discover this
rule and similar rules, then discovery is essential, since it is equivalent to
the practice of such a skill. If, on the other hand, the objective is to
master this one rule and not to learn the process of inducing such rules
from a set of examples, then exposition is a simple and efficient strategy

for training design. An expositive strategy has been strongly defended by Ausubel (1963, 1968) who views the meaningful organisation of subject matter for the trainee as one of the most important aspects of training. In 1963 he concluded a review of discovery learning by stating:

> Actual examination of the research literature allegedly supportive of learning by discovery reveals that valid evidence of this nature is virtually nonexistent... The different curriculum reform projects using discovery techniques have not attempted the well-nigh impossible task of isolating the effects of the discovery variable from the effects of other significant variables and, in most instances, have not even attempted to collect adequate control data with which to evaluate the efficacy of a given project as a whole (Ausubel, 1963, p. 56).

Many cognitive theorists of instruction are against Ausubel's position. Foremost amongst them is Bruner who emphasised the importance of discovery methods in cognitive development (Bruner, 1960). Similarly, Pask (1975, 1976) developed ideas for an instructional dialogue, named "conversation theory", in which the trainee was given control over both the type and sequence of training content which could be explored. It is perhaps obvious that a pure "discovery" method is impractical and that what is at stake is the balance between the trainer's and trainee's control over the instructional interactions in terms of what, how and when training material is explored. Gagné adopted an intermediate position preferring what he termed "guided discovery", although he firmly believed that training consisted of a preset menu of objectives and learning experiences through which the trainee must pass to achieve competence. Contemporary cognitive psychologists have generally seen learning itself as a problem-solving process (e.g. Bransford et al., 1989) about which the learner requires guidance. This is emphasised in the Collins and Stevens Inquiry Theory of Teaching discussed in Section 8.4. There is no reason why a mixture of these two strategies should not be used, as is evident in Brown and Palincsar's (1989) recent discussion of cooperative group training for improving comprehension skills. However, whilst the belief in discovery training is strong, Ausubel's assertion that such a contention has not been systematically tested, nor is it easy to do so, is still a telling criticism.

8.3 TYPES OF LEARNING AND TRAINING DESIGN

One psychological approach to the analysis of a task is to identify the types of learning which are involved. This is particularly useful if types of learning require different training methods or strategies, i.e. the design of training is different for each category of learning. If this criterion is met it means that, in principle, both analysis and design of training can be directly linked. The most well-known taxonomy of types of learning is that developed by Gagné and colleagues in a variety of publications from the 1960s onwards. In the intellectual domain, Gagné identified a hierarchy of types of learning which, despite criticism, has profoundly influenced those concerned with training, since it does make recommendations about both the analysis of tasks and the subsequent design of training. The relationship between Gagné's ideas and training design was addressed by Gagné and Briggs (1974, 1979), whilst Briggs and Wager (1981) have produced a self-instruction manual based on a systems approach to training design which covers many of Gagné's ideas. Gagné's types of learning are discussed later, together with those of Merrill who has elaborated types of learning in his Component Display Theory. Merrill's theory links types of learning to the development of training objectives and in this sense provides a refinement of Mager's prescriptions for the specification of training objectives (pp. 124–125).

The search for learning categories has a long tradition in psychology. Skinner made his well-known distinction between operant versus classical conditioning; Melton (1964) proposed six categories of learning involving conditioning, rote-learning, probability-learning, skill-learning, concept-learning and problem-solving. The work by Leith (1968) is less known, but is of interest since it addressed the instructional consequences of different learning categories, including the possible methods of facilitating learning. Leith (1968), cited in Duncan (1972), distinguished nine types of learning (see Table 8.1) which were expanded by Leith subsequently to 10, to include a category of self-evaluation. Presumably self-evaluation would be referred to as meta-cognitive skill nowadays.

Gagné's learning categories and conditions

Gagné's by now famous proposition is that all learning is not the same and varieties of learning can be distinguished in terms of the *conditions* necessary to promote them. His scheme is therefore more concerned with training design than the mechanisms of learning. Before reviewing this work, it has to be pointed out that various revisions have been made over the years. Gagné's main ideas are probably best presented in his book entitled *The Conditions of Learning* which was published initially in 1965 and underwent revision in the subsequent editions of 1970, 1977 and 1985. In his earlier publications, considerable prominence was given

Table 8.1   Suggestions for a taxonomy of learning (Leith, 1968)

Types of learning activities	Methods of facilitating learning
1. Stimulus discrimination	(a) Emphatic cues (b) Distinctive names (c) Fading
2. Response learning	(a) Practice with feedback (b) Tips on how to make the response (c) Errors to be avoided
3. Response integration	(a) Practice (b) Symbolic mediators (learner's own are best)
4. Trial and error learning	(a) Personal trials (b) Errors important to eliminate inappropriate responses (c) Feedback
5. Learning set formation	(a) Personal discovery (b) Feedback (c) Practice on each problem to criterion of mastery (d) Variety of problems (e) Making errors important (response elimination)
6. Concept learning	Trials with feedback to learner
7. Concept integration	(a) Structuring of sequence (b) Direct instruction/individual construction with feedback (c) Sometimes random presentation helpful
8. Hypothetico-deductive inference (problem-solving)	(a) Practice in framing and testing hypotheses (b) Feedback (c) Guidance
9. Learning schemata	Presentation of conflict situations needed to promote formation of higher-order structures

to his well-known learning hierarchy of eight types of skill. Subsequently this learning hierarchy was seen as an analysis of intellectual skill which in turn could be contrasted with other skill domains in a similar manner to that proposed by Bloom (pp. 206–207). The domain of cognitive strategies which was defined in his later work, at the time of the emergence of such notions in cognitive psychology, has an uneasy relationship with problem-solving which was the eighth and most complex type of learning in his learning hierarchy. In the mid-1970s, Gagné and Briggs (1974, 1979) became more concerned with the instructional implications of these distinctions and moved towards developing a theory of instruction. This aspect is taken up by Gagné and Dick (1983) and reflected in the title of the fourth edition of Gagné's 1985 book – *The Conditions of Learning and the Theory of Instruction* – and also in the recent third edition of *Principles of Instructional Design* by Gagné, Briggs and Wager (1988).

Learning outcomes, conceived of as acquired capabilities, are divided by Gagné into:

1. Intellectual skills
2. Verbal information
3. Cognitive strategies
4. Motor skills
5. Attitudes.

The five types of capability together with subskills in the intellectual domain are defined by Gagné and Briggs (1979) and illustrated in Table 8.2. These five categories correspond closely with those proposed by Bloom and colleagues. More recently, the distinction between declarative and procedural knowledge (Anderson, 1980) can be applied to Gagné's category of verbal information (concerned with facts and "knowing that") and the category of intellectual skills ("knowing how"). Whilst it is easy to agree on definitions of motor skills and attitudes, it is less clear what Gagné envisaged for the category of cognitive strategies since his explanation, (Gagné, 1985), contains two components which have different training implications. First cognitive strategies can be viewed as the mental processes underlying the performance of, e.g. reading, writing, problem-solving skill. Gagné quoted a mnemonic system which constitutes the basis of a cognitive strategy for retrieving information from memory. Second, cognitive strategies can be viewed as executive or higher-order control processes which determine the resources and lower-order strategies which are selected and used in the performance of a skill. In this latter sense, cognitive strategy resembles a metacognitive skill (Flavell, 1976) or a metacomponent as defined by Sternberg (e.g. 1985).

Table 8.2 Human capabilities with corresponding verbs and examples (from Gagné and Briggs, 1979)

Capability	Verb	Example
Intellectual skill		
Discrimination	Discriminates	Discriminates, by matching, the French sounds of "u" and "ou"
Concrete concept	Identifies	Identifies, by naming, the root, leaf, and stem of representative plants
Defined concept	Classifies	Classifies, by using a definition, the concept "family"
Rule	Demonstrates	Demonstrates, by solving verbally stated examples, the addition of positive and negative numbers
Higher-order rule (problem solving)	Generates	Generates, by synthesising applicable rules, a paragraph describing a person's actions in a situation of fear
Cognitive strategy	Originates	Originates a solution to the reduction of air pollution, by applying model of gaseous diffusion
Information	States	States orally the major issues in the presidential campaign of 1932
Motor skill	Executes	Executes backing a car into driveway
Attitude	Chooses	Chooses playing golf as a leisure activity

Undoubtedly, the exposition of the learning hierarchy of intellectual skill will remain one of Gagné's enduring contributions to training. In its early formulation (e.g. Gagné, 1975) the shift away from an emphasis on the pervasive mechanism of reinforcement to a focus on *what* had to be mastered and different learning outcomes was a significant step. In his learning hierarchy he not only distinguished eight types of learning but also the conditions for learning each (e.g. Gagné, 1970). These were divided into *internal* conditions, literally those conditions which must exist "in the learner", and *external* conditions which were concerned with the nature and organisation of training. Specification of the internal conditions of learning led Gagné to believe that different types of

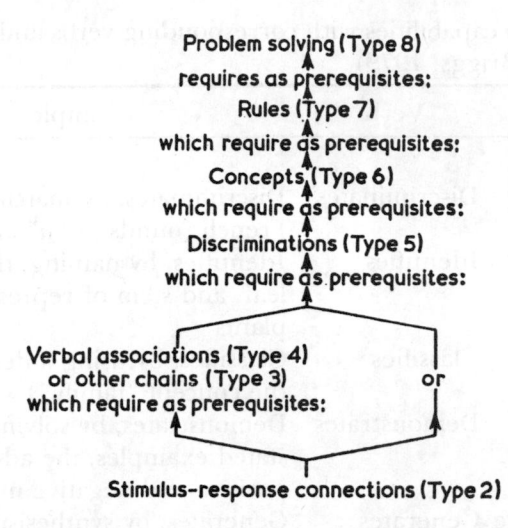

Figure 8.2   Gagné's (1970) learning hierarchy.

intellectual skill had prerequisite subskills. Thus he argued that types of learning higher in the learning hierarchy required as prerequisites the lower types of learning as illustrated in Figure 8.2. It can be seen that "problem-solving" requires as a prerequisite the "rules" used for solving problems to be learned which in turn require as a prerequisite that the "concepts" used in such rules are mastered and so on. The reader will notice that type 1 "signal learning" is missing from Figure 8.2 because Gagné was uncertain that this was a prerequisite for type 2 learning. Some indication of Gagné's revisions to his learning hierarchy can be gained from comparison of the eight learning types (Gagné, 1970), given in Figure 8.2, with the five types elaborated by Gagné (1985) in the intellectual domain which can be found in Table 8.2. In the later formulation some of the attractive simplicity of Gagné's original learning hierarchy is lost. Problem-solving, quite properly, is acknowledged to be no longer solely dependent on the acquisition of rules but is also contingent on learning cognitive strategies and factual information (i.e. capabilities outside of the intellectual domain). The contribution of each will depend upon the nature of the problem-solving task. Gagné and Briggs (1974) considered both the external and internal conditions necessary for learning intellectual skill (and its five subskills), cognitive strategy, verbal information, attitudes and motor skill. These external and internal learning conditions are combined and summarised in Table 8.3.

There are two important contributions to training which arise from Gagné's types of learning. Firstly, the different types of learning (both

Table 8.3 Types of learning and their associated conditions (Gagné and Briggs, 1974)

Type of lesson objective	Learning conditions
Intellectual skill	
Discrimination	Recall of S–R connections ("responses") Repetition of situations presenting "same" and "different" stimuli, with feedback Emphasis on distinctive features
Concrete concept	Recall of discrimination of relevant object qualities Presentation of several concept instances, varying in irrelevant object qualities Identification of concept instances by student
Defined concept	Recall of component concepts Demonstration of the components of the concept, *or* verbal statement of the definition Demonstration of concept by the student
Rule	Recall of component concepts or subordinate rules Demonstration or verbal statement of the rule Demonstration of rule application by student
Higher-order rule	Recall of relevant subordinate rules Presentation of a novel problem Demonstration of new rule in achieving problem solution
Cognitive strategy	Recall of relevant rules and concepts Successive presentation (usually over an extended time) of novel problem situations with class of solution unspecified Demonstration of solution by student
Information	
Names or labels	Recall of verbal chains Encoding (by student) by relating name to image or meaningful sentence
Facts	Recall of context of meaningful information Performance of reinstating fact in the larger context of information

Knowledge	Recall of context of related information
	Performance of reinstating new knowledge in the context of related information
Attitude	Recall of information and intellectual skills relevant to the targeted personal actions
	Establishment or recall of respect for "source" (usually a person)
	Reward for personal action either by direct experience or vicariously by observation of respected person
Motor skill	Recall of component motor chains
	Establishment or recall of executive subroutine (rules)
	Practice of total skill

within and outside the intellectual domain) can be used for classifying elements of performance during the sort of conventional task analysis described in Chapter 6. In this respect Gagné and Briggs (1974) provided examples of learning hierarchies. One of the most detailed is given by Rowntree (1988). He developed a hierarchy for the objective:

> State the time as so many hours o'clock or in terms of hours and minutes past, reading from a conventional 12-hour clock (e.g. '8 o'clock' or '4.37').

The resulting learning hierarchy, depicted in Figure 8.3, specifies the subskills which are prerequisites to the accomplishment of such an objective. In Gagné's terms these prerequisites are enabling objectives which involve lower types of learning. Stating the time in such a manner involves simple associations, discriminations, concepts and rules in Gagné's terms. It is perhaps surprising to find that such an apparently simple skill is dependent on so many subskills. Such an analysis would enable the trainer to identify what had to be learned. The development of training would entail comparison of the skills required against the pretraining competence of the trainee (e.g. a child or a person from another culture who might not have these clock reading subskills). Those which were performed unsatisfactorily would form the basis for the content of the training programme.

A second contribution of the learning hierarchy is that it dictates the sequence in which task components should be learned such that training proceeds from lower to higher order components. This has proved somewhat contentious. Evidence in favour of this proposition comes

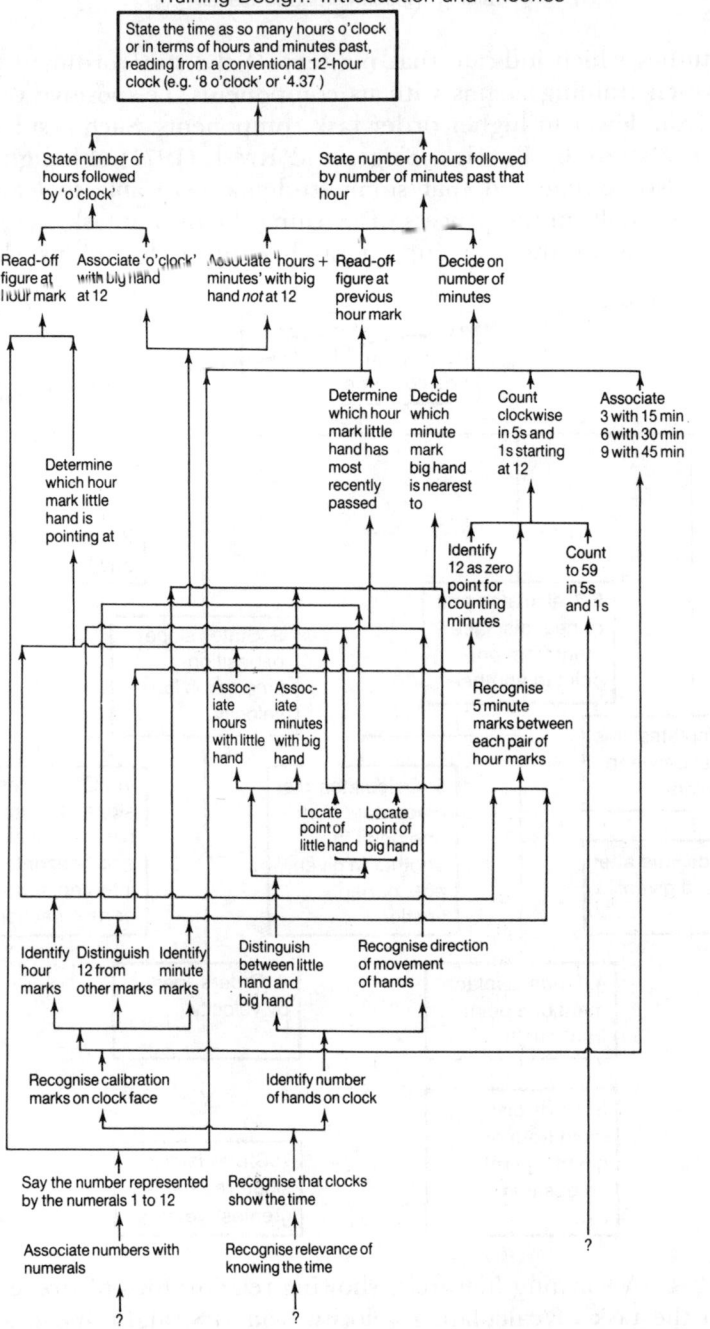

Figure 8.3 A learning hierarchy for "reading" the time of day (Rowntree, 1988).

from studies which indicate that mastery of the superordinate task is faster when training begins with its components, i.e. positive transfer occurs from lower to higher order task components. Such results were found in a study by Resnick, Siegel and Kresh (1971) although these authors also commented that some students were able to learn the subordinate skills in the process of learning the overall task.

Applications of the learning hierarchy approach and its claimed

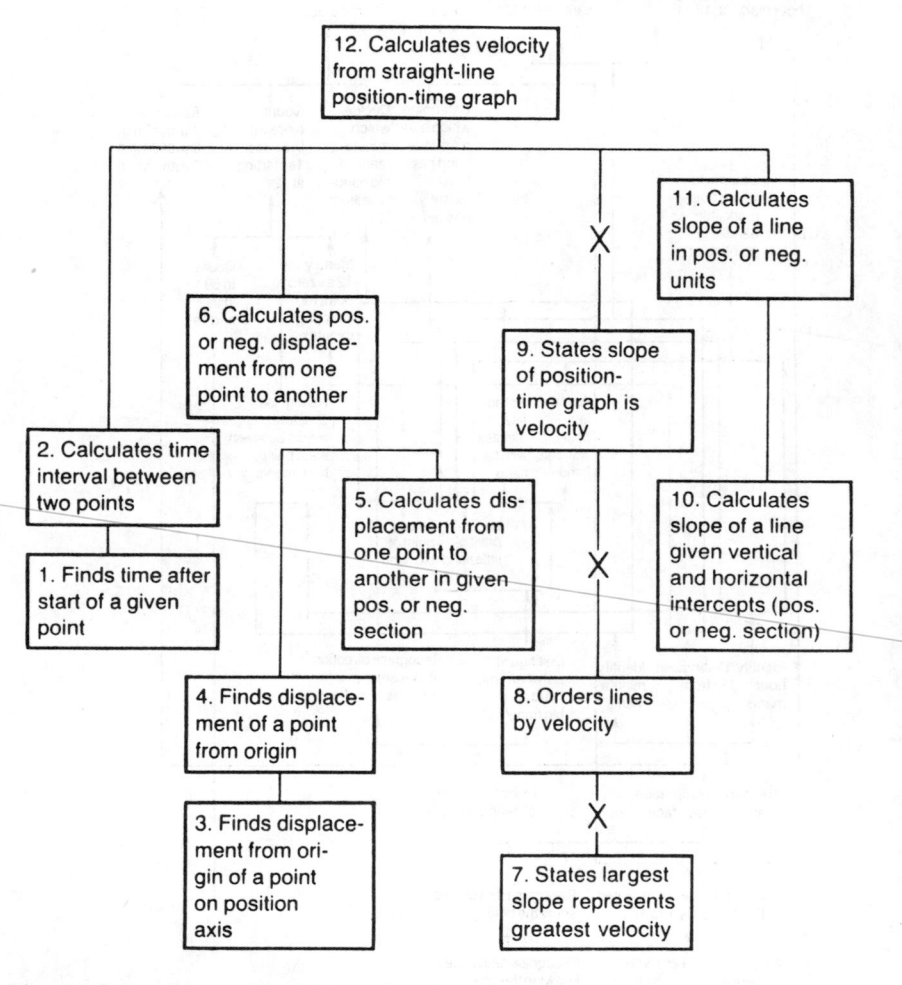

Figure 8.4 A learning hierarchy showing relationships of prerequisite skills to the task of calculating velocity from a straight-line graph of position and time (Gagné, 1985). (X indicates relationships which are not prerequisite.)

benefits are summarised by Gagné and Dick (1983) and Gagné (1985). An illustrative study is that by White and Gagné (1978). The skill of interest involved being able to calculate the velocity of an object from a graph of position against time given either the object's position or time. The learning hierarchy specified by Gagné and White was used to assess the component skills of students from courses in mathematics and science who had already mastered such a skill. It was found that virtually no students who were able to perform the higher skill, as defined in Figure 8.4, were *not* able to perform its lower-level components. The only exceptions were between components 12, 9, 8 and 7 (depicted by X in Figure 8.4). The reason given was that performance of these components involved primarily statements of verbal information which were outside the intellectual skill domain to which the hierarchy applied. A criticism of the study is that retention is used as an indicator of the sequence in which skills were learned originally. This may be misleading. A more convincing argument could be made from a comparison of different learning routes which were consistent and inconsistent with the learning hierarchy.

Gagné's learning hierarchy has received much attention and some criticism. In particular the notion of prerequisite subskills has generated much debate concerning what it means and how it should be tested (Bergan, 1980; Glaser and Resnick, 1972; Resnick, 1973; White, 1973). It is not entirely clear whether a subskill is a "part" of a skill and has to be combined with others to form the skill or whether, as Gagné seems to suggest, a subskill is a logical prerequisite to the acquisition of a more complex skill. Of course evidence of positive transfer from one subskill in the hierarchy to one at a higher level does not necessarily indicate a prerequisite relationship; it might just be that the lower-level one helps learning the high-level one. The reviews by Bergan (1980), Cotton, Gallagher and Marshall (1977) and White (1973) suggest that there is little evidence which is methodologically sound in support of Gagné's notion of prerequisite relationships in his learning hierarchy. From a more practical perspective, what is needed are further guidelines concerning *how* to analyse a task in order to identify subskills which correspond to Gagné's learning categories both within the hierarchy (i.e. in the intellectual domain) and outside (e.g. verbal information, cognitive strategy). Decomposing a task/skill into Gagné's types of learning is a more difficult activity than the final products of published analyses suggest. This is because it is unlikely that a unique solution exists in the analysis of any one task, and also the subskills identified by an analysis do not always fit neatly into Gagné's categories.

A theory of instruction has been developed by Gagné and Briggs

(1974, 1979) and elaborated subsequently by Gagné (1985). It attempts to link instructional events both to learning outcomes, which have been discussed previously, and to the internal learning processes. There are nine instructional events:

1. Gaining attention.
2. Informing learners of the objective.
3. Stimulating recall of prior learning.
4. Presenting the stimulus.
5. Providing "learning guidance".
6. Eliciting performance.
7. Providing feedback.
8. Assessing performance.
9. Enhancing retention and transfer.

It can be seen that these instructional events broadly follow an information-processing approach. As Gagné and Dick (1983) acknowledged, these suggestions are not unique and overlap with other theories of instruction. Perhaps they should be viewed as a framework to which psychological ideas concerning training design can be appended. All of these instructional events are involved for each piece of training content although how they are devised will depend upon the type of learning outcome. Recommendations concerning the instructional events needed for the five types of capability are given by Gagné and Briggs in Table 8.4.

Component Display Theory (Merrill, 1983)

Ideas from Merrill's previous studies concerned with the analysis and design of instruction (e.g. Merrill and Boutwell, 1973; Merrill et al., 1977) have been crystallised in what is termed Component Display Theory (CDT) (Merrill, 1983). CDT incorporates theoretical notions from Bruner, the RULEG system (Evans, Homme and Glaser, 1962), Gagné and others. Not surprisingly therefore, CDT provides a framework for integrating some well-known instructional principles. Merrill, as many others, has been strongly influenced by Gagné's ideas that different learning outcomes require different learning conditions. CDT is a significant development for a number of reasons; types of learning are defined by two dimensions – the type of performance required and the type of training content; types of learning are explicitly related both to the specification of training objectives and prescriptions concerning training design; these principles of training design have been applied to test construction (Ellis and Wulfeck, 1982) and to the development of computer-based training systems, such as TICCIT (Merrill, 1988). Merrill's theory, or more appropriately termed approach, is more narrow and detailed than Gagné's. It is restricted to the cognitive/ intellectual domain, although implications of the types of learning for training design are pursued into detailed prescriptions. This is done using a vocabulary, specific to CDT, which some might find technically unforgiving.

The aim of CDT is to provide advice for teachers and authors of training materials. At the heart of CDT is a performance–content matrix which identifies 10 types of learning. Unlike Gagné's learning hierarchy, this matrix is composed of two dimensions; one concerned with the level of performance and the other with the type of content. The three levels of performance are remember, use and find which can be applied to the four types of content: fact, concept, procedure and principle (Figure 8.5). This gives rise to 10 permissible combinations rather than 12 since a

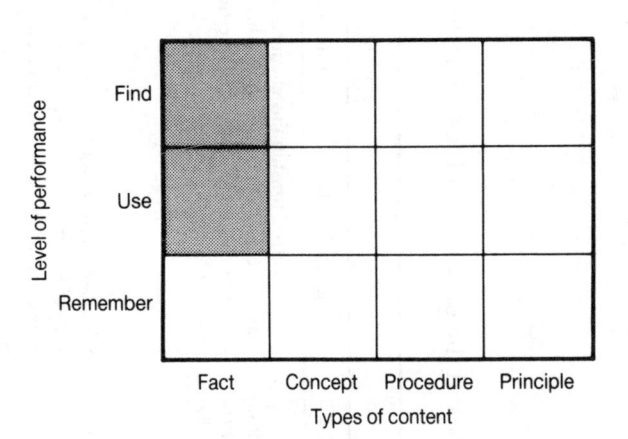

Figure 8.5   Performance–content matrix (Merrill, 1983).

fact has no abstract representation and therefore, according to Merrill, there are no "use-fact" and "find-fact" cells in the performance–content matrix. Merrill (1983) provided examples of each of the 10 performance–content cells, some of which are given below:

Remember-fact
  e.g. What is the value of pi?
Remember-concept
  e.g. What are the characteristics of a conifer?

Table 8.4 Instructional events and the conditions of learning they imply for five types of learned capabilities (Gagné and Briggs, 1979)

Instructional event	Type of capability				
	Intellectual skill	Cognitive strategy	Information	Attitude	Motor skill
1. Gaining attention	Introduce stimulus change: variations in sensory mode				
2. Informing learner of objective	Provide description and example of the performance to be expected	Clarify the general nature of the solution expected	Indicate the kind of verbal question to be answered	Provide example of the kind of action choice aimed for	Provide a demonstration of the performance to be expected
3. Stimulating recall of prerequisites	Stimulate recall of subordinate concepts and rules	Stimulate recall of strategies and associated intellectual skills	Stimulate recall of context of organised information	Stimulate recall of relevant information, skills and human model identification	Stimulate recall of executive subroutine and part-skills
4. Presenting the stimulus material	Present examples of concept or rule	Present novel problems	Present information in propositional form	Present human model, demonstrating choice of personal action	Provide external stimuli for model, demonstrating performance, including tools or action

guidance	to proper combining	hints to novel solution	to a larger meaningful context	observation of model's choice of action and of reinforcement received by model	feedback of performance achievement
6. Eliciting the performance	Ask learner to apply rule or concept to new examples	Ask for problem solution	Ask for information in paraphrase, or in learner's own words	Ask learner to indicate choices of action in real or simulated situations	Ask for execution of the performance
7. Providing feedback	Confirm correctness of rule or concept application	Confirm originality of problem solution	Confirm correctness of statement of information	Provide direct or vicarious reinforcement of action choice	Provide feedback on degree of accuracy and timing of performance
8. Assessing performance	Learner demonstrates application of concept or rule	Learner originates a novel solution	Learner restates information in paraphrased form	Learner makes desired choice of personal action in real or simulated situation	Learner executes performance of total skill
9. Enhancing retention and transfer	Provide spaced reviews including a variety of examples	Provide occasions for a variety of novel problem solutions	Provide verbal links to additional complexes of information	Provide additional varied situations for selected choice of action	Provide additional varied situations for skill practice
					Learner continues skill practice

Use-concept
   e.g. Is the mountain in this photograph an example of a folded mountain?
Find-concept
   e.g. Sort the rocks on this table into several different piles. Indicate the characteristics by which one of your classmates could sort them into the same piles.
Remember-procedure
   e.g. What are the steps in balancing a chequebook?
Use-procedure
   e.g. Demonstrate how to clean a clarinet.
Find-procedure
   e.g. Write a computer program that will index and retrieve recipes.
Remember-principle
   e.g. What happens when water evaporates? Explain in terms of molecule movement and heat.
Use-principle
   e.g. Below are pictures of two ocean vessels. One is floating very high in the water and the other is floating very low. Explain at least three different reasons that could account for this difference.
Find-principle
   e.g. Set up an experiment to assess the effect of tobacco smoke on plant growth. Report your findings (Merrill, 1983. Adapted from pp. 288–289).

Each type of performance–content can be linked with a particular form of training objective. Merrill adopted Mager's recommendation that for any objective to be adequately stated, it should cover the conditions, behaviour and criterion of performance. Merrill identified the generic form of the objective for each type of learning (Table 8.5). This table needs some explanation. In order to construct the appropriate objective, the reader moves from left to right along the corresponding row. Each of the three components of an objective (conditions, behaviour and criterion) is divided into two columns which represent those aspects which are fixed or necessary and those which vary according to the training situation. Those items which are underlined in the fixed conditions column indicate that they need specification for the training situation under consideration. Merrill provided some help with the following example of a remembering-fact type of objective which was stated as follows:

Given a drawing (column 1) of an eye (A) with the parts numbered in random order (column 2) the student will be able to recall the name of each part (B) (column 3), by writing the name opposite the number corresponding to that part (column 4) with no errors and no delay (column 5) as shown by one point for each part named correctly and one point subtracted from the score for each 10 seconds over 1 minute required to complete the exercise (column 6) (Merrill, 1983, p. 291).

In this example of an objective, it is noteworthy that the developer only has to define topic A, and then specify how the item is presented and how performance is scored. Thus Merrill envisaged that by using the generic form of the objective, the training developer can be said to *select* rather than *invent* the form of the objective.

CDT proposes that different forms of training are needed for each cell in the performance–content matrix. When the corresponding "presentations" (or training events) are used, then learning is optimised. Merrill distinguished between primary and secondary presentations. Primary presentations are divided into two dimensions: one dimension is concerned with the level of generality of the training material and the other with whether the instruction is of an expository or inquisitory nature. This results in four types of presentation:

1. Expository generality (e.g. telling the trainee a rule).
2. Expository instance (e.g. telling the trainee an example).
3. Inquisitory generality (e.g. asking the trainee about a rule).
4. Inquistory instance (e.g. asking the trainee about an example).

Training is made up of sequences of primary presentations which are supplemented by other instructional features (termed "secondary" presentations and interdisplay relationships). Some of the additional instructional features for the use-concept, use-principle and use-procedure objectives include:

help, e.g. in focusing attention on relevant attributes of a concept to be learned;
using alternative modes of representation;
fading the help provided during later stages of training;
providing feedback;
providing an adequate range of instances and levels of difficulty;
isolating the primary presentation form from other instructional material.

An examination of these instructional strategies plus other comments by Merrill suggest that these ideas have been formulated primarily from the concept-learning literature (e.g. Tennyson, Steve and Boutwell, 1975). Merrill (1983) stated that more than 50 studies have been conducted by himself and colleagues into aspects of CDT. However, it is not clear how CDT might be tested from a training perspective. Despite the claim that training recommendations (and "presentations") can be made for each of the performance–content distinctions, these are not explicit.

It has to be asked whether the exceedingly technical distinctions used

Table 8.5 Objectives corresponding to types of performance–content (Merrill, 1983)

	Conditions		Behaviour		Criterion	
	Variable[a]	Fixed	Fixed	Variable[b]	Fixed	Variable[c]
	Given:	*of/or:*	*the student will be able to:*	*by:*	*with:*	*as shown by:*
Use concept	Drawings Pictures Descriptions Diagrams	New examples	Classify	Writing Selecting Pointing Sorting	Some errors Short delay	
Use procedure	Word Materials Equipment Device	*Name* New *task*	Demonstrate etc.	Manipulating Calculating Measuring Removing	Some errors Timed or untimed	Check list
Use principle	Word Descriptions Drawings Figures	*Name* New *problem*	Explain or predict	Predicting Calculating Drawing Graphing etc.	Some errors Untimed	
Find concept	Drawings Pictures Descriptions Diagrams Objects	Referents from unspecified categories	Invent categories	Sorting and observing attributes Specifying attributes	Untimed High correlation when others use concept	
Find principle	Word Descriptions Drawings Figures	*Name* New *problem*	Explain or predict	Experiment Analysis Trial and error	Untimed Demonstration of utility	
Find procedure	Description Demonstration Illustration or	Desired *product* or	Derive steps			

principle	Illustration Observation	relationship	Analysis Observation Demonstration	Appropriate research design or scholarship
Remember fact	Drawings Pictures Diagrams Objects	A in any order Recall *B*	Writing Drawing Pointing Circling etc.	One point for each correct symbol / Within 10 sec / No errors
Remember concept	Word Symbol	*Name* State definition	Writing Circling Circling Circling Checking etc.	No delay / Few errors / One error for each characteristic
Remember procedure	Word Symbol Directions	*Name* State steps	Drawing Flow charting Listing Ordering etc.	Short delay / Few errors / One error each step
Remember principle	Word Symbol	*Name* State relationship etc.	Writing Drawing Formula Graph etc.	Short delay / Few errors / One error each relationship

a Variable condition refers to representation of stimulus materials given to the student.

b Variable behaviour refers to type of performance used by the student to show capability.

c Variable criterion refers to how a particular type of item will be scored.

by CDT are justified. Certainly the vocabulary will not be welcomed by practitioners. This criticism is particularly pertinent to the definitions and labelling of primary and secondary presentations and associated training events. One might argue that the four primary forms of presentation only sample two of a number of dimensions which are of relevance to training design. It is not evident why these two have been selected and form the focus of the theory.

An overriding strength of CDT is that it insists on a tight mapping and consistency between types of learning, training objectives, test items and instructional presentations. This has given rise to the Instructional Quality Profile which aims at ensuring that the objectives, tests and presentations are both adequate and consistent with each other in any training programme. The Instructional Quality Profile is discussed in Chapter 4, pp. 127–128. This has been developed by the Naval Personnel Research and Development Centre, San Diego into a useful manual which instructs trainers in how to develop training by applying principles from CDT (Ellis, Wulfeck and Fredericks, 1979).

8.4   OTHER THEORIES OF TRAINING DESIGN

The Algo-heuristic theory of instruction

The ideas of the Russian psychologist, Landa, were published in English in two books, one in 1974 – *Algorithmization in Learning and Instruction* (originally published in Russian in 1966) and the other in 1976 – *Instructional Regulation and Control: Cybernetics, Algorithmization and Heuristics in Education*. Many of these notions were embodied in a Russian book concerned with students' methods of reasoning in geometric proofs written by Landa and published as long ago as 1955. Landa emphasises the cognitive processes which underpin skill and many of his ideas were in advance of more contemporary notions of cognitive skill and the importance of procedural knowledge. These ideas, referred to as Landamatics, are carefully argued and consider the inter-relationships between the three components of training design which we discussed in Section 8.1, i.e. the trainee's characteristics, the nature of the training content, and the training methods and strategies (Figure 8.1). Summaries of the Algo-heuristic theory can be found in Reigeluth (1983, 1987a).

Like many of us, Landa (1983) lamented the shortcomings of conventional instruction:

1. Students are not taught processes (operations) at all because teachers themselves are not aware of them.

2. Students are taught the wrong make-up and/or system of operations (procedures).
3. Students are taught an incomplete repertoire and/or system of operations (procedures).
4. Students are taught particular rather than more general operations and their systems.
5. Students are taught uncertain, vague or ambiguous prescriptions, which leave unclear what specifically should be cognitively done in order to be able to solve problems. (Landa, 1983, p. 180; italics omitted).

From this list, it is evident that Landa ascribed a central role in his theory to what he termed "operations". These are equivalent to the mental or cognitive operations which transform knowledge into goal-directed behaviour or skill. In Anderson's terms it is the problem of compiling procedural knowledge from inadequate declarative knowledge. The essence of good training is to identify these mental operations and instil them into the trainee. Thus the Algo-heuristic theory is concerned with:

breaking down complex, unobservable, cognitive processes into more elementary but also unobservable cognitive operations that could be unambiguously executed by learners in the course of learning and performance and reliably produced by teachers in the course of instruction (Landa, 1983, p. 173; italics omitted).

Landa emphasised the importance of an analysis of the cognitive activities required in a task which coincides with one important message of this book. Landa stated that the Algo-heuristic theory was concerned with:

isolating them [operations], breaking them down into relatively elementary components, explicitly describing their composition and structure, creating prescriptions on the basis of descriptions, and directly managing and developing processes through the management and development of their known elementary components and their structures (Landa, 1983, p. 180; square parentheses added; italics omitted).

However as we discovered in Section 8.3 there are no easy methods for achieving this. Landa, not surprisingly, is also somewhat silent on this 64,000 dollar question.

According to Landa, basic cognitive operations are combined into either algorithmic or heuristic processes which underpin complex intellectual activity. An algorithmic process involves elementary operations which are combined in some "regular, uniform way under defined conditions to solve all problems of a certain class"; this contrasts with an heuristic process, which involves either nonelementary operations or elementary operations performed in a less regular or uniform manner. These algorithmic and heuristic processes are cognitive in nature and are different from, but analogous to, their motor counterparts, e.g. starting a car is an algorithmic motor process (no pun intended!). Analysing cognitive processes, which may be unconscious, into algorithmic or heuristic processes requires verification. Landa argued that verification might include: comparison of actual errors against those predicted on the basis of the hypothesised cognitive processes; computer simulation of these cognitive processes; and the implementation of training itself, which will indicate any variations between predicted and actual performance.

The Algo-heuristic theory is concerned with developing what are termed "prescriptions" (i.e. a set of instructions) for performers, trainees and trainers. The knowledge requirements of these three differ. The trainee has to master the cognitive processes of the task in the most expedient fashion, whilst the trainer requires knowledge not only of the nature of these processes, but also of how to train them. In some situations, it may not be possible to identify these covert processes, in which case the trainer can only manage the inputs to and outputs from the trainee during training. In such a situation, Landa suggested that some form of discovery method is inevitable, although he preferred the trainer to have more direct control over development of the appropriate cognitive processes. According to Landa, discovery methods using examples or trial and error learning are potentially useful if the nature of the interactions required can be made explicit. Discovery methods are often more valuable than expository ones, in which trainees are informed how to use algorithmic or heuristic processes. As we have discussed previously, this contention largely depends upon the nature of the training objectives. Landa, as others, preferred discovery methods because of the additional cognitive skills which are learned in the process of mastering the training material.

Landa (1987) provided an example of the use of Algo-heuristic theory in the development of training to identify types of lenses. Landa maintained, as is evident in his "lesson", that many complex skills can be reduced to simpler algorithmic processes. In this example, the key to training design was the specification, by the trainer, of an algorithm for the identification of types of lenses (Figure 8.6). This algorithm represented the terminal cognitive behaviours which had to be inculcated through training. The training material used a guided discovery process in which cognitive activities would be discovered and mastered through practice and then assembled using what Landa referred to as the snowball method. This method, as the name suggests, involves developing competence in the first cognitive process and then practising it, developing competence in the second and then practising the first and second cognitive processes and so on. Hence the cognitive processes involved in mastering parts of this algorithm are gradually assembled and then the trainee is able to practice all of the components until performance becomes "automatic".

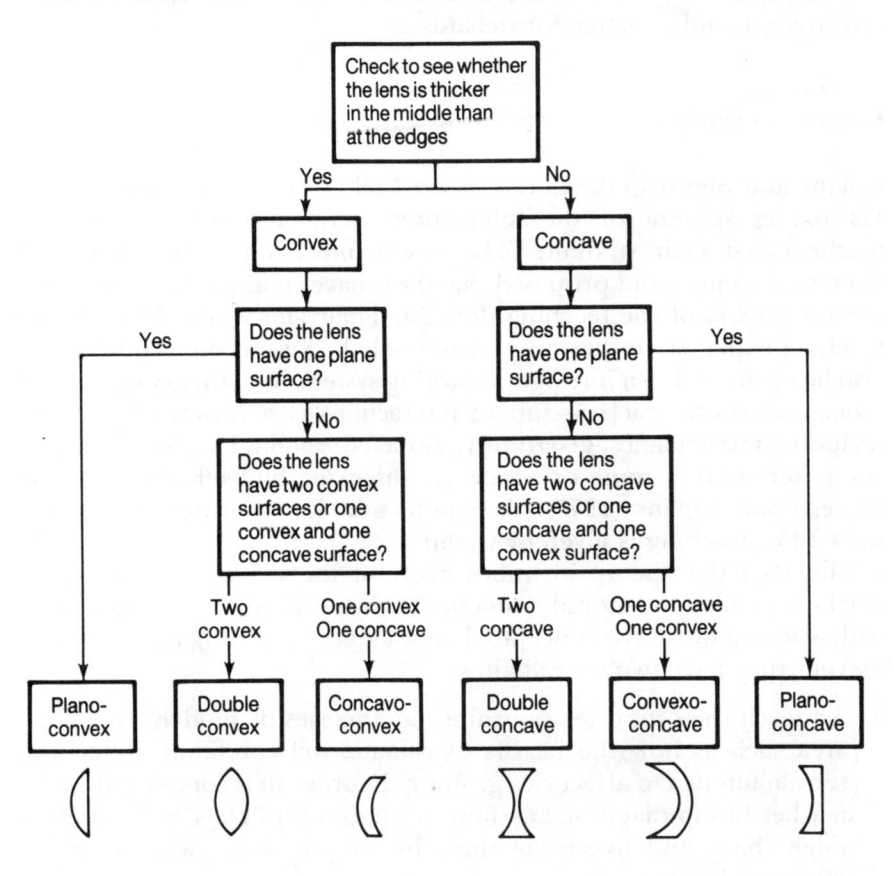

Figure 8.6   Algorithm for the identification of types of lenses (Landa, 1987).

The Algo-heuristic theory concentrates on the higher types of intellectual activity in Gagné's terms. It is more concerned with higher-level rules, problem-solving and cognitive strategies than factual learning and discriminations which occur at the lower levels of Gagné's learning hierarchy. It is important to remember that Landa's theory developed from studies of how students learned Russian grammar and geometry proofs, in which algorithmic and heuristic processes are prominent. However, Landa believed rightly that such processes are fundamental components of any complex skill. His emphasis on identifying the cognitive processes which underlie task performance and developing these through various training methods is in accord with much contemporary cognitive theory. How this should be achieved most effectively is still a matter for debate.

Inquiry teaching

Collins and Stevens (1982, 1983) and Collins (1985) have provided a fascinating account of the interactions between so-called "inquiry" teachers and their students. They were interested in the nature of Socratic dialogues and proposed that these have common features which are *independent* of the teaching domain. Their aim was to identify this teaching expertise so that it could not only be passed on to others, but also be captured in an intelligent tutoring system. The theory developed from analyses of teacher–student interactions in a variety of domains including mathematics, geography, moral education, law, medicine and computer science, some of which are discussed by Collins (1977) and Stevens and Collins (1977). A hypothetical lesson using the inquiry method of teaching is given by Collins (1987).

This cognitive theory identifies many of the strategies which good teachers employ in tutorial dialogue. Such tutorials are not concerned with teaching factual or conceptual knowledge. According to Collins and Stevens they have two overall aims:

1. To teach the causal relationships (i.e. theories or models) in a topic area such as how the factors of climate, soil condition, water and terrain interact to affect rice growing. In order to accomplish this, the teacher has to diagnose any misconceptions (or "bugs"!) the student might have and overcome them by various strategies, which are discussed below.
2. To enable the student to derive a new theory in a domain from a series of examples or cases.

The focus of the inquiry method is concerned with how to train problem-solving and cognitive strategies in Gagné's terms or how to train, what Merrill termed, "use-principles" and "find-principles", in his Component Display Theory. With respect to the debate concerning discovery versus expository methods, the inquiry method enables the student to discover all of the necessary and sufficient factors in a theory or discover how to test a theory and make a prediction from it. However, this does take place in a training situation in which exploration of the subject matter is controlled by the goals of the teacher. The teacher uses strategies such as asking questions and presenting examples in order to expose or correct the student's ideas. In one sense, this tutorial dialogue has some similarities with Skinner's notions of programmed instruction (Section 11.3), in which the student progresses at his or her own rate, is prompted to find the correct answers and any incorrect answers are corrected (Skinner, 1958). A major difference is the cognitive nature of the dialogue in the inquiry method of teaching. The teacher diagnoses and corrects the student's knowledge or "mental model". Inquiry teaching therefore crucially depends on the expertise of the teacher both in being fluent in the domain in question and being able to use appropriate strategies to diagnose the student's weaknesses and then correct them.

Formally, the theory of inquiry teaching is made up of three components:

1. The goals of the teacher.
2. The strategies used to achieve these goals.
3. The control structure which governs the dialogue between teacher and student.

As discussed previously, the main goals of the teacher are concerned with teaching a theory or teaching how to derive a theory. The former involves subgoals of correcting student's misconceptions about a theory and teaching how to make predictions from a theory. The latter involves teaching what questions to ask to construct a theory, teaching the nature of the theory and how to test it. The third component, the control structure, is broken down into four parts: an agenda which is maintained by the teacher and involves the goals and subgoals of the dialogue; priorities for adding goals to the agenda; selection of cases; and knowledge of the student. The rules which govern the priorities for adding goals to the agenda include dealing with:

errors of commission before errors of omission;
prior steps in the theory before later steps;
misconceptions which are easier to fix than more difficult ones;
more important factors in the theory than less important factors.

How cases are selected is also guided by some heuristics such as:

Selecting cases that illustrate more important factors before less important ones.

Selecting cases which lead to a significant generalisation. For example, in teaching about rainfall, countries may be selected such as S. California, N. Africa, W. Australia and N. Chile, which have little rainfall but are all on the western side of a continent in the latitude of 20 to 30 degrees. Selecting more important or frequent cases before less important or frequent ones.

The most significant contribution which this theory makes lies in its second component which concerns the strategies which expert teachers use to pursue their goals in a dialogue. These strategies are based on 24 rules which were identified by Collins (1977) and these have been elaborated in an appendix by Collins and Stevens (1982). In total there are 155 strategies (counting all variations) which cover the cases, questions and comments selected by the teacher during a dialogue. Collins and Stevens estimated that these strategies cover 80%–90% of a teacher's contributions to a dialogue to which has to be added strategies which encourage students to test hypotheses or to question authority. Ten of the most important strategies which teacher's use are given in Table 8.6 together with some examples.

Table 8.6 Some strategies of inquiry teachers (adapted from Collins and Stevens, 1982, 1983 and Collins, 1985)

1. *Selecting positive and negative examples*. Example: if a student is being taught the factors affecting whether a place has heavy rainfall or not, pick a case like the Amazon or Oregon where all the factors have values that lead to heavy rainfall

2. *Varying cases systematically*. This can be achieved in four ways, one of which is concerned with the variability of the factor as in this example: suppose Java has been identified as a place that is warm enough to grow rice, then pick a case like Japan which is much cooler but still grows rice

3. *Selecting counterexamples*. If a student forms an incorrect hypothesis then the teacher may select a counterexample which satisfies the student's hypothesis but results in an incorrect prediction. Counter-examples can be insufficient factors, unnecessary factors, irrelevant factors or incorrect values for a factor identified by the student. An example for an irrelevant factor is: suppose a student proposed that having high humidity was necessary for growing rice or predicts that Java grows rice because of the high humidity, then the teacher can ask about Egypt where the humidity is low but rice is grown, or the Congo where humidity is high but no rice is grown

4. *Generating hypothetical cases.* There are four kinds of hypothetical examples which parallel the four kinds of counterexamples (3 above). An example of the teacher constructing a hypothetical case to force the student to reconsider some insufficient factors is: suppose a student suggests they do not grow rice in British Columbia because it is too mountainous, ask the student "If British Columbia were flat could they grow rice then?" The answer is that they could not because of the cold temperature

5. *Asking students to form hypotheses.* There are various strategies for getting students to form hypotheses about the nature of factors involved and how they affect the dependent variable. These are called "identification strategies" by Collins and Stevens (1982) and include asking for a value of the dependent variable, asking for the formulation of a rule, asking for the similarities or differences between cases and asking for relevant, sufficient and necessary factors. An example of the teacher asking for similarities in factors between similar cases, in a dialogue concerning Peter Pan, is: what makes Peter Pan, Tinkerbell and Wendy good characters?

6. *Asking students to evaluate hypotheses.* Once the students have formed hypotheses there are various strategies for encouraging students to systematically test their hypotheses. These include asking if rules are correct, asking if factors are necessary, sufficient or irrelevant, asking if the values of factors are correct or incorrect. An example of the last type is: in discussing viral pneumonia, the teacher could ask if elevated respiratory rate, shaking chills, bloody sputum and severe pleural pain were correct or incorrect symptoms of such a diagnosis

7. *Asking students to make predictions and consider alternative predictions.* Example: if a student suggested that they grow rice in Nigeria because of warm temperature and heavy rainfall, then one might ask whether wheat or corn could also be grown there

8. *Entrapping students into revealing their misconceptions.* Entrapment strategies involve the teacher proposing incorrect hypotheses which aim to get students to reveal or find out possible misconceptions, e.g. by leading the student to make an overgeneralisation or a wrong prediction based on insufficient factors. Example: suppose a student is considering whether they grow rice in Florida, the teacher may ask if the warm climate would account for the inability to grow rice there

9. *Tracing consequences to a contradiction.* The teacher traces the consequences of a student's misconception to a conclusion which the student agrees is incorrect. This forces the student to reformulate his

theory into a more consistent one. Example: if the student asserted that rice could grow wherever there was a lot of rain, then the teacher might point out that it rained a lot in the southern part of Alaska and then ask the student about the climate, the terrain and the possibility of growing rice there until the student realised the contradiction with his proposal

10. *Encouraging students to question authority.* Too often students rely on the provision of the answer from a book or a teacher and it is useful to encourage students to construct their own theories and question what they read or are told

---

These strategies provide an insightful account of how expert teachers develop theories and reasoning skills in their students when the subject matter consists of causal relationships. These strategies can be applied to any domain although their relevance will vary. Tutorial dialogues in arithmetic emphasise theory development and involve strategies of case selection and counterexamples, whilst dialogues in geography and medicine focus on identifying factors and making predictions. An example of how some of these strategies fit together in a dialogue can be found in an Appendix from Stevens and Collins (1977), which the interested reader is recommended to consult. The most powerful aspect of Collins and Stevens work on the inquiry method is that they provide a most elegant *analysis* of the components of a Socratic dialogue between teacher and student. This analysis is descriptive rather than prescriptive. Nevertheless it is reasonable to assume that the components of the inquiry method, particularly the strategies, are from good teachers, are therefore desirable and should be passed on to other teachers. This seems eminently sensible, although as Collins (1985) conceded there is no evidence concerning the instructional effectiveness of the inquiry method. This is an unfortunate characteristic of all theories of instruction. Also further work is necessary in order to make the theory fully prescriptive. This should investigate the precise nature of the control structure for selecting and sequencing strategies as a consequence of the teacher's various goals and subgoals. This last criticism is somewhat harsh, since no other instructional theories meet such a criterion.

Collins (1985) summarised the inquiry method's advantages and disadvantages. It provides individualized training with the student actively involved which has both cognitive and motivational benefits. In addition, Collins believed that the inquiry method develops not only a "deep" understanding of the subject matter, but also many reasoning skills which are necessary for scientific thinking in other domains. On the negative side, it is slow, requires considerable resources, is difficult to implement with a class of students, and may result in negative reactions from students who have their misconceptions "exposed". Crucially, its effectiveness depends on the sensitivity and skill of the teacher who has to engage in a complex task – that of managing a tutorial dialogue using the inquiry method.

In conclusion, the inquiry method considers all three components of training design, discussed in Section 8.1. It explains how, in a tutorial, the teacher has to select and use teaching strategies in an ongoing manner as a consequence of the trainee's competence and the nature of the subject matter to be understood.

The ARCS model of motivational design

One of the most neglected yet important topics in training is how to motivate trainees to participate and perform well in a training pro- gramme. Identifying factors which affect motivation is important. Whilst the study of motivation has a long history in psychology, this work has not been, by and large, related to training. This can be confirmed either by a glance through review articles in training or instructional psychology in the *Annual Review of Psychology*, or by searching through the subject indices of texts concerned with training. Some exceptions, which include brief sections on motivation, are Goldstein (1974), Pintrich et al. (1986) and Wittrock and Lumsdaine (1977). Motivational aspects of training design cover diverse theoretical ideas, including attribution theory, equity theory, locus of control, expectancy theories, need for achievement, Hertzberg's two-factor theory and goal setting.

The ARCS model of motivational design is a brave attempt to synthesise some of these theoretical ideas concerning motivation into principles relevant to training design. Such a task is difficult, and inevitably theorists will complain of the boldness of the principles, whilst practitioners will argue that they still do not have sufficient guidance on how to implement them. Keller (1983) provided a general review of motivational aspects of training design and suggested that findings fell into four categories: interest, relevance, expectancy and satisfaction. Subsequently, Keller and Kopp (1987) changed the "interest" category to "attention" and the "expectancy" category to "confidence". Strategies for each of these categories of motivational design were identified. Some of the theoretical underpinnings of the 1983 version are less evident in the 1987 ARCS model. Consequently, the categories and strategies distinguished by both models are given in Table 8.7 together with brief

Table 8.7 Categories and strategies for motivational design (categories are labelled with letters and strategies with numbers)

Keller (1983)	ARCS Model (Keller and Kopp, 1987)
A. *Interest*	**A.** *Attention*
1. To increase curiosity, use novel, incongruous conflictual and procedural events. Attention is aroused when there is an *abrupt change* in status quo	1. *Perceptual arousal*. Gain and maintain student attention by the use of novel, surprising, or uncertain events in instruction
2. To measure curiosity, use anecdotes and other devices for injecting a *personal, emotional element* into otherwise purely intellectual or procedural material	2. *Inquiry arousal*. Stimulate information-seeking behaviour by posing or having the learner generate questions or a problem to solve
3. To arouse and maintain curiosity, give people the opportunity to learn more about things they *already know about* or believe in but also give them moderate doses of the unfamiliar and unexpected	3. *Variability*. Maintain student interest by varying the elements of instruction
4. To increase curiosity, use analogies to make the strange *familiar* and the familiar *strange*	
5. To increase curiosity, guide students into a process of question generation	
B. *Relevance*	**B.** *Relevance*
6. To enhance achievement striving behaviour, provide opportunities to achieve *standards of excellence* under conditions of *moderate risk*	4. *Familiarity*. Use concrete language and use examples and concepts that are related to the learner's experience and values
7. To make instruction responsive to the power motive, provide opportunities for *choice*, *responsibility* and interpersonal *influence*	5. *Goal orientation*. Provide statements or examples that present the objectives and utility of instruction, and either present goals for accomplishment or have the learner define them
8. To satisfy the need for affiliation, establish *trust* and provide opportunities for *no-risk, cooperative interaction*	6. *Motive matching*. Use teaching strategies that match the motive profiles of the students

C. Expectancy

9. Increase expectancy for success by increasing *experience* with success

10. Increase expectancy for success by using instructional-design strategies that indicate the *requirements* for success

11. Increase expectancy for success by using techniques that offer *personal control* over success

12. Increase expectancy for success by using attributional feedback and other devices that help students connect success to personal effort and ability

D. Outcomes

13. To maintain intrinsic satisfaction with instruction, use task-endogenous rather than task-exogenous rewards

14. To maintain intrinsic satisfaction with instructor, use unexpected, *noncontingent* rewards rather than anticipated, salient, task-contingent rewards (except for dull tasks)

15. To maintain intrinsic satisfaction with instruction, use *verbal praise* and *information* feedback rather than threats, surveillance or external performance evaluation

16. To maintain quantity of performance, use *motivating feedback* following the response

17. To improve the quality of performance, provide *formative (corrective) feedback* when it will be immediately useful, usually just before the next opportunity to practice

C. Confidence

7. *Expectancy for success.* Make learners aware of performance requirements and evaluate criteria

8. *Challenge setting.* Provide multiple achievement levels that allow learners to set personal standards of accomplishment and performance opportunities that allow them to experience success

9. *Attribution moulding.* Provide feedback that supports student ability and effort as determinants of success

D. Satisfaction

10. *Natural consequences.* Provide opportunities to use newly acquired knowledge or skill in a real or simulated setting

11. *Positive consequences.* Provide feedback and reinforcements that will sustain the desired behaviour

12. *Equity.* Maintain consistent standards and consequences for task accomplishment

descriptions. Keller and Kopp's suggestion that there are few differences between these models does not seem to be supported by the number and type of strategies listed in each (Table 8.7). Both models agree on the need to gain the trainee's attention (which is similar to the first instructional event in the Gagné–Briggs model of instruction) and to arouse and maintain the motivation of the trainee during the training programme. A variety of strategies are suggested for this purpose which are broken down into: getting the trainee's attention initially; establishing the relevance of the training material to the trainee's wider goals; giving the trainee sufficient confidence to engage in the training; and finally, rewarding the outcome of a trainee's efforts in order to maintain motivation. Seventeen strategies are discussed in the original version of the theory, which are reduced to 12 in the later version of the theory. Some examples of how each strategy might be implemented in different training situations can be found in Keller and Kopp (1987), although practitioners need more extensive guidelines and examples.

Keller and Kopp (1987) discussed how motivational design should be developed. They identified four stages. These are equivalent to the major stages in the Instructional System Development (ISD) models, which are discussed in Chapter 4. These four stages are:

1. Carrying out an audience analysis.
2. Specifying motivational objectives.
3. Selecting appropriate motivational strategies.
4. Evaluating them.

Keller and Kopp argued that the motivational design of a training programme involves a separate but complementary approach to that used for the cognitive aspects of training. They suggested that an audience analysis is needed to indicate in which areas the target trainees are lacking in terms of motivation, and therefore require support. Next comes the specification of objectives, although these are motivational ones rather than the skill/performance ones discussed in Chapter 4 of this book. For example, one motivational objective might be that trainees rate the training programme at least moderately interesting! The third stage of motivational design concerns the selection and use of appropriate strategies to achieve these motivational objectives. The fourth stage involves evaluation that the motivational objectives have been achieved in a fashion which is similar to the evaluation of behavioural objectives.

To its credit, the ARCS model concentrates on one aspect of training design, namely the trainee's motivation, which has been generally overlooked. It is often assumed, incorrectly, that a training programme which is well designed will be intrinsically motivating. This may be so although it is well nigh impossible to disentangle the motivational and cognitive aspects of a training programme. For example, the provision of feedback is assumed to have both an informational and motivational effect which cannot be separated satisfactorily. Also, some of the motivational design strategies identified by Keller and Kopp in the 1987 version such as inquiry arousal, familiarity and goal orientation, are closely related to cognitive aspects of training design.

REFERENCES

Anderson, J.R. (1980). *Cognitive psychology and its implications.* San Francisco: Freeman.

Ausubel, D.P. (1963). *The psychology of meaningful verbal learning: An introduction to school learning.* New York: Grune and Stratton.

Ausubel, D.P. (1968). *Educational psychology: A cognitive view.* New York: Holt, Rinehart and Winston.

Bergan, J.R. (1980). The structural analysis of behaviour. An alternative to the learning-hierarchy model. *Review of Educational Research,* **50**(4), 625–646.

Bransford, J.D., Vye, N.J., Adams, L.T. and Perfetto, G.A. (1989). Learning skills and the acquisition of knowledge. In Lesgold, A. and Glaser, R. (Eds) *Foundations for a psychology of education.* Hillsdale, NJ: Lawrence Erlbaum.

Briggs, L.J. and Wager, W.W. (1981). *Handbook of procedures for the design of instruction.* 2nd edition. Englewood Cliffs, NJ: Educational Technology Publications.

Brown, A.L. and Palincsar, A. (1989). Guided cooperative learning and individual knowledge acquisition. In Resnick, L.B. (Ed.) *Knowing, learning and instruction. Essays in honor of Robert Glaser.* Hillsdale, NJ: Lawrence Erlbaum.

Bruner, J.S. (1960). *The process of education.* New York: Randon House.

Bruner, J.S. (1966). *Towards a theory of instruction.* Cambridge, MA: The Belknap Press of Harvard University Press.

Campbell, J.P. (1971). Personnel training and development. *Annual Review of Psychology,* **22**, 565–602.

Collins, A. (1977). Processes in acquiring knowledge. In Anderson, R.C., Spiro, R.J. and Montague, W.E. (Eds) *Schooling and the acquisition of knowledge.* Hillsdale, NJ: Lawrence Erlbaum.

Collins, A. (1985). Teaching reasoning skills. In Chipman, S.F., Segal, A.W. and Glaser, R. (Eds) *Thinking and learning skills, Volume 2, Research and open questions.* Hillsdale, NJ: Lawrence Erlbaum.

Collins, A. (1987). A sample dialogue based on a theory of inquiry teaching. In Reigeluth, C.M. (Ed.) (op.cit.).

Collins, A. and Stevens, A.L. (1982). Goals and strategies of effective teachers. In Glaser, R. (Ed.) *Advances in instructional psychology, Volume 2.* Hillsdale, NJ: Lawrence Erlbaum Associates.

Collins, A. and Stevens, A.L. (1983). A cognitive theory of inquiry teaching. In Reigeluth, C.M. (Ed.) (op.cit.).

Cotton, J.W., Gallagher, J.P. and Marshall, S.P. (1977). The identification and decomposition of hierarchical tasks. *American Educational Research Journal,* **14**(3), 189–212.

Dewey, J. (1900). Psychology and social practice. *Psychological Review*, **7**, 105–124.

Dick, W. and Carey, L. (1985). *The systematic design of instruction*. 2nd edition. Glenview, IL: Scott Foresman and Company.

Donchin, E. (1989). The learning strategies project. *Acta Psychologica*, **71**, 1–15.

Duncan, K.D. (1972). Strategies for analysis of the task. In Hartley, J. (Ed.) *Strategies for programmed instruction: An educational technology*. London: Butterworths.

Ellis, J.A. and Wulfeck II, W.H. (1982). Handbook for testing in Navy schools. NPRDC SR-83–2, Naval Personnel Research and Development Center, San Diego, CA.

Ellis, J.A. Wulfeck II, W.H. and Fredericks, P.S. (1979). The Instructional Quality Inventory. II. User's manual. NPRDC SR-79–24. Naval Personnel Research and Development Centre, San Diego, CA.

Evans, J.L., Homme, L. and Glaser, R. (1962). The RULEG system for the construction of programmed verbal learning sequences. *Journal of Educational Research*, **55**, 513–518.

Flavell, J.H. (1976). Metacognitive aspects of problem solving. In Resnick, L.B. (Ed.) *The nature of intelligence*. Hillsdale, NJ: Lawrence Erlbaum.

Frederiksen, T.R. and White, B.Y. (1989). An approach to training based upon principled task decomposition. *Acta Psychologica*, **71**, 89–146.

Gagné, R.M. (1965, 1970, 1977). *The conditions of learning*. 1st, 2nd and 3rd editions. New York: Holt, Rinehart and Winston.

Gagné, R.M. (1975). Taxonomic problems of educational systems. In Singleton, W.T. and Spurgeon, P. (Eds) *Measurement of human resources*. London: Taylor and Francis.

Gagné, R.M. (1985). *The conditions of learning and theory of instruction*. New York: CBS College Publishing.

Gagné R.M. and Briggs, L.J. (1974). *Principles of instructional design*. New York: Holt, Rinehart and Winston.

Gagné, R.M. and Briggs, L.J. (1979). *Principles of instructional design*. 2nd edition. New York: Holt, Rinehart and Winston.

Gagné, R.M., Briggs, L.J. and Wager, W.W. (1988). *Principles of instructional design*. 3rd edition. New York: Holt, Rinehart and Winston.

Gagné, R.M. and Dick, W. (1983). Instructional psychology. *Annual Review of Psychology*, **34**, 261–295.

Glaser, R. (1976). Components of a psychology of instruction. Toward a science of design. *Review of Educational Research*, **46**, 1–24.

Glaser, R. and Bassok, M. (1989). Learning theory and the study of instruction. *Annual Review of Psychology*, **40**, 631–666.

Glaser, R. and Resnick, L.B. (1972). Instructional psychology. *Annual Review of Psychology*, **23**, 181–276.

Goldstein, I.L. (1974). *Training: Program development and evaluation*. Monterey, CA: Brooks/Cole.

Goldstein, I.L. (1980). Training in work organisations. *Annual Review of Psychology*, **31**, 229–272.

Gropper, G.L. (1974). *Instructional strategies*. Englewood Cliffs, NJ: Educational Technology Publications.

Gropper, G.L. (1975). *Diagnosis and revision in the development of instructional materials*. Englewood Cliffs, NJ: Educational Technology Publications.

Gropper, C.L. (1983). A behavioural approach to instructional prescription. In Reigeluth, C.M. (Ed.) (op.cit.).

Keller, J.M. (1983). Motivational design of instruction. In Reigeluth, C.M. (Ed.) (op.cit.).

Keller, J.M. and Kopp, T.W. (1987). An application of the ARCS model of motivational design. In Reigeluth, C.M. (Ed.) (op.cit.).

Landa, L. (1974). *Algorithmization in learning and instruction.* Englewood Cliffs, NJ: Educational Technology Publications.

Landa, L. (1976). *Instructional regulation and control: Cybernetics, algorithmization and heuristics in education.* Englewood Cliffs, NJ: Educational Technology Publications.

Landa, L. (1983). The Algo-heuristic theory of instruction. In Reigeluth, C.M. (Ed.) (op.cit.).

Landa, L. (1987). A fragment of a lesson based on the Algo-heuristic theory of instruction. In Reigeluth, C.M. (Ed.) (op.cit.).

Leith, G.O.M. (1968). Programmed instruction, acquisition of knowledge and mental development of students. Proceedings UNESCO seminar on programmed instruction, Paper ED/ENPRO/6, Varna, Bulgaria, UNESCO Paris.

Logie, R., Baddeley, A., Mané, A., Donchin, E. and Sheptak, R. (1989). Working memory in the acquisition of complex cognitive skills. *Acta Psychologica,* **71**, 53–87.

Mané, A.M., Adams, J.A. and Donchin, E. (1989). Adaptive and part-whole training in the acquisition of a complex perceptual-motor skill. *Acta Psychologica,* **71**, 179–196.

McKeachie, W.J. (1974). Instructional psychology. *Annual Review of Psychology,* **25**, 161–193.

Melton, A.W. (Ed.) (1964). *Categories of human learning.* New York: Academic Press.

Merrill, M.D. (1983). Component display theory. In Reigeluth, C.M. (Ed.) (op.cit.).

Merrill, M.D. (1987). An illustration of Component Display Theory. In Reigeluth, C.M. (Ed.) (op.cit.).

Merrill, M.D. (1988). Applying component display theory to the design of coursework. In Jonassen, D.H. (Ed.) *Instructional designs for microcomputer coursework.* Hillsdale, NJ: Lawrence Erlbaum.

Merrill, M.D. and Boutwell, R.C. (1973). Instructional development: Methodology and research. In Kerlinger, F.N. (Ed.) *Review of research in education. Volume 1.* Itasca, NY: Peacock.

Merrill, M.D., Richards, R.E., Schmidt, R.V. and Wood, N.D. (1977). *The instructional strategy diagnostic profile: Training manual.* San Diego: Courseware Inc.

Pask, G. (1975). *Conversation, cognition and learning.* Amsterdam/New York: Elsevier.

Pask, G. (1976). *Conversation theory. Applications in education and epistemology.* Amsterdam: Elsevier.

Pintrich, P.R., Cross, D.R., Kozma, R.B. and McKeachie, W.J. (1986). Instructional psychology. *Annual Review of Psychology,* **37**, 611–657.

Reigeluth, C.M. (Ed.) (1983). *Instructional-design theories and models. An overview of their current status.* Hillsdale, NJ: Lawrence Erlbaum.

Reigeluth, C.M. (Ed.) (1987a). *Instructional design theories in action: Lessons illustrating selected theories.* Hillsdale, NJ: Lawrence Erlbaum.

Reigeluth, C.M. (1987b). Lesson blueprints based on the Elaboration Theory of instruction. In Reigeluth C.M. (Ed.) (op.cit.).

Reigeluth, C.M. and Stein, F.S. (1983). The Elaboration Theory of instruction. In Reigeluth, C.M. (Ed.) (op.cit.).

Reigeluth, C.M., Merrill, M.D., Wilson, B.C. and Spiller, R.T. (1980). The elaboration theory of instruction: A model for sequencing and synthesising instruction. *Instructional Science,* **9**, 195–219.

Resnick, L.B. (1973). Hierarchies in children's learning. A symposium. *Instructional Science,* **2**, 311–362.

Resnick, L.B. (1976). Task analysis in instruction. In Klahr D. (Ed.) *Cognition and instruction.* New York: Wiley.

Resnick, L.B. (1981). Instructional psychology. *Annual Review of Psychology*, **32**, 659–704.

Resnick, L.B., Siegel, A.W. and Kresh, E. (1971). Transfer and sequence in learning double classification skills. *Journal of Experimental Child Psychology*, **11**, 139–149.

Rigney, J.W. (1978). Learning strategies: A theoretical perspective. In O'Neil, H.F. (Ed.) *Learning strategies*. New York: Academic Press.

Romiszowski, A.J. (1974). *The selection and use of instructional media*. London: Kogan Page.

Romiszowski, A.J. (1981). *Designing instructional systems*. London: Kogan Page.

Romiszowski, A.J. (1984). *Producing instructional systems. Lesson planning for individualized and group learning activities*. London: Kogan Page.

Romiszowski, A.J. (1986). *Developing auto-instructional materials: From programmed texts to CAL and interactive video*. London: Kogan Page.

Romiszowski, A.J. (1988). *The selection and use of instructional media*. 2nd Edition. London/ New York: Kogan Page.

Rowntree, D. (1988). *Educational technology in curriculum development*. 2nd edition. London: Paul Chapman Publishing Co.

Scandura, J.M. (1973). *Structural learning I : Theory and research*. London: Gordon and Breach Science Publishers.

Scandura, J.M. (1983). Instructional strategies based on the Structural Learning Theory. In Reigeluth, C.M. (Ed.) (op.cit.).

Scandura, J.M. and Brainerd, C.J. (Eds) (1978). *Structural/process models of complex human behaviour*. Leyden, Netherlands: Sijthoff.

Skinner, B.F. (1958). Teaching machines. *Science*, **128**, 969–977.

Snelbecker, C.E. (1987). Contrasting and complementary approaches to instructional design. In Reigeluth, C.M. (Ed.) (op.cit.).

Sternberg, R.J. (1985). General intellectual ability. In Sternberg, R.J. (Ed.) *Human abilities: An information processing approach*. 4th edition. New York: Freeman.

Stevens, A.L. and Collins, A. (1977). The goal structure of a Socratic tutor. *Proceedings of Association for Computing Machinery, National Conference*, Seattle, Washington.

Tennyson, R.D., Steve, M.W. and Boutwell, R.C. (1975). Instance sequence and analysis of instance attribute representation in concept acquisition. *Journal of Educational Psychology*, **67**, 821–827.

Wexley, K.N. (1984). Personnel training. *Annual Review of Psychology*, **35**, 519–551.

White, R.T. (1973). Research into learning hierarchies. *Review of Educational Research*, **43**, 361–375.

White, R.T. and Gagné, R.M. (1978). Formative evaluation applied to a learning hierarchy. *Contemporary Educational Psychology*, **3**, 87–94.

Wittrock, M.C. and Lumsdaine, A.A. (1977). Instructional psychology. *Annual Review of Psychology*, **28**, 417–459.

CHAPTER 9
Training methods

This chapter focuses on one of the three components of training design introduced in Section 8.1, namely training methods and strategies. Sections 9.1–9.4 are concerned with macro distinctions in the design of training such as when training interventions occur and their general nature. For example, one of the most powerful training methods is providing the trainee with some practice or attempts at "doing" the task coupled with knowledge of results or advice concerning the level of competence achieved. The ubiquitous nature of the log–log linear law of practice is discussed in Chapter 2 and practice is fundamental to both theories of skill acquisition (Chapter 2) and theories of instruction (Chapter 8). Different aspects of the design of practice are a central feature of this chapter. The remaining sections discuss: the effectiveness of breaking the task into parts for training purposes (Section 9.5); how training might be adaptive to the developing skills of individual trainees (Section 9.6); the spacing and duration of training sessions (Section 9.7); the benefit of overtraining (Section 9.8); and finally the design of training text (Section 9.9).

Some of the more traditional topics such as the role of feedback and the design of practice are covered by older texts (e.g. Holding, 1965; Stammers and Patrick, 1975). References for more detailed reading will be given in the discussion of each topic.

9.1 INTRODUCTION TO PRETRAINING, KNOWLEDGE OF RESULTS AND GUIDANCE METHODS

Distinctions in training methods, used in Sections 9.2–9.4, are not a set of mutually exclusive and exhaustive categories, but are rather high-level characterisations of different training methods. The appropriateness of training methods will be strongly influenced by the nature of the task to be trained and most tasks require a mixture of methods.

The first distinction which can be drawn between training methods is in the timing at which some training intervention occurs and in particular whether it is *before* or *during* the training programme. An introduction is necessary for any training programme and this may be supplemented by various pretraining techniques which are aimed at improving the trainee's subsequent understanding and assimilation of training material. Keller and Kopp's (1987) theory of instructional design emphasised the motivational aspects of such pretraining (Section 8.4), whilst in this section we are more concerned with its cognitive aspects. A second distinction in training methods is how information is provided to the trainee and when it occurs in relationship to the trainee's actions. The traditional training method which has developed from the behavioural tradition is to require the trainee to respond and to indicate afterwards the correctness of this behaviour. This paradigm has grown up in the verbal learning and motor skills literature, although it can be used in most training situations. A different training method is to demonstrate to the trainee the behaviour required. In this case, information is provided to the trainee *before* any behaviour is required. One example of this is an expert who acts as a model in a role-play situation and is observed by the trainee. Modelling as a training method stems from Bandura's (1977) ideas concerning the development of social behaviour through observation and imitation. Another approach to training design which provides the trainee with information prior to action is prompting or cueing which indicates to the trainee either the nature of the behaviour required or when it should be made. The range of tasks with which these techniques are used is more restricted than that associated with training either by practice with knowledge of results or by demonstration.

9.2 PRETRAINING

A trainee has to be given some introduction or advance information concerning the scope of a training programme. Such advance information can have not only cognitive benefits in the ease with which training material is subsequently assimilated, but also motivational benefits if the trainee understands what his or her goals are, the relevance of training etc.

Hartley and Davies (1976) reviewed the effects of four pretraining strategies, providing the trainee with:

pretests;
behavioural objectives;
overviews;
advance organisers.

It is difficult to distinguish overviews from advance organisers. Also whilst pretests are designed to measure pretraining performance, they do have beneficial learning side-effects. Here we will discuss evidence concerning the provision of behavioural objectives and advance organisers although studies which investigate these pretraining techniques face serious methodological problems which make generalisations difficult.

Behavioural objectives

In Chapter 4, the importance of specifying training objectives using Mager's prescriptions is discussed. These training objectives, specified in behavioural terms, are used for specifying the content and scope of training and also for determining that trainees have mastered the training material by being used for developing criterion measures of performance. Is it beneficial to provide trainees themselves with these objectives before training? Intuitively, the answer is yes, although reviews of the research are not so unequivocal in their conclusions (Duchastel and Merrill, 1973; Hartley and Davies, 1976; Wittrock and Lumsdaine, 1977). Variables which have been investigated include the specificity of the objectives and whether or not providing trainees with objectives affects the learning of material relevant or irrelevant to them. In summarising results from various studies, Wittrock and Lumsdaine concluded:

> In sum, the findings indicate that stating objectives to students often facilitates the learning of information directly relevant to them. ... The findings about the learning of information not directly relevant to the objectives are inconsistent, sometimes indicating that specific objectives narrow learning to directly relevant information (Wittrock and Lumsdaine, 1977, p. 422).

Training specialists would not consider the narrowing effect of providing the trainees with objectives to be a real disadvantage. Hartley and Davies (1976) added that behavioural objectives are of more use to average ability trainees rather than those at either end of the ability dimension. They also concluded that provision of such objectives to trainees does generally improve learning.

Advance organisers

The notion underlying the use of advance organisers is that in order to learn new information, the trainee has to have relevant concepts or schemata with which to integrate it and make it meaningful (Ausubel,

1960, 1963). Therefore advance organisers are needed if the trainee either does not possess the appropriate conceptual framework, or possesses it but does not recognise its relevance. Ausubel proposed that this conceptual framework can be provided to the trainee by an advance organiser which is at a "higher level of abstraction, generality and inclusiveness than the learning task". Two types of advance organiser exist: an *expository* organiser, which is used when totally unfamiliar material has to be learned and a *comparative* organiser, which distinguishes the similarities and differences between new and old knowledge.

Advance organisers were first used in order to improve learning from text. They were usually composed of prose. One of the first reported studies is by Ausubel (1960) in which a 500-word expository organiser was compared against an historical passage of the same length in helping college students to learn about the properties of steel from a text passage. The advance organiser discussed the similarities and differences between metals and alloys and their respective advantages and disadvantages, whereas the historical passage described methods for processing iron and steel but contained no concepts, according to Ausubel, which were relevant to learning the material. A group given the expository organiser before training was superior to another group given the historical passage in terms of retention after three days (mean scores 16.7 and 14.1 respectively). Ausubel considered that this difference would have been even greater if the group with the organiser had not had some prior knowledge of steel which offset to some extent the potential advantage of the organiser.

The research evidence concerning the effect of advance organisers has been the subject of much debate and a number of reviews (Barnes and Clawson, 1975; Hartley and Davies, 1976; Luiten, Ames and Ackerson, 1980; Mayer, 1979). Barnes and Clawson (1975) in a review of 32 studies concluded that "no clear patterns emerged regarding the facilitative effects of advance organisers", whilst Hartley and Davies stated that studies since 1967 "are not so overwhelmingly in favour of advance organisers". Luiten, Ames and Ackerson (1980) examined the "size of effect" rather than the statistical significance of findings from 135 studies and found that, generally, advance organisers were beneficial to learning and retention. Mayer (1979) attempted to reconcile the positive, negative and null effects of advance organisers by using assimilation theory to predict the conditions under which they should improve learning. Mayer reviewed the results from 44 studies, concluding that they were in agreement with assimilation theory and that:

> Advance organisers will result in broader learning when the material is
> potentially conceptual but appears unorganised or unfamiliar to the
> learner, when the learner lacks a rich set of related knowledge or abilities,
> when the organiser provides a higher level context for learning and when
> the test measures the breadth of transfer ability (Mayer, 1979, p. 161).

A fundamental methodological problem which plagues advance organiser studies is the definition and construction of an organiser. As we mentioned earlier, Ausubel believed that an organiser should be more abstract and general and in the case of expository organisers "provide relevant, proximate subsumers" for the trainee in learning the new material. However, these ideas have not been sufficient to restrict the nature of organisers, which varies remarkably between studies. What is needed is some means of linking the identification of the organiser to the analysis of the task to be trained, including the cognitive processes involved. A second methodological problem is how to construct an organiser which does not itself provide information relevant to training. Otherwise it might be argued that an advance organiser is not facilitating the assimilation of new training material but is rather itself part of the training material.

These difficulties and others can be illustrated by a contemporary example of the application of Ausubel's ideas to the training of a computer-based editing task (Patrick and Fitzgibbon, 1988). In learning to edit, it is easy to get "lost" in terms of appreciating the significance and status of a display and its relationship to other displays. A novice has no knowledge of the structure of the editing system, when to go where and how to accomplish this. Consequently, in the Patrick and Fitzgibbon study a "structural" display was given to one training group prior to some computer-based training concerning the editing task. This display or organiser, illustrated in Figure 9.1, was developed with a large dose of intuition. No guidelines were available concerning the systematic development or identification of the organiser from a task analysis. It was felt that the structural display complied with Ausubel's suggestions. Results indicated that the training group which had the structural display was superior in terms of speed and errors on a criterion editing task to both a control condition which had no display and also a condition which was presented with it *after* the training. The superiority of providing the structural display in *advance* of training suggested that the organiser improved the encoding of the training material although there are at least two explanations for this. Firstly, the organiser might have operated in the manner in which Ausubel and Mayer suggested and provided the trainees with some useful "conceptual scaffolding" to which the new material could be linked. Alternatively, the structural

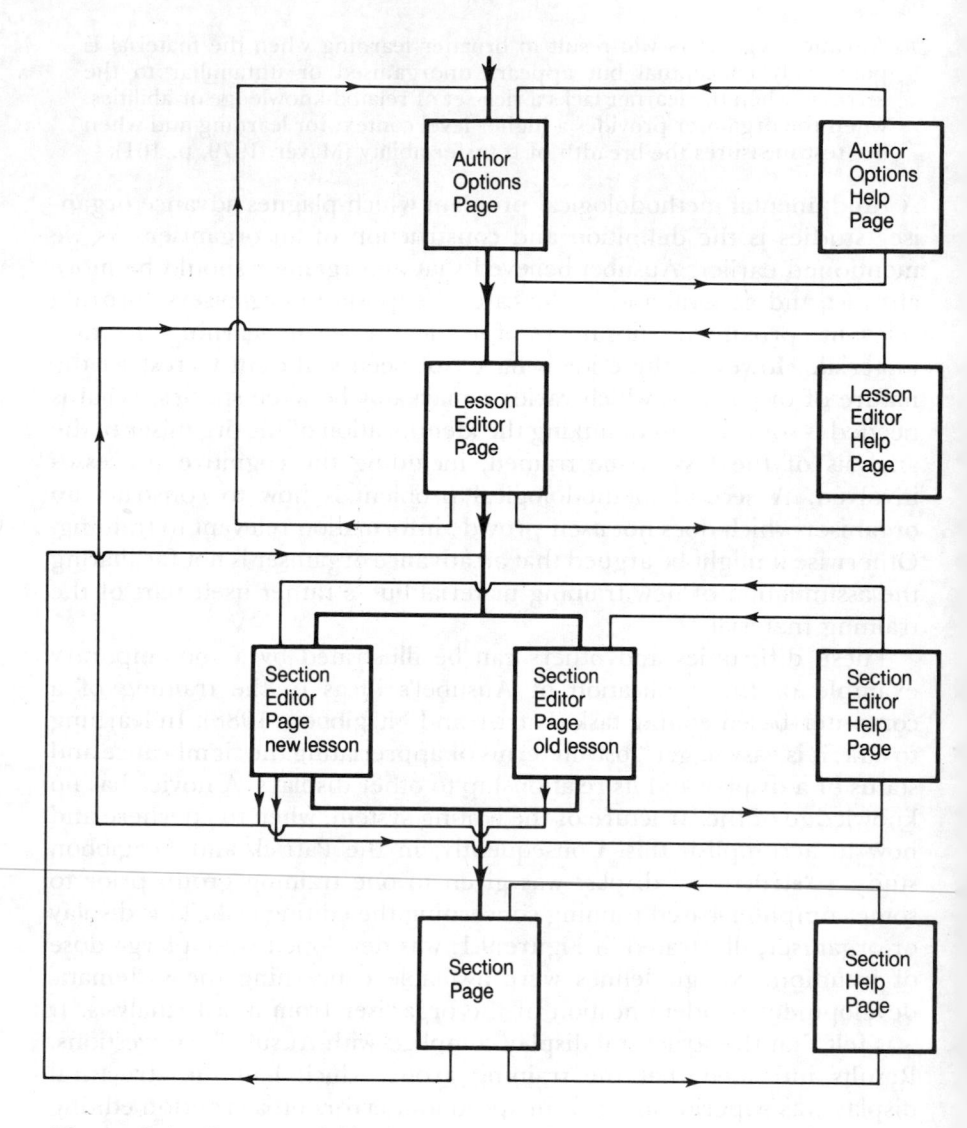

Figure 9.1 Structural display used as an advance organiser in training a computer-based editing task (Patrick and Fitzgibbon, 1988).

display may have enabled the trainee to direct his attention to, and focus resources on difficult parts of the training material. Necessarily, the display provided some task relevant information although the authors argued that this was not the reason for its beneficial effect. One cannot be certain. These difficulties are not unique to this study and apply to other studies of advance organisers.

In conclusion, advance organisers will generally be of benefit to training, even though theoretically we are less certain of how they should be designed and why they improve learning.

The Elaboration theory of instruction (Reigeluth et al., 1980; Reigeluth and Stein, 1983) builds upon Ausubel's ideas of advance organisers and extends them into a more general approach to training design. This theory prescribes that training should begin with an "epitome" which is progressively elaborated into various types and levels of description. An epitome is similar to an advance organiser except that it does not have to be at a higher level of abstraction and it may require substantial training. Reigeluth and Stein (1983) mentioned that one particular epitome had involved ten hours of training including practice exercises. The Elaboration theory can best be understood as analogous to the use of a zoom lens:

> A person starts with a wide-angle view, which allows him or her to see the major parts of the picture and the major relationships among those parts (eg the composition or balance of the picture), but without any detail.
> The person then zooms in on a part of the picture. Assume that instead of being continuous, the zoom operates in steps or discrete levels. Zooming in one level on a given part of the picture allows the person to see more about each of the major subparts. After having studied these subparts and their interrelationships, the person could then zoom back out to the wide angle view to review the other parts of the whole picture and to review the context of this part within the whole picture (Reigeluth and Stein, 1983, p. 340).

Hence Elaboration theory suggests that training should begin at a general level with an "epitome" and then gradually introduce greater detail in the manner indicated in Figure 9.2. At the end of each level of elaboration is a summariser and expanded epitome that indicates relationships between the original epitome, the current level of elaboration and a lower, more detailed level. How subject matter is divided into levels of elaboration is not made explicit, although Reigeluth argued that it will depend on the nature of the subject matter. He suggested that one can have different epitomes and elaborations for conceptual, theoretical and procedural subject matter, using some of the distinctions in subject matter structure made by Reigeluth, Merrill and Bunderson (1978). For example, a conceptual structure might be described by a parts-of or kinds-of hierarchy or some combination of both. If one was teaching an introductory course in statistics, i.e. conceptual subject matter in Reigeluth's terms, an example of an epitome and part of the first level elaboration for this conceptual material are given in

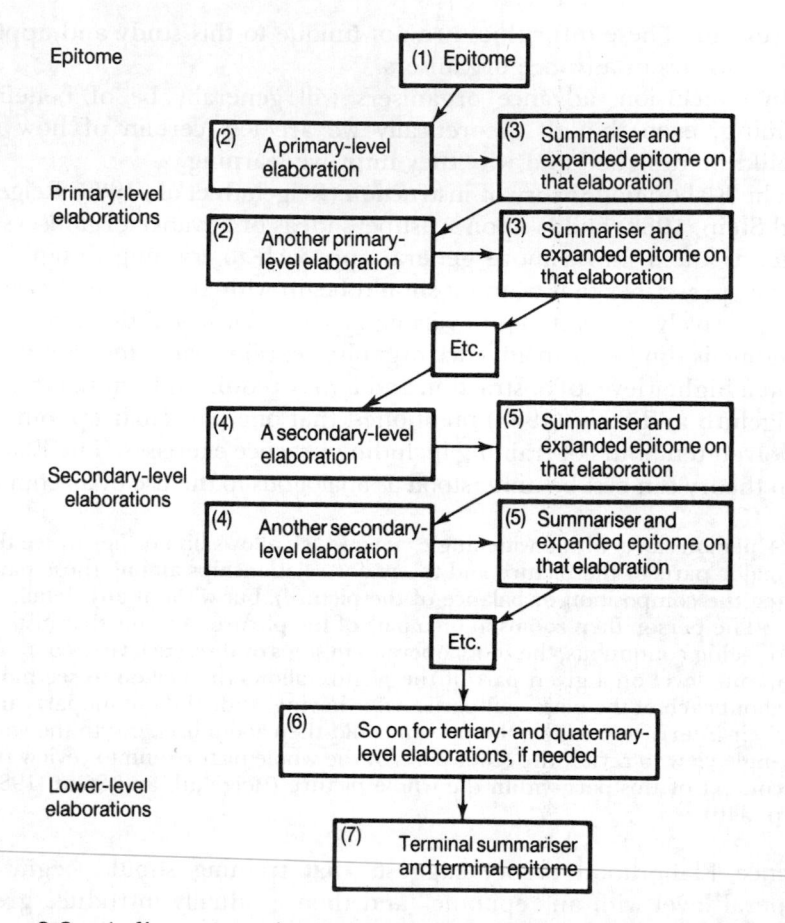

Figure 9.2 A diagrammatic representation of the Elaboration theory of instruction (Reigeluth et al., 1980).

Table 9.1a and b respectively. This elaboration is based on a kinds-of hierarchy.

Elaboration theory is aimed at the learning of facts, concepts, principles and procedures and presents some interesting speculation about the overall sequence of training. Like other theories of training design, it suffers from a lack of empirical evidence. What is needed is the development of training sequences which are consistent and inconsistent with the theory and their evaluation in terms of both qualitative and quantitative differences in the mental models developed by trainees.

Table 9.1 Conceptual content for an introductory course in statistics (adapted from Reigeluth and Stein, 1983)

(a) *Conceptual epitome*
  1. Organising content (concepts)
     Kinds of measures
     a. Elevation (or central tendency)
     b. Spread
     c. Proportion
     d. Relationship
     Kinds of methods
     a. Description
     b. Estimation
     c. Hypothesis testing
  2. Supporting content
     (Learning prerequisites for the aforementioned concepts)
     Practically all concepts in statistics can be viewed as elaboration
     on these concepts through the development of parts-of or
     kinds-of conceptual structures
(b) *Level 1 elaboration*
  1. Organising content (concepts)
     Kinds of measures

a.1 Mean	a.2 Median	a.3 Mode
b.1 Variance	b.2 Standard deviation	
c.1 Percent	c.2 Decimal	c.3 Fraction
d.1 r_s	d.2 r_{pb}	d.3 $r_\emptyset$

  2. Supporting content
     (Learning prerequisites for the aforementioned concepts)
     Additional elaborations would define kinds of methods for each
     kind of measure (e.g. methods of hypothesis testing for spread)

9.3 KNOWLEDGE OF RESULTS OR EXTRINSIC FEEDBACK

The most common and powerful method of training is to allow the trainee to perform the task and then to provide some information about the correctness of his/her action. This information, appropriately named knowledge of results, can be used to train a range of tasks, including throwing a ball, discriminating different aircraft at long distance and solving an arithmetic problem. Knowledge of results, coupled with some attempt at "doing" the task, provides a universal method for improving skill. This applies to any type of learning, as identified by Gagné and Merrill (Section 8.3), including the learning of facts, concepts, procedures, problem-solving, motor skills and cognitive strategies. Knowledge of results can be delivered in various ways, for example, by a trainer during on-the-job training or by written comments concerning the answer to a test performed at the end of training. The fundamental feature of this knowledge of results is that it provides the trainee with the discrepancy between actual and desired behaviour.

The importance of knowledge of results developed from reinforcement theories of learning which emphasised that reward should be presented after a correct response in order to strengthen the connection between stimulus and response. The first exposition of this principle was given by Thorndike (e.g. 1927) in his Law of Effect. However, gradually it became evident that rewards not only *motivated* the trainee but also provided *information* which could be used by the trainee to improve his or her next response. Consequently, a massive literature developed in the area of motor skill acquisition which investigated how and when to provide this knowledge of results in order to maximise learning. Reviews of this literature are available from Adams (1971), Annett (1961, 1969), Bilodeau (1966), and Salmoni, Schmidt and Walter (1984), whilst overviews can be found in Holding (1965) and Stammers and Patrick (1975). Adams (1987) provided a useful historical account of this topic. Whilst this literature has developed primarily in the context of simple motor tasks, knowledge of results is acknowledged to be a generalisable principle for promoting learning (e.g. Langley and Simon, 1981). In cognitive skill acquisition, in which a trainee is struggling to develop an appropriate mental model or discover and internalise rules for a problem solving task, knowledge of results can identify misconceptions, inappropriate rules or boundaries for their operation. In Anderson's (1982) ACT theory of cognitive skill acquisition, this type of feedback, coupled with practice, is important in facilitating some of the qualitative changes which occur before a skill becomes fully proceduralised. Even though feedback is as potent for learning cognitive as opposed to motor skills, it is much more difficult to provide for cognitive activities than for the more observable motor activities.

The terminology and distinctions used in discussion of knowledge of results can best be understood by returning to the motor skills literature where these ideas developed. Knowledge of results has been labelled feedback, information feedback, and of course, reinforcement. The terms knowledge of results and feedback are used interchangeably in this book.

Knowledge of results comes not only from *extra* information provided to a trainee about his performance during training but also from the visual, auditory and proprioceptive information associated with *normal* execution of the task. This led Annett (1961) to propose the important distinction between *intrinsic* and *extrinsic* knowledge of results. *Intrinsic* knowledge of results refers to information concerning performance which is available in the *normal* (i.e. nontraining) task situation. *Extrinsic* knowledge of results refers to additional information concerning performance which is supplied during training and is not available in the *normal* task situation. The value of providing such extrinsic knowledge of results was originally demonstrated by studies, which nowadays appear somewhat uninspiring, concerned with learning to draw lines of specified lengths whilst blindfold (Thorndike, 1927; Trowbridge and Cason, 1932). Thorndike (1927) found that telling one group of trainees "right" or "wrong" when performance was within one quarter inch of the target length improved learning in comparison to another group which received no such feedback. Trowbridge and Cason (1932) confirmed this result and extended it by demonstrating that provision of more precise quantitative knowledge of results when trainees were plus or minus one eighth of an inch of the target was superior to the qualitative statements of "right" and "wrong".

In these traditional experiments the only intrinsic knowledge of results which was available was provided by proprioception concerning the distance, location and rate of movement. The nature and amount of any intrinsic knowledge of results will depend upon the task in question. For example, a golfer will normally receive visual, proprioceptive and some auditory information for each swing of the golf club, plus a score for each hole which is aggregated into a total score for that round of golf. This is all intrinsic knowledge of results. Any additional information supplied by a coach concerning the swing of the club, the selection of club and tactics in the game is defined as extrinsic knowledge of results. This information will be withdrawn after training. Extrinsic knowledge of results can take many forms. A verbal statement of errors may be given; some video tape may enable the trainee to have a better view of his or her actions; and some "kinematic" knowledge of results might enable the trainee's actual movement pattern to be compared against an ideal pattern. Extrinsic feedback can be delivered either during performance of the task or at the end. For example, in training a missile operator to track a moving target, an auditory and/or visual signal might be given to indicate when the trainee is on target. Alternatively, some summary statement of accuracy, typically "time on target", might be given at the end of each attempt at tracking the target.

Howell (1956) provided an illustration of the powerful effect of extrinsic knowledge of results in training sprinters to improve their sprint starts. Interestingly, the key to a good sprint start is to generate an impulse pattern with the foot such that the impulse is immediate and

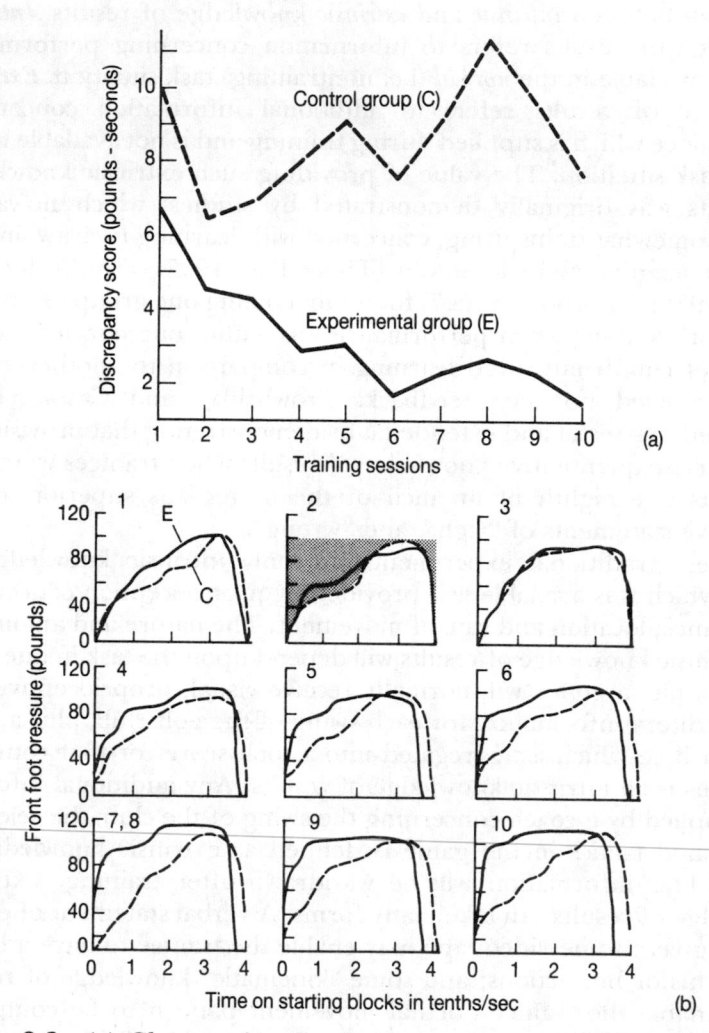

Figure 9.3 (a) Changes in average force–time graphs for a group of sprinters receiving knowledge of results compared with a control group over 10 training sessions. (b) Discrepancy between the actual and ideal impulse pattern for sprint starts over 10 training sessions. The discrepancy for the control group on the 2nd training session is shown as shaded area (Howell, 1956).

reaches its maximum on the first thrust before the front foot actually leaves the starting block. An ideal impulse pattern is described by a rectangular distribution of force plotted against time which is characteristic of champion sprinters. A means was developed of providing one group of novice sprinters with kinematic feedback concerning how closely their actual impulse pattern matched this ideal one. In contrast, a control group, equivalent to the experimental group in weight and impulse patterns on the first practice session, received the conventional coaching wisdom of the day. This involved an experienced coach's comments concerning quality of start, arm thrust, foot movement etc. The two groups were compared in quality of sprint starts over 10 training sessions spanning the period of one month. The increasing superiority of the experimental group which received the kinematic feedback is represented in Figure 9.3a. The impulse patterns of this group changed, so that by days 9 and 10 they resembled the ideal rectangular distribution, unlike those of the control group. This is reflected in Figure 9.3b which plots changes in discrepancy between the actual and ideal impulse patterns over the 10 training sessions. The experimental group's improvement by the tenth session is equivalent to a 77% improvement over performance on the first session. In contrast, the control group failed to make any improvement. This study has been cited as evidence of the powerful effect of extrinsic knowledge of results as a method of training design. This is not the whole truth, as the experimental group received in addition to knowledge of results some theoretical rationale for the ideal impulse pattern of the foot in a sprint start. This was felt, quite reasonably, to be necessary, presumably to enable the trainee to interpret the kinematic feedback, rather than just observe it and then have to infer the relationship between impulse pattern and sprint start. This theoretical explanation may have also contributed to the superiority of the experimental group, although by how much is impossible to say.

There are four significant principles which emerge from the literature concerning the use of knowledge of results as a training method for any type of skill. These are largely a matter of common sense.

Principle 1. Learning increases as practice with extrinsic knowledge of results increases until an asymptote is reached. This is consistent with the law of practice (Chapter 2), which involves the trainee receiving some form of knowledge of results. The only caveat that needs to be added is that there are occasions on which some extrinsic knowledge of results only improves *performance* during training and does not promote *learning*, which is evident when it is withdrawn (see Principle 2).

Principle 2. Extrinsic knowledge of results available during execution of the task may improve performance but not learning. This point was originally made by Miller (1953) who realised that providing a trainee with information

concurrent with doing a task might only serve as a crutch to performance rather than effect learning. Hence he labelled this type of
knowledge of results "action" feedback. One of the most frequently cited
studies which illustrates this phenomenon was carried out by Goldstein
and Rittenhouse (1954) in the context of training aerial gunnery. The
trainee had to track fast-moving target aircraft. A comparison was made
between a training condition which had a verbal summary of performance at the end of a series of practice sessions and another condition
which had a buzzer sound when the gun was on target. Whilst the buzzer
condition led to more rapid improvement in performance, there was a
decrement when the buzzer was removed and eventually the superiority
of this condition disappeared. In some follow up studies which examined
transfer to a similar type of gunnery task, there was evidence that the
condition trained with the concurrent buzzer experienced some difficulty in transfer. Other studies have found similar decrements on
withdrawal of knowledge of results after training particularly if *visual*
concurrent information is provided (Annett, 1959; Karlin, 1960; Lincoln,
1954; Patrick and Mutlusoy, 1982) although exceptions are available
(Fox and Levy, 1969; Robb, 1966). A variety of explanations have been
proposed to account for the negative effects of concurrent extrinsic
feedback. Ward and Senders (1966) suggested that it may interfere with
performance of the task; Lincoln (1954) proposed that it distracted
trainees from the cues which are important in performance of the task;
Annett (1970) proposed an intersensory effect, whereby visual and
proprioceptive feedback was summated in some way which distorted
recall. Notwithstanding which explanation is correct, Welford (1968)
provided a useful generalisation concerning this literature.

> A subject must have *some* cues to the results of his actions if he is
> to perform accurately at all and training procedures will be effective
> insofar as they help him to observe and use such cues as are inherent in
> the task for which he is being trained. They will fail insofar as they
> provide him with extra cues on which he comes to rely but which are not
> available when he changes from training to the actual job (Welford, 1968,
> p. 307).

In order to guard against this danger, extrinsic knowledge of results provided during training should be gradually faded out as training progresses.

*Principle 3. Extrinsic knowledge of results should be unambiguous, precise and
easily interpreted by the trainee in terms of the discrepancy between actual and
desired performance.* Most of these points are made in a review by
Wheaton et al. (1976). Complex or long-winded extrinsic feedback is
likely to confuse the trainee or be ignored. The effectiveness of extrinsic

feedback will be reduced if the trainee has to engage in inference or complex reasoning in order to interpret it. Also merely encouraging the trainee to try again or reminding him of the broad requirements of the task are unlikely to be useful. Similarly, evaluative comments such as "good" or "bad" are suboptimal for learning as they are not directed at the nature of the discrepancy between actual and required performance and how this might be eliminated. At the other extreme, there will be a limit beyond which increasing the precision of feedback information will not be helpful. In the training of motor skills, more precise knowledge of results facilitates learning (McGuigan, 1959), although this improvement does not occur with very precise feedback levels (Gill, 1975) and extreme precision is even detrimental (Rogers, 1974). Thus knowledge of results which indicates that a dart is 2.345 mm as opposed to 2 mm from a target is beyond the discriminative ability of any darts player!

It is straightforward to design knowledge of results which complies with Principle 3 for simple tasks. However, this is more difficult for problem-solving or reasoning tasks in which different strategies are available for tackling the task. Consider a trainee technician attempting to master fault-finding skills for a piece of equipment, or a student trying to understand and develop some geometry proofs. The trainer has initially to diagnose the trainee's weakness or misunderstanding before any feedback is provided (as emphasised in Collins and Stevens' Inquiry method of instruction). This may be problematic if different misconceptions on the part of the trainee can give rise to the same performance. Provision of appropriate feedback therefore depends upon the trainer or instructor having good diagnostic skills and being able to pinpoint the trainees' weaknesses. The same is true if a computer is used to provide some intelligent tutorial dialogue. This is discussed further in Section 11.5.

Principle 4. Extrinsic knowledge of results should occur before the trainee's next action or practice attempt. In the learning of simple motor skills, delay of extrinsic knowledge of results has not been particularly detrimental, unless it occurs after the trainee's next attempt at a task (Bilodeau, 1966; Welford, 1968). One might suspect that with more complex tasks, especially cognitive ones involving chains of reasoning, delay of feedback information will increase the risk that the trainee will forget to what aspects of performance it refers.

9.4 GUIDANCE

Guidance differs from extrinsic knowledge of results as a design method in the timing of information provided to the trainee. Guidance provides the trainee with information *prior* to action whilst knowledge of results, by definition, provides information *after* action. Guidance conveys advance information to the trainee concerning how to carry out part or all of the task. For example, a skilled motor mechanic might demonstrate how to dismantle the clutch on a car; a chess grandmaster might give some advice concerning tactics before a match or before a player's next move; and a gymnast might be manually guided through a complex movement pattern. Guidance differs from the pretraining methods discussed in Section 9.2 which are more general and do not provide specific prescriptions concerning future action. Guidance methods are part of everyday training practice, although they have received little evaluation. Providing the trainee with guidance, as opposed to allowing a trial and error exploration of a task, is likely to reduce major errors early in training. The effectiveness of guidance will depend upon both its informativeness with respect to the task and also how well the trainee is able to translate it into skilled performance. Guidance should provide the trainee with clear and unambiguous information, the same characteristics as elaborated for extrinsic knowledge of results in Principle 3, Section 9.3.

It is difficult to separate research concerning the effectiveness of guidance into neat piles. This is because the nature of guidance which is feasible depends upon the task. In addition, the questions addressed by research studies have varied. The term "guidance" was first used in the study of motor skills and forms of guidance were compared against knowledge of results methods. More recently, interest has centred on the development and organisation of knowledge during the acquisition of cognitive skills. An expert or a coach might provide advice to the trainee or create an environment in which the trainee can discover an appropriate mental model for performing the task. In these studies, the intention has been to study the development of expertise rather than to evaluate training methods.

The classic account of the early work concerned with guidance is given by Holding (1965). The rationale for training perceptual-motor tasks using guidance was to provide so-called "error free" training. This was believed to be important since errors committed early in learning tended to be repeated and therefore had to be "unlearned" (Holding, 1970). A rather different philosophy now exists in the training of cognitive tasks, since errors are seen as enabling the trainee to refine a concept, schema or mental model and to explore its boundaries or its range of application in novel situations. Holding (1965) differentiated four types of guidance: physical restriction in which physical movement is delimited by some device; forced response in which the required movement is executed passively; visual guidance where the trainee is shown the nature of the behaviour required; and verbal guidance which provides the trainee with some advice about what to do or what not to do or how to do it.

For our present discussion we will adapt Holding's distinctions into the following four types of guidance:

1. Physical guidance, which is relevant to the acquisition of motor skills and is a combination of Holding's categories of physical restriction and forced response. (It is a pity that some analogous method does not exist for cognitive skills which operates rather like a cognitive strait-jacket!)
2. Demonstrations, which include not only visual guidance but guidance using other modalities (e.g. auditory guidance). Demonstrations may involve modelling situations in which a person learns by observation or imitation of an expert (Bandura, 1977).
3. Verbal guidance or advice, which is a common training method although there is surprisingly little evidence concerning its effectiveness. One form of verbal guidance is prompting, which was used in Skinner's linear programmes in order to ensure that the trainee made the correct response (pp. 442–444).
4. Cueing, which is a type of guidance restricted to training for perceptual detection tasks. Formally, this category can be subsumed by the others although it is kept separate because cueing tells the trainee when a signal occurs, rather than what should be done next.

Physical guidance

There is a variety of reasons why some form of physical guidance might be used, particularly in the early stages of motor skill learning. Guiding the trainee's execution of a movement or restricting a movement in some way can be useful when learning a complex or dangerous motor skill. Hence a gymnast might be guided through a novel routine or a golfer's swing might be restricted by a harness. The earliest studies of this form of guidance were carried out with animals learning mazes in which either blind alleys were blocked off or the animals were physically transported through the maze in the correct fashion. This guidance produced reliable savings in training time compared to trial and error learning.

A set of experiments was carried out in the mid-1960s which evaluated the effectiveness of similar forms of physical guidance in human motor skill acquisition (Holding and Macrae, 1964, 1966; MacCrae and Holding, 1965a, b, 1966). Guidance methods were compared against knowledge of results methods. The tasks involved either simple position-ing movements or tracking. These studies demonstrated that physical guidance of one form or another can be as or more effective than training with knowledge of results. There were, however, a couple of exceptions in which guidance was worse. Stammers and Patrick (1975) suggested that these exceptions could be explained by differences between the training and test conditions. In other words, for physical guidance to be effective the trainee has to experience the same pro-prioceptive feedback during training as is normally available in task performance, i.e. the same intrinsic feedback. Physical guidance will be less effective the greater the mismatch between the movement sensations experienced during training and those experienced after training when guidance is withdrawn. Two further findings that emerged from these studies were:

(a) A small amount of physical guidance was more effective than a larger amount (Macrae and Holding, 1965b).
(b) The effectiveness of physical guidance as a training method increased with the complexity of the task (Macrae and Holding, 1966).

Demonstration

Labelling this category "demonstration" is somewhat unsatisfactory given the normal usage of the term. As defined here, demonstrations are training situations in which information is provided to the trainee prior to action, although verbal instructions and physical guidance are excluded. A demonstration typically provides the trainee with some visual guidance which shows the trainee what has to be achieved either directly (often referred to as "Sitting by Nellie" in industrial training), or indirectly through some symbolic coding. However, demonstrations are not restricted to the visual modality and an auditory demonstration can facilitate motor skill learning (Newell, 1981). Presumably, this is particu-larly useful where the task has an important auditory component, such as in playing a musical instrument or singing.

Demonstration as a training method has developed from two areas of psychology. One is concerned with motor skill acquisition, in which early errors were viewed as problematic (e.g. Kay, 1951) and visual guidance provided a means of reducing them. This type of demonstration is of benefit in the training of various athletic, ballet skills etc. A second area is that of social and developmental psychology, in which Bandura (1977) developed theoretical ideas concerning the importance of "modelling" or observational learning. He argued that by observation of a model, one can develop a cognitive representation, verbal or nonverbal, which can be used to guide future behaviour. These ideas have given a further impetus to the use of demonstration as a method of training motor skills (summarised by Adams, 1987). Modelling is potentially useful for training many skills and is important in the development of attitudes (Gagné, 1985). It has been used as a therapeutic method within clinical settings (Rachman, 1976).

The classic study of the effect of providing a demonstration using visual guidance is Von Wright's (1957) investigation of finger maze learning. The trainee had to learn to make a series of binary choices by following a diamond-shaped maze which moved towards him, although only a small part of it was visible at any one time. Three training conditions were used, which are represented in Figure 9.4. The aim was

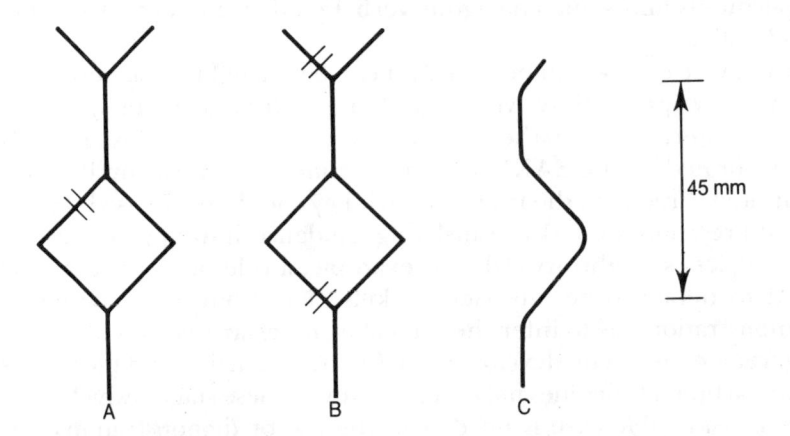

Figure 9.4 Part of the pattern of a maze as provided to three training conditions (Von Wright, 1957).

to learn to track the moving maze A and so avoid the incorrect paths as indicated in the upper half of the diamond on the left or the right. However, the trainee was unable to see which path was correct until after a choice had been made in the lower half of the diamond. One training condition used maze A, which therefore provided knowledge of results after the choice had been made (from the indication in the top of the diamond). Two visual guidance methods indicated the correct path to the trainee before a choice was made. In one guidance condition, the trainee was shown both the correct and incorrect alternatives (from the indication in the bottom of the diamond as in maze B). In the second guidance condition, only the correct path was seen as in maze C. These two visual guidance conditions had four guided trials before practising with maze A. The maze was learned to the criterion of two errorless runs. The results indicated that both visual guidance conditions were superior to the knowledge of results condition in terms of the number of trials to criterion and the number of errors made after the fourth trial. However, the visual guidance condition which could see the wrong alternative in addition to the correct one (i.e. maze B) was superior to the one which did not (i.e. maze C). Presumably, this was because trainees were forced into making a decision, rather than passively tracking the maze during the guidance trials. It should be noted that whilst Von Wright's task was maze learning and might appear to be a motor task, the correct path through the maze could be easily coded into a series of left and right commands. If this happened, then the *visual* aspect of the guidance might have been superfluous and some analogous verbal guidance might have been just as effective.

Guidance can vary in how easily it can be related to task performance. In Von Wright's study, visual guidance indicated unambiguously the correct alternative for the trainee to follow. Similarly, visual guidance incorporated in the SAKI keyboard trainer developed by Pask (1958) indicated directly to the trainee which key should be pressed. However, for more complex tasks, translating guidance into appropriate action may be less straightforward. For example, a role-play situation may be used to demonstrate interviewer skills. The trainee who watches the demonstration has to infer the critical or necessary aspects of interviewing, remember them, develop a suitable plan of action and then translate it into action. Difficulties may occur at any of these stages, which suggests that considerable care is needed in the use of demonstrations for the training of complex tasks.

Studies into the use of demonstrations as training techniques were carried out by Sheffield (1961) and Sheffield and Maccoby (1961).

Verbal guidance or advice

Information can be provided verbally to a trainee about how to carry out some future actions. It might be provided by the trainer or by a computer-based training system and it might be spoken or written. This advice might occur at the beginning of training or, preferably, in between the trainee's attempts at the task. Thus a foreman might describe how to dismantle part of an engine, a chess grandmaster might advise on the next chess move or an expert might suggest the next subgoal to pursue in a problem-solving task. This advice has to be both clear and usable, even for complex tasks. An expert, who provides advice often fails to understand that his conceptualisation of the task is quite different from the trainee's and that advice which to him might appear straightforward is not so to the trainee. Bainbridge (1989) illustrated how superficially simple instructions can require considerable inference and knowledge by the person attempting to follow them. We have all experienced such difficulties when attempting to interpret the "instructions" for operating a camera, or a piece of hi-fi equipment.

Hayes-Roth, Klahr and Mostow (1981) provided further illustration of the difficulties a trainee might experience in following conventional advice. They analysed the card game "hearts", and provided the following representative example of the sort of advice a trainee might receive:

> The goal of this game is to avoid taking points. In each round the deck of cards is initially dealt out among three or four players. Each player's cards constitute the player's hands. Play in a round consists of a series of tricks. Each player, clockwise in turn, plays once in a trick by moving a card from his or her hand into the pot. The player who has the two of clubs (2C) leads the first trick. Each player must follow suit if possible (i.e. must play a card of the same suit as that led). The player who plays the highest card in the suit led wins the trick and leads the next trick. A player who wins a trick takes all cards in the pot and is charged with any points that those cards have. Each heart has one point (hence the name of the game). The queen of spades (QS) has 13 points. The worst a player can do in any one round is take all but one point, in which case he or she takes 25 points. If the player takes 26 points (i.e. "shoots the moon"), every other player is charged with the 26 points. Shooting the moon is the best a player can do; taking 0 points is second best. You can prevent someone from shooting the moon by taking a point yourself. Whenever it is out, flush the queen of spades to make sure it isn't given to you (Hayes-Roth et al., 1981, p. 236).

The authors pointed out that this advice is made up of concept definitions (e.g. suit), behavioural constraints (e.g. each player must follow suit) and performance heuristics (e.g. if the queen of spades has not been played, then flush out the queen of spades). In order to use such heuristics, the player has to transform this advice into some plan of action and this may require several types of transformation on the advice given. For example, in order to use the heuristic concerning the queen of spades, the player has to know whether it has been played and then develop a plan to flush it out. One such plan might be to win the lead and then to lead spades. This might be a successful strategy under some circumstances but if the player has the king or an opponent has sufficient cards to protect the queen this may be unsuccessful. Consequently, the trainee has to operationalise advice into plans and then implement these in terms of actions, the outcomes of which lead to refinements of those plans. Advice for performing a complex task will inevitably be incomplete. The Hayes-Roth et al. example illustrates the discrepancy between conventional advice and advice which should be provided in a properly designed training programme. First, some analysis should have identified how the advice might be transformed by the trainee into procedural knowledge. This could then be addressed explicitly in training. Any conflicts between heuristics and the development of some meta-plan should be resolved before training. Second, the process of knowledge refinement as described by Hayes-Roth et al. depends upon the experience of trainees and their ability to diagnose the effect of their actions and reformulate knowledge appropriately. This occurs haphazardly in experiential learning and an organised training schedule should develop such skill more efficiently.

There is surprisingly little evidence concerned with the provision of advice or verbal guidance prior to and/or during training. Verbal pretraining which uses advance organisers or behavioural objectives, discussed in Section 9.2, has been found to be effective. These pretraining techniques only differ in degree from verbal guidance given prior to training which is more action-oriented. Even this distinction is not entirely satisfactory and there is a point at which they are inseparable. One of the earliest verbal guidance training studies, cited by Holding (1965), was a study by Wang (1925) using a traditional maze learning task. Verbal guidance given to trainees consisted of "turn to the left, keep going straight ahead, now turn right" etc. Verbal guidance conditions received 1, 2, 4, 8 or 16 trials with such advice, after which performance was compared against an untrained condition in terms of the number of trials required to learn the maze. The verbal guidance conditions saved at least 10 trials, although the amount saved did not vary with the number of guidance trials.

Not surprisingly, verbal guidance is particularly useful in learning a task which can be verbally coded. However, this advantage will only continue so long as skilled performance depends upon these verbal cues rather than other nonverbal cues in the task. Support for this comes from a study by Trumbo, Ulrich and Noble (1965) which manipulated directly the trainee's opportunity to utilise verbal coding. The task was one-dimensional pursuit tracking and performance was measured by an integrated absolute error score. A numerical code that described the path of the target was given to the trainees who rehearsed it before training. Although such verbal guidance reduced tracking error over the initial trials, neither this nor rehearsal of the numerical code affected retention after one week. This is consistent with the notion that verbal mediation of some perceptual-motor skills is important early in training, but that in later stages there is a greater dependence on the proprioceptive and visual cues intrinsic to the task. Alternatively, given a longer retention interval and a larger decrement in performance, verbal guidance might have been found to facilitate performance.

Another, somewhat different, traditional form of verbal guidance is known as "prompting". The most well-known example of prompting can be found in Skinner's linear programmes in which the trainee is almost given the correct answer before making it. This was done because of Skinner's insistence that the trainee must be positively reinforced after making the correct response. Prompting has also been successfully employed as a training method for paired-associate type tasks in which the trainee has to learn to associate a name or some other response with a particular stimulus. A trainee in a military establishment might have to learn a series of communication codes or how to discriminate types of ship, aeroplane, etc. Prompting provides the trainee with the stimulus and response terms which have to be associated by presenting them either simultaneously, or with the response just after the stimulus. Sometimes the trainee is asked to state the response. This form of verbal guidance prompts the trainee with the correct answer, typically a word, before an actual response is required. The effectiveness of prompting as a training technique has been compared with extrinsic knowledge of results. In a review, Aiken and Lau (1967) concluded:

> The data indicate that a variety of prompting procedures are equal or superior to a variety of confirmation [feedback] procedures in the learning of verbal paired-associates. The data are contradictory with regard to whether a combined prompting-confirmation procedure yields performance superior to either in pure form, though several researches indicated that prompting is superior to confirmation only early in learning (Aiken and Lau, 1967; p. 333; square parentheses added).

Prompting has been used successfully to train perceptual identification and discrimination skills in which a name has to be associated with a particular sound or visual signal. Training by prompting is better for learning complex sounds than training using practice coupled with knowledge of results, although this is not so clear-cut for visual identification tasks. Annett (1966) evaluated the effectiveness of prompting when the trainee had to learn to estimate a number of dots presented tachistoscopically. There was no difference in the effectiveness of prompting and knowledge of results training conditions although both of these were superior to a control condition which received no extra information about the task. Annett (1969) summarised the effect of prompting for training complex auditory pattern recognition. Many of the studies cited are not easily accessible in the literature and the following quotation from Annett (1969) is a good summary of their findings:

> Of particular interest is a series of studies by Swets (1962), and Swets, Harris, McElroy and Rudloe (1964) using computer-assisted instruction. Complex sound signals which could assume any of five different values along any of five dimensions constituted the material to be learned. The sounds were presented by a computer and the subject could enter a five-digit number, the name of the sound, on a teleprinter keyboard. A variety of tuition methods were available and subjects were given some freedom to choose the methods by which to learn. They could, for example, opt for a prompting mode in which the computer typed out the correct answer and then presented the tone, or they could opt for a test mode in which, after they had heard the sound and typed out an answer, the computer could give correct information along any one or all of the individual dimensions. It would also arrange to repeat the sounds or even to play back the sound corresponding to the subject's wrong answer.
>
> The main conclusion from these studies, an interesting one from the point of view of instructional technique, was that the students did not know what was good for them. Relating success to the amount of time spent by the subjects on each of the training modes, the simple prompting technique was found to be most efficient. Many subjects, however, tended to spend more time on the less efficient test modes, that is to say, attempting responses and getting various forms of knowledge of results ... An interesting postscript is provided by Sidley, Winograd and Bedauf (1965), also using complex sounds. In one case, the sounds remained audible during the subject's response and the consequent KR. In another case KR was, as in the Swets studies, provided only after each sound had ended. Improvement in the former case was 45 per cent and in the latter case was only 20 per cent. So once again we find the close temporal contiguity between the stimulus and its 'name' to be a potent factor in these forms of perceptual learning. Close contiguity would facilitate the 'specification' of an ephemeral signal (Annett, 1969, pp. 73–75).

This section has presented a smorgasbord of examples of training which involve some form of verbal guidance or advice being given prior to action. Tasks vary in the extent to which their performance is verbally mediated and this will determine the effectiveness of verbal guidance. In some tasks, such as riding a bicycle or time sharing between, say, cooking and a conversation, it will be impossible to generate verbal advice which prescribes adequately how to carry out the task.

Cueing

Formally, cueing can be subsumed under the two previous categories of demonstration and verbal guidance. However, it has been separated, since it is used for the training of perceptual detection tasks in which the person has to detect the occurrence of a signal against a "noisy" background. In addition, cueing is different from other training methods discussed so far since it informs the trainee *when* a signal is about to occur rather than the *nature* of the trainee's future action.

Radar or sonar operators have to be trained to detect signals which may be infrequent and difficult to detect. Similarly, industrial components have to be inspected or monitored on a production line in order to discover faulty items. Detecting flaws is necessary in the production of items such as photographic negatives, welding joints, chocolates and glassware. Cueing as a training method involves telling the trainee when a signal (e.g. an auditory signal or a defective item) is about to occur. The trainee is not required to make a response. The advantage of cueing is that it draws the trainee's attention to the signal, which can then be more fully "analysed" in terms of its characteristics. Such a training method has been evaluated against the provision of knowledge of results, where the trainee has to decide which was a signal and then was informed of the correctness of this decision. Aiken and Lau (1967) concluded that the training of auditory detection tasks by cueing was superior to practice coupled with knowledge of results. However, this superiority was reduced if the knowledge of results also informed the trainee of signals missed (i.e. false negatives). Annett and colleagues carried out a series of training studies of auditory detection and suggested that cueing enabled the trainee to build up a template concerning the characteristics of the signal more efficiently than trial and error practice with knowledge of results. This conclusion was reached in a review of five auditory detection training studies by Annett and Paterson (1967).

> Cueing seems to be an effective technique for providing the trainee with instances of the signal about which he can have very little doubt, thus enabling him to build up an image or template against which further instances can be assessed. It enables him, if you like, to build a "concept" of the signal. This could be achieved, although less efficiently, by knowledge of results. Auditory stimuli of the kind we have been using are ephemeral. By the time the subject learns that was or was not a signal he has already forgotten what he heard (Annett and Paterson, 1967, p. 426).

Performance of detection tasks is typically viewed in terms of signal detection theory. Annett and Paterson (1967) mentioned that knowledge of results tends not only to increase correct detections, but also incorrect ones (i.e. false alarms), whereas cueing improves sensitivity without an accompanying increase in false alarms.

Training visual as opposed to auditory detection by cueing has been less effective. Wiener and Attwood (1968) found knowledge of results superior to cueing, whilst Colquhoun (1966) found no difference between these training methods. Stammers and Patrick (1975) suggested that the difference in the effectiveness of cueing between auditory and visual detection tasks may lie in the fact that the auditory stimuli used in the studies have been relatively more difficult to detect than their visual counterparts.

9.5 PART- AND WHOLE-TASK TRAINING

Should a task be tackled as a whole during training or should it be broken up into parts which are trained separately? This simple question has been the subject of much discussion, from the first studies in 1900 and 1901 which were concerned with the learning of poetry, to those reported recently in the 1989 edition of *Acta Psychologica* which investigated the acquisition of a contemporary space aliens video game (Donchin, 1989; Mané and Donchin, 1989).

Sometimes it will be obvious that neither part nor whole training is appropriate. Some tasks are so simple and straightforward that any attempt to divide them into parts would be ridiculous. At the other extreme, some tasks are so complex, or require such a breadth of knowledge, that there is no alternative but to break them into parts which are mastered separately. Thus a trainee pilot does not initially practise the complete task of flying an aircraft even if it is in a simulated situation! Instead, part-task training is given on parts of flying such as procedures, stick control, navigation etc. Except for extreme examples, it is difficult to predict whether whole or part-task training will be more effective. An early review of the literature was carried out by McGeoch (1931) whose conclusion at that time is just as valid today:

> The conclusion regarding the whole–part problem that logically follows is that there is no inherently superior method: the absolute and relative efficiencies of any given method are the complex resultant of the pattern of experimental conditions in which many factors are differentially and reciprocally effective (McGeoch, 1931, p. 738).

The most quoted review of the part–whole literature was carried out by Naylor (1962) from which some training principles emerged which will be discussed later. More recent reviews have been carried out by Stammers (1982) for procedural tasks and by Wightman and Lintern (1985) for tracking and manual control tasks. Summaries of some of the literature can be found in Adams (1987), Holding (1965) and Stammers and Patrick (1975).

Traditionally, the answer to the part versus whole debate has been sought in the nature of the task. The trainee's knowledge and cognitive strategies which are brought to bear during training have been ignored. Hence the literature has been concerned almost exclusively with identifying dimensions of tasks which might be used to predict the efficacy of part- or whole- task training. The training principles which have resulted are not strongly supported, and one reason for this is the failure to consider the cognitive activities of the trainee. How does the trainee normally conceptualise and divide a complex task into parts? For some tasks stereotypes may exist which coincide with task divisions concerning structure, function, activity, etc. Whenever possible, divisions introduced by part-task training should coincide with the natural or existing ones made by trainees. Unfortunately, it is difficult to predict the trainee's conceptualisation of the task and therefore how any division into parts might take account of this. Also, a trainee's conceptualisation or mental model changes and evolves as skill develops during training. Qualitative changes occur during skill acquisition (Sections 2.4 and 2.5). One notion is that skill develops into a hierarchical form, such that subskills are gradually added to a trainee's repertoire and these subskills are controlled by a hierarchy of plans (Miller, Galanter and Pribram, 1960). Ideally part-task training should be designed to map onto these cognitive distinctions and accommodate such changes as they occur during training. Hence what constitutes a part would change during training to reflect the development of skill. Unfortunately, this cognitive approach to part-task training has not been taken up in the literature. It is, of course, difficult to identify the nature of such parts and how they will change. A promising study was carried out by Frederiksen and White (1989) which decomposed the skill required by a space video task into a series of goals and their associated strategies. These were taught effectively by a form of part-task training. This study is discussed later.

Part-task training is closely related to other training topics, namely, analysis, transfer and simulation. Identification of parts of a task should follow from an analysis of the whole task. However, the analysis methods discussed in Chapters 5–8 do not provide any indication or criterion as to which parts might profitably be trained separately. One exception is Gagné's hierarchical analysis of an intellectual task into various subskills, each of which is trained separately and forms the prerequisite for mastery of the next subskill (pp. 282–292). The question of part versus whole training also raises the issue of transfer, since the aim of any part training is to maximise positive transfer to performance of the *whole* task. This is possible, even though the trainee might never experience the whole task during training. Most part-task training regimes advocate some form of aggregation of the parts before transfer to the whole task after training. Finally the topic of simulation, discussed in Chapter 12, is closely related to the development of part-task training. If it is not desirable or feasible to train the task in the real situation, then some form of simulation is needed for training which often involves part-task methods. The advantages of part-task training, which we will discuss later, overlap with the advantages of using simulation (pp. 491–494).

Types of part-task training

What types of part-task training exist? Three principles have been used to identify types of part-task training:

The relationship between the part–whole.
The skills required by the part.
How the parts are practised and reassembled into a whole.

1. The relationship of the part to the whole task. A part-task may be a result of either *partitioning* or *simplifying* the whole task. Partitioning does not transform the part in any way which is the same as that which occurs in performing the whole task. One of the most obvious examples of partitioning is in team training, in which it is often desirable to train individuals separately on their own tasks before training them to put these together and to function as a team. Wightman and Lintern (1985) have divided partitioning further into *segmentation* and *fractionation*. Fractionation, in their terms, refers to part-tasks which are time-shared or performed simultaneously in the whole task, such as the control of pitch and roll whilst flying. Simplification occurs when some aspects of the whole task are transformed in order to make it easier for the trainee to master. Hence the speed of a moving target might be reduced, the symptoms to be diagnosed in a patient may be restricted to those associated with common ailments and an astronaut might practice in varying approximations to zero gravity. Such manipulations have to be designed carefully so that part-task training involving simplification results in positive transfer to performance of the full task. (Some adaptive training, which is discussed in Section 9.6, uses a simplified task that is progressively changed during training to match the trainee's increasing competence.) Of course, there is no reason why partitioning and simplification cannot be combined. For example, the whole task might be partitioned into parts, each of which is then simplified to produce simplified part-task training programmes, as opposed to simplified whole training.

2. The skill required by different parts. One obvious reason for using some part-task training is that different parts of a task may require different skills which in turn require different training methods. For example, parts involving perceptual detection, concept-learning, problem-solving, motor coordination and rule-following might be better trained separately. As a consequence, in military training establishments part-task training devices are frequently labelled concept trainers, principle trainers and procedural trainers. Gagné's (1985) five types of learning, together with the subskills he differentiated in the intellectual domain could identify parts of a task using different skills which therefore require different training conditions (pp. 282–292).

Mané, Adams and Donchin (1989) devised a part-task training regime which involved drills on three component skills of the overall task. The task was a computer-controlled video game in which the objective was to destroy a space fortress by firing missiles from a spaceship. The game required the development of both perceptual-motor and cognitive skills and is fully described by Mané and Donchin (1989). Part-task training involved: (a) two minutes practice of a double-button press in a time period similar to that in the game; (b) two minutes practice recognising and responding to either "friend" or "foe" mines; and (c) 10 minutes controlling the spaceship. The condition which received this 14 minutes part-task training prior to practice of the whole task was superior in scores during training to a condition which did not. In addition, the part-task training condition required about 21 minutes less practice to achieve the performance criterion where the fortress was destroyed at least as many times as the spaceship. Therefore the amount of time saved was more than the time required for the part-task training which represents a transfer ratio of greater than one from part- to whole-task practice.

Two other points of interest emerged from this study. First, the part-task training resulted not only in superior performance of components of the task which were practised during the part training, as might be expected, but also in improvements of other components. The reasons for such an effect deserves investigation, particularly if it could be replicated by other studies. Second, part-task training was superior to two adaptive training conditions in which the speed of the hostile elements in the game was reduced. This is illustrated in Figure 9.5 in which the whole, part and the two adaptive training conditions are compared at different stages of training in terms of game scores.

3. How the parts are practiced and reassembled into a whole. Traditionally, part-task methods are differentiated by the manner in which the parts

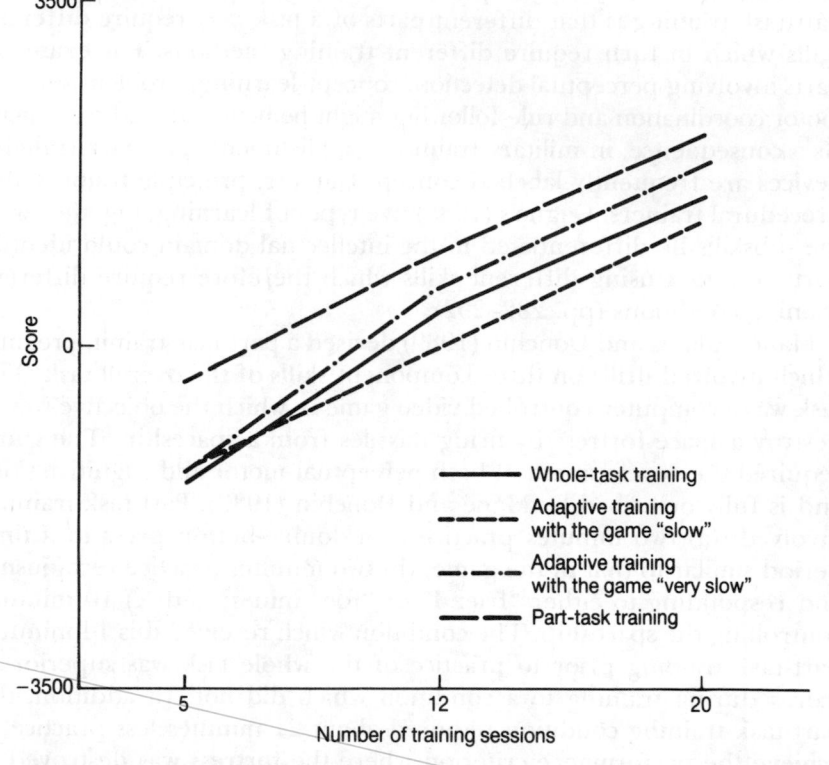

Figure 9.5 Four training conditions after 5, 12 and 20 training sessions on a computer-controlled space video game (Mané, Adams and Donchin, 1989).

are practised and put back together. Using this principle, there are four part-training methods although many variants of each exists.

(a) *Pure or isolated part.* Parts of the task are learned separately, either to some criterion or for a fixed number of trials. They are then combined in performance of the whole task.

(b) *Progressive part.* The first and second parts of the task are trained in isolation before being combined and practised together. A third part is then practised in isolation, and then combined and practised with parts one and two. Parts are therefore practised separately and added together until the whole task has been progressively assembled. Landa (1983) referred to this as the snowball method.

(c) *Repetitive part.* This is the same as the progressive part method, except that no pure-part training occurs before parts are practised together. Therefore part one is practised, then parts one and two, and then parts one, two and three and so on.

(d) *Retrospective part.* This is sometimes known as the reversed repetitive part method. Rather than beginning with the first part in a sequence, it involves practice of the last part, to which is then added the penultimate part and so on, with the remaining parts added in this reverse order. This method is similar to the notion of backward chaining advocated by Gilbert (1962).

Training principles and evidence

Evidence concerning the effectiveness of part versus whole training methods is generally inconsistent (e.g. Naylor, 1962). However, a wide range of tasks has been used and the suggestion was made by Naylor in his 1962 review that in order to make sense of the literature, characteristics of the tasks have to be taken into account. These task characteristics will affect the psychological demands upon the trainee, which will in turn influence whether whole or some form of part training is beneficial.

Two task characteristics or dimensions have been identified as important (Naylor and Briggs, 1963). The first is concerned with task "organisation" which:

> refers to the demands imposed on S [the trainee] due to the nature of the interrelationship existing among the several task dimensions (p. 217; square parentheses added).

Parts of a task may be interrelated by flow of information during performance. These inter-relationships may be straightforward, as when the output from one part provides the input to the next part and the two parts are always executed in the same sequence. On the other hand, some parts may have complex inter-relations of information flow and may be time-shared. The second dimension is task "complexity" which is defined as:

> the demands placed on S's [the trainee's] information-processing and/or memory storage capacities by each of the task dimensions independently (p. 217; square parentheses added).

These two task dimensions are combined to determine the difficulty of learning and the effectiveness of whole versus part training for any given task. Naylor and Briggs (1963) proposed two principles to guide the selection of training method:

Principle 1. For tasks of relatively high organisation as task complexity is increased, whole-task training should become relatively more efficient than the part-task methods.

Principle 2. For tasks of relatively low organisation (all task dimensions being independent), an increase in task complexity should result in a part-task method becoming superior to the whole-task method (Naylor and Briggs, 1963, p. 218).

These principles are appealing intuitively, since it might be expected that as the components of a task become more interdependent, they will be more difficult to train separately. Even if they are trained by part-methods, there may be some difficulty in integrating these parts into performance of the whole task, particularly where parts are time-shared. On the other hand, if the parts are not interdependent then part-methods are feasible and will become more effective as the parts become more complex. Surprisingly, there is only one direct test of these principles, in a study by Naylor and Briggs (1963). University students had to predict the number and location of aircraft carriers or submarines which appeared on a screen. Task complexity was varied in terms of the predictability of each type of information, whilst task organisation referred to the extent to which one type of information could be predicted by another. The results supported the two principles outlined above. There is further indirect support for Naylor and Briggs' Principle 1. Briggs and Waters (1958) demonstrated the increasing superiority of whole-task training as the interaction between the components of a tracking task increased. Adams and Hufford (1962) found some difficulties when the procedural and control parts of flight training had to be integrated after separate training, although these problems were quickly overcome. Knapp (1963) concluded a review of gymnastic and other sports skills by suggesting that whole-task training was preferable with part-task training being reserved for areas of weakness. Wightman and Lintern (1985) reviewed the evidence for tracking and manual control tasks which generally have high organisation and found little evidence in support of part-task training. One exception was for retrogressive part training when the parts involved partitioning the whole task and they were not time-shared. Part training for time-shared parts and simplified part training were not superior and, in some cases, were worse than whole-task training. Nevertheless, whilst part training was often not superior to whole training, it did usually result in at least some positive transfer. These results are generally consistent with Naylor and Briggs' predictions embodied in Principle 1.

The part–whole debate has been examined in the training of procedural tasks such as assembly tasks or start-up and shut-down procedures for plant and equipment. In Naylor and Briggs' terms, such tasks generally have low organisation, since the parts are a series of discrete units in which at most the output from one unit serves as the input to another one. Most procedural tasks that have been examined in the literature have low complexity. Therefore from Naylor and Briggs' Principle 2, one would not expect any difference between part and whole methods. This is indeed confirmed by the evidence. Cox and Boren (1965) compared part, retrogressive part and whole training for a 72 step procedure associated with the preparation for firing a missile. The results did not differ between the training methods. (The authors appear to consider their task of high organisation, although there is insufficient detail provided to verify this.)

One idea put forward by Sheffield and his colleagues is that part training should capitalise upon the natural segmentation of a task. Thus when parts are reassembled they are subject to a minimum amount of interference from each other. Stammers (1982) reported two studies which compared a variety of part methods with whole training for a 38 step procedure which was a simulation of the production of a food product. Part methods were designed to practice "natural" units of the procedure which in this case were equivalent to different subtasks. Part training was not superior to whole-task training. Two further studies concerned with learning a list of instructions found no advantage to part-task training, and in one of these, small amounts of part training had a detrimental effect on subsequent performance.

Annett and Kay (1956) have drawn attention to another aspect of a procedural task which they consider affects the selection of part or whole training methods. They were concerned with tasks which can be broken down into a series of signals which vary in predictability and require certain responses to be made. They suggested that a trainee's behaviour will, in some cases, influence the signals provided by a display such that it is difficult for the trainee to distinguish the contribution of his or her own actions from the changing behaviour of the system. Learning will therefore be difficult. In this situation, part-task training will be superior, since it permits the trainee to master parts of the task, which will in turn make subsequent signals in the series easier to learn because they will not be affected by the trainee's previous errors. When the person's actions do not influence the display (in Annett and Kay's terms, the task elements are then independent), such problems will not arise and whole training will be more appropriate. The principle proposed by Annett and Kay is:

> ... if the elements of a task are highly independent the task is best learned as a whole, but where elements are highly interdependent, they should be split up and the task learned in parts (Annett and Kay, 1956, p. 114).

This principle might appear to contradict the two principles proposed by Naylor and Briggs since it suggests that highly interdependent tasks should be trained by part methods whilst tasks with high organisation, according to Naylor and Briggs, require whole training. However, these task parameters are different. "High interdependence" refers to the interaction between the trainee's action and some displayed signal, whereas "high organisation" means that information from one part of a task facilitates performance of another part. Annett and Kay's principle is only applicable to a certain type of serial task and has not been tested empirically.

Part-training methods have been popular in industry, although the evidence reviewed so far does not strongly support their use. One exception is a study by Seymour (1966) of training the operation of a capstan lathe. This task was broken down into the following procedure:

1. Pick up component, insert in collet and lock collet.
2. Switch onto slow speed.
3. Wind in cross-slide tool.
4. Wind out cross-slide tool.
5. Switch on to full speed.
6. Operate six turret tool positions.
7. Switch off.
8. Unlock collet, remove component and place aside.

In one study, whole training was compared against isolated part and progressive part training. The isolated part condition had separate training on operating the turret and cross-slide until these were performed within a target time. Both of these operations were difficult to master (Seymour termed these parts "perceptually stringent"). The progressive part condition gradually assembled the parts in the standard fashion for this method, described earlier in this section. The results were in favour of the part-training methods, both of which resulted in fewer errors and faster machine cycle times than the whole method. The results of the two part methods were not significantly different from each other. Results from this study led to an increased use of part-training methods, particularly for manual repetitive industrial tasks. However, sometimes part methods were used inappropriately, as, for example, in the clothing industry (Toye, 1969; Victor, 1971). Part methods have to be carefully designed to avoid the problem of arbitrarily separating components of a skill and thus distorting them.

Earlier in this section a plea was made that parts should be constructed in a way which is psychologically meaningful, rather than on the basis of task characteristics per se. A recent study by Frederiksen and White

(1989) has taken a significant step in this direction. The authors argued that part training can be effective in a task with high organisation in Naylor's terms if it is possible to decompose the task in terms of the trainee's goals and build up the strategies needed to achieve these goals in a manner consistent with the development of skill for that task. They used the computer-controlled space fortress game described by Mané and Donchin (1989). From an examination of experts' performance, they identified three major goals:

1. To hit the fortress without being hit by the fortress.
2. To detect and destroy mines with as little disruption as possible to firing at the fortress.
3. To allocate resources so as to maximise the points scored in the game.

The strategies for achieving these goals were identified and a series of 28 "games" were devised which involved development of these strategies and associated skills and knowledge. These "games" were used in two training studies reported by Frederiksen and White, as indicated in Table 9.2. They were concerned with motor skill, ship control knowledge, strategies for manoeuvring the spaceship, integration (i.e. practising the parts together) and verbal information about some aspects of the task. The authors felt that the order in which the games were trained was largely obvious from the nature of the task. In Study 1, they commented:

> Determining a reasonable ordering for developing the subskills is relatively straightforward. Games involving the full strategy clearly have to be placed last in the instruction sequence, since learning the 'optimal' strategy requires knowledge of ship control, knowledge of game characteristics and basic motor skills. Similarly, games for developing ship control should follow the motor skills games since, in learning the ship control heuristics, one needs to be proficient in aiming and accelerating. This defines the ordering: motor skills, ship control heuristics and strategy development. There are fewer constraints on the location of information games within the instructional sequence (Frederiksen and White, 1989, pp. 141–142).

The two studies compared a part-training condition which used these games against a whole condition which practised the whole task. As can be seen from Figure 9.6, part training with the games resulted in superior performance in both studies. Those interested in these studies are advised to consult the published article in order to appreciate fully the design of them and the richness of their results. They serve to remind us that the identification and design of part-task training has to be undertaken with care, ingenuity and intelligence, rather than adherence to a set of training principles in a somewhat blinkered

Table 9.2 Twenty-eight training games to support skill and knowledge development for a space fortress video game (Frederiksen and White, 1989)

Study 1	Study 2
Objective: to hit the fortress without being hit by the fortress	*Objective*: (a) to detect and destroy mines with as little disruption as possible to firing at the fortress; (b) to allocate resources so as to maximise the point score
Developing motor skills – firing and aiming	*Developing skill in selecting resources*
1. Firing on the fortress	17. Selecting resources while playing the game
2. Aiming the spaceship while it is stationary	*Developing skill in identifying mines*
Developing ship control – stopping the spaceship	18. Pressing the I button with the correct interval
3. Slowing down and stopping the spaceship	19. Identifying friend and foe mines
Developing motor skills – aiming while moving	*Integrating mine identification and resource skills*
4. Aiming a moving spaceship from different distances	20. Identifying mines while selecting resources
5. Aiming and firing from different distances	21. Full game with stationary mine and no resources
6. Aiming and firing from different trajectories	22. Full game with stationary mine and resources
Developing ship control – changing trajectory	*Developing skill in tracking and shooting moving mines*
7. Making a 45° change in trajectory	23. Destroying moving mines
8. Slowing down while turning	*Integrating the full set of skills*
9. Turning through different angles by varying the thrust	24. Destroying moving mines while firing at the fort
10. Controlling the speed and trajectory of the spaceship	25. Selecting resources while shooting moving mines
11. Changing trajectories at corners of a hexagon	26. The full game without resources
Developing strategies	27. Almost the full game
12. Navigating the hexagon while aiming at the fort	
13. Navigating the hexagon while firing	
14. Navigating about the fortress while it is tracking	
15. Illustrating the fortress' tracking and firing zones	
16. The full game without mines and resources	

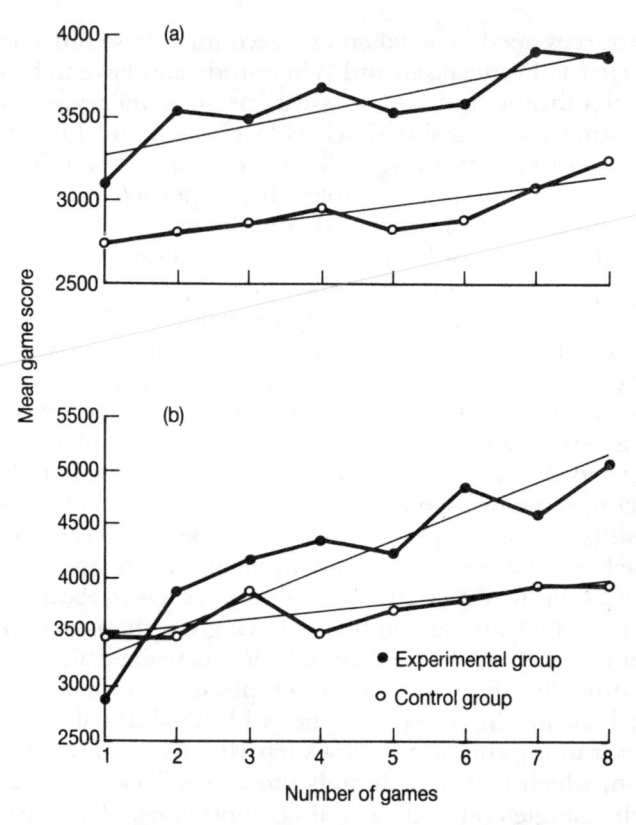

Figure 9.6 (a) Study 1: Average scores for the whole training group in the first eight games after training compared with the corresponding games in training for a part training group; (b) Study 2: Average scores for the whole versus part training groups over eight games at the end of training (Frederiksen and White, 1989).

fashion. However, even though Frederiksen and White's work refreshingly breaks the mould for part training, some caution is necessary in the interpretation of their results. First, as in other studies, it is difficult to determine how much training time should be given to the part-training condition in comparison to the whole-training condition. Designers of studies in this area face a dilemma. On the one hand, the amount of time spent training can be made equivalent between the different conditions in which case the amount learned will probably vary. On the other hand, a criterion of performance can be stipulated, as in the Frederiksen and White studies, in which case training time is likely to differ between the conditions. Also the costs of devising part-task training in terms of both time and resources need to be taken into account. These must have been considerable in the Frederiksen and White study and have to be weighed against the significant, but not massive, performance gains for part training. In other training situations, as Wightman and Lintern (1985) pointed out, part-task training will reduce costs when inexpensive devices can be used instead of complex and expensive pieces of equipment such as an aircraft or an aircraft simulator.

An interesting form of training which attempts to combine the advantages of part and whole methods is proposed by Gopher, Weil and Siegel (1989). Rather than breaking the whole task into parts for training, the whole task is used but different parts are *emphasised* during training. The potential benefit is that the problem of reintegrating parts into a whole can be avoided. Their study used the same space fortress video game as Fredericksen and White (1989). One "emphasis" manipulation concerned ship control and another involved mine handling. The emphasis manipulations used displays which provided additional knowledge of results for that aspect of the task to be emphasised (e.g. ship control). Each of these emphasis manipulations was assigned to one training condition whilst a third condition received both of them. Performance of the training conditions having emphasis manipulations were superior to a control condition which was trained with the whole task. Unfortunately, the value of the emphasis manipulations cannot be separated from the effect of the additional feedback supplied during these training conditions. Not surprisingly, the double-emphasis manipulation, which had considerably more feedback, was more effective than the single-emphasis training conditions. This study does demonstrate that it is feasible and beneficial to highlight important aspects to the trainee in whole-task training. In a task of such complexity as the space fortress game, the attention of trainees can be drawn to important parts and their efforts can be channelled into mastering them. This is likely to be particularly beneficial to low-ability trainees, which is indeed what the authors of this study found for the double-emphasis manipulation. Further research is necessary to determine whether emphasis manipulations within whole task training are superior to equivalent conditions using part-task training.

Finally, there is further evidence that part-task training is of benefit to low-ability trainees, presumably because they are less able to cope with the demands of the whole task. Clarke (1966) suggested that part training was of benefit to adult imbeciles. Nettelbeck and Kirby (1976) reported a study in which 30 females, with an IQ ranging from 48 to 83 on the Wechsler Adult Scale, were trained to thread an industrial sewing machine. This procedural task had 12 steps, as illustrated in Figure 9.7, and is of low organisation and low complexity in Naylor's terms

Step 1
Raise lever to release tension

Step 2
Thread over stand from rear

Step 3
Thread through peg

Step 4
Thread through upper and lower holes
of side peg

Step 5
Pass thread inside upper guard, around
tension wheel, over wire spring

Step 6
Thread under lower guard

Step 7
Thread back behind upper guard

Step 8
Thread through eye of mobile bar,
right to left

Step 9
Thread through upper guide

Step 10
Thread through lower guide

Step 11
Thread needle, left to right

Step 12
Lower lever

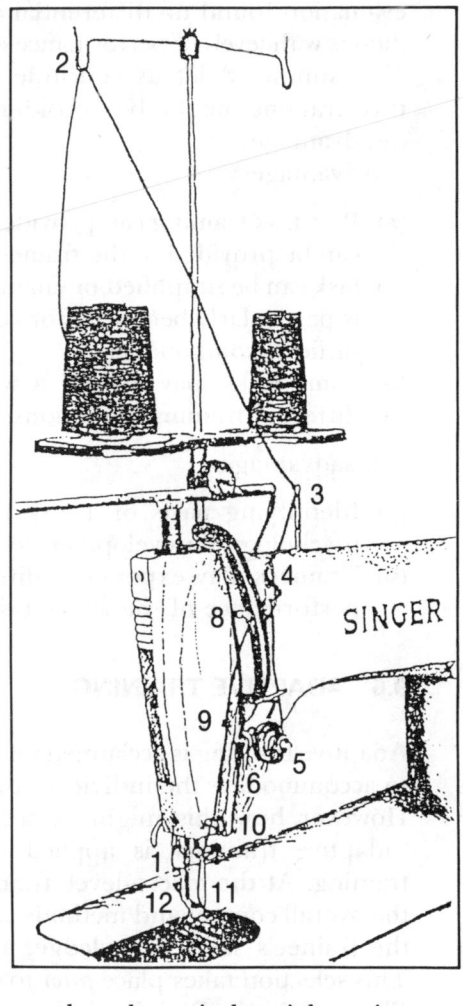

Figure 9.7 Twelve step procedure to thread an industrial sewing machine (Nettelbeck and Kirby, 1976). Steps 1–3, steps 4–5, steps 6–8, and steps 9–12 make up four parts in the part training conditions.

for normal ability trainees. Comparisons were made between part-, progressive part- and whole-training methods. Both forms of part training were superior to whole training in terms of both errors and time taken in achieving the criterion performance of four successive errorless trials. There were no significant differences between the part methods. One commendable feature of this study was that performance levels of the trainees were assessed one month after training. This longer-term evaluation found no differential decrements between the training conditions with levels of performance equivalent between the three conditions.

In summary, let us conclude with some of the reasons why part-task training might be considered and its possible advantages and disadvantages.

Advantages:

(a) Part-task training can provide a better training environment. Advice can be provided to the trainee more easily and characteristics of the task can be simplified or changed in order to promote learning. This is particularly beneficial for complex tasks or tasks which have some difficult components.
(b) Some tasks may involve a wide range of subskills which require different training conditions.

Disadvantages:

(a) Identifying parts of a task in a way which is consistent with the psychological development of skill for that task is problematic.
(b) Trainees may experience difficulties in reassembling the parts into performance of the whole task.

9.6 ADAPTIVE TRAINING

Adaptive training is acclaimed unanimously as desirable since it attempts to accommodate the individual differences of trainees during training. However how this might be achieved varies enormously. The term "adaptive training" is applied to both macro- and micro-levels of training. At the macro-level, training can be adaptive in the sense that the overall content and methods of training are selected to accommodate the trainee's skills, knowledge, aptitudes, abilities, cognitive style etc. This selection takes place *prior* to training and is the subject of much of Chapters 5–10. Training can also be adaptive at the micro-level where the task tackled *during* training is manipulated in some manner to take account of the strengths and weaknesses of the trainee. This latter, more restricted, meaning of the term "adaptive" is the main focus of the present section. Of course, macro- and micro-levels of adaptive training are not mutually exclusive. Thus training content and methods might be designed to accommodate the characteristics of a population of trainees (e.g. aged 40 and over) and within this training the difficulty of the task might be progressively changed to match the developing competence of each trainee.

Adaptive training, at the micro-level, is closely related to the topics of trainees' characteristics (Chapter 10) and automated training (Chapter 11). Fundamental to instruction is the notion that the presentation of training material should be responsive to the trainee's past and current performance, e.g. remedial training being provided to overcome a trainee's mistakes. Further, many have argued that trainees should be permitted to investigate the training material in whatever manner they wish. In this sense, training is adaptive because its exploration is governed by the preferences of trainees, and is known as learner control. This adaptive aspect of training has been facilitated by the involvement of a computer, and is discussed briefly later in this section and in Chapter 11.

Adaptive training contrasts with fixed or nonadaptive training in which the trainee practises the same task throughout the training period. Common sense dictates that this will be inefficient, since some parts of the task will be mastered more quickly than others. As learning progresses, it is advantageous if more time is devoted to mastering the remaining parts of the task which the trainee finds difficult. Thus during adaptive training, the task confronting the trainee changes dependent upon the nature and rate of learning (see Figure 9.8). In order to achieve this, Kelley (1969) specified that the following three components are required:

1. Some adjustable feature or dimension of the task or training materials which constitutes the adaptive variable.
2. Measurement of the trainee's performance.

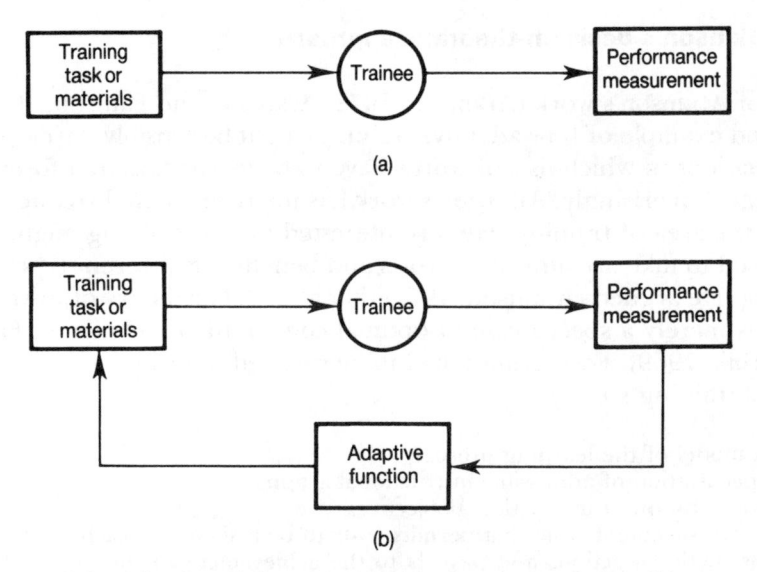

Figure 9.8   Fixed training (a) versus adaptive training (b).

3. Some adaptive function which relates changes in the adaptive variable as a function of the trainee's performance.

In principle, such adaptive training could be carried out by a human or machine although the difficulty of computing the adaptive function often makes it an impractical human task.

A variety of types of adaptive training has been investigated. What is feasible is dictated by the nature of the task and the adaptive variables available. In the following discussion, adaptive training is considered for both "discrete" and "continuous" tasks. Discrete tasks are usually self-paced. They involve a series of distinct responses such as when foreign words have to be translated into their corresponding meanings, or a series of perceptual codes require specified keyboard responses. In contrast, continuous tasks, such as vehicle control, are not self-paced and have a continuously changing perceptual pattern requiring an adjustive response. Adaptive training will be discussed for discrete tasks of both a verbal and motor nature. Training has been adaptive in the sense that the time available to master the various items or responses has been varied according to the trainee's learning. Hence adaptive training follows the trainee's progress, moving from easy to more difficult items so that more time is available to practise and learn the more difficult ones. This approach is exemplified in the work of Atkinson (e.g. 1972), Bartram (1988) and Lewis and Pask (1965).

R.C. Atkinson's decision-theoretic approach

Some of Atkinson's work (Atkinson, 1972; Atkinson and Paulson, 1972) is a good example of how adaptive training might be sensibly developed for situations in which lists of words have to be learned, as in a foreign language. Surprisingly, Atkinson's work has not been quoted frequently within the area of training. He was interested in how training might be optimised to take account of the costs and benefits of different types of training. He argued (Atkinson, 1972) that a model or theory of instruction was merely a special case of optimal control theory (Kalman, Falb and Arbib, 1969). Four criteria had to be satisfied in order to devise an optimal training strategy:

1. A model of the learning process.
2. Specification of admissible instructional actions.
3. Specification of instructional objectives.
4. A measurement scale that permits costs to be assigned to each of the instructional actions and payoffs to the achievement of instructional objectives (Atkinson, 1972, p. 922).

One simple illustration of this approach is given by Atkinson (1972) in learning a foreign language vocabulary. The training objective (criterion 3 above) was to maximise the rate of learning of a set of German–English items as measured by a delayed recall test. A simple model of the learning process (criterion 1 above) was employed to develop an optimal adaptive training strategy. Put simply, this model postulated that any item was either in a relatively permanent learned state P, or in a temporary learned state T, or not yet learned U. The assumption was that only items in state P would meet the training objective and therefore a strategy was derived for selecting and presenting items to the trainee which maximised the probability that items were moved into state P. This adaptive training involved computing the trainee's state of learning after every training session and selecting those items for presentation in the next session which maximised the level of learning. This was aptly named the "response-sensitive training strategy" and involved spending more time practising items which caused some difficulty. This form of adaptive training was compared against two conditions: a baseline condition in which items were selected randomly for presentation during training; and another condition in which the trainee determined which items should be examined and tested during training. The task involved learning seven lists of 12 German words arranged in a round-robin sequence, illustrated in Figure 9.9, with each list being examined

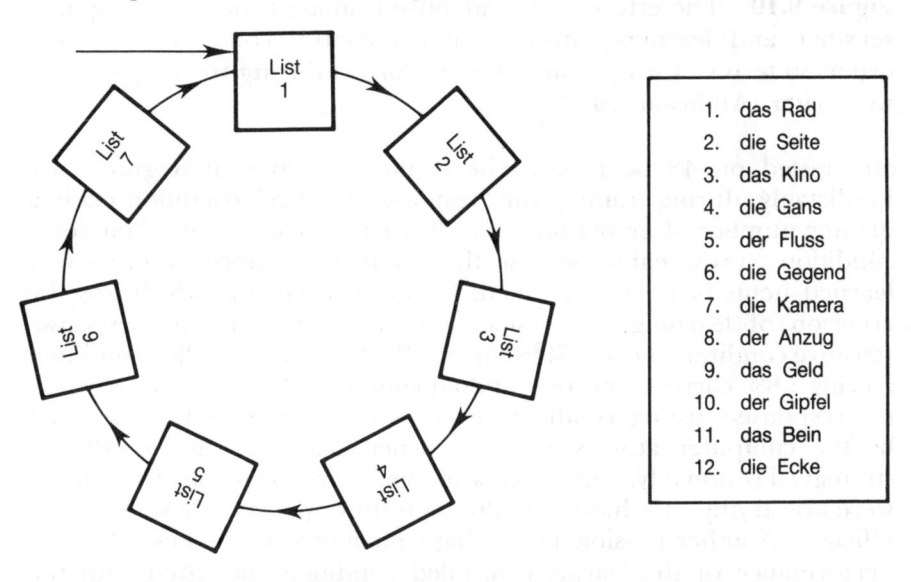

Figure 9.9 Sequence of presentation of lists and an example of 12 words on one list (Atkinson, 1972).

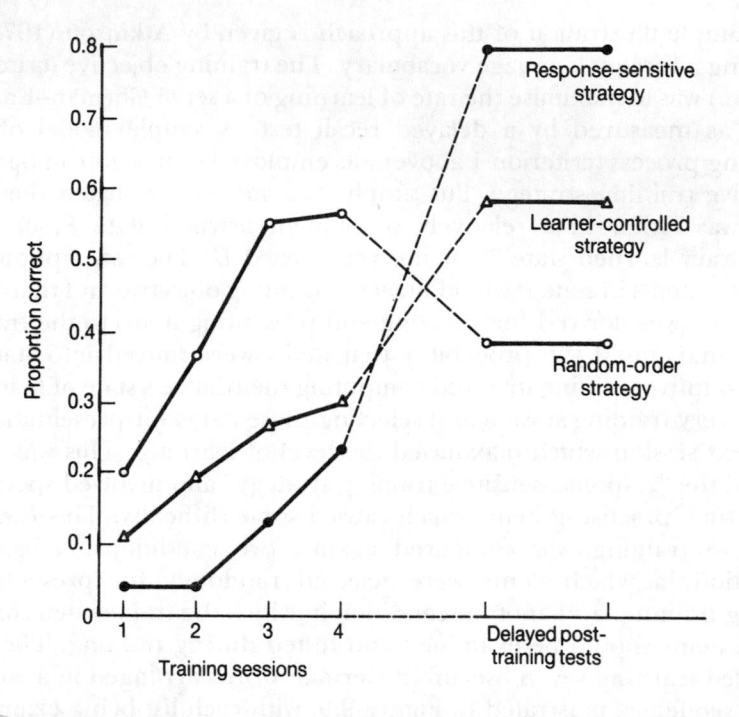

Figure 9.10 The effect of two adaptive training conditions (response sensitive and learner-controlled) and a control condition (random-order) in terms of proportion of items correct during training and one week later (Atkinson, 1972).

and tested on 48 occasions. The results are given in Figure 9.10. Predictably, during training the "response-sensitive" condition made a greater number of errors than the "learner controlled" and "random" conditions, presumably because there was less chance of previously learned items being re-presented. In the delayed test, which was the criterion of learning, the results were reversed with the response-sensitive condition scoring 79% correct, the learner-controlled condition scoring 58% correct, and the random condition 38% correct. Thus, in the response-sensitive condition, trainees having their efforts directed by the computer at mastering unlearned material was an efficient strategy. Presumably, the trainees in the learner-controlled condition were also trying to achieve this although they appear to have been less efficient. Another possible factor that contributed to the lower level of performance of the learner-controlled condition compared with the response-sensitive condition was the extra resources (memory, attention etc.) needed to select the items to study in addition to learning the task itself. Irrespective of this possibility, the important finding in this study was that *both* forms of adaptive training were superior to training which did not take account of the trainee's progress in learning the material.

Atkinson and Paulson (1972) compared two adaptive training schemes to teach 300 Swahili vocabulary items to college students. One scheme was based on the notion that learning has taken place after one correct response (i.e. an or-none basis), whilst the other was more complicated and involved updating estimates of both the difficulty of each item and the ability of each trainee after each training session. In the latter condition the authors pointed out that this necessitated entering the response data each evening in order to update the parameter estimates, which were then used to select item lists for each trainee to study the next day. Twenty training sessions of about an hour each were used. In each session, the trainee studied 50 Swahili–English pairs of words derived from the all-or-none strategy which were mixed randomly with another 50 pairs derived by the more complex adaptive strategy. Learning was assessed by a test a couple of days after training and by a delayed test after two weeks. Results indicated a considerable advantage for items trained using the more complex adaptive strategy in both the initial and delayed tests (Figure 9.11). Thus the more sensitive adaptive training was more successful at maximising learning. The authors also mentioned that the complex adaptive training was increasingly successful for groups of trainees starting later, since by then the parameters were more accurately estimated, as the database had expanded.

Keyboard skills

Many of the original ideas of adaptive training were proposed by Pask and colleagues (for a summary see Lewis and Pask, 1965). One area of interest was the learning of keyboard skills in which different combinations of signals on an eight-light display panel required a series of keys to be pressed. In this task, there was no simple spatial correspondence between the lights and the keys required. Lewis and Pask (1965) reported that only nine out of 10 trainees were able adequately to master eight combinations of four lights to achieve 75% accuracy over 40 problems. In subsequent studies, they investigated the use of part-task training methods which simplified the task into a series of subskills, which were taught using various forms of adaptive training. Training was adaptive by varying the mixture and difficulty of the subskills, either in some preset fashion, or on the basis of the trainee's level of performance. Adaptive training was generally superior to nonadaptive

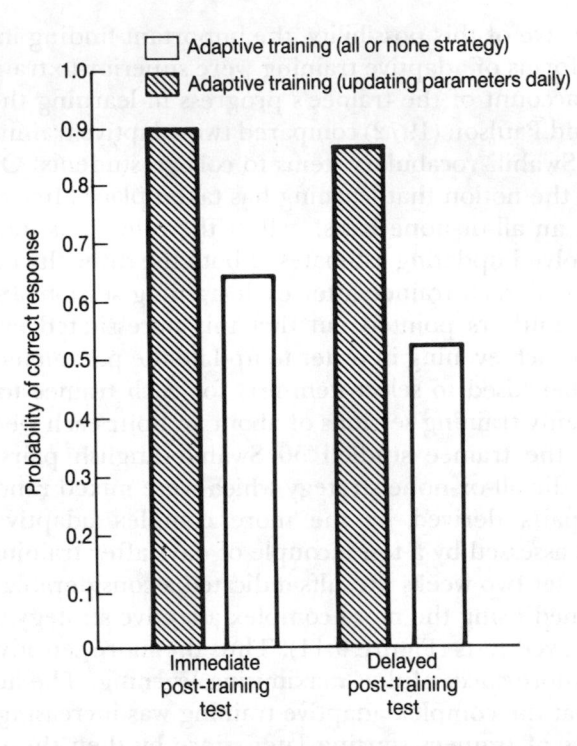

Figure 9.11 Probability of correct recall of Swahili words using two adaptive training strategies (Atkinson and Paulson, 1972).

training in terms of the number of training sessions required to meet some criterion level of performance. In addition, learner-controlled training was found to be inferior to machine-controlled adaptive training because trainees always spent too much time on the simple subtasks. Lewis and Pask (1965) concluded:

> They [the studies] do, however, all tell the same story, namely that adaptive controlled instruction gives significantly better results than fixed training sequences obtained from 'averaging out' the requirements of a representative sample of students (Lewis and Pask, 1965, p. 258; square parentheses added).

Bartram (1988) reported an industrial training study which capitalised upon the benefits of adaptive training. The study was concerned with training foreign destination coding operators in the Post Office. Their task involved classifying foreign mail into geographical categories (e.g. Austria zones 4 and 5) by entering a code on a keyboard. The speed at which the mail was presented was dictated by the operator's speed of categorisation. The objective of training was defined in exemplary fashion as:

> Trainees should be able to sort mail (simulated on the VDU) with an error rate of less than 1% and an average time per item of 1.8 seconds or less. This level of performance would need to be reached with around 50 or 60 hours of training distributed across three or four weeks (Bartram, 1988, p. 18).

The task was broken down into three parts which were trained using a backward-chaining strategy. These parts were:

A. Encoding the address and relating this to one of the geographical area names. This was a many-to-one mapping which required geographical knowledge and knowledge of all the area names.
B. Mapping the area name onto the corresponding chord pattern on a keyboard. This was a one-to-one mapping, although this part was significant since the trainee had to learn over 240 different area name chord patterns.
C. Executing the chord pattern as quickly as possible.

Training covered the following three phases in which the three parts (A, B and C above) were progressively assembled into the whole task in the following fashion.

Training phase   *Parts of task*

1. Keyboard familiarisation   C
2. Area name training   B–C
3. Address coding   A–B–C

A significant aspect of this study is that various types of adaptive training were employed in the different phases of training. In the first phase of training, concerned with keyboard familiarisation, "cumulative random" adaptive training was used initially until the full set of chords had been encountered. This was followed by "fixed" adaptive training which was intended to consolidate learning and improve accuracy. "Cumulative random" adaptive training, according to Bartram, involved selecting 16 of the easiest chords to start with and randomly sampling with replacement from this set of 16 until the trainee reached some predefined criterion of speed and accuracy. Then the set size was increased by another four items until performance reached the criterion and this continued in the same fashion until all the chords had been met. (If a criterion was not met, then the set was reduced by four items.) This was followed by "fixed" adaptive training that involved practising with a constant set of 10 chords with up to five chords being replaced after 10 training sessions. Thus training was adaptive in the manner in which items were selected for practice, dependent upon the trainee's pattern of learning.

The second phase of training was concerned with relating area names to chords. Each lesson covered up to 20 area names and within each lesson a set of six items was presented for practice using adaptive selection. Testing was also adaptive in this phase of training with test items being selected which had, for example, high error rates and poor reaction times. If the trainee failed to meet a criterion, then remedial training lessons were constructed to cover the items causing difficulty. The third and final phase of training used the whole task and involved adaptive principles which were similar to those used in the second phase of the study.

In Bartram's study, various types of adaptive training were used. This enabled the trainee's speed and accuracy to determine the rate at which new items and tasks were encountered during training. Bartram commented that:

> The choice of item selection "tactics" at different points in the training was dictated by the need to alternate between initial rapid developments of speed and confidence, then periods of consolidation and development of accuracy and then subsequent tests of competence (Bartram, 1988, p. 40).

The training manipulations in this study were part of one training programme which all trainees experienced. Therefore it is not possible to identify the effectiveness of these adaptive manipulations in comparison with others or a fixed training condition. However, Bartram does provide a description of the results of three groups of trainees. Overall the training was judged to be successful by the numbers of trainees who "passed" and their level of performance. Out of 65 trainees, 11 failed Phases 1 or 2 of training (three of these were for reasons not related to adequacy of performance) and a further five failed to pass one criterion in Phase 3. All of those who failed to complete the training course were over 40 years old. Trainees most likely to fail were identified as older and lacking experience.

Adaptive training requires a series of rules and criteria to be set which determine how the task is to be varied with respect to a trainee's performance. These rules and criteria have to be devised carefully. They will inevitably have imperfections initially and will need to be reviewed and adjusted in the light of the results of trainees. Hence the adaptive rules and criteria themselves should be adapted to the outcomes of training. (Self-improving is one feature of some intelligent tutoring systems mentioned in Section 11.5.) In the Bartram study the adaptive criteria were closely monitored and adjusted after the first group of trainees. Even though adaptive training is itself responsive to different trainees' levels of performance, there may be a need to employ different types of adaptive training for different populations of trainees (e.g. younger versus older workers).

Perceptual-motor control tasks

There is little evidence of the effectiveness of adaptive training for "continuous" perceptual-motor tasks, such as tracking or vehicle control, which require a continuously adjustive response to some target (Lintern and Gopher, 1978; Lintern and Roscoe, 1980). A similar conclusion was reached by Williges and Williges (1978) who commented that there was a dearth of unequivocal evidence of adaptive training's utility for motor control tasks. The review by Lintern and Gopher (1978) is critical of the methodology of various studies which claim to demonstrate the advantage of adaptive training. In this review a distinction is made between training which manipulates task difficulty by adapting either response variables or perceptual variables in tracking tasks. Response variables include the relationship between target and response movements (such as the order of control, gain, response lag and damping ratio). Perceptual variables refer to the characteristics of the target to be tracked which can be manipulated to increase tracking difficulty. Lintern and Gopher concluded:

> Adaptive training research has provided very little support, in comparison to the magnitude of the research effort, for the application of perceptual and response adaptations to applied training situations. The only unequivocal and statistically reliable data to demonstrate their effectiveness was obtained with an atypical control task (Gaines, 1967) and from a manually adapted task (Williges and Williges, 1976). Several of the experiments that apparently support AT [adaptive training] principles have methodological problems that are critical enough to discount the conclusions drawn from them. In general, the research related to perceptual and response adaptations has produced little conclusive evidence for or against AT (Lintern and Gopher, 1978, p. 535; square parentheses added).

In addition, whilst task difficulty has been manipulated in adaptive training of continuous perceptual-motor tasks, this has been done with a conspicuous absence of rationale. Adams (1987) pointed out that task difficulty has been treated as an independent variable in many studies whereas, in reality, it is a dependent variable affected by a multitude of psychological factors. What is needed is some analysis on psychological grounds which relates changes in difficulty to the natural development of skill such that positive transfer occurs from one part of the task to the next and ultimately to the whole task. Indeed this issue pinpoints the difficulty of devising adaptive training for perceptual-motor control tasks. How are changes in difficulty to be devised such that progression from training with one part will transfer positively to the next? This is extremely difficult for continuous perceptual-motor tasks, since the literature (discussed in Chapter 3) indicates that slight changes in control dynamics result in negative transfer. This is undoubtedly one major reason for the lack of success of adaptive training for this type of task.

Some evidence concerning the transfer of adaptive training to performance of the whole task comes from a study by Mané, Adams and Donchin (1989). A space fortress video game was used which involved both perceptual-motor and cognitive strategy components. In two adaptive training conditions, the speed of elements which were hostile to the spaceship was reduced at the beginning of training. Speed was then varied according to trainee performance. The adaptive training conditions differed in the degree to which the speed of the hostile elements was reduced. The "very slow" adaptive training condition was much better during training, but negative transfer occurred when tested with the normal task in which hostile elements moved at their usual pace. In contrast a "slow" adaptive training condition learned more than a control condition which practised the whole task normally. The "slow" adaptive training condition had a better game score and required less training time. Therefore care has to be taken that in devising adaptive training the nature of the task is not substantially changed from the actual task to be mastered. Otherwise no benefit will accrue from adaptive training. Of course, the problem remains of developing a theoretical basis for predicting how large a discrepancy is tolerable before negative transfer occurs. This danger is particularly acute with continuous perceptual-motor tasks, although it is a potential problem for any adaptive training regime.

Learner control

An old idea in training, which is being rediscovered under the recent labels of "hypertext" and "hypermedia", is that training can be adaptive by switching control from the trainer to the trainee. In the literature this topic is known as "learner control". One of the earliest and most famous studies of learner control was carried out by Mager (1961). He asked six adults to gain knowledge about electronics by requesting information from an instructor. No specific training objectives were given to trainees, although it was explained that they could request information, examples, demonstrations, problems, reviews and anecdotal material. It is amusing, and perhaps not surprising, that the trainees were initially somewhat perplexed about this training situation, presumably because it contrasted sharply with their normal training experiences. The study did not assess the effectiveness of learner control, which in any case would have been difficult because of the freedom allowed, but rather concentrated on the sequence and nature of information selected by trainees in comparison with the normal delivery of an instructor. Various discrepancies emerged. One was that trainees focused initially on the concrete aspects of "things" such as the vacuum tube, rather than the more abstract aspects of electron theory typically covered at the beginning of conventional courses. Mager concluded that:

> The results clearly suggest that the content sequence most meaningful to the learner is different from the sequence guessed by the instructor to be most meaningful to the learner (p. 412).

The literature concerning the effectiveness of learner control is conflicting and difficult to summarise because of variations between research studies in terms of the type of learner control, the type of task and the characteristics of trainees (Seidel et al., 1978). Perhaps most important is the type of learner control which has included control over: the speed of training or the amount of time permitted for the study of an item (e.g. Tennyson, Park and Christensen, 1985); the type and amount of training support and help (e.g. Merrill, 1980); and the sequence in which training material is studied (e.g. Gay, 1986). Mager's study permitted the trainee to control all of these aspects of training. In addition, learner control can occur at the macro-level in terms of an overall curriculum and the modules within it and/or at the micro-level where more specific information can be selected, say, with respect to each objective of a training module. Learner control is a feature of the TICCIT computer-based training system which is discussed in Section 11.4, pp. 453–456.

The aim of any form of learner control is to accommodate individual differences. The work of Pask, discussed in Section 10.2, related differences in cognitive style to the manner in which trainees selected material in what he termed a "free learning situation". Irrespective of the form of learner control, the critical question which has to be asked is whether trainees indeed know what's good for them. In other words, to what extent are trainees able to monitor their developing skills and knowledge, and diagnose their weaknesses (and which aspects are they particularly good at evaluating)? If they can, are they competent at selecting training material, explanations etc. which overcome these difficulties? (Some might argue that whether or not a trainee adopts this sort of approach to skill acquisition, which is a rational one from the trainer's perspective, is irrelevant because the one big advantage of learner control is its motivational value.) Unfortunately, we simply do not know the answers to these questions. There are hints that the more able trainee is likely to benefit from learner control which emerged from the evaluation of TICCIT, which provided learner control over various aspects of the training (see Section 11.4). Seidel et al. (1978) found that high performers tended to exercise more control over the sequence of training material for a COBOL course, although it was not possible to assess the effect of this on performance. With learner control of training, one might expect that it is even more important that adequate "signposts" and help are provided for trainees, particularly lower-ability ones, in order that they can navigate their way around the training material in a meaningful fashion. In this regard, Patrick and Evans (1983) found that the provision of an advance organiser was more beneficial when the learner, rather than the program, had control over the sequence in which small chunks of verbal information were learned. Interestingly, an "advance" organiser which was updated and presented during the training, was even more beneficial to a learner control condition.

Learner control of training raises many issues. Given the complexities of skill acquisition, it is a considerable challenge to decide how to engineer a training programme which is not only consistent with the development of skill but also provides the trainee with sensible choices. Training can vary along a continuum with at one extreme training being completely trainer-driven and at the other extreme, the trainee doing anything allowed by the training programme. In some cases, where for example, some subskills are logical or psychological prerequisites for the mastery of others (cf. Gagné, pp. 282–292), then some constraint is necessary within which the trainee can exercise choice. Currently, there is some enthusiasm for the trainee being allowed to "explore" what are termed "learning environments" in an unfettered fashion. Even in these the trainer has to decide the different ways in which material is structured which determine the trainees' options. Until more evidence is available, a middle course is desirable which attempts to provide the trainee with some control, whilst the training system ensures that this is not incompatible with the trainee's competence and other logical and psychological factors which may facilitate learning.

9.7 THE SPACING AND DURATION OF TRAINING

An important practical question concerns how to organise the sessions of a training programme. How long should the training sessions be? How much should they be spaced out? The literature has concentrated almost exclusively on the second question and has mostly investigated whether intervals between training sessions are desirable in comparison to none. This debate has been an old and vigorous one in psychology and is known as the issue of "massed" versus "distributed" training. Woodworth and Schlosberg (1954) devoted nine pages of their classic volume to this topic, which was reviewed subsequently by Bilodeau and Bilodeau (1961) in the context of motor skills. Little new evidence has emerged since that time and both Holding (1965) and Welford (1968) have provided overviews of the area.

Common sense suggests that for a person learning to drive a car, a training schedule of five minutes each week is just as ridiculous as one session lasting 12 hours. Within these extremes, practical considerations may also dictate what is acceptable. Over how long a period can training be distributed given that in most industrial and occupational contexts training causes some disruption to the normal work routine? Also there may be a deadline by which time the trainee has to be competent, due for example to the introduction of new technology or predicted staff shortages. These sorts of practical issues may dictate the nature of the training schedule, irrespective of which one produces better learning.

In the training of motor skills, massed training is not as inferior to distributed training as is often suggested in guidelines for training prac-titioners. Generally, massed training is worse than distributed training as measured by performance *during* training. However most, although not all, of this disadvantage disappears *after* training. Epstein (1949), cited by Woodworth and Schlosberg (1954), trained code substitution using 20 one-minute training sessions in which letters had to be substituted in a paragraph (e.g. g for a, t for b, etc.). One training group had no space between the sessions whereas the other group had one minute's rest. The speed of the spaced training group was higher during training although this apparent advantage reduced to only a small superiority in a retention test two weeks later, as can be seen from Figure 9.12.

It appears therefore that massed training depresses performance during training which does not reflect underlying levels of learning. Holding (1965) suggested that massed training produces a sort of "psychological fatigue". Intuitively, we are all aware of this phenomenon, particularly when learning tasks which are physically or mentally demanding. Even a short break during a training session is beneficial. After a rest, performance will improve when training is massed. For example, Ammons (1947) found that performance efficiency on a pursuit rotor increased from 18% to 43% if a rest period of 5 to 20 minutes followed an eight-minute continuous work period.

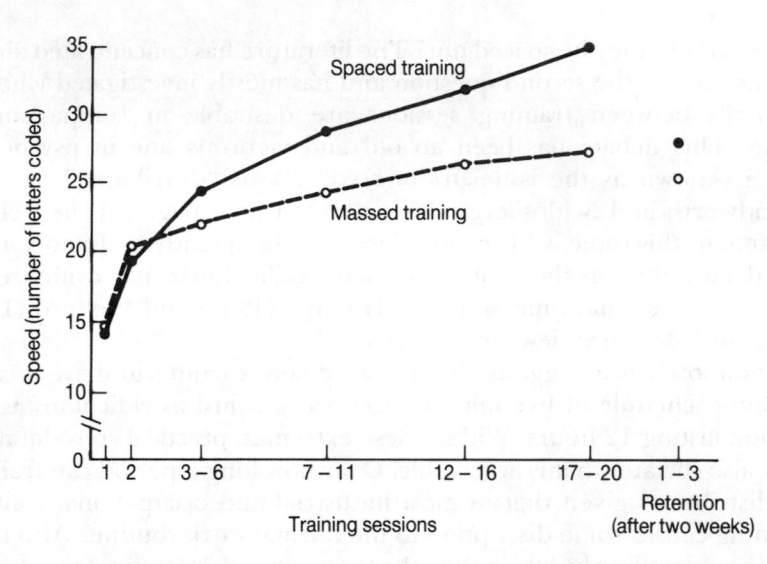

Figure 9.12 Massed versus distributed training of a coding substitution skill (Epstein, 1949).

A more recent study by Baddeley and Longman (1978) is one of the few which has investigated the effect of not only interval between training sessions but also the duration of each session. They argued rightly that the amount of training provided in a training session is an important variable which has largely been ignored. In their study, Post Office workers were trained in keyboard skills. The task involved typing alphanumeric codes using a typewriter keyboard. Seventy-two postmen were divided into four groups. Each training session was either one or two hours in duration and there were either one or two training sessions each day. Hence there were four training conditions. The (1×1) group was trained for one one-hour session each day, the (2×1) group for two one-hour sessions each day, whilst the (1×2) and (2×2) groups received two-hour training sessions either once or twice each day. Some of the results are summarised in Table 9.3. Both duration and frequency of training session had an effect although duration was more influential. The (1×1) group took less time to learn the task and was significantly faster after 60 hours training than either the (1×2) or (2×2) training groups (Table 9.3). The inferiority of the training condition that received the most training each day (i.e. two sessions of two hours each day) is quite striking. Even after 80 hours training, this group was worse in keystroke rate than the group receiving two one-hour training sessions each day. A commendable feature of this study was that retention was also measured after one, three and nine months. About

Table 9.3 The effect of frequency and duration of training session on acquisition of a typing skill (Baddeley and Longman, 1978)

	Training groups			
	(1 × 1)	(2 × 1)	(1 × 2)	(2 × 2)
Mean hours to learn	34.9	42.6	43.2	49.7
Mean rate of correct keystrokes (per min) after 60 hours training	79.31	73.43	71.12	64.78
Mean rate of keystrokes (per min) after 80 hours training		89.4	82.8	77.6

Note: the (1 × 1) group did not continue training after 60 hours.

30% of the typing skill had been lost after nine months although the authors did not consider this excessive. There was also a hint that the (2 × 2) training group was slightly worse than the other groups after this period of time.

From a practical perspective, this study demonstrates the advantage of a modest amount of training each day (i.e. 1 × 1 group) in comparison to a fairly large dose (i.e. 2 × 2 group). The effectiveness of each training hour is more in the (1 × 1) group than the (2 × 2) group. Against this has to be weighed the overall duration of the training period which is much shorter for the (2 × 2) group. Thus to complete 60 hours training would take 12 weeks for the (1 × 1) group, six weeks for the (1 × 2) and (2 × 1) groups and only three weeks for the (2 × 2) group.

The results of the Baddeley and Longman study are important in demonstrating the potency of the amount of training per session. The finding that one hour per day is optimal for learning should not be turned into a generalisation beyond the context of their study. The optimal combination of amount and frequency of training will vary according to the nature of the task, the trainees, the training programme etc. Further work should be carried out to determine the theoretical underpinnings for these practically significant training variables.

Let us conclude by considering some of the obvious factors which influence the effectiveness of different training schedules.

Memory. If the interval between training sessions is too long, then forgetting will occur, with the need for relearning. Also, if the trainee has to perform other similar tasks during this interval, then interference may occur. On the other hand, such intervals may be used for practice or rehearsal which will consolidate learning. In addition, the opportunity to "review" complex training materials has been demonstrated to assist retention. Two studies by Reynolds and Glaser (1964) were concerned with programmed learning for 10 topics in biology, covering 1280 "frames". They found that retention of one of these topics, namely mitosis, was considerably enhanced when two short reviews of this topic were interspaced between the learning of subsequent topics. The facilitating effect of allowing the trainee to review training material has been confirmed by other studies which are discussed by Ausubel and Robinson (1969). Also, review is part of the PQ4R study method advocated by Thomas and Robinson (1972), discussed on p. 410.

Anderson (1985) has pointed out that "encoding variability" is an important advantage of spaced training when words have to be learned. He cited a study by Madigan (1969) which found that the retention of words varied with the lag between the first and second presentations of a particular word. Recall was better the greater the lag and the greater the number of intervening items. One factor in this effect is "encoding variability" which suggests that retention is improved by studying the material in a variety of contexts. The greater the range of contexts, the greater the chance that one of these training contexts will match the context in which the trainee is tested. Retention improves as the similarity between training and testing contexts increases.

Warm-up. After any break from training, the trainee will have to "warm-up" and "reorient" to the task. This will take time. The longer the interval, the more time taken to warm-up which suggests that the interval between training sessions should not be too long.

Fatigue and motivation. It is difficult to differentiate the sort of "psychological fatigue" which occurs with massed training, discussed previously, from an increase in physical fatigue and a lack of motivation. All of these are potentially negative factors if the trainee is asked to work or concentrate for too long in a training session. These dangers can be avoided by the provision of relatively short breaks.

9.8 OVERTRAINING

The amount of training is one of the most potent variables which determines how much of a skill is retained, as discussed in Chapter 3. This has led some to argue that there is an advantage in "overtraining",

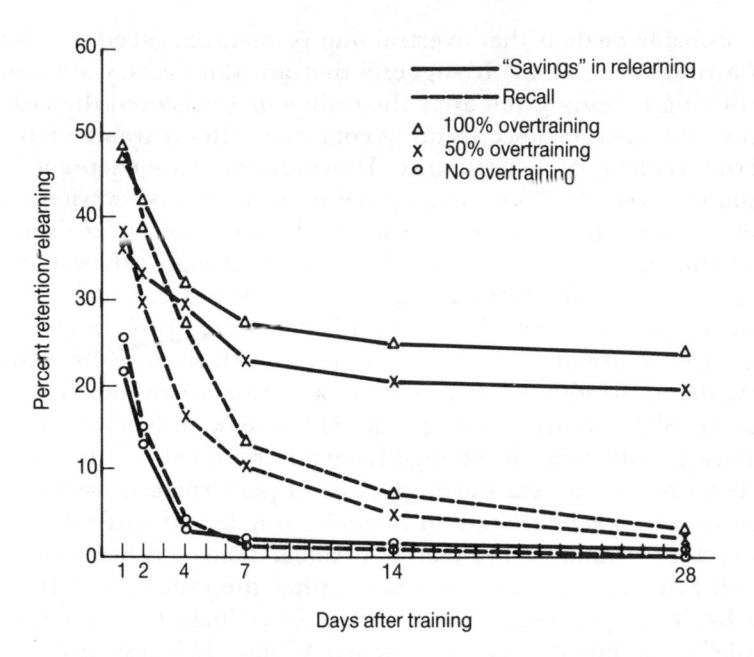

Figure 9.13 Different amounts of overtraining on retention of nouns (Kreuger, 1929).

since this will reduce skill loss. Consider a training situation in which it takes a trainee ten sessions to learn a task. Is there any advantage of providing the trainee with an extra five sessions, i.e. 50% overtraining? Will this improve retention by 50%?

Kreuger (1929) investigated these questions for a simple task in which 12 monosyllabic nouns had to be learned. The criterion of training was one perfect repetition of these nouns which took on average four or five "attempts". Three groups received 0%, 50% or 100% overtraining. Retention and relearning were measured after 1, 2, 4, 7, 14 and 28 days. The results are given in Figure 9.13. Overtraining was beneficial, although the improvement associated with an increase in overtraining from 50% to 100% was not as great as that from 0% to 50% overtraining. Thus whilst greater amounts of overtraining improve retention (and also reduce the time required to relearn), there are diminishing returns. How long after training the skill is assessed will determine whether and how much extra training effort is worthwhile. For example, after 28 days in Kreuger's study, the differences in retention between 0%, 50% and 100% overtraining were so slight that they might be judged trivial from a practical perspective.

It is probably evident that overtraining (sometimes called overlearning) is a misleading term. It suggests that an unnecessary amount of extra training is being given after the trainee has mastered the task. In one sense this is true, since training continues after a trainee has met some criterion level of performance. However, in another sense it is not overtraining, since learning takes place even after, say, a criterion of errorless performance has been reached. Hence what we are arguing about is the *criterion* of learning. Fitts (1962) strongly advocated that training should continue past an often arbitrary and minimal criterion of performance, since this increased resistance to stress, fatigue, and interference. Certainly, a training criterion which is equivalent to the first demonstration of satisfactory performance by the trainee is inadequate. Skill acquired during training has to be sufficiently versatile and robust to withstand the change from an organised training context to the less predictable real world domain. If performance has only just reached an acceptable level, then it will be fragile and easily disrupted unless further training takes place. A similar point has been made by Pask and Scott (1972) who questioned what the criterion of training should be. They proposed that in order for trainees to be considered "versatile" they should pass the "teachback" test. This test involves the trainee explaining or teaching another person (e.g. the trainer). Those with experience of teaching will understand that this is a much more stringent criterion, which ensures that the trainee has sufficient skill to be fluent with the subject matter.

9.9 THE DESIGN OF TRAINING TEXT

Training design covers not only the structure and organisation of the training programme, as discussed in previous sections, but also how it is presented to the trainee. Many writers have discussed presentation in terms of the different media used to "deliver" training (e.g. Briggs and Wager, 1981; Romiszowski, 1981). However, while media have some obvious practical implications, they are less important than the psychological aspects of training design. One remaining psychological issue to be discussed in this chapter is the presentation of training material when it is in the form of text. Text, in varying amounts, is likely to be involved in most training programmes, if only at the initial instruction stage. Research has examined the optimal organisation and layout of text and associated material. Reviews are available by Hartley (1978) and Wright (1977).

Text may come as either pre-instructions to the trainee or part of the training programme itself. In either situation, there are many factors which determine its effectiveness. It is useful to conceptualise the provision of text as part of the communication process between the trainer and the trainee. In designing effective text, it is important for the training designer to consider the aims of both the trainer and the trainee. On the one hand, the trainer may have various aims, such as drawing the trainee's attention to a particularly important issue; helping the trainee to understand a complex procedure; and enabling some information to be learned and remembered more easily. On the other hand, the aims of the trainee may be to search an operating manual to determine how to carry out a task or to understand the objectives and breadth of a training programme. The effectiveness of the design of training text is dependent upon how well it serves its varying purposes. It is therefore of doubtful value attempting to assess the effectiveness of different text designs per se. Generalisations concerning their effectiveness will be the result of many interacting factors.

The first possibility to consider is that the person for whom the text is designed may not participate in the communication process, i.e. the person fails to read the text. Wright, Creighton and Threlfall (1982) investigated factors which determined whether people read the instructions on 60 household items which varied in complexity of operation (e.g. video recorders, vacuum flasks). They found that not only did the type of item determine whether the instructions were read, but also the reader's assumptions about the simplicity of using a particular item. This suggests that the designers of instructions have to be much more aware of the attitudes of the audience for whom the instructions are designed. In addition, as Wright et al. observed, some people may dislike reading written instructions and may prefer to ask for information.

Assuming that the person reads the text, then we need to consider how difficulties can arise. A fairly obvious point is that the "readability" of the text should be adjusted to the appropriate reading level of the target population of trainees. This can be assessed by the use of measures of readability, reviewed by Klare (1974), such as the Flesch Reading Ease Score. However this and other measures do not take account of the difficulties created by the use of unfamiliar technical or abstract words. Wright (1977) has provided an excellent review of these and other text design issues and some of her recommendations, and those of others, are as follows:

Use common words and avoid long/technical ones.
Use words for their common meaning.
Write sentences in the active rather than passive tense.

(a)

Long-term training in basic knowledge required by specialist officers for their immediate jobs and for jobs in normal course of transfer or promotion.

(a) *Compulsory Training.* Certain classes of staff – sub-professionals, technical, special executive and departmental – are *required* as a condition of confirmed appointment or of advancement beyond the entry grade, to obtain specified qualifications by means of part-time study at external institutions. For this category a large degree of aid may be given within the following limits:

  (i) *Time Off*

  (A) *Day-time classes*
  Time off may be allowed to cover attendance during official hours at lectures, practical work, etc., including necessary travelling time. Time off during the day may be allowed for private study above six hours per week.

  (B) *Evening classes*
    (1) Time off during the day may be allowed for the number of hours by which attendance at evening lectures, etc., exceeds three hours a week.
    (2) Where private study is necessary, time off during the day may be allowed for the number of hours by which a combination of evening classes and private study exceeds six hours a week (if this is more favourable than (1)).

(Extracted from Estacode Vol. 2/amendment No. 5, sections Sc 1–5, April 1959.)

(b)

Outcomes

1 Claim under clause 5(a)(i)(A):
   Time off may be allowed to cover attendance (during official hours) at lectures, practical work, etc., *plus* necessary travelling time, *plus* time spent on private study in excess of six hours a week.

2 Claim under first part of clause 5(a)(i)(A):
   Time off may be allowed to cover attendance (during official hours) at lectures, practical work, etc., *plus* necessary travelling time. No extra allowance for private study.

Figure 9.14 (continued)

3 Claim under clause 5(a)(i)(B)(2):
  Add the time spent per week at evening classes to the time spent on private study, and deduct 6 hours. This gives the maximum amount of time off allowed during a week.
4 Claim under clause 5(a)(i)(B)(1):
  Deduct 3 hours from the amount of time per week spent at evening classes. This gives the maximum amount of time off allowed during the week.
5 No claim can be made for time off.

Figure 9.14 An extract of the regulations concerning time off for compulsory training programmes: (a) text versus (b) an algorithmic format (Lewis, Horabin and Gane, 1967).

Avoid long sentences and long prepositional phrases.
Separate different parts of the text by careful use of headings, spacing, and labels. Ensure that these are used appropriately and consistently. Draw attention to critical text and examples by highlighting them with boxes, colour etc.

Words are often not the best means of conveying meaning. Even sentences which are grammatically correct can be ambiguous. Information, particularly of a technical nature, can often be better presented to the trainee by the use of illustrations, diagrams and the like. However, these can also be a source of ambiguity unless designed carefully. One has to remember that illustrations and diagrams use conventions and symbols which are often shorthand expressions of complex ideas and relationships. There will be a communication failure if the trainee does not appreciate and share the assumptions made by the text designer. In this book, various types of illustration are used; graphs indicate quantitative relationships or trends; tables enable numerical data to be expressed clearly; and network diagrams represent complex and/or hierarchical relationships. (Networking is also a type of technique for improving learning strategies, discussed in Chapter 10.3, pp. 418–419.)

Flow charts are an effective means of representing the relationships between decisions and actions. Instructions concerning a procedure, such as filling out a tax return or operating some equipment, are usually more comprehensible when presented in the form of a flow chart or an algorithm. Lewis, Horabin and Gane (1967) provided various examples of how instructions that are written in a tortuous and dense style can become comprehensible when translated into an algorithm, as in Figure 9.14. In this book some of the models concerned with stages in the development of training, discussed in Chapter 4, adopt this format, as does Figure 6.2 which is concerned with testing malfunctioning equipment.

The obvious benefit of flow charts has been corroborated by various research studies.

Another representation which is particularly appropriate for complex explanations of, say, the functioning of a piece of equipment, is a schematic diagram. This enables the location and shape of parts of equipment to be indicated clearly. Imagine trying to explain how the rather old-fashioned speedometer in Figure 9.15 works without the aid of such a diagram. Finally, some diagrams, called pictograms, avoid the use of words and, through illustrations, instruct the person in a series of actions and their associated effects. An obvious example is the use of

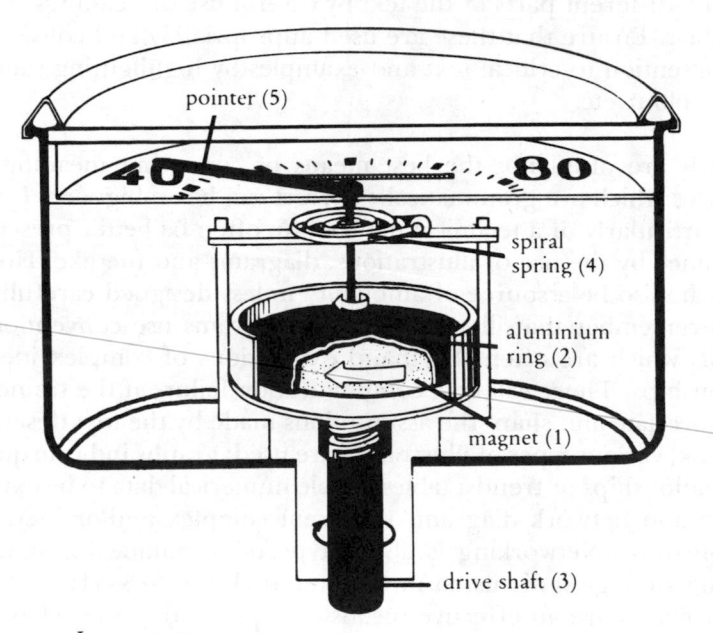

In summary:
- when the car moves, the drive shaft (3) rotates the magnet (1).
- the rotation of the magnet (1) produces a magnetic field which twists the ring (2).
- attached to the ring is a pointer (5) which indicates the speed of the car.

Figure 9.15 Schematic diagram of how a speedometer works (from Patrick et al., 1986).

pictograms to depict the operating procedures for cameras, which has the additional advantage of avoiding the need for any translation of text into different languages. A pictogram illustrating how to switch on a machine and what happens subsequently is given in Figure 9.16, from Barnard and Marcel (1984). In a similar vein, over the last decade, there has been a trend for computer interfaces to consist of icons which can be manipulated directly by the user.

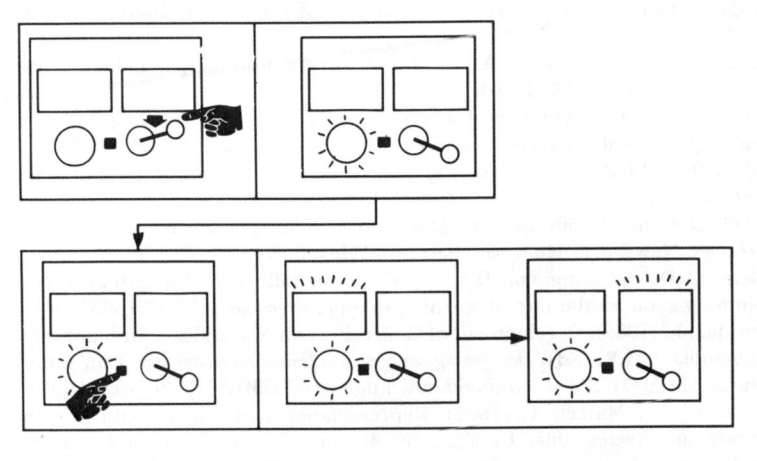

Figure 9.16   A pictogram illustrating the actions to switch on a machine and their associated effects (from Marcel and Barnard, 1979).

REFERENCES

Adams, J.A. (1971). A closed-loop theory of motor learning. *Journal of Motor Behaviour*, **3**, 111–149.

Adams, J.A. (1987). Historical review and appraisal of research on the learning, retention and transfer of human motor skills. *Psychological Bulletin*, **101**(1), 41–74.

Adams, J.A. and Hufford, L.E. (1962). Contributions of a part-task trainer to the learning and relearning of a time-shared flight manoeuvre. *Human Factors*, **4**, 159–170.

Aiken, E.G. and Lau, A.W. (1967). Response prompting and response confirmation. A review of recent literature. *Psychological Bulletin*, **68**, 330–341.

Ammons, R.B. (1947). Acquisition of motor skill: II. Rotary pursuit performance with continuous practice before and after a single rest. *Journal of Experimental Psychology*, **37**, 393–411.

Anderson, J.R. (1982). Acquisition of cognitive skill. *Psychological Review*, **89**(4), 369–406.

Anderson, J.R. (1985). *Cognitive psychology and its implications*. 2nd edition. New York: Freeman.

Annett, J. (1959). Learning a pressure under conditions of immediate and delayed knowledge of results. *Quarterly Journal of Experimental Psychology*, **11**, 3–15.

Annett, J. (1961). The role of knowledge of results in learning: A survey. Navtradevcen Report No. 342–3. New York: US Naval training Device Center.

Annett, J. (1966). Training for perceptual skills. *Ergonomics*, **9**, 459–468.

Annett, J. (1969). *Feedback and human behaviour*. Harmondsworth: Penguin.

Annett, J. (1970). The role of action feedback in the acquisition of simple motor responses. *Journal of Motor Behaviour*, **2**, 217–221.

Annett, J. and Kay, H. (1956). Skilled performance. *Occupational Psychology*, **30**, 112–117.

Annett, J. and Paterson, L. (1967). Training for auditory detection. *Acta Psychologica*, **27**, 420–426.

Atkinson, R.C. (1972). Ingredients for a theory of instruction. *American Psychologist*, **27**, 921–931.

Atkinson, R.C. and Paulson, J.A. (1972). An approach to the psychology of instruction. *Psychological Bulletin*, **78**, 49–61.

Ausubel, D.P. (1960). The use of advance organisers in the learning and retention of meaningful verbal material. *Journal of Educational Psychology*, **51**, 267–272.

Ausubel, D.P. (1963). *The psychology of meaningful verbal learning*. New York: Grune and Stratton.

Ausubel, D.P. and Robinson, F.C. (1969). *School learning. An introduction to educational psychology*. New York: Holt, Rinehart and Winston.

Baddeley, A.D. and Longman, D.J.A. (1978). The influence of length and frequency of training session on the rate of learning to type. *Ergonomics*, **21**, 627–635.

Bainbridge, L. (1989). Development of skill, reduction of workload. In Bainbridge, L. and Quintanilla, S.A.R. (Eds) *Developing skills with information technology*. Chichester: Wiley.

Bandura, A. (1977). *Social learning theory*. Englewood Cliffs, NJ: Prentice-Hall.

Barnard, P. and Marcel, T. (1984). Representation and understanding in the use of symbols and pictograms. In Easterby, R. and Zwaga, H. (Eds) *Information design*. Chichester: Wiley.

Barnes, B.R. and Clawson, E.U. (1975). Do advance organizers facilitate learning? Recommendations for further research based on an analysis of 32 studies. *Review of Educational Research*, **45**(4), 637–659.

Bartram, D. (1988). The design and evaluation of a computer-based training system for foreign destination coding desk operators. In Patrick, J. and Duncan, K.D. (Eds) *Training, human decision making and control*. Amsterdam: Elsevier.

Bilodeau, I.McD. (1966). Information feedback. In Bilodeau, E.A. (Ed.) *Acquisition of skill*. New York: Academic Press.

Bilodeau, E.A. and Bilodeau, I.M. (1961). Motor skills learning. *Annual Review of Psychology*, **12**, 243–280.

Briggs, L.J. and Wager, W.W. (1981). *Handbook of procedures for the design of instruction*. 2nd edition. Englewood Cliffs, NJ: Educational Technology Publications.

Briggs, C.E. and Waters, L.K. (1958). Training and transfer as a function of component interaction. *Journal of Experimental Psychology*, **56**, 492–500.

Clarke, A.D.B. (1966). *Recent advances in the study of subnormality*. London: National Association for Mental Health.

Colquhoun, W.P. (1966). Training for vigilance. A comparison of different techniques. *Human Factors*, **8**, 7–12.

Cox, J.A. and Boren, L.M. (1965). A study of backward chaining. *Journal of Educational Psychology*, **56**, 270–274.

Donchin, E. (1989). The Learning Strategies Project. *Acta Psychologica*, **71**, 1–15.

Duchastel, P.C. and Merrill, P.F. (1973). The effects of behavioural objectives on learning. A review of empirical studies. *Review of Educational Research*, **75**, 250–266.

Epstein, B. (1949). *Immediate and retention effects of interpolated rest periods on learning performance*. New York: Teaching College Continuing Education.

Fitts, P.M. (1962). Factors in complex skill training. In Glaser, R. (Ed.) *Training research and education*. New York: Wiley.

Fox, P.W. and Levy, C.M. (1969). Acquisition of a simple motor response as influenced by the presence or absence of action visual feedback. *Journal of Motor Behaviour*, **1**, 161–180.

Frederiksen, J.R. and White, B.Y. (1989). An approach to training based upon principled task decomposition. *Acta Psychologica*, **71**, 89–146.

Gagné, R.M. (1985). *The conditions of learning and the theory of instruction*. 4th edition. New York: CBS College Publishing.

Gaines, B.R. (1967). Automated feedback trainers for perceptual-motor skills. Final Report to Ministry of Defence, Cambridge: University of Cambridge.

Gay, G. (1986). Interaction of learner control and prior understanding in computer-assisted video instruction. *Journal of Educational Psychology*, **78**, 225–227.

Gilbert, T.F. (1962). Mathetics: The technology of education. *Journal of Mathetics*, **1**, 7–73.

Gill, D.L. (1975). Knowledge of results precision and motor skill acquisition. *Journal of Motor Behaviour*, **7**, 191–198.

Goldstein, M. and Rittenhouse, C.H. (1954). Knowledge of results in the acquisition and transfer of a gunnery skill. *Journal of Experimental Psychology*, **48**, 187–196.

Gopher, D., Weil, M. and Siegel, D. (1989). Practice under changing priorities: An approach to the training of complex skills. *Acta Psychologica*, **71**, 147–177.

Hartley, J. (1978). *Designing instructional text*. London: Kogan Page.

Hartley, J. and Davies, I.K. (1976). Preinstructional strategies: The role of pretests, behavioural objectives, overviews and advance organisers. *Review of Educational Research*, **46**(2), 239–265.

Hayes-Roth, F., Klahr, D. and Mostow, D.J. (1981). Advice taking and knowledge refinement. An iterative view of skill acquisition. In Anderson, J.R. (Ed.) *Cognitive skills and their acquisition*. Hillsdale, NJ: Lawrence Erlbaum.

Holding, D.H. (1965). *Principles of training*. Oxford: Pergamon.

Holding, D.H. (1970). Repeated errors in motor learning. *Ergonomics*, **13**, 727–734.

Holding, D.H. and Macrae, A.W. (1964). Guidance, restriction and knowledge of results. *Ergonomics*, **7**, 289–295.

Holding, D.H. and Macrae, A.W. (1966). Rate and force of guidance in perceptual-motor tasks with reversed or random spatial correspondence. *Ergonomics*, **9**, 289–296.

Howell, M.L. (1956). Use of force–time graphs for performance analysis in facilitating motor learning. *Research Quarterly*, **27**, 12–22.

Kalman, R.E., Falb, P.L. and Arbib, M.A. (1969). *Topics in mathematical system theory*. New York: McGraw-Hill.

Karlin, L. (1960). Psychological study of motor skills. Phase I. Navtradevcen Report No. 558–1. New York: US Naval Training Device Center.

Kay, H. (1951). Learning of a serial task by different age groups. *Quarterly Journal of Experimental Psychology*, **3**, 166–183.

Keller, J.M. and Kopp, T.W. (1987). An application of the ARCS model of motivational design. In Reiguluth, C.M. (Ed.) *Instructional-design theories in action: Lessons illustrating selected theories*. Hillsdale, NJ: Lawrence Erlbaum.

Kelley, C.R. (1969). What is adaptive training? *Human Factors*, **11**, 547–556.

Klare, G. (1974). Assessing readability. *Reading Research Quarterly*, **10**(1), 62–102.

Knapp, B. (1963). *Skill in sport. The attainment of proficiency*. London: Routledge and Kegan Paul.

Kreuger, W.C.F. (1929). The effect of overlearning on retention. *Journal of Experimental Psychology*, **12**, 71–78.

Landa, L. (1983). The Algo-heuristic theory of instruction. In Reigeluth, C.M. (Ed.) *Instructional-design theories and models. An overview of their current status.* Hillsdale, NJ: Lawrence Erlbaum.

Langley, P. and Simon, H.A. (1981). The central role of learning in cognition. In Anderson, J.R. (Ed.) *Cognitive skills and their acquisition.* New York: Lawrence Erlbaum.

Lewis, B.N., Horabin, I.S. and Gane, C.D. (1967). *Flow charts, logical trees and algorithms for rules and regulations. CAS Occasional Paper No 2.* London: HMSO.

Lewis, B.N. and Pask, G. (1965). The theory and practice of adaptive teaching systems. In Glaser, R. (Ed.) *Teaching machines and programmed learning, II, Data and directions.* Washington: National Education Association of the United States.

Lincoln, R.S. (1954). Learning a rate of movement. *Journal of Experimental Psychology*, **47**, 465–470.

Lintern, G. and Gopher, D. (1978). Adaptive training of perceptual-motor skills: Issues, results and future directions. *International Journal of Man-Machine Studies*, **10**, 521–551.

Lintern, G. and Roscoe, S.N. (1980). Adaptive perceptual-motor training. In Roscoe, S.N. (Ed.) *Aviation psychology.* Ames: Iowa State University Press.

Luiten, J., Ames, W. and Ackerson, G. (1980). A meta-analysis of the effects of advance organisers on learning and retention. *American Educational Research Journal*, **17**, 211–218.

Macrae, A.W. and Holding, D.H. (1965a). Method and task in motor guidance. *Ergonomics*, **8**, 315–320.

Macrae, A.W. and Holding, D.H. (1965b). Guided practice in direct and reversed serial tracking. *Ergonomics*, **8**, 487–492.

Macrae, A.W. and Holding, D.H. (1966). Transfer of training after guidance and practice. *Quarterly Journal of Experimental Psychology*, **18**, 327–333.

Madigan, S.A. (1969). Intraserial repetition and coding processes in free recall. *Journal of Verbal Learning and Verbal Behaviour*, **8**, 828–835.

Mager, R.F. (1961). On the sequencing of instructional content. *Psychological Reports*, **9**, 405–413.

Mané, A.M. and Donchin, E. (1989). The space fortress game. *Acta Psychologica*, **71**, 17–22.

Mané, A.M., Adams, J.A. and Donchin, E. (1989). Adaptive and part-whole training in the acquisition of a complex perceptual-motor skill. *Acta Psychologica*, **71**, 179–196.

Marcel, A. and Barnard, P. (1979). Paragraphs of pictographs: the use of non-verbal instruction for equipment. In Kolers, P.A., Wrolstrad, M.E. and Bouma, H. (Eds) *Processing of visible language.* Volume 1. New York: Plenum Press.

Mayer, R.E. (1979). Twenty years of research on advance organisers: Assimilation theory is still the best predictor of results. *Instructional Science*, **8**, 133–167.

McGeoch, G.O. (1931). Whole-part problem. *Psychological Bulletin*, **28**(10), 713–739.

McGuigan, F.J. (1959). The effect of precision, delay and schedule of knowledge of results on performance. *Journal of Experimental Psychology*, **58**, 79–84.

Merrill, D.M. (1980). Learner control in computer-based learning. *Computers and Education*, **4**, 77–96.

Miller, R.B. (1953). Handbook on training and training equipment design. Report No. 53–136, Wright-Patterson Air Force Base, Wright Air Development Center.

Miller, C.A., Galanter, E. and Pribram, K.H. (1960). *Plans and the structure of behaviour.* New York: Holt, Rinehart and Winston.

Naylor, J.C. (1962). Parameters affecting the relative effectiveness of part and whole training methods. A review of the literature. Report No. 950–1. New York: US Naval Training Devices Center.

Naylor, J.C. and Briggs, G.E. (1963). Effects of task complexity and task organisation on the relative efficiency of part and whole training methods. *Journal of Experimental Psychology*, **65**, 217–224.

Nettelbeck, T. and Kirby, N. (1976). A comparison of part and whole training methods with mildly mentally retarded workers. *Journal of Occupational Psychology*, **49**, 115–120.

Newell, K.M. (1981). Skill learning. In Holding, D.H. (Ed.) *Human skills*. Chichester: Wiley.

Pask, G. (1958). Electronic keyboard teaching machines. *Education and Communication*, **24**, 336–348.

Pask, G. and Scott, B.C.E. (1972). Learning strategies and individual competence. *International Journal of Man-Machine Studies*, **4**, 217–253.

Patrick, J. and Evans, P. (1983). Advance organizers and learner control of sequence in recall of topic attributes. *Human Learning*, **2**, 269–277.

Patrick, J. and Fitzgibbon, L. (1988). Structural displays as learning aids. *International Journal of Man-Machine Studies*, **28**, 625–635.

Patrick, J. Michael, I. and Moore, A. (1986). *Designing for learning—some guidelines*. Birmingham: Occupational Services Ltd.

Patrick, J. and Mutlusoy, F. (1982). The relationship between types of feedback, gain of a display and feedback precision in acquisition of a simple motor task. *Quarterly Journal of Experimental Psychology*, **34A**, 171–184.

Rachman, S.J. (1976). Observational learning and therapeutic modelling. In Feldman, M.P. and Broadhurst, A. (Eds) *Theoretical and experimental bases of the behaviour therapies*. London: Wiley.

Reigeluth, C.M. and Stein, F.S. (1983). The elaboration theory of instruction. In Reigeluth, C.M. (Ed.) *Instructional-design theories and models. An overview of their current status*. Hillsdale, NJ: Lawrence Erlbaum.

Reigeluth, C.M., Merrill, M.D. and Bunderson, C.V. (1978). The structure of subject matter content and its instructional design implications. *Instructional Science*, **7**, 107–126.

Reigeluth, C.M., Merrill, M.D., Wilson, B.C. and Spiller, R.T. (1980). The elaboration theory of instruction: A model for sequencing and synthesising instruction. *Instructional Science*, **9**, 195–219.

Reynolds, J.H. and Glaser, R. (1964). Effects of repetition and spaced review upon retention of a complex learning task. *Journal of Experimental Psychology*, **55**, 297–308.

Robb, M. (1966). Feedback and skill learning. *Research Quarterly*, **39**, 175–184.

Rogers, Jr, C.A. (1974). Feedback precision and postfeedback interval duration. *Journal of Experimental Psychology*, **102**, 604–608.

Romiszowski, A.J. (1981). *Designing instructional systems*. London: Kogan Page.

Salmoni, A.W., Schmidt, R.A. and Walter, C.B. (1984). Knowledge of results and motor learning. A review and critical reappraisal. *Psychological Bulletin*, **95**(3), 355–386.

Seidel, R.J., Wagner, H., Rosenblatt, R.D., Hillelsohn, M.J. and Stelzer, J. (1978). Learner control of instructional sequencing within an adaptive tutorial CAI environment. *Instructional Science*, **7**, 37–80.

Seymour, W.D. (1966). *Industrial skills*. London: Sir Isaac Pitman and Sons Ltd.

Sheffield, F.D. (1961). Theoretical considerations in the learning of complex sequential tasks from demonstration and practice. In Lumsdaine, A.A. (Ed.) *Student response in programmed instruction*. Washington, DC: National Academy of Science – National Research Council.

Sheffield, F.D. and Maccoby, N. (1961). Summary and interpretation of research on organisational principles in constructing filmed demonstrations. In Lumsdaine, A.A. (Ed.) *Student response in programmed instruction*. Washington, DC: National Academy of Science – National Research Council.

Sidley, N.A., Winograd, E. and Bedauf, E.W. (1965). Stimulus identification overlap in learning to identify complex sounds. *Journal of the Acoustical Society of America*, **38**, 11–13.

Stammers, R.B. (1982). Part and whole practice in training for procedural tasks. *Human Learning*, **1**, 185–207.

Stammers, R. and Patrick, J. (1975). *The psychology of training*. London: Methuen.

Swets, J. (1962). Learning to identify nonverbal sounds: An application of a computer as a teaching machine. Technical Report No. 789–1. US Naval Training Device Center.

Swets, J.A., Harris, J.S., McElroy, L.S. and Rudloe, H. (1964). Further experiments on computer-aided learning of sound identification. Technical Report No. 789–2. US Naval Training Device Center.

Tennyson, R.D., Park, O.C. and Christensen, D.L. (1985). Adaptive control of learning time and content sequence in concept learning using computer-based instruction. *Journal of Educational Psychology*, **77**, 481–491.

Thomas, E.L. and Robinson, H.A. (1972). *Improving reading in every class. A sourcebook for teachers*. Boston, MA: Allyn and Bacon.

Thorndike, E.L. (1927). The law of effect. *American Journal of Psychology*, **39**, 212–222.

Toye, M. (1969). A rethink on basic skills. *Industrial Training International*, **4**, 112–119.

Trowbridge, M.H. and Cason, H. (1932). An experimental study of Thorndike's theory of learning. *Journal of Genetic Psychology*, **7**, 245–260.

Trumbo, D., Ulrich, L. and Noble, M.E. (1965). Verbal coding and display coding in the acquisition and retention of tracking skill. *Journal of Applied Psychology*, **49**, 368–375.

Victor, J.E. (1971). What's wrong with analytic training? *The Bobbin*, **12**, 40–52.

Von Wright, J.M. (1957). A note on the role of guidance in learning. *British Journal of Psychology*, **48**, 133–137.

Wang, G.H. (1925). The influence of tuition in the acquisition of skill. *Psychological Monographs*, **34**, 154.

Ward, J.L. and Senders, J.W. (1966). *Methodological studies of tracking behaviour. The effect of various supplemental information feedback*. Cambridge, MA: Bolt, Beranek and Newman.

Welford, A.T. (1968). *Fundamentals of skill*. London: Methuen.

Wheaton, G., Rose, A.M., Fingerman, P.W., Karotkin, A.L. and Holding, D.H. (1976). Evaluation of the effectiveness of training devices: Literature review and preliminary model. Research Memo 76–6. US Army Research Institute for the Behavioral and Social Sciences, Washington.

Wiener, E.L. and Attwood, D.A. (1968). Training for vigilance. Combined cueing and knowledge of results. *Journal of Applied Psychology*, **52**, 474–479.

Wightman, D.C. and Lintern, G. (1985). Part-task training for tracking and manual control. *Human Factors*, **27**, 267–283.

Williges, B.H. and Williges, R.C. (1976). Manual versus automatic adaptive skill training. *Proceedings of the 5th Symposium on Psychology in the Air Force, Springfield, VA*. National Technical Information Service, US Department of Commerce.

Williges, R.C. and Williges, B.H. (1978). Critical variables in adaptive motor-skills training. *Human Factors*, **20**, 201–214.

Wittrock, J.M. and Lumsdaine, A.A. (1977). Instructional psychology. *Annual Review of Psychology*, **28**, 417–459.

Woodworth, R.S. and Schlosberg, H. (1954). *Experimental psychology*. London: Methuen.

Wright, P. (1977). Presenting technical information: A survey of research findings. *Instructional Science*, **6**, 93–134.

Wright, P., Creighton, P. and Threlfall, S.M. (1982). Some factors determining when instruction will be read. *Ergonomics*, **25**, 225–237.

CHAPTER 10
The trainee

So far in this book we have discussed two components of training design: the nature of the training content (Chapter 8) and various training methods (Chapter 9). The third component, identified in Figure 8.1, is the characteristics of the trainee(s) that have to be considered in the design of any training programme. Trainees vary in terms of past experience, knowledge, skills, attitudes, age etc., all of which can influence how new or related skills are mastered. To use the jargon term, the trainer should be aware of the characteristics of the "target population" of trainees and training should be designed to accommodate them. This raises the rather thorny question of which characteristics are sufficiently important to demand the attention of the training designer. To reiterate the point made in Chapter 1, there are three criteria that any characteristics or variables have to satisfy: robustness, generality and practical significance. Sadly, few pass this test.

The importance of the trainee's past experience, knowledge and skills is implicit in much of the discussion in this book and these threads are drawn together in Section 10.1. Traditionally, the search for important trainee characteristics began with the study of individual differences such as IQ, age, personality and ability. A great deal of effort was expended on examining the relationship of these variables to learning, although the results were disappointing, with the notable exception of the consistent effect of age (Section 10.2). In the 1960s and 1970s this search went forward under the banner of "Aptitude Treatment Interaction" (ATI) research (e.g. Cronbach and Snow, 1977). The philosophy underlying ATI research was that the effectiveness of different training variables (methods, pace, style etc.) would depend upon the aptitudes of the trainee. This approach, which was enthusiastically advocated by Cronbach (1967), has produced weak and inconsistent results which do not lead to training recommendations for practitioners. ATI research, together with the effect of the trainee's style on learning and performance, are discussed in Section 10.2.

One reason for the disappointing results of research into both individual differences and ATI, according to the more recent cognitive tradition in psychology, is that variables manipulated by these approaches are gross descriptions of a trainee's cognitive or affective state. The argument is, rather like a reductionist one, that in order to explain and predict how a person learns and reacts to variations in training, it is necessary to measure detailed cognitive processes rather than rolling these up into one global index in which the effects of component processes become submerged. As a consequence even variables such as anxiety are now being analysed in terms of the cognitive processes which they affect (Tobias, 1987). In addition, since the mid-1970s, considerable interest has focused upon *how* the trainee goes about learning and the cognitive strategies which are used, or need to be used, to master training material. This approach is known as the "learning strategy" movement, which grew out of experimental/cognitive psychology (Section 10.3). This has given an interesting twist to the search for important trainee characteristics, although most of this work is restricted to the comprehension and retention of facts and concepts in text.

Finally, some approaches to training cannot be put easily into pigeon-holes because they use a variety of principles of training design. This is the case of behaviour role-modelling (discussed in Chapter 12) because it is an example of the use of simulation, although many other features contribute to its effectiveness. At the end of this chapter, the reciprocal teaching method developed by Brown and Palincsar (e.g. 1989) is discussed. This approach uses some learning strategies, and is sensitive to the trainee's needs, although it does have many other important features which make its inclusion here somewhat arbitrary.

10.1 EXPERIENCE, SKILLS AND KNOWLEDGE

Any training should take account of the experience, knowledge and skills of the trainees. Broadly, this can be achieved by suitable modifications to either the *content* or the *design* of the training programme or, indeed, both.

Put simply, the *content* of training is determined by a sort of subtraction process. Any relevant skills and knowledge possessed by a trainee are subtracted from those which are needed to perform the task or job; that which remains specifies the content of training. Occasionally, this process is built into the method of analysis itself, such as Hierarchical Task Analysis, where the extent to which tasks are analysed depends upon the trainee's lack of knowledge and skills. Other techniques analyse the job or task without reference to any potential trainee or group of trainees (e.g. McCormick's Position Analysis Questionnaire, Flanagan's Critical Incident Technique) and it is the responsibility of the trainer to ensure subsequently that the content of training is modified suitably for any trainee(s). In the subtraction process, an important question facing the developer of training is whether or not the target population of trainees is sufficiently homogeneous in terms of skills and knowledge to receive the same training content. If some trainees already have some of the target skills, then there is little point in them experiencing this part of the training programme. In this manner the overall content of training can be adapted to the existing knowledge and skills of trainees by ensuring that trainees only experience relevant training "modules".

Accommodation to the trainee's skills can also take place at a more micro-level *during* training, within, say, a training "module". In principle any form of individualised training can allow this to happen (see the features of a closed-loop training system, pp. 448–451). The much heralded advantage of programmed instruction, computer-based training, and intelligent tutoring systems, discussed in Chapter 11, is that training is sensitive to the needs of individual trainees. Further explanation and advice can be tailored to the level of competence and understanding of each trainee. (This is also done by a good human tutor.) In addition the sequence in which training material is presented and its level of difficulty can be made to suit the needs of individual trainees. For example in the adaptive training discussed in Section 9.6, the computer monitored how well each trainee learned items (words or key presses) and then selected and presented those items which had not yet been mastered. In this way, adaptive training is able to accommodate not only variations in the order in which items are learned by trainees, but also different learning rates.

The trainee's experience, knowledge and skills will also affect the *design* of training exercises. Ausubel stressed the importance of relating new information to existing knowledge which, according to him, enabled new information to be assimilated more easily. One method of achieving this is to provide the trainee with an advance organiser prior to training, a topic discussed in Section 9.2. Reigeluth and Stein's Elaboration theory of instruction (pp. 323–325) adopts a similar perspective and suggests that training material should be introduced progressively and elaborated in increasing detail as a training programme unfolds. Also many of the learning strategies, discussed in Section 10.3, improve learning and retention by requiring trainees to use their existing knowledge and experience to elaborate and organise new information.

Functional context training

The term "functional context training" is used occasionally in the literature (e.g. Caro, 1973; Montague, 1988), although I have to confess to being uncertain of the meaning of the term. What is certain is that it is highly desirable and beneficial to use this technique, method, set of principles or whatever "it" might be. Duncan and Gray (1975) have performed some useful detective work in tracing its origins and they have discussed various training studies, including their own, which use it. Their discussion and that by Montague (1988), confirms my suspicion that functional context training is a rather diffuse set of ideas, and can mean many things. One aspect appears to be that it is "performance-oriented", (Montague, 1988) and "contains safeguards against inclusion of topics that lack functional significance" (Shoemaker, 1960, cited by Duncan and Gray, 1975). The concern underlying these points is that training content may not be relevant to the job in question; instructors may provide a lot of abstract theory (declarative knowledge) which cannot be related to performance of the task (procedural knowledge). One message of this book is that carrying out a proper analysis before developing training should minimise such problems.

Other important aspects of functional context training can be integrated by the notion that *the trainee should develop new skills by relating them to both previous ones and to the future performance situation*. This interpretation is conveyed in the following quotations concerning features of functional context training:

> All new knowledge is acquired on the foundations of old knowledge (Sticht et al., 1986, pp. 175–176, cited by Montague, 1988, p.130).

> A meaningful and relevant context is provided for the learning of novel and abstract material (Shoemaker, 1960, cited by Duncan and Gray, 1975, p. 84).

> Aircraft manoeuvres such as descending turns are taught to under-graduate level instrument flight trainees within the functional context of a simulated instrument approach, rather than as an exercise, per se, ... (Caro, 1973, p. 505).

> ... establishing a need to know certain instructional material before that material is presented (Herbert, F.J., in the Appendix to Brown et al., 1959, cited by Duncan and Gray, 1975, p. 85).

Duncan and Gray (1975) identified the same ideas as being important in functional context training which they used to guide their development of training for petroleum refinery operators:

1. that the information presented in the course of instruction must mean something to the trainee in the sense that he can connect it to his previous experience, inside or outside of refineries; and

2. that the information presented in the course of instruction must be placed in the context of those operations and procedures which are necessarily performed in the control of refineries (p. 87).

Hence functional context training emphasises that the significance of new training material is established before it is encountered, one consequence of which is that trainees should proceed from whole to part training so that they can appreciate the breadth of training and how parts fit together (cf. Reigeluth and Stein's Elaboration theory, pp. 323–325). Functional context training is of benefit because of its positive cognitive and motivational effects. It is closely related to Ausubel's notion that new information is more easily assimilated when the trainee has some relevant "conceptual scaffolding" and knows where the new information fits. This is also motivating as is knowledge of the goal of training and how "lessons" relate to parts of the trainee's job.

10.2 INDIVIDUAL DIFFERENCES

The argument that individual differences are relevant to training is a simple one. Nearly all of the findings discussed in this book are generalisations based on the average score of a sample of trainees (or learners), e.g. the power law of practice discussed in Chapter 2. By definition, some scores are above average and others below average. How much of this variation can be attributed to individual differences between the persons used in these studies? Are individual difference variables of age, IQ and personality related to the rate of learning and, if so, can any handicaps be overcome? In a nutshell, the answer to the first question is that not much variation can be pinned down systematically to individual differences, and that which can occurs in the early stages of training and disappears later on. Training, it seems, has a levelling effect. This is consistent with the notion, discussed in Chapter 7, that a task-specific ability becomes more important in the later stages of skill acquisition, or in Anderson's terms, a unique rule structure is developed as procedural knowledge. The answer to the second question is that personality effects have not been demonstrated, despite a couple of exceptions (Leith, 1969, 1982), and IQ, almost by definition, has an impact for some tasks, although large variations in IQ are necessary to produce reliable differences in performance. Even then, training can be designed to cope with these difficulties. Some of the most compelling evidence of individual differences is associated with research into the effect of age. This work has built up gradually over the last 40 years and is particularly important to training for two reasons. Firstly, the longevity of the population is increasing. Secondly, the rate of technological change in society means that the nature of jobs has changed, and is continuing to do so, resulting in an increasing need for retraining. Thus maintenance personnel have been retrained to deal with electronic rather than electromechanical devices; process control operators are no longer physically involved in the manufacturing process, which is now largely automated, but are involved in more of a monitoring and supervisory role. New skills have also been developed to cope with developments in information technology which have affected daily life. Therefore an important issue concerns how well the older person or worker can be trained to cope with these changes.

Age

Is there a deterioration in basic cognitive capabilities with increasing age? If so, does this affect the efficiency of learning new skills? Can training be designed to circumvent such problems? These questions which concern retraining the older person form the focus of this section. First, let us examine whether basic capacities deteriorate with age before discussing whether training programmes can accommodate and overcome them.

Sadly, there is overwhelming evidence that basic cognitive capacities do deteriorate with age, although more recent reviews suggest that decrements in capacity are smaller and occur later than was originally thought (e.g. Birren and Schaie, 1985). Talland (1968) demonstrated that persons between 77 and 89 years old remembered less than half the number of three-letter words compared with a group between 20 and 25 years old in an immediate recall test. Older people find it more difficult to ignore irrelevant features of a task (Rabbitt, 1965), whilst those over 55 years of age find it difficult to adapt when information about a task is transformed in some manner, such as by a mirror (Welford, 1958). Older people need relatively more time to discriminate cards or weights as the number of alternatives increases (Crossman and Szafran, 1956). Salthouse, Kausler, and Saults (1988) examined the correlations between age (ranging from 20 to 79 years) and performance on eight basic cognitive tasks including verbal and spatial memory, geometric analogies, series completion and speed of matching digits and numbers. There was a negative correlation between age and level of performance on all eight measures.

These limitations with increasing age are likely to retard the older person's learning of some tasks and partly explains the "slowing of responding" that characterises the older person's performance of complex tasks (Welford, 1958). Important questions are whether the age-related deficit increases with the complexity of the task and, if so, whether it can be overcome with practice. These questions were addressed by Jordan and Rabbitt (1977) in a study of the difference in response time between 12 elderly persons (average of 69 years) and 12 young persons (average of 20 years). Three studies were conducted in which the complexity of the mappings between displayed stimuli and responses varied as indicated in Figure 10.1. Two-choice, four-choice

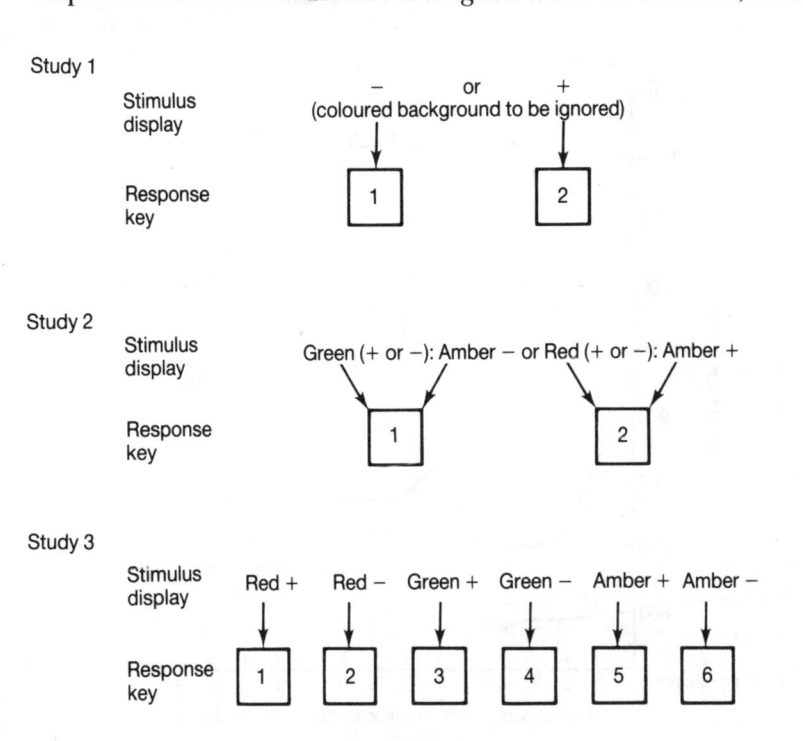

Figure 10.1 Schematic diagrams of stimulus–response mappings used in three studies by Jordan and Rabbitt (1977).

and six-choice tasks were used in Studies 1, 2 and 3 respectively. The elderly group was slower than the younger group and this difference increased with the complexity of the task used in the studies. Study 3 is particularly interesting since practice was given over four blocks of trials. Complexity was varied by changing the manner in which the stimulus–response pairing varied from one trial to the next. For example, on successive trials, the person might respond to the same stimulus display, a display in which the shape changed but the colour remained the same or a display in which both colour and shape changed. The first situation simply involves repetition and therefore no change from one trial to the next. The last situation is the most complex, since both shape and colour change and have to be "processed" by the person in order to find the correct response on the next trial. Differences in response time between the elderly and young groups over the four practice sessions are given in Figure 10.2. The initial decrement for the elderly group increases as complexity increases. It is striking, however, that the elderly group

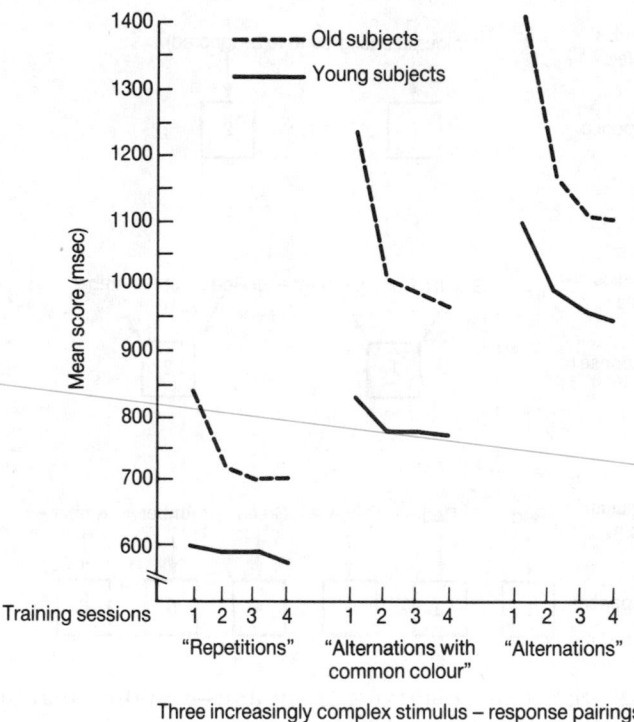

Figure 10.2 Learning curves for elderly and young persons over four training sessions (Jordan and Rabbitt, 1977, Study 3). The three sets of data refer to the complexity of the changes which occurred from one trial to the next. In "repetitions" there was no change, whereas in "alternations with common colour" shape changed and in "alternations" both shape and colour changed making it the most difficult condition.

improves more rapidly than the young group until the age decrement is approximately a constant amount after a period of practice. This suggests that whilst increasing complexity affects older persons more than younger ones, this decrement reduces with practice until it reaches a fixed amount.

So far we have established that there are reductions in the efficiency of basic psychological processes which are related to age. Therefore it should be no surprise to find age-related decrements or difficulties associated with mastering tasks which require such processes. One problem with examining this proposition is that tasks in studies have not been devised because they require such processes but because they were of applied interest. Even if tasks were used which did require such processes, age-related effects may not be found. One reason is that performance may not be sufficiently dependent upon those processes to produce differences in rate of learning. Another reason is that older persons may have compensatory strategies which, in effect, means that they are superior at other aspects of a task that compensate for their handicap in those aspects related to basic processes. Neither of these issues has received sufficient attention in the literature. Salthouse (1989) discussed the possibility that older persons use such compensatory mechanisms to maintain their level of skill at bridge, chess and typing although interpretation of the evidence is not straightforward.

Various studies have demonstrated age-related problems in training. A sustained research programme was carried out by Belbin and her colleagues on problems of training the older worker (Belbin, 1964; Belbin and Belbin, 1972; Newsham, 1969). Some of this work is discussed in detail later. Czaja and Drury (1981) were interested in age-related effects in an industrial inspection task. They used a simulated task which consisted of detecting faulty characters in a set of 74 characters displayed on a slide. They found post-training differences between three groups of persons aged 20–35 years, 36–50 years and 51–65 years. Both search time and classification errors increased with age. A review by Salthouse (1989) mentioned some lesser known studies, including two by Thorndike et al. (1928) concerned with writing and learning a language. In one study young adults (average of 22 years) were found to be faster than middle-aged adults (average of 41 years) in wrong-hand writing after 15 hours practice. The results of a second study, which was concerned with learning Esperanto, were less clearcut. The middle-aged group improved as much as the young group on all measures of language proficiency except one concerned with oral directions. Another age-related training effect, according to a study by

Smith, Kliegl and Baltes (1987), again cited by Salthouse (1989), was that young adults were better at learning a mnemonic skill.

Belbin (1964) described some, by now, famous studies of how training might be adapted to cope with the needs of older trainees. One study was concerned with problems of training letter sorters at the London Postal School. The main problem was that many trainees were not sufficiently competent after training. During the nine months preceding the study, 128 of 533 trainees had failed the training course and, significantly, the failure rate was 27% for those over 40 years in comparison with 18% for the others. The task that had to be learned involved associating the names of streets with their correct postal district in the London area and subsequently sorting letters into a 48-box frame using their postal districts such as "Battersea S.W.11", "foreign" and "W.2". In total the trainee had to know the position of 635 places in London in terms of their geographical location and their corresponding pigeon-holes in the frame. The objective of training was that the trainee was able to sort 500 incompletely addressed cards "at the rate of thirty-three a minute with fewer than fifteen errors".

Problems of training these letter sorters were examined by a mixture of observation of, and discussion with trainees, together with experimental studies and pilot training schemes. One major problem was how trainees could learn to associate the address with the correct postal district. In the traditional training method each trainee was provided with a pack of cards which had an address on one side of each card and its postal district on the reverse side. Thus trainees could refer to these "prompts" when they were unsure of the correct postal district. Belbin noted that this created a memory problem because during practice, typically, the trainee read the card, turned it over, read the prompt, searched for the postal district in the frame, and then put the card in the correct pigeon-hole. Belbin suggested that turning the card over to read the cue on the back interfered with learning the pairing between the address and its location in the frame. Hence by the time the trainee had put the card in its correct pigeon-hole in the frame, the trainee "would forget which place he was putting there". The first solution tried by Belbin was to minimise early errors by heavily prompting the trainee where to put each card (for example coloured card to same coloured box). As might be expected, this was unsuccessful, since it resulted in improved performance but little learning. Eventually, after a series of experiments on different aspects of training, a modified training programme was designed. This involved the use of six "learning" packs of cards which represented a sort of cumulative part training. For example, one pack was concerned with locations on the frame, another pack presented common postal districts whilst another pack covered districts which were easily confused. The final training programme incorporated various other changes such as longer practice sessions, a reduction in so called "extraneous" lectures and an emphasis on enabling the trainee to make a correct decision and act on it. According to Belbin the revised training programme compared favourably with the traditional one. However there was an increase in the failure rate of trainees which Belbin attributed to shortcomings in the training of instructors. It is not possible to disentangle the effects of the different modifications used in the training programme which is a criticism of most applied training studies. Belbin's account is a rich documentation of problems associated with training the older person and how they might be overcome by carefully modified training procedures.

Newsham (1969) summarised recommendations for training the older worker which emerged from Belbin's postal study and other related investigations. These are listed in Table 10.1. Overall, these recommendations emphasise that using what are essentially principles of good training design is even more important for the older trainee. Thus training should proceed cautiously, providing sufficient time to master one part before proceeding to the next and minimising the extent of any "cognitive gymnastics" which are required of the trainee. Newsham (1969) stressed the importance of the older trainee's confidence and attitudes. Generally, the older trainee is less risky in decision-making and may have considerable anxiety associated with retraining. This partly explains the reluctance of older persons to take up retraining, which is not helped by the stereotype that they are more rigid and difficult to train. Newsham (1969) found that a higher proportion of older rather than younger persons left either during training or soon afterwards. (The training study by Bartram, discussed on pp. 362–365, suggested that age was an important determinant of success during training.) However, this trend reverses at some point after training, since it is found that older trainees "survive" longer in a job than younger trainees. Newsham suggested that there were critical periods of adjustment for older trainees which occurred both during and after training, lasting several weeks.

Older people tend to be more cautious, which is why in paced tasks, they opt for accuracy rather than speed. A subsidiary finding of the Jordan and Rabbitt study, discussed earlier, was that the elderly group was generally more accurate than the young group, making fewer errors in responding to complex stimuli. Similarly Belbin and Belbin (1972) described the progress of 50-year-old Mrs Chatton in learning a high speed sewing machine skill whereby "at every stage she showed a

Table 10.1 Problems of learning for the older trainee (Newsham, 1969)

Difficulties increase with age	Suggestions as to how the training could be suitably adapted for the older learner
1. When tasks involve the need for short-term memory	(a) Avoid verbal learning and the need for conscious memorising. This may often be accomplished by making use of "cues" which guide the trainee (b) When possible, use a method which involves learning a task as a whole. If it has to be learned in parts, these parts should be learned in cumulative stages (a, a + b, a + b + c, and so on) (c) Ensure consolidation of learning before passing on to the next task or to the next part of the same task (importance of self-testing and checking)
2. When there is "interference" from other activities or from other learning	(a) Restrict the range of activities covered in the course (b) Employ longer learning sessions than is customary for younger trainees (i.e. not necessarily a longer overall time, but longer periods without interruption) (c) To provide variety, change the method of teaching rather than the content of the course. A change of subject matter may lead to confusion between the subjects
3. When there is need to translate information from one medium to another	(a) Avoid the use of visual aids which necessitate a change of logic or a change in the plane of presentation (b) If simulators or training devices are to be used, then they must be designed to enable learning to be directly related to practice

4. When learning is abstract or unrelated to realities

    (a) Present new knowledge only as a solution to a problem which is already appreciated

5. When there is need to "unlearn" something for which the older learner has a predilection

    (a) Ensure "correct" learning in the first place. This can be accomplished by designing the training around tasks of graduated difficulty

6. When tasks are "paced"

    (a) Allow the older learner to proceed at his own pace
    (b) Allow him to structure his own programme within certain defined limits
    (c) Aim at his beating his own targets rather than those of others

7. As tasks become more complex

    (a) Allow for learning by easy stages of increasing complexity

8. When the trainee lacks confidence

    (a) Use written instructions
    (b) Avoid the use of production material too soon in the course
    (c) Provide longer induction periods. Introduce the trainee very gradually both to new machinery and to new jobs
    (d) Stagger the intake of trainees
    (e) If possible, recruit groups of workmates
    (f) Avoid formal tests
    (g) Don't give formal time limits for the completion of the course

9. When learning becomes mentally passive

    (a) Use an open situation which admits discovery learning
    (b) Employ meaningful material and tasks which are sufficiently challenging to an adult
    (c) Avoid a blackboard and classroom situation or conditions in which trainees may in earlier years have experienced a sense of failure

disposition to pause for extra checks and inspections". The older person's predisposition towards accuracy rather than speed could be of benefit in many jobs. Another point for the training designer to consider is that an older person brings a greater range of both general and specific skills to any training situation. This may either facilitate or hinder the acquisition of new skills.

The training designer therefore has to be aware of the potential problems of the older trainee and design training to overcome these difficulties. It is likely to be an exceptional situation in which this is not possible.

Ability and intelligence

Persons with different abilities will differ in their acquisition of skill to the extent that either the training method or the task requires those abilities. This rather obvious statement follows from the definition and concept of ability which are discussed in detail in Section 7.2. Therefore persons of low verbal ability will not do well if confronted by verbal instructions concerning how to operate a piece of equipment. Also studies carried out by Fleishman and colleagues, described in Section 7.2, have identified the changing ability requirements of some tasks at different stages of training. This information has been used not only to predict differences in the rate of learning for groups varying in the level of required abilities, but also to modify the training programme to take account of these changes in ability requirements.

In learning complex tasks, less able trainees are likely to be disadvantaged by training situations which are unstructured. There are more courses of action available to trainees in performing complex tasks and the less able may be more easily distracted by irrelevant information leading to an inefficient strategy (e.g. Dale, 1958). Some interesting results concerning ability level emerged from a study by Duncan (1971) which investigated the training of a complex fault-finding task. The task involved locating a fault in a chain of components in which the probability and cost of failure of each component varied. Sixty persons were trained and split into six groups which were tested after 6, 58 or 182 days on either the original task or a transfer task which involved a different set of costs and probabilities of failure. The main finding was that whilst retention declined, transfer remained at the same low level. These results were re-examined in terms of high- versus low-ability persons, ability in this case being defined by initial, unaided performance on some fault-finding problems. It emerged that the high-ability group did not deteriorate over the three retention intervals and were better at the transfer task on each occasion in contrast to the low-ability group. Duncan interpreted these results as evidence that the high-ability group learned a general strategy concerning how to solve problems of this type, whilst the low-ability group only learned the specific algorithm for solving the training task and therefore showed poor transfer and decreasing retention.

The notion that there is a strong relationship between general measures of ability, such as intelligence, and the rate of learning was abandoned some years ago (e.g. Woodrow, 1946; Gagné, 1967). Intelligence is not a unitary concept and involves various cognitive activities. Consequently, intelligence is only a useful index of trainability when the task to be mastered imposes similar requirements on a trainee as a conventional intelligence test. From a training perspective, perhaps the most important facet of measured intelligence is the ability to tackle a task within a limited time period.

There is evidence that large differences in IQ (40 points or more) are necessary before clear differences emerge between normals and retardates in learning verbal tasks (Zeaman and House, 1967). Also Clarke (1966), in a survey of the trainability and employability of adult imbeciles (IQ, 20–50), concluded that, with special training programmes, such individuals could be trained to perform many routine perceptual-motor tasks at normal levels of competence. A study by Clarke and Hermelin (1955) demonstrated that it was possible to train imbeciles in the tasks of bicycle pump assembly, cutting insulated wire to an exact length, and soldering four coloured wires to an eight-pin television plug. Training was effective but it took much longer and performance during the initial stages was particularly slow and inaccurate. It has also been found that even with these very low IQ adults, transfer and retention does occur given an appropriately tailored training programme. Clarke (1966) proposed the following principles be used for training adult imbeciles for industrial tasks, some of which are the same as those principles discussed previously for training the older worker.

Use incentives.
Use part-task training, ensuring that parts are trained in the sequences required in the actual task.
Ensure that the correct movements are made early in training, by, for example, guidance.
Space out training sessions.
Overtrain.

Emphasise accuracy rather than speed early in training.
Ensure that the tools and materials for carrying out the task are clearly arranged.

Trainee strategies and styles

The book *A Study of Thinking* by Bruner, Goodnow and Austin (1956) was an important landmark for two reasons. Firstly, it demonstrated the importance of viewing learning as an *active* process rather than the passive one which was the dominant behaviourists' perspective at that time. Secondly, it was found that persons adopted different strategies or styles when given some choice in tackling a task.

Using a concept discovery task, Bruner et al. attempted to externalise

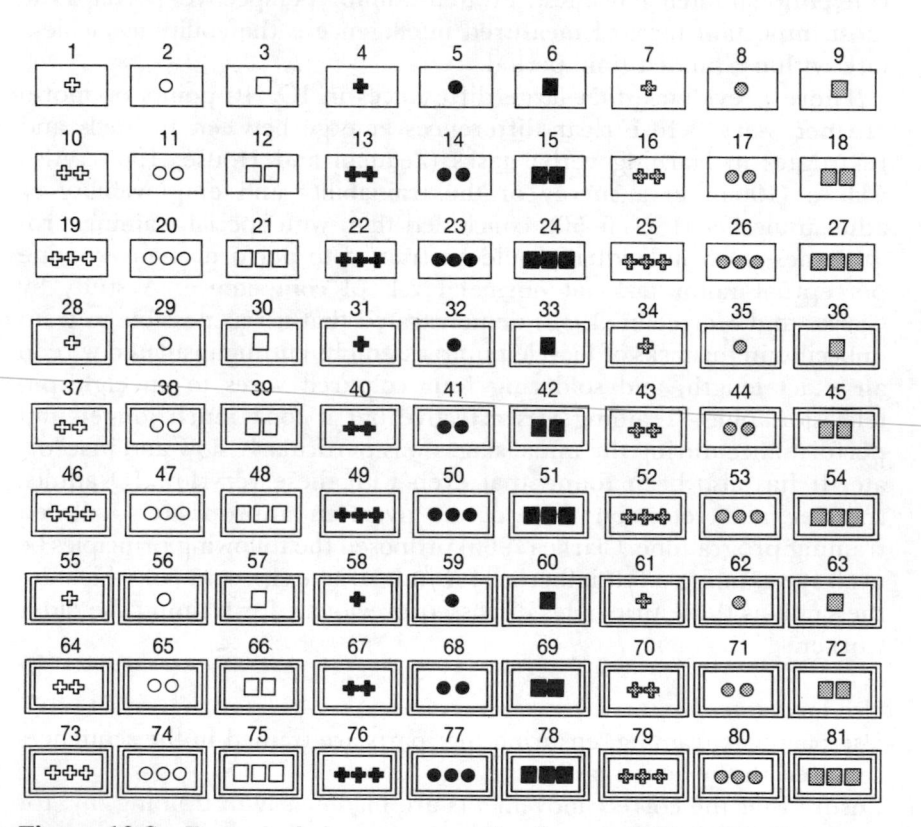

Figure 10.3   Four cards in a concept discovery task (Bruner, Goodnow and Austin, 1956). Open figures are in green, solid figures are in black, and shaded figures are in red.

the person's thinking and reasoning processes. It was termed a "selection" task because the person had to select an item, in this case a card from an array of 81 cards (Figure 10.3). The task involved the person discovering the concept which another person had defined, by selecting cards containing various attributes and being informed whether the card was a positive or negative instance of the concept. The four attributes that could be involved in the concept were number, shape, colour and number of borders, each of which had three possible values. For example consider three cards in Figure 10.3: "one green circle with one border" – card 2; "three red crosses with two borders" – card 49; and "two red crosses with two borders" – card 40. If the concept that the person is attempting to discover is "red crosses with two borders", then the cards 40 and 49 are positive instances of the concept and the card 2 is a negative instance. (In total there are three positive and 78 negative instances for this concept.) The task begins with the person being shown a positive instance of the concept and then having to discover the concept by requesting whether particular cards are positive or negative instances until sufficient information has been collected to state the concept. Bruner et al. recorded the sequence of cards examined en route to discovering the concept. From this information a person's strategy was inferred. Four basic strategies were identified made up of two main types and two subtypes:

1. *Focusing strategies.* The person focused on the attributes and changed them until the concept was found.
   (a) *Conservative focusing.* Here the person took the first positive instance as a focus and then systematically changed one attribute at a time as each card was selected. For example, given that "three green squares with two borders" is a positive instance, the person might decide to test whether the number of shapes is relevant by selecting "one green square with two borders". If this card is a negative instance then the concept must include three shapes. In this way the person need only make as many selections as there are attributes in order to discover the concept.
   (b) *Focus gambling.* This is a more risky strategy in which more than one attribute is changed at a time.
2. *Scanning strategies.* The person tests hypotheses about the concept rather than changing attributes systematically.
   (a) *Simultaneous scanning.* This is the ideal solution which is impossible psychologically. The person has to bear in mind all possible concepts and then eliminate those inconsistent with the first positive instance, and then select the next instance that eliminates

the maximum number of remaining concepts, proceeding in this fashion until only one concept is left.

(b) *Successive scanning.* This is a common strategy where the person adopts an hypothesis and then attempts to "prove" it usually by selecting positive instances. The hypothesis is only revised when a couple of negative instances are encountered. This strategy is inefficient, not only because hypotheses are tested one at a time but also because examining positive instances provides less information than examining negative ones.

The impact of Bruner et al.'s work cannot be overestimated. Even though it had a rather rough ride at the time, it gradually changed not only the nature of the questions asked by research studies, but also how they were investigated. Ironically, the focusing and scanning strategies can even be used to characterise the practice of scientific research, some scientists forming hypotheses and then attempting to substantiate them, others being more content to change variables and examine their effect. Certainly focusing and scanning represent rather different ways of approaching a problem-solving task and more recently Morrison (1985) has provided some evidence that they correlate with quality of performance of a fault-finding task. Because Bruner et al.'s work raised new possibilities, it also raised some researchers' hopes that this approach might offer a handle on individual differences, both in performance and learning. The sort of questions asked were: Are general strategies or styles adopted by different persons in performing or learning a task? Do they have implications for training?

Some research in the 1960s and 1970s was devoted to answering these questions. The simplicity of the notion that different persons have different cognitive styles or strategies which need to be identified, has had, and still does have amongst my students, great appeal. Alas the dividends of this research have been small, and it is not perhaps surprising that the complexity of human psychology cannot be captured adequately by a simple dimension of cognitive style or strategy. Nevertheless, this research did lay the foundations for examining in more detail the qualitative differences between "good" and "poor" learners and readers, a subject which has flourished in the past 10 years (e.g. Bereiter and Scardamelia, 1989).

Messick (1976) listed as many as 19 cognitive styles or strategies. Four well-known ones are:

Reflective–impulsive. This dimension was identified by Kagan (e.g. Kagan, Pearson and Welch, 1966) and refers to the extent to which persons adopt accuracy versus speed in situations which allow a trade-off.

Field dependence–independence. This is probably the most well-known cognitive style, identified by Witkin (1976). It refers to the extent to which a person organises and analyses new information (field-independent) as opposed to a more global, less analytic approach (field-dependent). It is tested by the classic embedded figures test.

Surface versus deep processors. This dimension was identified by Marton and Saljo (1976) from an analysis of what students remembered from text passages and how they reported reading them. A "deep" approach which is desirable "goes beyond" the words of the text and attempts to understand fully the intention and implications of the material. A "surface" approach, as its name suggests, fails to do this.

Holist versus serialist. These distinctions were made by Pask (e.g. Pask and Scott, 1972) and are explained below.

The last two distinctions are of particular interest, since they are concerned with *how* persons tackle the task of learning. The surface–deep distinction by Marton and Säljö gave impetus to a body of research in the educational context, summarised by Ramsden (1985). It relates to some of the learning strategies, discussed in Section 10.3, which are aimed at improving the manner in which readers process material, by, for example, providing "orienting tasks" such as answering questions.

Some of Pask's work provides a good illustration of the cognitive style approach (Pask and Scott, 1972; Pask, 1976). Few summaries of Pask's work exist, partly because of the technical complexity of some of the publications (e.g. Pask, 1975), although a useful résumé is given by Holloway (1978). Pask was interested in how persons tackled what he termed a "free learning" situation, which he created for subject matter domains that could be represented by some sort of hierarchical structure. For example, Pask and Scott (1972) devised two domains concerning fictitious Martian creatures: the Clobbits and the Gandlemullers. The Gandlemullers lived in the Martian swampland and had three subspecies: the Gandlers, the Gandleplongers and the Plongers, that were further subdivided as illustrated in Figure 10.4. A person learned about this fictitious zoological taxonomy by requesting information from a set of cards. On the front of each card was specified the type of information which could be found on the reverse (such as a picture of what a subspecies looked like; its habitat; its physical characteristics). Analysis of how persons set about learning this sort of task, and the protocols which they produced when they were asked to "teachback" what they had learned, led Pask to make his now famous distinction between holists and serialists. Holists are more interested in discovering the overall structure of the subject matter and are "global" in their

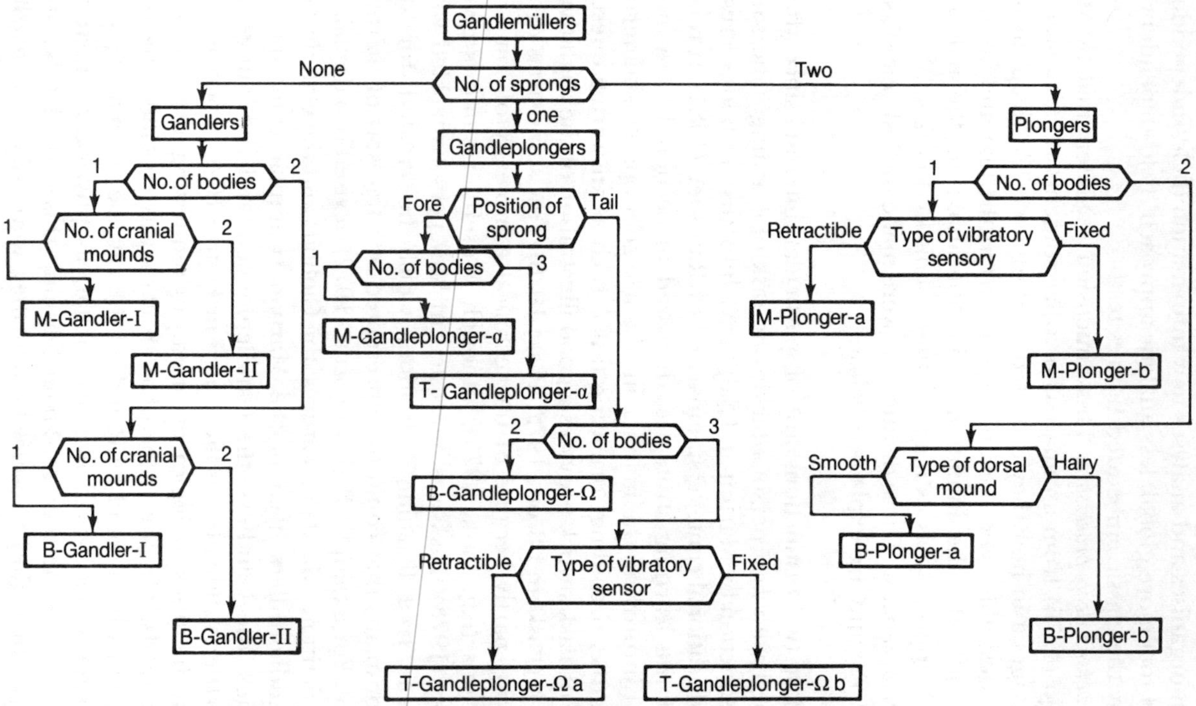

Figure 10.4 The Gandlemuller taxonomy (Pask and Scott, 1972).

approach to learning. In contrast, serialists proceed in a "step by step" fashion, accumulating a lot of detailed information in a systematic fashion, and consolidating knowledge in one area before proceeding to the next. Thus, with respect to the Gandlemullers, the holists had a good understanding of the structure and relationships between subspecies, whereas the serialists tended to focus on detail and speculate less about the relationships between the subspecies. Serialists tended to fail to see the "wood from the trees" because of the amount of information collected, whereas holists failed to recall some of the detail accurately. Pask interpreted these differences in terms of the degree of uncertainty that different persons are comfortable with whilst learning a task; serialists are only able to tolerate a low level of uncertainty, which accounts for their proceeding in a step-by-step fashion. However, as Holloway (1978) pointed out, there are different types of uncertainty: uncertainty about structure and uncertainty about detail. It may be that holists are unable to tolerate uncertainty about the structure of a domain in contrast to serialists who can. The converse applies to uncertainty about the detail of a domain.

Studies by Pask (e.g. Pask, 1975) investigated the learning of other tasks, whose structure could also be represented by relationships between nodes, termed an "entailment structure". There were more restrictions concerning how the learner could proceed than in the "free learning" situation. The learner's progress was monitored by which "nodes" in these structures were interrogated and the type of information requested. Multiple-choice tests were also given during learning to identify the current level of understanding of parts of the domain. Serialists tended to aim to master material concerning adjacent nodes in contrast to holists who were more wide-ranging in their approach.

These ideas have immense appeal, although the reliability, generalisability and potency of these effects have not been demonstrated sufficiently to make them an everyday feature of training design. A prerequisite of the holist–serialist distinction is that the subject matter can be structured and segmented in some hierarchical fashion such as a kinds-of, or parts-of hierarchy. One important finding of Pask's work from a training perspective is that there were drawbacks with both cognitive styles in terms of the extent to which the subject matter was mastered. The holist fails to master sufficient detail, whereas the serialist does not learn the overall structure of the material. Both types of learner therefore require the intervention of the trainer or training system to ensure that full mastery is accomplished.

Aptitude Treatment Interaction (ATI)

In the preceding sections we have discussed various individual differences which affect the nature and rate of learning. Ideally, training should be designed to accommodate these individual differences between trainees. The ultimate consequence of this is that different training methods may be necessary for different trainees. In this way, training can be adapted to individual differences and each trainee can experience the optimal training programme. This approach was advocated enthusiastically by Cronbach (1967), which began the search for what were known as Aptitude Treatment Interaction (ATI) effects. ATI research is reviewed by Cronbach and Snow (1969), whilst Cronbach and Snow (1977) have provided a comprehensive review of all aspects of this research.

What is meant by the term aptitude treatment interaction? Both aptitude and treatment were defined broadly by Cronbach and Snow (1977) as follows:

> ... 'aptitude' is here defined as any characteristic of a person that forecasts his probability of success under a given treatment (p. 6).

> We also give 'treatment' a broad meaning. It covers any manipulable variable. Instructional studies vary the pace, method, or style of instruction. Classroom environments and teacher characteristics are also treatment variables of interest. Even where a characteristic cannot be manipulated (e.g. teacher sex), the student's experience can be manipulated by an assignment policy (p. 6).

ATI can be explained by reference to Figure 10.5. In Figure 10.5a, there is no interaction between the training treatment and the trainee's characteristics. Those versed in analysis of variance will recognise this because the two lines in the graph are parallel. What this means is that, irrespective of the level of any trainee's aptitude/characteristic, training treatment A is always superior to training treatment B. Consequently, all trainees should be given treatment A. It should be noted that outcome is defined in any way which is significant to the aim of training which includes measurement of learning, costs in the widest sense, and any aggregation of the two. In Figure 10.5b there is one type of ATI effect, known as a disordinal interaction. (Disordinal interaction indicates that the lines cross over rather than just diverging or converging which is an ordinal interaction.) In this situation, training treatment A is better for some trainees, whilst training treatment B is better for others. This is represented in Figure 10.5b by the dotted cut-off line which passes through the intersection of the lines of the graph. Trainees with levels of

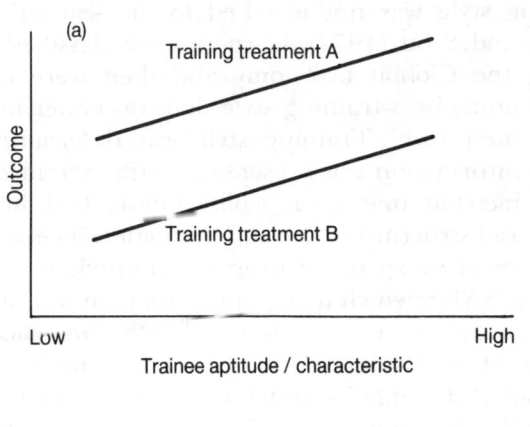

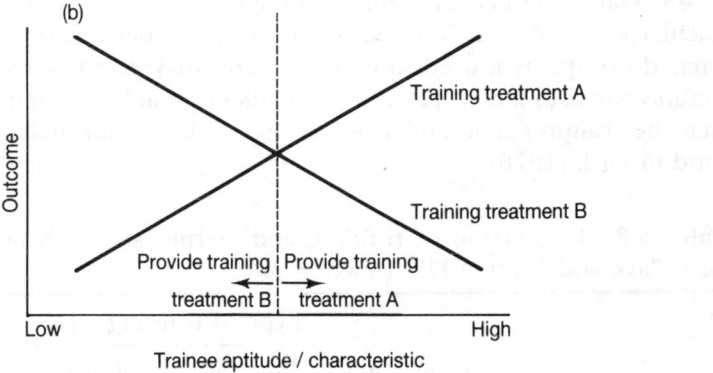

Figure 10.5 Relationships between training treatments and trainee aptitudes/characteristics.

the aptitude/characteristic which are lower than the cut-off level should receive training treatment B, whereas those with higher levels should receive training treatment A. Consequently, individual differences in aptitude are being used to determine which "type" of training a trainee should experience.

Anxiety is one aptitude which has been found to interact with different training treatments (Sieber, O'Neil and Tobias, 1977; Tobias, 1977). Generally, highly anxious trainees perform better when the training is highly organised and structured. However, evaluation itself depends upon whether trainees are subject to test anxiety and if they are, then performance is depressed. In the preceding section, Pask's distinction between holists and serialists was discussed (Pask, 1976; Pask and Scott, 1972). This work also identified an ATI effect, since learning suffered if training style was not matched to the learner's style. In the study by Pask and Scott (1972), learners were classified as holists or serialists using the Clobbit taxonomy and then were taught the Gandlemuller taxonomy by a training style that was either matched or mismatched with their own. Training style was determined by the sequence in which information was presented, so that serialists received initially low-level facts in one area, whilst holists had information concerning the overall structure of the subject matter. There was also a difference in the type of background information provided in the holist and serialist training styles, which makes interpretation of the results of this study problematic. However it was found that the "matched" groups (i.e. serialist/serialist and holist/holist) were better than the "mismatched" groups (i.e. serialist/holist and holist/serialist) not only in their test results for the Gandlemuller taxonomy but also when they were asked to "teachback" what they had learned to the experimenter. The mismatched groups produced more errors and their test results were considerably worse (Table 10.2). Further evidence that learning deteriorates when the training style and the learner's style are mismatched can be found in Pask (1976).

Table 10.2 Interaction of training and learner styles on average test score (Pask and Scott, 1972) (max. = 30)

Type of learner style	Type of training style	
	Serialist	Holist
Serialist	29	8.5
Holist	19	30

One of the main problems with ATI effects is their inconsistency. Some studies find an ATI effect whilst others do not, and generally there has been difficulty in replicating results, as noted by Cronbach and Snow (1977). These authors are widely quoted in their statement that no ATI effects "are so well confirmed that they can be used directly as guides to instruction". However, the overall conclusions of their massive review were critical of the research carried out rather than the ATI approach itself, about which they remained optimistic. However, there are no signs today that ATI research, as traditionally conceived, is improving its record and unfortunately, despite considerable research, the overall findings have been disappointing. Carroll (1967) anticipated this state of affairs in his comments on Cronbach's (1967) conference paper by stating:

... I predict that the study of instructional methods and individual differences is going to be extremely difficult and frustrating, even if it is "most interesting" psychologically. Cronbach has already pointed to the inconsistency and inconclusiveness of the available research literature. It is, then, possible that research will never be able to come up with a sufficiently solid set of conclusions to justify being adopted in educational practice. Or, it may turn out that even though differentiation of instructional method is possible in an actuarial sense, the net gains are not of impressive magnitude. In many cases, the cost of differentiating instruction may be too high to suit the practical school administrator, particularly if it involves elaborate and expensive equipment or extensive teacher retraining. "Reality teaching" in this field may be painful (p. 41).

10.3 LEARNING STRATEGIES

A trainee uses various cognitive strategies to learn the content of a training programme. Cognitive strategies which facilitate learning and retention are termed "learning strategies". Trainees vary in the extent to which they use these strategies and if they do, how efficiently they deploy them. Is it not possible to identify these learning strategies and either train or encourage trainees to use them? This question was posed in the 1970s and generated much excitement, since traditional training and education programmes had ignored such issues. Arguments were made that the *processes* of learning had received little attention in comparison with the *products* of learning and yet *how* the trainee goes about learning, determines the success or not of training. Evidence in support of this proposition comes from a vast number of experimental studies which demonstrated that learning and retention could be improved dramatically when the learner organised and elaborated new information rather than being a passive recipient. For example, the use of mnemonic techniques has a powerful effect on the retention of factual information. This sort of evidence gave rise to some over-optimistic hopes that training in effective learning strategies would enable students or trainees to get more from poorly designed education or training programmes. Some imagined that after being equipped with effective learning strategies, trainees might operate somewhat like vacuum cleaners in picking up new skills and knowledge. Not surprisingly, such unrealistic hopes were disappointed, although some progress was made in developing practical interventions designed to improve learning strategies for a certain type of task, namely, reading and understanding text.

The origins of the learning strategy movement can be traced back to the notion of study skills. Robinson (1946) developed what was known as the SQ3R approach which was intended to improve the understanding and retention of ideas in text passages. It was recommended that the student should: *survey the content of a chapter to identify the main areas; develop *questions which the text might answer; and then *read the material whilst attempting to answer these questions. The last two Rs in SQ3R refer to *recalling what has been read and then *reviewing it. A more recent version of this study technique is the PQ4R method developed by Thomas and Robinson (1972). The stages in this method are *preview, *questions, *read, *reflect, *recite and *review. The main difference between PQ4R and the SQ3R method is the extra R concerned with reflection. In reflecting, the learner is encouraged to generate examples, whilst reading, in order to relate new information to previous knowledge. There is considerable experimental evidence to justify the use of the headings employed by these study skill techniques.

Learning strategies and orienting tasks

It is important to clarify the nature of learning strategies and their implications for training. One of the most penetrating accounts of learning strategies is provided by Rigney (1978). Rigney observed that the traditional approach to training has been to provide training content and hope that the appropriate cognitive (i.e. learning) strategies will be generated by the trainee. Rigney provided the following definition of cognitive strategy:

> Cognitive [i.e. learning] strategy will be used to signify operations and procedures that the student may use to acquire, retain, and retrieve different kinds of knowledge and performance. These operations and procedures may be cognitive information processing, as in mental imagery, or may be cognitively controlled, as in skimming through a textbook to identify major points. Cognitive strategies involve representational capabilities of the student (reading, imagery, speech, writing, and drawing), selectional capabilities (attention and intention) and self-directional capabilities (self-programming and self-monitoring) (Rigney, 1978, p. 165; square parentheses added).

Skilled or expert learners share the same general characteristics of experts in other domains. They are able to select what to attend to, select appropriate strategies for tackling the training materials or tasks, and monitor and regulate their cognitive processes (e.g. Glaser and Bassok, 1989). Rigney suggested that training should develop appropriate learning strategies by the provision of what he termed "orienting tasks".

As the term suggests, these tasks "orient" the trainee to adopt and develop appropriate strategies for learning the task. The distinction between learning strategies and the orienting tasks that are designed to develop them is an important one. Learning strategies are covert and not open to direct manipulation. They can only be influenced indirectly by the manipulation of what Rigney has labelled "orienting tasks". Thus activities engaged in by the trainee such as summarising, questioning, notetaking, rereading, reviewing and following the instructions of the trainer are examples of orienting tasks designed to nudge the trainee to develop appropriate learning strategies. Therefore the role of the training designer is to select and develop appropriate orienting tasks for different training materials. However, no matter how well conceived the orienting task, the possibility remains that the trainee will deliberately or unintentionally fail to develop an appropriate learning strategy.

Rigney used two dimensions to distinguish how orienting tasks might vary (Table 10.3). The first dimension concerns whether the orienting

Table 10.3 Learning strategies and orienting tasks (adapted from Rigney, 1978)

Nature of learning strategy	Control of orienting task	
	Trainee assigned	Training system assigned
Detached	A	B
Embedded	C	D

task is under the control of either the trainee or the training system (i.e. trainer, automatic device). In the former case the trainee might instruct himself in how to go about the task, which in turn may influence the learning strategy used. Such self-instruction is an orienting task which may or may not be successful. A trainee may be unaware of the learning strategies which he uses, and the orienting tasks which induce these strategies. This state of affairs may be less haphazard if the training system has control over the orienting task, although, again, there is no way of guaranteeing that the trainee will adopt suitable cognitive strategies.

The second dimension of orienting tasks identified by Rigney, concerns whether the learning strategy is independent of the training material (i.e. is "detached") or not (i.e. is "embedded"). The SQ3R and PQ4R study techniques, discussed previously, are orienting tasks in Rigney's terms that are designed to develop "detached" learning strategies. This is because the study techniques can be trained independent of any specific material and, in theory, can be applied to any learning from text. The same philosophy underpins the orienting tasks used in Dansereau's learning strategy training programme which is discussed later in this section. In contrast an orienting task might produce a learning strategy that is "embedded" in the training material and is not separable from it. Hence during training a trainee might be confronted with: questions interspersed in the text that are designed to encourage the information to be processed in a particular manner; instructions to use a mnemonic or some imagery in order to facilitate the encoding and retention of information; and an analogy which pinpoints the similarity between a new principle and one already known. These are all examples of orienting tasks that develop learning strategies which are closely linked to some specific training material, i.e. are "embedded". Another example, in an industrial training situation, is provided by Marshall, Duncan and Baker (1981). They were interested in training operators to diagnose plant failures. In one training condition information concerning various indicators was "withheld" until requested by the trainee. The "orienting task" of requiring trainees to request information enabled the trainer to ensure that the trainees were using the diagnostic rules provided during training and also applying them in the optimal sequence.

Evidence concerning the potential effectiveness of the learning strategy approach to training comes from two sources:

1. Laboratory studies of individual strategies in which certain treatments result in superior learning and/or retention.
2. Training or education programmes which bring together various learning strategies. These applied intervention programmes either train these learning strategies directly or embed them within the training/educational materials.

These two sources of evidence are discussed in the following two sections.

Individual learning strategies

There is a vast literature concerning how learning and retention can be improved by different orienting tasks. This discussion will necessarily be highly selective. Reviews of some of this evidence can be found in Dansereau (1978, 1985), Holley and Dansereau (1984a, b), Jonassen (1988), Weinstein (1978), and Weinstein and Mayer (1986). It has already been pointed out that the term learning strategy was first used in the 1970s. Rothkopf (1970) used the term "mathemagenic" to refer to those activities which literally "gave birth to learning". Also Wittrock (1974) pointed to the importance of "generative" activities during learning in which the learner establishes new relationships and conceptual structures between new information and previous knowledge. Undoubtedly, retention is better when the learner is active in organising and elaborating new information.

The distinction between orienting tasks and learning strategies has already been discussed although it is a distinction which is not observed in much of the literature. Below are some common orienting tasks designed to improve learning strategies, typically for prose materials and relatively straightforward comprehension tasks:

Mnemonics	Analysis of key ideas
Notetaking	Categorising
Paraphrasing	Elaborating
Analogies	Integration and differentiation
Questions	Reviewing
Summarising	Underlining
Images	Instructions
Networking	Rehearsal

These orienting tasks may produce either "detached" or "embedded" learning strategies in Rigney's terms, depending upon how they are used. The same type of orienting task can fulfil different functions depending upon the training situation. Thus embedding questions in text may direct the trainee's attention to important material and therefore have a directional function. Alternatively, questions might be designed to encourage material to be processed in a particular manner (e.g. what are the similarities and differences between materials X and Y?). This has led some writers to categorise orienting tasks in terms of their function. Weinstein and Mayer (1986) defined and contrasted eight categories of learning strategies covering rehearsal, elaboration, organisation, comprehension monitoring and motivation (Table 10.4). However, these distinctions are not clearcut and there is some overlap between categories.

Questions. Questions can be inserted in training text in order to improve how trainees process and remember new information. Reviews have considered the effect of question type, position and frequency (Prosser, 1978; Rickards and Denner, 1978). This literature is complex and difficult to summarise. Generally, it is found that the insertion of relevant questions after some text, improves comprehension and recall

Table 10.4 Eight categories of learning strategies (Weinstein and Mayer, 1986)

1. *Rehearsal strategies for basic learning tasks* – such as repeating the names of items in an ordered list. Common school tasks in this category include remembering the order of the planets from the sun and the order in which Shakespeare introduces the characters in the play *Hamlet*.
2. *Rehearsal strategies for complex learning tasks* – such as copying, underlining or shadowing the material presented in class. Common school tasks in this category include underlining the main events in a story or copying portions of a lesson about the causes of World War I.
3. *Elaboration strategies for basic learning tasks* – such as forming a mental image or sentence relating the items in each pair for a paired-associate list of words. Common school tasks in this category include forming a phrase or sentence relating the name of a state or its major agricultural product, or forming a mental image of a scene described by a poem.
4. *Elaboration strategies for complex tasks* – such as paraphrasing, summarising, or describing how new information relates to existing knowledge. Common school tasks in this category include creating an analogy between the operation of a post office and the operation of a computer, or relating the information presented about the structure of complex molecules to the information presented about the structure of simple molecules.
5. *Organisational strategies for basic learning tasks* – such as grouping or ordering to-be-learned items from a list or a section of prose. Common school tasks in this category include organising foreign vocabulary words into the categories for parts of speech, or creating a chronological listing of the events that led up to the Declaration of Independence.
6. *Organisational strategies for complex tasks* – such as outlining a passage or creating a hierarchy. Common school tasks in this category include outlining assigned chapters in the textbook, or creating a diagram to show the relationship among the stress forces in a structural design.
7. *Comprehension monitoring strategies* – such as checking for comprehension failures. Common school tasks in this category include using self-questioning to check understanding of the material presented in class and using the questions at the beginning of a section to guide one's reading behaviour while studying a textbook.
8. *Affective strategies* – such as being alert and relaxed, to help overcome text anxiety. Common school tasks in this category include reducing external distractions by studying in a quiet place, or using thought stopping to prevent thoughts of doing poorly from directing attention away from the test and towards fear of failure.

of information that is related to these questions. However, the exact nature of this effect and the reasons for it are still a matter of debate.

An alternative to the trainer embedding questions in training materials is to ask or train the trainees to generate their own questions. One of the earliest investigations of whether trainee-generated questions improved recall was a study by Frase and Schwartz (1975). Students were required to recall facts from a passage of text after either generating questions, answering questions generated by a fellow student or studying alone in the conventional manner. It was found that both generating questions and answering questions improved recall, but only of information directly related to the questions. Information not directly related to the questions was no better recalled than when studying alone. Frase and Schwartz also found that increasing the number of questions generated by students from five to 10 did not increase recall significantly, although this finding is likely to depend upon many features such as the nature and amount of the training material.

Wong (1985) reviewed 27 studies which evaluated the effectiveness of trainee-generated questions. Wong found considerable variation in the type of question which the trainee was asked to generate. Questions were aimed at clarification, constructing some high-level understanding, relating new information to prior knowledge, and monitoring one's own comprehension whilst reading or being in a tutorial. Generally all of these types of question were effective at improving scores on measures of both recall and understanding. According to Wong, studies which failed to demonstrate the benefits of self-questioning suffered from one or more methodological problems:

> insufficient training prior to administering posttraining tests, lack of explicitness or direct instruction on generation of questions, and insufficient processing time allowed students to read given passages and to generate questions (Wong, 1985, p. 250).

Analogies. An analogy points to the similarities between two experiences, ideas or devices and is potentially useful therefore in helping us to understand something "new" in terms of something "old". In the last decade, psychologists have suggested that much learning is achieved by analogical reasoning. Rumelhart and Norman (1981) argued that learning by analogy underpinned the development of new schemata. More recently, Collins and Gentner (1987) have argued that analogies can be used to construct a new "mental model" in an unfamiliar domain, although this process is difficult and can result in misconceptions and incorrect inferences. Different analogies can have powerful effects on the way in which people understand and think about new situations.

This is well illustrated by Gentner and Gentner (1983) who found that the pattern of inferences made about problems concerning electricity depended upon which analogy of electricity was adopted: either, what they termed, a "water-flow" or a "moving crowds" analogy.

Science writers have long recognised the power of providing the reader with an analogy to understand a new principle or device. Curtis and Reigeluth (1984) analysed 216 analogies which they discovered in 26 science textbooks. They found that the majority of these analogies were aimed at explaining how something functioned, for example, the principle of feedback being explained in terms of how a thermostat functions. However, the majority of analogies were not accompanied by any explicit description of how the analogy was relevant or should be used. This is risky because, by definition, an analogy is concerned with the *similarities* between something "new" and something "old". The designer intends that the *differences* between them should be ignored, although this may not be so unless the analogy is made explicit.

Like questions, analogies can be provided by the trainer or they can be self-generated by the trainee. The risk is even greater in the latter case that an inappropriate analogy might be generated or the trainee might fail to appreciate the boundaries of the analogy or when it should be used. Providing the trainee with an analogy depends upon some careful analysis of the new task or subject matter having been undertaken. An analogy needs to be selected so that it maximises the similarities between the new and old task, situation, idea, etc.

Mnemonics and associated techniques.   In any training situation, we would all like to be able to learn and remember new information better and more easily. A trainee salesman has to remember different selling techniques; students have to remember information given in lectures; actors have to remember their "lines"; and some military personnel have to be fluent in Morse code or semaphore signals. It is not surprising therefore, that the study of techniques which "improve" memory have a long history. We constantly encounter advertisements promising to provide us with a "super-power" memory which will enable us to perform some amazing memory feat.

Mnemonics and similar techniques attempt to fulfil these dreams. The principles on which they are based are quite straightforward and have been known for many years. William James, as usual, was one of the first to articulate these principles when he said:

> In mental terms, the more other facts a fact is associated with in the mind, the better possession of it our memory retains. Each of its associates

becomes a hook to which it hangs, a means to fish it up by when sunk beneath the surface. Together they form a network of attachments by which it is woven into the entire tissue of our thought. 'The secret of a good memory' is thus the secret of forming diverse and multiple associations with every fact we care to retain. But this forming of associations with a fact, what is it but *thinking about* the fact as much as possible? Briefly, then, of two men with the same outward experiences and the same amount of more native tenacity, the one who thinks over his experiences most, and weaves them into systematic relations with each other, will be the one with the best memory (James, 1908, p. 294).

Associations between facts can take many forms. Perhaps the most simple mnemonic is to associate a new fact with a familiar one which one will never forget. Evidently, when Bertrand Russell visited New York in 1951, he was reported to have told a newsreporter that he could easily remember that his room number at his hotel was 1414 because it had the same digits as the square root of 2.56 (i.e. 1.414)! Clearly the utility of this highly individual mnemonic will depend upon what the person is familiar with and finds meaningful. Alternatively, an association can embellish the item to be remembered by providing some extra mental imagery which is both vivid and points to its important aspects. For example, in order to remember a dog and a bicycle, one could evoke an image of a dog riding a bicycle, which should be quite memorable! Here one is associating two items which have to be remembered through the same imagery. Such imagery might be either provided to the trainee by a photograph, diagram etc. or the trainee might be instructed to produce his or her own imagery.

Other forms of elaboration which can be used to improve learning and retention are discussed by Weinstein (1978) and Mayer (1980). A trainee may relate new information to existing knowledge (integrative elaboration) or compare two new concepts (comparative elaboration). Just adding information which is unusual or interesting is an aid to memory. For example, pretend that you wish to remember that the boiling point of water is influenced by atmospheric pressure. One way would be to remember that it is impossible to get a decent cup of tea at the top of Mount Everest! There atmospheric pressure is low and tea boils at a low temperature; totally unsuitable for making tea.

One of the most powerful principles expounded in any psychological textbook on memory is the effect of organisation. It is perhaps stretching James' notion of association a bit far but essentially organisation is concerned with associating bits of information in some way. Thus it is easier to remember 200 words of poetry than 200 words of prose, which are in turn easier to remember than 200 nonsense syllables (Lyon, 1914). This is because of the differing degrees of meaningfulness and organisation of these materials. Organisation can be imposed on information provided during training either by the trainee or by the trainer, training text etc. Either form of organisation will improve retention dramatically which is confirmed by many laboratory studies in psychology, too numerous to cite. Even putting a list of items to be remembered into a set of categories will facilitate recall. For example a list of hazardous substances could be categorised in terms of their effects or a list of your new employees could be grouped according to their different jobs. Any *meaningful* organisation of items will improve their recall.

One class of techniques, which are orienting tasks in Rigney's terms, bring together many of these principles in order to improve the retention and comprehension of prose materials. They have been labelled "spatial learning strategies" (Holley and Dansereau, 1984a) because each one of these techniques requires the trainee or reader to represent the ideas, concepts etc. diagramatically. As we will discuss later, emphasis on the spatial nature of these learning strategies is somewhat misleading. These techniques vary in terms of both the rules and vocabulary which the reader uses to "analyse" or represent the passage and also the type of material to which they can be applied. Holley and Dansereau (1984b) described one such technique, named "networking", in which readers analysed and mapped out the relationships between the concepts and ideas in a textbook. An example of such a map which was constructed from part of a nursing textbook concerned with the discussion of wounds is given in Figure 10.6.

The relationships identified in this networking technique are: parts-of (p), and types-of (t), relationships in a hierarchy; chains (l) which include lines of reasoning, causal sequences; and clusters which involve characteristics (c), definitions and analogies. Thus in the discussion of wounds there are two parts (p), one of which breaks wounds down into four types (open, closed, accidental and intentional), each of which has its own characteristics (c) (Figure 10.6). Readers can be trained in the use of this networking technique which they can apply to analyse the structure of passages in textbooks. Assuming the relevance of such a technique to some text, it is very unlikely that it would not be of benefit since it forces the reader to organise, summarise and represent the main ideas. However, its benefit will depend on the extent to which it makes the reader attend to and analyse important parts of the materials in a way which would not have occurred spontaneously. Whilst the spatial aspect of such an orienting task may exert some influence on retention, and we know that spatial representation can be powerful, it is impossible, or at least exceedingly difficult, to separate its effect from the cognitive

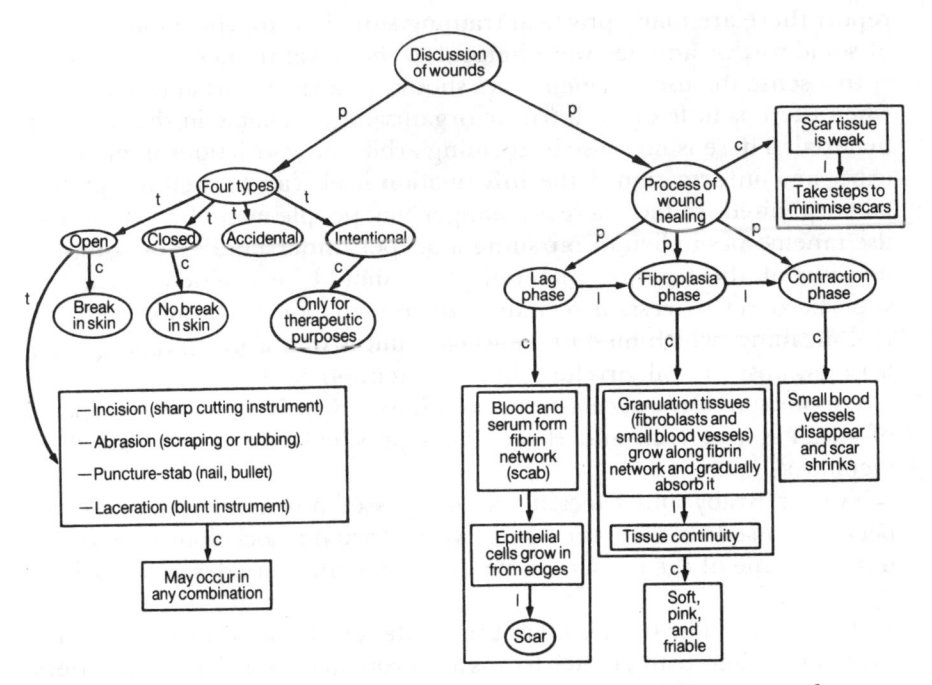

Figure 10.6 Example of the application of networking to a chapter from a nursing textbook (Holley et al., 1979).

activities of categorising, organising and summarising which the technique requires. A number of techniques sharing the same philosophy as "networking" include relational mapping between concepts (Schallert, Ulerick and Tierney, 1984) and mapping ideas in text (Armbruster and Anderson, 1984). The differences between these kinds of techniques lie in the nature of their distinctions and how these distinctions are represented. A problem which is particularly acute for this type of orienting task, is the relevance of these preset distinctions to both the goals of the reader and the nature of the materials.

It is difficult to leave this topic without mentioning some of the traditional and much-loved mnemonic techniques which inevitably creep into most student textbooks. In case some training practitioners are beginning to think that this is rather academic, it is worthwhile trying to rescue our cause by citing a report by Braby and Kincaid (1978) which was concerned with the use of mnemonics in training materials for the US Navy. Their aim was to encourage the use of mnemonics by writers of technical training materials by describing nine types of mnemonic, their potential application and how they should be developed. In their report there are many practical training situations in which mnemonics of some sort or another were helpful to the naval trainee.

In a sense the use of mnemonics should be a last resort and only used when there is little or no intrinsic organisation available in the training material. There is no sense in forming arbitrary associations in order to learn new information if the information itself can be well integrated and organised. In fact there is a danger that people might be tempted to use mnemonics in lieu of pursuing a deeper understanding or comprehension of the training material. This should be avoided, since the superficial yet successful recitation of information is no substitute for real meaning, which might take longer, but is well worth pursuing, not least because it will produce better retention in the long run. Also mnemonics are only necessary in situations in which accuracy and speed of recall is essential, and there is no possibility of using some aide memoire.

Two of Braby and Kincaid's nine types of mnemonic have already been discussed: namely the use of verbal/visual associations and visual images. Some of the remaining types of mnemonic are described below.

1. First letter.   The trainee takes the first letter of each key word that has to be remembered and either forms an acronym or reorders these letters to produce a meaningful word.

Example: A trainee technician has to remember the following shutdown procedure:

(a) *S*top the main motor.
(b) *T*urn off the mains isolator.
(c) *E*nsure mould is fully closed.
(d) *P*urge the machine if necessary.

The word "STEP" might be remembered to cue the steps of this procedure. If the procedure could be executed in any sequence then other words such as "PETS" or "PEST" might be remembered depending upon which one could be more easily associated with this shutdown procedure.

2. Acrostic.   An acrostic is a series of words, usually a sentence, each of which starts with the first letter of the words to be recalled.

Example: Presumably we all remember what "*R*ichard *o*f *Y*ork *g*oes *o*ut *i*n *v*ain" stands for?

3. Alliteration.   The trainee uses the same letter or sound in a series of words in order to remember some key points.

Example: (from Braby and Kincaid). The following navigational rule can be remembered by the mnemonic:

Rule	Mnemonic
Keep the *r*ed buoy	*R*ed
on the *r*ight	*R*ight
when *r*eturning	*R*eturning
from sea	

4. Rhyme. This needs no explanation except to point out that most of us use a rhyme in remembering the number of days in a month.

5. Method of loci. Trainees are encouraged to visualise placing the items to be remembered in different locations (loci), perhaps along a familiar route such as from home to work. Since the locations can be recalled, so can the items.

Example: Trainees have to learn the procedure for inserting tools into an injection moulding machine. They do this by imagining their usual walk from the car park to their office and creating an image at each location which links that location with a step in the procedure. For example, at the security gate the trainee who has to remember "prepare tool for lifting and changing" might imagine a large tool being unwrapped and preventing the gate from opening. If the second step in the procedure is to "attach the tool to a hoist", then the trainee might imagine a large crane-like hook protruding from the door of the reception room! By rehearsing this imaginary walk from the security gate to the canteen with the associated actions, the trainee will be able to remember the procedure. Try it if in doubt!

6. Pattern. (from Braby and Kincaid). Any pattern or regularity in the information can be used to remember it.

Example: Navy recruits who have to remember the Morse code numbers 1–5 should notice that number 1 is one dot and four dashes, number 2 is two dots and three dashes, and so on, up to number 5 which has five dots.

7. Peg word. Various peg word or peg list mnemonic systems exist. One common peg word system uses a rhyme to link peg words and numbers:

One is a bun	Six are sticks
Two is a shoe	Seven is heaven
Three is a tree	Eight is a gate
Four is a door	Nine is a line
Five is a hive	Ten is a hen

One – Bun

1. Take charge of this post and all government property in view.

Sentry on giant bun overlooking post "taking charge" of post

Two – Shoe

2. Walk my post in a military manner, keeping always on the alert, and observing everything that takes place within sight or hearing.

Walking past in military manner wearing well shined shoes

Three – Tree

3. Report all violations of orders I am instructed to enforce

George Washington chopping down cherry tree and then reporting "violation" to his father.

Four – Door

4. Repeat all calls more distant from the (guard house) quaterdeck than my own.

Sentry repeating call from guard house with door open.

Five – Hive

5. Quit my post only when properly relieved.

New sentry relieving old sentry who is being chased by bees from hive.

Six – Sticks

6. Receive, obey and pass on to the sentry who relieves me, all orders from the commanding officer, command duty officer, officer of the day, officers of the deck, and officers and petty officers of the watch only.

New sentry being given orders (on scrolls that look like sticks) from the sentry relieving him.

Seven – Heaven

7. Talk to no one except in line of duty.

Silent angel/sentry

Eight – Gate

8. Give the alarm in case of fire or disorder.

Sentry giving alarm with open gate behind him.

Nine – Line

9. Call the (corporal of the guard) officer of the deck in any case not covered by instructions.

Sentry calling officer of the deck.

Ten – Men

10. Salute all officers and all colors and standards not cased.

Men saluting officer.

Figure 10.7 Examples of the use of peg-word mnemonics (from Braby and Kincaid, 1978).

The rhyme is learned and each of the items to be remembered is "hooked" onto a peg word, for example, by forming a strong image between the item and the peg word.

Example: (from Braby and Kincaid). Naval recruits have to remember the duties of a sentry. How some of these duties are "hooked" onto the peg word in an imaginative manner are illustrated in Figure 10.7.

Learning strategy training programmes

The common aim of learning strategy training programmes is to improve *how* trainees learn. However, they vary enormously in terms of their specific objectives, training methods, theoretical basis, skills taught and the type of evaluation carried out. For a full discussion of these issues the reader should consult a useful review of four programmes by Campione and Armbruster (1985). Most learning strategy training programmes are restricted to the acquisition of information from text. They all raise the same fundamental training and transfer issues which are discussed in Chapters 2 and 3. What is the expertise of skilled learners? To what extent is this expertise domain-dependent? How can this expertise be taught in order to maximise its transfer potential? In this section Dansereau's learning strategy training programme, which was one of the first to be developed and evaluated, will be discussed (Dansereau, 1978; Dansereau et al., 1979; Dansereau, 1985). Its philosophy is similar to Weinstein's elaboration training programme (Weinstein, 1978; Weinstein and Underwood, 1985) in that learning strategies are taught in a "detached" fashion (in Rigney's terms) by a training programme devoted exclusively to teaching them.

Much of Dansereau's work is published in technical reports and a good summary is available in Dansereau (1985). Learning strategies are divided into two types: *primary* strategies which operate directly on the materials to be remembered and *support* strategies which maintain the trainee's concentration, mood etc., which are prerequisites for learning (Figure 10.8). The primary strategies are similar to those advocated by the SQ3R study technique (p. 410), although Dansereau argued that the problem with SQ3R is that no training is given in how to develop and implement these strategies. As can be seen from Figure 10.8, primary strategies are either concerned with comprehension/retention or retrieval/utilisation. Both of these primary strategies involve the trainee proceeding through five steps: *u*nderstanding the text, *r*ecalling the information, *d*igesting it, *e*xpanding upon it and finally *r*eviewing misconceptions about it. These five stages when linked with one of the

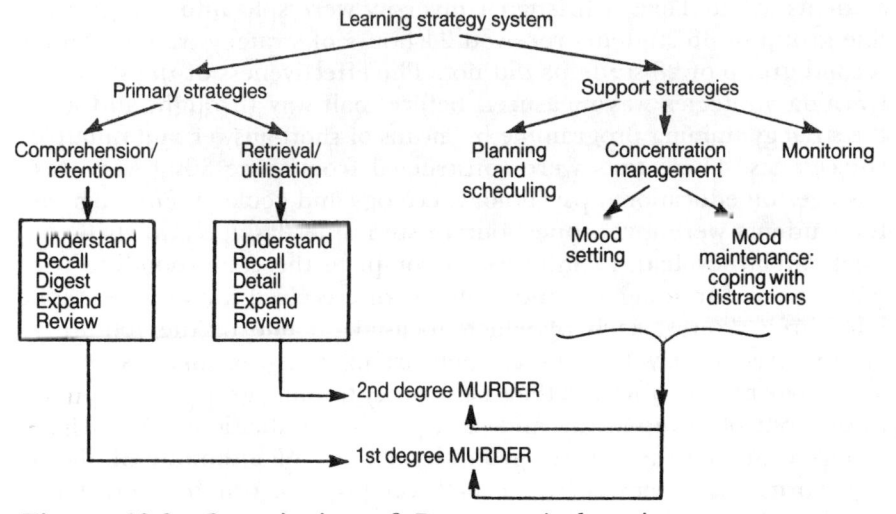

Figure 10.8 Organisation of Dansereau's learning strategy system (Dansereau, 1985).

secondary strategies concerned with setting the *m*ood give rise to the acronym MURDER. First degree MURDER represents the comprehension/retention strategies and second degree MURDER the retrieval/utilisation strategies. Dansereau (1985) detailed the following three substrategies which were used in the recall stage of first degree MURDER:

1. *Paraphrase/imagery.* Trainees are involved in summarising the text and developing mental images associated with the ideas and concepts in it.
2. *Networking.* Trainees are taught how to represent the organisation of text using a set of relationships as described and discussed previously (pp. 418–419).
3. *Analysis of key concepts.* This activity involves defining and identifying important concepts in the text and inter-relationships between them. It complements the networking activities.

The support strategies are a reminder that irrespective of how good training might be, it will be doomed to failure unless the trainee is in the correct frame of mind, is motivated, is concentrating, and is planning and monitoring his or her learning activities. Various techniques are used for these purposes.

One evaluation of the first degree MURDER learning strategy training programme was reported by Dansereau et al. (1979). Undergraduate students at the Texas Christian University were split into two groups: one group of 38 students received 24 hours of strategy training and a second group of 28 students did not. The effectiveness of the students' learning strategies was measured before, half-way through, and after the strategy training programme by means of short-answer and multiple-choice tests. These tests were constructed from three 3000 word text passages on educational psychology, ecology and geology. For each test the students were given one hour to study the passage and then one week later they had 45 minutes to complete the corresponding test. After the mid-training test, the students who received training were split into three groups, each of which focused on one of the following: paraphrase/imagery techniques, networking and the analysis of key ideas. The results indicated that the strategy training group was superior to the control group at the mid- and post-test evaluations. Overall this group outscored the control group by about 20% although all of this superiority was achieved by the half-way point of training and it was mostly reflected in better short answers. Comparison of the three training subgroups which received different strategies in the second half of training, revealed that: networking was the best strategy and improved scores from mid-test to post-test; analysis of key ideas had no effect; and paraphrase/imagery had a slightly negative effect. In such an applied study it is not possible to disentangle the reasons for these effects. Presumably, if all students in the training group had been taught networking in the second half of training then the overall score of the training group would have improved from mid- to post-test. A supplementary finding of the study was that students who received strategy training reported a greater improvement in their attitudes and study habits than another group of students which did not receive such training.

Dansereau (1985) concluded that this, and a second similar evaluation study, pointed to the benefits of learning strategy training for text-processing tasks. This conclusion was also supported by studies which have demonstrated the effectiveness of individual strategies. The improvements in learning found in Dansereau's evaluation studies occurred despite the fact that the tests were not specifically designed to measure the contribution of the different strategies which had been trained. More microscopic evaluation studies would improve our understanding of the relative contributions of the different primary and secondary learning strategies. Further questions also need to be addressed. To what extent are some of these learning strategies normally adopted by the better trainees? How do these strategies vary both with the type of subject matter and the experience of different trainees? Dansereau (1985) acknowledged the need for more fine-grained work in this area. He also raised two other basic questions concerned with the transfer and retention of learning strategies. The intention of such a learning strategy training programme is that trainees will apply these learning strategies in similar training situations. Discussion of the transfer issue in Chapter 3 of this book suggests that positive transfer, particularly of cognitive skills, often does not take place even when it is expected to do so. One reason is that trainees find it difficult to judge when certain skills are applicable and how they should be adapted to a new situation. Dansereau indicated that his students had similar difficulties in adapting their learning strategies to different types of text. This suggests that it may be more profitable to try and identify these learning strategies and train each of them in a more embedded fashion. Finally, as with most cognitive skills, there is little evidence about how well learning strategies are retained following long periods of no practice.

Brown and Palincsar's reciprocal teaching

A much quoted recent approach to the training of reading comprehension skills has been developed by Brown and Palincsar (1989), and Palincsar and Brown (1984), named "reciprocal teaching". It is of interest because it not only uses some learning strategies, but also brings together many principles of training, including more contemporary ones, into an approach which the developers claim is "more than the sum of the parts". Whilst one trend has been to analyse the cognitive processes involved in learning in finer and finer detail, this approach seems to buck this trend, preferring not to decompose training into a set of different activities and examine the effect of each. Some impressive evidence is provided that reciprocal teaching can produce considerable benefits, even for poor readers, and that its effects generalise and are sustained over periods of, in some cases, at least six months. Useful reviews of reciprocal teaching are provided by Collins, Brown and Newman (1989) and Glaser and Bassok (1989).

Brown and Palincsar (1989) explained reciprocal teaching as follows:

> Reciprocal teaching takes place in a cooperative learning group that features guided practice in applying simple concrete strategies to the task of text comprehension. ... An adult teacher and a group of students take turns leading a discussion on the contents of a section of text that they are jointly attempting to understand. The discussions are free ranging, but four strategic activities must be practiced routinely: *questioning, clarifying,*

summarizing, and predicting. The dialogue leader begins the discussion by asking a question on the main content and ends by summarizing the gist. If there is disagreement, the group rereads and discusses potential candidates for question and summary statements until they reach consensus. Summarizing provides a means by which the group can monitor its progress, noting points of agreement and disagreement. Particularly valuable is the fact that summarizing at the end of a period of discussion helps students establish where they are in preparation for tackling a new segment of text. Attempts to clarify any comprehension problems that might arise are also an integral part of the discussions. And, finally, the leader asks for predictions about future content. Throughout, the adult teacher provides guidance and feedback tailored to the needs of the current discussion leader and his or her respondents (p. 413).

Reciprocal teaching has many features and from a training perspective some of its important ones are:

1. It trains students in the use of four learning strategies which are embedded within the learning task, that of reading comprehension. These strategies, which are directed toward comprehension monitoring, are questioning, clarifying, summarising and predicting (i.e. anticipating the next part of the text). The first three of these are similar to traditional learning strategies discussed previously. However unlike the learning strategy training programme by Dansereau et al. (1979), these are not trained separately from the learning task. Brown and Palincsar put great emphasis on the fact that these strategies are being taught within a goal-directed activity and context, that of understanding a particular piece of text.

2. The teacher models the use of these strategies. The students observe the teacher and can also ask questions about the teacher's questions etc. Gradually, as the students become more confident and competent to use these strategies, the teacher takes less of the lead and less of a modelling role and adopts more of a monitoring role of the group's activities.

3. The teacher provides individual students with feedback concerning their strategies and suggests how they might be improved.

4. Reciprocal teaching takes place within a cooperative group situation which provides advice, encouragement and support for the individual.

5. Students not only practise their own strategies but they learn to evaluate those of others. Collins et al. (1989) suggested that this forces them to make explicit what they consider to be the qualities of good strategies (e.g. questioning, summarising), which not only helps the development of their own skill, but enables it to transfer more freely to other contexts.

Brown and Palincsar (1989) summarised the findings of some of their studies concerned with the use of reciprocal teaching. Some notable features of the studies were: reciprocal teaching was used in an applied setting with students; the teaching was usually spread across a four-week programme; students' progress was measured by multiple indicators including qualitative changes in the group's discussions, immediate post-training tests of the retention of discussed text and also novel text, and long-term retention and transfer of reading comprehension. Brown and Palincsar reported remarkable improvements which, on average, ranged from 30% to 40% correct at the beginning of the training to 70%–80% correct after four to 15 days of the training programme. In this sort of research, as discussed in previous chapters, it is always difficult to identify what to evaluate the effect of training against. Palincsar and Brown (1984) used a variety of control groups; one being tested in the same manner but having no training, and another receiving training from the teacher who guided the student to the answers in the text. The superiority of the learning scores for the group receiving reciprocal teaching was considerable both during and after training. In a more recent study (Brown et al., work in progress) two more stringent control groups were used: in one, the teacher modelled how to use the four

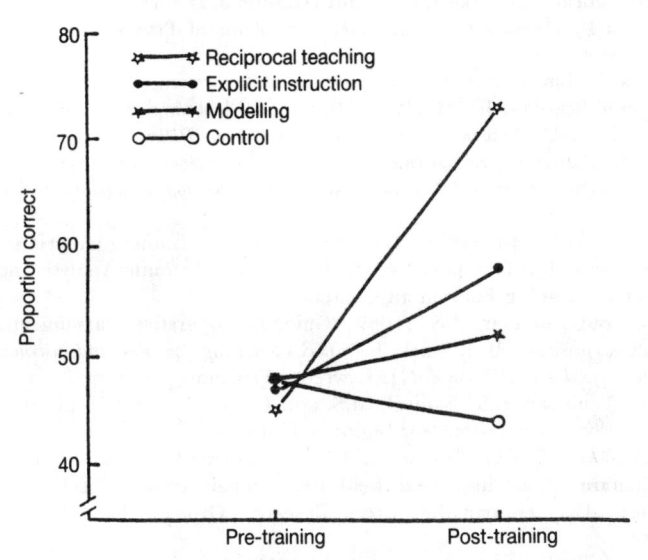

Figure 10.9 The effect of different approaches to training reading comprehension in three groups of matched junior high school students (from Brown et al., work in progress, cited by Brown and Palincsar, 1989).

learning strategies (i.e. only one part of reciprocal teaching) and in another, the teacher discussed the learning strategies and then the students practised using them in pencil and paper exercises (termed explicit instruction). The results are represented in Figure 10.9. The improvement in reading comprehension for the students trained in reciprocal teaching was significantly more than that of the two control groups which received some training. Another control group which had no training was worst of all.

Brown and Palincsar, in their final assessment of what reciprocal teaching has accomplished and what remains to be achieved, confessed that little is known about *how* these skills are acquired. Also they suggested that in the future more complex comprehension tasks should be used in conjunction with longitudinal studies which assessed qualitative developments in this skill.

REFERENCES

Armbruster, B.B. and Anderson, T.H. (1984). Mapping: Representing informative text diagramatically. In Holley, C.D. and Dansereau, D.F. (Eds) (op.cit.).

Belbin, E. (1964). *Training the adult worker*. Problems of Progress in Industry No. 15. London: HMSO.

Belbin, E. and Belbin, R.M. (1972). *Problems in adult retraining*. London: Heinemann.

Bereiter, C. and Scardamelia, M. (1989). Intentional learning as a goal of instruction. In Resnick, L.B. (Ed.) *Knowing, learning and instruction. Essays in honor of Robert Glaser*. Hillsdale, NJ: Lawrence Erlbaum.

Birren, J.E. and Schaie, W. (1985). *Handbook of the psychology of ageing*. 2nd edition. New York: Van Nostrand.

Braby, R. and Kincaid, J.P. (1978). Use of mnemonics in training materials: A guide for technical writers. TAEG Report No 60. Orlando, FL: Training Analysis and Evaluation Group, Naval Training Equipment Center.

Brown, A.L. and Palincsar, A.S. (1989). Guided, cooperative learning and individual knowledge acquisition. In Resnick, L.B. (Ed.) *Knowing, learning and instruction. Essays in honor of Robert Glaser*. Hillsdale, NJ: Lawrence Erlbaum.

Brown, A.L., Palincsar, A.S., Samsel, M.S. and Dunn, D. (work in progress). Bringing meaning to text. Early lessons for high-risk first graders.

Brown, G.H., Zaynor, W.C., Bernstein, A.J. and Shoemaker, H.A. (1959). Development and evaluation of an improved field radio repair course. Technical Report 58. Washington, DC: Human Resources Research Office, The George Washington University.

Bruner, J.S., Goodnow, J.J. and Austin, G.A. (1956). *A study of thinking*. New York: Wiley.

Campione, J.C. and Armbruster, B.B. (1985). Acquiring information from texts: An analysis of four approaches. In Segal, J.W., Chipman, S.F. and Glaser, R. *Thinking and learning skills, Volume 1, Relating instruction to research*. Hillsdale, NJ: Lawrence Erlbaum.

Caro, P.W. (1973). Aircraft simulators and pilot training. *Human Factors*, **15**, 502–509.

Carroll, J.B. (1967). Instructional methods and individual differences. In Gagné, R.M. (Ed.) (op.cit.).

Clarke, A.D.B. (1966). *Recent advances in the study of subnormality*. London: National Association for Mental Health.

Clarke, A.D.B. and Hermelin, B.F. (1955). Adult imbeciles: Their abilities and trainability. *Lancet*, **2**, 337–339.

Collins, A., Brown, J.S. and Newman, S.E. (1989). Cognitive apprenticeship: Teaching the crafts of reading, writing, and mathematics. In Resnick, L.B. (Ed.) *Knowing, learning and instruction. Essays in honor of Robert Glaser*. Hillsdale, NJ: Lawrence Erlbaum.

Collins, A. and Gentner, D. (1987). How people construct mental models. In Holland, D. and Quinn, N. (Eds) *Cultural models in language and thought*. New York: Cambridge University Press.

Cronbach, L.J. (1957). The two disciplines of scientific psychology. *American Psychologist*, **12**, 671–684.

Cronbach, L.J. (1967). How can instruction be adapted to individual differences? In Gagné, R.M. (Ed.) *Learning and individual differences*. Ohio: Merrill.

Cronbach, L.J. and Snow, R. (1969). Individual differences in learning ability as a function of instructional variables. Unpublished report. Stanford: School of Education, Stanford University.

Cronbach, L.J. and Snow, R.E. (1977). *Aptitudes and instructional methods. A handbook for research on interactions*. New York: Wiley.

Crossman, E.R.F.W. and Szafran, J. (1956). Changes with age in the speed of information intake and discrimination. *Experimentia Supplement*, **4**, 128–135.

Curtis, R.V. and Reigeluth, C.M. (1984). The use of analogies in written text. *Instructional Science*, **13**, 99–117.

Czaja, S.J. and Drury, C.G. (1981). Ageing and pretraining in industrial inspection. *Human Factors*, **23**, 485–494.

Dale, H.C.A. (1958). Fault-finding in electronic equipment. *Ergonomics*, **1**, 356–385.

Dansereau, D.F. (1978). The development of a learning strategy curriculum. In O'Neil, H.F. Jr (Ed.) *Learning strategies*. New York: Academic Press.

Dansereau, D.F. (1985). Learning strategy research. In Segal, J.W., Chipman, S.F. and Glaser, R. (Eds) *Thinking and learning skills, Volume 1: Relating instruction to research*. Hillsdale, NJ: Lawrence Erlbaum.

Dansereau, D.F., Collins, K.W., McDonald, B.A., Holley, C.D., Garland, J., Dickhoff, G. and Evans, S.H. (1979). Development and evaluation of a learning strategy training program. *Journal of Educational Psychology*, **71**, 64–73.

Duncan, K.D. (1971). Long-term retention and transfer of an industrial search skill. *British Journal of Psychology*, **62**, 439–448.

Duncan, K.D. and Gray, M.J. (1975). Functional context training. A review and an application to a refinery control task. *Le Travail Humain*, **38**, 81–96.

Frase, L.T. and Schwartz, B.J. (1975). Effect of question production and answering on prose recall. *Journal of Educational Psychology*, **67**, 628–635.

Gagné, R.M. (1967). *Learning and individual differences*. Ohio: Merrill.

Gentner, D. and Gentner, D.R. (1983). Flowing waters or teeming crowds: Mental models of electricity. In Gentner, D. and Stevens, A.L. (Eds) *Mental models*. Hillsdale, NJ: Lawrence Erlbaum.

Glaser, R. and Bassok, M. (1989). Learning theory and the study of instruction. *Annual Review of Psychology*, **3**, 631–666.

Holley, C.D. and Dansereau, D.F. (Eds) (1984a). *Spatial learning strategies: Techniques, applications, and related issues*. New York: Academic Press.

Holley, C.D. and Dansereau, D.F. (1984b). Networking: The technique and the empirical evidence. In Holley, C.D. and Dansereau, D.F. (Eds) (op.cit.).

Holley, C.D., Dansereau, D.F., McDonald, B.A., Garland, J.C. and Collins, K.W. (1979). Evaluation of a hierarchical mapping technique as an aid to prose processing. *Contemporary Educational Psychology*, **4**, 227–237.

Holloway, C. (1978). Learning and Instruction. Open University, Cognitive Psychology, Block 4, Units 22–23. Milton Keynes: Open University.

James, W. (1908). *Psychology*. Holt.

Jonassen, D.H. (Ed.) (1988). *Instructional designs for microcomputer courseware*. Hillsdale, NJ: Lawrence Erlbaum.

Jordan, T.C. and Rabbitt, P.M.A. (1977). Response times to stimuli of increasing complexity as a function of ageing. *British Journal of Psychology*, **68**, 189–201.

Kagan, J., Pearson, L. and Welch, L. (1966). Conceptual impulsivity and inductive reasoning. *Child Development*, **37**, 583–594.

Leith, G.O.M. (1969). Personality and learning. In Dunn, W.R. and Holroyd, C. (Eds) *Aspects of educational technology, II*. London: Methuen.

Leith, G.O.M. (1982). The influence of personality on learning to teach: Effects and delayed effects of microteaching. *Educational Review*, **34**(3), 195–204.

Lyon, D.O. (1914). The relation of length of material to time taken for learning and the optimum distribution of time. *Journal of Educational Psychology*, **5**, 1–9; 85–91; 155–163.

Marshall, E.C., Duncan, K.D. and Baker, S.M. (1981). The role of withheld information in the training of process plant fault diagnosis. *Ergonomics*, **24**(9), 711–724.

Marton, F. and Säljö, R. (1976). On qualitative difference in learning: I – Outcome and process. *British Journal of Educational Psychology*, **46**, 4–11.

Mayer, R.E. (1980). Elaboration techniques that increase the meaningfulness of technical text. An experimental test of the learning strategy hypothesis. *Journal of Educational Psychology*, **72**(6), 770–784.

Messick, S. (Ed.) (1976). *Individuality in learning: Implication of cognitive styles and creativity for human development*. San Francisco: Jossey-Bass.

Montague, W.E. (1988). Processing and learning by designing the learning environment. In Jonassen, D.H. (Ed.) *Instructional designs for microcomputer courseware*. Hillsdale, NJ: Laurence Erlbaum.

Morrison, D.L. (1985). The effect of cognitive style and training on fault diagnosis performance. *Programmed Learning and Educational Technology*, **22**, 132–139.

Newsham, D.B. (1969). *The challenge of change to the adult trainee*. Training Information Paper 3. London: HMSO.

Palincsar, A.S. and Brown, A.L. (1984). Reciprocal teaching of comprehension-fostering and monitoring activities. *Cognition and Instruction*, **1**, 117–175.

Pask, G. (1975). *Conversation, cognition and learning. A cybernetic theory and methodology*. Amsterdam: Elsevier.

Pask, G. (1976). Styles and strategies of learning. *British Journal of Educational Psychology*, **46**, 128–148.

Pask, G. and Scott, B.C.E. (1972). Learning strategies and individual competence. *International Journal of Man-Machine Studies*, **4**, 217–253.

Prosser, G.V. (1978). The role of relevant active questions in learning based upon successive presentations. *Instructional Science*, **7**, 359–383.

Rabbitt, P.M.A. (1965). An age decrement in the ability to ignore irrelevant information. *Journal of Gerontology*, **20**, 233–8.

Ramsden, P. (1985). Student learning research: Retrospect and prospect. *Higher Education Research and Development*, **4**, 51–69.

Rickards, J.P. and Denner, P.R. (1978). Inserted questions as aids to reading text. *Instructional Science*, **7**, 313–346.

Rigney, J.W. (1978). Learning strategies: A theoretical perspective. In O'Neil, H.F. Jr (Ed.) *Learning strategies*. New York: Academic Press.

Robinson, F.P. (1946). *Effective study*. New York: Harper Row.

Rothkopf, E.Z. (1970). The concept of mathemagenic activities. *Review of Educational Research*, **40**, 325 336.

Rumelhart, D.E. and Norman, D.A. (1981). Analogical processes in learning. In Anderson, J.R. (Ed.) *Cognitive skills and their acquisition*. Hillsdale, NJ: Lawrence Erlbaum.

Salthouse, T.A. (1989). Ageing and skilled performance. In Colley, A.M. and Beech, J.R. (Eds) *Acquisition and performance of cognitive skills*. Chichester: John Wiley.

Salthouse, T.A., Kausler, D.H. and Saults, J.S. (1988). Investigation of student status, background variables, and the feasibility of standard tasks in cognitive ageing research. *Psychology and Ageing*, **3**, 29–37.

Schallert, D.L., Ulerick, S.L. and Tierney, R.J. (1984). Evolving a description of text through mapping. In Holley, C.D. and Dansereau, D.F. (Eds) (op.cit.).

Shoemaker, H.A. (1960). The functional context method of instruction. *IRE Transactions on Education*, E-3, 52–57.

Sieber, J.E., O'Neil, H.F. Jr. and Tobias, S. (Eds) (1977). *Anxiety, learning and instruction*. Hillsdale, NJ: Lawrence Erlbaum.

Smith, J., Kliegl, R. and Baltes, P.B. (1987). Testing the limits and the study of age differences in cognitive plasticity. The sample case of expert memory. Unpublished manuscript. Berlin: Max Planck Institute for Human Development and Education.

Sticht, T.G., Armstrong, W.B., Hickey, D.T. and Coyler, J.S. (1986). Cost of youth: Policy and training methods from the military experience. San Diego: Applied Behavioral and Cognitive Sciences Inc.

Talland, G.A. (1968). Age and span of immediate recall. In Talland, G.A. (Ed.) *Human ageing and behaviour*. New York: Academic Press.

Thomas, E.L. and Robinson, H.A. (1972). *Improving reading in every class. A sourcebook for teachers*. Boston: Allyn and Bacon.

Thorndike, E.L., Bregman, E.O., Tilton, J.W. and Woodyard, E. (1928). *Adult learning*. New York: Macmillan.

Tobias, S. (1977). Anxiety-treatment interactions: A review of research. In Sieber, J.E., O'Neil, H.F. Jr and Tobias, S. (Eds) (op.cit.).

Tobias, S. (1987). Learner characteristics. In Gagné, R.M. (Ed.) *Instructional technology: Foundations*. Hillsdale, NJ: Lawrence Erlbaum.

Weinstein, C.E. (1978). Elaboration skills as a learning strategy. In O'Neil, H.F. Jr (Ed.) *Learning strategies*. New York: Academic Press.

Weinstein, C.E. and Mayer, R.E. (1986). The teaching of learning strategies. In Wittrock, M.C. (Ed.) *Handbook of research on teaching. Third Edition*. New York: Macmillan.

Weinstein, C.E. and Underwood, V.L. (1985). Learning strategies: The how of learning. In Segal, J.W., Chipman, S.F. and Glaser, R. *Thinking and learning skills, Volume 1, Relating instruction to research*. Hillsdale, NJ: Lawrence Erlbaum.

Welford, A.T. (1958). *Ageing and human skill*. Oxford University Press for the Nuffield Foundation.

Witkin, H.A. (1976). Cognitive style in academic performance and in teacher–student relations. In Messick, S. (Ed.) (op.cit.).

Wittrock, M.C. (1974). Learning as a generative process. *Educational Psychologist*, **11**, 87–95.

Wong, B.Y.L. (1985). Self-questioning instructional research: A review. *Review of Educational Research*, **55**(2), 227–268.

Woodrow, H.A. (1946). The ability to learn. *Psychological Review*, **53**, 147–158.

Zeaman, D. and House, B.J. (1967). The relation of IQ and learning. In Gagné, R.M. (Ed.) (op.cit.).

CHAPTER 11
Computers and training

Computers not only create training problems, but can be used to solve them. For example, introduction of a new word-processing system into an office means that clerical and secretarial staff require retraining. This might be supplied by a computer-based tutorial package accessible from the normal word-processing station. In this solution the computer-based training is said to be "embedded" within the existing computer facilities for normal work. This is often a sensible and cost-effective training solution, particularly for organisations which have new or upgraded computer facilities.

The most important point to make about using computers for training is that the technology per se does not guarantee that the quality of training is good. We have all probably experienced so-called computer-based tutorial packages associated with a new editor or software package which do not merit use of the term "training". Typically, they constitute a few statements of what is in the new software, but barely scratch the surface in training people how to use it. Even though such a criticism would receive almost unanimous support, there is nevertheless a deep-seated belief, not confined to practitioners, that the more advanced the technology employed in training then the better training will be. Unfortunately, this is just not true. What is important is *how* the technology or media for providing training is used. A computer's potential can be wasted if it is used as an expensive "page turner" of training text which has no facility for interacting with the trainee and providing intelligent advice. There are some examples of "programmed learning" textbooks which provide good training because considerable care and attention has been paid to what the trainee has to learn, how this is segmented and structured into learning exercises with accompanying feedback, and what "remedial" pages the trainee should read given certain difficulties. Therefore what matters is not the technology per se, but the extent to which the principles of both training generally and training design in particular have been used in the development of training.

This argument should not be taken to imply that new technology does not offer the training designer new opportunities which can improve further the design of training. A computer can be used to drive a complex simulation or evaluate a trainee's answer almost instantaneously. Both situations would be difficult, if not impossible, without a computer's involvement. Interactive video techniques similarly offer new possibilities. These media, sometimes inappropriately labelled training "methods", provide both opportunities and constraints in the development of training, but reference to them does not enable the value of training to be gauged. Yes, a training designer has to decide whether to use a lecture, video, training manual, audio tape, computer-based training, group discussion etc., or any combination of these. However, the selection of delivery method(s) is of secondary significance, apart from the obvious, in comparison to how intelligently training has been engineered. Hopefully, these remarks will serve to dampen the enthusiasm with which every innovation in the technology of training is greeted in some parts of the training community. Technology per se is no panacea.

This chapter discusses the different functions which a computer can fulfil in training (Section 11.2), besides the tutorial one which has already been mentioned. The remaining sections of this chapter reflect the historical development of computers as training devices and some of the different labels which have been used to describe this role. The story begins with the "programmed instruction" or "programmed learning" movement in the 1950s which produced the important notion of a "teaching machine". What is meant by programmed instruction, its different forms and the theoretical ideas from which it developed are discussed in Section 11.3. As the ingenious, but limited, automated devices of this movement were replaced by computers, the term "computer-based training", and various synonyms, were used in the 1960s and 1970s. Section 11.4 discusses different configurations of computer-based training, the use of computer-based training for a variety of tasks, and evaluation studies. More recently, in the late 1970s and in the 1980s the term "intelligent tutoring systems" was used, which reflected the desire to make such training more "intelligent" (in a sense discussed in Section 11.5). Despite the lofty aims of intelligent tutoring systems, some of the best examples remain research demonstrations, rather than training solutions that have been implemented and subjected to careful evaluation.

11.2 ROLES FOR COMPUTERS IN TRAINING

Computers have four main roles in training:

1. Provision of training.

2. Development of training.
3. Management of training.
4. Research into training.

The first and most well-known role for a computer in training is where it presents some training material to a trainee, in other words it provides the training programme. One example of this role is in adaptive training, discussed in Section 9.0, in which there is a continuous evaluation of trainee performance accompanied by subsequent modification of the training material that is presented. It is often the closed-loop, fast and flexible features of such a computer-based training environment which commend this role for a computer. Sections 11.3–11.5 provide further examples in which a computer provides all or part of a training programme.

A second role for a computer is in the development of training, although this is much less frequent than its primary role of providing training. To understand this second role, it is necessary to remind ourselves of the stages in the development of training, which are described by the Instructional Systems Development (ISD) models discussed in Chapter 4. Broadly, the development of training involves specifying training objectives, elaborating training content by means of some analysis of the task, and designing/developing the training materials. Theoretically, a computer might be used for any of these development activities either directly, by performing these activities itself or indirectly, by supporting a person to do them. Rigney and Towne (1969) described a rather unusual use of a computer which analysed a task or subject matter in order to derive the content of training. Whilst it is straightforward for a computer to present a predetermined job analysis questionnaire to a person and analyse it subsequently, it is more difficult to capture the expertise associated with using less formal analysis techniques (e.g. Hierarchical Task Analysis).

There are many examples where the computer is involved indirectly in the design of training materials, some of which are concerned with training the trainers to use the IPISD model (pp. 117–120). A computer-based training package might train the trainers in the use of different training methods. Authors of training materials can be trained in how to construct good test items, how to specify objectives adequately, or how to monitor and assess the level of reading difficulty of training text. It is possible for a computer program itself to generate a training package. This is particularly cost-effective when a lot of training programmes have to be devised for different versions of the same task or class of tasks. An example of this is given by Braby et al. (1978), where a lot of training was designed for US Navy personnel to recognise sets of symbols, e.g. electronic symbols on schematic diagrams, symbols on maps and weather charts. In order to satisfy this training need, the AUTHOR package was developed which automatically organised and output information in a form suitable for the training of symbol recognition. AUTHOR was able to generate pretests, tutorial exercises, criterion tests and suggestions for refresher training. Hence it was a general purpose computer-aided authoring system aimed at generating training for any symbol recognition task. Because its scope was restricted to this type of task, it was feasible to develop an algorithm for producing training material based on the same set of learning and training design principles. Part of this algorithm is represented in Figure 11.1, together with the training principles that it uses. A human author had to prepare and enter information into AUTHOR about the set of symbols to be trained and also had to review the material before it was finally produced automatically.

The principle of devising general purpose computer-based aiding systems for activities in the development of training is a good one. In practice it is difficult to accomplish this unless either the development activity is a restricted one (e.g. producing multiple choice test items) or a class of task is carefully selected as in the Braby et al. AUTHOR example. With a wide range of either training development activities or tasks, it is difficult to specify training solutions which are generalisable and context-independent.

A third role for a computer in training is in the management of one, or more, training courses. This is labelled "computer-managed training" or "computer-managed learning" (CML). In this role, a computer may schedule trainees through various training exercises performed off-line, record progress, administer tests and provide summaries of trainees' progress to course instructors. This administrative role is particularly useful in large-scale organisations which have a high turnover of trainees and schedule many training programmes. This macro-management role should not be confused with the micro-management role which takes place when a computer provides a conventional interactive training programme. Some management does occur at this micro-level, since the computer prescribes different learning routes or training materials on the basis of the trainee's competence. At the macro-management level the computer is only a record-keeper and administrator and is not involved in fine-grained decisions about learning.

Many conventional computer-based training programmes have associated with them a computer-based management facility. Computer-based training modules in different areas of statistics were developed at

Leeds University in the UK, by Hartley (1975), which had such a facility. Teachers in statistics could "programme" different courses for their students by varying the routing between modules, contingencies between them and advice provided. It was possible for the teacher to derive a cumulative record of the progress of a "class" of students or to get more detailed information on any one student's performance. Typically, such computer-managed learning systems enable students to log onto the system and return to the point at which they previously finished their study. Records are not only valuable to students and teachers, but also to the authors who developed the various modules. In this way, modules can be revised and updated to take account of any difficulties encountered by students. Thus, a computer-based management system enables training development and evaluation of training to proceed together in an iterative manner. In the Leeds University example, the computer-based management system operated at different levels ranging from the student in one course, to the teacher at one University, up to a central unit which was able to monitor and change any aspects of the system. Such a management system can coordinate, monitor, advise and test trainees on different training courses in the same organisation. There is no reason in principle why this could not be extended to a regional or national level. A computer could administer aptitude tests, keep up-to-date information on the labour market's present and future manpower requirements, provide trainees with details of relevant training courses, monitor their progress etc.

The fourth role for a computer is to support research into training. This is not our concern here, although it will be noted that many research studies cited in this book, besides those in computer-based training, utilise a computer.

11.3 PROGRAMMED INSTRUCTION

The terms "programmed instruction" or "programmed learning" are used more or less interchangeably to refer to a movement in the 1950s and 1960s which advocated the construction of "programmed" training materials, often presented by some sort of "teaching machine". This movement was heavily influenced by Skinner's (1954) paper "The Science of Learning and the Art of Teaching", in which Skinner criticised the educational establishment for not employing the learning principles of reinforcement in the practice of teaching. Subsequently, one part of the programmed learning movement became devoted to the implementation of Skinnerian principles in the design of what became

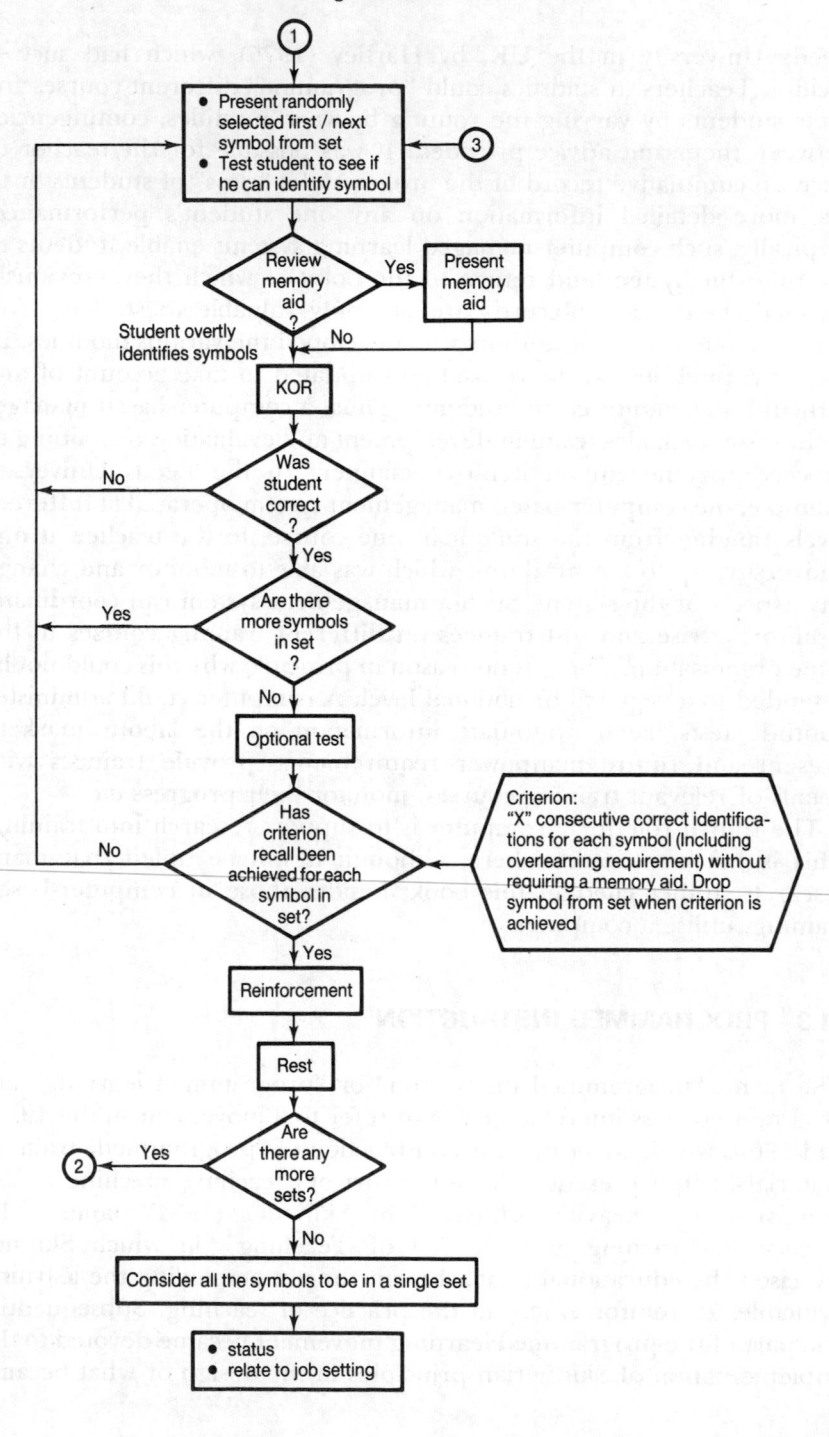

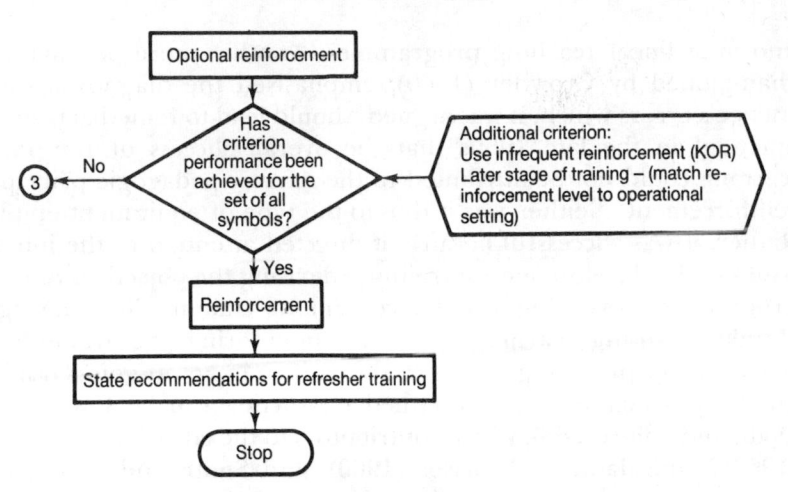

Optional reinforcement

Has criterion performance been achieved for the set of all symbols?

No → ③

Additional criterion:
Use infrequent reinforcement (KOR) Later stage of training – (match reinforcement level to operational setting)

Yes

Reinforcement

State recommendations for refresher training

Stop

1. Relate training clearly to meaningful and job related tasks.

2. Show differences between similar individual features of symbols. Do this before associating these symbols with identification responses.

3. Break up the total list of symbols into smaller sets when any of the following conditions exist:

   (a) A long list of symbols is to be learned.

   (b) Material is complex for students.

   The size of the set for each student should vary according to how much each of the factors departs from the normal situation for each condition.

4. Present the associated item (or meaning) immediately after the symbol in time as the basis for this kind of training.

5. Randomise the order of the presentation of the symbols to the student so that all symbols will be learned equally well.

6. Use mnemonics (associating recall of symbols with imagery, rhymes or rhythms) for difficult to recall symbols. Provide mnemonics which will cause an affective reaction in the student. Also provide directions for the student to develop his own mnemonics.

7. Allow for self-paced practice with knowledge of results (KOR).

8. Prevent decay of recall by (1) requiring the student to overlearn the original associations and (2) ensuring periodic refresher training.

9. Test for correct identification of symbols by measuring overt performance by the student.

10. Provide self-paced training that can be adapted to the individual student's needs. Both rate and level of learning depend upon the characteristics of the individual student.

11. Use immediate KOR and frequent reinforcement in the early stages of training. In later stages of training, match the KOR and reinforcement levels that exist in the operational setting.

Figure 11.1 Part of an algorithm for the design of AUTHOR which provided computer-aided authoring of training material for symbol recognition (Braby et al., 1978).

known as linear teaching programmes. Another more pragmatic part, championed by Crowder (1960), emphasised the diagnostic value of trainee's errors which, it was argued, should lead to remedial training. It emerged in the late 1960s that the overall success of programmed learning could not be attributed to the narrow pedagogic principles of reinforcement. Neither was it due to the type of equipment employed. Rather, it was successful because it directed attention to the important issues in the development of training: devising the objectives of training programmes, breaking up the content of training into manageable chunks, devising learning exercises, monitoring the trainee's competence, and providing advice to the trainee in an on-going fashion. A good introduction to programmed instruction can be found in Kay, Dodd and Sime (1968), whilst contributors to the edited texts by Coulson (1962), Lumsdaine and Glaser (1960), and Smith and Moore (1962) provide a representative sample of the ideas and evidence current at that time.

The origin of teaching machines is attributed to Sidney Pressey at Ohio State University (Pressey, 1926, 1927). He developed the "Test-Rater" which was intended to remove the burden of marking student's answers in the conventional fashion. Students who had to answer a sheet of multiple-choice questions were given a "punchboard" in which the rows of a matrix of holes represented the questions and the columns, the answer choices. The student pushed a metal stylus through the hole corresponding to his or her chosen answer to a given question. If the answer was correct, the stylus passed through whereas if it was incorrect, it did not. The student continued until the correct answer was found. It was discovered that whilst this device was developed for testing purposes it also resulted in learning. Subsequently, Pressey devised machines which enabled the student to proceed only when the correct answer was achieved and which counted the student's errors. Studies by him demonstrated that these early machines provided effective teaching.

Linear and branching programmes

From Skinner's perspective, Pressey's devices were inadequate because they were not designed with respect to the principles of learning. Errors, according to Skinner, should be avoided so that correct answers could be positively reinforced. In addition, trainees should be required to *construct* a response rather than just recognise the answer from a set of alternatives. These principles gave birth to the development of *linear programmes*, so called because all students followed the same sequence of training materials. The main characteristics of a linear programme are:

1. The material to be learned is divided up into small steps or frames.
2. Each frame provides information and requires the student to make a response.
3. Immediately after a response is made, the correct answer is given to the student.
4. The frames are constructed so that approximately 95% of students will provide the correct answer at their first attempt.
5. Students proceed at their own pace.

An example of part of a linear programme for high-school physics, from Skinner (1958), is given in Table 11.1 together with part of Skinner's commentary. Whilst this programme is simple, perhaps too simple from the trainee's perspective, its construction is quite difficult. One reason for this was Skinner's insistence on reinforcing a correct response, which meant that very small steps, together with various cues and prompts, were used to ensure that trainee's gave the correct answer. Many argued that these prompts meant that the learning situation was no longer analogous to Skinner's operant conditioning paradigm. Examples of the sort of cues and prompts used in linear programmes are:

Rhyming. Example: Man and woman are joined in matrimony at the CERE****. (Answer: ceremony.)
Grammatical construction. Example: Just as copper expands when it is heated, so also iron ____ when it is heated. (Answer: expands.)
Contrast. Example: RECUR has only *one* ____ but OCCUR has ____. (Answer: c; two cs.)
(Examples from Leith, 1966, pp. 50–51.)

Construction of a linear programme was also difficult because Skinner believed that complex behaviour had to be "shaped" from simpler forms which were scheduled to approximate more and more closely to that which was required.

Branching programmes, as their name suggests, provide different routes through the training materials, dependent upon the trainee's competence at various points in the programme. In a branching programme, there is typically more information in each frame in comparison to a linear programme. Questions at the end of the frame are diagnostic, indicating whether the trainee is ready for some new information, or whether some remedial explanation is necessary. When an incorrect answer is provided, alternative "branches" are available for remedial instruction and the one selected will depend upon the nature

Table 11.1 Part of a linear programme in physics, together with commentary (adapted from Skinner, 1958)

Sentence to be completed	Word to be supplied
1. The important parts of a flashlight are the battery and the bulb. When we "turn on" a flashlight, we close a switch which connects the battery with the ___.	Bulb
2. When we turn on a flashlight, an electric current flows through the fine wire in the ___ and causes it to grow hot.	Bulb
3. When the hot wire glows brightly, we say that it gives off or sends out heat and ___.	Light
4. The fine wire in the bulb is called a filament. The bulb "lights up" when the filament is heated by the passage of a(n) ___ current.	Electric
5. When a weak battery produces little current, the fine wire, or ___, does not get very hot.	Filament
6. A filament which is less hot sends out or gives off ___ light.	Less
7. "Emit" means "send out". The amount of light sent out, or "emitted", by a filament depends on how ___ the filament is.	Hot
8. The higher the temperature of the filament the ___ the light emitted by it.	Brighter Stronger
9. If a flashlight battery is weak, the ___ in the bulb may still glow, but with only a dull red colour.	Filament
10. The light from a very hot filament is coloured yellow or white. The light from a filament which is not very hot is coloured ___.	Red

Commentary. "Technical terms are introduced slowly. For example the familiar term "fine wire" in frame 2 is followed by a definition of the technical term "filament" in frame 4; "filament" is then asked for in the presence of the non-scientific synonym in frame 5 and without the synonym in frame 9. In the same way "glow", "give off light", and "send out light" in early frames are followed by a definition of "emit" with a synonym in frame 7. ... in frame 3 the words "heat and" preempt the response "heat", which would otherwise correctly fill the blank" (Skinner, 1958, p. 974).

of the trainee's mistake. Crowder, to whom is usually credited the development of branching programmes, has described various types of branching, one of which is represented in Figure 11.2. This is a branching programme for a "scrambled" textbook in which there are

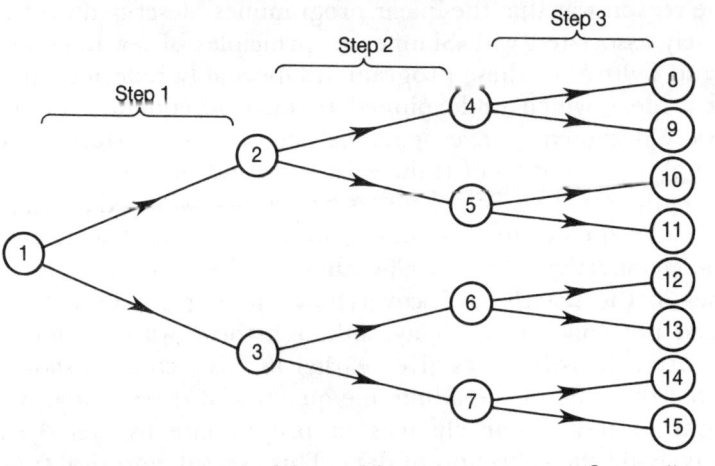

Figure 11.2 One type of branching programme for a "scrambled" book (adapted from Crowder, 1962). The numbers represent page numbers.

two choices at each of three steps. The textbook is said to be scrambled because the pages are not studied in the normal sequence, but in a sequence dictated by the answer given to the question posed by each "frame". A computer can overcome the somewhat awkward nature of such scrambled books.

Crowder's enthusiasm for branching programmes grew out of his work concerned with training technicians how to find faults in equipment. He believed that incorrect answers should be elaborated to explain how and why mistakes occurred. Whilst Crowder used multiple-choice questions in his branching programmes, there is no reason why, as in more "intelligent" tutoring systems, the trainee should not construct his or her own answer. The intelligence lies in the automatic device being able to read and interpret the answer in a human-like fashion. One obvious advantage of a branching programme is that it should be better able to cope than a linear programme with the varying abilities of trainees. The use of different branches not only enables training to be tailored more closely to trainee's needs, but also avoids some of the boredom and lack of motivation experienced with linear programmes.

Evaluation of programmed instruction

Many intense battles were fought between the 1950s and the early 1970s concerning which type of programmed instruction was superior and why. One reason was that the linear programmes, described previously, were closely associated with Skinnerian principles of learning and the success and failures of these programmes inevitably reflected upon the theoretical ideas which underpinned them. Consequently, evaluation studies were designed to investigate the need for: small step size; overt responding; minimisation of trainee's errors; and immediate confirmation (i.e. reinforcement). Some studies deliberately violated a prescribed programmed sequence to determine how important that sequence was. From the perspective of the 1990s, these studies are now but minor skirmishes in the search to discover how training can be automated. They need not concern us today, although those who are interested should consult the references given earlier in this section. It should not go unstated that one of the admirable qualities of these studies was an enthusiasm to test minor changes in programme by well-designed studies involving the collection of data. This careful empirical tradition compares rather favourably with the lack of detailed evaluation of some of the more recent intelligent tutoring systems.

The basic problem in evaluating any programmed instruction is in fact a problem common to the evaluation of any training programme. What should it be compared against? Programmed instruction could be compared against some conventional form of training or against a teacher, perhaps even an above average one. But is this fair? Because many factors are confounded in such comparisons, interpretation of such evaluation studies is problematic. These factors include the following:

Information is presented visually in programmed instruction whereas a teacher also uses the auditory modality.
Motivation may be increased by the novelty of the programme.
It is difficult, if not impossible, to equate fairly the amount of time spent learning in programmed instruction with that in a conventional teaching course.
It is difficult to match students in their ability.
More time is taken to define and structure the subject matter in programmed instruction than in conventional courses.

Notwithstanding these problems of interpretation, many evaluation studies have been carried out together with a number of reviews of them. The results of 112 evaluation studies which compared programmed with conventional instruction are summarised in Table 11.2, from a review by Hartley (1966).

For whatever reason, programmed instruction is superior to conventional instruction in terms of time taken to learn and test results at the

Table 11.2　The results of 112 studies comparing programmed with conventional instruction (Hartley, 1966)

Measures recorded	Number of studies recording these measures	Programmed instruction group		
		Significantly superior	Not significantly different	Significantly worse
Time taken	90	47	37	6
Test results	110	41	54	15
Retest results	33	6	24	3

Note: Figures in the first column differ because not all measures were recorded in each of the studies.

end of training although retest results are more evenly balanced. However, Hartley himself cautioned that some of the studies in his review had small numbers of students, short programmes and little data on long-term retention.

Cost–benefit analysis is also part of the evaluation equation. This is carried out infrequently, if at all, and then only in a half-hearted manner. Systematic cost–benefit analyses are not only missing from evaluations of programmed instruction, computer-based training and intelligent tutoring systems but also from evaluations of more conventional training courses. Hartley (1972), from an analysis of 10 studies, provided some indication of the estimated savings of industrial applications of programmed instruction in 1972 money (Table 11.3).

Important features of programmed instruction

The programmed instruction movement laid the foundations for automated training which in the late 1960s onwards capitalised upon the power and flexibility which computers afforded. Four of the most important features of programmed instruction were:

1. The shift from an open-loop to a closed-loop training system. Accompanying this was specification of the functions required by a training system (automated or not).

Table 11.3 The cost–benefits of programmed instruction (Hartley, 1972)

Investi-gations	Cost of programme	Cost of conventional instruction	Estimated savings
1	—	—	20%–50% of training time
2	$218 per student hour	$309 per student hour	29% of instruction, 27% of trainee time
3	—	—	$90,000 in training to date ($30/man)
4	£1500	£1500	£1500 per year
5	£20,000	—	1 week's training time, approx. £10,000 per year
6	£12,500	—	8.2% of training time, £24,700 after 2 years
7	—	—	3 hours per supervisor, $90,000 per course
8	£550	—	£1275 annually
9	£13,500	—	£1000 for every three courses
10	—	—	10 weeks trainee time Labour turnover reduced from 70% to 30%. Retention of skilled labour

2. The definition of training objectives together with a more systematic organisation of the training material.
3. A perspective of the trainee as an active participant in training rather than a passive one.
4. The development of self-contained training "packages".

1. Open-loop versus closed-loop training systems. Most traditional training systems are of the open-loop variety, depicted in Figure 11.3. The difference between this and the more desirable closed-loop type of training system is evident from comparison of Figures 11.3 and 11.4 (Kay, Dodd and Sime, 1968). In an open-loop training system, information is taken from a "subject matter store" which may be a book, some notes or even the trainer's memory and is then "displayed", visually and/or aurally, to the trainee. Such a system is likely to be ineffective. The trainer is unable to judge *what* to select from the subject matter store and *how* to display it to the trainee. This is because the trainee's current level of understanding is not known. The relevance of information in

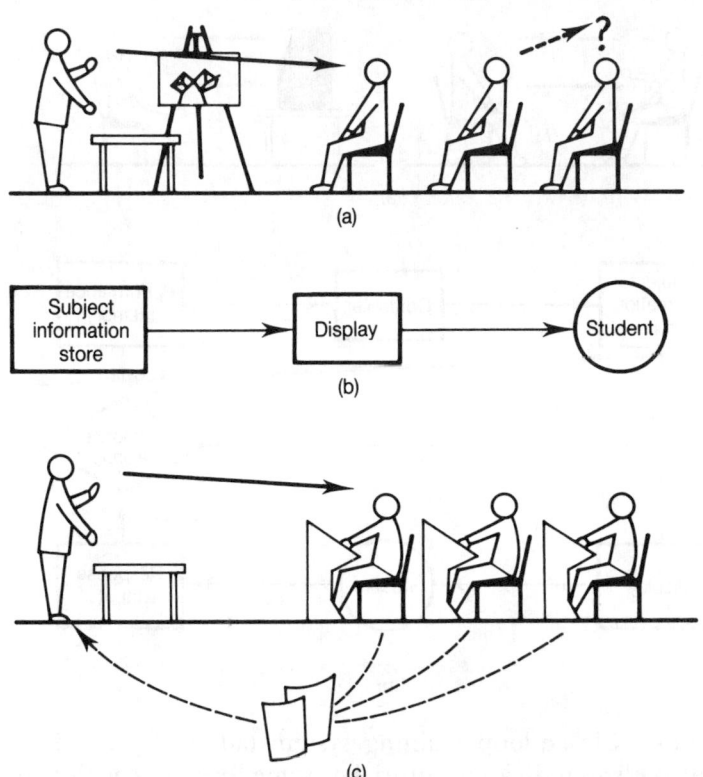

Figure 11.3 Open-loop training system (adapted from Kay et al., 1968). (a) With traditional lectures, films, videos, there is no feedback to the teacher. (b) Flow of information in an open-loop training system. (c) Feedback derived from occasional examinations is too late to control information provided during training.

the subject matter store to the trainee can only be based on a guess rather than knowledge of the trainee's actual requirements. If information in the subject matter store is irrelevant or becomes out of date, this may go unnoticed. These problems are intrinsic to the conventional lecture or talk with demonstration given to a group of trainees. Sadly, such open-loop training systems are as prevalent today as they were when these issues were originally raised in the 1960s. The remedy lies in closing the "loop" in the training system, (Figure 11.4), so that trainees' difficulties can be detected and at least in principle, overcome. The extra components in a closed-loop training system are:

Response from the trainee. A trainee responds to some training material presented.

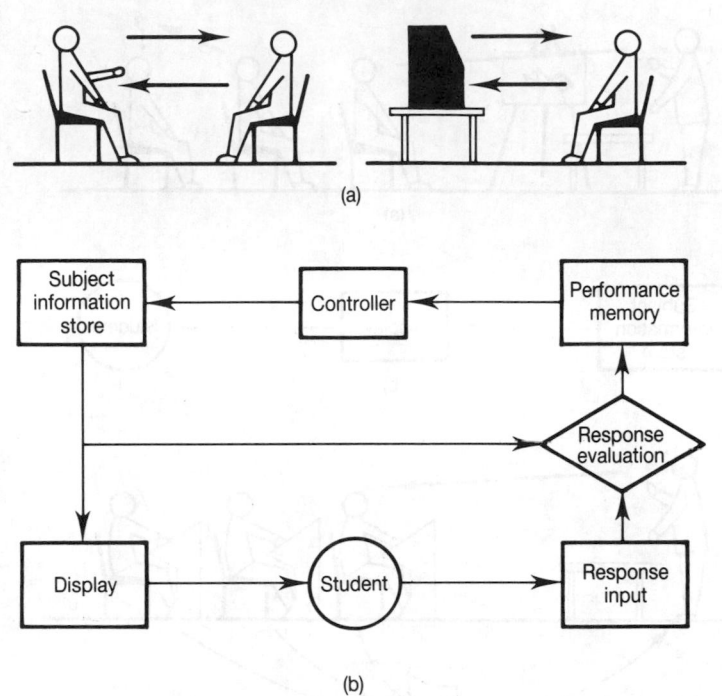

Figure 11.4 Closed-loop training system (adapted from Kay et al., 1968). (a) With an individual tutorial or some form of teaching machine, feedback to the trainer (or machine) is immediate which is used to control subsequent interaction. (b) Flow of information in a closed-loop training system.

Evaluator. The trainee's response is evaluated with respect to the correct or ideal answer. The implications of different errors may be diagnosed at this stage.

Performance memory. A history of the trainee's past performance is stored and is accessible.

Controller. Subsequent training material is selected from the subject matter store on the basis of rules in this component which link the trainee's response, its correctness and the trainee's past performance.

Whilst the components of a closed-loop training system are derived from the programmed instruction movement, these components, with different labels, can be found at the heart of more technologically advanced training discussed later in this chapter. The "evaluator" function is important and in these early days it was fulfilled by comparison of the trainee's answer with a list of predefined alternatives. The "controller" function is equally important. The sophistication of the "teaching expertise" which is embedded in this function will determine its effectiveness. At the crudest level, a trainee's answer is judged to be acceptable, thus enabling the next "frame" of information to be presented. Alternatively, if an error is made, the trainee's misunderstanding can be diagnosed and some remedial training can be provided involving further explanation, examples etc. In this manner a closed-loop training system provides the opportunity for training to be tailored to a trainee's individual needs, a feat impossible with an open-loop training system.

By now it should be evident that the components of closed-loop training cannot be conveniently divided into those performed by "human" and those by "machine". Each component can be fulfilled by human, machine or some combination of both. The requirements of closed-loop training can be met by a one-to-one tutorial, programmed instruction embodied in a book, and a teaching machine. The hardware (human or otherwise!) is relatively unimportant in comparison with the quality of the training expertise embodied in components of the "loop" (Figure 11.4). Fundamental decisions concerning the content and design of training have to be resolved before the appropriate "delivery" mode is selected. Only then is it sensible to consider whether information should be stored and displayed on video, in printed form or in some auditory form. A trainee's response might be written down, selected via a button or touch-sensitive screen. The evaluator function may be performed by the trainer, the teaching machine or even the trainee as can the memory and controller functions.

Programmed instruction's enduring contribution to training has been to focus attention on the importance of a closed-loop training system which enables training to be controlled on the basis of the trainee's current understanding and level of competence.

2. Definition of training objectives and training content. Programmed instruction forces the developer of training to make explicit the training objectives and also to consider the structure, sequence and content of the "frames" or parts of the training programme. Writing a programmed learning text or a program to drive a teaching machine or a computer-based tutorial is a marvellous discipline for exposing many inconsistencies and inadequacies which would normally remain unnoticed in the preparation and delivery of, say, a lecture. Programmed instruction has to be devised such that training can stand alone and proceed without constant interruption and improvisation from the trainer. The rigours which programmed instruction imposes on the development and design of training is a major reason for its success.

3. The trainee as an active participant. By definition, all forms of programmed instruction require the trainee to respond to some training exercise, question etc. These training exercises can be viewed as "orienting tasks", discussed in Chapter 10, which force the trainee to engage in at least some processing of the material presented. The extent to which exercises or questions "orient" the trainee to organise and assimilate new information in a useful fashion, will influence the amount of learning. Almost any interaction between the trainee and the new material is preferable to none. Naturally, the quality and relevance of this interaction will determine its effectiveness. Questions concerning the nature of a trainee's interaction are important in evaluating not only programmed instruction but also a tutorial with a human tutor.

4. Training can be packaged. Programmed instruction demonstrated the advantage of being able to package training in a teaching machine or programmed text. Training packages can be distributed to trainees in their locations and they can be studied when time permits. These advantages became more forceful with the advent of powerful computers and the development of local, national and international computer networks. One disadvantage of packaging, which is in essence the disadvantage of developing any systematic training, is that it is expensive and the high development costs of such training have to be recouped from its wide distribution and use on more than an occasional basis.

Summary

For those who may be still uncertain of the nature of the beast called "programmed instruction", let us conclude with a summary of its main features from Wallis, Duncan and Knight (1966):

> Instruction, or training, is 'programmed' when the subject-matter or content of the course displays the following defining characteristics:
> (a) There is a clear-cut statement of objectives, i.e. of 'terminal performance'.
> (b) The material to be learned has been itemised and is presented serially in identifiable steps, i.e. frames.
> (c) The actual sequence of frames which any student encounters is controlled according to rules derived from the particular programming technique employed.
> (d) Frequent and unambiguous responses from every student are required throughout the whole sequence.

(e) Feedback of information about the correctness or otherwise of responses is given to the student before the next frame is presented.

(f) A 'response comparator' is implicit in (e) above to judge between actual and desired (i.e. 'correct') responses. This function can be performed by the student or by a device (Wallis et al., 1966, p. 2).

11.4 COMPUTER-BASED TRAINING

Four roles for computers in training were identified in Section 11.2, of which the most important is when the computer is a provider of training material. Various terms have been used to refer to this role. "Computer assisted learning" (CAL) and "computer assisted instruction" (CAI) were terms used interchangeably in the 1970s, and primarily reserved for educational contexts. The term "computer-based training" (CBT) was used in connection with industrial, occupational and military contexts. Distinctions between these terms are superficial since the subject matter of learning in both educational and training contexts may often be the same (p. 3–4). The conventional role of a computer as a provider of training, contrasts with its role as a manager of training, labelled "computer managed learning" (CML), which was discussed in Section 11.2. It is useful to envisage the degree of computer management as varying along a continuum. CML is at one extreme where the computer may administer a series of training courses and record trainees' progress and test results. At the other extreme lies classical CAL or CBT, where computer management is minimal, although some does occur because different training is prescribed on the basis of trainees' answers *during* the training programme.

Two of the earliest and most ambitious computer-based educational programmes were PLATO and TICCIT, although the philosophy underpinning each was different. PLATO (Programmed Logic for Automatic Teaching Operation) was developed at the Computer-based Education Research Laboratory at the University of Illinois from the 1960s onwards and has undergone many revisions up to the present day. Smith and Sherwood (1976) stated that:

> The system now has 950 terminals located in universities, colleges, community colleges, public schools, military training schools, and commercial organisations ... The users have access to more than 3,500 hours of instructional material in more than 100 subject areas (p. 344).

From the perspective of the 1970s, PLATO had considerable technological facilities including:

graphical and animated representations;
student interaction via a touch-sensitive screen;

a communication network between the authors of lessons;
the TUTOR author language which was aimed at assisting the development of lessons;
a library of lessons which was accessible to users of the system.

The instructional quality of the lessons was variable since they depended upon the expertise and enthusiasm of the authors. The system did not offer guidelines on how lessons should be written and in this sense had a laissez-faire philosophy.

TICCIT (Time-shared Interactive Computer Controlled Information Television) was another major CAL system which was developed in America in the 1970s. In contrast to PLATO, it prescribes how the subject matter should be structured and the nature of the student's interaction with it. How this is accomplished derives from Merrill's Component Display Theory, discussed in Section 8.3, which developed alongside Merrill's involvement in the TICCIT project (Merrill, 1988). TICCIT is aimed mainly at concept learning. Great emphasis is placed upon the fact that TICCIT is a learner-controlled CBT system, the keyboard for which is represented in Figure 11.5. The student is able to

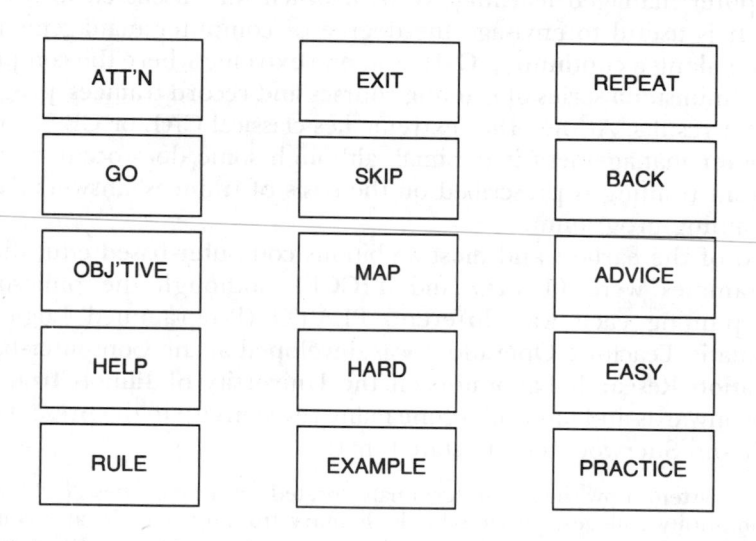

Figure 11.5   The learner control keys in TICCIT (fom Merrill, 1988).

select rules, access examples of these rules, and practice using them by pressing the bottom three keys of the 15 learner-control keys (Figure 11.5). Examples of the use of these keys and the "map", "rule/help" and "advice" keys for a lesson concerning grammar are given in Figure 11.6,

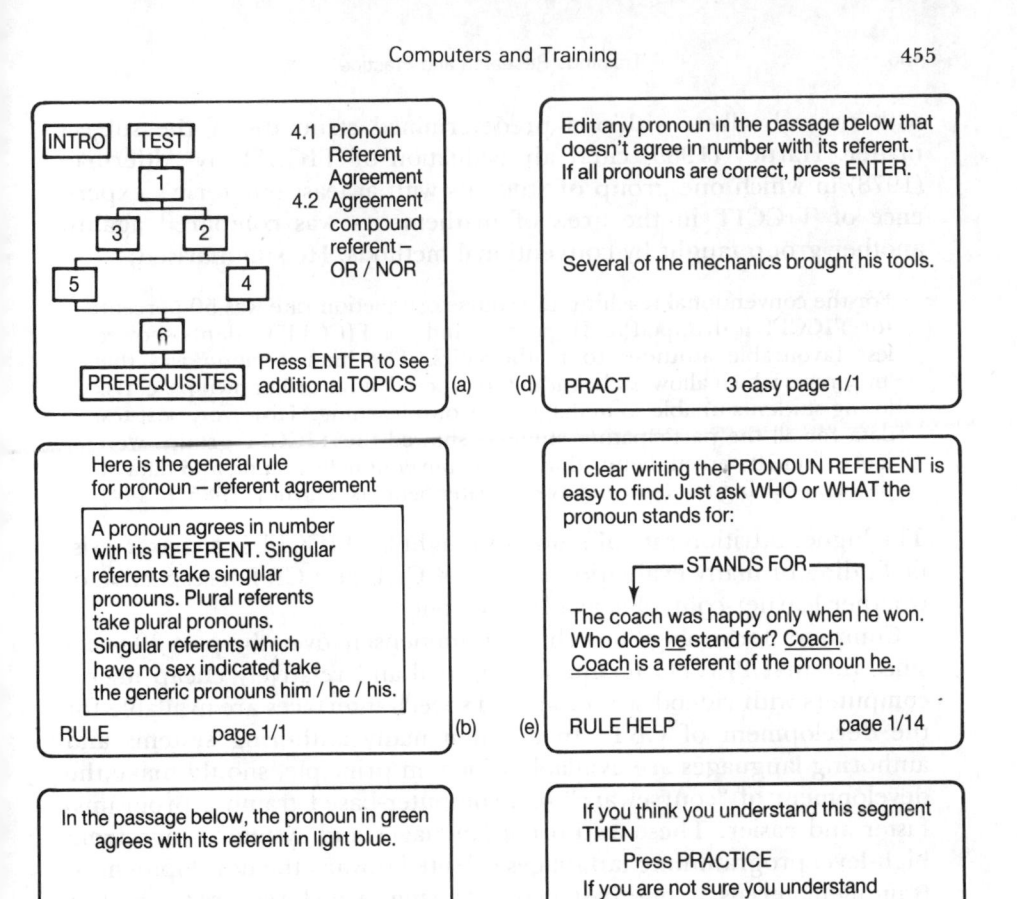

Figure 11.6 Sample displays of an English grammar lesson from TICCIT: (a) Lesson map; (b) rule; (c) example; (d) practice; (e) rule help; (f) advice (from Merrill, 1988).

from Merrill (1988). The difficulty of the material is varied by use of the "hard" and "easy" keys; how parts of a lesson fit together is accessed by the "map" key; comments on a student's performance and next selection can be obtained from the "advice" key; and the objective of the current lesson is displayed by the "obj'tive" key. TICCIT therefore invites the student to plan his or her own course of study and provides the student with control, albeit within a predetermined structure of the subject matter. Hartley (1985) cited an evaluation of TICCIT by Alderman (1978) in which one group of students with at least one term's experience of TICCIT in the area of mathematics was compared against another group taught by conventional methods. He summarised:

> For the conventional teaching the course completion rate was 50 percent; for TICCIT it dropped to 16 percent and the TICCIT students showed less favourable attitudes to mathematics. The interpretation was that 'programs which allow each student to proceed at his or her own pace, risk losing students unable to manage their own learning.' However, post-test data for all the participating students showed the TICCIT groups were more than 10 percent better than those conventionally taught, and data on problem-solving tests showed even greater benefits (Hartley, 1985, p. 144).

The higher attrition rate of students taught by TICCIT is a characteristic finding of many evaluation studies of CAL and CBT irrespective of whether learner-control is available or not.

Computer technology has changed immensely over the past 30 years since the first PLATO terminal. Powerful and relatively cheap microcomputers with videodisc and limited speech interfaces are available for the development of CBT. In addition many authoring systems and authoring languages are available which, in principle, should make the development of "courseware" (i.e. computer-based training programs) faster and easier. These authoring languages and systems range from high-level programming languages oriented toward the development of training materials, to highly structured systems which require the author to input information in a series of formats (e.g. objectives, information items, test items), from which a lesson is "created" by the system. Despite all of these advances, the bottleneck still remains the same: a lack of expertise in how to create good training programmes, coupled with the fact that any training development is still a labour-intensive activity.

Criteria for computer involvement

Before considering CBT in more detail, a fundamental question needs to be addressed. When should a computer be used in a training programme? This question is difficult to answer, because whilst what a computer can and cannot do is more or less a matter of fact, judging when to use a computer involves a value judgement. Seltzer (1971), in attempting to make these value judgements explicit, suggested three criterion statements:

(a) If the computer poses a unique solution to an important problem in the instructional process, then it should be used regardless of the cost involved.

(b) If the computer is more efficient or effective and the cost of its use to instruct is minimal, then it should be used...

(c) If the cost of development and use of the computer in instruction is relatively high with the relative efficiency or effectiveness only marginal, then the computer should not be used in the instructional process (p 375).

In these statements, Seltzer uses the terms, "unique solution", "more efficient or effective" and "cost" which are more difficult to judge than might at first appear. Uniqueness is a function not only of qualitative but also quantitative advantages provided by a computer. Assessment of this is unlikely to be value free. Estimating not only the potential advantages of different training "solutions", but also the cost–benefit of computer involvement are quite problematic. Systematic evaluation studies of CBT, particularly of a fine-grained nature, are rare. The cost of hardware at the time of Seltzer's writing was high and even though it is much reduced today, the cost of software development remains significant. Estimates for the development of one hour of CBT range from 200 to 400 hours, with some reduction if a suitable authoring system is available. In educational establishments, where the ethic of academic exchange is still strong, high development costs can be spread through transfer of software between institutions. In industrial contexts, commercial competition makes this less feasible and in addition, the training manager inevitably has to produce a more precise estimate of potential training benefit.

There are many training programmes in which a computer can be claimed to satisfy Seltzer's first criterion, that of providing a "unique solution". A computer is virtually the only means of driving a complex dynamic simulation of, say, a nuclear power plant or a national economy. Such simulations depend upon the speed and flexibility which a computer offers. In a complex domain, it is possible for the trainee to access different representations of the subject matter with the press of a button. Thus in the training of fault-finding, trainees might access circuit diagrams, definitions of the function of components, pictures of the physical location of components and the causal relationships between system variables. In addition, complex calculations can be performed quickly both in the evaluation of trainee performance and in the generation of new training material to be presented.

Seltzer's second criterion is in essence concerned with the cost–benefit or cost-effectiveness of using a computer for training. The benefit of

CBT has to justify its cost. Cost will be minimal when new CBT programmes do not have to be developed and existing ones can be utilised. The next best scenario, mentioned at the beginning of this chapter, is where CBT can be "embedded" within, or "piggyback" onto existing or newly acquired computer facilities which may be used, for example, to control a complex plant or to provide an accounting or stock control system. The classic example is when banking and administrative systems become computerised, and the new tasks and procedures required of clerks can be trained by means of a CBT package embedded in the system itself. Such a case study (and success story) was reported by Simmons (1975). British Airways upgraded their worldwide reservation system to a computer-based system involving new procedures, the use of VDUs etc. A training solution was embedded in this new system such that the user terminal could also function as a training device. Despite some initial scepticism from employees, the CBT was effective and eventually carried the day with substantial savings of:

over 2,000 hotel nights, over 500 man days of travelling time and over 750 man days of teaching time (Simmons, p. 290).

There is no reason why such applications should not become commonplace as computer networks are extended both within and between large organisations.

Configurations of CBT

The term CBT is misleading if it suggests one, uniform type of training. It is a mistake to attempt to characterise CBT per se, because there are as many configurations of CBT as there are different training solutions. One means of differentiating variations in CBT is to recall the functions in a closed-loop training system which were discussed in the context of programmed instruction in Section 11.3. These functions included a subject matter store, a display, an evaluator of responses, a performance memory, and a controller of material provided to the trainee (see Figure 11.4 and pp. 448–451 for a description). The computer can fulfil all or some of these functions, or indeed just part of one function. Therefore many configurations of CBT exist.

Crawford and Crawford (1978) reported an interesting CBT study in which, whilst the computer fulfilled all functions, prime interest focused on the feasibility and effectiveness of using an interactive graphic simulation of part of an anti-submarine aircraft system. The task involved simple procedural and perceptual-motor skills. Trainees were able to input commands via a touch panel on a PLATO IV terminal and the simulation would respond in a similar manner to the real equipment (Figure 11.7). The CBT also provided training material, practice, tests and feedback. The study found that three hours of this CBT was superior to eight hours of conventional training using a workbook. The feasibility of using an interactive simulation within the CBT was therefore demonstrated together with its effectiveness. Such training was considerably cheaper than using a full-scale realistic simulator.

Some of the most convincing applications of CBT are where a computer is used for the fast generation and display of simulated material, sometimes involving the modelling of complex relationships.

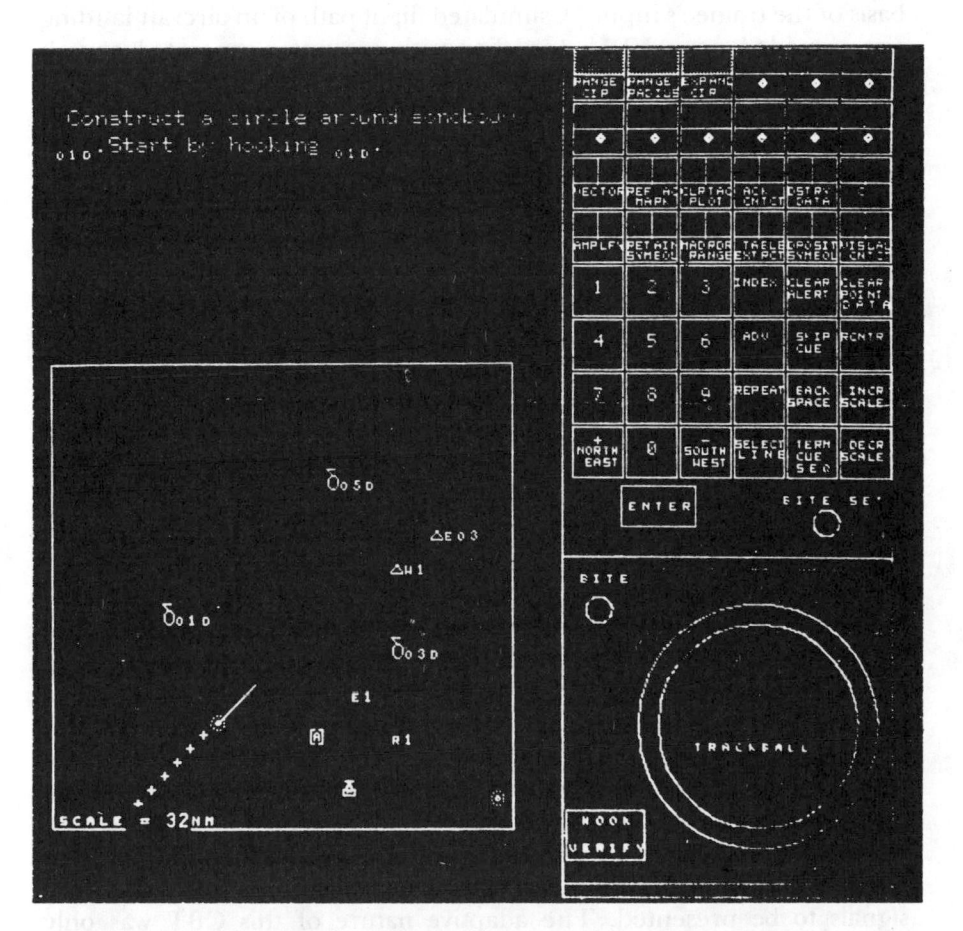

Figure 11.7 Simulation of the control panel of an anti-submarine aircraft using a PLATO IV screen (Crawford and Crawford, 1978).

In the late 1970s a flight simulator was developed at the US Naval Training Equipment Center, Orlando, in which a trainee pilot could "fly the plane" either from a display of computer generated images or from images generated by a camera moving over a terrain model (literally a small-scale model of the land). The computer-generated images were therefore just one part of the overall task display within the full-scale simulator. In the training of letter sorters in the US Postal Service, computer-generated simulations of different envelopes and styles of handwriting were displayed to trainees. Breaux (1976) reported a CBT system for air traffic controllers in which the computer was totally responsible for generating and controlling the simulated displays on the basis of the trainee's input. A simulated flight path of an aircraft landing was provided on a VDU, together with computer-generated speech from the pilot which responded to the speech input of the trainee.

CBT is therefore not a unitary concept. Any training function can, in principle, be fulfilled by a computer, a human, or a mixture of both. Generalisations about CBT will inevitably be misleading, unless notice is taken of differences in the configuration of CBT and the varying roles which a computer can fulfil in the provision of training.

Tasks and CBT

The aim of this section is to dispel any notion that use of CBT is restricted to particular types of task. Just as the configurations of CBT can vary widely, so can the tasks for which CBT is employed. There is no reason why some form of CBT cannot be used for training any type of task, which will become evident from the following selective review, based in part on an account by Patrick and Stammers (1977).

(a) *Perceptual identification.* Auditory and visual identification have been trained in a series of studies by Swets and colleagues using computer-based training (Swets et al., 1966; Swets et al., 1962; Weisz and McElroy, 1964). These studies were more research-oriented than application driven and were aimed not only at identifying optimal training methods for this type of task, but also examining the feasibility of using a computer-based system. A computer generated the signals, recorded the trainees' responses, provided feedback or knowledge of results concerning the accuracy of performance and selected future signals to be presented. The adaptive nature of this CBT was only possible because of the computer's involvement although this feature did not produce better learning than a simple presentation of stimulus response pairs. It was found in the Weisz and McElroy study that a combination of cueing and feedback training methods were optimal. In training for this task, the speed with which a computer evaluated a response and generated subsequent training material satisfies Seltzer's criterion of "uniqueness" for computer involvement.

(b) Perceptual-motor skills. The examples of adaptive training of key-board skills, discussed in Section 9.6, are also examples of CBT. The study by Bartram (pp. 362–365) described computer-based training for letter-sorters which used an adaptive cumulative-part training regime. Many CBT packages are available for improving "discrete" perceptual-motor skills such as typing, editing etc. Gaines (1967, 1969) was one of the first to demonstrate the feasibility of automating training for "continuous" perceptual-motor tasks, such as tracking. The processing power provided by a computer is useful in modelling the complex dynamics of a control system, evaluating a trainee's performance, and adjusting the difficulty of the trainee's task in an adaptive manner.

In order to "stack" aircraft which are waiting to land at an airport, pilots have to be trained to fly what are known as "holding patterns". Aircraft are usually stacked at 1000 feet intervals and fly in an oval pattern within a horizontal space of approximately 7 by 10 miles (Figure 11.8a). This is a straightforward task with no wind but the "ideal" holding pattern changes in accordance with the direction and speed of the wind (Figure 11.8b). Studies by Finnegan (1977), Trollip and Ortony (1977) and Trollip (1979) investigated CBT for this task using the PLATO IV system. The trainee had to "fly" the plane by means of a hand controller which was linked to the computer, whilst observing simulated flight and navigation instruments on the VDU. The CBT system calculated the ideal holding pattern for a specified wind condition and compared it against the current pattern being flown by the trainee. A built-in "instructor" provided feedback such as "you are turning too fast" etc. At the end of flying each holding pattern, the trainee was presented with a picture of the ideal pattern with the pattern (s)he actually flew superimposed upon it. This was accompanied by a verbal analysis of mistakes and possible reasons for them by the "instructor". When the trainee was competent at flying one type of holding pattern, a more difficult type was selected for training. Two important results emerged concerning the CBT used in these studies:

the CBT resulted in faster training with fewer errors in comparison with more conventional training;

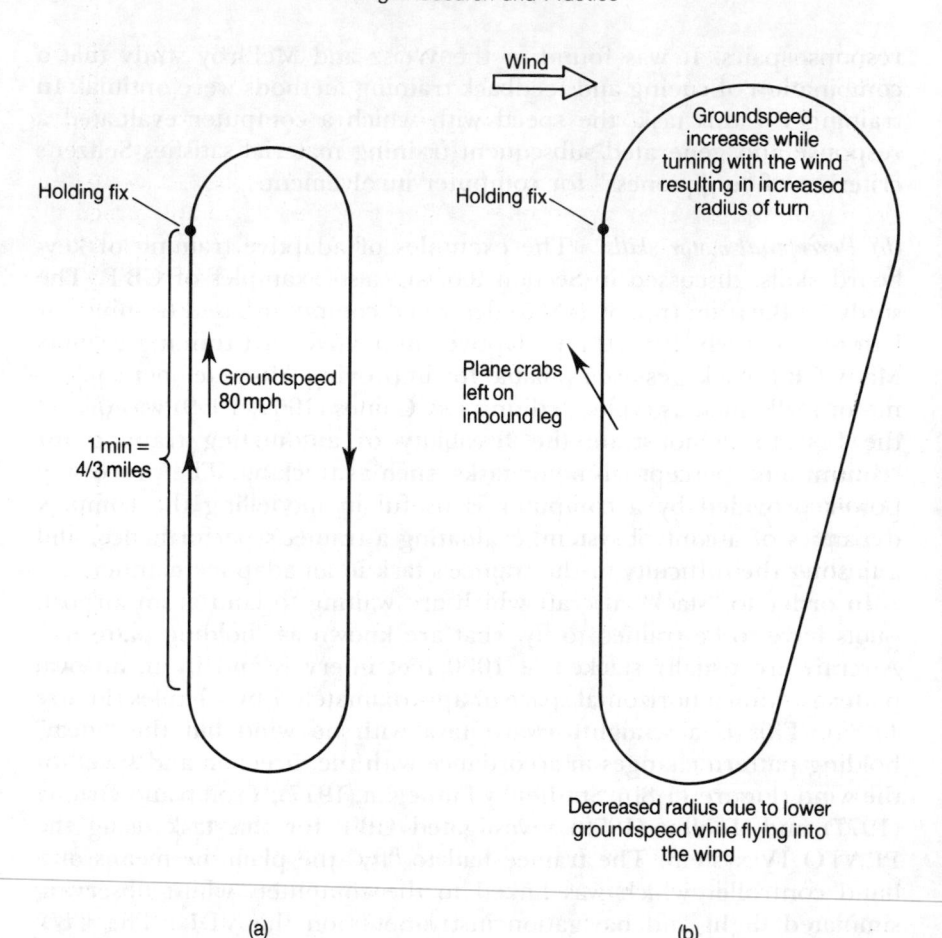

Figure 11.8   Flying a holding pattern with (a) no wind and (b) a crosswind (from Finnegan, 1977).

this superiority was found in transfer tests using both the GAT-2 trainer (a realistic simulator) and also an actual aeroplane.

(c) Basic intellectual skills.   This title refers to tasks involving factual information, concepts and rules, i.e. the basic intellectual skills in Gagné's learning hierarchy excluding the more complex types such as problem-solving. Training for these tasks can be found in many introductory courses in both education and industrial training. TICCIT is a CBT system aimed at concept and rule learning. The syllabuses in disciplines, such as mathematics, biology and chemistry, require that

facts, discriminations and simple concepts be mastered. Some of the early applications of PLATO were directed to this end (e.g. Chabay and Smith, 1977). CBT for basic skills programmes using PLATO were successfully introduced into three Illinois prisons (Plato Corrections Project Staff, 1978). Suppes and Morningstar (1969) reported on the evaluation of two CBT programmes. One involved "drill and practice" for elementary mathematics (e.g. counting, addition, division, fractions) and was implemented for schools in the California area between 1966–1968. The second programme concerned tutorial material for elementary Russian (e.g. grammar, syntax) which was used in schools in Mississippi between 1967–1968. Evaluation of the mathematics programme indicated that conventional methods were as successful as CBT, although CBT was advantageous in schools which were less affluent, where presumably teacher quality and training were more problematic. CBT of Russian was more of an unqualified success with students who used CBT having higher exam scores and a lower attrition rate than those trained by conventional methods.

In industry, both induction training and the initial stages of training for many technical jobs are concerned with the acquisition of facts and concepts. Two studies compared CBT with conventional programmed instruction for technician training (Schwartz and Haskell, 1966; Schwartz and Long, 1967). Trainees using CBT had no better examination scores, although training time was reduced by 10%–15%. Trainees' reactions were favourably disposed to CBT, which at the time of these studies could not be assumed because CBT was a novel mode of training. More recently, Friend and Patrick (1988) described CBT for induction training of chemical plant apprentices which covered the visual appearance, location and function of different pieces of plant equipment. Learner control permitted the trainee to select one of 18 CBT modules organised in a two-dimensional matrix, one dimension representing the piece of equipment and the other dimension the type of information. Whilst the main aim of the study was to investigate the relationship between learning sequence and the manner in which knowledge was organised and represented, this CBT was effective.

(d) Management tasks. A range of tasks can be subsumed under the title of "management" training. The most well-known applications of CBT have attempted to improve the decision-making of "managers", using computerised "games". Military commanders can be trained in strategic decision-making by interacting with simulated battlefield scenarios. Similarly, the decision-making skills of the business manager can be assessed by comparison against an "ideal" or "correct" pattern and

subsequently improved using some CBT. In one project, sponsored by the National Development Programme for Computer Assisted Learning between 1973–1978 in the UK, CBT was devised to improve managers' perceptions of their own assumptions and those of others in decision-making situations. The computer not only provided a simulation of a business situation but evaluated the consistency and accuracy of the managers' judgements.

More unusual is the application of CBT to the training of social skills, although this is restricted to interactions which can be formalised, for example, by a set of rules. Spencer et al. (1975) used PLATO to train US naval officers in the nature of the feedback which could be provided to subordinates during social interaction. CBT provided a tutorial in which trainees (i.e. officers) were given examples of both the nature of the feedback which was permissible and when it could be provided.

(e) Problem diagnosis. Performance in problem diagnosis tasks is well-suited to a computer-based training solution. The most commonly studied problem diagnosis task is that of fault-finding, although clinical diagnosis, in which a doctor diagnoses a patient's illness has also been investigated. These tasks have some common features. A problem state, i.e. a set of symptoms, is "displayed" to the diagnostician. These symptoms have to be interpreted and, in the light of this, further information gathered (e.g. results of tests) until the problem can be diagnosed. The aim of the diagnostician is to interpret the symptoms and "interrogate" the system (a piece of equipment or a patient), as efficiently as possible in order to arrive at the solution quickly and without error. Such a task might require various cognitive activities from application of rules/heuristics to reasoning about the causal relationships between variables in the system.

There are various advantages to using some form of CBT for problem diagnosis. The first, and most obvious, is that it is possible to simulate such a task in a manner which preserves its psychological requirements and yet gains the advantages accruing from the use of a simulation. Both "patients", emergency situations or hazardous equipment can be simulated and trainees' diagnosis and management strategies can be evaluated without the dangers associated with the real situations. The time pressure of an emergency situation can also be preserved by the simulation. Such a study is reported by Taylor (1975) in which hospital patients and emergency situations were simulated and trainees' performance evaluated against "ideal" diagnoses and patterns of care. The second advantage of CBT is that a simulation can be devised to expose the trainee to a greater range of problem diagnosis situations than might normally occur in the real situation. De Dombal, Hartley and Sleeman (1969) found the patient populations available in hospitals too specialised, which led them to train clinical diagnosis using an audio-visual display with a teleprinter as the trainee's terminal. Thirdly, the computer can provide flexibility in the manner in which the task is represented to the trainee (Patrick and Stammers, 1981). A fault-finding task can be displayed by an abstract representation of interconnected units (Rouse, 1979), a functional diagram, a picture of the actual equipment and a circuit diagram. The fast generation of alternative representations by a computer can be claimed to provide a "unique solution" in Seltzer's terms and one suspects that this is of considerable instructional benefit. Alternative representations of a task are incorporated in the AIDE system (Towne and Rigney, 1979) and more recently in Lind's multilevel flow modelling of complex systems (Lind, 1990).

A fourth advantage is that evaluation of trainee performance during a complex problem diagnosis task can be problematic without the involvement of a computer. Performance may have to be evaluated against some "ideal" model involving calculations concerning probability, cost, efficiency etc. in order to provide the trainee with some feedback information. ACTS (Adaptive Computer Training System) was devised by Crooks, Kuppin and Freedy (1978) to improve troubleshooting skills by enabling trainees to test components, replace parts and diagnose faults in a simulated electronic circuit. The decision-making of a trainee was evaluated in terms of cost, probability of success and information gain by comparison against the model of an expert's decision-making. The computer carried out such calculations quickly and provided the trainee with feedback concerning the utility of his actions. Duncan and Gray (1975) proposed that fault-finding be evaluated with respect to all the feasible faults consistent with a particular symptom pattern (termed the "consistent fault set"). Inadequate performance included premature diagnoses, redundant questions and extra questions. A computer can not only be used to provide such feedback information during fault-finding, but can also provide advance information about the wisdom of a projected choice by the fault-finder, i.e. feedforward information.

For all these reasons, problem diagnosis is a type of task for which CBT offers substantial benefits.

In conclusion, computer-based solutions have been used for training perceptual identification skills, perceptual-motor skills, basic intellectual skills, supervisory skills, and the skills of fault-finding and clinical diagnosis. This list is not exhaustive and CBT has also been used for tasks which involve the acquisition of procedures and principles. CBT can not only be used for different types of task, but it can exist in different configurations, even alongside conventional training. It is misleading to characterise CBT as one form of training. It needs to be viewed as providing a potential solution to a training problem and therefore has to be judged by how well it accomplishes this.

Evaluation of CBT

Evaluation of CBT has not been carried out systematically. Some investigations of CBT were feasibility studies and the fact that training was implemented was considered a success. When evaluation of CBT has been carried out it has typically involved comparison with a more conventional method. This is unsatisfactory for two reasons. Firstly, it ignores the different roles and configurations of CBT which have been discussed previously. Ideally, evaluation studies should be more fine-grained and should include comparison of different configurations of CBT. Secondly, global comparisons of CBT with conventional methods are confounded by just the same set of factors which were problematic in the evaluation of programmed instruction (pp. 446–447). It is difficult to make comparisons between CBT and conventional training which can be justified as "fair".

If these difficulties were not enough, evaluations of the cost effectiveness of CBT have themselves been the subject of considerable debate. Fielden (1977) illustrated the subjectivity and complexity of costing CBT and criticised any notion that costing was straightforward. Fielden (1977) concluded:

> Cost judgements are far from simple and when they are applied in a dynamic qualitative environment, where the nature and impact of the change is unclear, they will continue to require added explanation and require greater qualification (Fielden, 1977, p. 200).

This conclusion was substantiated by a review of CBT evaluation studies in the US military by Orlansky and String (1979). This review criticised some of the costing criteria and measures of effectiveness which were used. The review covered 30 studies (some of these were of CML), which were carried out since 1968. The CBT which was the focus of these evaluation studies varied considerably in terms of the number of trainees (a couple to 50), the duration of the training (one day to one week), and the nature of the training content (e.g. theoretical material, vehicle repair tasks). Orlansky and String's conclusions were divided into general criticisms, and more specific findings concerning both the effectiveness and the cost of CBT. Their conclusions can be summarised as follows:

1. *General criticisms*

   Only eight out of 30 evaluation studies reported data on both cost and effectiveness.

   Even these eight studies used data and costs which were incomplete "with respect to costs of program management, maintenance and repair, instructional support, and other factors important in determining life-cycle costs." (Orlansky and String, p. 3).

   All studies used measures of trainee achievement and did not include measures of transfer to the job.

   Trainee attitudes were often measured and, whilst these may have been interesting, they did not relate directly to either the cost or effectiveness of CBT.

   The comparison of CBT with conventional training was confounded by self-pacing, computer support and the revised nature of the training material.

2. *Effectiveness*

   Trainee achievement using CBT was about equivalent to that found using conventional training in most evaluation studies. It was superior in one-third of the studies although this superiority was of little practical significance. This superiority was partly because trainees were kept in CBT courses until they achieved a specified level of performance.

   CBT resulted in about 30% reduction in training time in comparison with conventional training.

   CBT was associated with a slightly higher rate of attrition.

   Trainees preferred CBT but trainers did not.

3. *Costs*

   Data on costs of training were insufficiently detailed to permit comparisons of different types of training.

   The data concerning costs which are needed for any training course relate to:

   1. Training design and development.
   2. Implementation and delivery of training.
   3. Management and administration of training.
   4. Trainee costs.

   Evaluation studies had various "gaps" in their data on costs.

   (Adapted from Orlansky and String, 1979.)

The cost of CBT is generally understated. One means of defraying its high development costs is the use of general purpose CBT systems. Such systems can either provide wide access to shared lessons, as in the statistics modules developed at the University of Leeds, or support the development of CBT for different examples of the same type of task. The latter option is attractive although difficult to achieve. One example of this, which was discussed earlier, is the AUTHOR system which supported the training of symbol recognition. Similarly, the training of troubleshooting skills for various pieces of equipment has been carried out using the AIDE system (Towne and Rigney, 1979) which seems also to have been named the GMTS (Generalized Maintenance Trainer Simulator). This is a general purpose system which enables difference pieces of equipment to be simulated. The system is "programmed" to contain images of equipment (modules, boards etc.), circuit diagrams, faults and their associated symptoms, and relationships between all of these. The trainee investigates a simulated fault using a touch pen to access the current state of an indicator, to change a switch setting, or to replace a component. This interaction terminates when the trainee believes that the fault has been diagnosed and rectified. Towne (1981) reported that this general purpose training system had been used for a radar repeater, a shipboard communication system and a satellite communication system. Some evidence concerning the effectiveness of such training has involved transfer to the actual equipment. Another advantage of such a CBT system is that it enables the trainer to learn about both the diagnostic strategies employed by trainees, and the effectiveness of different interventions provided during training. In this manner research and training proceed hand-in-hand.

Besides underestimating the cost of CBT, other factors required to develop CBT successfully are often overlooked. Trade union attitudes concerning the computer-based storage of trainee records are important. In addition the development and implementation of CBT requires a variety of skills which are rarely available in the correct mixture. Programming, technical and training skills are needed, together with knowledge of the domain for which training is being developed. Computer operators, programmers and technicians are necessary to develop and maintain the software and hardware. In order to manage these additional and yet complementary inputs, training departments require some reorganisation. It is not easy to anticipate the change in resources which CBT brings and some typical problems are summarised by Spencer et al. (1975) in the development of CBT for interpersonal skills:

There were many unknowns ... the capabilities of the PLATO IV system ... and the feasibility of training social skills using computer assisted instruction ... Some problems occurred. For a major portion of the contract period, there was only one terminal ... Also, explanation of the PLATO system and the TUTOR language seemed to follow a trial and error mode ... The PLATO system's periodic breakdown was also a problem area ... Finally the PLATO capabilities had some significant shortcomings. Specifically, the inability to interpret open-ended responses constrained the simulation and practice potential of the training materials.

11.5 INTELLIGENT TUTORING SYSTEMS

The desire that CBT should be more "intelligent" has led to the development and labelling of so-called Intelligent Tutoring Systems (ITSs). Alternatively, these have been described as Intelligent Teaching Systems or Intelligent Computer Assisted Instruction (ICAI). This is an important area of cognitive science where cognitive psychology and techniques of artificial intelligence have been brought to bear on training problems. The aim has been to develop automated training resembling that of a good (i.e. intelligent) human tutor. Whilst progress has been made, the aim of developing a completely intelligent tutor, except in a very restricted domain, remains a goal which will not be achieved for some considerable time. Most ITSs are research-oriented feasibility projects and have not been implemented and evaluated in the normal manner as training solutions to applied problems.

There has been a surge of interest in ITSs during the last 15 years. Naughton (1986) provided an introduction to the application of artificial intelligence to training issues. The book *Intelligent Tutoring Systems* by Sleeman and Brown (1982) is a good source for descriptions of many important ITSs. More recently Wenger (1987) has provided an authoritative text on the subject and other useful sources include: Lawler and Yazdani (1987); Polson and Richardson (1988); Psotka, Massey and Mutter (1988); and Self (1988).

Two issues are addressed in the following sections. Firstly, what is an ITS and how can it be distinguished from CBT and programmed instruction? Secondly, some of the more famous ITSs are discussed in order to illustrate their main characteristics.

Aims and features of ITSs

Comparison of the capabilities of programmed instruction and computer-based training with those of a human tutor finds many "intelligent" features missing. The aim of ITSs is to rectify this and create more intelligent automated training. Typically, a number of criticisms of conventional CBT are made. Some of these, e.g. that conventional CBT is an expensive "page turner", are not critical of CBT per se, but rather of the manner in which it is configured. The following criticisms are more significant:

1. Conventional CBT programs do not have any explicit expertise in the domain. They do not "know" how to do what the trainee is being taught except in a very restrictive sense. They are unable to demonstrate how to do e.g. a geometry proof.
2. Interaction with the trainee takes place by recognition of a set of restricted codes which is far removed from a natural language dialogue with a human tutor.
3. The development of CBT has to break material into frames, specify remedial frames and anticipate all of the trainee's answers and routes through the material. This is difficult, if not impossible, in complex domains.
4. Training materials are prestructured and are not capable of being generated to cope with, say, a trainee's request.
5. Conventional CBT does not make inferences about the trainee's expertise in a domain except in a rudimentary fashion (e.g. a list of correct and incorrect answers).

The difference between CBT and ITSs is a matter of degree. There is no clear division between them. For example, adaptivity is an important feature of ITSs. However, some CBT systems are adaptive and modify their training materials in the light of a trainee's level of competence. In CBT this is usually accomplished by an algorithm which specifies the relationship between the trainee's responses and how the training material should be changed, e.g. in terms of level of difficulty. However, these algorithms or teaching rules are not themselves adaptive, i.e. capable of being changed in the light of experience. Self-improvement is a feature of some intelligent tutoring systems (e.g. Kimball, 1982). Similarly, the extent to which ITSs and CBT diagnose a trainee's weaknesses or misconceptions is also a matter of degree. ITSs strive for a "deep" understanding of the trainee's knowledge, for example, by using the strategies of good tutors' identified by Collins and Stevens and discussed in Section 8.4. In contrast, conventional CBT only has a "surface" understanding of the trainee's knowledge, possibly in terms of the number of lessons accessed coupled with the percentage of correct answers on some post-tests.

One early and authoritative account of the nature of an ITS was given by Hartley and Sleeman (1973). They suggested that an ITS should have the following four features:

1. *A representation of the teaching task.* This comprises the knowledge, skill etc. which has to be trained. More recently, this is known as *domain expertise.* Anderson (1988) has discussed different approaches to structuring and representing this expertise.

2. *A representation of the trainee.* The knowledge, skill of the trainee is inferred on the basis of his or her current and past performance. This is assembled into what is referred to nowadays as a *student model.* Van Lehn (1988) has described different types of student model.

3. *A set of teaching operations.* This constitutes the training events or methods which can be used. So, for example, the trainee may be allowed to exercise "learner-control" over the pace or sequence of the training material. Irrespective of whether "learner-control" is available the training system may have: different types of example and explanation; different questions coupled with varying forms of advice or feedback; and different training exercises which can be generated.

4. *A set of means–ends guidance rules.* Hartley and Sleeman stated that "these are decision rules which state the conditions under which the teaching operations [3], should be used with an individual student during his learning" (p. 216). These rules therefore control the interaction between the system and the trainee, e.g. "if the trainee gets 75% or more of the questions concerning topic X correct, then proceed to train topic X+1".

Features 3 and 4 above, proposed by Hartley and Sleeman, are normally subsumed under the title "teaching expertise". An ITS can therefore be said to have three main features: domain expertise (i.e. *what* has to be mastered), a student model (i.e. a representation of the trainee's current level of competence) and some teaching expertise (i.e. *how* training should be designed). (The reader will recognise these as equivalent to the three components of training design discussed in Section 8.1.) The nature of these features and their interactions will determine the degree of intelligence possessed by any training system, whether this is labelled CBT or an ITS. One might argue that these features are not new and existed, or were implicit, in descriptions of programmed instruction and a closed-loop training system (Section 11.3, pp. 448–451). In programmed instruction, a "controller" had rules which governed the sequence of training material which was a primitive form of teaching expertise. Also the "evaluator" and "performance memory" functions involved some domain expertise and a student model, even though these were implicit in the manner in which the training material was structured. Consequently, ITSs differ from programmed instruction and CBT in their determination to make the domain expertise and student model explicit. However, the degree of intelligence of *any* form of automated training can only be assessed from a careful examination of how its components are formulated rather than reference to any global label.

A fourth feature frequently cited for an ITS is its user interface. A trainee is able to interact with a human tutor in a relatively flexible and unconstrained manner. This is unlike conventional CBT in which interaction is via a set of menus and the program is only able to recognise simple anticipated inputs rather than complex spontaneous messages. The interface needs to be more tolerant of both spelling mistakes and syntactic errors and ideally it should be able to sustain a natural language dialogue. In addition the trainee should be permitted to switch goals during a tutorial and this need should be recognised by the system, in a similar fashion to a human tutor.

The overall aim of an ITS is to design these four features such that they capture the expertise of a human tutor. It is not surprising that this aim has not been achieved, except for very restricted tasks, if one considers the magnitude of what is involved. Essentially one is faced with the difficulty of analysing a complex cognitive task, that of human tutoring, and identifying the types of knowledge involved, alternative representations of each type of knowledge and some control structure which specifies how these interact in dynamic fashion. The enormity of this task is beyond our current capabilities, a fact acknowledged by Naughton (1986), O'Shea and Self (1983) and more recent writers on this topic. In case some readers are not convinced of this, possibly because of the somewhat exaggerated claims made for ITSs, then it is worth describing Millward's 1979 article "Teaching a computer to teach" which spelled out why the goal of a fully automated and intelligent training system is so difficult to achieve. According to Millward there are three main components in an intelligent tutorial:

1. The types of knowledge used.
2. The tutor's problem-solving skills to diagnose the student's difficulties.
3. Natural language communication.

Prescribing how these three components inter-relate is a major problem. Millward identified the following six types of knowledge used by a human tutor which also interact in subtle ways:

1. Knowledge of the subject matter to be taught (i.e. domain expertise).
2. Everyday knowledge about the world.

3. Knowledge about the student's knowledge and abilities (i.e. a student model).
4. The tutor's knowledge about his own knowledge.
5. Knowledge about how to teach and communicate (i.e. teaching expertise).
6. Knowledge of social conventions.

It is very easy to underestimate the range of sources which provide information even for the normal categories of knowledge discussed in relation to ITSs (i.e. categories 1, 3 and 5). For example, Millward pointed out that a tutor's knowledge of a student's knowledge and abilities, not only comes from formal explicit records (e.g. essay marks) but also from the tutor's knowledge concerning the student's linguistic competence, socioeconomic background, past history etc. Similarly, the tutor's knowledge about how to teach also involves making intuitive judgements, for example, sensing that a student is getting confused. In addition to the standard three types of knowledge (domain expertise, a student model and teaching expertise), a tutor uses everyday knowledge, knowledge about his own knowledge and knowledge of social conventions. A good tutor will often draw on some common world knowledge shared by the student in the attempt to elucidate a concept or provide an analogy. How is this world knowledge to be captured and represented in an ITS, especially if requirements for it cannot be anticipated? There are also social conventions which guide a tutorial dialogue and these need to be specified. Even when these six types of knowledge have been identified, decisions have to be taken concerning how each type is represented and interrelated. The ultimate aim of ITSs to emulate a human tutor will remain to be accomplished as long as the analysis of complex skills continues to be problematic.

Let us conclude these general remarks with Millward's summary of the nature of a tutorial:

> The higher level goals of a tutor are guided by the problem solving component interacting with a model of the student. A difference between the tutor's model of the student's subject-matter knowledge and the tutor's own subject-matter knowledge generates a proposition to be transmitted to the student. The knowledge-of-teaching component is called to suggest a way to transmit this proposition; for example, ask a leading question, provide a hint, suggest an analogy, or tell the student the idea outright. Once the specific form of the proposition has been selected, the discourse generator constructs a sentence to accomplish the higher level goal.
>
> The student's comments, answers, and questions are parsed into a representation that can be compared with existing knowledge systems. Assuming the student's comment is relevant to the subject matter, it is stored as a new piece of evidence about the student's knowledge ... Both

the production and interpretation of discourse invoke stupendous problems ... For communication to occur, both the tutor and the student must
have a number of types of knowledge to refer to, including models of each
other's knowledge states (pp. 108–109).

Examples of ITSs

Most ITSs have been developed to illustrate how one or more of
the features of a human tutor might be captured. They have been
developed in various domains to train aspects of, for example, mathematics, programming, language, geography and engineering. A large
number of ITSs have been concerned with diagnostic skills in both
industrial and medical contexts. This is because such skills are not only
important and interesting but the tasks can be simulated in a manageable fashion.

The aim of this section is to provide a flavour of this work by
examining briefly some of the landmarks in the development of ITSs.
The following three ITSs are discussed:

1. SCHOLAR (Carbonell, 1970).
2. BUGGY (Brown and Burton, 1978).
3. SOPHIE I, II and III (Brown, Burton and De Kleer, 1982).

In addition the development of GUIDON and related systems (Clancey,
1982; Richer and Clancey, 1987) has had a major impact on the thinking
in this area.

SCHOLAR, developed by Carbonell (1970), is recognised as the first
ITS. It was developed to train factual knowledge concerning the
geography of South America rather than any skills or procedural
knowledge. This included facts like "Uruguay is a country", "Argentina
is in South America and is between latitude −22 and −55". An
important aspect of SCHOLAR was its *generative* nature, such that the
factual material and its sequencing was not predetermined by the
designer but could be generated by the system as required. This was
achieved by representing the facts as a semantic network, which at that
time was considered to be similar to how a person's knowledge would be
organised. Figure 11.9 shows part of the semantic network which
represented the domain expertise of SCHOLAR. The nodes in this
network were concepts, such as countries, and the lines represented
relationships between them, e.g. part-of. SCHOLAR produced an
answer to a question, not by consulting a list of factual statements and
trying to select one, but by inference using the semantic network. Thus
"What is the latitude of Uruguay?" would lead it to find the node

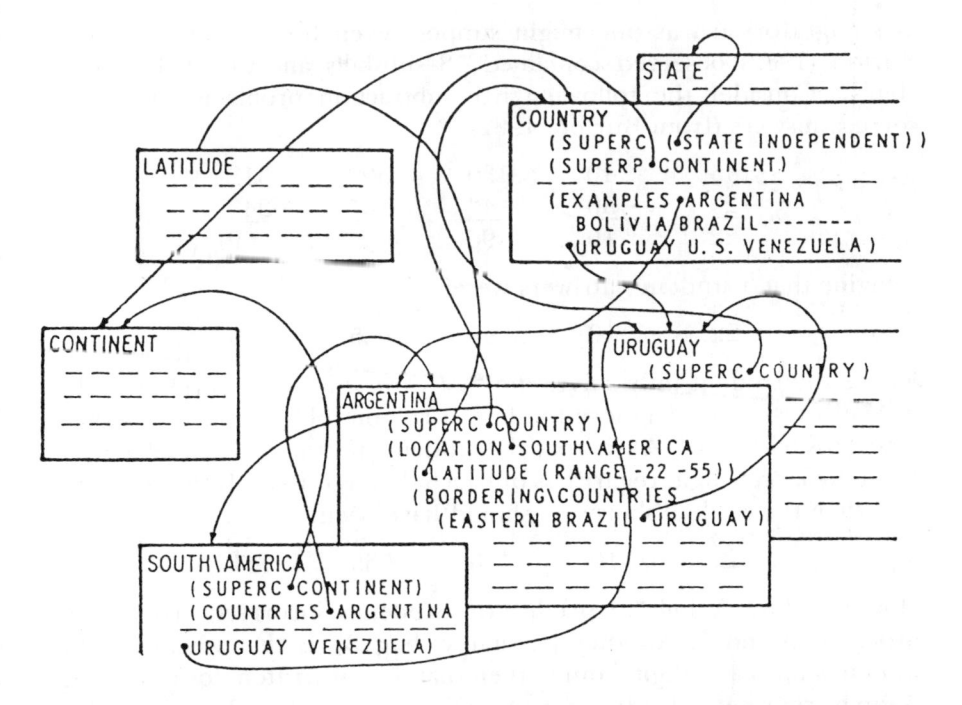

Figure 11.9 Part of the semantic network used by SCHOLAR (Carbonell, 1970).

"Uruguay" and then search for the latitude relationship. In this way it was able to answer questions posed by the trainee and also generate its own questions. A crude model of the trainee's competence was developed by flagging nodes on the network which were known by the trainee. SCHOLAR regulated the amount of information it gave in response to a question by restricting its answer to adjacent nodes in the network and properties which were tagged as important. With further prompting it would extend its answers to more distant nodes and less important information. This gave it some human-like qualities even though its teaching expertise was rather limited.

BUGGY was developed by Brown and Burton (1978) in order to train teachers to diagnose students' mistakes in doing simple problems of addition and subtraction. The philosophy underlying BUGGY was that students often suffered from an underlying misconception (a "bug"), which resulted in systematic mistakes being made in how arithmetic procedures were performed. Therefore teachers had to be trained to diagnose these "bugs" and then correct them. This diagnostic task is not as straightforward as one might suppose even for subtraction which Burton (1982) observed contained 58 subskills and about 110 basic "bugs". Consider the following five subtraction problems with their correct answers (from Burton, 1982):

$$
\begin{array}{ccccc}
45 & 40 & 139 & 500 & 312 \\
-23 & -30 & -43 & -65 & -243 \\
\hline
22 & 10 & 96 & 435 & 69
\end{array}
$$

Imagine that a student's answers were:

$$
\begin{array}{ccccc}
22 & 10 & 96 & 565 & 149
\end{array}
$$

Hence the student only solves the first three problems correctly. The teacher's task is to diagnose the bug(s) responsible for these mistakes. One possibility (bug A), is that the student subtracts the smaller digit from the larger digit, regardless of which digit is on top. If this were the case then the student's answers should have been:

$$
\begin{array}{ccccc}
22 & 10 & 116 & 565 & 131
\end{array}
$$

However, bug A fails to predict the student's incorrect answers for problems 3 and 5. Another possibility (bug B), is that whenever the student subtracts a digit from 0, then that digit is written down (i.e. bug B can be represented as $0 - n = n$). In this example, bug B predicts all of the student's answers, both correct and incorrect, and is therefore judged to be the source of the student's mistakes. BUGGY works by finding the bug which provides the best match to a set of answers and then decides whether the evidence is sufficiently compelling to diagnosis that bug as the source of the student's difficulties. The domain expertise is based on an analysis of the subskills required in simple arithmetic and how they can go wrong. This is represented as a kind of "bug catalogue" which is consulted by BUGGY. The student model is defined by the subskills which the student can and cannot perform correctly.

In its basic format, BUGGY selects a bug and then simulates its effect on some arithmetic problems. The teacher, who is actually the trainee, asks BUGGY to solve further problems using the bug. The teacher makes a diagnosis when confident to do so. An example of the protocol from a team of teachers using BUGGY is given in Figure 11.10. Further versions of BUGGY are described by Burton (1982). DEBUGGY diagnosed bugs in a student's answers off-line and IDEBUGGY is an interactive version of it.

It might come as some surprise that even basic arithmetic skills can be so complex and difficult to diagnose. There are a number of factors which complicate such a task. Firstly, different bugs may produce the same answers to problems and therefore questions have to be derived in such a manner that the maximum number of potential bugs are eliminated at each stage of the diagnostic process. Secondly, there is "noise" in a student's answers, since they will not always be consistent; a lapse or slip may occur which is nonsystematic and is not the result of a "bug". Thirdly, multiple bugs may occur which are considerably more difficult to diagnose. BUGGY's "intelligence" stems from a thorough *analysis* of the tasks of addition and subtraction which provides it with a near exhaustive catalogue of bugs (at least single ones). In complex domains, proceeding in this manner presents a formidable problem because of the immense resources required and the fact that one can never be sure that all of the trainee's possible problems have been anticipated (see pp. 93–94 for a related discussion in the context of the transfer of fault-finding).

Brown and Burton (1978) reported that BUGGY was used to analyse a subtraction test given to 1325 students in grades 4, 5 and 6. BUGGY was able to identify the bugs of about 40% of the students. Of the remainder, 40% used essentially correct procedures and 20% could not be diagnosed by BUGGY, presumably because the errors were random or a result of multiple bugs. Interestingly, the most common bug was when borrowing from a column where the top digit is 0, the student writes 9, and does not continue borrowing from the column to the left of the 0 (i.e. 206 − 37 = 269). The next two most common bugs were those mentioned in the example discussed earlier; always subtracting the smaller digit from the larger one irrespective of position; writing down N when subtracting N from zero. From a training perspective, this type of information is exceedingly useful. The frequency and nature of errors, and perhaps how they vary according to age, would warn teachers of potential problems and enable training to focus its resources on those areas of potential difficulty.

SOPHIE (*SOPH*isticated *I*nstructional *E*nvironment) is undoubtedly the most well-known ITS and is a testimony to some of the ways in which artificial intelligence can not only enrich automated training but also some of the formidable difficulties involved. SOPHIE I, II and III are three versions developed over a five-year period from 1973 at the University of California and subsequently at Bolt, Beranek and Newman, in Cambridge, Massachusetts. They are concerned with training the skills for troubleshooting electronic circuits. An account of the features and developments of SOPHIE can be found in Brown, Burton and De Kleer (1982). Further details of SOPHIE II are provided by Brown, Rubenstein and Burton (1976), whilst Burton and Brown (1978) have discussed general issues concerning the development of a natural

Protocol of a Team Using BUGGY

WELCOME TO BUGGY.
I HAVE CHOSEN A BUG. HERE IS AN EXAMPLE OF THE BUG.

```
 17
 +5
 13
```

The system presents an example in which the student does not get the right answer.

NOW YOU CAN GIVE ME PROBLEMS TO DETERMINE THE BUG.

```
 18        43
 +6       +79
 15        23
```

The team generates problems that are answered by the "student". Notice that the team's test problems are similar to the initial example generated by BUGGY. This is usually a poor diagnostic strategy as it may leave other symptoms of a bug undiscovered.

Got the bug!

The team forms an initial hypothesis and tells the system they have discovered the bug. The system now asks the team to describe the bug and then tests them on their understanding. Asking for a description forces the team to verbalise their sometimes fuzzy idea of what the bug is and often makes them realise how ill-defined or vague their idea actually is. In the present system, the descriptions are saved but no attempt is made by the system to understand them.

PLEASE DESCRIBE THE BUG.

Student adds the number to be carried into the last column worked in.

This cryptic description is typical of those we have observed. Describing bugs in English is surprisingly difficult. What the team is trying to say is that if a column adds to more than 9, the units digit and the carry digit are added together and the result is written as the answer.

The hypothesis does account for the observed behaviour. Unfortunately, it is not the student's bug.

HERE ARE SOME PROBLEMS TO TEST YOUR THEORY ABOUT THE BUG. WHAT IS:

```
 21
 +39
 51
```

To ensure that the team has found the correct bug, the system produces several problems for the team to solve. At present, BUGGY has a heuristic problem generation programme that gives a broad range of "different problems".

The team's hypothesis is revealed as incorrect by the rest of the five test problems. BUGGY presents its answer and then allows the team to enter more problems.

THAT'S NOT THE BUG I HAVE.
USING MY BUG:

```
  21
+ 39
  15
```

TRY GIVING ME SOME MORE EXAMPLES

```
|    51        99      68
| + 1707     | 90    + 9
     21        36      23
```

After failing the test, the team gives a greater range of problems, specifically those using bigger numbers. How is it that 51 + 1707 can add up to 21? By broadening the scope of example problems they are able to re-evaluate their initial hypothesis, dismiss it, and develop another one that is complete and consistent with respect to the new errors.

| Got the Bug!

PLEASE DESCRIBE THE BUG YOU THINK I HAVE.

The student is adding all the digits together.

HERE ARE SOME PROBLEMS TO TEST YOUR THEORY ABOUT THE BUG.
WHAT IS:

```
    33     1091       8       28      90
  + 99      + 60    + 34     + 70    + 6
|   24        17      15       17      15
```

This time the team's hypothesis passes the test and they are given the description of the bug stored in the procedural network.

VERY GOOD, MY DESCRIPTION OF THE BUG IS:
THE STUDENT ALWAYS SUMS UP ALL THE DIGITS WITH NO REGARD TO COLUMNS.

Note: Those lines typed by the team are indicated by a vertical line | in the left margin.

Figure 11.10 Example of a teacher's interaction with BUGGY in diagnosing a "bug" in addition (Brown and Burton, 1978).

language interface, which is probably SOPHIE's most impressive feature.

The basis of SOPHIE I is a simulation of one power supply circuit. The trainee has to diagnose a fault in the circuit and in so doing engages the system in a fairly unconstrained dialogue. SOPHIE can not only answer questions posed by the trainee as he or she is trying to diagnose the fault but also evaluates the trainee's hypothesis and comments on the benefit of measurements requested by the trainee. In addition, it can calculate the effects of any modifications of the circuit the trainee wishes to make. It is important to note that in building this, and any other training device, decisions have to be made concerning the optimal design of training. In SOPHIE the philosophy is to enable the trainee to take the initiative and to explore a learning environment. This raises general questions concerning the effectiveness of this approach and how well the trainee utilises the facilities provided. Another issue is that SOPHIE concerns one type of power supply circuit, albeit a nontrivial one, and this is a limiting factor, given that the ambitious aim of SOPHIE is to improve reasoning in general troubleshooting skills. In the absence of an analysis of how circuits vary and the extent to which they require different skills, it is difficult to predict its transfer value, except in an empirical fashion.

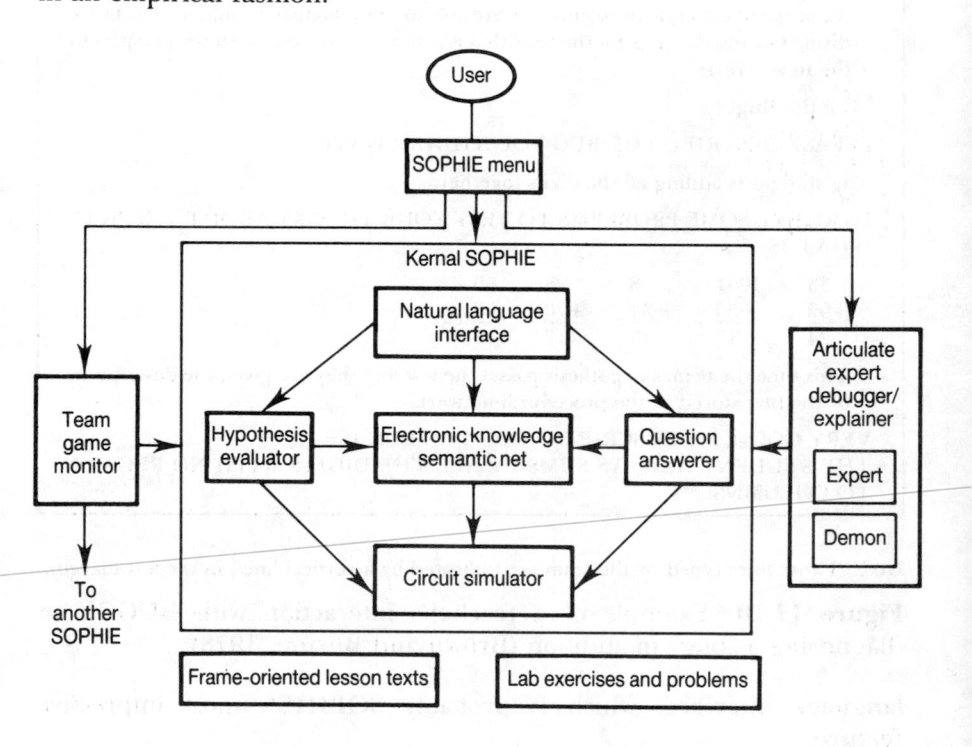

Figure 11.11 SOPHIE II system (Brown, Rubenstein and Burton, 1976).

The components of SOPHIE II are represented in Figure 11.11. Two changes from SOPHIE I were the addition of what was called an "articulate expert" and a game situation in which one team inserted a fault and the other team attempted to locate it. The "expert" provided a model or demonstration of not only the steps involved in tackling a fault, but also the reasoning and deductions at each step. The questions that arise here are how many reasoning strategies could be used for this task, which ones were used by the expert and to what extent did these coincide with the trainee's preferred or naturally adopted strategy? A drawback with SOPHIE II was that it was unable to follow up trainee's errors, in the manner of a good tutor, or adopt the strategy used by the trainee. SOPHIE III was developed to overcome some of these difficulties and it was better able to reproduce the reasoning behaviour of both real experts and novices. It also coped with a greater range of electronic circuits. For a full description the reader should consult Brown et al. (1982).

SOPHIE has clearly demonstrated the potential of artificial intelligence techniques in automated training. It is an environment which provides a variety of facilities and supports a flexible dialogue with the trainee. However, despite the many person-years involved in its development, Brown et al. described some of its limitations. One important limitation of SOPHIE III's expert was the assumptions it had to make in order to diagnose a fault. Two of these were that only one fault, rather than multiple faults, existed and that all of the ways in which the circuit could fault were known (although this is quite difficult to be certain about even for the relatively simple circuit used by SOPHIE). Finally, the developers of SOPHIE literally ran out of computer "space", even though SOPHIE is dedicated to training only one type of task, in one domain etc.

Most ITSs are demonstrations of the feasibility of using artificial intelligence in training devices, rather than training solutions to applied problems. One exception is the Recovery Boiler Tutor (Woolf et al., 1987) which has been used to train operators in the control of paper mills. SOPHIE, despite its immense development cost, has seen little use as a training system. Also few ITSs have received more than a rudimentary evaluation. Littman and Soloway (1988) estimated that about 20 evaluations of ITSs have been reported in the literature although most of these are informal and use criteria concerning whether the ITS behaves in the way that it should rather than whether it changes the trainee's behaviour. Also, it is an exceptional situation in which the sort of ITSs discussed in this chapter are cost-effective, given the massive development effort required. Perhaps the most important warning, which is in line with the thrust of this book, is that a prerequisite for the development of ITSs is an understanding of how an expert performs the task which only comes through some analysis of the task/skill. Whilst developing an ITS is itself an activity which generates ideas about how experts *may* function, validation is only possible through the fine-grained analysis of human expertise. This is one major reason given by Brown et al. (1982) why work on SOPHIE was discontinued:

> the intellectual issue was our increased awareness that we did not really know what it meant to "understand" how a complex piece of equipment works. In particular we did not know what mental models the experts had of a given system's functioning, nor did we know how these were learned, for they certainly weren't explicitly taught (p. 279).

The way forward for those concerned with the development of training seems to be in the use of artificial intelligence in a more restricted manner where parts of human expertise can be captured easily and the benefits are clear. In this way smaller ITSs can enrich existing training systems, thus making the transition from developmental systems to commonplace training solutions.

REFERENCES

Alderman, D.L. (1978). Evaluation of the TICCIT computer assisted learning system in the community college. Final Report. Princeton, NJ: Educational Testing Service.

Anderson, J.R. (1988). The expert module. In Polson, M.C. and Richardson, J.J. (Eds) (op.cit.).

Braby, R., Parrish, W.F., Guitard, C.R. and Aagard, J.A. (1978). Computer-aided authoring of programmed instruction for teaching symbol recognition. TAEG Report No 58. Orlando, FL: Training Analysis and Evaluation Group, Department of the US Navy.

Breaux, R. (1976). Training characteristics of the automative adaptive ground controlled approach radar controller training system. Technical Report NAVTRAEQUIPCEN 52. Orlando, FL: Naval Training Equipment Center.

Brown, J.S. and Burton, R.R. (1978). Diagnosing models for procedural bugs in basic mathematical skills. *Cognitive Science*, **2**, 155–192.

Brown, J.S., Burton, R.R. and De Kleer, J. (1982). Pedagogical, natural language and knowledge engineering techniques in SOPHIE I, II and III. In Sleeman, D.H. and Brown, J.S. (Eds) (op.cit.).

Brown, J.S., Rubenstein, R. and Burton, R. (1976). Reactive learning environment for computer assisted electronics instruction. Report No 3314. Cambridge, MA: Bolt, Beranek and Newman Inc.

Burton, R.R. (1982). Diagnosing bugs in a simple procedural skill. In Sleeman, D.H. and Brown, J.S. (Eds) (op.cit.).

Burton, R.R. and Brown, J.S. (1978). Intelligent CAI: An author and for a natural language interface. Report No 3913. Cambridge, MA: Bolt, Beranck and Newman.

Carbonell, J.R. (1970). AI in CAI: An artificial-intelligence approach to computer-assisted instruction. *IEEE Transactions on man-machine systems*, **11**, 190–202.

Chabay, R. and Smith, S.G. (1977). The use of computer-based chemistry lessons. *Journal of Chemical Education*, **54**, 745–747.

Clancey, W.J. (1982). Overview of Guidon. In Barr, A. and Fergenbaum, E.A. (Eds) *The handbook of artificial intelligence, Volume 2*. Los Altos, CA: Morgan Kaufman.

Coulson, J.E. (Ed.) (1962). *Programmed learning and computer-based instruction*. New York: Wiley.

Crawford, A.M. and Crawford, K.S. (1978). Simulation of operational equipment with a computer-based instructional system: A low cost training technology. *Human Factors*, **20**, 215–224.

Crooks, W.H., Kuppin, M.A. and Freedy, A. (1978). Application of adaptive decision aiding systems to computer-assisted instruction. Adaptive computer training system. Report No. TR-78–A6, (AD-AO56900) Alexandria, Virginia: US Army Research Institute for the Behavioral and Social Sciences.

Crowder, N.A. (1960). Automatic tutoring by intrinsic programming, In Lumsdaine, A.A. and Glaser, R. (Eds) *Teaching machines and programmed learning*. Washington: NEA.

Crowder, N.A. (1962). Intrinsic and extrinsic programming. In Coulson, J.E. (Ed.) (op.cit.).

De Dombal, F.T., Hartley, J.R. and Sleeman, D.H. (1969). A computer-assisted system for learning clinical diagnosis. *The Lancet*, January 18, 145–148.

Duncan, K.D. and Gray, M.J. (1975). Scoring methods for verification and diagnostic performance in industrial fault-finding problems. *Journal of Occupational Psychology*, **48**, 93–106.

Fielden, J. (1977). The financial evaluation of NDPCAL. *British Journal of Educational Technology*, **3**(8), 190–200.

Finnegan, J.P. (1977). Evaluation of the transfer and cost effectiveness of a complex computer-assisted flight procedures trainer. Technical Report ARL-77–7/AFOSR-77–6. Illinois: Institute of Aviation.

Friend, C. and Patrick, J. (1988). Strategies and representation in learner controlled training. In Patrick, J. and Duncan, K.D. (Eds) *Training, human decision making and control*. Amsterdam: Elsevier.

Gaines, B.R. (1967). Teaching machines for perceptual motor skills. In Unwin, D. and Leedman, J. (Eds) *Aspects of Educational Technology*. London: Methuen.

Gaines, B.R. (1969). Adaptively controlled instruction for a tracking skill. In Bresson, F. and De Montmollin, M. (Eds) *Programmed learning research: Major trends*. Paris: Dunod.

Hartley, J. (1966). Research report. *New Education*, **2**(1), 29–35.

Hartley, J. (1972). Evaluation. In Hartley, J. (Ed.) *Strategies for programmed instruction: An educational technology*. London: Butterworth.

Hartley, J.R. (1975). Some experiences with individualised teaching systems. In Hooper, R. and Toye, I. (Eds) *Computer assisted learning in the United Kingdom: Some case studies*. London: Council for Educational Technology.

Hartley, J.R. (1985). Some psychological aspects of computer-assisted learning and teaching. *Programmed Learning and Educational Technology*, **22**(2), 140–149.

Hartley, J.R. and Sleeman, D.H. (1973). Towards more intelligent teaching systems. *International Journal of Man-Machine Studies*, **5**, 215–236.

Kay, H., Dodd, B. and Sime, M. (1968). *Teaching machines and programmed instruction*. Harmondsworth: Penguin.

Kimball, R.A. (1982). A self-adapting, self-improving tutor for symbolic integration. In Sleeman, D. and Brown, J.S. (Eds) *Intelligent tutoring systems*. New York: Academic Press.

Lawler, R.W. and Yazdani, M. (Eds) (1987). *Artificial intelligence and education, Volume One: Learning environments and tutoring systems*. Sussex: Lawrence Erlbaum.

Leith, G.O.M. (Ed.) (1966). *A handbook of programmed learning*. Birmingham: University of Birmingham.

Lind, M. (1990). Representing goals and functions of complex systems. An introduction to multilevel flow modelling. Report 90–D-381. Copenhagen: Institute of Automatic Control Systems, Technical University of Denmark.

Littman, D. and Soloway, E. (1988). Evaluating ITSs: The cognitive science perspective. In Polson, M.C. and Richardson, J.J. (Eds) (op.cit.).

Lumsdaine, A.A. and Glaser, R. (Eds) (1960). *Teaching machines and programmed learning. A source book.* Washington, DC: National Education Association of the United States.

Merrill, M.D. (1988). Applying component display theory to the design of coursework. In Jonassen, D.H. (Ed.) *Instructional designs for microcomputer coursework.* Hillsdale, NJ: Lawrence Erlbaum.

Millward, R. (1979). Teaching a computer to teach. *Behavior Research Methods and Instrumentation,* 11(2), 102–110.

Naughton, J. (1986). *Artificial intelligence: Applications to training.* Sheffield: Manpower Services Commission.

Orlansky, J. and String, J. (1979). Cost-effectiveness of computer-based instruction in military training. IDA Paper P-1375. Arlington, VA: Institute for Defense Analyses and Technology Division.

O'Shea, T. and Self, J. (1983). *Learning and teaching with computers: Artificial intelligence in education.* Brighton: Harvester Press.

Patrick, J. and Stammers, R. (1977). Computer assisted learning and occupational training. *British Journal of Educational Technology,* 8, 253–267.

Patrick, J. and Stammers, R. (1981). The role of computers in training for problem diagnosis. In Rasmussen, J. and Rouse, W.B. (Eds) *Human detection and diagnosis of system failures.* New York: Plenum.

Plato Corrections Project Staff. (1978). Computer-based education has been introduced in three Illinois prisons. *American Journal of Correction,* 40, 1.

Polson, M.C. and Richardson, J.J. (Eds) (1988). *Foundations of intelligent tutoring systems.* Hillsdale, NJ: Lawrence Erlbaum.

Pressey, S.L. (1926). A simple device which gives tests and scores – and teaches. *School and Society,* 23, 373–376.

Pressey, S.L. (1927). A machine for automatic teaching of drill material. *School and Society,* 25, 549–552.

Psotka, J., Massey, L.D., and Mutter, S. (Eds) (1988). *Intelligent tutoring systems: Lessons learned.* Hillsdale, NJ: Lawrence Erlbaum.

Richer, M.H. and Clancey, W.J. (1987). GUIDON-WATCH: A graphic interface for viewing a knowledge-based system. In Lawler, R.W. and Yazdani, M. (Eds) (op. cit.).

Rigney, J.W. and Towne, D.M. (1969). Computer techniques for analysing the microstructure of serial section work in industry. *Human Factors,* 11, 113–122.

Rouse, W.B. (1979). Problem solving performance of maintenance trainees in a fault diagnosis task. *Human Factors,* 21, 195–203.

Schwartz, H.A. and Haskell, R.J.J. (1966). A study of computer assisted instruction in industrial training. *Journal of Applied Psychology,* 50, 360–363.

Schwartz, H.A. and Long, H.S. (1967). A study of remote industrial training via computer-assisted instruction. *Journal of Applied Psychology,* 51, 11–16.

Self, J. (Ed.) (1988). *Artificial intelligence and human learning. Intelligent computer aided instruction.* London: Chapman and Hall.

Seltzer, R.A. (1971). Computer-assisted instruction – what it can and cannot do. *American Psychologist,* 26, 373–377.

Simmons, L.M.H. (1975). Computer assisted learning in British Airways. In Hooper, R. and Toye, I. (Eds) *Computer assisted learning in the United Kingdom,* London: Council for Educational Technology.

Skinner, B.F. (1954). The science of learning and the art of teaching. *Harvard Educational Review,* 24, 2.

Skinner, B.F. (1958). Teaching machines. *Science*, **128**, 969–977.

Sleeman, D. H. and Brown, J.S. (Eds) (1982). *Intelligent tutoring systems*. New York: Academic Press.

Smith, S.G. and Sherwood, B.A. (1976). Educational uses of the PLATO computer system. *Science*, **192**, 344–352.

Smith, W.I. and Moore, J.W. (1962). *Programmed learning: Theory and research*. New York: Van Nostrand.

Spencer, G.J., Hausser, D.L., Blaiwes, A.S. and Weller, D.R. (1975). Use of computer-assisted instruction for interpersonal skill training – A pilot study. Report No NAVTRAEQUIPCEN 73–C-0133–1 (AD-A009361). Orlando, FL: US Naval Training Equipment Center.

Suppes, P. and Morningstar, M. (1969). Computer-assisted instruction. *Science*, **166**, 343–350.

Swets, J.A., Harris, J.R., McElroy, L.S. and Rudloe, H. (1966). Computer-aided instruction in perceptual identification. *Behavioral Science*, **11**, 98–104.

Swets, J.A., Millman, S.H., Fletcher, W.E. and Green, D.M. (1962). Learning to identify nonverbal sounds: An application of a computer as a teaching machine. *Journal of the Acoustic Society of America*, **31**, 928–935.

Taylor, T.R. (1975). Computer assisted learning in clinical decision making. In Hooper, R. and Toye, I. (Eds) *Computer-assisted learning in the United Kingdom*. London: Council for Educational Technology.

Towne, D.M. (1981). A general purpose system for simulating and training complex diagnosis and troubleshooting tasks. In Rasmussen, J. and Rouse, W.B. (Eds) *Human detection and diagnosis of system failures*. New York: Plenum.

Towne, D.M. and Rigney, J.W. (1979). A developmental microprocessor-based system for OJT and JPA management in electronics maintenance. Report No NAVTRAEQUIPCEN-76–C-0023. University of Southern California, Los Angeles: Behavioral Technology Laboratories.

Trollip, S.R. (1979). The evaluation of a complex computer-based flight procedures trainer. *Human Factors*, **21**, 47–54.

Trollip, S.R. and Ortony, A. (1977). Complex skill training in computer-assisted instruction. *Instructional Science*, **6**, 135–149.

Van Lehn, K. (1988). Student modelling. In Polson, M.C. and Richardson, J.J. (Eds) (op.cit.).

Wallis, D., Duncan, K.D. and Knight, M.A.G. (1966). Programmed instruction in the British Armed Services. London: HMSO.

Weisz, A.Z. and McElroy, L.S. (1964). Response and feedback techniques for automated training of visual identification skills. Technical Report NAVTRADEVCEN 789–3 (AD 447882). New York: US Naval Training Devices Center.

Wenger, E. (1987). *Artificial intelligence and tutoring systems*. Los Altos, CA: Morgan Kaufman.

Woolf, B., Blegen, D., Jansen, J.H. and Verloop, A. (1987). Teaching a complex industrial process. In Lawler, R.W. and Yazdani, M. (Eds) (op.cit.).

Chapter 12
Simulation

Synonyms of the verb "to simulate" are "to represent" and "to mimic" according to dictionary definitions. A simulation therefore represents or mimics something. That something might be a task, a relationship of some kind, a phenomenon (e.g. a rainbow), a piece of equipment, behaviour, a situation or some cognitive activity. What is simulated and how this is accomplished is dictated by the purpose of the simulation. Simulations are used for three main purposes:

1. *To carry out research.* The design of a new building, manufacturing process or piece of equipment can be tested by a simulation. The efficiency of procedures for evacuating an aeroplane can be compared in a simulated emergency. A scientist can investigate complex physical, chemical and biological relationships through computer-generated models or simulations. The common aim in all these situations is to examine some aspect of whatever is simulated. The same is true in the context of training when it is sometimes not possible to analyse the real task. Instead, a simulated version of the task is analysed in order to determine the skills required and to develop a training programme. In this instance the simulation is a source of data and provides an opportunity to analyse the nature of the task. (For a further discussion of this use of simulation, read Section 5.2, pp. 147–150.)
2. *To assess proficiency.* Job applicants are sometimes presented with simulated tasks in order to assess their level of performance. Trainee pilots may be assessed in a full-scale flight simulator to determine whether they can proceed to training with an actual aeroplane. Some of the skills of process control operators are used infrequently in their jobs and so levels of performance might be evaluated using simulated plant to determine whether refresher training is necessary.
3. *To train.* A simulation (or simulator) is often designed to enable training to take place. A task or part of a task is simulated and combined with principles of training design to produce a training programme. Computer-based training for perceptual identification, problem diagnosis, perceptual-motor, and various other tasks is discussed in Chapter 11. In all of these tasks a simulation was used for training and in almost all of them this was generated by a computer.

487

The power and speed of a computer enables it to produce multiple and complex simulations extremely quickly. On the other hand, simulations can be provided by paper and pencil, cardboard cut-outs, metal or wood mock-ups and photographs. Simulations can vary enormously, even when training the same type of task, as in the case of troubleshooting where a simulation might be either an abstract representation of the connections between components on a VDU (e.g. Rouse, 1981), a surface replica of the actual equipment which is computer-controlled, and a pack of cards indicating the state of equipment components (Bond and Rigney, 1966).

Our concern in this chapter is the use of simulation for the purpose of training. This topic has been of much concern to military training where both individuals and teams have to become skilled not only at firing guns and complex weapons systems but also at strategic manoeuvres in battlefield situations. Training using simulations has played a large part in the development of such skills. Aviation has recognised the need to train pilots using flight simulators (sometimes called trainers) ever since Edward Link developed his first flight simulator in 1929, although systematic studies of the benefit of training using these simulators were not carried out until 1949 onwards. Training in both military and aviation contexts has been at the forefront of research and development into simulations. Using simulators as part of training does not always involve expensive hardware. Management training uses simulated situations and behaviours in order to examine and improve decision-making, interpersonal, leadership and other "managerial" skills.

Four basic questions will be addressed in this chapter which are relevant to the use of simulation in any training context:

1. What is the aim of simulation and what are its main features?
2. Why is simulation needed for training?
3. How are simulations designed to maximise learning?
4. What varieties of simulation are used?

12.1 AIM AND FEATURES OF SIMULATION

The more general term simulation is preferred in this chapter since it covers not only simulators that involve the use of equipment, but also other simulations that do not, e.g. role play. In training, a distinction is drawn between training "on-the-job" and "off-the-job". As the terms indicate, the former refers to training a person in the actual work situation, which is often not possible or desirable, whilst the latter involves some training outside the normal work situation. It can be argued that any form of training which occurs "off-the-job" inevitably involves some form of simulation. In this broad sense, simulation can be viewed as an attempt to represent some characteristics or features of the real task and to incorporate them into an effective training environment away from the job. The key issue, therefore, is to devise simulation training so that it will result in high positive, preferably perfect, transfer of training when the person performs the task in the normal work situation. This, of course, is the goal of any training programme.

Gagné (1962) and Leplat (1989) have both adopted this perspective and have provided very useful introductions to this topic. Gagné emphasised that a simulator (and in our terms a simulation) has three important features:

1. A simulator attempts to *represent* a real situation in which operations are carried out.
2. A simulator provides its users with certain *controls* over that situation.
3. A simulator is deliberately designed to *omit* certain parts of the real operational situation.

Gagné's first point stresses that a simulation should enable a trainee to perform a task (an operation in his terms), which represents the one carried out in the normal work situation. The nature of the task should be preserved in the simulation such that the psychological demands made of the trainee correspond as closely as possible with those in the real situation. In this way transfer from the simulation will be maximised. (This is termed psychological fidelity which is discussed later in Section 12.4.) This does not mean that every last switch or colour has to be represented in a simulation unless they are significant to performance of the task. Even then the mode of operation of a switch can be changed so long as its functionality is preserved (i.e. what it controls and its control relationship). Similarly, changing the coding of five keys from 1–5 to A–E does not normally constitute a significant change to any task.

One simple means of assessing whether a simulated task is a good representation of the actual task is to apply Mager's prescriptions (discussed in Section 4.5). In other words, a task can be specified as a goal or objective to be achieved using Mager's three criteria:

the *activity* (physical or cognitive) performed by the trainee;
the *conditions* in which the activity is carried out (e.g. tools, environmental conditions, stress);

the *standards* of performance which have to be achieved (e.g. speed, accuracy).

These three aspects of a task provoke a series of questions concerning how well the simulated task represents the real task. Is the simulated task carried out to the same standards? Does it involve the same or comparable conditions? The most important question to be asked is whether the simulated task requires the same physical or cognitive activities as the real task, i.e. it uses the same type of skill. Hence if a person has to be trained to track a target using a velocity control, then there is no point in the simulated task involving distance or acceleration control which will only result in negative transfer to the real task. Similarly, if a person has to be trained to use qualitative reasoning to diagnose a fault in an electronic circuit (cf. White and Frederiksen, 1987), then the simulation should not allow the trainee to use other strategies such as pattern matching or heuristic methods. A similar recommendation was made by Cormier (1987), in the context of the design of aircraft simulators, who stated that the "essential cue-response relationships" should be preserved in the simulated task. These exhortations that the psychological demands or skill requirements of a task should be maintained in a simulation are endorsed unanimously in the literature (e.g. Leplat, 1989). However, accomplishing this is difficult, particularly for complex tasks, because identifying the nature of skill is still more a matter of an art than a science (Section 7.3). We will return to this issue in Section 12.3.

Gagné's second point is that a simulation permits the user or trainer some *control* over the task. Batsmen, table tennis and tennis players can be "thrown" balls by a simulator which can be varied in terms of speed, direction etc. The number and nature of targets on a weapon system simulator can be controlled so that the trainee moves from simple to more complex versions of the task. Other dimensions of the task might be controlled in order to create a good training environment (see Section 12.2).

Gagné's third feature of a simulation is that some parts of the real situation are omitted. Our previous discussion has implied that this is because these parts are either unimportant to the nature of the task and therefore need not be represented, or they are not practicable to simulate for some reason (e.g. danger, cost).

Training using simulation involves all of the normal stages of training development: specification of training objectives; analysis of a job/task; and design of a training programme. As with any training, the goal is to maximise positive transfer to the job/task after training. The only additional consideration which a simulation brings is how to represent the task and omit certain features so that transfer to the real task is maximised. The topic of transfer is therefore central to discussion of the design of simulation.

12.2 REASONS FOR SIMULATION

It is often not desirable or possible to train persons in the operational situation, i.e. on-the-job. It has previously been mentioned that a simulation can offer various advantages such as providing extra instructional features, improving safety and reducing costs. These and other reasons for the use of simulations in training are discussed below.

1. Inaccessibility of tasks in the operational situation. There are at least two ways in which real tasks may be inaccessible for training purposes. Firstly, they may not exist! Before new equipment or plant is commissioned and becomes operational, various persons will require training, necessarily involving some simulation. Secondly, the operational situation may preclude opportunities for training, such as when astronauts have to be trained to "fly" a space vehicle and make a lunar landing.

2. Costs and consequences of error. Errors occur during training, particularly in its early stages. These errors may be either too costly or too dangerous for training to take place in the operational situation. Trainee surgeons are not let loose initially on real patients, just as trainee pilots practise in a simulator rather than the actual aeroplane, until satisfactory proficiency is attained. Nuclear power plant operators are trained on realistic large-scale simulators which are driven by computer-controlled models of the actual plant. Even with the use of simulators, training cannot totally avoid use of the operational situation, even if it does have potential dangers. Johnson (1968) reported that:

> during the twenty-four months prior to June 1967 airlines lost eight jets and twenty-six crew members during training flights.

Even with less hazardous and complex tasks, errors can be costly. Trainees may: produce incorrectly sized components; weld joints unsatisfactorily; and fail to detect flawed items on a production line. With large scale manufacturing, any of these errors could result in costly losses in both quality and quantity of production. Simulation, therefore, offers a more tolerant environment in which training can take place.

3. Lower costs of simulation.   The costs of flight and maintenance simulators are substantially lower than using the operational equipment. Various estimates of these savings have been made. Chatelier, Harvey and Orlansky (1982), in a review of these estimates, stated that:

> flight simulators can be operated at costs that vary from 5 to 20 per cent of what it would cost to operate comparable aircraft; the median value is 12 per cent (p.5; underlining omitted).

In the discussion of transfer of training in Chapter 3, it is pointed out that cost savings alone are not compelling evidence unless the transfer effectiveness of simulators is also known. Chatelier et al. considered this issue and concluded:

> pilots trained in simulators needed less time in aircraft to perform acceptably than pilots trained only in aircraft; the amount of flight time saved was about one-half of the time spent in the simulator ...
>
> Since flight simulators save about 50 per cent of the time needed by pilots to train in aircraft and cost only 12 per cent as much to use (median values in both cases), it is clear that flight simulators are cost-effective, compared to the use of aircraft alone for training. The amount of such savings ... were large enough to amortize the procurement cost of flight simulators within two years or less (p.7; underlining omitted).

A similar but less favourable picture emerged for the use of maintenance simulators although the authors could find only one study (Cicchinelli et al., 1980), that provided a complete comparison of the costs of a simulator and the actual equipment.

One has to remember that the cost-effectiveness figures cited above are not just a reflection of the effect of the simulators per se, but also their instructional features which are critical in determining their transfer value. In other words, simulation is just one aspect of a training environment and it is therefore misleading to attribute the outcome of training to this one feature. Similar caution has been urged with respect to the evaluation of any training which is inevitably the consequence of many interacting factors.

4. Provision of advice.   A simulation can be designed so that the trainee is provided with advice concerning the correctness of his or her actions. This advice, either knowledge of results (extrinsic feedback) or guidance, may be impossible to provide on-the-job in a satisfactory manner. Provision of this extra information, as discussed in Section 9, will improve learning substantially. It should be noted that in this situation an instructional feature is added to the simulation in order to promote skill acquisition.

5. *Manipulation of the dimensions of a task.* It is frequently desirable to manipulate the complexity and temporal dimensions of tasks during training in order to facilitate the acquisition of skill. The real task might be so complex that training is designed to expose the trainee to a series of simplified versions which gradually approach its true complexity. This idea is compatible with the notion that skill in tracking begins with distance control and gradually progresses to velocity and later acceleration control (Fuchs, 1962). In a different context, a similar idea has been proposed recently by White and Frederiksen (e.g. 1987). They suggested that in training people to reason about, for example, an electrical circuit, a series of more complex models of how a circuit works should be introduced. Models promote qualitative reasoning initially, with increasingly complex ones eventually leading to quantitative reasoning.

It is sometimes desirable to speed up, slow down, or even stop a simulated task during training. Emergencies, rare diseases in patients and unusual faults in equipment occur, by definition, infrequently. This means that training in the real situation cannot cover the full range of possibilities that a person has to be trained to deal with. Therefore simulations are "programmed" with a full range of faults or emergencies, thus providing the trainee with what has been termed "collapsed experience". Some start-up and shut-down procedures in the process control industries take a long time, due to the slow response characteristics of plant. These tasks in their operational context are not only infrequent, but have long periods of inactivity between steps of a procedure. Again, simulations can be used in training in order to speed up the evolution of the task. The reverse is sometimes necessary for a high-speed task. Simulated tasks can be slowed down to allow the trainee to master the parts before speed is developed gradually. Finally, being able to "freeze" or "playback" a trainee's performance of a simulated task can be helpful in providing both the trainer and trainee with an opportunity to analyse performance in detail.

6. *Reducing the stress of a task.* An operational task might be stressful for a variety of reasons and it might be considered desirable to eliminate or reduce any stress in order to make the task easier to learn. The conditions in which the task has to be performed might be stressful, e.g. low lighting, heat, noise and vibration. During war, many military tasks are carried out in conditions which expose their performers to the severe stress of possible death or injury. Stress also comes from the demands of the task itself and therefore a reduction in its complexity or difficulty, discussed in the preceding point 5, will also reduce the level of stress. Whilst training that involves reduced stress in comparison with

the operational situation may seem sensible from an instructional perspective, it has a major drawback. Failure to incorporate stress in a simulated task may result in poor transfer of training to the real task. A common finding is that the supposed high level of skill achieved by, for example, tank crews, breaks down under battlefield conditions. This is one reason why some military training exercises expose trainees to the hazards of real ammunition.

7. *Part-task simulation.* The reasons for using some part-task simulations are the same as those discussed in Section 9.5 concerning part-task training generally. Parts of a task may require different skills and therefore need different training conditions. The procedural aspects of flying might be trained by one part-task simulator and the display-control relationships by another. Alternatively, it might be desirable to simplify one part of a task and to develop skill by using a series of part-task simulations which gradually approximate closer to the actual part. Part-task simulations vary from relatively expensive simulators to simple paper-and-pencil mock-ups. Typically, after part-task training, some training which uses the whole task is desirable, although for some tasks this can be short. For example, Adams and Hufford (1962) found that part training of an aircraft manoeuvre only resulted in a decrement in comparison with whole training on the first attempt at the whole task. On the second attempt there was no difference. One can envisage a range of part-task and whole-task simulations being used in a complex domain with the trainee progressing from one to another. This can provide not only cost savings, but also instructional advantages.

12.3 DESIGN OF SIMULATION

By discussing the design of simulation for training, one has to be careful not to imply that a set of principles exist that are separate from those which apply to the development of any training programme. The major issues of analysing a task/skill and designing training, which are discussed in the preceding chapters of this book, are just as relevant to the development of simulations for training purposes. Unfortunately, this obvious point is not reflected in the literature, where many of the features of simulation design are no more than those involved in the development of training generally. Nevertheless the question of how to design simulations does bring at least one issue into sharper focus. It will be remembered that the aim of any simulation used for training is to maximise transfer to the real task in its normal context. The key issue therefore is to decide what characteristics or features of the task should be *represented* in the simulation in order to achieve high transfer of training. The simulation has to represent the task to the trainee in such a way that the psychological or skill requirements of the task are not changed significantly. The trainee should have to deploy the same cognitive activities in performing the simulated task as the actual task. This leads us to the 64,000 dollar question of how a simulation can be designed to do this if it is not an exact copy of the real situation. Which features are superficial and can be omitted? Which features are more fundamental and affect the cognitive activities used to carry out the task? These questions are particularly important in the design of simulations for training. There are two solutions:

To assess transfer of training.
To compare the simulated and real tasks in psychological terms.

1. A transfer of training study. This is the empirical solution where evidence is collected using the typical transfer of training design, discussed in Chapter 3. One group of trainees that has been trained using the simulation is tested on the operational task and compared against another group that did not experience the simulation. The early literature concerning transfer from flight simulators to real aircraft was reviewed by Valverde (1973) and similar issues in the development of simulators for training maintenance and fault-finding skills were discussed by Fink and Shriver (1978).

However, whilst such empirical evidence exists, there are several problems associated with carrying out transfer of training studies. If one takes an extreme position, on each occasion a new simulation is introduced or an old one is changed, a transfer study has to be performed to ascertain its value. This is a lot of work which may also be expensive. Another difficulty which arises, for example, in the context of evaluating a flight simulator for an advanced aircraft is getting a control group of trainees with the satisfactory level of experience against which an experimental group can be compared fairly (Adams, 1979). On the one hand, the training value of a flight simulator will be underestimated if the control group has some related prior flying experience, and yet on the other hand, trainees in this group have to be able to fly to generate performance measures for comparison purposes! Another major problem with a transfer of training study, particularly for evaluating an expensive simulator, is that the evidence which it provides is rather late! Indeed there is some irony in carrying out such a transfer study which is well captured in the following quotation from Adams (1979):

The subjects of an experimental group must fly the aircraft well on the first flight after simulator training. If not, they would not be allowed to fly, and so there would be no measures and no experiment. The experiment cannot be done unless rather high positive transfer is an implied guarantee. It is a strange experiment where positive outcome is a precondition (p. 713).

These difficulties associated with transfer studies can be reduced by devising a comprehensive research simulation which permits simulation design to be evaluated for training different tasks. This approach was adopted in the development of the AWAVS flight simulator (an *Aviation Wide Angle Visual System*) at the Naval Training Equipment Center, at Orlando (Collyer and Chambers, 1979). One aim was to determine the importance of various parameters in the visual system (e.g. types of image, field of view) to transfer of training. From research studies it was hoped to identify the features of types of task that should be represented in a simulator to maximise transfer from training with the simulator. In this situation a full-scale comprehensive simulator was used to identify how smaller, less realistic, simulators might be designed to support training for each type of task. One type might require a very realistic visual image for high transfer, whilst another might not. Because there were so many simulator variables to evaluate, this would have resulted in a large number of conventional research studies to determine their importance. Therefore some clever research designs devised by Simon (e.g. 1979) were used to isolate those simulator variables that were likely to be most influential, thus reducing the number of studies necessary.

2. *On the basis of psychological principles.*   The second means of determining the design of a simulation is to employ a psychologist! The outcome of such a strategy, leaving aside the competence of the psychologist, depends upon how well the skill involved in the real task can be pinpointed and captured in the simulated task. This in turn depends upon techniques for analysing tasks/skills (Chapters 5–8) and principles concerning transfer of training (Chapter 3). Whilst psychological knowledge and analysis techniques enable us to have a fairly good shot at designing a simulation, it is not possible to be certain, particularly of more fine-grained details, without carrying out a transfer study. Rose, Evans and Wheaton (1987), took a more optimistic view and have reported the development of the Device Effectiveness Forecast Technique (DEFT). This technique uses various "dimensions" to evaluate a simulator design and predict the effectiveness of learning and transfer. It is embodied in a computer-based model with which a person interacts via a series of menus. The person is prompted for information (e.g. a

rating of the extent to which a trainee can already meet a training objective) and an assessment of predicted simulator effectiveness is given. The authors reported that a validation of this approach is planned.

So far our discussion has been concerned with simulation design in order to maximise transfer. There is another subsidiary but important aim in designing a simulation which, if overlooked, will endanger this main goal of transfer. Both the trainees and also the trainers have to accept that the simulation has sufficient face validity. Both trainees and their instructors need to have a positive attitude to the simulation and be motivated to participate in training with it. Baker and Marshall (1989) have discussed these issues in the context of simulator training for both the off-shore oil industry and the nuclear power industry. One can conceive of a simulation which incorporates psychological aspects of the real task that is so different in appearance that those using it fail to take training with it seriously.

Fidelity of simulation

In any discussion of simulation, and particularly simulators, the topic of "fidelity" inevitably arises. It has been studiously avoided so far because it arguably has little to contribute except yet another label. We have already discussed the relationship between the simulated and real task, emphasising that the former must involve the same psychological activities as the latter. In the technical jargon, this is known as "psychological fidelity", although sometimes this term is also used to indicate the extent to which "trainees perceive training equipment as being a duplicate of the operational equipment and task situation" (Fink and Shriver, 1978, p. 25). These two views of psychological fidelity differ and the former is used here because trainees may be influenced by surface characteristics of a simulation and may be poor judges of how much a simulation requires the same psychological processes as the operational situation. A second, less important type of fidelity, can be defined from an engineering perspective as:

> The duplication of physical and functional characteristics of operational equipment within very tight tolerance specifications. These tolerances are usually close to the limit of engineering skill and often beyond those of production capability (Miller, 1953).

Traditionally, the degree to which a simulation represents the real situation, i.e. its fidelity, has been interpreted from this engineering perspective as the degree of realism and physical fidelity of the training

device. The drive to duplicate the appearance and feel of real equipment has been very strong, not in the training community, but in
industry generally. Very often an aircraft simulator is rated by an
experienced pilot in how well it "operates" with respect to the actual
aircraft and this rating is influential in determining the design of the
simulator. However, not only is high physical fidelity expensive, but it is
not always necessary. High transfer of training can occur without it, so
long as the simulation contains that elusive quality of high psychological
fidelity. Of course, the problem is specifying and predicting the psychological fidelity of a simulation on a priori grounds. Otherwise the
definition of psychological fidelity becomes circular because it can be
defined only by whether or not a simulation design produces transfer of
training.

In the case of simulators, increasing their "engineering" fidelity
inevitably implies an increase in cost. How does transfer of training vary
as a function of degree of engineering fidelity? How do these variables
interact with the cost of a simulation? Miller (1954) speculated about the
relationships between the degree of engineering fidelity, cost and
transfer of training which are represented in Figure 12.1. The transfer
of training function rises steeply initially and then levels off as engineering fidelity increases. In contrast, the costs of simulation rise slowly
initially, but any increase between medium and high fidelity is associated

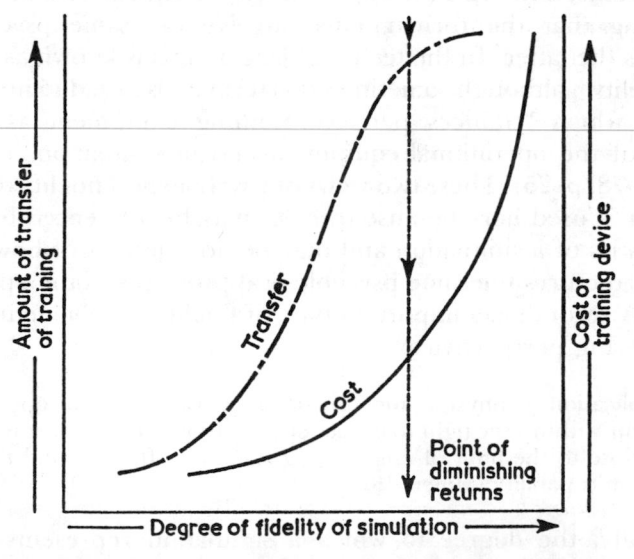

Figure 12.1 Miller's hypothetical relationships between simulator
fidelity, transfer and simulator cost (adapted from Biel, 1962).

with a large increment in cost. Miller suggested that there was a point of "diminishing returns" that represented the highest transfer to cost ratio, i.e. where the two curves are furthest apart. This rather neat idea is not based on any evidence and therefore should be treated with caution. What Miller's relationship fails to take account of is the context of the training study and what amount of transfer is necessary. For some tasks perfect transfer is required on the trainee's first attempt at the task (e.g. a lunar landing). Therefore a pragmatic approach is to increase fidelity until either acceptable transfer is achieved or unacceptable cost is reached. A more fundamental problem with Miller's proposition is the suggestion that transfer of training increases with the degree of engineering fidelity of the simulator. As he acknowledged, psychological fidelity is the critical determinant of transfer and therefore, assuming a one-to-one ratio between transfer and psychological fidelity, it is possible to infer the relationship between engineering and psychological fidelity. However, this relationship is not consistent with the findings for some tasks. High transfer can be achieved with simulations of low physical fidelity when training cognitive tasks and procedures. Also predicting the relationship between simulator design and transfer for other tasks is more problematic than Miller's relationships suggest.

These problems can be illustrated by reference to a continuing debate in aviation concerning the value of motion cues in flight simulators (e.g. Caro, 1979; Hays and Singer, 1989; Koonce, 1979; Lintern, 1987). This question is particularly important because of the costs involved. Lintern (1987), who strongly criticised a recommendation by Gebman et al. (1986) that a forthcoming simulation system for the US Air Force should have motion systems, pointed out that the extra 6% costs for them amounted to 24 million dollars, or three million dollars per simulator. Traditionally, the transfer of training evidence concerning motion cues in flight simulators has suggested that they add little and can be reduced or eliminated with no adverse effect (e.g. Jacobs and Roscoe, 1975; Martin, 1981; Pohlmann and Reed, 1978). As Caro (1979) pointed out, this conflicts with evidence that motion in a simulator changes a pilot's performance in that simulator (e.g. Levison and Junker, 1977). A convincing resolution proposed by Caro (1979) was that studies had failed to take account of both the nature of the motion cues and the nature of the task being trained. Certain motion cues would be relevant to some tasks and not others. In this regard a distinction was made between *manoeuvre* and *disturbance* motion, the latter being attributed to some factor outside the pilot's control, e.g. turbulence, engine failure. Transfer of training studies had used manoeuvre motion, whereas disturbance motion was associated with pilot's changing behaviour in the simulator. Caro went on to discuss both the tasks and types of aircraft for which these different motion cues had a prima facie case of being relevant. For example, manoeuvre motion generally only provides the pilot with confirmation of information available from instruments, whereas disturbance cues can alert a pilot to the need to deal with problems, e.g. engine failure. Therefore the motto of this story is that searching for generalisations about the importance of simulated features per se without careful examination of the task/skill is rather risky.

The degree of physical fidelity or realism has been shown to be unimportant for training both procedures and cognitive tasks. The evidence concerning procedural tasks is particularly strong and straightforward. Prophet and Boyd (1970) compared the training of start-up and shut-down procedures using a Mohawk aircraft and a cockpit mockup made of plywood and photographs. They found pilots who used the cheap simulation to be just as proficient as those trained in the actual aircraft. A well-known study by Cox et al. (1965) compared various simulations, differing in degree of physical fidelity, in their effectiveness at training army personnel to operate a 92-step procedure on a control panel. Training included the real equipment (costing 11,000 dollars), a realistic simulator (costing 1000 dollars), cheap cardboard models, photographs and a reduced size drawing. There were no differences between groups trained with these different devices in terms of training time, post-training performance and retention. These findings have been replicated by Grimsley (1969) and more recently by Johnson (1981). Therefore a procedure can be trained just as well with low cost, low physical fidelity simulations as with expensive, high physical fidelity simulations. The only requirement is that the simulation enables each step of the procedure to be represented adequately to the trainee.

One might expect that cognitive tasks could be trained effectively using low-physical-fidelity simulations because the observable physical aspects of these tasks are, by definition, unimportant. Decision-making, problem-solving and reasoning tasks can usually be represented adequately in simple ways, perhaps using paper and pencil. Fault-finding skills can be trained using simulations with low physical fidelity so long as the fault-finder's moves in examining a piece of equipment and collecting information about symptoms can be represented adequately. Marshall et al. (1981) used a simulated control panel made up of magnetic tiles mounted on a magnetic board to represent specific plant instruments and their readings. Various simulated fault-finding exercises were used to train operators to diagnose malfunctions in an oxidisation plant. Alternatively, paper-and-pencil exercises can be used for training this type of skill. Such approaches become inadequate when the "problem space" which has to be simulated is dynamic, complex and requires multiple formats, and trainees' interventions need to be both represented and evaluated. This is the reason that some form of computer-based training is ideally suited for problem diagnosis tasks, as discussed in Section 12.4.

Management, business and war "games" provide simulations in which cognitive tasks can be performed for various purposes, including training. Some of these are discussed by Goldstein (1986) and Hays and Singer (1989). Such "games" provide the "players" or trainees with experience in making decisions and learning about how their outcome is affected by other players' decisions, organisational factors, time and the like. For example, players might receive hypothetical yet realistic data on the finance, sales and production figures of a hypothetical company and then play out different courses of action with an instructor evaluating their decisions and providing feedback. Goldstein (1986) cited the Looking Glass, Inc. (McCall and Lombardo, 1982) as one of the most carefully designed simulations which aimed to improve the development of management teams.

> Looking Glass, Inc. is a hypothetical medium-sized glass manufacturing corporation. . . . For a simulation, Looking Glass is quite realistic. Complete with annual report, plausible financial data and a variety of glass products, the simulation creates the aura of an authentic organization. Participants are placed in an office-like setting, complete with telephones and an interoffice mail system. The positions actually filled in the simulation are the top management of the corporation, including four levels ranging from president to plant manager. . . . The company consists of three divisions whose environments vary according to the degree of change, with one division's environment being relatively placid, another turbulent, and the third a mixture of the two.
>
> Lasting six hours, the simulation is intended to be a typical day in the life of the company. It begins by placing each participant face-to-face with an in-basket full of memoranda. Together with background information common to all participants, this information, which differs somewhat from division to division, level to level, and position to position, constitutes the stimulus. Participants spend the rest of the day responding to these interlocking sets of stimuli, acting and interacting as they choose. Contained in the collective in-baskets of the 20 participants are more than 150 different problems that participating managers might attend to. The problems vary in importance, and they also vary, realistically, in how apparent or hidden they are to the one or more individuals who ought to be concerned about them. Also true to life, the number of problems far exceeds the time available to deal with them (Kaplan, Lombardo and Mazique, 1983, p. 29).

Kaplan, Lombardo and Mazique (1983) evaluated 17 managers who had used the Looking Glass, Inc. They concluded that qualitative improvements in various dimensions of managers' work had taken place which were still evident some months after the simulation exercise. Such data are not only difficult to secure but are often subjective, resting on self-appraisal. Indeed, assessment of whether a manager's skills improve in the job as a consequence of training is a difficult, if not impossible, task to perform satisfactorily. Simulated games not only provide a safe environment, but also enable a person's strategies and decision-making to be "exposed" and evaluated with modifications and alternatives being practised. (This is not that dissimilar to how Bruner et al. externalised the different strategies involved in a concept attainment task.) Managers are forced to attend to the criteria on which decisions are based and these can be debated, factors which have not been taken into account can be identified and instructors can intervene as they deem necessary. The focus of such games can be extended from an organisation or company to the international level in order to train politicians and diplomats. For example, the Yugoslav Dilemma (Swezey et al. 1984) is a computer-based simulation of a seven-day international, military and political crisis in which participants attempt to solve problems and learn about the consequences of their actions (Hays and Singer, 1989).

Level of skill acquisition

Simulation, as any form of training, should be designed to accommodate the trainee's increasing level of competence during training. Most simulations and simulators are designed to enable trainees who already have some competence at the task to have further practice. In Anderson's terms the skill has been compiled but needs proceduralisation and fine tuning. Gagné (1954) was one of the first to suggest that simulators be used only in the later stages of skill acquisition. It was argued that expensive simulators were unnecessary when the trainee was struggling to understand the nature of the task and simple training aids would suffice. The only exception which Gagné made was for motor skills where it is necessary for a simulator to reproduce the control movements faithfully in order to avoid problems of negative transfer.

In principle, there is no reason why different types of simulation should not be designed to accommodate the qualitative and quantitative changes in performance which occur as skill is developed (Chapter 2). As usual Miller, as long ago as 1954, was the first person to articulate this highly desirable state of affairs (Miller, 1954). Of course, these ideas apply to the design of any training programme and not just to simulation. In the first stage of skill acquisition (Fitts' cognitive stage), simple simulations (pictures, diagrams, mock-ups) could be used to familiarise the trainee with the nomenclature and location of the displays and controls involved in the perceptual-motor tasks that were prevalent in the 1950s and 1960s. Miller suggested that the relationship between different controls and displays should also be capable of being simulated. In the second stage of skill acquisition (Fitts' associative phase), the trainee should be able to practise coordinating movements and also making anticipations in the same manner as that required by the operational task. In the final stage of skill acquisition (Fitts' autonomous phase), simulation should support high levels of practice of the task at high speeds and under heavy workloads or in low signal-to-noise ratios. Miller's notions are still relevant to the training of perceptual-motor tasks today and generally remind us that ideas of skill acquisition do have important implications for training design. Finally, it should be remembered that no simulation per se will effect training unless it also includes the more general principles of training design discussed in Chapters 8 and 9.

12.4 VARIETIES OF SIMULATION

In principle, simulations can be used for training any type of task and it is often advantageous if these simulations are computer generated, possibly within a computer-based training system. Studies which adopt this approach for perceptual identification and discrimination tasks, perceptual motor tasks, management tasks, problem-solving and tasks requiring basic intellectual skills are discussed in Section 11.4. Therefore one means of classifying types of simulation is in terms of the nature of the task that is simulated.

Alternatively, types of simulation can be distinguished on the basis of *what* is simulated. It has been mentioned that any simulated task attempts to represent the actual task in such a way that the psychological activities of the person performing it are preserved. There are many aspects of a task and its situation which may be simulated. Some tasks involve interaction with equipment and therefore simulations (or rather simulators) are required to represent the equipment and how it "behaves". For other tasks involving human–human interaction (e.g. social and supervisory tasks), it is necessary that simulations represent human behaviour. Both of these types of simulation are potentially useful for training.

Simulation of equipment

A number of reviews of simulators for training are available including the previously mentioned one by Gagné (1962). The use of simulators as training devices has been discussed in military contexts (Knight and Sharrock, 1983), in the nuclear power industry (Stammers, 1979) and for maintenance training (Fink and Shriver, 1978). The leading area of development has been that of aircraft or flight simulators, reviews of which have been mentioned previously (e.g. Valverde, 1973). Some ideas from the design of flight simulators have been applied to other areas, such as the design of simulators for training ship-handling skills. It is surprising, as Stammers and Patrick (1975) remarked, that simulators are not widely used for training people to drive cars. A variety of car simulators has ranged from simple representations of the car's controls and displays with a film of traffic situations being shown, to realistic cars, or parts of cars, which provide dynamic interaction with the trainee's actions effecting changes in the visual display (Schori, 1970). These have not gained wide acceptance in driving schools. One suspects that this is partly due to difficulties in both instructor and trainee acceptance. Also there is the risk of negative transfer for control skills developed by car simulators which do not respond in exactly the same manner as the trainee's actual car.

A major factor affecting the use of simulators is their cost. Simulators are generally cheaper than the real equipment, although sometimes their additional features for instructional control can make them more expensive. Despite the fact that generally costs are reduced for simulators, they are still substantial, e.g. aircraft simulators, nuclear power plant simulators. The availability of low-cost stand-alone micro-computers has provoked researchers to investigate when low physical fidelity can still result in high transfer of training. For example, studies by both Crawford and Crawford (1978), which simulated an interactive antisubmarine control panel, and Trollip (1979), which simulated an aircraft flying a holding pattern, demonstrated the feasibility of high transfer with low cost, low physical fidelity systems using computer terminals. Crawford and Crawford (1978) calculated that the delivery cost of their PLATO-based simulation training was 102 dollars per trainee, which compared favourably against 321 dollars per trainee for conventional training. Savings were estimated to be significant, since 200 pilots were trained each year. Even further savings could have been made if comparable CBT applications were available to utilise the remaining time on the PLATO terminals.

Not all equipment-oriented simulations pose major cost problems.

Some simple and cheap forms of simulation have been used for training tasks which occur in dentistry and the clothing industry. In these instances it is the *material* being worked upon that is simulated rather than any equipment. Dental students are trained to drill teeth using "phantom heads" which has some obvious advantages! Basic sewing skills in the clothing industry have been taught using paper and other cheap material, although Toye (1969) warned that negative transfer may occur unless the characteristics of the real and simulated fabrics were highly similar.

Simulation of behaviour

One of the most well-known training studies of a simple industrial task was carried out by Lindahl (1945). The task involved operating by means of a foot control a cutting machine which sliced discs from a tungsten rod. Lindahl decided that the "skill" of the task resided in the pattern of foot movements and so a technique was developed for recording these movements. Trainees practiced making the appropriate foot movements whilst viewing simulations of the ideal and various incorrect movement patterns. Eleven weeks of this training produced a level of proficiency better than that of workers who had been performing the task for five months.

The training of social and supervisory skills can involve simulating the behaviour of a person in specified situations which the trainee has to learn to deal with. Service and retail industries develop training for customer contact or customer liaison skills through simulating inter-personal interactions. This applies to the jobs of waiters, sales clerks, airport check-in clerks and customer advisors. It also includes those persons who are trained to deal sympathetically with the onslaught of complaints by frustrated customers, which makes some of us even more frustrated! In training these interpersonal skills, trainees are asked to "role play" with another person who simulates the behaviour of a "customer" according to some script. The situation is acted out, some-times being video recorded, and then it is analysed by the trainer with appropriate comments and suggestions being provided. Variants of this simple format exist; a range of behaviours might be covered for different situations; and the trainee and "customer" might swap roles in order to expand the trainee's understanding of the situation.

More recently this sort of role-playing has been incorporated into a wider training approach termed behaviour role-modelling. Behaviour role-modelling was developed by Sorcher and Goldstein (1972), and

Goldstein and Sorcher (1974) as an application of Bandura's theory of social learning to the training of supervisory skills. Since then it has been examined enthusiastically in the context of training various managerial skills. Bandura's theory assigns a central role to the observation of a model in the learning of social behaviours. A person acting as model is observed and imitated and Bandura suggested that this was affected by the processes that determined how the model was observed and how important characteristics were attended to; how the model's behaviour was remembered; how subsequent behaviour was performed and practised by the observer; and how the motivational/reinforcement contingencies which affect the production of these behaviours were arranged. Goldstein and Sorcher (1974) criticised the practice of management training much of which involved changing managers' attitudes and telling managers what they should attempt to achieve rather than training managers in specific behaviours. Behaviour role-modelling consists of the following steps:

1. A model (e.g. an expert) demonstrates the behaviour and skills the trainee has to learn. For example, this might cover how a supervisor deals with an employee who is absent frequently. The demonstration may be live or on a video tape.
2. The trainee is encouraged to rehearse and practise the model's behaviour.
3. Feedback or reinforcement from the trainer, and possibly other trainees, is provided as the trainee's behaviour approximates closer to the behaviour of the model.

Modifications to this basic format have been examined. Decker (1980, 1982) demonstrated the beneficial effect of providing trainees with guidelines and practice concerning how to attend to, code, and mentally rehearse the key behaviours of the model. Generally the main points (termed "learning points") are presented to the observer/trainee (cf. Latham and Saari, 1979) and trainees should attend to them during both the demonstration and their subsequent practice of the behaviours. A further study by Decker (1983) investigated the optimal conditions for behaviour rehearsal, concluding that the presence of one or two observers combined with videotaped feedback was best. This might have been due to either the nature of the feedback or the number of rehearsals observed by trainees, both of which varied between conditions in this study.

McGhee and Tullar (1978) raised concerns about the lack of evidence concerning the effectiveness of behaviour role-modelling as a training technique. Latham and Saari (1979) carried out a field evaluation, using the technique to train 20 first-line supervisors from an international company. Training sessions took two hours each week for nine weeks. They covered nine topics concerning problems which a supervisor might have to deal with, e.g. disciplinary action, motivating a poor performer. The behaviour role-modelling for each training session was as follows:

a) introduction of the topic by two trainers (attentional processes);
b) presentation of a film that depicts a supervisor model effectively handling a situation by following a set of 3 to 6 learning points that were shown in the film immediately before and after the model was presented (retention processes);
c) group discussion of the effectiveness of the model in demonstrating the desired behaviours (retention processes);
d) practice in role-playing the desired behaviours in front of the entire class (retention processes, motor reproduction processes); and
e) feedback from the class on the effectiveness of each trainee in demonstrating the desired behaviours (motivational processes) (Latham and Saari, 1979, p. 241).

A group which received training was evaluated against a control group which did not. Evaluation used the following measures: the trainees' reactions after training; a post-test six months afterwards requiring verbal descriptions; a post-test three months afterwards requiring behaviour which was rated; and ratings of job behaviour prior to and after training. Trainees' reactions to the training were highly favourable and the behaviour role-modelling group was superior in performance to the control group on all other evaluation measures. This effect due to behaviour role-modelling was further substantiated because these differences disappeared after the control group received the same training one year later (although the data are not reported in the paper). A similar study by Russell, Wexley and Hunter (1984) used behaviour modelling to train supervisors of a car supplies manufacturing company. In contrast to Latham and Saari's study, training effects were only observed in trainees' reactions and verbal responses in a post-test with no difference between the training and control groups in rated behaviour and job performance.

Differences between studies in the effect of behaviour role-modelling are not surprising given the variations in how not only training, but also evaluation can take place. Evaluation of transfer to job performance for any training is exceedingly difficult and relies mainly on ratings of dimensions of job performance, with all of their associated problems of rating error, opportunity bias etc. Also, behaviour role-modelling is not exactly a technique, but is better described as an approach that uses many well-established training principles (demonstration, practice and feedback). Therefore it would be very surprising if it was not effective.

Studies of a fine-grained nature, such as those carried out by Decker, should reveal how different aspects of this approach to training can be improved, particularly for different tasks.

Finally, the most unusual simulation, which cannot be classified easily, is when the trainee uses mental imagery to both represent and practice a task. It is certainly the cheapest training method! In fact there is some evidence that it can work. A much cited study was conducted by Prather (1973) in which some pilots were trained by a sort of mental simulation. Trainee pilots listened to tape recordings whilst they sat in simulated cockpits, and mentally practised the manoeuvres for landing an aircraft without overtly responding. Afterwards their rated competence at landing was superior to other trainees who did not receive this form of training. Further evidence of the benefit of mental practice comes from a rather different study by Mackay (1981) which compared covert and overt practice at speaking unfamiliar sentences as quickly as possible. He found some advantage for mental practice in both acquisition and transfer. (Mackay has developed a theory of skill acquisition which explains the effect of such mental practice and this is discussed in Section 2.4.) The possible effect of mental practice has long been recognised by sports trainers who instruct athletes and gymnasts to mentally rehearse their activities in preparation for a competition. However any effect may be due to motivational rather than cognitive factors. Annett (1989) has discussed this and other explanations of the effects of mental practice. For skills which are verbally mediated, such as carrying out a procedure, it is not suprising that mental rehearsal will have some beneficial effect, assuming that the person has reached a reasonable level of competence beforehand. If skill is viewed as a hierarchy of subroutines, then one can imagine that rehearsal of the subroutines and the circumstances under which particular ones are selected is likely to be of benefit. However, it is less clear how this might work for skills which are not verbally mediated. Further research should address this intriguing topic which is of both theoretical and practical importance to training.

References

Adams, J.A. (1979). On the evaluation of training devices. *Human Factors*, **21**, 711–720.

Adams, J.A. and Hufford, L.E. (1962). Contributions of a part-task trainer to the learning and relearning of a time-shared flight manoeuvre. *Human Factors*, **4**, 159–170.

Annett, J. (1989). Training skilled performance. In Colley, A.M. and Beech, J.R. (Eds) *Acquisition and performance of cognitive skills*. Chichester: Wiley.

Baker, S. and Marshall, E. (1989). Simulators for training and the evaluation of operator performance. In Bainbridge, L. and Quintanilla, S.A.R. (Eds) *Developing skills with information technology*. Chichester: Wiley.

Biel, W.C. (1962). Training programs and devices. In Gagne, R.M. (Ed.) *Psychological principles in system development*. New York: Holt, Rinehart and Winston.

Bond, N.A. and Rigney, J.W. (1966). Bayesian aspects of trouble-shooting behavior. *Human Factors*, **8**, 377–383.

Caro, P.W. (1979). The relationship between flight simulator motion and training requirements. *Human Factors*, **21**, 493–501.

Chatelier, R.R., Harvey, J. and Orlansky, J. (1982). The cost-effectiveness of military training devices. Working Group for Simulators and Training Devices. TTCP-UTP-2.

Cicchinelli, L.F., Harmon, K.R., Keller, R.A. and Kottenstette, J.P. (1980). Relative cost and training effectiveness of the 6883 three-dimensional simulator and actual equipment. AFHRL-TR-80–24. Texas: Air Force Human Research Laboratory, Brooks Air Force Base.

Collyer, S.C. and Chambers, W.S. (1979). AWAVS, A research facility for defining flight trainer visual system requirements. Orlando, FL: Naval Training Equipment Center.

Cormier, S.M. (1987). The structural processes underlying transfer of training. In Cormier, S.M. and Hagman, J.D. (Eds) *Transfer of learning. Contemporary research and application*. San Diego: Academic Press.

Cox, J.A., Wood, R.D. Jr, Boren, L.M. and Thorne, H.W. (1965). Functional and appearance fidelity of training devices for fixed procedures tasks. HUMRRO Technical Report 65–4. Alexandria, VA: Human Resources Research Office.

Crawford, A.M. and Crawford, K.S. (1978). Simulation of operational equipment with a computer-based instructional system: A low cost-training technology. *Human Factors*, **20**, 215–224.

Decker, P.J. (1980). Effects of symbolic coding and rehearsal in behaviour-modeling training. *Journal of Applied Psychology*, **65**, 627–634.

Decker, P.J. (1982). The enhancement of behaviour modeling training of supervisory skills by the inclusion of retention processes. *Personnel Psychology*, **35**, 323–332.

Decker, P.J. (1983). The effects of rehearsal group size and video feedback in behaviour modeling training. *Personnel Psychology*, **36**, 763–773.

Fink, C.D. and Shriver, E.L. (1978). Simulators for maintenance training: Some issues, problems, and areas for future research. AFHRL-TR-78–27. Texas: Air Force Human Resources Laboratory, Brooks Air Force Base.

Fuchs, A.H. (1962). The progression-regression hypothesis in perceptual-motor skill learning. *Journal of Experimental Psychology*, **63**, 177–182.

Gagné, R.M. (1954). Training devices and simulators: Some research issues. *American Psychologist*, **9**, 95–107.

Gagné, R.M. (1962). Simulators. In Glaser, R. (Ed.) *Training research and education*. University of Pittsburgh Press. Reprinted in 1965. New York: Wiley.

Gebman, J.R., Stanley, W.L., Barbour, A.A., Berg, R.T., Birkler, J.L., Chaloupka, M.G., Goeller, B.F., Jamison, L.M., Kaplan, R., Kirkwood, T.F. and Batten, C.L. (1986). Assessing the benefits and costs of motion for C-17 flight simulators: Technical appendices. (N-2301–AF). Santa Monica, CA: Rand Corporation.

Goldstein, I.L. (1986). *Training in organizations: Needs assessment, development and evaluation*. Monterey, CA: Brooks/Cole.

Goldstein, A.P. and Sorcher, M. (1974). *Changing supervisory behavior*. New York: Pergamon Press.

Grimsley, D.L. (1969). Acquisition, retention and retraining: The effects of high and low fidelity in training devices. Technical Report 69–1, HUMRRO. Alexandria, VA: Human Resources Research Organisation.

Hays, R.T. and Singer, M.J. (1989). *Simulator fidelity in training system design. Bridging the gap between reality and training.* New York: Springer-Verlag.

Jacobs, R.S. and Roscoe, S.N. (1975). Simulator cockpit motion and the transfer of initial flight training. Proceedings of the Human Factors Society 19th Annual Meeting. Santa Monica, CA: Human Factors Society.

Johnson, S.L. (1981). Effect of training device on retention and transfer of a procedural task. *Human Factors,* **23**, 257–272.

Johnson, W.L. (1968). Flight simulation and airline pilot training. In Rolfe, J.M. (Ed.) *Vehicle simulation for training and research.* Report No R442. Farnborough: RAF Institute of Aviation Medicine.

Kaplan, R.E., Lombardo, M.M. and Mazique, M.S. (1983). A mirror for managers: Using simulation to develop management teams. Technical Report Number 13. Greensboro, NC: Center for Creative Leadership.

Knight, M.A.G. and Sharrock, D. (1983). Simulators as training devices: Some lessons from military experience. Proceedings of the conference on simulators. Conference Publication No 226. London: Institution of Electrical Engineers.

Koonce, J.M. (1979). Predictive validity of flight simulators as a function of simulator motion. *Human Factors,* **21**, 215–223.

Latham, G.P. and Saari, L.M. (1979). Application of social-learning theory to training supervisors through behavioural modeling. *Journal of Applied Psychology,* **64**, 239–246.

Leplat, J. (1989). Simulation and simulators in training: Some comments. In Bainbridge, L. and Quintanilla, S.A.R. (Eds) *Developing skills with information technology.* Chichester: Wiley.

Levison, W.H. and Junker, A.M. (1977). A model for the pilot's use of motion cues in roll axis tracking tasks. Report AMRL-TR-77–40. Ohio: Aerospace Medical Research Laboratory, Wright-Patterson Air Force Base.

Lindahl, L.G. (1945). Movement analysis as an industrial training method. *Journal of Applied Psychology,* **29**, 420–430.

Lintern, G. (1987). Flight simulation motion systems revisited. *Bulletin of the Human Factors Society,* **30** (12) 1–3.

MacKay, D.G. (1981). The problem of rehearsal or mental practice. *Journal of Motor Behaviour,* **13**, 274–285.

Marshall, E.C., Scanlon, K.E., Shepherd, A. and Duncan, K.D. (1981). Panel diagnosis training for major-hazard continuous-process installations. *The Chemical Engineer,* February.

Martin, E.L. (1981). Training effectiveness of platform motion: Review of motion research involving the advanced simulator for pilot training and the simulator for air-to-air combat. Report No AFHRL-TR-79–51. Arizona: Air Force Human Resources Laboratory, William Air Force Base.

McCall, N.W. Jr and Lombardo, M.M. (1982). Using simulation for leadership and management research: Through the Looking Glass. *Management Science,* **28**, 533–549.

McGhee, W. and Tullar, W.L. (1978). A note on evaluating behaviour modification and behaviour modeling as industrial training techniques. *Personnel Psychology,* **31**, 477–483.

Miller, R.B. (1953). Handbook on training and training equipment design. Report No 53–136. Ohio: Wright Air Development Center, Wright-Patterson Air Force Base.

Miller, R.B. (1954). Psychological considerations in the design of training equipment. Report No 54–563. Ohio: Wright Air Development Center, Wright-Patterson Air Force Base.

Pohlman, L.D. and Reed, J.C. (1978). Air-to-air combat skills: Contribution of platform motion to initial training. Technical Report AFHRL-TR-78–53. Arizona: Air Force Human Resources Laboratory, Williams Air Force Base.

Prather, D.C. (1973). Prompted mental practice as a flight simulator. *Journal of Applied Psychology*, **57**, 353–355.

Prophet, W.W. and Boyd, H.A. (1970). Device-task fidelity and transfer of training: Aircraft cockpit procedures training. Technical Report 70–10. Alexandria, VA: Human Resources Research Organisation.

Rose, A., Evans, R. and Wheaton, G. (1987). Methodological approaches for simulator evaluations. In Cormier, S.M. and Hagman, T.D. (Eds) *Transfer of learning. Contemporary research and applications*. New York: Academic Press.

Rouse, W.B. (1981). Experimental studies and mathematical models of human problem solving performance in fault diagnosis tasks. In Rasmussen, J. and Rouse, W.B. (Eds) *Human detection and diagnosis of system failures*. New York: Plenum Press.

Russell, J.S., Wexley, K.N. and Hunter, J.E. (1984). Questioning the effectiveness of behaviour modeling training in an industrial setting. *Personnel Psychology*, **37**, 465–481.

Schori, T.R. (1970). Driving simulation: An overview. *Behavioral Research and Highway Safety*, **1**, 236–248.

Simon, C.W. (1979). Application of advanced experimental methodologies to AWAVS training research. Technical Report NAVTRAEQUIPCEN 77–C-0065–1. Orlando: Naval Training Equipment Center.

Sorcher, M. and Goldstein, A.P. (1972). A behavioural modeling approach in training. *Personnel Administration*, **35**, 35–41.

Stammers, R.B. (1979). Simulation in training for nuclear power plant operators. Report No 12. Karlstad: Ergonomrad AB.

Stammers, R.B. and Patrick, J. (1975). *The psychology of training*. London: Methuen.

Swezey, R.W., Streufert, S., Criswell, E.L., Unger, K.W. and Van Rijn, P. (1984). Development of a computer simulation for assessing decision-making style using cognitive complexity theory. SAIC Report No 84–04–178. McLean, VA: Science Applications International Corporation.

Toye, M. (1969). A rethink on basic skills. *Industrial Training International*, **4**, 112–119.

Trollip, S.R. (1979). The evaluation of a complex computer-based flight procedures trainer. *Human Factors*, **21**, 47–54.

Valverde, H.H. (1973). A review of flight simulator transfer of training studies. *Human Factors*, **15**, 510–523.

White, B.Y. and Frederiksen, J.R. (1987). Qualitative models and intelligent learning environments. In Lawler, R.W. and Yazdani, M. (Eds) *Artificial intelligence and education, Volume 1: Learning environments and tutoring systems*. Hillsdale, NJ: Lawrence Erlbaum.

CHAPTER 13
Evaluation

Training, including education, is a multi-billion pound/dollar activity. It is not unreasonable for people to ask questions of the sort: Did a training programme "work"? Was it worthwhile? Did the investment justify the results? Can the training be improved? All of these questions lead us to the topic of evaluation. Before they can be answered, it is necessary to define the questions more carefully. First of all, it matters why the question is being asked or for what purpose information is to be gathered. A lecturer might be interested in whether students enjoyed a course; a head of department might be concerned that students had completed a programme of study and achieved a specified level of competence; an administrator might be interested in the number of students, their entry/exit grades, and the cost of one course in comparison with another; and the researcher might be concerned with the effectiveness of one training manipulation in comparison with another. Secondly, and closely linked to the purpose of evaluation, the criteria necessary for answering the question have to be identified. Is evaluation interested in trainees' reactions, course grades, costs etc.? Thirdly, it has to be decided how information about criteria is to be collected and analysed in order to answer the question posed. Evaluation techniques or "methods" include: a questionnaire to assess trainees' reactions; a post-test to measure skill and knowledge; a cost-effectiveness formula; and a research study designed to identify the effectiveness of a particular training variable. These three issues will be discussed in this order, namely, the aims of evaluation (Section 13.1), the criteria of evaluation (Section 13.2) and different evaluation approaches including methods and techniques (Section 13.3).

Many writers have lamented how little evaluation of training is carried out. Phillips (1990) cited a survey of management training carried out in 1977 in which only 24% of 3100 executives reported that change in job behaviour was measured; 52% relied on feedback from trainees; and only 1.8% calculated the return on their training investment. This is consistent with the opinion of most commentators that training is evaluated too infrequently, and even when it is, this is confined to the measurement of trainees' reactions. Whilst trainee reactions are important and should be taken notice of, they are rarely the most relevant

513

criterion for evaluation, irrespective of the evaluator's motive. This lack of evaluation is rather surprising, given the scrutiny which other forms of investment receive in organisations and companies. Also, evaluation methodologies are well established and have seen few changes in the last decades, unlike other areas of training which are more responsive to changing psychological perspectives. This puzzle has to be taken seriously. Yes, many practical problems do exist; trainees may disperse to distant locations after training; measuring subtle changes in skill as manifested in job behaviour is exceedingly difficult; and assessing either the value of different attitudes or the costs of aspects of training involve many assumptions. Another possible explanation is that, typically, evaluation is not an activity which is integrated into the process of training development as it should be. It occurs, if at all, as a separate activity, carried out by persons not involved in training, which means that it is not planned to occur at the right time and evaluators may not even be aware of the training needs and objectives that led to the development of the training programme. Unfortunately, it also has to be said that a lack of political will to evaluate training exists in many organisations. Persons who are responsible for organising and developing training lack any incentive to find out the extent to which a training programme is effective, or put another way, is ineffective. It is the author's opinion that evaluation is perceived as a means of eradicating problems rather than improving training. This point was captured by a phrase I encountered recently in a student's thesis which concluded that evaluation in organisations was perceived "more as a weed-killer than a plant fertiliser". This sums it up perfectly.

Evaluation is well documented by a number of texts and therefore this chapter is more concerned with providing a general framework for evaluation and accompanying signposts rather than covering in detail what can be found elsewhere. Evaluation issues in the context of training are discussed by Goldstein (1986) and different approaches or models of evaluation of training are described by Hamblin (1974), Kirkpatrick (1967), and Warr, Bird and Rackham (1978). Borich and Jemelka (1981) provided a useful account of historical trends and different approaches/models used in evaluation. However, before discussing different approaches, it is necessary to return to our first point in this chapter, namely, that evaluation is undertaken for different purposes.

13.1 AIMS AND DEFINITIONS OF EVALUATION

Evaluation of training has to be defined broadly in order to encompass its many roles and forms, some of which have already been mentioned.

Evaluation is any attempt to obtain information concerning the effect or value of training in order to make decisions about any aspect of the training programme, the persons that have been trained and the organisations (local, national or international) responsible for providing that training. However, even this broad definition is too narrow to cover the CIRO framework for evaluation of training proposed by Warr, Bird and Rackham (1978). The acronym CIRO stands for:

Context evaluation   Obtaining and using information about the current operational context in order to determine training needs and objectives.

Input evaluation   Obtaining and using information about possible training resources in order to choose between alternative "inputs" to training.

Reaction evaluation   Obtaining and using information about trainees' expressed current or subsequent reactions in order to improve training.

Outcome evaluation   Obtaining and using information about the outcomes of training in order to improve subsequent training ... (p. 20).

Both the "C" and "I" activities fall outside the definition of evaluation used here since they are not concerned with the effects or value of training, but rather the development of training itself. "C" involves the activities of analysing a job/task and identifying training needs and objectives (discussed in Chapters 4–7). "I" represents training design (Chapters 8–12) plus consideration of resources in its widest sense. The "R" and "O" activities do fall within our definition of evaluation.

Cronbach (1969) provided an illuminating account of evaluation in the educational context which is just as applicable to the training context. Most importantly, he distinguished between three aims of evaluation in terms of the types of decisions for which evaluation is used. Goldstein (1986) also adopted this perspective in his definition of evaluation which was:

... the systematic collection of descriptive and judgmental information necessary to make effective training decisions related to the *selection*, *adoption*, *value*, and *modification* of various instructional activities (p. 111; italics added).

Distinguishing between the aims or goals of evaluation, as mentioned earlier, is particularly helpful because with them are associated different evaluation approaches, criteria and methods. There is some overlap but this perspective does enable one to disentangle the many recommendations concerning evaluation which can be found in the literature. Cronbach's three aims have been adapted and a fourth added in order to produce the following aims, or types of decision, underlying the evaluation of training:

1. *Training programme improvement.* This covers revision of the *content* and *design* of a training programme plus revision of any practical aspects of the programme.
2. *Decisions about trainees.* Further training may be planned on the basis of individual trainee's needs and some selection and grouping may occur, e.g. in terms of career paths within an organisation. Also trainees have to be debriefed concerning their strengths and weaknesses.
3. *Administrative and organisational decisions.* These involve judgements of quality and value using various indicators at different levels of training (e.g. the trainee, the training course, the training system).
4. *Training research.* The aim is to identify which manipulations or variables improve training.

The need to make different evaluation decisions leads to different approaches, criteria and methods being selected. This has not been recognised sufficiently in the evaluation literature concerned with training. One type of evaluation is sometimes advocated exclusively because the different aims of evaluation are not perceived. Also, apparently conflicting views and definitions of evaluation can be reconciled by reference to the type of evaluation decision that needs to be made. For example, training research involves the use of "scientific methodology" so that one can be certain whether a training variable has an effect or not. This is judged by whether the variable passes the conventional test of statistical significance after a research study, using the experimental method, has been conducted. It is important in such a study that the results are not contaminated by other factors, against which principles of sampling and experimental control offer some protection. This sort of evaluation study is unsuitable for an administrator who is concerned with value for money invested in training and, at most, may collect global scores of trainees at the end of various courses. In contrast, decisions and feedback concerning individual trainees require more fine-grained information, indicating strengths and weaknesses in different dimensions of performance. In this case, evaluation does not, and cannot, use the normal experimental methodology because it is carried out on an individual basis.

Before considering the different approaches to evaluation, let us consider the different effects of training that can be evaluated. These effects are the criteria by which training can be judged. It is not a matter of which criteria are correct, but rather which ones are relevant to the aim(s) of the evaluation. After this has been established, it is necessary to decide how these criteria are to be assessed and measured. Evaluation can employ many methods of data collection and also sources of information, which are discussed in Section 5.2, in the context of task analysis. These same methods (e.g. interview, questionnaire, observation) and sources of information (e.g. job incumbent, supervisor) are used in the assessment of training criteria for evaluation purposes. Further, this assessment has itself to satisfy the criteria of reliability and validity discussed in Section 5.3. In other words, whatever is measured has to be done in a manner which is consistent (i.e. is reliable from one occasion to another or from one observer to another) and accurate (i.e. valid).

13.2   CRITERIA FOR EVALUATION

The effects of training have been divided into four types: reactions, learning, job behaviour and results (Kirkpatrick, 1967) and reactions, immediate outcomes, intermediate outcomes and ultimate outcomes (Warr, Bird and Rackham, 1978). Hamblin (1974), in an excellent discussion of evaluation for training practitioners, identified five types, or what he termed *levels*, of training effects:

1. Reactions.
2. Learning.
3. Job behaviour.
4. Organisation.
5. Ultimate value.

These five levels of training are represented in Hamblin's cycle of evaluation model, Figure 13.1. Before discussing each of these levels, let us consider Hamblin's model. First, Hamblin envisaged that training (T) leads to training effects, E1 to E5, such that lower-level effects are prerequisites for effects at higher levels. He argued that these five effects are rather like a chain which can snap at any of its links. For example, learning (E2) has to occur before there is a possibility that it can be translated into some effect on job behaviour (E3). Even if learning does occur, changes in job behaviour may not. Similarly, changes in job behaviour (E3) are necessary before any organisational effects (E4) can be manifested. This idea is quite neat, although it breaks down for the link between E1 and E2 since learning may occur despite, for example, a trainee's poor opinion of a training course. Also, whether or not there is a prerequisite link between E4 and E5 will depend upon

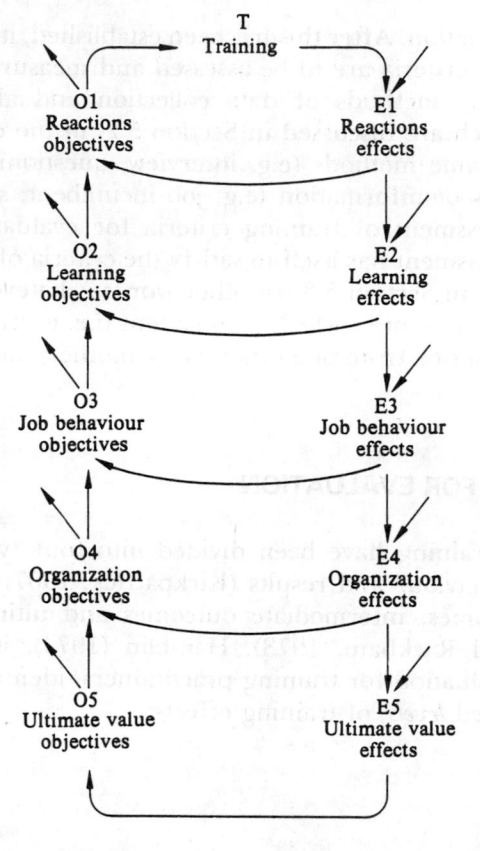

Figure 13.1 Hamblin's cycle of evaluation model (Hamblin, 1974).

the nature of the "ultimate" effects to be evaluated. These are discussed later. Secondly, in Hamblin's model (Figure 13.1), training effects are represented on the right-hand side and their corresponding objectives, against which they are evaluated, on the left-hand side. Thirdly, the reader may be curious about the "extra" arrows in Figure 13.1 which leave each objective and return to each training effect. These arrows represent factors which are not directly related to the training. Thus a trainer may try to achieve a "reactions objective" (O1) not only by good training, but also by a good standard of cuisine and entertainment on a residential training course! Similarly trainees' reactions (E1) will be affected by not only the training course, but also by factors both within and outside the trainer's control (e.g. the weather). The same logic applies to the other levels in Hamblin's evaluation model. Finally, evaluation is conceptualised by Hamblin, and many others, as a means by which training is regulated and controlled. The evaluator has to identify any training effects (E1–E5) that were not achieved, or in Hamblin's terms where the chain has snapped, and suggest modifications which can be made to mend it. If training effects are attained, then so too are their corresponding objectives, represented by the horizontal, right-to-left arrows in Figure 13.1.

1. Reactions

The trainees' reactions to training are important, particularly to the trainees! However, from the training manager's perspective they are not as important as whether learning and job behaviour effects have taken place. Each trainee's reactions, attitudes etc. are complex and a result of many factors such as training content and methods, other trainees, the training context, location etc. and the trainee's perceived success at achieving some of the goals of training. These reactions will vary throughout the training course, some being transitory in nature. Therefore it has to be decided not only what aspects of these reactions are of interest, as specified in the "reactions objectives", but also when they should be assessed. A questionnaire, using rating scales, is undoubtedly the most popular method of assessment and this can be supplemented by interview and informal discussion.

If we return to the different aims of evaluation, then it is evident that trainees' reactions do not have a high priority. They are of little concern to training research, being regarded correctly as too "soft" an index of training, whilst they are rarely of interest to the administrator unless attitudes to training are desperately unfavourable. Even decisions concerning modification of a training programme are driven more by the achievement of learning and changes in job behaviour than trainees' reactions.

2. Learning

Arguably, the most important question addressed by any evaluation of training is whether trainees have acquired the skills and knowledge for which the training programme was developed. These are specified by the training objectives, discussed in Section 4.5, and both the content and design of training are geared to enabling them to be achieved. In one sense, if trainees fail to achieve the necessary skills and knowledge, then it can be said that it is the training system that has failed, rather than the trainee, and requires modification.

Obviously, any evaluation of learning has to assess carefully and precisely the nature of the skills and knowledge that should have been acquired. This may involve the many different types of learning which are discussed in Section 8.3, with respect to both Gagné's taxonomy and Merrill's Component Display Theory. Training objectives should be sufficiently detailed and performance-oriented that they not only capture the different types of skill to be acquired, but also what constitutes persuasive evidence that they have actually been met (viz. Mager's prescriptions in Section 4.5).

Any evaluation of skill acquisition has to be carried out with care to ensure that any assessment is both reliable and valid. Firstly, as discussed in Section 1.1, it is important to be aware of the distinction between learning and performance. Only the latter can be measured directly. Learning has to be inferred from the measurement of performance and so care has to be taken that performance is a true reflection of the effect of training and is not affected by extraneous factors. Secondly, an important question concerns *when* this assessment should take place. Undoubtedly, evaluation is necessary at the end of training, using some "post-test", although this is never sufficient. Ideally, training should be developed in the knowledge of how long trainees are expected to retain their skills and at what levels. This should be specified in the training objectives such that it is evident when after training skills should be reassessed, not least to determine whether refresher training is required. Some skills and knowledge can deteriorate rapidly over short time intervals, whilst others are quite resistant to decay, as discussed in Section 3.7. Many factors affect the degree of skill loss, including the amount of training (Section 2.3) and overtraining (Section 9.8).

Again, the reason why evaluation of skill acquisition is to be carried out will determine how it is assessed. If the aim is to improve the training programme or make decisions concerning each trainee, then fairly detailed information needs to be collected concerning how many trainees achieved which training objectives to what standards of performance. Many dimensions of performance have to be assessed in order to pinpoint which aspects of either the content or design of the training programme require improvement. This is why, if training improvement is one's aim, some evaluation of both the group and individual trainee's progress during training, is likely to be valuable in identifying ineffective parts of the training programme. In contrast, an administrator's aim is likely to be served by global measures of trainees' post-test performance, sometimes supplemented by a pre-test measure. This is unlikely to be sufficient for a training researcher who is interested in being able to state unequivocally that a particular training variable (e.g. amount of training,

training method) was or was not responsible for any change in pre-test to post-test performance. This requires the use of suitable research designs which enable the effects of many factors surrounding a training programme to be disentangled from the training variable of interest. This issue is discussed later in this chapter.

3. Job behaviour

For occupational training it is critical that skill and knowledge acquisition are translated into appropriate changes in job behaviour. Even outside the occupational context, the aim is for persons to acquire skills which can be performed without the trainer's support in their natural setting, whatever that might be, e.g. a sportsperson competing in a race. Therefore evaluation of job behaviour, level 3 in Hamblin's terms, is closely associated with the topic of "transfer of training" (Chapter 3). The objective of training is to maximise transfer to the "real" situation and this depends not only upon psychological principles governing transfer, but also on the accuracy of the task analysis which laid the foundations for the training programme.

In addition to the technical difficulties of ensuring that training is geared to producing changes in job behaviour, there may be practical difficulties in assessing this. There is no problem when each trainee (i.e. job incumbent) performs one task and this can be measured directly. However, this is often not possible, particularly for tasks of a team nature or those requiring interactions with other persons, possibly at different times, and in different locations, e.g. some social and supervisory tasks. Further, trainees may disappear after training to remote locations or to different parts of an organisation, making access difficult and sometimes costly. Another potential practical difficulty is that trainees must have the *opportunity* of putting their training to good effect and this will be determined by the nature and range of their job activities. Obviously, an evaluator needs to ensure that sufficient opportunity has been available for a trainee to demonstrate the effect of training by improving job behaviour.

4. Organisation

It is hoped that any training effects on job behaviour will be translated into beneficial effects upon the organisation within which the trainee works. Hamblin distinguished between more immediate organisational effects, i.e. this level 4, from what he termed "ultimate" effects, in level 5. This distinction is somewhat fuzzy, although it attempts to differentiate the large number of possible organisational effects in terms of "local" ones from those more concerned with an organisation's "ultimate" objectives (e.g. profit). More "local" organisational effects include improvements to:

quality and quantity of production;
safety;
damage to equipment;
absenteeism;
labour turnover;
attitudes to work, job satisfaction etc.;
running costs;
improvements in work methods.

5. Ultimate value

Undoubtedly, the ultimate value of training to organisations is judged mainly in terms of its financial effect and this could be projected up to effects on national and international economies. Generally cost-effectiveness studies of training are few in number and poor in quality. Some cost-effectiveness studies are discussed concerning computer-based training (Section 11.4) and simulation (Chapter 12). Naturally, evaluation involving cost-effectiveness can be very important in persuading organisations to invest in both training and retraining their personnel. However, there are both practical and technical difficulties facing such evaluations. Collecting all of the relevant data concerning both "cost" and "effectiveness" is problematic, not least because of the various assumptions which have to be made (e.g. in the calculation of not only training development costs but also improvements in production attributable solely to training). Also, a situation may arise whereby the cost of evaluation itself exceeds the financial return from the training. Cost-effectiveness is discussed further with respect to the administrator's view of evaluation (Section 13.3).

Some will balk at the notion that the ultimate value of training can be captured adequately by reference to the pound, dollar etc. This of course is the problem currently facing many educational institutions, at least in the United Kingdom, which are being forced to justify the provision of education in terms of its "value" rather than retiring to trusted phrases such as "it teaches people to think" and "it broadens experiences". Some argue that it is not appropriate to attempt to carry out cost-effectiveness evaluations. Disentangling educational effects from others is itself a nightmare let alone costing their benefits over, possibly, a lifetime. Similar problems face evaluation of "ultimate" training effects, some of which may be concerned with the promotion of "human good". Hamblin took an optimistic view and suggested that most organisations attempt to promote at least some "human good" through training although they are constrained by the degree of financial pressure under which they have to operate.

> ... hospitals, schools, prisons, police forces, armies, welfare organisations, and even Government departments may all give priority to some kind of measurement of *human good* over purely financial criteria, though the extent to which they are able to do this will depend on the amount of financial pressure placed on them at particular times. Even business organisations, which purport to exist solely in order to make profit, may, in times of prosperity, carry out some activities (including training) which are not geared towards any financial goal, although they may still try to *rationalize* these activities in financial terms. ... So the *hard-headed view*, which would automatically equate *ultimate value* with *costs*, may in some cases be quite mistaken (Hamblin, 1974, p. 22).

Finally, it should be mentioned that sometimes the phrase "validation of training" is used in the context of evaluation. A distinction is drawn between internal and external validation. The Department of Employment's *Glossary of Training Terms* (1971) defines these as follows:

1. Internal validation:
   A series of tests and assessments designed to ascertain whether a training programme has achieved the behavioural objectives specified.
2. External validation:
   A series of tests and assessments designed to ascertain whether the behavioural objectives of an internally valid training programme were realistically based on an accurate initial identification of training needs in relation to the criteria of effectiveness adopted by the organisation (p. 32; italics omitted).

Internal validation is concerned with evaluating that certain learning outcomes have been achieved by training (Hamblin's level 2). External validation goes further and addresses Hamblin's levels 3–5. The notion of validation should not be confused with the very different use of the term "validity" which is used in connection with the design of evaluation studies, where different factors can threaten both internal and external validity. This topic is discussed later in this chapter.

13.3 APPROACHES TO EVALUATION

Any evaluation of training has to select both criteria and methods of assessment in order to achieve its aim. Four main aims of evaluation were identified in Section 13.1 in terms of the type of decision for which evaluation is employed. These decisions are broadly associated with different approaches to evaluation, as follows, although there is some overlap:

1. *Training programme improvement*: systems approach, research/scientific approach, naturalistic approach.
2. *Trainee-oriented decisions*: ad hoc.
3. *Administrative decisions about training*: cost-effectiveness approach; statistical approach.
4. *Decisions concerning the effect of training manipulations/variables*: research/ scientific approach.

On the one hand, decisions concerning how to improve a training programme may involve a variety of approaches to evaluation. For example, it is common to employ the systems approach in conjunction with the research approach. On the other hand, if evaluation is concerned with pinpointing the effect of one training manipulation or variable, then there is little alternative but to carry out a research study, either in the laboratory or in an applied setting. Differences between approaches to evaluation are explored below in the context of the decisions which they attempt to serve.

Training programme improvement

Many writers regard improvement of the training programme as the most important aim of evaluation. For example Cronbach (1969) stated:

> The greatest service evaluation can perform is to identify aspects of the course where revision is desirable (p. 364).

Improvement of the training programme is the explicit concern of any *systems approach* to the development of training. Various ISD models are discussed in Chapter 4 which view the development of training as a system which can be broken down into its functions. Evaluation has an important function because it provides the feedback which allows the system to control and regulate itself. Training development can be adaptive through the information supplied by evaluation, e.g. by revising training materials in the light of trainees' difficulties in particular areas of the programme. As a consequence of evaluation data, it might be necessary to change the training objectives, the training content or the design of training in order to improve training and enable training to achieve its objectives. No training programme will ever be perfect on its first implementation and it requires continual revision and fine tuning. From this perspective, evaluation provides the training manager with the means of controlling and regulating training and ensuring that training accomplishes what it sets out to. This view is the same as that adopted by Hamblin (1974):

> The purpose of evaluation is *control*. The control of training is in effect the management of training: the process of collection, analysis, and evaluation of information, leading to decision-making and action. ... The purpose of evaluation is to create a feedback loop, or a "self-correcting training system" (Rackham, Honey and Colbert, 1971). A well-controlled training programme is one in which weaknesses and failures are identified and corrected by means of negative feedback, and strengths and successes are identified and amplified by means of positive feedback (p. 11).

The systems approach emphasises that evaluation is an integral part of the development of training; it is not some add-on activity. In order to carry out an evaluation, information is necessary concerning training needs, training objectives and also the content of the proposed training programme. There should be a direct mapping between these elements and the dimensions of performance selected for evaluation. In other words, evaluation should be directed at those aspects of knowledge/skill defined by the training needs/objectives which the training programme is attempting to fulfil. Some of these links are discussed by Borich (1979) in the context of a six-stage model for evaluation which is represented in Figure 13.2. The first stage involves collecting and reviewing any information concerning the needs and objectives of training, and presumably this includes any task/job analysis. The second stage is concerned with "structured decomposition" which is, according to Borich, a systematic method of "breaking down a complex training programme into its constituent parts", as indicated in Figure 13.2. The nature of the training programme should not only link to the training needs/objectives but also to the dimensions of performance to be evaluated (stage 3). These dimensions selected for evaluation have to be both relevant and comprehensive with respect to the skills/knowledge which the trainees should have acquired. From these dimensions, questions are formulated (stage 4), then data are collected and subjected to analysis by statistical methods (stage 5) and finally conclusions are reached concerning each dimension of the trainee's performance (stage 6).

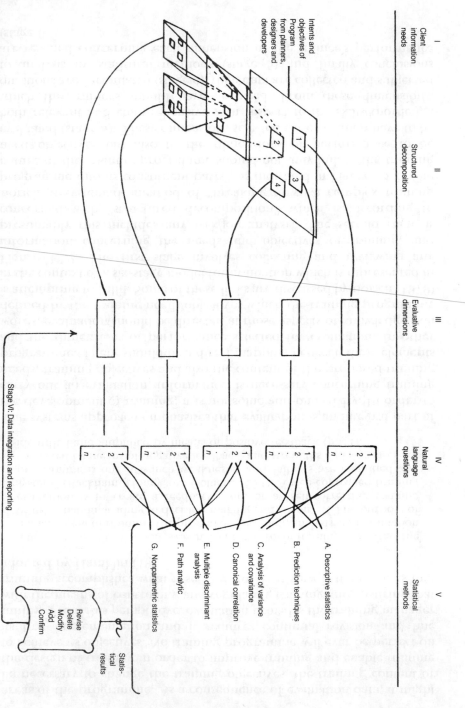

Figure 13.2 A six-stage model for evaluation (Borich, 1979).

The systems approach to evaluation requires detailed information about a range of criteria in order to ensure that training is achieving its objectives and, if not, to determine what modifications are necessary. As Borich's model indicates, an average score of trainees' performance on some post-test will inevitably be inadequate because the evaluator will be unable to diagnose problem areas of the training programme. This is one reason why both multiple criteria and multiple dimensions of these criteria are useful. In addition, evaluation *during* training is likely to provide information which is indicative of trainees' sources of difficulty.

In any systems approach to the evaluation of training a distinction is drawn between *formative* and *summative* evaluation (Scriven, 1967). Formative evaluation takes place prior to conducting training and is equivalent to pilot testing the programme. In contrast, summative evaluation occurs after all, or at least some, training has been completed. Formative and summative evaluation are stages specified in Briggs and Wager's ISD model described on pp. 120–121, and they can also be found in other ISD models, although not under these labels.

In a general sense, formative and summative evaluation share the same function, that is, they both aim to enable training materials to be revised and improved. However, with formative evaluation this takes place when the training materials are in various embryonic forms. The specific purpose is to test not only their potential effectiveness, but also the feasibility and practicability of the overall training programme and specific training modules. In contrast, summative evaluation is concerned with whether the training has "worked" and training objectives have been met. Another difference between these types of evaluation is in the methods they employ. Formative evaluation is an iterative process, initially using informal methods and, sometimes, finishing with a more formal method. Dick (1977) described three stages of formative evaluation which vary in scale and degree of formality: preliminary evaluation, small group evaluation and field trial evaluation. Initially, the training developer explores a preliminary draft of the training materials with a person from the target population and notes any difficulties with the instructions, timing, explanations, equipment etc. After revision, the draft training materials are tested on a small group of trainees and then, after further revision, a field trial is conducted which attempts to evaluate the training in a situation which resembles the "real" one as closely as possible. At this last stage it is desirable for the evaluation to be conducted formally and in a similar fashion to the intended summative evaluation after training.

Formative evaluation uses criteria concerning trainees' reactions and learning. Summative evaluation uses not only these criteria, but also changes in job behaviour and organisational effects. In the worst scenario, none of these criteria may be available for a variety of practical reasons. With no information concerning the effect of training, is there any means of conducting an evaluation? Well, certainly not in terms of the definition of evaluation used in this chapter. However, as a last resort, it is possible to accomplish some evaluation by using the systems approach. It will be remembered that there are stages in the development of training which are specified by the ISD models discussed in Chapter 4. These stages and the sequence between them are necessary, but not sufficient, conditions for an effective training programme. So, given no other information, the evaluator can assess, firstly, whether the development of the training programme was in accord with these stages, and secondly, whether each of these stages was tackled by an appropriate method, technique or set of principles. Whilst this information is no substitute for an assessment of training outcomes, it is better than none at all.

The systems approach is not the only approach to evaluation when training programme improvement is the prime aim. It is sometimes necessary to evaluate the criteria by means of a research study. This may be required to settle some dispute regarding the optimal method of training which cannot be resolved by an examination of the research literature on the subject. The research approach to evaluation is discussed later in this chapter.

Other approaches to evaluation might also be needed to answer other more practical questions. One might wish to know whether the trainers, training equipment and trainees kept to the training schedule, whether there were any unanticipated issues which arose during training, and whether there were any breakdowns in communication between those responsible for implementing training. These sorts of issues require a more open-ended, less formal approach which can be found in *naturalistic* evaluation, discussed by Borich and Jemelka (1981). These authors, citing Guba (1978), suggested that naturalistic evaluation differed from other approaches to evaluation in terms of two dimensions:

(a) the degree to which the investigator manipulates conditions antecedent to the inquiry; and
(b) the degree of constraint imposed on the behavior of subjects involved in the inquiry (p. 187).

Borich and Jemelka discussed five models which might be used in the naturalistic approach to evaluation:

1. *The responsive model* (Stake, 1975). This is an informal and unconstrained assessment by an evaluator who responds to the requirements

of those persons who have undergone "the programme" and in the light of this, strikes up a dialogue with the programme developers. Evaluation is "responsive" in just about any way.

2. *The judicial model.* Again, as the name suggests, the evaluation proceeds along the lines of a hearing in a court of law, with preparatory stages, calling of witnesses and the like.

3. *The transactional model* (Rippey, 1973). This is discussed by Wagner and Seidel (1978) in the context of training. Transactional analysis can enable problems in the development or implementation of training to be addressed by those involved who express opinions about the nature of the problems and a consensus is reached concerning how they can be resolved.

4. *The connoisseurship model.* As the name suggests evaluation is carried out by the judgement of a connoisseur or expert, rather akin to a consultant who might make an overall judgement of the quality of a training programme.

5. *The illumination model* (Parlett and Hamilton, 1978). This evaluation adopts an anthropological approach. "Investigators observe, inquire further and then seek to explain", again, in an unfettered fashion. It focuses on how an innovatory programme takes place, rather than its products, and it seeks to expose tacit assumptions and unexpected characteristics of the programme.

These possible models associated with naturalistic evaluation are at the opposite extreme to research-oriented evaluation. They have to be employed cautiously, recognising the problems of subjectivity, value judgement, error and the like. Nevertheless, it has to be admitted that the success of any training programme, especially more conventional "courses", cannot be captured totally by the extent that anticipated effects are achieved.

Trainee-oriented decisions

Evaluation of training can focus on individual trainees' records, using any of the criteria discussed previously. The training manager or the trainee's supervisor may wish to select further training for a trainee on the basis of his or her profile of scores obtained during the training programme. Alternatively, the aim may be just to provide the trainee with knowledge of results concerning levels of performance. Again, to do this satisfactorily, a variety of detailed, multi-dimensional assessments of performance is necessary.

The systems approach to evaluation focuses on the training system's objectives and whether these have been achieved by a group of trainees. This emphasis ignores the trainee's personal objectives which may be quite different. The acquisition of skill might be valued by the trainee or training might be viewed only as a means to some further goal, such as a job, financial reward etc. Hamblin (1974) described these and other goals which may be valued by the trainee and related them to his five criteria or levels of evaluation: trainees' reactions (E1), learning (E2), job behaviour (E3), organisational effects (E4) and ultimate value (E5) (Figure 13.3). The ultimate value of training for the trainee is defined by his or her personal goals, which cover many dimensions besides financial return. Some goals may be achieved by: the experience or entertainment value of the course; the learning it promotes; and the effect which passing the course and securing some "ticket" bestows.

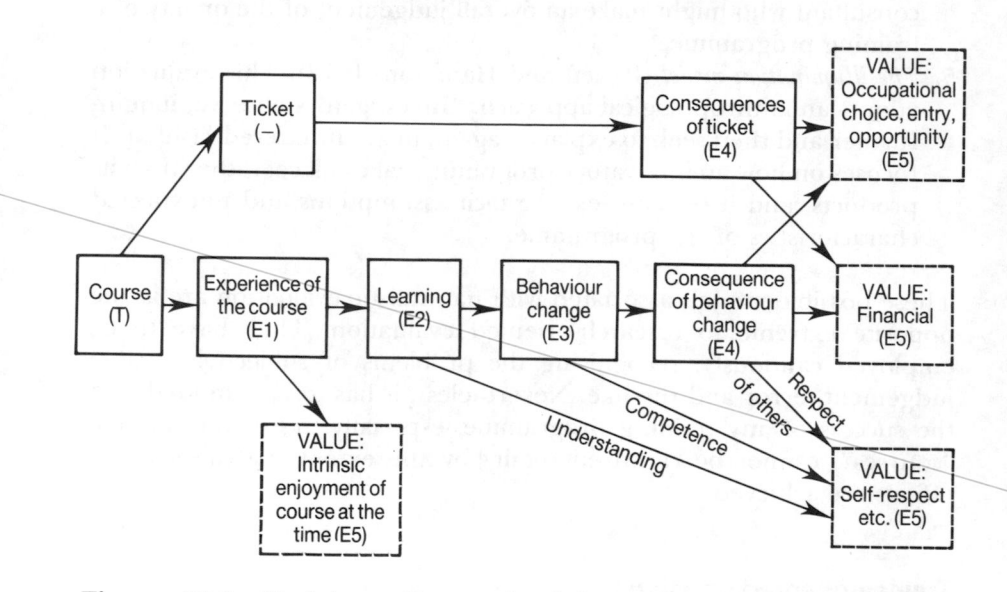

Figure 13.3 Training effects valued by trainees (Hamblin, 1974, adapted from Burgoyne, 1973).

Administrative decisions about training

Administrators may use various aggregated assessments of trainees' scores, pass rates, throughput, cost, and relate these, via regression and other statistical methods, to other factors such as the number of instructors, the number of trainees per course and broad characteristics of the nature of training in order to make judgements concerning the allocation of resources. Nowadays, the call for cost-effectiveness is becoming louder and more persistent. Both the "effect" side, and the "cost" side of this equation provide serious problems for the evaluator, plus the overall logic involved in such an evaluation. In order to compare "costs", "benefits" and "effects", they have to be measurable. Some would argue that measuring some of the effects of training and educational programmes is not possible, e.g. the long-term, qualitative outcomes. However if we accept that measurement is feasible, then two options are available. On the one hand both "costs" and "benefits" can be quantified using the same scale, presumably financial costs, and then compared. The problem here is how these translations into pounds, dollars etc. are calculated and the associated assumptions that are necessary. On the other hand, evaluation can list the "costs" and "effects" using different scales of measurement, and then a value judgement has to be made to determine whether the latter can be justified by the former. This latter option might arise in two circumstances. A company or organisation may have some existing training for a particular job/task and the question is whether the "new" training is more cost-effective than the "old". This is easier when either the costs or the effects are the same for the two training programmes being compared although a value judgement is still necessary. A second circumstance is where the company has no existing training for that job/task. In this situation, as Fielden and Pearson (1978) observed in the context of computer-based training:

> there is an add-on cost for a claimed extra benefit and an overall assessment becomes an exercise in value judgement (p. 130).

Further, Fielden and Pearson (1978) rightly concluded that:

> cost effectiveness techniques are of little help in making the value judgement of whether an extra benefit is worth the extra cost. Cost analysis can help with the identification and measurement of costs, but cost-effectiveness has nothing to add (p. 117).

Even identification and measurement of the costs of training is not straightforward. Accountants and economists can puzzle us by distinguishing between "direct", "marginal", "opportunity" and "fixed costs". The costs of training can be easily overlooked and underestimated. Costs are involved in all of the main stages of training development.

1. *Planning and analysis costs* involved in deciding on the need for, and nature of a training programme and obtaining information to make these decisions. For example:

job/task/skill analysis;

expenses of subject matter experts;

obtaining existing training materials, documentation and information concerning critical tasks.

2. *Design and development costs* involved in preparing and producing training materials, equipment etc. For example:

pilot testing of materials;

renting, leasing or purchasing equipment;

training of instructors.

3. *Implementing, evaluating and revising training* involve costs. For example:

preparation, production and revision of training materials;

administrative and instructor costs;

trainee costs;

evaluation costs;

costs of buildings, land etc.

If, despite these difficulties, one decides that the cost-effectiveness of training has to, and can be tackled, then Schmidt, Hunter and Pearlman (1982) have provided a formula for calculating its financial impact. Schmidt et al. argued correctly that the evaluation of training programmes by a research study and accompanying statistical methods does not support an administrator's decision-making which is better served by calculation of their impact in terms of pounds/dollars. They suggested that this could be accomplished by adaptation of a methodology which they had used previously to assess the economic impact of valid selection procedures on work force productivity. They explained their suggestions in the context of the following example.

Imagine that there are 200 computer programmers in an organisation and that one half of this group is given training and the other half is not. The cost of training is 500 dollars per trainee; training occurs out of work time and therefore incurs no extra costs of "lost" work; supervisors rate the quality of programs produced over a six-month period, not knowing which programmers received training. The mean rating of those trained is 55 versus a mean of 50 for those who were not, and the standard deviation for both groups is 10. A conventional *t*-test confirms that there is a significant difference between the means with a value of 3.53, df=198, $p<0.001$. Schmidt et al. provided the following formula for calculating the financial impact of training as:

$$\Delta U = TNd_tSD_y - NC$$

Each of these terms is as follows:

1. ΔU is equivalent to the financial impact of the training programme.
2. T is the number of years duration of the training effect on performance. In this example this is estimated to be two years.
3. N is the number of personnel trained (i.e. 100).
4. d_t is the true difference in job performance between the average trained and untrained employee in standard deviation units. In this example the gain in performance is:

$$\frac{\text{Average of trained group} - \text{Average of untrained group}}{\text{Standard deviation}} = 0.50 \text{ standard deviation units}$$

However Schmidt et al. pointed out that this figure assumes perfect reliability of ratings and therefore needs adjustment to take account of interrater reliability which they argued is likely to be about 0.60, providing a value of $d_t = 0.50/\sqrt{0.60} = 0.65$. Further they suggested that in some cases d_t could be estimated from the results of relevant published studies, although they admitted that d_t is the most difficult term to estimate in their formula and may be considerably lower than their estimate of 0.65.

5. SD_y is the standard deviation of job performance in pounds/dollars of the untrained group. The reader should consult Schmidt et al.'s original discussion concerning methods for doing this, their assumptions and relative advantages. Suffice it to say that estimation of this parameter is difficult and open to dispute. They argued that one rule of thumb was to use 40% of annual salary. In this example Schmidt and Hunter found a value of 10,413 dollars for SD_y using another method.

Therefore in this example the financial impact of training is as follows:

$$\Delta U = 2(100)(0.65)(\$10,413) - (100)(\$500)$$
$$= \$1,303,690.$$

Schmidt et al. argued that if this example is realistic then the impact of training is greater than psychologists have realised. However, dramatic changes in the estimated financial impact of training can be produced by modest changes in the values of parameters in the equation. For example, if d_t were only 0.25 and the cost per trainee was 1000 dollars, then the financial impact would be 420,650 dollars. Inevitably, both the terms in such an equation and how they are estimated are the subject of much debate.

Decisions about training variables: the research approach

Evaluation of training can use what is loosely termed here "the research approach". This is appropriate not only for carrying out research into training, but also evaluating the effect of a training programme systematically. The research approach refers to use of the "scientific method" which involves the steps of identifying the problem and developing a hypothesis; designing an experiment to test this hypothesis; conducting the experiment and collecting data; testing the hypothesis by analysing the data; and reaching a conclusion. This approach dominates research in the social and biological sciences. Students of psychology, biology, economics etc. receive training in the principles of experimental design and statistical analysis in order to carry out "scientific" studies. The aim of these studies is to discover the cause–effect relationships or "laws" which connect variation in the independent variable (e.g. type of training) to variation in the dependent variable (e.g. some aspect of the trainee's performance). Put symbolically:

$$Y = f(X)$$

where Y is the dependent variable or the aspect of performance being assessed. With respect to evaluation of training, Y is equivalent to the criteria selected by the researcher: trainees' reactions, learning, job behaviour etc. X is the independent variable which is being manipulated by the researcher or trainer. Hence X may be concerned with the presence/absence of training, a range of "types" of training and any of the training variables discussed in this book. A study is carried out to establish whether Y is a function of X, in other words, whether changes in Y (e.g. trainee's reactions/learning) are attributable to changes in X (e.g. the presence/absence of training or the nature of training). After data have been collected, the principles and techniques of statistical analysis provide the researcher with a means of scrutinising the data and finding out whether there is sufficient evidence to claim that a relationship between X and Y exists. However, statistical analysis only examines patterns amongst data and no matter how sophisticated, it provides no guarantee that variation in Y, or lack of it, is a true reflection of the manipulation of X. This can only be achieved by a proper *design* of the study which enables the researcher to be confident that such variation is not attributable to other variables and that the design is *valid*.

There are many factors which jeopardise the validity of the design of research studies. This topic has received detailed and exhaustive treatment in many texts and it is not possible, or necessary, to reiterate all of the subtleties of this literature. Some of the main issues which are relevant to training are discussed here with references provided for the interested reader to pursue. The classic and most authoritative account of sources of invalidity and how these might be overcome by appropriate research designs is given by Campbell and Stanley (1966). Subsequently, Bracht and Glass (1968) and Cook and Campbell (1976) have made further contributions to this debate. Introductions to this topic in the context of the experimental approach to science are provided by Neale and Liebert (1973) and Christensen (1977) and in the context of training by Goldstein (1986). Our discussion in the remainder of this chapter will cover: the definition of types of invalidity; sources of invalidity; and how different sources of invalidity can be overcome.

Campbell and Stanley's (1966) exposition of validity was motivated by the disillusionment, at that time, with use of the experimental model in education. However they maintained that the only means of resolving educational disputes or identifying improvements in teaching practices was through the use of carefully designed experiments. (A similar line is taken by Goldstein, 1986, and Hinrichs, 1976, in the context of training.) Campbell and Stanley made the now famous distinction between *internal* and *external* validity.

> *Internal validity* is the basic minimum without which any experiment is uninterpretable: Did in fact the experimental treatments make a difference in this specific experimental instance? *External validity* asks the question of *generalizability*: To what populations, settings, treatment variables, and measurement variables can this effect be generalized? Both types of criteria are obviously important, even though they are frequently at odds in that features increasing one may jeopardize the other. While *internal validity* is the sine qua non, and while the question of *external validity*, like the question of inductive inference is never completely answerable, the selection of designs strong in both types of validity is obviously our ideal. This is particularly the case for research on teaching [and training], in which generalization to applied settings of known character is the desideratum (Campbell and Stanley, 1966, p. 5; square parentheses added).

The distinction between internal and external validity of experiments has been much quoted. Internal validity is concerned with whether or not the effect of some independent variable on the dependent variable was identified correctly by the experiment, whereas external validity is concerned with generalisation of the findings to other populations of people, situations, contexts and treatments. However, the distinction between internal and external validity is a little more tricky and subtle than might at first appear. For example, consider an experiment in which the true effect of a training programme was actually attributable to the person who tested the trainees rather than the training itself.

Table 13.1   Threats to the internal and external validity of training studies (adapted from Bracht and Glass, 1968; Campbell and Stanley, 1966; Cook and Campbell, 1976)

Internal validity	External validity
1. *Intervening events* Any events occurring between the first (e.g. pre-test) and second (e.g. post-test) measurement of performance which might contaminate the effect of training, e.g. trainees receiving information relevant to training between the pre- and post-test	1. *Population validity* *Accessible versus target populations* The population of trainees accessible to the study has certain characteristics which may not be the same as those of the complete population of trainees of interest to the investigator
2. *Maturation* Changes in performance due to the trainees changing in some way, e.g. growing older, wiser	2. *Interaction of the effect of the training with some characteristics of the trainees* e.g. Aptitude Treatment Interaction effects in which the effect of, say, training methods varies as a function of trainees' aptitudes
3. *Testing* When a trainee is tested more than once, one test may have a transfer effect to the second one (either a positive or negative effect)	3. *Ecological validity* *Describing the training completely* A prerequisite for replication and generalisation of findings is that all aspects of the training situation or study are made explicit
4. *Instrumentation* How a trainee's performance is measured may change from one test to another, e.g. different rating scales or different observers can produce such a confounding effect	4. *Multiple treatment interference* When trainees receive multiple training conditions their reaction is not necessarily the same as when they experience only one
5. *Statistical regression* The difference between training groups which are high and low on some measure of performance on one occasion, will ⌐luce on the second occasion. This statistical phenomenon is	5. *The reactive effect of pre-testing* A pre-test may increase or decrease trainees' responsiveness to

Differential selection

Trainees receiving different training manipulations may differ on some important variable (e.g. ability, experience, age) which will influence their performance scores

7. *Differential loss of trainees*
Different kinds of trainees might drop out of one training group in comparison with another group. Differences between the scores of the remaining trainees in the groups will be affected by such trends

8. *Selection–maturation interaction*
This occurs when, for example, training groups are composed of different kinds of persons who mature at different rates

9. *Diffusion or imitation of the training treatment*
Information which is only provided to the training group may become available to the control group, e.g. when trainees are in the same organisation

10. *Compensatory equalisation of treatments*
When training produces beneficial effects, some administrators may decide that the control group should also experience the training

11. *Trainees' knowledge of their group membership*
If trainees have a knowledge of which training group they are in, they may be motivated to improve performance or they may be resentful and not bother to try

12. *Misuse of statistical techniques and misinterpretation of results from them*
Data from an experiment is subjected to statistical analysis. The analysis needs to be appropriate in terms of both the investigator's question and the assumptions of the technique. Further, the output of a statistical technique needs careful interpretation (e.g. a correlation coefficient)

6. *...*
Trainees' knowledge that they are participating in a study may influence their behaviour (e.g. the Hawthorne effect). The *novelty* of the training treatment may have an effect rather than the treatment itself. Also the expectations of the trainer and person testing the trainee can bias the data collected

7. *Other conceptual misinterpretations*
The training variable has to sample adequately the range of values of interest, e.g. if amount of training is of interest, then high, medium and low amounts need evaluation in the experiment. Also the dependent variable needs to be selected so that it is sensitive to the effects of the training variable. Finally, any cause and effect relationship found in the experiment must be unambiguous and not attributable to some other theoretical variable. For example, the reason that knowledge of results improves performance may be due to its informational or motivational value

(This is known in psychology as the experimenter effect.) One's first inclination is to view this as a contaminating or confounding variable which threatens the internal validity of the study and yet Campbell and Stanley would have classified this effect under external validity as did Bracht and Glass (1968). Also Cook and Campbell (1976) identified this kind of factor as a source of what they termed "construct invalidity", which they acknowledged was part of Campbell and Stanley's original definition of external validity. The experimenter effect can be argued to fall within the realm of external validity because it affects any attempt to generalise the finding to other situations in which different persons are involved in the testing of trainees' performance. However, as mentioned previously, it is also a confounding variable which affects the correct interpretation of the results of the study and therefore apparently is a source of internal invalidity. In order to sort out these problems of definition, one has to return to Campbell and Stanley's original distinctions. They viewed factors of internal invalidity as ones which *directly* affected the process of observation or measurement, i.e. they produced an effect which was summed with the effect of the treatment, in our case training. In contrast, factors of external validity are concerned with the treatment effect being affected by another factor in some circumstances but not in others. This is difficult to explain, although for those familiar with analysis of variance, it can be described as the difference between a contaminating factor which has a main effect (internal validity) and one which has an interaction effect (external validity). This careful distinction has not always been preserved in some textbooks on this topic.

Before considering some of the factors associated with these two types of validity, the reader needs to be warned of some further distinctions. Cook and Campbell (1976) identified a special form of internal validity as "statistical conclusion validity" which refers to:

> the validity of conclusions we draw on the basis of statistical evidence about whether a presumed cause and effect covary (p. 223).

Also Bracht and Glass (1968) divided external validity into "population" and "ecological" validity. The former is concerned with generalisations to populations of persons, whereas the latter is concerned with the "environment" of the experiment and the conditions under which an effect is found, such as the nature of the treatment, the context and the dependent variables.

Factors affecting both the internal and external validity of the design of training studies are summarised in Table 13.1. Let us consider some of these in the context of a simple example. Imagine that a training programme is implemented and its effect is gauged by the difference between trainees' performance before and after training. This simple and popular design can be represented as:

| PRE-TEST | TRAINING PROGRAMME | POST-TEST |

There are various threats to the validity of such a design which mean that the change in performance between pre- and post-test may not be attributable to the effect of the training programme. The reader might care to consider the sources of invalidity described in Table 13.1, in the context of this example. Obviously other events may occur between the pre- and post-test which obscure the effect of the training programme (internal validity factor 1, Table 13.1); the trainees may change in some way between pre- and post-test assessment (internal validity factor 2); trainees may become practised at being assessed (internal validity factor 3); the pre- and post-tests may not be equivalent (internal validity factor 4). There are also potential sources of external validity, although further information is necessary to determine whether they constitute a problem. For example, the group of trainees may be highly experienced and not representative (external validity factor 1); training might be administered by one poor trainer (external validity factor 7); and so on. The first four sources of internal invalidity can be overcome by the use of a control group which does not receive training, represented as follows:

| PRE-TEST | NOTHING | POST-TEST |

Comparison of the training and control groups' change in scores from pre- to post-test enables the investigator to eliminate the four factors threatening internal validity that are mentioned above. The possibility that the trainees are not representative of the "target population" (external validity factor 1) can be overcome in various ways. First, the investigator has to ensure that trainees are being selected from a population which is representative in terms of, for example, experience, individual differences etc. Second, trainees used in the study should be selected randomly and also allocated randomly to either the training or the control group.

These solutions may be feasible when the training study is carried out under laboratory conditions. However, the use of a control group and randomisation procedures are often not possible when carrying out an experiment in an applied context. Yet, ironically, studies of this nature are highly desirable in order to learn the extent to which findings can be generalised to real training situations. Both Campbell and Stanley (1966) and Cook and Campbell (1976) have provided a comprehensive discussion of validity associated with experiments in field settings and how some problems can be overcome by the use of so-called "quasi-experimental designs". Some of these designs involve time series analysis. Many of them and the accompanying statistical analyses are moderately complex. However, if we return to our discussion of the aims of evaluation, it is more likely that these designs are of interest to the researcher than the practitioner or training manager. In other words, if the aim is to increase our understanding of training variables and their interactions, then this is only possible if systematic studies are carried out.

To the problem of experimental design facing the training researcher have to be added the considerable practical difficulties of conducting research in an applied context. These include confidentiality, sensitivity to the organisation's constraints concerning how the study is designed and carried out, and persuading those in authority of the value of rigorous evaluation. The researcher faces further challenges in selecting the appropriate evaluation criteria and also gaining access to measure them. By now some may consider that rigorous training research in an applied setting is too demanding. However, as Wolfe (1951) pointed out, there are a few compensations which are just as apt over forty years later.

> Despite the difficulties faced by a psychologist conducting research on training, he can proceed with the knowledge that if his studies are properly designed they will have two values. The first is practical: research can increase the effectiveness of specific training programs. The second value is more fundamental. Present knowledge of the principles of learning is largely of a qualitative nature. Properly conducted research will contribute quantitative information on the limits of each principle, its optimal conditions of application, and the nature of its interaction with others (p. 1284).

REFERENCES

Borich, G.D. (1979). A systems approach to the evaluation of training. In O'Neil, H.F. Jr (Ed.) *Procedures for instructional systems development*. New York: Academic Press.

Borich, G.D. and Jemelka, R.P. (1981). Evaluation. In O'Neil, H.F. Jr (Ed.) *Computer-based instruction. A state-of-the-art assessment*. New York: Academic Press.

Bracht, G.H. and Glass, G.V. (1968). The external validity of experiments. *American Educational Research Journal*, **5**, 437–474.

Burgoyne, J.G. (1973). The evaluation of managerial development programmes with special reference to the Manchester Business School. Unpublished PhD thesis. University of Manchester.

Campbell, D.T. and Stanley, J.C. (1966). *Experimental and quasi-experimental designs for research*. Chicago: Rand McNally.

Christensen, L.B. (1977). *Experimental methodology.* Boston: Allyn and Bacon.

Cook, T.D. and Campbell, D.T. (1976). The design and conduct of quasi-experiments and true experiments in field settings. In Dunnette, M.D. (Ed.) *Handbook of industrial and organizational psychology.* Chicago: Rand McNally. (Reprinted in 1983 by Wiley.)

Cronbach, L.J. (1969). Evaluation for course improvement. In Anderson, R.C., Faust, G.W., Roderick, M.C., Cunningham, D.J. and Andre, T. (Eds) *Current research on instruction.* Englewood Cliffs: Prentice-Hall.

Department of Employment (1971). *Glossary of training terms.* London: HMSO.

Dick, W. (1977). Formative evaluation. In Briggs, L.J. (Ed.) *Instructional design: Principles and applications.* Englewood Cliffs, NJ: Educational Technology Publications.

Fielden, J. and Pearson, P.K. (1978). *The cost of learning with computers. The report of the financial evaluation of the National Development Programme in Computer Assisted Learning.* London: Council for Educational Technology.

Goldstein, I.L. (1986). *Training in organizations: Needs assessment, development and evaluation.* Monterey, CA: Brooks/Cole.

Guba, E. (1978). Toward a methodology of naturalistic inquiry in educational evaluation. Los Angeles: Center for the Study of Education, University of California.

Hamblin, A.C. (1974). *Evaluation and control of training.* London: McGraw Hill.

Hinrichs, J.R. (1976). Personnel training. In Dunnette, M.D. (Ed.) *Handbook of industrial and organisational psychology.* Chicago: Rand McNally. (Reprinted in 1983 by Wiley.)

Kirkpatrick, D.L. (1967). Evaluation of training. In Craig, R.L. and Bittel, L.R. (Eds) *Training and development handbook.* New York: McGraw Hill.

Neale, J.M. and Liebert, R.M. (1973). *Science and behavior. An introduction to methods of research.* Englewood Cliffs, NJ: Prentice-Hall.

Parlett, M. and Hamilton, D. (1978). Evaluation as illumination. In Hartley, J. and Davies, I.K. (Eds) *Contributions to an educational technology, Volume 2.* London: Kogan Page.

Phillips, J.J. (1990). *Handbook of training evaluation and measurement measures.* London: Kogan Page.

Rackham, N., Honey, P. and Colbert, M. (1971). *Developing interactive skills.* Northampton: Wellens Publishing.

Rippey, R.M. (1973). *Studies in transactional evaluation.* Berkeley, CA: McCutchan.

Schmidt, F.L., Hunter, J.E. and Pearlman, K. (1982). Assessing the economic impact of personnel programs on workforce productivity. *Personnel Psychology,* **35**, 333–347.

Scriven, M. (1967). The methodology of evaluation. In Tyler, R., Gagné, R.M. and Scriven, M. *Perspectives of curriculum evaluation.* AERA Monograph Series on Curriculum Evaluation, No 1. Chicago: Rand McNally.

Stake, R.E. (1975). Program evaluation, particularly responsive evaluation. Occasional Paper No 5. Kalamazoo, MN: The Evaluation Center, Western Michigan University.

Wagner, H. and Seidel, R.J. (1978). Program evaluation. In O'Neil, H.F. Jr (Ed.) *Learning strategies.* New York: Academic Press.

Warr, P., Bird, M. and Rackham, N. (1978). *Evaluation of management training.* Farnborough: Gower Press.

Wolfe, D. (1951). Training. In Stevens, S.S. (Ed.) *Handbook of experimental psychology.* New York: Wiley.

Subject index

Author index